HEMINGWAY: A BIOGRAPHY

Books by Jeffrey Meyers

Fiction and the Colonial Experience
The Wounded Spirit: A Study of "Seven Pillars of Wisdom"
T. E. Lawrence: A Bibliography
Painting and the Novel
A Reader's Guide to George Orwell
George Orwell: The Critical Heritage
George Orwell: An Annotated Bibliography of Criticism
A Catalogue of the Library of Siegfried Sassoon
A Fever at the Core: The Idealist in Politics
Married to Genius
Homosexuality and Literature, 1890–1930
Katherine Mansfield: A Biography
The Enemy: A Biography of Wyndham Lewis
Wyndham Lewis: A Revaluation
Hemingway: The Critical Heritage
D. H. Lawrence and the Experience of Italy
D. H. Lawrence and Tradition
The Craft of Literary Biography
Disease and the Novel, 1860–1960
Wyndham Lewis *by Roy Campbell (editor)*

Hemingway

A BIOGRAPHY

Jeffrey Meyers

MACMILLAN

Copyright © Jeffrey Meyers 1985

First published in the United States 1985 by Harper & Row, Publishers, Inc., New York

First published in the United Kingdom 1986 by
MACMILLAN LONDON LIMITED
4 Little Essex Street London WC2R 3LF
and Basingstoke

Associated companies in Auckland, Delhi, Dublin, Gaborone, Hamburg, Harare, Hong Kong, Johannesburg, Kuala Lumpur, Lagos, Manzini, Melbourne, Mexico City, Nairobi, New York, Singapore and Tokyo

British Library Cataloguing in Publication Data

Meyers, Jeffrey
    Hemingway: a biography.
    1. Hemingway, Ernest — Biography   2. Novelists,
    American — 20th century — Biography
    I. Title
    813'.52   PS3515.E372/

    ISBN 0-333-42126-4

Printed in Great Britain by
Richard Clay (The Chaucer Press) Ltd,
Bungay, Suffolk

For Iris Murdoch and John Bayley

Contents

Illustrations

Maps

Acknowledgments

In "The Christmas Gift" Hemingway wrote: "The most complicated subject that I know, since I am a man, is a man's life," and in this biography I have tried to do justice to the complexity of his character and his work. I am pleased to acknowledge the assistance I received from a great many people and institutions. I had generous hospitality as well as valuable information from Jack Hemingway, Patrick Hemingway, Gregory and Valerie Hemingway; Christopher and Frances Dorman-O'Gowan; Bonte Durán; Antony, Margaret and Alane Mason. Robert and Lynn Piper provided a refuge while I was working in Washington. Mario Menocal, Jr. wrote more than one hundred perceptive pages about the Cuban period, and Anne Rabinowitz sent me the manuscript and correspondence of her father, Dr. Lawrence Kubie. Valerie Meyers was an expert editor and indexer.

Jo Hills of the Hemingway Collection at the John F. Kennedy Library, Jean Preston of the Firestone Library at Princeton University, Ralph Franklin and David Schoonover of the Beinecke Library at Yale University, allowed me complete access to their superb collections of Hemingway letters and manuscripts and guided me through the complex task of reading them. A fellowship from the American Council of Learned Societies and a University of Colorado grant-in-aid enabled me to spend a year in London writing the book.

For other personal interviews I would like to thank: Durie Shevlin Appleton, Elicio Arguelles, Tillie Arnold, Constance Bessie, Gerald Brenan, Matthew Bruccoli, Evangeline Bruce, Toby and Betty Bruce, Lewis Clarahan, Marguerite Cohn, Bill and Annie Davis, Luis Miguel Dominguín, Joseph Dryer, Ernesto Durán, Jane Durán, Afdera Franchetti Fonda, Michael Foot, M. P., M. R. D. Foot, Brian Gaisford, John and Carol Hemingway Gardner, Martha Gellhorn, John Groth, Patricia Hemingway, John Hersey, Bill and Bunny Horne, Joris Ivens, Jane Joyce, Joseph Losey, Forrest MacMullen, Robert Manning, Pedro Menocal, Wallace Meyer, Madelaine Hemingway Miller, Antonio Ordóñez, Fernanda Pivano, George Plimpton, Bud Purdy, Michael Reynolds, Alfred Rice, Thorwald Sánchez, Jr., Tina Sánchez, Dr. George Saviers, Charles Scribner, Jr., George Seldes, Dr. Richard Selzer, Irwin Shaw, Marian Smith, Lucy Durán Sowe, Clara Spiegel, Dr. Randall Sprague, Dr. Belinda Straight, Michael Straight, Harry Sylvester, Peter Viertel, Edward Wagenknecht, William Walton, Lael Wertenbaker, Milton Wolff and Fred Zinnemann.

For letters about Hemingway I am grateful to: Nicholas Angell, Carlos Baker, Correlli Barnett, Lord Blyth, Philip Bonsal, Dr. Wayne Brandstadt, James Brasch, Dr. Eugene Brody, William Buckley, Leonard Bushkoff, Reginald Cartwright, Dr. James Cattell, Herbert Channick, Julia Child, Charles Collingwood, Barnaby Conrad, Dr. Sheldon Cooperman, Fleur Cowles, Malcolm Cowley, Jenny Craig, Roald Dahl, Penny Dedman, Mary Dickens, Scott Donaldson, Dr. Scott Earle, Sarah Gamble Epstein, Leslie Fiedler, Paul Fusco, Ava Gardner, Isabel Gattorno, John Gehlmann, Walter Gellhorn, Lavinia Graecen, Ian Gray, C. Z. Guest, Raymond Guest, General Sir John Hackett, E. R. Hagemann, Dr. Edward Hager, Emily Hahn, James Halbe, Nigel Hamilton, Audre Hanneman, Field Marshal Lord Harding, Harold Hayes, Robert Helmle, Andree Hickok, Robert Hickok, Peggy Percival Howden, Laura Huxley, Ralph Ingersoll, Dr. Peter Isaacson, Robert Joyce, Julia Gamble Kahrl, Alfred Kazin, Lord Keith, Nancy Keith, Bernice Kert, Helen Kirkpatrick, Phillip Knightley, Leonard Krieger, Robert Lewis, Pia Lindstrom, Polly Loxton, Ada MacLeish, Norman Mailer, André Masson, T. S. Matthews, John McNeil, Dr. Bernard Meyer, Caroline Moorehead, Oscar Morency, Dr. John Moritz, Maurice Neville, Stella Norton-Dawson, Felipe Orlando, Thelma Pelkey, J. F. Powers, John Raeburn, Julius Rodman, Lillian Ross, Herbert Ruhm, Karl Ryavec, Lars Schmidt, Günther Schmigalle, William Seward, Roger Sharrock, Joseph Sigman, Frances Fitzgerald Smith, S. W. Speiser, Sir Stephen Spender, Robert Stephens, Nancy Streeter, Elaine Strutt, Hugh Thomas, Brian Urquhart, Linda Wagner, Benjamin Weissman, Sven Welander, William Wetherby, William White, Earl Wilson, Dr. Leonard Wilson, Air

Marshal Sir Peter Wykeham, Delbert Wylder, Dr. Irvin Yalom, Philip Young, Denis Zaphiro, Bronislaw Zielinski.

I received useful material from the following institutions: Boss & Co.; Bryn Mawr College; Canadian Broadcasting Company; Jonathan Cape Ltd.; Department of Justice; Department of State; Department of the Treasury; Farrar, Straus & Giroux; Magnum Photos; *Miami Herald;* Ministry of Defence, London; School of Journalism, University of Missouri; University Archives, University of Missouri at Kansas City; Arnoldo Mondadori Editore; National Archives, Washington, D.C.; National Gallery of Art, Washington, D.C.; Netherlands Consul General, New York; Netherlands Filmmuseum; Oberlin College Archives; *Panorama,* Milano; *People Weekly;* Procter & Gamble; Paul Raymond Publications; *Rendezvous; Student; Toronto Star;* Trinity College, Hartford; United Nations; F. W. Woolworth, Toronto.

I also read Hemingway's unpublished papers at or from: Amherst College Library; Colby College Library; Dartmouth College Library; Houghton Library, Harvard University; Lilly Library, Indiana University; Knox College Library; Library of Congress; University of Maryland Library; National Library of Australia; Newberry Library; New York Public Library; Oak Park High School Library; Oak Park Public Library; University of Reading Library; Southern Illinois University Library; I Tatti, Settignano; Humanities Research Center, University of Texas; University of Virginia Library; Washington University Library, St. Louis. And I did research at the BBC Sound Archives; the British Medical Association Library; Imperial War Museum, London; *Jewish Chronicle* Library, London; King's College Library, London University; Manchester University Library; Public Record Office, Kew; Royal Military Academy Library, Sandhurst.

For those that love the world serve it in action,
Grow rich, popular and full of influence,
And should they paint or write, still it is action.

YEATS, "Ego Dominus Tuus"

1

A Midwestern Boyhood
1899–1917

> Civil war is the best war for a writer.
> *Green Hills of Africa*

I

Both of Hemingway's grandfathers fought in the Civil War and the family was proud of its military traditions. Ernest Hall, a tall man with gray eyes and dark hair, was born in Sheffield in 1840 and had some comical troubles with constipation on the ship that brought him from England in his late teens. In August 1861 he left the family cattle farm in Dubuque and enlisted in the First Iowa Volunteer Cavalry. He furnished his own horse and saddle, and agreed to serve for three years. In Warrensburg, Missouri, in April 1862, Hall received a gunshot wound in the left thigh.[1] The bullet remained lodged in his leg, rendering him incapable of riding on horseback; and he was discharged with one-tenth disability a year after his enlistment. When offered a military pension by the government, he proudly refused it: "I gave my services to my adopted country. I did not sell them."[2] Hall later cultivated the appearance of an English gentleman—complete with muttonchop whiskers and white Yorkshire terrier—and prospered in the wholesale cutlery business in Chicago.

In a letter about his grandfather, Hemingway expressed three ideas that recurred throughout his life—martial prowess, selfish women and suicidal men—and characteristically exaggerated Hall's military career. Hemingway wrote that Hall, who had a strong English accent, had been taken for a Union spy and beaten up while on a business trip in the South. He had fought for four years and was badly wounded, but hated

1

killing and never allowed the war to be spoken of in his presence. He was a strong man, and controlled his daughter's wilfulness, selfishness and conceit. Dying in unbearable pain, Hall planned to kill himself with a pistol he kept under his pillow. But Hemingway's father removed the bullets and Hall tried to shoot himself with the unloaded gun. Ernest, who was six at the time, thought it was a cruel thing for his father to have done.[3]

Across the street from Hall lived Grandfather Hemingway, a soldier and a patriot who loved to recall his victories. Anson Tyler Hemingway, descended from a Ralph Hemingway who had lived in Roxbury, Massachusetts, as early as 1633, was born in East Plymouth, Connecticut, in 1844. He came to Chicago at the age of ten when his father was sent west by Seth Thomas to open a wholesale clock business. Anson enlisted as a private in 1862 with the board of trade regiment of the 72nd Illinois Infantry. He was promoted to lieutenant by President Lincoln in 1864 and raised Negro troops for an infantry regiment in Natchez, Mississippi.[4]

After the war Anson attended Wheaton College in Illinois, worked for ten years as general secretary of the Chicago YMCA and became a friend of the evangelist Dwight Moody. Anson was a formal, serious and deeply religious man who was active in the temperance movement and deacon of the First Congregational Church. He had four sons and two daughters, all of whom attended Oberlin College in Ohio. He later established a prosperous real estate business in Oak Park, a suburb ten miles west of Chicago, and built the house at 439 North Oak Park Avenue where Ernest Miller Hemingway was born on July 21, 1899.[5]

Ernest's father, Clarence Edmonds Hemingway, who used to shape bullets with an old army mold that Anson brought back from the war, killed himself in 1928 with Anson's Union Army pistol. Anson's grandchildren were brought up on heroic tales of the Civil War and always attended the Memorial Day parades to watch him march in full uniform. Anson saved great mounds of newspaper clippings about the war and replayed battles with Confederate veterans while vacationing in the South.[6] Anson's glorification of the Civil War was reinforced by Dr. William Barton, pastor of the First Congregational Church, who wrote numerous books about the war. Inspired by Anson and Barton, Ernest began in boyhood to read military histories and to study the photographs of Mathew Brady, whose morbid details stimulated his imagination. At Christmas 1914, Anson gave Ernest an inscribed copy of Lasalle

Pickett's *The Bugles of Gettysburg,* and Ernest claimed that his grandfather took him to see D. W. Griffith's epic *The Birth of a Nation* (1915)
thirty times. In 1918 Ernest boasted to his friends and upset his family
with a tall story about an affair with and engagement to Mae Marsh, who
had starred in the film. In 1918, when *Oak Leaves,* the town newspaper,
published the story of Ernest's war wound and citation for valor in Italy,
they included a photograph of Anson in his blue dress uniform. Hemingway, who maintained a lifelong interest in the war and had twenty-
six books on the subject in his library, always spoke about the Civil War
to his sons with reverence in his voice. When his eldest son, Jack, led
a company of Negro military policemen after World War Two, Hemingway said they reminded him of Anson's troops.[7]

In *For Whom the Bell Tolls* (1940) the hero, Robert Jordan, compares his grandfather's adventures in the American Civil War to his own
experiences in the Spanish Civil War. His grandfather's military
achievements and his father's "cowardly" suicide are linked and contrasted—as they actually were in Hemingway's life and mind. Jordan's
doubt about his courage is inherited from his father, his resolution
(symbolized by the saber—"bright and well-oiled in its dented scab-
bard")[8] from his grandfather. In his eulogy of the commander of the
American battalion in the Spanish Civil War, Hemingway compared
Milton Wolff to the wartime President: "tall as Lincoln, gaunt as Lincoln, and as brave and as good a soldier as any that commanded batta-
lions at Gettysburg."[9] He compared his own irregular exploits in World
War Two to those of John Mosby's Confederate cavalry. The title *Across
the River and into the Trees* was based on the last words spoken by
General Stonewall Jackson.

Ernest was also fascinated by the wars and heroes at the turn of the
century: the Spanish-American War (1898); the Boer War (1899–1902);
and the Russo-Japanese War (1904–05), which inspired him to collect
military cartoons. Ernest loved to read the Old Testament when he was
a boy because it was so full of battles. He remembered going with Anson
to meet Teddy Roosevelt, who greeted them with a hearty handclasp
and a high squeaky voice. There are some striking similarities between
Teddy Roosevelt, who glorified his own exploits and became President
two years after Ernest was born, and Hemingway, who modeled himself
on the hero of San Juan Hill. Both men had tremendous energy, personal magnetism, boastful self-confidence and a boyish joy in ordinary
experience. Both advocated the strenuous life, and placed great empha-

sis on bodily fitness and physical strength. Both were pugnacious and belligerent, and became experienced boxers. Both were keen naturalists who hunted big game in the American West and in East Africa. Both were men of letters who became men of action, and heroes who generated considerable publicity. Hemingway, following in the tradition of his grandfathers and of Teddy Roosevelt, went to five wars: in Italy, Turkey, Spain, China and France.

II

The atmosphere of Oak Park and the influence of Hemingway's parents were as important as the events of his childhood. Frank Lloyd Wright, an Oak Park contemporary who built one of his houses across the street from the Hemingways, wryly described the genteel, strait-laced, rigidly Protestant tone of the village (there was only one Catholic church), in which men wore silk hats to Sunday worship: "Oak Park's other name was 'Saint's Rest.' So many churches for so many good people to go to, I suppose. The village looked like a pretty respectable place. The people were good people most of whom had taken asylum there to bring up their children in comparative peace, safe from the poisons of the great city. The village streets were generously shaded. It had a village government of its own, too, accounting to some extent for its subsequent growth."[10] Wright's biographer emphasizes the smugness of that particularly Puritan suburb, which "denied Chicago" and had no saloons or poor people: "The community held a high opinion of itself: its residents were Oak Parkers, not Chicagoans, though many worked in the city. Their activities centered in their churches, their schools and their civic organizations. Oak Parkers were white, Protestant, provincial, exclusive, and prosperous; they shunned urban political corruption, happy that Austin Street, which separated the city from their 'dry' suburb, was the point, as the Congregationalist minister Bruce [i.e., William] Barton put it, where 'the saloon stops and the Church steeples begin.' "[11]

Wright moved to Oak Park just after his marriage in 1889, opened his studio in 1895, had designed twenty-nine buildings by 1909 and was held in high esteem by his neighbors. But Wright, like Hemingway, failed to conform to the strict conventions of the town and outraged the respectable residents in 1909 by running off with a married woman.

Hemingway's sister Carol remembered that all adult conversation about Wright would suddenly cease when she entered the room.

The church, as Wright suggested, was the dominant influence in the town and in the Hemingway household. Ernest's sister Sunny wrote: "We were a religious family. We always said the blessing before meals. We had morning family prayers, accompanied by a Bible reading and the singing of a hymn or two. . . . Our family expected to go to church each Sunday."[12] As a child, Ernest, who sang in the choir and was photographed with high collar and slicked-down hair, was confused by the homonyms of a Protestant hymn. He thought the congregation was singing about "Gladly, the cross-eyed bear" and was eager to see this willing but strabismic animal. The Sabbath was strictly enforced at home; all games and play were forbidden. When the children were spanked by their father, they had to kneel down and ask God's forgiveness.

William Barton, pastor of the church and father of Bruce Barton, the advertising man and author, had wide interests and was a good salesman for God. Barton often spoke from the pulpit about Lincoln and about the archeological discovery of Tutankhamen, which led Hemingway's father to complain: "we always hear about them in Church, but what about the Bible?" The pastor was also patriotic and militaristic. When America entered the Great War in April 1917 he urged Ernest and the other high school graduates to join the army. (The less popular minister of the Second Congregational Church opposed the war and eventually lost his position.)[13]

Ernest's sisters remained religious throughout their lives, but as an adult he attempted to eradicate in himself every vestige of Oak Park. In 1918 Ernest had tried to reassure his mother about his religious beliefs: "Don't worry or cry or fret about my not being a good Christian. I am just as much as ever and pray every night and believe just as hard so cheer up! Just because I'm a *cheerful* Christian ought not to bother you."[14] During his expatriate years in the 1920s, when Gertrude Stein called him ninety percent Rotarian, Hemingway confessed that he was still lousy with Christian precepts and inhibitions.[15] His fictional hero Nick Adams also regretted the imposition of religious precepts: "You had this fake ideal planted in you and then you lived your life to it."[16] Hemingway escaped from Oak Park in his youth and tried to replace it with Michigan and Montana, Paris and the Veneto. But he always retained his hard-working, self-reliant, conscientious, anxious and guilt-ridden Protestant heritage.

III

Hemingway's mother, Grace Hall, was born in Chicago in 1872 and brought up in the Episcopal Church. According to family tradition, she had scarlet fever when she was seven years old and was completely blind for several months.[17] Though there is no medical connection between scarlet fever and blindness, Grace remained permanently sensitive to light and often rested her eyes in a darkened room. Hemingway claimed that he habitually woke up at sunrise because of his "thin eyelids." He always blamed his weak eyes on his mother, though his farsighted father had to hold books at arm's length in order to read them.

Grace had blue eyes, blond hair, bold features and a ruddy complexion. She was the first girl in town to ride the precarious high-wheeled bicycle, and twice during her childhood traveled with her parents to visit England. She first met "Ed" Hemingway, who lived across the street, during her second year at Oak Park High School. Grace, a talented contralto, studied with a well-known voice teacher in New York during 1895–96, was offered a contract by the Metropolitan Opera and made her singing debut at Madison Square Garden. But she abandoned her promising career because the stage lights hurt her eyes and Ed wanted to marry her. At the time of her marriage in the First Congregational Church on October 1, 1896, Grace had fifty voice pupils, charged eight dollars an hour and earned as much as a thousand dollars a month. Ed, just starting his medical practice, made only fifty dollars a month.

Ed Hemingway, a year older than Grace, attended Oberlin College during 1890–93, played on the college football team, but did not graduate. He later wrote that at Oberlin he learned "an appreciation of Christian sincerity among fellow men and no[t to] compromise with a known evil influence."[18] He studied at Edinburgh University and earned his degree at Rush Medical College in 1896. He was an extremely busy doctor and became medical examiner for three insurance firms and the Borden Milk Company, head of the obstetrical department at the Oak Park hospital, inventor of laminectomy forceps, president of the Oak Park Physicians Club and the Des Plaines Medical Society. He delivered more than three thousand babies during his career, including his own six children: Marcelline in 1898, Ernest in 1899, Ursula in 1902, Madelaine in 1904, Carol in 1911 and Leicester in 1915.

All the Hemingway children were born at home; Grace feared the babies would be mixed up in the hospital.[19]

Ed Hemingway was six feet tall, with wide shoulders, a hawk nose and a beard that covered his weak chin. Nervous, quick-moving and sharp-eyed, he impressed Ernest's boyhood friends as a rather fierce character. Bill Smith remembered that Ed was "big, dark and hairy, looked very formidable, almost forbidding. I thought he looked cruel." Carl Edgar recalled: "He was a very arbitrary, very gruff man. He and Ernest did not get along then or at any other time and I think home was none too attractive to Ernest."[20] A female classmate, however, saw Ed's gentle but shabby side: "Dr. H. was a dear, but his wife never saw to it that he was well groomed any more than she did her son, and he too had a slightly seedy and unkempt air. It always seemed to explain his not being too successful as a doctor, for everyone liked him." Ed's son Leicester described him in the 1920s as "a haggard father who showed the strain by hurrying through everything and then fretting about it long afterward."[21] To Edward Wagenknecht, he seemed terribly tense and ready to fly to pieces.

When Ed was courting the rather reluctant Grace, he promised that she would never have to do housework—and kept his word. He always prepared the children's breakfast and served Grace in bed. He bought the groceries, did most of the cooking, took care of the laundry and managed the servants—despite his medical responsibilities. Grace—who seemed pampered, spoiled and selfish—hated dirty diapers, sick children, housecleaning, dishwashing and cooking. Though Grace was a mediocre cook (her best dish was pork chops fried in cornflakes), she made all the furniture for her cottage in Michigan. In times of emotional crisis, she would rush to her room, draw the shades and announce that she had a sick headache. The children, well cared for by the cook, the nursemaid and (later on) the older sisters, did not feel neglected by their mother, who remained free to pursue her artistic interests. Hemingway later hired servants and freed himself from domestic household duties in Key West and Havana as his mother had done in Oak Park.

The Oak Park neighbors described Grace as a tall, buxom, old-fashioned woman who wore ankle-length dresses, gave voice lessons, organized concerts, painted pictures and was dramatically preoccupied with her public performances and artistic career. But the neighbors' view (reinforced by Hemingway) of the snobbish, self-centered, pretentious and overbearing woman needs correction, for she was also attractive, energetic, stimulating, imaginative and idealistic. Ernest's perceptive high school teacher Fannie Biggs saw Grace in a positive, even sensual light: "Thinking of his mother's exuberant vitality, the rich curves of her every move, the warmth of her vital personality, I wondered if Ern would find a wife with the lush motherhood he knew."[22]

The marriage of Grace and Ed was essentially happy. Though the two high-strung personalities, hedonistic and spartan, often got on each other's nerves and welcomed temporary separations, they rarely quarreled. Ed depended on her vitality, Grace on his solidity; Ed worshipped her and Grace loved him. He enjoyed pleasing her and willingly, sacrificially, gave in to her wishes. As the Italian priest says in *A Farewell to Arms:* "when you love you wish to do things for. You wish to sacrifice for. You wish to serve."[23]

IV

Ernest Hemingway was named after his maternal grandfather, Ernest Hall. Like the pseudonymous George Orwell, who said "it took me nearly 30 years to work off the effects of being called Eric,"[24] Hemingway always hated his Christian name. He associated it with the naive, even foolish hero of Oscar Wilde's play *The Importance of Being Earnest* (1895), and considered it bourgeois, expressionless, unimaginative. So he gave himself—and all his friends—facetious nicknames. He was Wemedge, Taty, Stein, Hemingstein and even Hemorrhoid before he finally became the patriarchal Papa.[25]

Grace kept detailed scrapbooks of the early lives of all her children and on Ernest's birth date announced, in characteristic style, that the birds sang their sweetest songs to welcome the little stranger to this beautiful world. She breast-fed her first son, kept him in her bed and recorded that he was happy to sleep with his mother and lunched all night.[26] When Ernest was seven weeks old he took the first of twenty annual summer trips to Walloon Lake in northern Michigan. Two weeks later he had a minor operation while Grace was in Chicago. The sight of his left eye was defective from birth and he developed a definite myopia by the time he was ten. He went through school without eyeglasses, squinting to focus on distant objects and to protect his eyes from bright lights. He was rejected by the army because of defective vision, and later claimed (though there is no evidence for this) that he hurt his eye while boxing with professionals in Chicago.

Hemingway's earliest memory describes the carefully preserved relics of his parents' lives. They are sexually suggestive and associated with birth, boyhood, marriage, home, family traditions and personal legacies: "the earliest thing [I] remember [was] . . . the attic of the house where I was born and my mother and father's wedding-cake in a tin box hanging from one of the rafters, and, in the attic, jars of snakes and other specimens that my father had collected as a boy and preserved in alcohol."[27] Another boyhood memory suggests the fear of his bearded father: "he used to dream about a furry monster who would grow taller and taller every night and then, just as it was about to eat him, would jump over the fence."[28]

Marcelline, who was born a year before Ernest and resembled her mother, was Grace's favorite child. It was customary in the Victorian era to dress boys in girls' clothing and keep their hair long, and Grace was determined to have her handsome children appear as twins. For the first three years of Ernest's life he was dressed, like Marcelline, in fluffy, lace-trimmed dresses and flowery hats. Several writers have attempted to link Hemingway's assertive masculinity to the feminine finery of his infant years. Though Ernest's long hair was not cut until 1906, it seems clear that he graduated into boy's clothing before he was aware of being dressed as a girl. In this respect he was quite different from the Soviet Foreign Minister Chicherin, whom Hemingway observed in a gaudy, compensatory uniform at the Genoa Conference in 1922: "The boy who was kept in dresses until he was twelve years old always wanted to be a soldier."[29]

Grace recorded early manifestations of Ernest's aggressive, self-confident and courageous character as well as his tendency to exaggerate his own exploits: "[He] delights in shooting imaginary wolves, bears, lions, buffalo, etc. Also likes to pretend he is a 'soldser.' . . . He storms and kicks and dances with rage when thwarted and will stand any amount of rough usage when playing. . . . He is perfectly fearless after the first time bathing in the lake. . . . When asked what he is afraid of, he shouts out 'fraid a nothing' with great gusto." When he was five years old he claimed to have stopped a runaway horse single-handed.

After Ernest Hall died in May 1905, Grace used her inheritance to build a rather grand fifteen-room, two-story, gray stucco and wood-trimmed house at 600 North Kenilworth Avenue in Oak Park. The house had a large fireplace, a picture window and a long covered porch. Grace designed the thirty-square-foot music room, with high ceiling and balcony, where she taught her children and pupils and gave her impressive musical performances. Ed had his waiting room, medical office and collection of stuffed animals on the ground floor. Ed's brother Willoughby, a missionary-doctor in China, sent the family exotic objects —Oriental pottery and Tibetan prayer wheels—which were also displayed in the house.

One of Ernest's earliest letters, written to Marcelline on June 9, 1909, expressed his lifelong interest in competition, violence, action and punishment: "Our room won in the field day against Miss Koontz room. Al Bersham knocked two of Chandlers teeth out in a scrap and your dear gentle Miss Hood had Mr. Smith hold him while she lickt him with a raw hide strap."[30] The following year Grace, who liked to paint marine landscapes in Nantucket and took one of her adolescent children to the island every fall, spent September there with Ernest and then showed him the historic sites of Boston. But Ernest felt she was snobbish about her eminent English ancestors, and did not enjoy either the trip east or the exclusive company of his mother.

Hemingway had four sisters (and, later, four wives). His favorite was his next-youngest sister, Ursula, the only small one in the family, who resembled Ernest in looks and character. She comforted him during the difficult period of readjustment after the war and was the only member of the family he kept in touch with until the end of his life. His third sister, Sunny, a tomboy and an athlete, appeared in three of his stories: as the softball player Helen in "Soldier's Home," as Dorothy in "Fathers and Sons" and as "Littlest," who helps Nick run away from the game warden in "The Last Good Country." The youngest girl, Carol, was ordered around by the imperious older children and found it difficult to follow them through Oak Park High School. Leicester, sixteen years younger than Ernest, did not know his older brother well until the 1930s.

The two sides of Ernest's character came from his two parents, and he could say, as Goethe did:

> From father have I the stature
> For earnest living without fail,
> From mother this uncaring nature,
> This joy telling a tale.

He inherited the temperament and artistic talent of his mother, the looks and sporting skills of his father. Grace was ambitious for all her children, asked them to define their goals and urged them all to succeed. Ed was extremely rigid; he saw everything as black or white, and refused to recognize the gray ambiguity. Both parents, when Ernest was a boy, were foes of dirt and disorder. They brought up their children to follow strict schedules, stand inspection and be scrupulously neat and tidy.

Inevitably, there were (slightly comical) adolescent rebellions. Once, Hemingway claimed, when he would not eat vegetables, "no matter how much they whipped me," he became constipated, got piles and refused to move his bowels for nine days. At the age of fifteen, eager for manhood and chafing against his mother's restraint, he pleaded for long trousers—every little shrimp in the class had them—and complained that his tight pants were just about to split.

Another source of conflict was Grace's insistence that Ernest take cello lessons and join the family chamber orchestra. Hemingway, who believed he had no talent for the instrument and could not have become a cellist if he played for a hundred years, claimed that Grace kept him out of school for a year to study music. Marcelline denies this and points out that Ernest, though no Casals, was eager to succeed, reached a modicum of competence and liked music well enough to play the cello in the high school orchestra until his senior year. (Marcelline, in fact, was the one who was kept back for a year, so the two children could go through school together and graduate at the same time. She naturally missed her friends and resented her mother's decision.) Another classmate recalls that Ernest, in a subversive moment, "broke a string on his cello *purposely,* to cause a commotion!"[31] But even Hemingway admitted that the study of musical technique was good preparation for a writer, and used this knowledge to create the carefully contrapuntal structure of *For Whom the Bell Tolls.* Scott Fitzgerald exaggerated Ernest's resistance to the importance of the musical training during his genteel childhood when he said that the adult "Hemingway was still rebelling against having been made to take cello lessons when growing up in Oak Park."[32]

The father's world, by contrast, was in the open countryside just west of Oak Park and in the wilds of Michigan. Ed, practical and energetic, could mold bullets, can fruit, make candles and cook pies. He liked physical activity and felt resentful if any of his children took time to dream or think. Ernest loved to read, but when Ed saw him absorbed in a book he would urge his son to develop his boxing and hunting skills. Ed, who liked to save people and kill animals, incited Ernest toward an endless destruction of fauna: if it moved, they killed it. When a neighbor reprimanded Ed for hunting wild fowl out of season, he irritably shouted: "Never mind the law, madam. Shoot the birds!"[33]

Ernest could hunt all day on the unplowed land that was filled with wildflowers. He stocked the Des Plaines reservoir with pickerel and secretly watched them grow big. He praised his father's fast wing shots, hunted snipe with him in the spring and skated on the frozen ponds in winter. When he was ten years old, shooting quail with his father in southern Illinois, he fired his own rifle, retrieved Ed's dead bird and claimed it as his own:

> I picked the quail up, reloaded the gun, wiped my nose and set out to find my father. I was sick of not hitting any.
> "Did you get one, Ernie?"
> I held it up.
> "It's a cock," he said. "See his white throat? It's a beauty."
> But I had a lump in my stomach that felt like a baseball from lying to him and that night I remember crying with my head under the patchwork quilt after he was asleep because I had lied to him. If he would have waked up I would have told him, I think. But he was tired and sleeping heavily.[34]

Hemingway, as if following a Renaissance tradition, always went to expert teachers to absorb what he wanted to know. He learned about the Civil War from his grandfathers; woodcraft, trout fishing and shooting from his father; military tactics from Chink Dorman-Smith and Buck Lanham; journalism from William Bolitho and Lincoln Steffens; politics from Clemenceau, Lloyd George and Mussolini; writing from Anderson, Stein, Pound, Ford and Fitzgerald; art from Miró, Pascin and Picasso; bullfighting from Juanito Quintana and Sidney Franklin; investments from Gus Pfeiffer; deep-sea fishing from Bra Saunders; big-game hunting from Philip Percival. His extensive experience was reinforced by wide reading and he himself became a great teacher. He taught his friends, wives and children to fish and shoot; Jack became a superb fly fisherman, Patrick a white hunter and Gregory a champion wing shot. Finally, Hemingway's precepts taught three generations how to write novels and he became the preeminent model for the American artist in action.

V

If the gentility, church and cello of Oak Park represented the world of the mother, the wilderness around the family cottage on Walloon Lake, an extension of the prairies, stood for the realm of the father. Ed, who suffered from hay fever in the city, left his medical practice and spent his summers at the cottage. The family traveled there by lake steamer from Chicago to Harbor Springs, Michigan, and then by train around the bay to Petoskey and down to the lake. The interests and values Ernest developed there remained permanent: a passion for hunting and fishing, an obsession with violence and courage.

The photographs of Ernest in Michigan recall Huckleberry Finn; he appears in a fringed and tattered buckskin shirt and trousers, with bamboo fishing pole, oversized straw hat and heavy basket. His early letters, like his later ones, count, record and boast of his catches and kills. When he was about six, he locked a sleeping porcupine in the woodshed of the schoolhouse and then savagely hacked it to pieces with an ax.[35] In Michigan Ernest also started the long series of accidents that would plague him throughout his life (see Appendix I). As a young child he fell while running downhill with a stick in his mouth, rammed it into his throat and gouged out part of his tonsils. He also hooked his own back while fishing from a boat on the lake.

Marcelline described the rough and isolated cottage that was planned by Grace and built in 1900:

> It consisted of a living room with window seats on each side of the huge brick fireplace, a small dining room, kitchen, and two bedrooms. There was a roofed-over porch with a railing, and a hooked, hinged double gate across the front steps, which led down to the lake. The outside was white clapboard and the interior white pine. No plumbing, of course. A well was dug to the right of the cottage in the front yard. Visiting and communication were by water.[36]

In 1902 a kitchen wing was built and four bedrooms—three of them in an annex—were added. Ernest preferred to sleep outside in the back yard. When he woke in the night he heard the wind in the hemlock trees outside the cottage and the waves of the lake coming in on the shore.

Ernest's nurse remembered his secret, omnivorous reading: "Each

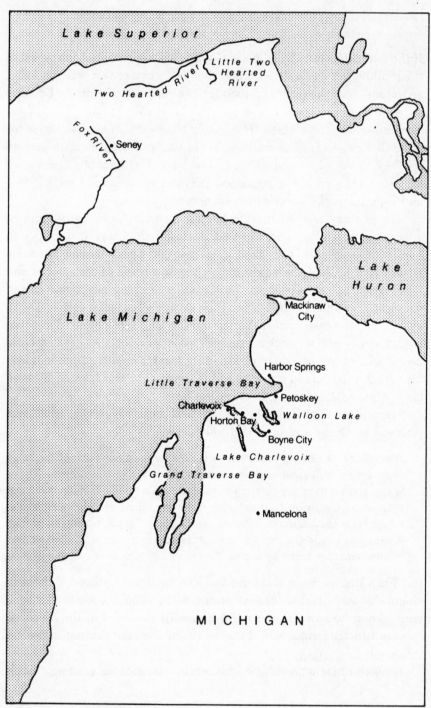

1. *Northern Michigan*

evening I'd search his cabin and take away all the books. When I'd tuck him in, he'd say good night, as sweet as could be, then in the morning I'd find books stuffed under the mattress, in the pillowcase, everywhere. He read all the time—and books way beyond his years."[37] While recovering from his war wound in the Milan hospital, he substituted bottles for books.

A significant incident (later fictionalized in "The Last Good Country") took place in 1915 when Ernest shot a protected blue heron. He carried the dead bird under his shirt and left it in his boat; but the game warden found it, went to Ernest's house and threatened to arrest him. Ernest, who had been questioned about the bird, first hid in the woods and then sought the aid of his paternal uncle George. But George Hemingway refused to help the boy, forced Ernest to turn himself in, to plead guilty and to pay the fine. Uncle George, with the same hardhearted rectitude, refused to give Ed money just before he killed himself in 1928.

In the Michigan story "Indian Camp," George is contrasted to Nick Adams' doctor-father and portrayed unsympathetically. The Indian woman in labor "bit Uncle George on the arm and Uncle George said, 'Damn squaw bitch!' and the young Indian who had rowed Uncle George over laughed at him."[38] In "Three Shots" Nick becomes as terrified of the wilderness as he had been of the game warden. Nick fires his gun to summon his father and his uncle (who again appears under his own name) and tries to justify his childish behavior with an unconvincing lie about a threatening animal:

> "Damn that kid," Uncle George said as they rowed back. "What did you tell him to call us in for? He's probably got the heebie-jeebies about something." Uncle George was an enthusiastic fisherman and his father's younger brother. . . . "I know he's an awful coward," his father said, "but we're all yellow at that age."
> "I can't stand him," George said. "He's such an awful liar."[39]

In this story the father, provoked by Uncle George, accuses the son of cowardice. In *For Whom the Bell Tolls,* by contrast, the son, nervous before battle, accuses the father of cowardice. Though Hemingway successfully tested his courage throughout his life, he feared that he might, like his father, succumb to suicide. Hemingway thought Uncle George's accusation of cowardice was unjust, but believed that the art of lying was part of his training as a writer. He boasted to gullible people of his Indian blood and his Indian daughters, and made up true-to-life stories like "Indian Camp" (which never actually took place) about a wife's gory childbirth and a husband's savage suicide.

When Ernest reached adolescence, he worked for long hours during the summer vacation making horseshoes at the forge of Jim Dilworth and harvesting hay, alfalfa, potatoes and beans at the family's forty-acre farm across the lake. Bill Smith, a boyhood friend, recalled: "Hem's father expected a very great deal from him on the farm the Hemingways bought across from their summer cottage. . . . To Hemingway chores of that kind were pretty much torture and that probably accounted for much of the friction with his father."[40]

Hemingway met the extraordinary orphaned siblings Kenley, Bill and Katy Smith in 1916. They lived with their maternal aunt in St. Louis and spent their summers two miles from the Hemingways, at Horton Bay. Their brilliant father taught physics and mathematics at Tulane University and had written a book arguing that Christ never actually existed. Kenley, ten years older than Bill, had entered Harvard at fourteen and gone into the advertising business. Katy "was about five feet, three inches, blonde, slim, with tiger colored eyes."[41] She was a roommate and close friend of Hemingway's second wife, Pauline Pfeiffer, at the University of Missouri and was fiercely loyal to Pauline when Hemingway left her to marry Martha Gellhorn. Katy married Hemingway's friend John Dos Passos, and met a violent death in 1947.

Hemingway claimed romantic attachments to Katy Smith and to the Indian girl Prudy Boulton, who "did first what no one has ever done better." But his sexual experience was severely restricted by religious training, timidity and the dread of venereal diseases, which had been drilled into him, with more force than truth, by Dr. Hemingway: "His father had summed up the whole matter by stating that masturbation produced blindness, insanity, and death, while a man who went with prostitutes would contract hideous venereal diseases and that the thing to do was to keep your hands off of people."[42] The son and the father had a strong sexual rivalry. Ed had impressive collections of snakes and guns, outshot Ernest, forced him to work on the farm, accused him of cowardice and produced numerous children while fiercely repressing his son's awakening desires.

In "Ten Indians" Nick's father takes cruel pleasure in telling his son about the infidelity of his Indian girlfriend. In "Fathers and Sons" Nick's only emotional outlet is a retributive fantasy with the weapon his father had given him. When his father punished him, he felt resentful, impotent and angry: "he had sat inside the woodshed with the door open, his shotgun loaded and cocked, looking across at his father sitting on the screen porch reading the paper, and thought, 'I can blow him to hell. I can kill him.' "[43]

Hemingway retained the childhood pattern of changing houses every year. He always moved west from Florida and Cuba, when the heat and hurricanes became oppressive, to Wyoming and Idaho; and he continued in the Rockies the rough outdoor life of his youth in Michigan. Throughout his life Hemingway associated intellect, art and culture with the aesthetes of the 1890s, with homosexuals and with the sissified music pupils of his mother. He outwardly suppressed the sensitive side of his nature and chose instead to cultivate a virile image. He wrote about the Indians and violence of Michigan, rather than the stuffy culture of Oak Park, because he wished to remember and recreate his father's world.

VI

Ernest's career in Oak Park High School, one of the best in the country, was characterized by the frenetic extracurricular activity that teenage students value more highly than academic achievement, as well as by juvenile attempts at writing that compensated for his failure to achieve athletic distinction. Edward Wagenknecht, the class valedictorian, who became an English professor, recalled the more attractive aspects of his friend. He said Ernest resented restraint and always wanted to do exactly as he pleased: "Hemingway was a handsome, friendly, and courteous boy who seemed equally enthusiastic about the sermons of the famous Dr. William E. Barton at the First Congregational Church (which was the family temple), and the performances of the Chester Wallace Players at the Warrington Theater. I have since read that he was lonely in high school, that he had once run away from home, and that he was sometimes regarded as a 'tough guy.' . . . There was nothing in my contacts with Hemingway to cause me to suspect this." Wagenknecht added that Ernest (who never ran away from home) was sometimes quite daring in class. When a teacher named Evans acquired a new toupee, Ernest wrote in the newspaper that Evans had stood on his head, and as Shakespeare said, "Verily, there is something that sticketh closer than a brother."[44]

Lewis Clarahan, a close friend and hiking companion, saw the harsher side of Ernest's character: "He was exceedingly competitive towards everyone including his friends and would not allow any restrictions on his activities from them or from his family or the school. . . . He was always aggressive and competitive, doing what he wanted to do and enlisting recruits for that purpose."[45] A girl in his class thought the exceptionally good-looking, brown-eyed, six-foot-tall boy "was egotistical, dogmatic and somewhat obnoxious. On the other hand, he unquestionably had 'personality plus.' "[46]

Ernest managed the track team, competed on the swimming, water polo and football teams, joined the debating club, played in the orchestra, wrote for the newspaper, was the class prophet and, in powdered wig, acted the part of Richard Brinsley Sheridan in the senior play, *Beau Brummel*. Ernest's mock review of his own performance is filled with puns and private jokes: "Hemingstein felt queer before the play and acted as he felt. He gave his best to the development of the drama but knocked the class out of the class play. A noble character until his death."[47] The yearbook said: "None are to be found more clever than Ernie," who was destined for (but never reached) the University of Illinois.

Ernest went to his first prizefight in about 1916 and soon became a keen boxer. He took part in a serious fist fight against another gang of boys at Walloon Lake and knocked little Lew Clarahan unconscious in an Oak Park match. In the spring of 1917 Ernest gave his family one of the more realistic accounts of his amateur fights. He said that after sparring for a minute, he was knocked out and awoke to find a friend rubbing his face with a wet sponge.[48] His later stories of boxing in Chicago, getting his nose broken and coming back for more punishment were all fantasies, contrived to toughen his image. But even as a youth, he reacted quickly and capably in a crisis. On February 3, 1917, the town newspaper, *Oak Leaves*, reported that "three girls who were riding the dumbwaiter in the lunchroom of Oak Park High School 'were flying to destruction when Ernest Hemingway . . . saw and realized the danger. He grabbed the rope and was jerked off his feet and his bare hands engaged and blocked the pulley at the top' until four other boys ran to his assistance and pulled the girls back to safety."[49]

Though Ernest rescued maidens in distress, he did not seem seriously interested in girls. In a late scrapbook, Grace wrote that at age fifteen he put on long pants, took dancing lessons and had his first sweetheart, Dorothy Davies. But Lewis Clarahan emphasized that Ernest "did not care to date and seemed to avoid girls, except at parties he was obliged to attend." Hemingway blamed his parents and Marcelline, and adopted a cavalier attitude toward his lack of social life. He said he was not allowed to ask a girl to a school dance until after his deservedly unpopular sister had been invited. Since attractive girls had to be asked well in advance and Marcelline was not invited until just before the event, Ernest said the hell with it, and gave up.[50]

During his last two years of school Ernest focused his energy on writing and became the favorite of his English teachers. Some of the classes were held in the elegant, oak-paneled English Club room, where the students sat in leather armchairs beneath a beamed ceiling. Margaret Dixon read the leading literary magazines and was very up-to-date. Her blunt honesty and realism provided an antidote to the smug complacence that sometimes prevailed at the school: "She had a temper and her class was never a dull place. She was an outspoken liberal. Again and again, she expressed in her classroom her admiration for Woodrow Wilson."[51] Another classmate contrasted two inspiring teachers:

Miss Dixon I remember as a dynamic and expressive type of woman. She was dark complexioned, about medium height and weight, rather on the masculine side, particularly in her mannerisms. She had a great amount of nervous energy and was a tireless worker. I remember her as always talking fast and loud. She directed the class plays and also some of the drama club shows. Fannie Biggs was a tall slender woman, sort of prim and somewhat affected in her manner of speaking. She had a rather thin, angular nose and face, wore glasses, and had her hair done up in a pompadour style. She was on the blond side, charming but firm and somewhat requiring as an instructress but a good personality and likeable.[52]

Ernest and his athletic friends on the *Trapeze,* the school newspaper, imitated sportswriters, especially Ring Lardner—who wrote for the *Chicago Tribune* under the name "Line O'Type"—in their mannerisms, fast talk and colloquial style. Since Ernest's weekly column devoted a good deal of space to his own exploits, he received even more exposure than the star athletes. His first three stories, printed in *Tabula,* the school magazine, were no better than any adolescent efforts, but they reveal some early literary influences. The double death in "The Judgment of Manitou" suggests Kipling's "At the End of the Passage"; the surprise ending in the boxing story "A Matter of Color" suggests O.

Henry; the savage vengeance in "Sepi Jingan" suggests the adventure tales of Jack London. Despite his extensive activities, Ernest's scholastic record in his senior year was surprisingly good: he was exceptional in English, history, algebra and law; good in zoology and chemistry; average in Latin and geometry.[53]

Ernest's grades would certainly have allowed him to enter college (two-thirds of the Oak Park class continued their education), and his family urged him to follow his father to Oberlin and pursue a career in medicine. Marcelline, who was an accomplished singer and pianist, a good student and the commencement speaker, did go to Oberlin—though she left after a year because of poor health. But Ernest, who later claimed the money intended for his education was spent in 1919 on building his mother's new cottage across the lake, had other plans. America had entered the war in the spring of 1917 and he was eager to join the army and fight the Germans.

According to Fannie Biggs, Ernest felt his parents had failed to support him in school: "Toward both parents at that time Ernest had a grudge because the other boys had so much more endorsement from their parents. . . . 'Neither of my parents would come to school for *me* no matter *how right* I was. I'd just have to take it.' " Yet when his father bandaged his friend's injured hand, "there was no doubt of his pride and affection."[54]

Hemingway also exaggerated his mother's faults and his own unhappiness in his love letters to his fourth wife, Mary Welsh. He felt Grace's main fault developed as a child when she was spoiled after her mother's death and as an adult when she abandoned her musical career. Grace was phony enough to have achieved a certain success. She had no conscience and was absolutely ruthless. He also told Mary that he had been disturbed by his parents' quarrels, which led his father to revise his will. Both parents burdened him with family responsibilities he could not deal with. He was happiest, in Oak Park, when his mother was in the hospital with typhoid fever. The children escaped her discipline and never visited the "bitch."[55] In fact, Grace's mother died in 1895, when Grace was an adult of twenty-three. And unless Grace was contagious, Ed almost certainly would have insisted that the children visit their mother in the hospital.

Hemingway's recollections of his youth were usually unreliable. After his father's suicide Hemingway—who always portrayed himself as a victim and had to find a scapegoat for all his problems—created a retrospective view of his childhood in which the castrating Grace dominated her cowardly husband and drove him to self-destruction. In "The Doctor and the Doctor's Wife" Grace is portrayed as self-righteous, overbearing and insensitive. In "Now I Lay Me" she burns her husband's precious collection of stone axes and Indian arrowheads— though this fictional event never actually took place and Ed retained his treasures until the end of his life.

The recollections of his family and friends, however, reveal that Hemingway's youth was certainly not unhappy. When Grace died in 1951, he guiltily remembered all the things about her that he admired. Like most sons, he respected his parents but was shrewd enough to perceive their major faults: Grace's selfishness, Ed's rigidity. Hemingway gave the most convincing view of his early life in an enthusiastic letter of 1945 about the physical pleasure he found, when he left the confines of Oak Park, in the museums, whorehouses, bars, gambling dens, football fields, swimming pools and grand hotels of Chicago:

I remember always how exciting it was when I was a kid and the Art Institute where I first saw pictures and made [me] feel truly what they tried to make you feel falsely with religion and the old South State Street whore-house district where we used to go and Hinky Dink's the longest bar in the world and the beer cellars and Wurz n'Zepps and the crap games we gambled in on Saturday nights with me or Jack Pentecost handling dice for the money of all our gang and the cold rides in cars to play foot-ball and the feel of the field under your spikes when you came out fast to warm up and the noise of the crowd you never thought of or looked at or heard from then on, and the taste of hot-dogs with mustard and a pickle in a smooth laquered bun up at Northwestern when we would come out from swimming meets, and the Drake [Hotel] which was Whites, Boodles and all Class its-self then.[56]

2

Kansas City and the War
1917–1918

> War groups the maximum of
> material and speeds up the
> action and brings out all
> sorts of stuff that normally
> you have to wait a lifetime
> to get.
>
> HEMINGWAY TO FITZGERALD

I

Hemingway's father thought his son too young to fight in the war and
Ernest wanted to work for a year before going to Oberlin (like Marcelline) or to the University of Illinois. He liked writing for the high school
Trapeze and was fortunate to get a job on one of the best newspapers
in the country through his uncle Tyler Hemingway, who worked in the
lumber business and was a close friend of Henry Haskell, the chief
editorial writer of the *Kansas City Star.* Hemingway described his
departure in October 1917 for the rough big city—a strong contrast to
respectable Oak Park—in an emotional passage in *For Whom the Bell
Tolls* where the son exchanges roles with the father: "His father had
kissed him good-by and said, 'May the Lord watch between thee and
me while we are absent the one from the other.' His father had been
a very religious man and he had said it simply and sincerely. But his
moustache had been moist and his eyes were damp with emotion and
Robert Jordan had been so embarrassed by all of it, the damp religious
sound of the prayer, and by his father kissing him good-by, that he had
felt suddenly so much older than his father and sorry for him that he
could hardly bear it."[1] When Hemingway crossed the Mississippi, "the

river seemed to move solidly downstream, not to flow but to move like a solid, shifting lake, swirling a little where the abutments of the bridge jutted out."[2]

Hemingway began work in mid-October and lived at first with Uncle Tyler at 3705 Walnut Street. But he found the family atmosphere too reminiscent of Oak Park and moved, a few weeks later, to the small and rather dismal attic lodging of Carl Edgar (a Walloon Lake friend who worked for a fuel oil company) at 3516 Agnes Avenue, an unfashionable part of town. In "Summer People" Hemingway portrayed Edgar as hopelessly in love with Katy Smith: "He was ugly to look at and everybody liked his face. . . . [He] was awfully nice. He had been nicer to Nick than anybody ever had."[3] Hemingway earned $60 a month and paid $35 a month for his room and two meals a day.

He soon became friendly with another *Star* reporter, Ted Brumback, the son of a prominent judge in Kansas City. Brumback had lost an eye in a golfing accident, but had been accepted by the American Field Service and had driven an ambulance in France from July to November 1917. One night, after work, Hemingway took Brumback back to his room and read Browning's poems out loud for hours while they drank Italian red wine. Hemingway, who looked forward to joining the army, enlisted almost immediately in the Missouri National Guard and spent six months training with them.

Like Mark Twain, Stephen Crane, Theodore Dreiser and Sinclair Lewis, Hemingway was a journalist before he became a novelist. The most famous newsman on the *Star* was Lionel Moise, a capable, tough, drinking and brawling ladies' man, whom Hemingway admired for his writing skill as well as for his violent way of life:

Lionel Moise was a great re-write man. He could carry four stories in his head and go to the telephone and take a fifth and then write all five at full speed to catch an edition. There would be something alive about each one. He was always the highest paid man on every paper he worked on. If any other man was getting more money he quit or had his pay raised. He never spoke to the other reporters unless he had been drinking. He was tall and thick and had long arms and big hands. He was the fastest man on a typewriter I ever knew. He drove a motor car and it was understood in the office that a woman had given it to him. One night she stabbed him in it out on the Lincoln Highway half way to Jefferson City. He took the knife away from her and threw it out of the car. Then he did something awful to her [broke her jaw]. She was lying in the back of the car when they found them. Moise drove the car all the way into Kansas City with her fixed that way.[4]

Hemingway, who had been well tutored by his high school teachers, continued his excellent education on the *Star*. The newspaper took pride in training its own men and its famous handbook of style had a distinct influence on Hemingway's innovative prose. It advocated short sentences, short paragraphs, positive, vigorous English; emphasized authenticity, selectivity, compression, precision, clarity, immediacy. Hemingway acknowledged: "Those were the best rules I ever learned for the business of writing. I've never forgotten them."[5]

Hemingway was known in Kansas City as a big, good-natured, conscientious boy. But his Oak Park background made him unusually timid and hesitant with strangers. He lacked the necessary brashness of a newspaper reporter, and felt shy and awkward when questioning people about their personal lives.[6] Yet he had enormous energy, always wanted to be where the action was, loved to ride in ambulances and squad cars, and gradually developed a brash demeanor. He would get up at seven o'clock, reach the office by eight and rush around town to cover his assignments until one in the afternoon. He would then take twenty minutes for a quick lunch and work until six—an hour past his official time. He returned home exhausted and (he complained to his family) had no opportunity to meet young ladies.

Hemingway was responsible for the "short-stop run": the police station, where he covered crime; the railroad station, where he followed tips, met shady characters and interviewed traveling celebrities; and the hospital (up a long hill from Union Station), where he checked on violent crimes, accidents and deaths. The *Star* was then fighting the corrupt city administration. The politicians on the hospital board had grafted $27,000 since the start of the fiscal year, and there were no chemicals to develop the x-rays, or antiseptics for the patients. Hemingway, the doctor's son, noted the criminal conditions that prevailed during epidemics of meningitis and smallpox. Brumback reported that Hemingway found and identified a smallpox victim who was isolated by the fearful crowd in the railroad station. When "no one made a move, he himself picked up the man in strong arms and carried him out of the station. Then he ordered a taxicab and took him personally to the General hospital, charging the expense to The Star."[7]

Thirteen of Hemingway's unsigned stories have been identified and reprinted. They anticipate his later fictional interest in boxing, crime, violence, heroism, suicide and death. They describe a Russian office boy who is also a bantam fighter; an accidental gun fight between revenue officers and city detectives (which Hemingway observed from under a Ford); sudden death in the hospital emergency room; strikers driving a laundry truck over a cliff (the law-abiding Hemingway reported a rock-throwing striker to the police). Several of the stories concern methods of military recruiting.

He was enthusiastic about his work and liked to be able to get inside information. In youth, as in manhood, he was fascinated and stimulated by danger, and told his brother Leicester: "My luck was a big fire. Even the firemen were being careful. And I got inside the fire lines where I could see what was going on. It was a swell story. . . . Sparks fell all over everything. I had on a new brown suit that got burnt full of holes. . . . Never risk anything unless you're prepared to lose it completely— remember that."[8] While covering a suicide story for the *Star,* he managed to "interview the girl in the case. . . . I had the regular police star that we keep for emergencies, and so she told me everything she knew."[9]

The clichés in Hemingway's news stories—under "the glare of the surgeon's light, he dangles on a little thread of life, while the physicians struggle grimly"—were redeemed by a passage on the forms of violence in a big city: "It's razor wounds in the African belt and slugging in the wet block. In Little Italy they prefer the sawed-off shotgun. We can almost tell what part of the city a man is from just by seeing how they did him up" and by an effective simile in a recruiting story: "The tank lurches forward, climbs up, and then slides gently down like an otter on ice."[10]

Hemingway was more interested in feature stories and revealing character through action than he was in factual reporting. He later said that his most impressive *Star* story, "Mix War, Art and Dancing," was "very sad, about a whore." But the story, which never explains why the woman was excluded from a fashionable dance, does not actually state she was a whore. In this brief, significant vignette Hemingway tried out, for the first time, his seminal idea that a skilled writer may omit things he knows, yet make the reader feel them as strongly as if he had actually stated them. He also introduced, in a rather crude form, the techniques of counterpoint (the contrast between the people outside and inside the dance hall) and of compressed repetition, which he would later bring to perfection:

> Outside a woman walked along the wet street-lamp lit sidewalk through the sleet and snow. . . .
> Outside the woman walked along the wet lamp lit sidewalk. . . .
> The woman walked along the wet sidewalk through the sleet.[11]

Hemingway evoked the atmosphere of Kansas City during the last year of the war in two minor short stories and an interchapter of *In Our Time*. In "A Pursuit Race" (1927), an advance man for a burlesque show breaks down with drink and drugs. In the ironically titled "God Rest You Merry, Gentlemen" (1933), which has a far-fetched simile in the opening sentence: "In those days . . . Kansas City was very like Constantinople," an incompetent doctor is unable to deal with a religious fanatic's attempt to castrate himself.

Interchapter VIII, based on an incident that took place in Kansas City on November 19, 1917, subtly connects urban violence with the war. It is related to his news story of the gun fight between revenue agents and detectives and to his description in interchapter III of shooting Germans as they come over the wall in Mons. In this taut vignette a Kansas City policeman, Jimmy Boyle, kills two unidentified Hungarians who have robbed a cigar store at two o'clock in the morning. His partner, Drevitts, fears there will be trouble, but he is reassured by the murderer, who insists there will be no difficulty because the victims are crooks and "wops." Boyle claims "he can tell wops a mile off "; and his false identification, which reflects the racial hostility of Irish and Italians in Kansas City, will be accepted by his superiors in order to justify the deaths of the Hungarians.

II

Ernest felt "there hadn't been a real war to go to since Grandfather Hemingway's shooting at the Battle of Bull Run."[12] He had reached maturity in Kansas City and was eager to enlist, but was rejected by the army because of defective vision. Following Brumback's example, he volunteered as a Red Cross ambulance driver in December 1917, was accepted for service and left the *Star*, after seven months, on April 30,

1918. He arrived in New York in early May, was commissioned as a second lieutenant and marched in the parade of volunteers that was reviewed by President Wilson.

Hemingway, in high spirits just before he left for Europe, caused an emotional explosion in Oak Park by announcing his "engagement" to the famous film star Mae Marsh. His preposterous letter, characteristic of many others he sent to friends, seriously upset his naive and sentimental parents. They were shocked by the very idea—let alone the actuality—of their son's impulsive engagement to a cinematic temptress, by his gesture of sexual independence, and by the gulf that had opened between parents and son since his departure for Kansas City. Grace felt wounded and feared that Ernest's rash act might ruin the future happiness she envisioned for the cozy couple: "I must have been a very poor success as a Mother, that you refused to give me your confidence. When I asked you about the girls you have never mentioned any girl to me, and now you speak of an engagement. . . . You may come home disfigured and crippled; would this girl love you then? A marriage ceremony should be followed by constant companionship in a little home nest, a bit of heaven roofed over and walled in, for just two loving souls."[13] When Hemingway finally explained that his engagement was merely a fantasy, Ed, furious but relieved, exaggerated their suffering: "Your wire explaining the 'joke' which has taken five nights sleep from your mother and father received about half hour ago. —So glad to receive it, hope you have written to your dear mother, who was broken hearted."[14]

Hemingway finally shook himself free from family restraints and on May 23 sailed with Ted Brumback for Bordeaux on a French Line ship, the *Chicago*. There was nothing much to do on the transport ship but play poker and craps. According to rumor, the *Chicago* was supposed to be safe from attack because German spies used it for travel, but Hemingway was delighted at the prospect of encountering enemy submarines. Bill Horne, who had graduated from Princeton, met Hemingway just before the voyage and clearly recalled his first impression: " 'He is like a wild horse!' Proud. Free as all outdoors. Head up, wary of strangers."[15]

When Hemingway reached Paris the city was under a bombardment that marked the last great German offensive of the war and final attempt to break through the front at Amiens. The loud and ominous sound from the firing of the super-*Kanon*, which bit huge slabs from the

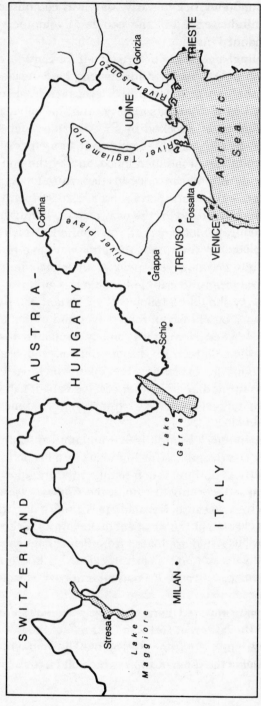

2. *The Italian Front, 1917–1918*

houses, occurred randomly but regularly, forcing the population into the fetid air of bomb shelters. Hemingway, by contrast, was excited by the barrage, commanded a cab driver to take him and Brumback where the shells were falling, and planned to wire a great story back to the *Star*. They spent an hour chasing around the city before they finally caught up with a shell burst, which hit the façade of the Madeleine church and chipped off a chunk of stone.

In early June, after two frenetic days in Paris, Hemingway traveled to Milan. On the day he arrived, an ammunition factory exploded in the nearby Lombard countryside. He had to carry mutilated corpses and human fragments detached from the barbed-wire fence that surrounded the factory, as if he were working at the hospital in Kansas City: "Arriving where the munition plant had been, some of us were put to patrolling about those large stocks of munitions which for some reason had not exploded, while others were put at extinguishing a fire which had gotten into the grass of an adjacent field, which task being concluded, we were ordered to search the immediate vicinity and surrounding fields for bodies. We found and carried to an improvised mortuary a good number of these and, I must admit, frankly, the shock it was to find that these dead were women rather than men."[16]

Two days after the explosion Hemingway was posted to an ambulance unit at Schio, east of Lake Garda. He drove the top-heavy, blunt-nosed Fiats for three weeks; contributed a humorous parody of Ring Lardner to the camp newspaper, *Ciao;* and briefly met John Dos Passos, who also drove ambulances and would later become a close friend. But Hemingway wanted to get close to the fighting against the Austrians and volunteered to run a Red Cross canteen on the Piave front, in northeast Italy. During a brief leave at Mestre, across the lagoon from Venice, Hemingway, still extremely shy, became acutely embarrassed when approached by a whore at the officers' brothel.

Though he was close to the front, Hemingway was a noncombatant with a rather inglorious job: "I would be sitting out in front of a dug out in a nice trench 20 yards from the Piave River and 40 yards from the Austrian lines listening to the little ones whimper way up in the air. . . . What I am supposed to be doing is running a posto di ricovero. That is, I dispense chocolate and cigarettes to the wounded and the soldiers in the front line."[17] In "A Way You'll Never Be," one of the three superb stories Hemingway wrote about the war, Nick Adams, who arrived before American soldiers fought in Italy, is ironic about his purely propagandistic role: "I'm supposed to have my pockets full of cigarettes and postal cards and such things. I should have a musette full of chocolate. These I should distribute with a kind word and a pat on the back. But there weren't any cigarettes and postcards and no chocolate. So they said to circulate around anyway. . . . If they see one American uniform that is supposed to make them believe others are coming."[18]

Despite his trivial though useful duties, Hemingway enjoyed the masculine comradeship of war and the brave commitment to battle. In church, the hymn "Some day the silver cord will break" had made him realize that he must someday die; but in the war, a constant test of courage, this remote prospect became a distinct reality. In *Death in the Afternoon* he defined bravery as "the ability to ignore possible consequences." In *Men at War,* a decade later, he said that imagination, the essential quality for a writer, was fatal for a soldier; and he defined cowardice as "almost always simply a lack of ability to suspend the functioning of the imagination. Learning to suspend your imagination and live completely in the very second of the present minute with no before and no after is the greatest gift a soldier can acquire. It, naturally, is the opposite of all those gifts a writer should have."[19] Hemingway later admitted that he had been scared to death after being wounded in the war.

III

Hemingway was seriously wounded at midnight on July 8, 1918, at Fossalta di Piave. This wound was—with his divorce from Hadley Richardson in the 1920s, his participation in the Spanish Civil War in the 1930s and his African plane crashes in the 1950s—a major turning point of his life. His objective, subjective and fictional versions of what actually happened illuminate the full significance of this event.

According to a contemporary Red Cross report, probably written by Hemingway's superior Captain Jim Gamble, "Hemingway was wounded by the explosion of a shell which landed about three feet from him, killing a soldier who stood between him and the point of explosion, and wounding others."[20] The shell was a muzzle-loaded Austrian trench mortar—a five-gallon can filled with explosives and scrap metal—fired from across the river. Ted Brumback, in a letter to Ed Hemingway written on July 14, six days after the event, stated that Hemingway, though badly wounded and nearly killed, had acted heroically: "An enormous trench mortar bomb hit within a few feet of Ernest while he was giving out chocolate [in the trenches]. The concussion of the explosion knocked him unconscious and buried him with earth. There was an Italian between Ernest and the shell. He was instantly killed while another, standing a few feet away, had both legs blown off. A third Italian was badly wounded and this one Ernest, after he had regained consciousness, picked up on his back and carried to the first aid dug-out. . . . Although some 200 pieces of shell lodged in him none of them are above the hip joint."[21] Hemingway later told Malcolm Cowley that the third Italian, whom he had carried back to the dugout, was dead.

Bill Horne, who saw Hemingway soon after he was wounded, explained that he "was picked up by the Austrian searchlights and took several big machine gun slugs [in his legs] while carrying a wounded Italian soldier back from the advanced listening post to the front line."[22] Though Horne differed from Brumback about whether Hemingway carried the Italian back to the first aid dugout or to the front line, he confirmed his courage and added that he fully deserved the Silver Medal for Valor: "Ernie acquitted himself with distinction and won real glory. The Italians were pretty generous with the Croce di Guerras— I have three, I think—but they were damn tough and tight about awarding the Medaglia d'Argento al Valore.—Believe me, you had to be damn near killed, in a most honorable way, to get that."[23]

The official Italian citation read: "Gravely wounded by numerous pieces of shrapnel from an enemy shell, with an admirable spirit of brotherhood, before taking care of himself, he rendered generous assistance to the Italian soldiers more seriously wounded by the same explosion and did not allow himself to be carried elsewhere until after they had been evacuated."[24] Giovanni Cecchin speculates that despite Gamble's favorable report of 1918, Hemingway's heroism was not mentioned in Charles Bakewell's *Story of the American Red Cross in Italy* (1920) because the authorities felt he had unnecessarily exposed himself to danger.[25]

Though Hemingway's bravery is indisputable, there is some doubt about several other points: the number of wounds he sustained, his Catholic "baptism," the discrepancies in his own accounts. Sceptical critics have asked how anyone could have known the precise number of wounds in his gory, mutilated legs except by counting the shrapnel fragments that had been removed. (When told about a man who had been wounded in seventeen places, Katherine Mansfield's cousin Elizabeth Russell replied: "I didn't know a man had seventeen places!")[26] Yet W. R. Castle, the American Red Cross representative in Italy, reliably told Ed Hemingway on July 20 that his son "received 237 separate wounds in his leg[s]. All but ten of these wounds are superficial."[27] These calculations were confirmed in a letter of July 19 from Brumback to Ernest, which said even the Italian doctor "decided that over 200 perforations were no exaggeration."

Hemingway was carried on a stretcher for three kilometers to a dressing station. While he waited two hours in a roofless stable for an ambulance to arrive, he was given shots of morphine and anti-tetanus, and had about twenty-eight fragments removed from his legs. He was then taken to the field hospital in Fornaci, before being evacuated to the base hospital in Milan. In Fornaci, a Florentine priest, Don Giuseppe Bianchi, passed by the wounded men, murmuring holy words and anointing them. There was no need for the priest to give Hemingway extreme unction; he was not in mortal danger and was recovering from his wounds. Bianchi's perfunctory ceremony was not (as Hemingway later conveniently claimed) a formal baptism into the Catholic Church.

Hemingway gave numerous and somewhat contradictory descriptions of his wound. His first account, in a cavalier yet reassuring letter to his family on August 18, 1918, reduced the number of wounds by ten to 227. It also suggested that he was able to carry the wounded soldier, though wounded himself, because he was in a state of shock and did not feel intense pain until after he had staggered 150 yards to the dugout:

> The 227 wounds I got from the trench mortar didn't hurt a bit at the time, only my feet felt like I had rubber boots full of water on. Hot water. And my knee cap was acting queer. The machine gun bullet just felt like a sharp smack on my leg with an icy snow ball. However it spilled me. But I got up again and got my wounded into the dug out. I kind of collapsed at the dug out. The Italian I had with me had bled all over my coat and my pants looked like somebody had made currant jelly in them and then punched holes to let the pulp out. . . . We took off my trousers and the old limbs were still there but gee they were a mess. They couldn't figure out how I had walked 150 yards with a load with both knees shot through and my right shoe punctured in two big places. Also over 200 flesh wounds.[28]

When his father first heard of the wound he said the "Great Physician" would care for Ernest.

At the time of his wound Hemingway was tremendously idealistic (he had been in Italy for a very short time and had not seen the horrors of the western front) and seems to have genuinely believed all the war propaganda. He echoed Matthew 20:16 and patriotically told his parents: "We all offer our bodies and only a few are chosen, but it shouldn't reflect any special credit on those that are chosen. They are just the lucky ones. . . . The mother of a man that has died for his country should be the proudest woman in the world, and the happiest."[29] These high-minded sentiments provide a powerful contrast to the bitter disillusionment expressed in *A Farewell to Arms.* "The truth about war," he later observed, "was lacking to me when I needed it most."[30]

Hemingway, conscious of the fame he might achieve for his exploits in Italy (which were described in the Oak Park newspaper), called his war experience "the next best thing to getting killed and reading your own obituary." (He would take great pleasure in reading his own death notices after he was nearly killed in two African plane crashes.) In his Spanish War dispatches he confessed: "In the war that I had known, men often lied about the manner of their wounding. Not at first; but later. I'd lied a little myself in my time."[31] His contemporary accounts were generally accurate, but later versions (in which he acquired an aluminum kneecap) were exaggerated into myth.

Apart from the extensive traumata in his legs and knees, Hemingway suffered another significant wound. He claimed he was shot twice through the scrotum and had to rest his testicles—which remained intact—on a pillow.[32] Other soldiers in his ward had seriously damaged genitals and those who were mutilated inspired the wound of Jake Barnes in *The Sun Also Rises.* Jake's wound is not described in the novel; but the account of Frederic's wound in *A Farewell to Arms*—like the personal descriptions of Joyce Cary and George Orwell—is close to what actually happened.

Cary "felt as if [his] brains were blown to pieces"; Orwell had "the sensation of being *at the centre* of an explosion."[33] Hemingway gave Guy Hickok, a journalist friend whom he met in 1922, a metaphorical account of his wound that foreshadowed his description in the novel: "There was one of those big noises you sometimes hear at the front. I died then. I felt my soul or something coming right out of my body, like you'd pull a silk handkerchief out of a pocket by one corner. It flew all around and then came back and went in again and I wasn't dead any more."[34] The feeling that his soul was floating out of his body recurs in a sensory passage in *A Farewell to Arms,* written at the height of his artistic powers. Like Cary and Orwell, he stoically conveys a sense of "posthumous" reflection, of returning from death. In contrast to Hemingway's letter of August 18, where the knees were shot through but "the old limbs were still there," Frederic Henry reaches down to touch his knee and is horrified to find it "wasn't there":

> Through the other noise I heard a cough, then came the chuh-chuh-chuh-chuh—then there was a flash, as when a blast-furnace door is swung open, and a roar that started white and went red and on and on in a rushing wind. I tried to breathe but my breath would not come and I felt myself rush bodily out cf myself and out and out and out and all the time bodily in the wind. I went out swiftly, all of myself, and I knew I was dead and that it had all been a mistake to think you just died. Then I floated, and instead of going on I felt myself slide back. I breathed and I was back. . . .
>
> I sat up straight and as I did so something inside my head moved like the weights on a doll's eyes and it hit me inside in back of my eyeballs. My legs felt warm and wet and my shoes were wet and warm inside. I knew that I was hit and leaned over and put my hand on my knee. My knee wasn't there. My hand went in and my knee was down on my shin. I wiped my hand on my shirt and another floating light came very slowly down and I looked at my leg and was very afraid.[35]

Hemingway again referred to his wound in a moving speech he gave in 1937 when his film, *The Spanish Earth,* was privately shown in Hollywood to raise money to buy ambulances for the Spanish Loyalists. He described his feelings when hit, noted that the pain occurred after the wound and emphasized that modern ambulances were needed to save the lives of the wounded: "At the moment that it happens, unless the bullet or the shell fragment hits a nerve, and even then it may numb it, it is not very painful. It is more like being knocked down by a club. You can be clubbed in the belly or the legs or the neck or the shoulders or the feet or almost anywhere. If you're clubbed in the head you don't know any more about it at the time. But in about half an hour, when the shock has worn off, the pain starts and when the pain really gets going you will truly wish you were dead if the ambulance is slow in getting there."[36]

The last significant description of his wound appeared in a letter to the critic Harvey Breit in January 1951, after Hemingway had suffered many more accidents and injuries. Written in the detached, stoical style of his story "A Natural History of the Dead," this letter takes pleasure in stressing the grisly details. His catalogue of horrors began when he put his hand on his knee, found it was not there and felt his hand slide into the wound; when he covered his testicles, was wounded in the scrotum and feared blindness after a grenade exploded; when bullets shattered bones and caused terrible head injuries. While reluctant to glorify wounds, he believed that serious injuries purified men who endured them, enabling them to transcend the brutal and destructive side of war.[37]

Yet the tone of Hemingway's letters of 1918 is extremely positive and the photographs in the Milan hospital show a proud and happy young man, well on the way to recovery. For Hemingway had proved his heroism in action and experienced a close encounter with death without suffering any permanent injuries. His behavior under fire gave him confidence in his courage and in his capacity to act bravely under stress. The wound made him aware not only that he could die, but also that he could survive. It made him feel invincible, made him live intensely, made him want to challenge fate rather than submit to it. He had endured the trench mortar and machine gun fire, and thought nothing could kill him.

Hemingway's experience at Fossalta led him to divide men into those who had been wounded and those who had not. Like Cantwell in *Across the River*, "he only loved people . . . who had fought or been mutilated."[38] His close friendships with men like Gianfranco Ivancich were based on their common exploits in war. He said they had both fought, been wounded and led partisan troops; that these experiences had forged a strong bond between them.[39] Though he was never a soldier (Proust spent more time in the army than Hemingway), he had the combatant's hatred of the safe staff officer and believed you could not judge a man until you had seen him in action.

Hemingway's wound, far from being psychologically traumatic (as Philip Young has argued in an influential book), had an extraordinarily positive effect on his life. His wound, for which he received the Medaglia d'Argento al Valore, was of course a mishap, a mistake, a misfortune. He had been hurt—and had survived—by chance. Yet he was able to transform what began as the commonplace distribution of chocolate and cigarettes into something glorious and noble. Like Jake Barnes and

Frederic Henry, his later heroes are wounded men: Harry Morgan has an amputated arm, Robert Jordan has a fractured leg, Robert Cantwell has a misshapen hand, Santiago has Christ-like wounds in his body. Hemingway, who once remarked that "Napoleon taught Stendhal how to write,"[40] saw most clearly when he lived most intensely. He believed you "have to be hurt like hell before you can write seriously."[41]

IV

On July 17, after nine days in the field hospital, Hemingway, the first American to be wounded in Italy, was moved to the Ospedale Maggiore. The Red Cross hospital was located on the fourth floor of a beautiful old mansion, with a gate and courtyard, at 19 via Alessandro Manzoni, near the cathedral in Milan. The hospital had sixteen single bedrooms, which could hold double that number in an emergency, several bathrooms, a kitchen, and well-equipped anesthetic and operating rooms. The nurses lived in ten bedrooms on the floor below, which had an office, drawing rooms, library, kitchen and porch.

Hemingway's parents would have been hurt if they had known that the nurses found their son "impulsive, very rude, 'smarty,' and uncooperative. He gave the impression of having been badly spoiled. He always seemed to have plenty of money which he spent freely for Italian wine and tips to the porter who brought it."[42] There was a great row when the head nurse found his wardrobe filled with empty cognac bottles. Hemingway, healthy and eager to recover, began the kind of physical therapy described in "In Another Country": "My knee did not bend and the leg dropped straight from the knee to the ankle without a calf, and the machine was to bend the knee and make it move as in riding a tricycle." The main psychological effects of his concussion did not occur until he returned home, when he suffered long nights of insomnia and could not bear to have the lights out. He fictionalized and perhaps intensified his nightmare fears in "Now I Lay Me," where Nick felt "if I ever shut my eyes in the dark and let myself go, my soul would go out of my body. I had been that way for a long time, ever since I had been blown up at night and felt it go out of me and go off and then come back."[43]

The main attraction—and most effective therapy—at the hospital was a lovely American nurse, Agnes von Kurowsky, with whom Hemingway quickly and inevitably fell in love. Agnes, seven years older than her patient, was born in Germantown, Pennsylvania, of a German father and an American mother who was the daughter of a general. Agnes had spent her early childhood on army posts in Alaska and Vancouver. She was fluent in French and had worked as a professional librarian in Washington, D.C., before training as a nurse at Bellevue Hospital in New York. In 1918 she was twenty-six years old, tall, slender and shapely, with chestnut hair and blue-gray eyes. She had arrived at the newly opened Milan hospital a week before Hemingway, who was one of the first patients to be admitted.

Henry Villard, a fellow patient, remembered Agnes as "a tall girl, doubly attractive so far from home, cheerful, quick, sympathetic, with an almost mischievous sense of humor. . . . [She] was easily the most scintillating of the nurses. . . . Sympathetic and tactful, fresh and pert and lovely in her long-skirted white uniform, moving lithely about her tasks . . . she radiated zest and energy."[44] Bill Horne, who visited his friend at the hospital, said Agnes was "a nice, cheery American woman. And Ernie at that time [was] one of the best looking, big strong men you could want to see. So they fell in love—very very much. . . . She was a nice girl—a very bright spot of America in northern Italy in 1918. She truly loved Ernie, I'm sure."[45] Agnes volunteered for unpopular night duty so she could spend more time with her pampered patient. Hemingway was always moved by women's soft, sensual hair. In *A Farewell to Arms* he described Agnes—the model for Catherine Barkley—and recreated the intimate atmosphere of her nightly visits by comparing her hair to shining water: "Miss Barkley was quite tall. She wore what seemed to me to be a nurse's uniform, was blonde and had a tawny skin and gray eyes. I thought she was very beautiful. . . . She had wonderfully beautiful hair and I would lie sometimes and watch her twisting it up in the light that came in the open door and it shone even in the night as water shines sometimes just before it is really daylight."[46]

In 1971 Agnes recalled that Hemingway was always in good spirits:

> He was worried about his leg. He was afraid they'd amputate. You know when he got there, they had him in an Italian emergency hospital for a while. The first few days, he was using a pen knife to dig out the pieces of shrapnel. He was still doing it when he got home, he said in a letter. But they saved his leg. . . . I never saw him down in the dumps when he was in the hospital. . . . Of course he had gone against his orders at

the front. When he saw his striker [servant] fall, he went out to get him. He had gone against his orders. . . . He drank brandy all the time. I think he slept very well.[47]

In the late fall of 1918, Marcelline, watching a Pathé newsreel in Chicago about the hospital in Milan, was astonished when "suddenly, in the silent film, Ernest appeared. He was in uniform, sitting in a wheelchair on the hospital porch, being pushed by a pretty nurse."[48]

Hemingway was the only one allowed to call her Ag. As he recovered under her care and moved from bed to wheelchair to crutches to cane, they visited the Duomo, La Scala and the Café Cova, strolled through the Galleria, took open carriage rides around town and went to the races at San Siro. When she was transferred to Florence during October and November, and to Treviso in December to help fight an influenza epidemic, she carried his photograph and wrote to him almost every day. Her letters are extremely affectionate; she writes that she is lonesome, misses Hemingway, dreams of him, loves him, wishes they could marry in Italy: "Old dear, consider yourself severely hugged and a kiss implanted on your left eye. . . . I think everyday of how nice it would be to feel your arms around me again. I am so proud of you and the fact that you love me, that I want to blurt it all out. . . . If this hits you about Xmas time, just make believe you're getting a gift from me (as you will someday). And let me tell you I love you."[49]

Hemingway boasted to his soldier-friend Chink Dorman-Smith that it took a trained nurse to make love to a man in a splint, and portrayed Frederic and Catherine as lovers in his novel. But Agnes gave a quite different version of the love affair with her shy admirer and insisted: "I think Hemingway and I were very innocent at that time—very innocent—both of us. In those days we were all pretty innocent."[50] The fact that she later jilted Hemingway suggests that she was not sufficiently committed to sleep with him: her "gift" would come after marriage. Agnes, who deeply resented the identification with Catherine Barkley and the implication that she had been Hemingway's mistress, later maintained that their relationship was not serious. But it is clear from her letters that she was (as Bill Horne said) very much in love with Hemingway and that she planned to marry him when he recovered, returned to America and found a job.

In September 1918, during a trip to Stresa on Lake Maggiore, Hemingway met the centenarian Count Greppi, a distinguished diplomat, who was the model for Count Greffi in *A Farewell to Arms*. In late October, three and a half months after he was wounded, he obtained permission to return to the front. The Italians were preparing to rout the Austrians and win the war in the battle of Vittorio Veneto. Brumback wrote afterwards to Hemingway's family that he had "just recovered from the jaundice. His sickness was due to a perfectly natural, but rather foolhardy desire to visit the front and see all his friends at work. How he prevailed on the doctor to let him come out there I don't know. But at any rate he arrived when the Italian offensive was at its full height. The excitement and the strain were too much for him in his run down condition"[51]—and he immediately returned to the hospital in Milan.

Hemingway's inglorious withdrawal from the war marked the beginning of his compensatory lies about his achievements in battle. In a newspaper interview of January 1919, he claimed that he had stayed at the front until the armistice. On an Oak Park American Legion form, he specifically but inaccurately stated that he had been a first lieutenant in the 69th Infantry, Brigata Ancona, of the Italian army during the Monte Grappa offensive of October 26–November 2, 1918. He sometimes varied this story by maintaining that he had served with the *Arditi,* a body of daredevil volunteers who later became the core of the Fascist squadrons. The *Arditi* legend, repeated in his postwar conversations and speeches, in his war fiction, and in letters and interviews throughout his life, eventually took root and was accepted as the truth. His behavior, though genuinely heroic, was not sufficient to satisfy his ideal self-image and craving for adulation. The accident suffered by a noncombatant while handing out chocolate had to be transformed into action with the elite shock troops who had followed D'Annunzio in the Great War.

Hemingway saw Agnes for the last time in Treviso on December 9. He spent Christmas week in Taormina, overlooking the sea in Sicily, as the guest of Jim Gamble, who was supposed to be heir to the Procter & Gamble fortune. The two friends got on well together and Gamble offered to support Hemingway for a year while they lived and traveled in Italy. Hemingway was inclined to accept this generous offer. But Agnes—who understood his attraction to money and feared that he would be corrupted by wealth—insisted that he refuse: "He would have accepted that invitation. I don't think that would have worked out. It wasn't the place for a young fellow. . . . I sent him home. He hated me for that. I told him he'd never be anything but a bum if he started travelling around with somebody else paying all the expenses. . . . He was very fascinating to older men. They all found him very interesting."[52]

Agnes may have sensed that Gamble's fascination was based on a homosexual attraction to Hemingway. A revealing passage in *Death in the Afternoon* about disillusion with a homosexual friend suggests why Hemingway accepted her advice: "The friend, who was a little older, he had met only recently, but they had become great friends and he had accepted his friend's invitation to come abroad as his guest. His friend had plenty of money and he had none and their friendship had been a fine and beautiful one until tonight. Now everything in the world was ruined for him."[53]

Hemingway gave up a year in Italy and returned to America in January 1919 with the understanding that Agnes would marry him. But the marriage did not take place. After he left, Agnes fell in love with Lieutenant Domenico Caracciolo, the heir to a Neapolitan dukedom: "He was very gentle, a gentle, nice soul—much more interesting to me than a nineteen-year-old." By comparison, Hemingway, who had not yet begun to make his way in the world, may have seemed provincial and immature. According to Henry Villard, Agnes thought Hemingway "was hasty, impulsive—not to say impetuous. He really didn't know what he wanted. He hadn't clearly thought out anything."[54]

After Agnes jilted Hemingway in March 1919, she revised her feelings and pretended she had never been in love with him: "He was so furious when I wrote him that I was too old for him and that he ought to look around. . . . I don't think I was ever crazy mad about him. He was a very attractive person. He had wit and you could enjoy his company."[55] Hemingway gives the essence of Agnes' letter in "A Very Short Story," which accurately portrays their courtship, love letters and plans for marriage: "She was sorry, and she knew he would probably not be able to understand, but might some day forgive her, and be grateful to her, and she expected, absolutely unexpectedly, to be married in the spring."[56]

But Agnes did not marry the Italian. Caracciolo's family considered Agnes (despite her "von") an unsuitable title-hunter and forced him to break off their engagement. Agnes sent Hemingway a sad letter from Rome in June 1919 saying that she had fallen out with her lieutenant, that she was very distressed and that Hemingway was now revenged

for what she had done to him. Finally, after a three-and-a-half-year gap
in the correspondence, Agnes sent a regretful letter when she heard of
his marriage to Hadley Richardson: "There has always been a little
bitterness over the way our comradeship ended, especially since I got
back [to America and another nurse, Elsie Macdonald] read me the very
biting letter you wrote her about me."[57]

Agnes' unexpected rejection had a devastating effect on Hemingway. The emotional wound was as painful as the physical injury. It led
to a desire for revenge (which is childishly inverted in "A Very Short
Story" when the hero contracts gonorrhea from a girl in Chicago) and
to a need to "show" Agnes that he was worthy of her love. Her rejection
may have driven Hemingway to strive for success as a writer and to
recreate Agnes as Catherine in *A Farewell to Arms.* In the novel,
though not in actual life, the submissive Catherine becomes the hero's
mistress and is "punished" by death in childbirth.

The most influential woman in Hemingway's life, apart from his
mother, was Agnes von Kurowsky. She first taught him, when he was
young and vulnerable, to accept the care and protection of a woman.
Harry's recollections in "The Snows of Kilimanjaro"—which concern
Agnes, not Hemingway's first wife, Hadley, whom he could and did
"cure himself of loving"—suggest the profound effect of her rejection:
"He had written her, the first one, the one who left him, a letter telling
her how he had never been able to kill it. . . . How everyone he had slept
with only made him miss her more. How what she had done could
never matter since he knew he could not cure himself of loving her."
The trauma of her betrayal, for that is how he interpreted it, forced him
into instinctive self-protection. For the rest of his life he guarded himself against betrayal and loneliness by conducting a liaison with a future
wife during his current marriage; when he had ensured his own emotional security, he abandoned his wife before she could leave him.

With Agnes, Hemingway also established a pattern of falling in love
during war. When he was endangered or hurt, the woman would share
his peril and help him recover. His affair with Martha Gellhorn developed while their hotel was under bombardment in Madrid, and he fell
in love with Mary (who nursed him after a car accident) during the
London blitz. This emotional pattern of war and love influenced his
affairs and marriages, and structured his novels from *A Farewell to
Arms* to *Across the River.*

Like Tolstoy, who believed in emotional inspiration and told Turgenev, "before I am able to write anything, I must first of all experience the fever of love," Hemingway believed "the best writing is certainly when you are in love."[58] He had, in fact, a new woman for each of his major works. Agnes provided the emotional inspiration for *A Farewell to Arms,* Duff Twysden for *The Sun Also Rises,* Pauline Pfeiffer for *Green Hills of Africa,* Jane Mason for "The Short Happy Life of Francis Macomber," Martha Gellhorn for *For Whom the Bell Tolls,* Adriana Ivancich for *Across the River* and Hadley Richardson for *A Moveable Feast.*

V

Hemingway formed one of his closest and most significant friendships while recuperating in Milan. At the Anglo-American Club on the Italian Armistice Day, November 3, 1918, Hemingway met Captain Eric Edward (Chink) Dorman-Smith of the Fifth Northumberland Fusiliers.[59] He was then a temporary major on light duty, commanding British troops in Milan and recovering from a severe gastric illness. When a waitress rushed in with the news that the war against Austria was over, both men felt they had been reprieved and Chink said: "So we are to go on living!"

Chink's father—an Irish Catholic country gentleman and squire of Bellamont, a magnificent eighty-acre estate in County Cavan—had been a major in the Boer War. Chink, born in 1895, had gone from Uppingham School and the Royal Military College at Sandhurst to the front at Mons[60] and temporarily commanded a battalion at Passchendaele. Six feet tall and very thin—with blue eyes, black hair and a clipped red moustache—he had "the game cock walk of the professional British soldier."[61] He was wounded three times between December 1914 and August 1915, and won the Military Cross at Ypres on June 16, 1915 for conspicuous gallantry under fire.[62] Chink was not at all the conventional type of bluff, strait-laced soldier. He was gentle, quiet, introspective, intellectual; he admired wit and puns, could be both charming and caustic.[63]

Hemingway was wearing his Red Cross uniform when they met, but (sensitive about his noncombatant status and impressed by the kind of reticent, stoical soldier he had always wanted to be) wildly exaggerated his military and sexual exploits. He told Chink that he had been badly wounded leading *Arditi* storm troops on Monte Grappa and (when he returned from Taormina with Jim Gamble) that "he'd seen nothing of Sicily except from a bedroom window because his hostess in the first small hotel he stopped in had hidden his clothes and kept him to herself all week."[64] Chink thought Hemingway looked like his youngest brother, Reginald, and called him Popplethwaite; Hemingway made himself Chink's unofficial aide-de-camp and became "the best possible companion." They had long drinking bouts and, as Hemingway recalled in an early poem, fascinating literary discussions:

> Always talking. Talking
> of your trade and my trade and the Empire and people we
> knew and bulls and horses, places we had been and plans
> and projects and the necessity for money, overdrafts and how
> to handle tailors, the Empire again and the great good in
> drinking, shooting, and when drunk I boasted and you never
> minded.[65]

The two men, who felt intellectual sympathy and looked at the world in much the same way, had youth, wounds and the war as their common bond. An acquaintance who met the young Hemingway in Paris noticed that he admired the British military virtues, and deliberately adopted the style and manner of the professional soldier. Hemingway was "more European than American in get-up. Could have been taken as a young guards officer."[66]

Chink went skiing, fishing, hiking and bull running with Hemingway in Switzerland, Germany, Italy and Spain from 1919 to 1925 (when he was transferred from Cologne to England); he stood godfather to Hemingway's first son and became Ernest's closest friend. John Dos Passos, who walked through Andorra with Chink in 1924, confirmed: "Chink turned out to be a splendid fellow. Public school and Sandhurst. Stiff as a ramrod and chary of words, but a good walker who enjoyed scenery, just the kind of reliable man you would want to climb a mountain with." Chink said of Hemingway: " 'He was a likely lad.' Always in the past tense."[67]

Chink clearly inspired Hemingway's imagination. He frequently referred to Chink and to the adventures they shared in his journalism, poetry, stories and nonfiction from 1923 until the end of his life.[68] Hemingway tended to idealize men of action who had professional skills that he himself did not possess: hunters, soldiers and matadors.

Like Philip Percival in Africa, Gustavo Durán in the Spanish Civil War, Buck Lanham in World War Two and Antonio Ordóñez during the "dangerous summer" of bullfights in 1959, Chink became Hemingway's ideal hero.

In the year and a half since leaving high school in a protected, religious suburb, Hemingway had traveled far and had many crucial experiences. Oak Park, for all its limitations, prepared him well for the demands of journalism and war, though not of love. He had profited from contact with the lower depths of city life, from concentrated training as a writer and from knowledge of newspaper reporting. He had been to New York and known comradeship with his fellow volunteers. In Milan and at the front he had met Europeans, discovered a new culture and come close to death. All these experiences helped him shed his midwestern provincialism and achieve new self-confidence and sophistication. His physical wound gave him an opportunity to reflect on violence and war, which he would turn to advantage in his fiction. He had fallen in love and suffered the pain of betrayal. To his parents and to Agnes he may still have seemed a youth, but the new depth of bitterness belied his boyish appearance. He had come to admire the stoic military virtues that were epitomized in his first adult friend, Chink Dorman-Smith. But the transition to peace would be more difficult to endure than the war.

3

Hadley
1919–1921

> And we'll never love anyone
> else but each other.
>
> *A Moveable Feast*

I

Hemingway faced formidable problems of readjustment when he returned home at the end of January 1919. After the stimulation of Europe, the excitement of war, the trauma of his wound and the pleasure of love, Oak Park and Michigan, though restful, seemed tame and dull. He was having trouble with his leg and endured another operation. He was lonely, and missed Italy and Agnes. At times he felt stifled, depressed, half-alive.

He was still in his teens, but had come into maturity while away from home. He had outgrown the religion and morality of his self-righteous parents and sanctimonious town. Yet he had to conform to them—and regress to a childlike role—when he came back. During the first few months he was not interested in college, girls, jobs, writing or the future. War had been his university and he had gained enormously from that experience, but it had not prepared him for a profession and had alienated him from the high school friends who had gone to college. He had written some stories in the Milan hospital and desperately wanted to be a writer, but found it difficult to express the significance of his extraordinary adventures. He had not yet developed his talent and had all his stories rejected. So he returned to newspaper work, the only kind of job he had ever had.

He had acted bravely under fire and accepted his wound without bitterness, but was still insecure about his noncombatant role. He continued for months to wear his Red Cross uniform, with high polished boots and Italian cape. He became doubtful about his heroism and, when urged to speak publicly, began to lie about his exploits. When he left Milan he had planned to marry Agnes, and wrote to her frequently. But in mid-March he received her letter of rejection. He was physically sick for several days and then tried to cauterize her memory with other girls. It was probably at this point that he lost his perilous balance and began to suffer the delayed psychological effects of shell shock.

Hemingway sailed from Genoa on the *Giuseppe Verdi* on January 4, 1919, stopped for three days in Gibraltar and Algeciras, and had a stormy but pleasant crossing. The detailed description of his wound (in a letter to his parents) had been printed in *Oak Leaves* on October 5; and stories of his exploits, medals, recovery and arrival in New York on January 21 appeared in the *Kansas City Star* and the *Chicago American*. The former reporter made good copy. He was the first American to be wounded in Italy and the first to come home; he had absorbed an astonishing quantity of metal and had proved his courage; he was tall and strong, handsome and articulate, positive and patriotic; he had sustained serious injuries (which were obvious from his limp) but was getting well; and he had interesting stories to tell when there was still keen public interest in the warriors. From his high school days to his dramatic death he had the ability to attract publicity. Interviewed by the *New York Sun* on January 22—"Has 227 Wounds, But Is Looking for Job"—he stoically said "the slugs from the shell felt like the stings of wasps as they bore into him" and was ready for any newspaper that "wants a man that is not afraid of work and wounds."

He was met at the Chicago train station by his father and Marcelline, who later noted the changes in her brother after the war: "He was on crutches. I brought him meals in bed when he had bad times after he came home. . . . He had the same enthusiasm (avidly excited about life and guns and thrills and people) but after a while [when he received Agnes' letter] he was disillusioned—not *at once*. He changed more after he hurt others more (divorces, etc.) later."[1]

Hemingway collected $1,400 in insurance payments for his wounds, lived mainly at home and did not have to work for a year. He spent his mornings in bed, his afternoons visiting the high school, browsing in the library or reading on his front porch. On February 19 some grateful members of the Italian community of Chicago gave a party in his honor at the Hemingway home. Ernest spoke some Italian and, as the wine flowed, his teetotal father tried as best he could to join the merriment. In March and April Hemingway accepted eight speaking engagements in churches, clubs and schools from Evanston to Gary, Indiana, and was paid about ten dollars a talk. His address to the enthusiastic Oak Park High School assembly was successful. On March 22 the *Trapeze* reported that he lectured in uniform, carried a captured Austrian revolver and gas mask, and held up his punctured and blood-stained trousers as proof of his tale.

Hemingway was committed more to art than to action (though action stimulated his art), more to legend than to truth. When opportunity offered, he was capable of heroism; when it did not, he escaped into mythomania. He followed the tradition of Mark Twain and frontier humor (which he had exploited in his high school days), of exaggerated exploits and tall tales. In "Soldier's Home," the most accurate portrayal of his feelings just after the war, Krebs is ashamed of his own need for mendacity: "To be listened to at all he had to *lie*, and after he had done this twice he, too, had a reaction against the war and against talking about it. . . . His lies were quite unimportant lies and consisted in attributing to himself things other men had seen, done or heard of, and stating as facts certain apocryphal incidents familiar to all soldiers."[2] But later, when boasting and prevarication were more a sign of gregarious self-confidence than of insecurity, Hemingway defended interesting lies as a vital expression of the writer's imagination: "It is not *unnatural* that the best writers are liars. A major part of their trade is to lie or invent and they will lie when they are drunk, or to themselves, or to strangers. They often lie unconsciously and then remember their lies with deep remorse. If they knew all other writers were liars too it would cheer them up. . . . A liar, in full flower . . . is as beautiful as cherry trees, or apple trees when they are in blossom. Who should ever discourage a liar?"[3]

His parents wanted him to attend the University of Wisconsin, but he refused. In Paris, when he discovered that all his literary friends had been to good eastern universities, he came to regret his decision. After his father's death, he invented the story that he had wanted to go to college and was unable to do so because his mother had selfishly spent the money in the summer of 1919 on Grace Cottage, across Walloon Lake, instead of sending him to Princeton. In fact, he was too restless to settle down; after all he had been through, formal education seemed superfluous. Grace did not spend the money intended for the children's education in order to have privacy and a place to play music, for as Hemingway well knew, Ursula went to Carleton College in Minnesota and Carol to Rollins College in Florida.

His father did, however, persuade Hemingway to have his tonsils (damaged in the childhood throat accident) removed by a medical school friend and specialist, Dr. Wesley Peck. The operation was successful, but Hemingway liked to hold grudges—real or imaginary. In "Indian Camp," he portrayed his father as professionally cool and callous (a strong contrast to the squaw's husband) during her difficult Caesarean birth: " 'I haven't any anaesthetic,' his father said. 'But her screams are not important. I don't hear them because they are not important.' " Though Ed did not perform the tonsil operation, Hemingway told Bill Smith that he had "always held it against his father for taking out his tonsils without an anaesthetic."[4]

His mental state deteriorated after the initial euphoria of homecoming and his psychological problems became more serious than his medical ones. Hemingway explained that when he got off the train at Seney, Michigan, in the summer of 1919, "I can remember the brakeman saying to the engineer, 'Hold her up. There's a cripple and he needs time to get his stuff down.' I had never thought of myself as a cripple. But since I heard I was I stopped being one. . . . [But] I was hurt very badly; in the body, mind and spirit and also morally. . . . The true gen [information] is I was hurt bad all the way through and I was really spooked at the end." After the war, he said, his favorite sister, Ursula, "would drink something light with me until I went to sleep and then she would sleep with me so I would not be lonely in the night. We always slept with the light on except she would sometimes turn it off if she saw I was asleep. . . . At that time I could not sleep without a light on" because he had been wounded in the dark and associated darkness with death.[5]

Gradually, with the help of restorative fishing trips with high school friends in the wild scenery of the upper peninsula of Michigan—lovingly described in "Big Two-Hearted River"—Hemingway renewed his interest in women and in writing. The two always were joined in his life. In the summer of 1919, at Horton Bay near Walloon Lake, Hemingway met a seventeen-year-old, red-haired high school girl, suggestively named Marjorie Bump. She was the daughter of a hardware dealer in

Petoskey and waited on tables during the summer. She was a freckled, pudgy, cute, smiling girl who looked young and vulnerable. Friendly and likable, she was very much in love with Hemingway. His unsatisfactory romance with Marjorie inspired two sour Nick Adams stories, "The End of Something" and "The Three-Day Blow" (in which Nick discusses the break-up with a friend, based on Bill Smith). But a crucial passage in the first story, written in 1925 when his love for his first wife was disintegrating, is more closely related to the fictional portrayals of the end of his marriage to Hadley ("we aren't going to have any fun, anyway") in "Cat in the Rain" and "Out of Season" than to his brief liaison with Marjorie:

> "It isn't fun any more. Not any of it."
> She didn't say anything. He went on. "I feel as though everything was gone to hell inside of me. I don't know, Marge. I don't know what to say."
> He looked at her back.
> "Isn't love any fun?" Marjorie said.[6]

At the end of the summer season Hemingway stayed in Michigan at the house of neighbors, the Dilworths, and slept with a woman for the first time. She was several years older than Hemingway and worked as a waitress. *She* (not the Indian girl Prudy Boulton) did first what other women probably did better—after Hemingway had acquired more sexual experience. Her initiation inspired the shocking, graphic description in "Up in Michigan" which Gertrude Stein considered unprintable, which Bill Bird printed privately in *Three Stories and Ten Poems,* which Horace Liveright excluded from the trade edition of *In Our Time,* and which appalled and horrified Hemingway's parents and sisters—partly because he portrayed a woman's desires and gave the real names of Jim and Liz Dilworth to the lustful characters in the story: "One of Jim's hands went inside her dress and stroked over her breast and the other hand was in her lap. . . . 'You mustn't, Jim. You mustn't.' Neither Jim nor Jim's big hand paid any attention to her. The boards were hard. Jim had her dress up and was trying to do something to her. She was frightened but she wanted it. She had to have it but it frightened her."[7]

In November Hemingway moved to Potter's rooming house at 602 State Street in Petoskey, a few streets up from Lake Michigan. The town, with its broad and handsome main street, lined on both sides with brick and stone buildings, became the setting for his satiric parody *The*

Torrents of Spring. (Braun's restaurant on Howard Street was the model for Brown's Beanery in the novel.) He made new friends there: Grace Quinlan, a fourteen-year-old schoolgirl, and Dutch Pailthorp, a big, red-headed, outgoing fellow who was the son of a judge and had attended The University of Michigan. Pailthorp worked for Woolworth's in Toronto when Hemingway lived there, and admired his friend's manliness and sporting skills.

Hemingway spent long hours at his desk in Petoskey and wrote a crudely crafted story, "The Passing of Pickles McCarty, or The Woppian Way" (a bad pun on Appian Way). This tale described an Italian boxer, fighting under an Irish name, who gives up a championship fight, joins the *Arditi* on the Italian front, achieves victory in battle and cannot return to his tame career in the ring. The autobiographical story portrays the tough Hemingway, stifled by Oak Park, who gives up journalism to join the Red Cross, wins a medal and is overwhelmed by banal conditions when he comes home. On December 4, 1919, Hemingway, hopeful despite unremitting disappointments, told Bill Smith that George Horace Lorimer, the editor of the popular *Saturday Evening Post* (with whom Scott Fitzgerald would soon have great success), had returned another story, unpromisingly titled "Wolves and Doughnuts"; and that another editor, Charles McLean of *Popular Magazine,* had not yet returned "The Woppian Way": "Hope to God he may buy it. Non hearage from him is a good sign at any rate. A better sign would be a large check."[8]

Hemingway's final war lecture at the Petoskey Public Library on Mitchell Street produced extraordinary results. He impressed one member of the audience, the stunning Harriet Connable, who came from Petoskey, was a friend of Grace Hemingway and was married to the highly successful manager of the Woolworth stores in Canada. Ralph Connable was born in Chicago in 1873, moved to Toronto in 1915 and expanded Woolworth's from ten to a hundred stores. He was also famous as a practical joker: "His favorite escapade was to dress like a woman and walk into the men's locker rooms of the staid Lambton Golf Club. While men shouted and tried to hide behind doors, Connable would whisper, 'I'm looking for my gentleman friend.' "[9] The Connables had a son, Ralph, Jr., who was a year younger than Hemingway and had been lame since birth. They were looking for a tutor and companion to live with the young man while they spent a winter month in Palm Beach. The Connables felt their son would be stimulated by Heming-

way's experience and interest in sports, and offered him a job that
allowed time to continue his writing.

The position, which paid $50 a month and all expenses, was de-
scribed by Ralph Connable in a kind letter of January 12, 1920:

> You were to make your home at our house, devote your time to your
> literary studies and work undisturbed. The work you would do for me
> would be by your talks and association, to give Ralph the right slant on
> life, especially as to his sports and pleasures. . . . I wanted to be sure that
> he had the right companionship in the evenings, and my plan was to
> supply you with the necessary funds to pay for such entertainments and
> sports as you felt would lead him along the right channel.
>
>   The fact that he has never taken much interest in athletics is due to
> an injury he sustained at birth, and his right hand and limb are not fully
> developed—they are in length but not in strength, and I was very
> anxious to get someone to interest him in athletics so he would over-
> come this handicap.[10]

Hemingway accepted the job and in mid-January 1920 moved into the
splendid gray stone mansion at 153 Lyndhurst Avenue in Toronto. The
following month Ed Hemingway (who did not seem to realize that
Ralph was nineteen) offered some old-fashioned paternal advice:
"Write to me often dear boy and if Ralph needs a walloping, now is the
time while his folks are away to pound respect into him. Much love from
yours lovingly, Daddy."[11]

Connable was a powerful figure in Toronto. When he returned to
the city in February, he kept his promise to introduce Hemingway to
friends on the *Toronto Star Weekly*. Gregory Clark, a five-foot-tall ex-
infantry major who was then features editor, was not greatly impressed
by the raw young man: He "was wearing a short leather coat and a
peaked cap and was carrying a walking stick. He walked, I noted, with
a slight limp. . . . He was a large, rather heavy, loose-jointed youth, with
a flushed face, dark loose hair, and a big red mouth. He perspired easily.
. . . He appeared to be shy, anxious and restless. When he spoke, he
could not pronounce the L. . . . He had a queer, explosive way of
describing things."[12] Clark was sceptical of Hemingway's claims to military and journalistic experience, but the novice proved himself by
showing his medals and writing creditable stories. The two men went
skiing and fishing that winter (when Hemingway began his habit of
shadow boxing during conversations), and eventually became good

friends. Clark, who understood both sides of Hemingway's character, thought "a more weird combination of quivering sensitiveness and preoccupation with violence surely never walked this earth."[13]

Like Clark, the editor, J. H. Cranston, did not see Hemingway "as likely to develop into anything out of the ordinary." But because of Connable's recommendation, he gave Hemingway a chance to write human interest stories that would provide weekend entertainment for the mass reader. He paid a maximum of ten dollars a story and Hemingway earned only $150 during his first year. Hemingway published eleven stories between February and mid-May, when he returned to Walloon Lake for the summer, and sent another twenty-two stories to the *Star Weekly* from the time he moved to Chicago in October 1920 until he left for Europe as a reporter for the *Daily Star* in December 1921.

Hemingway's boyish but lively pieces had a mildly humorous, satiric or didactic element and an insider's point of view. They concerned the rental of paintings, free shaves, a critique of the mayor, store thieves, fox ranching, whiskey smuggling and wedding gifts. His articles on camping, fishing and boxing allowed him to follow the strong tutorial instinct that reached its apotheosis in "Big Two-Hearted River." (He continued to write popular articles on blood sports in magazines like *Esquire* and *Sports Illustrated* until the end of his life.)

Hemingway sought powerful sensations in boxing matches, as he later did in bullfights. Cranston noted three important aspects of Hemingway's character: his craving for experience, need to test his body and desire to show his courage: "There was nothing Hemingway would not do just for the sheer excitement of it and he had eaten—or said he had —all kinds of things, slugs, earthworms, lizards, all the delicacies that the savage tribes of the world fancy, just to get their taste."[14] Bill Smith reported that Hemingway, in a similar fashion, "would walk over the shards of broken glass to show them all how tough the soles of his feet were. 'He cut his foot in a couple of places, but he made it.' "[15]

In Chicago, as in Kansas City, Hemingway wrote about big-city crime and violence: "The Wild West Is Now In Chicago," "Plain and Fancy Killings, $400 Up." On April 15, 1921, Hemingway told his father: "They hanged Cardinella and Cosmano and some other Wop killer today. . . . Cardinella is a good man to swing I guess. Passed the [Cook] County Jail this morning and there was a big crowd standing outside waiting for the event."[16] This incident inspired interchapter XV of *In Our Time:* an objective, realistic account of the guards' callousness, the priests' inadequacy and Sam Cardinella's cowardice (Sam responds to the injunction to "Be a man" by emptying his bowels). Hemingway is disgusted by this event, where everyone behaves badly, but his vignette does not—like Orwell's more compassionate essay "A Hanging" —question the justice of capital punishment.

II

Hemingway's second postwar summer on Walloon Lake, where he celebrated his twenty-first birthday, led to an open clash with his mother that had been threatening to erupt ever since his return from Italy. In 1920, at the age of forty-eight, Grace, under pressure, was experiencing severe emotional problems connected with the physiological changes of menopause. Hemingway claimed that Grace hated him because he opposed the construction of her cottage; but if he voiced any objections, she ignored them. In the spring of 1920 Hemingway, wishing to escape the constrictions of family life and to gain new experience (as Eugene O'Neill and Jack London had done), planned to become a stoker on a ship from San Francisco to Yokohama. But, as Ted Brumback explained: "I talked eloquently about the inestimable opportunity such a trip would give you in the writing game, [but] your mother is against it as she wants you to go to college."[17]

A Chicago friend, who served with Hemingway in the Red Cross and knew Grace, observed that she had a strong will that her son, still striving to attain emotional and financial independence, found difficult to resist: "She was a very powerful woman and she insisted that what she wanted done had to be done. As I recall, she tried to force music on to Ernest, and I don't think he gave a damn about it. . . . After 1921 or 1922 I always had the feeling he didn't want to have the power his mother had behind his back pushing him into things he didn't want to do."[18] And Hemingway recalled, shortly after Grace's death, the radical misunderstanding that existed between the war veteran and the domineering mother who could not fathom his psychological problems and still insisted on treating him as a boy. His mother criticized him for drinking and for not thinking seriously about his future. He told her that he had had some bad experiences and would work out his problems if she left him alone. How could he say he had had such a bad time, Grace remarked, since by his own admission he'd spent most of his time in hospitals?[19]

A relatively trivial incident caused the inevitable crisis, just after his birthday on July 21. At midnight, Ursula, Sunny and two girlfriends decided to go out for a late picnic; they persuaded Hemingway and Brumback to come with them, and returned at three in the morning. While they were gone (without their parents' permission) the girl-friends' mother "raised hell" at the Hemingway house and accused the boys of seductive intent. "The air was BLUE with condemnations," Sunny said. "Our innocent picnic was judged to have been a disgraceful orgy. Ernie and his guest [Brumback] were blamed unmercifully be-cause they were older and should have had more sense."[20]

Ernest was not allowed to defend himself or explain that he had gone out to chaperone the girls. Grace, in an attempt to snatch her son from the hellfire that surely awaited him, gave him a lecture and drove him out of the house. She castigated him for all the crimes she felt he had committed during the past eighteen months—idleness, hedonism, parasitism, wantonness, selfishness, seduction, irreligion, corruption and disrespect. Unless you "come to yourself; cease your lazy loafing and pleasure seeking," Grace said, "stop trying to graft a living off anybody and everybody; spending all your earnings lavishly and waste-fully on luxuries for yourself; stop trading on your handsome face to fool little gullible girls, and neglecting your duties to God and your Savior . . . there is nothing before you but [moral] bankruptcy. . . . Do not come back until your tongue has learned not to insult and shame your mother."[21] Ed Hemingway, alerted in Oak Park to the domestic turmoil in Michigan, strongly supported Grace and told Ernest to stay away from the summer house until formally invited to return. Unless Ernest got a job and developed a greater sense of responsibility, he warned (in an odd mixture of high and low diction), "the Great Creator will cause him to suffer a whole lot more than he ever has so far."[22] From his parents' viewpoint Hemingway was and would continue to be—even after he achieved literary fame—a disgrace to the family. He did not attend college, did not get a job after the war, drank openly in a teetotal home. Later on, he wrote obscene books, got divorced three times, abandoned his own faith and converted (for a decade) to Catholicism —the religion (according to Oak Park Protestants) of immigrants, serv-ants and drunkards.

Hemingway, who had faced Austrian bullets but did not have the courage to challenge his mother, portrayed their postwar conflicts in "Soldier's Home." In that story her stifling maternal love is more difficult to bear than her hostility: " 'Don't you love your mother, dear boy?' 'No. . . . I don't love anybody.' . . . It wasn't any good. He couldn't tell her, he couldn't make her see it. It was silly to have said it. He had only hurt her. . . . 'I'm your mother,' she said. 'I held you next to my heart when you were a tiny baby.' Krebs felt sick and vaguely nauseated."[23] In "Soldier's Home" the mother confronts but does not comprehend her son. She exerts pressure on him to start work, which he has no desire to do, and expresses herself in the language of religion, which he has rejected. Krebs, lacking affect (with girls as with parents), wounds his mother, who resorts to emotional blackmail and creates a scene. She cries, reminds him of her maternal care during his infancy and asks him to pray—which he cannot do. (This scene echoes Stephen Dedalus' refusal to pray at his dying mother's bedside, which Buck Mulligan tauntingly refers to at the beginning of *Ulysses*.) The deceptions he practices at home (the title of the story suggests an impersonal institution rather than a domestic refuge) uncomfortably remind him of the lies he and others have been forced to tell in order to sensationalize for home consumption the dull reality of war.

III

In October 1920 Hemingway moved into the large flat of Bill Smith's brilliant and handsome older brother, Kenley, at 100 East Chicago Avenue. He and his wife, Doodles, had sublet it from Dorothy Aldis, a patroness of the arts who was traveling in Europe. Hemingway later remembered, with nostalgia and bitterness: "Hot nights along the lake when I was poor in the summer after the war, and the boarding houses and the tenements we used to live in and when [we] had money able to send out to the chinamen's for lovely food. Then we got tired of liveing dirty and five of us rented Mrs. Aldis's apartment, just off [the] lake, was very nice and we had good cook and lived fine and could walk to work. . . . I haven't gone [back] because it would be rude to go and not see my mother and I can't stand to see her."[24]

After Christmas, when the sublet ended, they moved to a comfortable seven-room flat, with a cook, at 63 East Division Street. Hemingway enjoyed life in Chicago; he saw boxing matches and opera, played

tennis and went dancing. Kenley, who worked in advertising, introduced Hemingway to his first well-known author, Sherwood Anderson. He had just returned from six months in Paris, urged Hemingway
to live there and in November 1921 wrote generous letters of introduction to Pound, Stein and Sylvia Beach, as well as to Lewis Galantière:
"Hemingway is a young fellow of extraordinary talent and, I believe, will get somewhere. He has been quite a wonderful newspaper-
man."[25] At Kenley's house, Hemingway also heard Carl Sandburg
read from work he had recently published in Harriet Monroe's magazine, *Poetry*.

An unfortunate quarrel spoiled Hemingway's friendship with Kenley in the summer of 1921. Don Wright, one of the bachelor tenants in
the flat, was having an affair with the slovenly Doodles, who told Hemingway about it. Hemingway, still sexually naive, was furious and
wanted to punch Wright; but Bill Smith held Hemingway back so that
Kenley would not discover his wife's betrayal. Hemingway talked about
the affair, and was blamed for his meddling indiscretion when word got
back to Kenley. Y. K. Smith was a boy wonder, Hemingway said, who
had entered Harvard at the age of fourteen. But he was naive and
foolish in his personal affairs, and had a great deal of trouble with
women.[26]

In December 1920, while living with the Smiths, Hemingway, who
had been unemployed since leaving Toronto in May, answered an ad
in the *Chicago Tribune*. He was hired at $40 a week (raised to $50 in
January) as assistant editor of *Co-operative Commonwealth*, a "Magazine of Mutual Help" published each month by the Cooperative Society
of America. The magazine, which had a circulation of 65,000, printed
about twenty pages of advertisements and eighty pages of editorials and
human interest stories. Much of it was written by Hemingway. The
five-column, sixteen-page issue of October 1921, for example, contained a short story and several articles advocating aspects of the international cooperative movements, from laundry to banking, with special
emphasis on activities in Belgium.

One of Hemingway's articles, "Will You Let These Kiddies Miss
Santa Claus?," was a shamelessly sentimental piece on the effects of
non-cooperation in families. He quotes an official of the Court of Domestic Relations in Chicago, which handled the financial problems of
four thousand women each month: "The wives come here because the
husbands refuse to support them. The court makes an allotment out of

the husband's wages. This goes to the wife. But still many of them are destitute."[27] The editor, pleased with Hemingway's work, half-promised to send him to Rome to study the cooperative movement and write editorials from Europe.

But the owner, Harrison Parker, an advertising man with political ambitions, perpetrated an enormous fraud, manipulated trusts and swindled money out of unsophisticated dupes. When the whole enterprise collapsed, the *Nation* reported:

> The Cooperative Society of America, a colossal venture in frenzied finance, was adjudged bankrupt by Judge Evan A. Evans in the United States District Court in Chicago, October 6 [1921]. Newspaper reports indicate that the liabilities of the Society were $15,000,000, and that the assets seizable by the receiver do not amount to more than $50,000. . . . During the 2½ years of the life of The Cooperative Society of America at least half a dozen subsidiary concerns were organized by the trustees of the principal company, and assets were deftly shifted from one company to another, until millions vanished.[28]

Hemingway left in June 1921, before the collapse, in order to spend the summer in Michigan. He later told Charles Fenton: "I worked until I was convinced it was crooked; stayed on a little while thinking I could write and expose it, and then decided to just rack it up as experience and the hell with it."[29] If Hemingway had persisted with the exposé, he would have had a major journalistic scoop and saved the contributors a great deal of money.

In February 1921, while Hemingway was still working for *Co-operative Commonwealth,* he was offered a regular job on the *Toronto Daily Star* by the managing editor, John Bone. Hemingway asked Greg Clark's advice and was told to say he was earning $75 a week (instead of $50) and to ask for $90. Hemingway asked for $85, but did not come to an agreement with the newspaper at that time. In November 1921, after he had left *Co-operative Commonwealth,* had married Hadley Richardson and was unemployed (apart from occasional articles he was sending to the *Star*), Hemingway wrote again to Bone, saying that he was going to live in France. They agreed that he would become their European correspondent, paid by the word for what he wrote in Paris and at $75 a week plus expenses when he was traveling to cover specific stories.

IV

Hemingway met Hadley Richardson in early November 1920 when he was living in Kenley Smith's flat on East Chicago Avenue. She had been a classmate and close friend of Kenley's sister, Katy, at the Mary Institute in St. Louis and was invited to Chicago just after the death of her mother. Hadley came from a comfortable background, but had had a tragic early life. A year older than Agnes and eight years older than Hemingway, she was born in St. Louis in November 1891. She was the youngest of six children, two of whom died in infancy. As a small child she fell out of a window, suffered a serious back injury and was brought up as an invalid. Her mother was interested in theosophy and psychic phenomena; her father entered the family pharmaceutical business and, after financial reverses, shot himself in 1903, when Hadley was twelve. She toured Europe in the summer of 1909 with her mother, who chose Hadley's clothes from a utilitarian viewpoint. She entered Bryn Mawr that autumn but left after one year, with her mother's encouragement, after failing a course. Hadley's sister died in the summer of 1910 when her clothes caught fire. In her teens, Hadley apologetically told Hemingway, she had a lesbian friendship with a Mrs. Rapallo: "being very suggestible I began to imagine that I had all this low sex feelin' and she for me—quite sure now it was nothing."[30]

Hadley was a talented pianist who fell in love with her teacher, Harrison Williams, and was rejected by him—as Hemingway had been by Agnes. She gave concert performances in St. Louis, but abandoned her musical career because of her lack of physical stamina—just as Grace had because of her weak eyes. Hadley's oppressive mother died (like Grace's father) of Bright's disease in the fall of 1920 and left her with a trust fund of about $3,000 a year. Her mother's death allowed Hadley to shed the role of dependent invalid and to live her own life.

Hadley was tall and beautifully built, with reddish gold hair and high cheekbones. Talented, charming, poised and friendly, she immediately impressed Hemingway, who said: "There's the girl I'm going to marry."[31] Hadley was just the kind of woman his parents would approve of; she shared a passionate interest in music with Grace and was well liked by everyone. Though Marcelline described Hemingway in 1920 as "more like a boy of sixteen than a man approaching his twenty-first birthday," Sunny felt his war experience made him unusually mature.

He seemed to develop quickly during his year of courtship, became more conscious of his appearance, and acquired more polish and better taste in clothes. Carol's statement that the couple's difference in age was not apparent is confirmed by the photographs of the wedding.[32]

Hadley had a kind and tender temperament, was intelligent and well-read. She and Hemingway were frank with each other and discussed Havelock Ellis' descriptions of sexual behavior during their courtship. Hadley gave him French lessons on the boat to Europe and said: "Ernest's French was far from perfect and never got much better. But he could put himself over and could understand."[33] Edmund Wilson described Hadley as "wholesome and level-headed"; Max Eastman was less enthusiastic and hinted at future problems when he called her "a likeable though not alluring girl, rather on the square side, vigorously muscular and independent; I think of her as a natural-born 'hiker.' "[34]

Hemingway, who brought Hadley out of her sheltered existence, gave her self-confidence and introduced her to outdoor life, said she was the wife who liked to ski and really *do* things. He admired Hadley as a good sport who hobbled on a sprained ankle to watch a football game. During their difficult hike over the St. Bernard Pass with Chink Dorman-Smith, Hadley stoically endured pain and discomfort. Three years after their marriage Hemingway paid his well-rounded wife his highest compliment and told Bill Smith that she fished like a man, with genuine rather than simulated interest. She knew as much about boxing as she did about music, and was a good drinker.[35]

Their courtship was conducted mainly by correspondence, with Hemingway in Chicago and Hadley in St. Louis. The trials of separation —with Hadley as with his later wives—always intensified his feelings and stimulated his love. Hadley wrote dull, devoted and reassuring letters. She complained that they both felt "So low and droopy and not able to stop missing each other [for] a few minutes and whisk a good time out of somebody else." In a letter of December 17, 1920, she confessed her love and was responsive and passionate. She also foreshadowed her tolerance of his adultery and disastrous submission to his will:

Consider yourself plenty, plenty loved enough my dear—only consider too that I could be so nice and concrete about it close to you. . . . About our being simpatica—yes dear I never did love anyone so much. I couldn't get along without you Ernest unless you had to have someone else—then that would have to be tho I can't see it now. . . . I am crazy about you and there never was such a heavenly person and I love you. . . . I am wanting the best for you and am going to do pretty nearly what you want.[36]

Things did not always go so well when they were together. While listening to Rimsky-Korsakov's *Scheherazade* in Kenley's apartment, "Ernest pulled Hadley over beside him on the sofa and announced, posing majestically, that they were the prince and princess. Hadley was embarrassed nearly to tears by this childish display and was appalled at Ernest's enjoyment of it." At their engagement party in St. Louis on June 21, Hadley, unintentionally stressing how close he had been to death, announced that Hemingway "was the first American *killed* in Italy."[37]

Hadley's friends were struck by the liveliness and excitement that Hemingway generated. Though Hemingway, eager to be first, would always walk ahead of her instead of holding the door in a gentlemanly fashion, Hadley felt "nobody could be more gracious and more charming, or get into the center of another person's heart." When asked about his sexual performance, she discreetly said: "Women have been enthusiastic."[38] Despite their difference in age, Hemingway was, from Hadley's point of view, a most attractive husband. Both came from the same upper-middle-class midwestern background and were seriously interested in art. Hemingway impressed her with his boyish charm, extraordinary strength, good looks (Clark Gable with biceps) and swirling military cape; his skill in boxing and fishing; his dedication to writing; and his courageous war record. Though much older than Hemingway, Hadley was not a substitute mother and sometimes wondered if she would not prefer him as her papa.

Since Hadley's parents were dead and she did not want a St. Louis wedding that would be dominated by her officious sister, they were married in Horton Bay, Michigan. Though Hadley was Episcopalian and Hemingway nominally Congregationalist, the ceremony took place in the Methodist church on September 3, 1921. Hadley's sister almost held up the proceedings by insisting that the word "obey" be stricken out. The preparations prior to church reminded Hemingway of dressing rooms before fights and football games, and he wondered if he would feel the same way if he were going to be hanged. Bill Smith was best man. Ed and Grace, Ursula, Carol and Leicester, Bill Horne, Carl

Edgar, Howell Jenkins (a Red Cross friend), Dutch Pailthorp, Katy Smith, Harriet and young Ralph Connable assisted Hemingway through the ordeal.

The couple spent the two-week honeymoon at the Hemingway family cottage and after the wedding (as in *A Farewell to Arms*) "it was a long row across the lake in the dark."[39] Hadley remembered that it was an *awful* honeymoon. They both got food poisoning and influenza, and all she could recall, when they first went to the cottage, was being sick. During the honeymoon Hemingway, still insecure, took Hadley into Petoskey and introduced her to Marjorie Bump and several other old girlfriends to show her how much they missed him.

Because of the quarrel with Kenley Smith, Hemingway and Hadley were unable to move into his apartment as originally planned and had to live instead in a dreary flat in the 1300 block of North Clark Street. Hadley's uncle Arthur conveniently died in October and left an unexpected legacy of $8,000, which, with her trust fund, supported them in Chicago and in Europe. Hemingway, who had no job when they married, arranged with the *Toronto Star* in November to become their European correspondent. The Hemingways had been buying lire and planned to go to Italy, but they followed Sherwood Anderson's advice and moved to Paris, the center of avant-garde writing in English as well as in French. In November 1921, shortly before sailing to Europe, Hemingway was formally presented with the Italian Medaglia d'Argento al Valore by General Armando Díaz at a banquet in Chicago.

The postwar years marked his transition from Agnes to Hadley, from the betrayal of love to the commitment of marriage. Both women were considerably older than Hemingway; both were extremely attractive in a similar sort of way: with soft features and good figures; both wrote the same kind of conventional love letters. But Agnes, a well-traveled professional nurse, took the dominant role when Hemingway was wounded, dependent upon her care and sexually innocent. Hadley, who had led a sheltered and rather tragic life, was submissive (or pretended to be). Agnes, sophisticated and self-confident, was well aware of his youthful limitations; she had a good job and was not yet ready for marriage. In love with but not fully committed to Hemingway, she was more calculating than Hadley and thought she could do better with an Italian nobleman than with a wounded boy. Hadley, brought up as an invalid and prepared for the life of a spinster, had been completely dominated by her mother. She had been rejected by the only man she had ever loved and, at twenty-nine, must have feared it was too late for her to marry. Unlike Agnes, who had spent three solid months with the immobilized patient and knew him very well, Hadley had spent only six weeks with him during their ten months of courtship. Though aware of his occasional gaucheness, she was grateful for his love and thoroughly committed to her husband. With Hadley, Hemingway achieved everything he had hoped for with Agnes: the love of a beautiful woman, a comfortable income, a life in Europe.

4

Paris
1922–1923

It was a pleasant café, warm
and clean and friendly.

A Moveable Feast

I

Unlike Henry James and T. S. Eliot, Hemingway did not become an expatriate because of the cultural vacuum in America. He did not become absorbed in English society and letters, as James and Eliot did, but was attracted to the Latin civilization of Italy, Spain and France. He wanted to recapture the excitement of his wartime adventures and gain new experience in Europe. But he remained American, wanted to write American prose and, in his early years, learned from American authors. He had obtained a good job in Paris, which in the early 1920s was a cheap and interesting place to live and work. It provided a good climate for literary experimentation; many of the best writers in English lived in Paris and numerous little magazines receptive to the work of new authors were published there.

Unlike D. H. Lawrence, whose restlessness always propelled him to new destinations, Hemingway both appreciated the discoveries of a journey and extracted the maximum physical pleasure from the place where he lived. He was not a deracinated exile and gained enormously from his stimulating exposure to alien cultures. He lived intermittently in Paris from December 1921 until March 1928, but was away from the city for about half that time. He became fluent, if not perfect, in French as well as Spanish and Italian. He understood others, expressed himself clearly and developed an extensive technical vocabulary in subjects that particularly interested him: sports, bullfighting, war. He nourished a special fondness for certain places and fixed them in the imagination of his readers: Paris and Spain in the twenties, Key West and Kenya in the thirties, Havana and Venice in the forties.

The Hemingways sailed from New York on the *Leopoldina,* stopped briefly in Vigo (where he wrote an article on Spanish tuna fishing) and arrived in Paris on December 22, 1921, in time for their first Christmas dinner in Europe. They miscalculated the price of the meal and did not have enough money with them to pay the bill, so Hadley was forced to wait nervously while Hemingway returned to their room for more cash. They stayed first at the Hôtel Jacob, on the street of that name; and on January 9 moved to a rather depressing flat at 74 rue Cardinal Lemoine, just off the treeless, cobblestoned Place Contrescarpe. It is still a dreary part of Paris, filled with drunkards and deadbeats. Orwell, who lived in the nearby rue du Pot de Fer in the late 1920s, captured the decrepit atmosphere of that working-class quarter: "It was a very narrow street —a ravine of tall, leprous houses, lurching towards one another in queer attitudes, as if they had all been frozen in an act of collapse."[1] A photograph of the fourth-floor rear, two-room flat, up a dark and narrow spiral stairway with a shared faucet and toilet on each landing, confirms that it was grim. (The Hemingways' own bathroom was a recessed closet with slop jar.)

But Hemingway—who was inexperienced in Paris, wanted their money to last as long as possible and was intoxicated by the romance of bohemian life—found it gay and cheerful. He told Dos Passos: "We pay 250 francs [$18] a month. It is on top of a tall hill in the oldest part of Paris and directly above a fine place called the Bal du printemps. . . . The noise of the accordion they dance to you can hear if you listen for it, but it doesn't intrude."[2] And to Katy Smith, eager for news in Chicago, he suggested that they were living in absolute luxury. He said their comfortable apartment was larger than the one they had on North Clark Street in Chicago. It had an open fireplace, a large French bed, pleasant dining and dressing rooms, and a kitchen with thousands of pots and pans hanging on the walls.[3] They actually had a maid who shined these pots in the morning and returned to cook dinner at night. Hemingway, who had not yet developed a taste for luxuries, said the flat would not be uncomfortable to anyone used to a Michigan outhouse. Though Hadley never complained, she had been brought up in comfort and must have found the accommodations rather depressing.

The cramped and noisy flat disturbed Hemingway's work. At the beginning of 1922 he rented a small writing room in a hotel on the rue Mouffetard where, according to the legend started by Hemingway and accepted by scholars, Paul Verlaine had died.[4] In fact, the dissipated, homosexual poet died (in 1896) at 39 rue Descartes, near the Panthéon. Hemingway's mythic connection with Verlaine (whose work was not important to him) was meant to suggest his sympathetic fellowship with an artist who had lived in poverty and suffered neglect. It amused Hemingway, after he had achieved wealth and fame, to give the misleading impression that he had once been as poor as Verlaine.

But the Hemingways were not poor, for at that time $3,000 a year was a lot of money in Europe. He calculated that two people could live well and travel on five dollars a day, which would leave a comfortable residue of $1,200. In Germany, where the currency was wildly inflated, they had four days of full room and board in Freiburg for eighty cents each. In Paris, with fourteen francs to the dollar, their hotel was one dollar a night, a complete dinner cost fifty cents and they could afford to dine every week on *tournedos* and observe the Joyce family at a nearby table in an expensive restaurant, Michaud's. Though their apartment was cheap, they ate well, bet money on bike races and horses at Enghien and Auteuil, went skiing in Switzerland and Austria, traveled extensively in northern Italy, spent long summers following the bullfights around Spain and bought a painting by Miró in 1925. The only thing they could not afford was new clothes for Hadley. Gertrude Stein, like Hadley's mother, advised her to buy Stein's own brand of steerage wear for comfort and durability. Hemingway illogically agreed that by "never buying [Hadley] any new clothes, you could save and have luxuries." Hadley acquiesced, as always, to his wishes. But one of her friends disapproved of his lack of consideration and exclaimed: "Hadley's a perfect fool to take it. Her clothes are falling off. She can't even show herself on the street. And it's her money."[5]

Since Hemingway felt his mother had dominated his father, he was determined to maintain the upper hand in his own marriage. Dos Passos noted that Hemingway used to make Hadley watch the six-day bike races throughout the night: "Right from the beginning Hem was hard on his women." Hadley, who accepted her husband's sporting enthusiasms if not his personal intransigence, later recalled Zelda Fitzgerald (who never got on well with Hemingway) saying with a smile, "I notice that in the Hemingway family you do what Ernest wants." Ernest didn't like that very much but it was a perceptive remark. He had a passionate, overwhelming desire to do some of the things that have since been written about, and so I went along with him —with the trips, the adventures. He had such a powerful personality; he could be so enthusiastic that I became caught up in his notions too. It could work in reverse, that persistence. Once he took a dislike to someone you could absolutely never get him back [to them]. If he took exception to anyone that was it; there was no reasoning with him about it. He eventually turned on almost everyone we knew, all his old friends.[6]

It was fortunate that Hadley was submissive, for Hemingway could be a difficult man to live with. He was silent at breakfast as he thought about his writing, absent and absorbed in his work during the day and, when writing well, withdrawn at night. He felt that sexual and creative energy—spilling sperm and spilling ink—came from the same vital source, that both could be exhausted in the same way and that the first must be conserved if the second was to flow: "I have to ease off on makeing love when writing hard as the two things are run by the same motor."[7] He had a Hindu attitude about the finite number of orgasms and the need for sexual conservation, and sagely advised the young Allen Tate: "Don't make too much love while you're young; save some up for middle age."

Hemingway, remembering writers like Maupássant and Nietzsche, also adopted the Romantic idea that venereal disease could inspire creativity: "A man can't really be a good writer unless he has had syphilis." He cultivated a taste for the low life and prostitutes of Montmartre, but told Max Eastman that he felt disgusted by his attraction to these girls. His swaggering Introduction to the privately printed sexual *Memoirs of Kiki* provides a sharp contrast to Kiki's description of the novelist, who seemed to have retained some of his choirboy innocence after several years in Paris: "I saw Ernest again, looking more like a first-communion lad and friendlier than ever; I wondered if he was still a virgin."[8]

Hemingway's own sexual fantasy, recounted to the alcoholic Scott Fitzgerald, combined sport and sex. In the dream, which suggested that Hemingway tried to be monogamous but was essentially adulterous, his mistresses were more like the nine muses than real sexual partners:

I wonder what your idea of heaven would be—A beautiful vacuum filled with wealthy monogamists, all powerful and members of the best families all drinking themselves to death. . . .

To me heaven would be a big bull ring with me holding two barrera [front-row] seats and a trout stream outside that no one else was allowed to fish in and two lovely houses in the town; one where I would have my wife and children and be monogamous and love them truly and well and the other where I would have my nine beautiful mistresses on 9 different floors.[9]

Though Hemingway was inspired by passion and believed "the best writing is certainly [done] when you are in love," he also felt he had to have some emotional and psychic safeguards in order to write. He saw his wife as a cure for loneliness, the occupational hazard of a writer, but (like many other men) thought love made him vulnerable. During their courtship he told Hadley that she could hurt him terribly; his love for her was a chink in his armor and she could thrust a sword into it whenever she wished.[10] He felt the ideal conditions for writing were a completely loyal wife, a less committed involvement—which guarded him against an Agnes-like betrayal—on his part, and a superficial discontent (illness or argument) that provided the requisite stimulation.

Paris was filled with many phonies and poseurs, and a few genuine writers: "the Freaks who would never do anything," as Jean Rhys said, and "the Freaks who just possibly might." Hemingway, who believed "you'll lose it if you talk about it," defined himself in opposition to the legions of American bohemians in Paris: "They are nearly all loafers expending the energy that an artist puts into his creative work in talking about what they are going to do and condemning the work of all artists who have gained any degree of recognition. By talking about art they obtain the same satisfaction that the real artist does in his work. That is very pleasant, of course, but they insist upon posing as artists."[11]

He insisted that his own life, though apparently hedonistic, had followed a steady course of education and discipline, for he could not give himself up to pleasure if he had not completed his daily work. If he was not writing well or not writing at all, he became miserable and bad-tempered. "Let those who want to, save the world," he proclaimed in *Death in the Afternoon*, "the great thing is to last and get your work done." He was confidently aware of his literary powers long before the world recognized them; he would breakfast at the Café Dôme and read his stories to anyone who would listen; and, as Morley Callaghan said, "he was willing to be ruthless with himself or with anything or anybody that got in the way of the perfection of his work."[12]

Though Hadley was often alone, and sometimes had a difficult time with the self-absorbed Hemingway and the dreary flat, she enjoyed her new life and was basically happy. She improved her French, learned to cook, played the piano and traveled around Europe. In January 1922, soon after they got settled, they bought new ski equipment and went on a two-week holiday with Chink Dorman-Smith in Chamby, five miles northwest of Montreux, in the Swiss Alps. Chink, exaggerating his own innocence and Hadley's brazenness, noted that "they were very much in love and used to disturb my bachelorhood at breakfast coffee by reciting, blow by blow, the events of their nights." The tall mountain pines reminded Hemingway of aisles in a cathedral and he later used Chamby as the setting for the final chapters of *A Farewell to Arms*.

They met Chink in Chamby again in May, went trout fishing and mountain climbing, and walked over the St. Bernard Pass, through deep snow and without adequate boots, into Italy. Chink recalled their unusual reversal of roles: "Hadley had refused to be parted from her toilet bottles. A furious Hem declined to carry them. For the sake of peace I stuffed them into my already heavy rucksack. . . . Hem developed a form of mountain sickness and Hadley had to help him on. . . . The journey became something of a nightmare, with Hem sick, Hadley worried and myself carrying two packs forward at a time and returning for the odd one."[13]

A far graver crisis—and major turning point in their marriage—occurred in mid-December 1922 when Hadley traveled from Paris to Lausanne to join Hemingway for another ski holiday. She brought with her all the manuscripts, typescripts, copies and carbons of his unpublished work, which included material written in Petoskey in 1919, some "good stories about Kansas City" and his latest efforts.[14] The suitcase containing all this material was stolen from the compartment of Hadley's train while it was still in the Gare de Lyon. Despite extensive searches, nothing was ever recovered.

Hemingway gave the earliest substantial account of this event in a letter of December 6, 1924. He told Bill Smith that she had put the suitcase filled with manuscripts in her compartment, left to see if her trunk was on the train, and returned to find the suitcase was gone. She was afraid to tell him about it for several days, and when she did, he took it very hard. In the "Miami" draft of *Islands in the Stream* (deleted from the published novel), he said there were eleven stories, a novel and poems, that she went out on the quay to buy a London paper and a bottle of Evian water.[15]

Hadley naturally found it difficult to confess her inexcusable negligence. While she was crying and stammering, Hemingway wrote in the *Islands* draft, he imagined all the worst things she could have done. He thought she must have either deceived him or fallen in love with another man. The Spanish painter and soldier Luis Quintanilla, who first met Hemingway in 1931, heard that Hemingway, forced to guess the worst, exclaimed: "Then you've slept with a Negro, tell me!"[16] When she finally blurted out the truth, he found it difficult to believe that she had actually taken the originals *and* all the copies.

Hemingway gave various descriptions of his response to the loss of the manuscripts. In 1951 he told Charles Fenton that he "felt so badly about the loss that [he] would almost have resorted to surgery in order to forget it"; and the still-guilty Hadley agreed with him: "so deeply had Ernest put himself into this writing that I think he never recovered from the pain of this irreparable loss." Marcelline confirmed: "He was absolutely sick. It nearly killed him."[17] He adopted a less wounded, more stoical attitude when writing *A Moveable Feast* in the late 1950s. He idealized Hadley in that memoir, did not want to blame her for the loss and said: "Chink had taught me never to discuss casualties. . . . It was probably good for me to lose [my] early work. . . . There was only one thing to do; to start over." Critics from Cowley (1949) to d'Amico (1980) have followed this later line of reasoning and argued that it "was even a stroke of good fortune for Hemingway, since the loss enabled him to begin over again and concentrate, as Gertrude Stein had advised."[18] But this *felix culpa* theory ignores the terrible psychological effects on Hemingway, who felt, for a time, that he would never write again. It also mistakenly assumes that it was better for him to lose than to retain the stories, better to begin over again than to revise and improve his early work. Scholars would now give a great deal to have examples of his apprentice fiction.

Hemingway was so deeply shocked and hurt by the loss that he immediately took the long journey from Lausanne to Paris to determine if Hadley had left anything at all behind. She had not. The fact that she had been so careless about his most precious possession—the tangible expression of his deepest thoughts and feelings—had brought the copies (instead of leaving them in a safe place) and had shown so little understanding of his life as a writer dealt the first disastrous blow to their marriage. The loss was irrevocably connected in Hemingway's mind with sexual infidelity, and he equated the lost manuscripts with lost love. He tried to forgive her, but could not; and it was Hemingway, not Hadley, who eventually fell in love with someone else. Ezra Pound, for one, believed that she was jealous of his writings and had lost them deliberately.[19] Hemingway now had something to hold against her—for he never forgot an injury—and would later use it to justify his callous behavior. The loss of his creative work when he was in Lausanne probably influenced his fictional portrayal of the loss of Catherine Barkley's baby in Montreux. In the novel he vicariously got rid of the unwanted infant just as Hadley (subconsciously, if not deliberately) got rid of the manuscripts that had kept them apart, day and night.

II

Hemingway's genius for friendship flowered in Paris. His mature character was fully formed; the rough edges were softened by contact with Hadley, who soothed his bitterness and restored the confidence he had lost with Agnes. His physique and character were at their very best during the years before he had achieved literary fame. He was then quite a different man from the swaggering hero of the thirties, the drunken braggart of the forties or the sad wreck of the late fifties. The flawed public persona of the older writer is so well known that readers scarcely recognize the early Hemingway; the brash egoistic image is so firmly entrenched that they fail to see the gentler, more introspective aspects of his personality—the compellingly attractive yet paradoxical mixture of sensitive charm and physical force. As Luis Quintanilla observed of his complex nature: "Ernest was noble, a good friend, generous, passionate in his ideas and feelings, sentimental at times, extremely reflective and cautious; but, above all, very, very complicated."[20]

In 1922, before he had replaced gentleness with toughness, Hemingway was a tall, handsome, muscular, broad-shouldered, brown-eyed, rosy-cheeked, square-jawed, soft-voiced young man. He was resolute in danger, as the dumbwaiter accident in high school and the trench mortar explosion in Italy had proved. He seemed innocent despite his experience, and retained his breezy midwestern cordiality. He focused all his attention on the person he was talking to and listened intently to what was said. The vitally important evidence of his son Jack must be balanced against the negative anecdotes of Hemingway's later life: "The essential [point] that is always missed is the great sense of fun he exuded and how much fun it was to be with him. His enormous appetite for life flowed over everyone around him."[21]

Gerald Murphy called Hemingway "an enveloping personality, so physically huge and forceful, and he overstated everything and talked so rapidly and so graphically and so well that you found yourself agreeing with him." Archibald MacLeish felt Hemingway "could exhaust the oxygen in a room just by coming into it."[22] Allen Tate, who thought "even his malice had a certain charm," said he and most others were compelled by the force of Hemingway's personality to do whatever he wanted. Tate (like Hadley) went night after night to the bike races though they did not interest him. Hemingway's overwhelming yet subtle power appealed not only to intellectuals but also to waiters, barmen, boxers and cowboys. Dos Passos observed that after only one day at the rough Nordquist ranch in Wyoming, "Hemingway already had the ranch hands under his thumb. They thought he was the most wonderful guy they'd ever met."[23] His acute insight allowed him to be both sympathetic about people's inner feelings and cruel about their weaknesses. Donald Ogden Stewart stated: "He was charismatic; and it was for this very reason that the mean streak startled you so when it came to the surface." Hemingway justified this aspect of his character when he wrote of his fictional hero Harry Morgan: "Since he was a boy he never had no pity for nobody. But he never had no pity for himself either."[24]

In the one year between February 1922 and January 1923 Hemingway formed some of his most important and influential friendships, if not his most enduring ones. (Though he spoke French and was acquainted with the artists Masson, Miró, Pascin and Picasso, his closest friends were American or British.) In February 1922 he met Ezra Pound; in March, Gertrude Stein, Sylvia Beach, James Joyce, Guy Hickok; in April, William Bird, Max Eastman, Lincoln Steffens, Max Beerbohm; in July, Wyndham Lewis; in October, Charles Sweeny and Henry Strater; in November, William Bolitho; in January 1923, Robert McAlmon; in February, Edward O'Brien. Between 1923 and 1925 Hemingway added to his circle of friends Morley Callaghan, Ford Madox Ford, Jean Rhys, John Dos Passos, Harold Loeb, Donald Ogden Stewart, Evan Shipman, Nathan Asch, Archibald MacLeish, Ernest Walsh, Duff Twysden, Scott Fitzgerald, Sara and Gerald Murphy. These friends would drink and travel with him, stimulate and teach him, paint and publish him.

Hemingway soon found that many of his friends had graduated from Ivy League colleges and were extremely well educated. Pound had been at the University of Pennsylvania; Stein at Radcliffe; Dos Passos and Waldo Peirce at Harvard; Bill Horne, Strater, Loeb and Fitzgerald at Princeton; MacLeish, Murphy and Donald Stewart at Yale. Hemingway, who was highly intelligent, began to educate himself with an intensive course of reading. The authors who were most important to him when he began to write serious fiction were Tolstoy, Dostoyevsky, Turgenev; Stendhal, Flaubert, Maupassant; Kipling, Conrad, Joyce, D. H. Lawrence; Twain, James, Crane, Anderson, Stein, Pound and Eliot. Five writers outside the American tradition—Tolstoy, Kipling, Joyce, D. H. Lawrence and (later) T. E. Lawrence—had (as we shall see) a profound effect on his work.[25]

A paradoxical aspect of Hemingway's friendships was the relation between his occasional but distinct anti-Semitism (which appears most notably in his animus against Robert Cohn in *The Sun Also Rises*) and his large number of Jewish friends: girls, writers, agents, publishers, painters, bullfighters, bibliographers, lawyers, fishermen, photographers, doctors, soldiers, art historians, journalists and critics.[26] Hemingway's expression of sympathy for pogrom victims in his Kansas City article "Kerensky, the Fighting Flea" suggests that his anti-Semitism developed after he had left Oak Park (for no Jews lived in that town). The workmen in Kiev, he wrote, "made a cross of ice and set it up on the frozen river. It fell over and they blamed the Jews. Then the workmen rioted, breaking into stores and smashing windows." Hemingway's fashionably hostile feelings about Jews probably began when he entered artistic circles in Paris and met wealthy Jews who lived (as Hemingway himself did) on unearned income and seemed to him to exploit, rather than contribute to, the world of art and literature. His hostility, though sometimes vociferous, was actually quite mild, for he spent a good deal of time with Jewish friends, established professional relations with them and told Harvey Breit that the only very rich people who were generous with money were Jews.[27]

Hemingway tended to form four kinds of relationships. In America, while still a novice, he formed equal friendships with high school classmates, fishing companions, war comrades and newspaper colleagues. In the early twenties, before he established his literary reputation with

The Sun Also Rises in 1926, he quickly became the good companion of struggling younger writers and the disciple of older authors who recognized his talent and helped his career. After 1926, he emphasized his originality as a writer and repudiated his literary benefactors. After 1937, when he quarreled with Dos Passos, he had no close literary friends. As he said of Harry Morgan, he had "an ability to make people like him without ever liking or trusting them in return, while at the same time convincing them warmly and heartily of his friendship."[28] During the last two decades of his life he repudiated his equals and dominated his inferiors.

III

Hemingway met Ezra Pound by chance in Sylvia Beach's bookshop soon after he returned from skiing in Chamby in early February 1922. Pound, fourteen years older than Hemingway, had been living in Europe since 1907 and in Paris since 1920. He was a close friend of Joyce, Lewis, Ford and Eliot; he had just finished editing *The Waste Land* and had been instrumental in the publication of *Ulysses,* which appeared on February 2. He had published a number of influential volumes of poetry, had begun the *Cantos* and was well connected with all the avant-garde magazines in Chicago, New York, London and Paris. Hemingway described Pound—who wore a moustache and goatee, had a staircase of russet hair, and adopted a mode of bombastic and bohemian behavior—as tall, with a patchy red beard, fine eyes and strange haircuts. Lewis, who had a wary rivalry with Pound, called him "an uncomfortably tensed, nervously straining, jerky, reddish-brown American."[29] Both Pound and Hemingway were passionately devoted to their art and soon established a dynamic creative sympathy. They liked each other personally, shared the same aesthetic aims and admired each other's work. Pound was an unofficial minister of culture who acted as midwife for new literary talent. Hemingway, who at this time of his life was most responsive to constructive criticism, was intensely interested in technique: of poetry and prose as well as of boxing and bullfighting. He came to Pound as a pupil and allowed the poet to assume his favorite role as teacher. Pound, the first significant writer to recognize Hemingway's talent, did everything possible to help him achieve success.

Pound's studio on the rue Notre Dame des Champs—well lighted, heated by a stove and decorated with Japanese paintings—was a meeting place for expatriate artists. A brilliant catalyst, Pound introduced Hemingway to Lewis, Ford, Ernest Walsh, John Peale Bishop, Malcolm Cowley, Derek Patmore and Henry Strater. The two of them played tennis and, as Hemingway explained to Sherwood Anderson, "I've been teaching Pound to box with little success. He habitually leads with his chin and has the general grace of the crayfish or crawfish. He's willing but short winded. Going over there this afternoon for another session, but there ain't much joy in it as I have to shadow box between rounds to get up a sweat."[30] The ex-cellist even tolerated Pound's bassoon music. They toured northern Italy together in February 1923 and the Hemingways rented a flat on Pound's street in January 1924. Hemingway defended Pound in one early poem, "The Soul of Spain," and borrowed the title and some lines of two others—"The Age Demanded" and "Blood is thicker than water"—from Pound's "Hugh Selwyn Mauberley."

Early and late, in "Homage to Ezra" (1925) and his affectionate portrait in *A Moveable Feast*, Hemingway praised Pound's generosity, his character and his poetry:

> We have Pound the major poet devoting, say, one-fifth of his time to poetry. With the rest of his time he tries to advance the fortunes, both material and artistic, of his friends. He defends them when they are attacked, he gets them into magazines and out of jail. He loans them money. He sells their pictures. He arranges concerts for them. . . . He advances them hospital expenses and dissuades them from suicide. And in the end a few of them refrain from knifing him at the first opportunity. . . .
>
>   Ezra was kinder and more Christian about people than I was. His own writing, when he would hit it right, was so perfect, and he was so sincere in his mistakes and so enamored of his errors, and so kind to people that I always thought of him as a sort of saint. He was also irascible but so perhaps have been many saints.[31]

Hemingway learned a great deal about how to achieve a compressed and precise Imagist style from Pound, and gratefully but uncharacteristically acknowledged his literary debt. He said Pound had taught him more about "how to write and how not to write" than any son of a bitch alive; and he insisted, in a letter to Ford, that "any poet born in this century or in the last ten years of the preceding century who can honestly say that he has not been influenced by or learned greatly from the work of Ezra Pound deserves to be pitied rather than rebuked."[32] Pound "was the man I liked and trusted the most as a critic then," he said in *A Moveable Feast*, "the man who believed in the *mot juste*—the one and only correct word to use—the man who had taught me to distrust adjectives." Hemingway's aesthetic assertion: "Prose is architecture, not interior decoration, and the Baroque is over," clearly shows the beneficial influence of Pound.[33]

Pound was indefatigable in helping Hemingway publish his early work. The first six chapters of *in our time* appeared in the "Exiles" number of *The Little Review* (Spring 1923), edited by Pound and Margaret Anderson; that book was one of six works constituting "The Inquest into the state of contemporary English prose, as edited by Ezra Pound"; Hemingway's "Neothomist Poem" was published in Pound's magazine *Exile* (Spring 1927); his early poems were reprinted in Pound's *Profile* (1932) and *Active Anthology* (1933). Hemingway also acknowledged Pound's kindness and genius in his tributes to the *Cantos* (1933) and to *Ezra Pound at Seventy* (1955).

Hemingway was a close friend until the poet moved from Paris to Rapallo in 1924. He saw Pound for the last time a decade later in Paris, when Joyce, convinced that Pound was mad and genuinely frightened of him, asked Hemingway to accompany him to a dinner at which Pound behaved very strangely. Hemingway quickly surpassed Pound's prestige and power in the literary world, but remained loyal to Pound during the poet's days of tribulation and penance at St. Elizabeth's Hospital. With MacLeish, Frost and Eliot, he was instrumental in securing Pound's release in 1958. Two years before Pound was freed, Hemingway sent him a check for a thousand dollars, which the grateful poet placed in a plexiglass paperweight as a reminder of "yr magnanimous glory." Pound and Joyce were the only literary friends with whom Hemingway never quarreled. At the end of his life Pound said: "Hemingway did not disappoint me. . . . I never saw him save at his best."[34]

IV

On December 3, 1921, five days before the Hemingways sailed for France, Sherwood Anderson wrote Gertrude Stein an enthusiastic letter and said the young author could inform her about the current trends in American literature: "Mr. Hemingway is an American writer instinctively in touch with everything worth while going on here, and I know you will find Mr. and Mrs. Hemingway delightful people to know."[35] In March they walked over to Stein's comfortable flat at 27 rue de Fleurus (between the Jardin de Luxembourg and the Boulevard Raspail), which was filled with Cubist paintings.

Stein was the Amy Lowell of Paris: she weighed two hundred pounds and was ugly, rich, poetic and domineering. Though Hemingway later compared her to a monolithic Buddha, called her "Lard-Ass" and speculated that each of her great breasts must weigh at least ten pounds, he found her attractive when they first met. He transformed her from a Jew into an Italian and concentrated—as he always did with women—on her sensual hair: "Miss Stein was very big but not tall and was heavily built like a peasant woman. She had beautiful eyes and a strong German-Jewish face that also could have been Friulano and reminded me of a northern Italian peasant woman with her clothes, her mobile face and her lovely, thick, alive immigrant hair." Hadley thought Stein's dark-skinned, prune-faced, hairy-lipped companion, Alice Toklas, resembled "a little piece of electric wire, small and fine and very Spanish looking, very dark, with piercing dark eyes."[36]

Stein, like Hemingway's father, had been trained as a doctor, though she did not complete her medical degree. But the striking resemblance to his mother made the presence of Grace immediately apparent. Grace was born in 1872; Gertrude, who was old enough to be his mother, in 1874. Both had the same imposing, statuesque appearance. Both, according to Hemingway, had emotional problems that were connected to their change of life and that provoked their quarrels with him. His comment on Stein applies perfectly to Grace, for he said that he had been loyal to that old bitch until the menopause affected her judgment and she threw him out of the house. Both women had formidable, overbearing characters: Stein "had such a personality that when she wished to win anyone over to her side she would not be resisted."[37] Both were highly talented and extremely egocentric. Both were frustrated artists who felt irritated by their thwarted careers and lack of recognition. Stein had managed to publish only three of her books since 1909 and her magnum opus, *The Making of Americans,* had remained in her desk drawer since 1911. Both women competed with Hemingway (always a mistake) and were angry when he surpassed their achievement. Grace rejected him in 1920; Gertrude rejected him in 1925. Hemingway regretted their quarrels and even remembered them fondly after Gertrude died in 1946 and Grace in 1951. Most significantly, Hemingway tried to work out with Gertrude some of the strong Oedipal feelings he had for Grace: "I always wanted to fuck her and she knew it and it was a good healthy feeling and made more sense than some of the talk."[38] Such forbidden desires could be safely expressed because he knew he could not actually sleep with a lesbian any more than he could sleep with his mother.

Their friendship ripened quickly as the unusually docile "Hemingstein" came under the powerful influence of Gertrude Stein. He liked her paintings and brandies and cakes and conversation; she liked him (Hadley was always shunted off to speak to Alice) and treated him like a promising child—a role he could not tolerate for long. She urged him to get out of journalism, which would drain away his creative energy; he was grateful for this good advice and followed it as soon as he could. She spoke enthusiastically about bullfights, expressed her admiration for the matador Joselito and encouraged him to visit Spain. When his first child was born, he asked Gertrude to be godmother. (The beautiful Bumby later recalled: "My earliest memories of Stein and Toklas were of two of the ugliest creatures I could conceive.") She taught him about the rhythm of prose and the repetition of words. When she disapproved of his early work, she commanded him to "begin over again and concentrate." She wrote the first (brief but favorable) review of his first book in November 1923. He deferred to her judgment and in August 1924 boyishly, dutifully confessed: "It used to be easy before I met you. I certainly was bad, gosh, I'm awfully bad now but it's a different kind of bad."[39] Gertrude liked this respectful attitude very much. He even played Pound to her Hemingway and published her apparently unpublishable work when Ford was absent and he became assistant editor of the *Transatlantic Review*. Since there was only one sewn and bound manuscript of *The Making of Americans*, Hemingway (not Alice) was entrusted with the job of amanuensis. He may have been the only person who read this supremely boring book to the very end.

Despite this promising beginning, with admiration and gratitude bestowed on both sides, the seeds of discord were sown from the very start. Alice was jealous of their friendship, for Stein and Toklas—though rivaled by Sylvia Beach and Adrienne Monnier, Janet Flanner and Solita Solano, Nathalie Barney and Romaine Brooks, Hilda Doolittle and

Bryher, Margaret Anderson and Jane Heap—were the leading literary lesbians. Toklas' "cruel erotic demands were much to Stein's taste. . . . In exchange she acted as Stein's willing secretary and social slave." Hemingway, who was perfectly aware of their sexual relationship and had a number of conversations with Gertrude on this subject, was able to write his lesbian story, "The Sea Change," with some authority. Stein openly defended lesbianism, contrasted it to vicious homosexuality and believed women "do nothing that they are disgusted by and nothing that is repulsive and afterwards [i.e., after sex] they are happy and they can lead happy lives together."

In a fascinating but unconvincing scene in *A Moveable Feast*, Hemingway explained that his relations with Stein ended when he unintentionally overheard a degrading and disgusting sexual quarrel between Stein and Toklas: "I heard someone speaking to Miss Stein as I had never heard one person speak to another; never, anywhere, ever. Then Miss Stein's voice came pleading and begging, saying, 'Don't, pussy. Don't. Don't, please, don't. I'll do anything, pussy, but please don't do it. Please don't. Please don't, pussy.'"[40] During this suggestively understated incident, which parodies Stein's repetition, Hemingway portrays himself as if he were entirely innocent, and had just discovered the shocking nature of their sexual relationship.

But the reasons for their quarrel were aesthetic as well as personal. According to Hadley, it was Stein, not Hemingway, who broke off relations: "I arrived with the baby one day, as usual, to stop in at Gertrude and Alice's apartment and chat for a few minutes. And Alice came to the door and she said, 'I'm very sorry. Gertrude can't see you today.' It was just a complete dismissal. And I know of no explanation. . . . It was very curious and quite sudden." Hemingway blamed the break on Alice's jealousy (when he did not blame it on Gertrude's menopause) and admitted there was not much of a future in friendship with "great women." Stein, who was fond of insisting "Twentieth century literature *is* Gertrude Stein," desperately wanted disciples.[41] But she taught Hemingway by telling him what to do rather than by showing him how to do it. Her work did not, like Hemingway's, have significant content based on extensive experience, and she remained stagnantly trapped by her own self-defeating technique. "She disliked the drudgery of revision," Hemingway said, "and the obligation to make her writing intelligible." When Hemingway went well beyond what she had achieved and created fiction that was entirely his own, she became intensely jealous of his literary success. Hemingway foreshadowed his own destructive tendency when he wrote of Stein: "She had, or Alice had, a sort of necessity to break off friendships and she only gave real loyalty to people who were inferior to her. She had to attack me because she learned to write dialogue from me just as I learned the wonderful rhythms in prose from her."[42]

As more of Stein's work began to appear in print, her stylistic faults and intellectual limitations became all too apparent. Wyndham Lewis categorically demanded: "Miss Gertrude Stein should get out of english," and launched an attack on "Trudy" in *Time and Western Man* (1927) that permanently damaged her literary reputation: "It is a little difficult to understand how she could be so stupid. . . . Creaking, groaning, and repeating itself in an insane iteration, it grows, flowers heavily, ages and dies. . . . Slab after slab of this heavy, insensitive, common prose-song churns and lumbers by. . . . It is mournful and monstrous, composed of dead and inanimate material." A few years later, her reputation as an art critic was devastated by Georges Braque: "Miss Stein understood nothing of what went on around her. . . . Miss Stein obviously saw everything from the outside and never the real struggle we were engaged in. For one who poses as an authority on the epoch it is safe to say that she never went beyond the stage of the tourist."[43]

The sharp decline in Stein's reputation, which remained secure only as long as she did not publish her work, made it all the more galling for Hemingway—after he had developed his mature style and content—to be denigrated by Lewis as well as by Harold Acton and Nathalie Barney as a dependent and derivative disciple.[44] Though Hemingway maintained "it goes against my digestion to take shots at anyone who's ever been a friend no matter how lousy they get to be finally," he began to fire at Stein before she unleashed her massive barrage in 1933. In a chapter called "The Making and Marring of Americans" in *The Torrents of Spring* (1926), a parody of Anderson that made Stein very angry, Hemingway wrote: "Gertrude Stein. . . . Ah, there was a woman! Where were her experiments in words leading her?" [45] His poem of that year, "Portrait of a Lady," alluded to her unwillingness to work at revision and said: "Gertrude Stein was never crazy / Gertrude Stein was very lazy." *The Sun Also Rises* countered her *mot* about the Lost Generation with a hopeful epigraph from Ecclesiastes. In a humorous version of "The True Story of My Break with Gertrude Stein," which made news in *The New Yorker* in 1927, Hemingway gave a version of Stein's *froi-*

deur that was quite close to Hadley's account: "I would come to the door of Gertrude Stein's house and ring the bell nobody would answer. . . . Occasionally a maid would come to the door and say, 'No, Miss Stein (or *Mademoiselle Stein,* as the maid called her in French) is not at home *(pas chez elle).*'"[46]

These clever cracks were more than sufficient to provoke the most massive attack on Hemingway since the Austrian trench mortars in 1918. Stein enjoyed ordering Basket, her pampered white poodle, to "Play Hemingway, be fierce." But she had also studied his weaknesses and knew how to hurt him. Her *Autobiography of Alice B. Toklas* (1933) stabbed at Hemingway's most vulnerable points and was all the more wounding because of the core of truth at the heart of each bitter accusation. Hemingway prided himself on his courage; Stein said he was "yellow." He believed he had created an original style; she demoted him to dull-witted disciple "who does it without understanding it, in other words who takes training." He boasted of his sporting skills; she said: "Hemingway was teaching some young chap how to box. The boy did not know how, but by accident he knocked Hemingway out." He felt he had stamina and endurance; she said Hemingway "was easily tired. He used to get quite worn out walking from his house to ours." He boasted of his toughness; she said: "Ernest is very fragile, whenever he does anything sporting something breaks, his arm, his leg, or his head." He thought he was sophisticated and cosmopolitan; she reduced him to an Oak Park provincial and said he was "ninety percent Rotarian." Anderson would not retaliate, but he enjoyed Stein's revenge and praised her for slicing "such big patches of skin off Hemmy with your delicately held knife."[47]

Hemingway, who was supposed to have sent her the legendary wire: "A bitch is a bitch is a bitch," defended himself in a letter to Pound and then launched his own prolonged counterattack. He resented being called a mere epigone of Anderson and Stein and correctly predicted that they would be remembered as teachers rather than as writers. He denied the charge that he was a derivative author, and said that Stein had given him a great deal of useful advice as well as a lot of shit. He had always been fond of Stein and loyal to her, and had kept her work in the *Transatlantic Review* when Ford refused to print another word of it.[48]

In two Introductions written in 1934, the year after the *Autobiography* was published, Hemingway made gratuitous slurs on Stein's lesbianism ("a woman who isn't a woman") and her exploitation of his name to help the sale of her memoirs.[49] The attack continued the following year, when the quarrel became notorious and one critic noted that Hemingway "went all the way to Africa to hunt and then when he thought he had found a rhinoceros, it turned out to be Gertrude Stein." In *Green Hills of Africa* he scorned the charge that he was yellow; condemned her malice and self-praise, her inability to write dialogue and her need to attack the man who had taught *her* how to write. In *For Whom the Bell Tolls* (1940) Robert Jordan clumsily parodied Stein's well-known phrase, punned on the meaning of her German name (stone) and repeated: "A rose is a rose is an onion. . . . An onion is an onion is an onion . . . a stone is a stein is a rock is a boulder is a pebble."[50] In the *Paris Review* interview conducted at the end of his life, Hemingway still found it necessary to deny her influence and repeat the charge that *The Sun Also Rises* had taught her to write dialogue.

Since Hemingway outlived Stein by fifteen years, he had the last word in the quarrel that was protracted beyond the grave. In three intriguing chapters of *A Moveable Feast* he condemned her jealousy of the only two contemporaries he admired: "If you brought up Joyce twice, you would not be invited back. . . . Her dislike of Ezra [who called her "an old tub of guts"], skillfully and maliciously put, [was] invented years later." And he accused her of precisely his own fault: "I cannot remember Gertrude Stein ever speaking well of any writer who had not written favorably about her work or done something to advance her career except for Ronald Firbank and, later, Scott Fitzgerald."

Since Stein had a strong maternal hold on Hemingway, the loss of her friendship and viciousness of her attack caused a profound and permanent wound. It forced him to return repeatedly to that bitter quarrel in many of his writings from 1926 until the very end of his life. A letter of July 1948 (two years after her death) summarized his extraordinarily complex feelings and honestly emphasized the sexual aspects of their relationship: his love for her, her sensual hair, her lesbianism and Alice's jealousy:

> I always loved her very much and as you said I never counter-punched when she left herself wide open. . . . I liked her better before she cut her hair and that was sort of a turning point in all sorts of things. She used to talk to me about homosexuality and how it was fine in and for women and no good in men and I used to listen and learn.[51]

V

The den mother of the petulant pack of expatriates—who competed, exploited and quarreled bitterly with each other—was the good Sylvia Beach. She had grown up in Princeton, spent two years in Spain, done Red Cross work in Serbia and, after the war, opened Shakespeare and Company, which sold and lent English-language books. Her shop rivaled Pound's studio and Stein's salon as a gathering place for writers. It was located at 12 rue de l'Odéon, a street that extends from the Boulevard St.-Germain toward the façade of the theater and is still lined with bookshops. Beach published *Ulysses,* idolized Joyce and sold his books as if they were saints' medals in a cathedral. Hemingway wrote that "Sylvia had a lively, sharply sculptured face, brown eyes that were as alive as a small animal's and as gay as a young girl's, and wavy brown hair that was brushed back from her fine forehead."[52]

A photograph of Sylvia and Hemingway, with heavily bandaged head, taken in March 1928 after his accident with a falling skylight, captures the essence of their relationship. Part of the shop's name—"eare and Comp"—appears in faint letters above the door and Joyce's photo can be seen on a shelf in the window (between the two assistants). On the mild spring day she wears a tied scarf, tailored suit, white stockings and patent leather shoes. He is conservatively dressed in a rumpled double-breasted suit and thick unpolished shoes, and cautiously carries a topcoat. Sylvia gazes with girlish admiration at his white badge of courage while he stares directly at the camera with a look of sardonic resignation.

Sylvia, who was always kind to Hemingway, introduced him in March 1922 to Joyce: "He was tall and thin and he had a moustache and a small beard that grew straight up and down on his chin and he wore thick, thick glasses and walked with his head held very high."[53] Joyce's unusual face was hollowed out, with jutting brow and jaw, like a carved primitive mask. He liked to play the amusing Irishman and was learned, witty, humane. He had an unaffected love of good food and plentiful drink, and took Hemingway on his alcoholic sprees. The timid, weak-eyed genius would get into a drunken argument with a stranger he could scarcely see and then tell his huge companion: "Deal with him, Hemingway! Deal with him!" Hemingway, who frequently had to carry the Irishman home after an evening's drinking, recalled that Nora Joyce would open the door and angrily exclaim: "Well, here comes James Joyce the writer, drunk again with Ernest Hemingway."[54] Joyce, who envied his friend's physical strength, extensive travels and violent experience, asked Hemingway in 1933 if his own books "were too suburban. He said that was what got him down sometimes. Mrs. Joyce said, 'Ah Jim could do with a spot of that lion hunting.' "

Though Hemingway made occasional cracks about Joyce's feebleness, conceit and need for admiration, his friendship with Joyce, as with Pound, transcended literary rivalry. He was furious when Samuel Roth pirated *Ulysses* and paid Joyce no royalties; and thought the Nobel Prize of 1930 should have been awarded to Joyce or Pound instead of to Sinclair Lewis: "Jim Joyce was the only alive writer that I ever respected. He had his problems but he could write better than anyone I knew. Ezra was nice and kind and friendly and a beautiful poet and critic. G[ertrude] Stein was nice until she had the menopause. But who I respected was Mr. Joyce."[55]

Joyce read Hemingway's manuscripts (a rare privilege for a young author); Hemingway studied Joyce's works and used the techniques in his own work. *Dubliners* (1914)—not the stories of Anderson and Stein —provided the model for the thematically connected and structurally unified stories of *In Our Time*. Joyce taught him how to pare down his work to the essentials and to suggest rather than state his meaning. Hemingway's story "Indian Camp" first appeared in the *Transatlantic Review* (1924) under the Joycean title "Work in Progress"; there was an echo of *Ulysses* in "Soldier's Home," and the sexual soliloquies of Marie Morgan and Dorothy Hollis in *To Have and Have Not* were clearly based on those of Molly Bloom.

In March 1922 Hemingway also formed a less vital but more equal friendship with Guy Hickok, whom he met at the weekly luncheon meetings of the Anglo-American Press Association. Hickok was born in Mecca, Ohio, in 1888, worked as a teenager on *McClure's* magazine when Willa Cather was on the staff, attended Oberlin College (like Ed Hemingway), and was church and political editor of the *Brooklyn Eagle* before he was sent to Paris as bureau chief. He "was quiet, modest to the point of often being diffident, straight as an arrow, with strong convictions between right and wrong but very tolerant of the weakness and disreputable traits in others."[56] His feature articles on Hemingway appeared in the *Eagle* in 1925 and 1928. Lincoln Steffens' *Autobiography* describes a conversation in the *Eagle* office when Hemingway, who liked to boast of his sexual exploits, gloomily said there was no sure contraceptive. The kindly journalist Krum, who appears briefly as Jake Barnes' friend in *The Sun Also Rises*, seems to be based on Hickok.

In March 1928, when the value of the dollar doubled after a huge devaluation of the French franc, the two friends took a ten-day car trip through Mussolini's Italy in Hickok's old Ford. They drove down the Riviera coast to Pisa, through Florence to Rimini on the Adriatic, back across northern Italy to Genoa and up to Ventimiglia on the French border. During the trip they accidentally lunched at a bordello, transported a Fascist who insisted on riding on the running board of their car and had to pay an extortionate fine for dirty license plates. Hemingway first described this journey in a newspaper article, "Italy—1927." He then published it as a story, in which Hickok appears as Guy, "Che Ti Dice La Patria?" The title was taken from a patriotic slogan of D'Annunzio.

VI

Wyndham Lewis described his dramatic introduction to Hemingway in July 1922 when he pushed open the door to Pound's studio and saw "a splendidly built young man, stripped to the waist, and with a torso of dazzling white, standing not far from me. He was tall, handsome, and serene, and was repelling with his boxing gloves—I thought without undue exertion—a hectic assault of Ezra's. After a final swing at the dazzling solar plexus (parried effortlessly by the trousered statue) Pound fell back upon his settee. The young man was Hemingway." In *A Moveable Feast* Hemingway distorted Lewis' motives and asserted: "I wanted us to stop but Lewis insisted we go on, and I could see that, knowing nothing about what was going on, he was waiting, hoping to see Ezra hurt."[57] Hemingway failed to see that Lewis—who was extremely fond of Pound and certainly did not want to see him injured —was absorbed in the energy and design of the fight. Hemingway, notorious for beating up much older or weaker men in friendly boxing matches, revealed his own aggressive feelings for Pound, a serious literary competitor, by transferring them to Lewis.

Hemingway also distorted Lewis' character after meeting him with Archibald MacLeish in December 1927, just after the appearance of Lewis' vitriolic *Time and Western Man*. Hemingway, who had recently published *The Sun Also Rises,* had doubts about the dialogue of the English Brett Ashley, but Lewis assured him that his ear for speech was good and there was no occasion for anxiety. MacLeish recalled: "I took Lewis to lunch in Paris and got Hemingway to come along. Walking back to the Left Bank E.H. said: 'Did you notice? He kept his gloves on all through lunch.' . . . Since I hadn't and since he hadn't the question became lurid and memorable. But even as early as that Hemingway had decided not to care for him." Hemingway had undoubtedly heard about Lewis' notorious "paranoia" and decided to contribute his share to the legend that was partly created by Lewis' enemies. In *Across the River* Hemingway approves of the vigilant Colonel Cantwell, who sits defensively but securely at a table in a Venetian restaurant and "had both his flanks covered and rested solidly against the corner of the room."[58] But when Lewis, who also liked to sit in a corner with his back to the wall, behaved in a similar fashion, Hemingway criticized his strange habits. Hemingway, like Lewis, created his own legend and was aggressive, hypersensitive, eager for recognition and intolerant of criticism. The two colossal egos were bound to clash.

Lewis had established his reputation before the war as the leader of the Vorticist group of painters as well as one of the most lively and stimulating forces in modern literature. He published his classic novel, *Tarr,* in 1918. Hemingway, who was intensely jealous of Pound's long-standing friendship and passionate advocacy of Lewis' work, took an instant dislike to both his painting and his writing. He was rather intimidated by Lewis, who, unlike Pound, had no interest in helping Hemingway. In 1925, when Pound was planning an issue dedicated to Lewis in Ernest Walsh's *This Quarter,* Hemingway gratuitously warned Walsh that Pound was trying to unload Lewis' rubbish in the little magazine. He exclaimed that Lewis was a rotten artist and writer, that his reputation was based on publicity. Lewis was finished and dead, and could never be revived by a tribute in *This Quarter.*[59]

When Lewis' *Paleface* (first published in his magazine *The Enemy* in September 1927) blasted the exaltation of Indian and Negro primitivism in Anderson's *Dark Laughter* (1925) and D. H. Lawrence's *Mornings in Mexico* (1927), and praised Hemingway's satiric parody of Anderson in *The Torrents of Spring,* Hemingway trimmed his sails to suit the prevailing current. On October 27 he responded enthusiastically to Lewis' work: "I am very glad you liked *The Torrents of Spring* and thought you destroyed the Red and Black enthusiasm very finely in

Paleface. That terrible ——— about the nobility of any gent belonging to another race than our own (whatever it is) was worth checking. Lawrence you know was Anderson's God in the old days—and you can trace his effect all through A[nderson]'s stuff. . . . In fact *The Torrents of Spring* was, in fiction form, performing the same purgative function as *Paleface.*"

The very next month, however, Hemingway discovered that Lewis had attacked his own work, exposed his foolish indebtedness to Stein, mocked Walsh's praise of Hemingway and launched a powerful assault on Pound in "The Revolutionary Simpleton" chapter of *Time and Western Man.* Angered by these treacherous attacks (a mere warm-up for Lewis' massive onslaught on Hemingway in 1934), Hemingway once again changed his mind about Lewis. He renewed his own attack, in a letter to Pound, on Lewis' fascistic political ideas, unconvincingly accused him of stealing *Paleface* from *The Torrents of Spring* and suggested that Lewis had (noncreative) syphilis:

> Have been reading works of your good friend Wyndham in which it appears that [the] principal fault of mine is Blood Lust—destruction of Bulls—Men—Women doubtless too and no doubt Dogs—(see bitches). It appears that I've been urged on to this by you, you son of a bitch, who forced poor old Hem into these Bloody deeds through yr Influence. (And you always protesting against my youthful violence.) Well well.
> Shit, Shit. Fascist! . . .
> You it seems are a parasite. Wyndham is a true genius and original artist. The poor bird got a god knows how many page piece (Essay) entitled *Paleface* out of a book called *The Torrents of Spring.* For the old spyrochetes (or however you spell the little fellows) after speeding up the brain and production will finally lead to a decline of some sort. Or has he never had syph? If not, we may get a lot more numbers of The Enemy.[60]

Hemingway changed his tack again in October 1932. He repressed Lewis' attack on his work, remembered only the praise in *Paleface,* told Jonathan Cape that Lewis had written favorably about *The Torrents of Spring* and suggested that Cape ask Lewis to write the preface to the English edition of *Torrents.*

Hemingway's hostility was exacerbated anew by Lewis' witty and incisive chapter on his work in *Men Without Art* (1934)—a title probably influenced by Hemingway's *Men Without Women* (1927). Lewis' influential essay (like Stein's *Autobiography,* published the previous

year) criticized the very things Hemingway prided himself on: his originality, sophistication and fictional heroes. It also shot barbs into his most
vulnerable spots: his embarrassing indebtedness to Stein, his lack of
political awareness and his passive characters who have the soul of a
dumb ox: "This brilliant Jewish lady has made a *clown* of him by teaching Ernest Hemingway her baby-talk! . . . [She has] strangely hypnot-
ized him with her repeating habits and her *faux-naif* prattle . . .
[though] he has never taken it over into a gibbering and baboonish
stage as has Miss Stein." Lewis continued his argument by implying,
rather unfairly, that Hemingway's characters reveal his own lack of
ideology and intelligence: "Hemingway invariably invokes a dull-witted, bovine, monosyllabic simpleton, a lethargic and stuttering dummy
. . . a super-innocent, queerly-sensitive, village-idiot of a few words and
fewer ideas." His characters are *"those to whom things are done,* in
contrast to those who have executive will and intelligence."[61] Lewis'
criticism enraged the victim. He read the essay in the Shakespeare and
Company bookshop and seemed to confirm the charge that he was
anti-intellectual by punching a vase of tulips on Sylvia's table and sending the fragments flying across the room.

In his fury, Hemingway failed to notice that Lewis also praised his
work. In *Rude Assignment* he said: "I have always had a great respect
for Hemingway. . . . He is the greatest writer in America and (odd
coincidence) one of the most successful"; while in Canada, he taught
and lectured on *For Whom the Bell Tolls.* Hemingway's cruelty in *A
Moveable Feast* was a mean response to Lewis' intelligent criticism:
"Wyndham Lewis wore a wide black hat, like a character in the quarter,
and was dressed like someone out of *La Bohème.* He had a face that
reminded me of a frog, not a bullfrog but just any frog, and Paris was
too big a puddle for him. . . . I do not think I had ever seen a nastier-
looking man. . . . Lewis did not show evil; he just looked nasty. . . . The
eyes had been those of an unsuccessful rapist."[62]

The most vicious portrait in *A Moveable Feast* is horribly effective
(in America, Lewis is still remembered more as an unsuccessful rapist
than as a great artist) but morally dishonest. The portrait ostensibly
reflects Hemingway's view of Lewis on their first encounter in Paris in
July 1922 ("this was how he seemed to me on the first day I ever met
him"), but it is not an accurate view of Lewis at that time. It is actually
influenced by Hemingway's hostility *after* the publication of "The
Dumb Ox" in 1934. Lewis had abandoned his wild bohemian dress in

1914 and had a major reputation in 1922, before Hemingway had published his first story. Yet he portrays Lewis as a fake bohemian and an insignificant writer. Lewis may have seemed frog-like after his four serious operations in the mid-1930s, but in 1922 he was still a strikingly handsome man and a great success with numerous beautiful, rich and artistic women. He was not (like Kreisler in *Tarr*) a rapist. In Hemingway's portrait, Lewis neither says nor does anything that is unpleasant: Hemingway imputes all the base motives to him. He tells Hadley that Lewis is nasty and she implicitly agrees with his judgment without meeting Lewis.

Finally, Hemingway repeats and exaggerates a discreditable anecdote about Lewis as a pedantic and mechanical "Measuring Worm," which he picked up, second hand, from Stein, who had been condemned by Lewis and was not a disinterested witness. Hemingway's portrait of Lewis also exposed his own weaknesses, for both writers frequently pilloried people who had tried to help them and used their discarded benefactors as satiric victims.

Despite all this, Hemingway's attitude to Lewis—as well as to other friends he attacked—was not entirely negative. His feelings were too complex to be expressed entirely in black and white. His magnanimity overcame his animosity—for he was a generous man—when Lewis was impoverished during the summer of 1944 and desperate to secure a portrait commission in St. Louis. After the young Marshall McLuhan approached Edna Gellhorn, then Hemingway's mother-in-law, and suggested that Lewis would be the best artist for the job, she phoned Hemingway in Cuba to ask about Lewis' credentials. Hemingway, mollified by Lewis' admiring account of him in *Blasting and Bombardiering* (1937), spoke of the author of "The Dumb Ox" in the highest terms and urged Mrs. Gellhorn to do anything she could for him. Thanks to his old enemy, Lewis got the commission.

The same pattern of jealousy, hostility and generosity marked Hemingway's friendship with the minor *littérateur* Robert McAlmon. William Carlos Williams portrayed him as Jack Murry in *A Voyage to Pagany* (1928), and described "the firm, thin-lipped lower face, jaw slightly thrust out, the cold blue eyes, the long, downward pointing, slightly-hooked straight nose, the lithe, straight, athletic build."[63] McAlmon, like all the Paris friends, was older than Hemingway. He was born in 1896, grew up in California and came to Paris after the war. He was a homosexual and had married a lesbian in 1921. His wife, who wrote under the name Bryher, was the daughter of the English ship-ping millionaire Sir John Ellerman. When she left McAlmon to live with Richard Aldington's wife (and Pound's ex-fiancée), Hilda Doolittle, Ell-erman settled $75,000 on her husband, who was then called Robber McAlimony. He went on and partially paid for Hemingway's first trip to Pamplona in the summer of 1923; and his private press, Contact Editions, published Hemingway's first book, *Three Stories and Ten Poems,* in October 1923, when Hemingway was unable to place his work anywhere else.

McAlmon, who had a loose and caustic tongue, satirized Heming-way's transition from boxer to bullfighter: "Before leaving Paris, Hem-ingway had been much of a shadow-boxer. As he approached a café he would prance about, sparring at shadows, his lips moving, calling his imaginary opponent's bluff. Upon returning from Spain, he substituted shadow-bullfighting for shadow-boxing. The amount of imaginary cape work and sword thrusts he made in those days was formidable." McAlmon knew Hemingway well, was perceptive and saw the paradox-ical aspects of his character:

> At times he was deliberately hard-boiled and case-hardened. Again he appeared deliberately innocent, sentimental, the hurt, soft, but fairly sensitive boy trying to conceal hurt, wanting to be brave, not bitter or cynical but being somewhat both, and somehow on the defensive, suspi-cions lurking in his peering analytic glances at a person with whom he was talking. He approached a café with a small-boy, tough-guy swagger, and before strangers of whom he was doubtful, a potential snarl of scorn played on his large-lipped, rather loose mouth.[64]

McAlmon's alcoholism, homosexuality and malice inevitably led to the rupture of their precarious relationship. Unlike Hemingway's friendship with Pound, Stein, Joyce, Beach and Hickok, his connection with McAlmon was based not on mutual respect, but on McAlmon's money and his willingness to help Hemingway. He told friends that McAlmon, always irresponsible and unpleasant when drunk, ruined their comradely evenings. Hemingway always found it hard to watch his publisher vomit after his fourth whiskey. When McAlmon spread the nasty rumors that Hemingway had beaten Hadley when she was pregnant and (in a perfect reflection of his own marriage) that Heming-way was a fairy and his second wife, Pauline, a lesbian, Hemingway threatened to beat that thin, disappointed, half-assed, fairy ass-licking, fake-husband, literary type.[65] The long-delayed showdown came when Jimmy Charters opened his new Parisian bar in 1934. Hemingway accused McAlmon of malicious gossip, escorted him out to the street and smashed his passive opponent with a short left hook. Yet, as Morley Callaghan explained, McAlmon "was wrong in thinking Ernest, in his success, had forgotten about him and wouldn't lift a hand to help him. Within a year, back in New York, I was to learn that Hemingway had [tried to] persuade Perkins at Scribner's to publish a book of McAlmon's."[66]

5

European Reporter
1922–1923

> He had seen the world change;
> not just the events.
>
> "The Snows of Kilimanjaro"

I

Hemingway made a successful assault on the literary beachhead soon after reaching Paris and established his reputation among the best writers before he had actually published any fiction. At the same time, fortified by marriage and stimulated by travel, he worked as a reporter during his first two years in Europe while making the difficult transition from journalism to art. His job with the *Toronto Star Weekly* gave him freedom to travel and to write about the stories that interested him. He was not a foreign correspondent, responsible for reporting the news of the day, but a feature writer who interpreted events and mailed in his stories.

Hemingway, who believed that "it's very hard to get anything true on anything you haven't seen yourself,"[1] traveled nearly ten thousand miles by train during his first year in Europe. His travels to report on the Genoa Conference in April 1922, the Greco-Turkish War in October, the Lausanne Conference in November and conditions in the French-occupied Ruhr in April–May 1923 were interspersed with frequent pleasure trips. Apart from the two journeys to Chamby in January and May 1922, he and Hadley toured the Black Forest in August (when he first grew a moustache), skied near Lausanne in December, visited Rapallo in January 1923, toured northern Italy in February, skied in Cortina in March and April, and traveled around Spain in May and July.

Hemingway was always searching for fresh experience: new countries and cultures; new excitement in sports and bullfighting; new places to hunt and fish; new wives and new wars.

Hemingway's journalism reflected his travels. He wrote stories on the conferences and the war as well as on French Royalists, Italian Fascists and some of the leading political figures of the time: Chicherin, Hamid Bey, Poincaré, Clemenceau and Mussolini. He also contributed many articles of social commentary on life in Europe: on the cost of living, currency exchange and German inflation as well as on Swiss resorts, French clothes, rug vendors, night life, Russian émigrés, the Legion of Honor and a flight from Paris to Strasbourg. Finally, he wrote of his sporting activities: fishing, skiing, lugeing and bobsledding. Pound admired his genial debunking of received ideas. Most colleagues, early and late, noticed that Hemingway, while thoroughly professional, was cynical about his journalism and always reserved the best material for his fiction: "He didn't give a damn about it, except that it provided some much needed funds and gave him an association with other writers."

Hemingway's careful observation of international politics and war, his close contact with seasoned reporters and soldiers, his need to make his own way without education or money, his desire to pit himself against obstacles, fight for his beliefs and take charge of the situation, inevitably brought out the aggressive and violent aspects of his character. "To know a man nowadays," Malraux observed, "is above all to know the element of the irrational in him, the part he is unable to control."[2] Hemingway had a short fuse and a bad temper, liked to be considered a tough guy rather than a writer. He wrote that a man in a rage is like an animal, that bullying is the first step toward cowardice, but he himself preyed on the weaknesses of others. In conversation, in letters and in print, he attacked Victorian morality, his mother and all castrating women, competing writers, hostile critics, phonies and fags. He hated social refinement, which he considered artificial and false, and defined the writer in opposition to intellectuals (like Henry James), aesthetes (like Marcel Proust) or invalids (like Franz Kafka). Hemingway was perhaps the first major writer to combine athletic skill and literary talent.

Hemingway often acted out his aggressive attitudes and believed: "When that moment [the time to fight] arrives, whether it is in a barroom fight or in a war, the thing to do is to hit your opponent the first punch and hit him as hard as possible."[3] Since Hemingway was a powerful man—he was six feet tall and weighed two hundred pounds—his punches, frequently directed at weaker opponents, had disastrous and discreditable results. In January 1922 he sparred with Lewis Galantière, who, when he first arrived in Paris, had taken him to lunch and helped him find his way around the city. After a few rounds, Galantière stopped, took off his right glove and put on his spectacles. Hemingway continued to shadow box, suddenly struck out, hit Galantière in the face and broke his glasses.

This ugly pattern—transforming a friendly match into a brutal assault, beating a weaker man, attempting an irrelevant justification—recurred during the Lausanne Conference in November 1922. A journalist remembered:

> With G. Ward Price, veteran correspondent of the London *Daily Mail*, we all met in the baths at Spa, where there is a gymnasium. Boxing gloves were hanging there and Price, then about 40 odd, I should say, suggested he would like to spar with someone. Hemmie immediately accepted and although he even then outweighed Price by 20 or 30 pounds and was only in his early twenties, he began to slug Price unmercifully. He knocked Price down, bloodied his nose and cut his lip. Afterwards Hemmie remarked, "I never liked guys who wear monocles."

His behavior with Price was even more callous than with Galantière. He considered the monocle a sign of intolerable affectation and in "The Snows of Kilimanjaro" condemned the Rumanian Dadaist Tristan Tzara, "who always wore a monocle." As if to atone for his inexcusable behavior, Hemingway praised the pugilistic skill of the dandified Ward Price in an article of 1935 and made the unusual admission that (while exhausted and hung over) he had been beaten by Price in boxing: "The very debonair, handsomely built, tall, one hundred and eighty pound, perfectly conditioned Price would stick the finest left hand I've ever seen out of the professional ring in your correspondent's puss for a period of a half an hour."[4]

Hemingway, who later used a giant tuna as a punching bag when he could not find a human victim, repeated his brutal behavior on at least four other occasions. In April 1924 he explained to Harold Loeb that he felt like "blasting the hell" out of the young architect Paul Fisher—the impulse had been simply too strong to resist. In 1934 he punished McAlmon for his malicious gossip. In May 1935 he knocked out the wealthy publisher Joseph Knapp. And in February 1936 he beat up the poet Wallace Stevens.

II

Hemingway's first major assignment was the Genoa Economic Conference—the first international gathering since the 1919 peace talks at Versailles. His trip to postwar Italy began ominously and led to a minor reenactment of the trench mortar wound. After the janitor had forgotten to adjust the safety valve, the hot-water heater in his bathroom in the Hotel Gênes exploded and fragments of metal wounded his torso. Max Eastman, who reminded Hemingway of a jolly midwestern college professor, said with some exaggeration that it "blew [Hemingway] halfway down the hall."

Another journalist, George Seldes—who saw no signs of Hemingway's injuries or his nascent genius—thought he was a good reporter. He was confident but not arrogant, sure of himself but eager to learn from older men, attractive and well liked by his colleagues. Lincoln Steffens found him "a charming companion. Big and strong, handsome, he was physically alive, mentally forever at play." Steffens and Seldes "gave him a quick course in cablese," Seldes recalled, "and within a week Hemingway mastered it. He came in one night and said: 'Stef, look at this cable: no fat, no adjectives, no adverbs—nothing but blood and bones and muscle. It's great. It's a new language.' Hemingway's writings after the 1922 Genoa experience are considerably changed."[5]

Since Hemingway felt Machiavelli's *The Prince* could be used as a textbook for all conferences, he did not report the discussions of war reparations and disarmament. He focused instead on the personalities of the leading statesmen and shrewdly revealed their radical limitations. The Soviet Foreign Minister, Georgi Chicherin (whose delegation, fearing bombs, stayed on the Riviera at Santa Margherita), was obsessed by his gaudy uniform; Maxim Litvinov had a ham-like face; Karl Wirth, the German chancellor, looked like the tuba player in a Bavarian band. Hemingway did, however, recognize and respect a capable and intelligent statesman like Walther Rathenau.

The Genoa Conference allowed Hemingway to judge the postwar leaders and to observe the turbulent conditions in Italy just before the Fascist takeover. During 1920–22 a civil war raged in Italy between the Fascists and the Socialists, in which three hundred of the former and three thousand of the latter were killed in riots. After a no-confidence vote, the nation had no government for several weeks in July 1922.

3. *Greece and Turkey, 1922*

When a general strike was declared the following month, the Fascists aligned themselves with the police and public opinion, which called for authoritarian rule. The successive governments—weak, confused, paralyzed—could not control the economic chaos or the civil war, and took no action when the Fascists mobilized their cohorts. The March on Rome, which established the Fascist government in October 1922, was neither a revolution nor a *coup d'état*. It was actually "a comfortable train ride, followed by a petty demonstration, all in response to an express invitation from the monarch."[6]

Hemingway returned to Italy with Hadley in June 1922 for a disappointing visit to his war sites: Schio, Lake Garda, Mestre and Fossalta. He also interviewed Mussolini, then editor of the influential *Popolo d'Italia* in Milan. He called Mussolini "a big, brown-faced man with a high forehead, a slow-smiling mouth, and large, expressive hands" and quoted his prediction: "We have force enough to overthrow any government that may try to oppose or destroy us." At this time, Hemingway still admired anyone who had been under fire in the war and took Mussolini's word about his own heroic exploits: "as soon as Italy entered the war [he] enlisted in the crack 'Bersagliere' [sharpshooters] corps as a private. [He was] severely wounded in the fighting on the Carso plateau and several times decorated for valor." But during World War Two, in the patriotic Introduction to his anthology *Men at War*, he radically revised his view of Mussolini's military career, made rare use of psychoanalytic terminology and accused the dictator of the kind of fear he himself had experienced in the Great War: "I have often thought that all his martial bombast and desire for military glory was a defense mechanism, formed against his own knowledge of how frightened he had been in the world war and the ignominious exit he had made from it at the first opportunity."[7]

Hemingway's second interview with Mussolini, which took place in Lausanne in November 1922 after the Duce had seized power, was more perceptive and showed how Hemingway's political ideas had matured in five months. He now saw beneath Mussolini's mask, said: "there is something wrong, even histrionically, with a man who wears white spats with a black shirt," called him "the biggest bluff in Europe" and concluded: "you will see the weakness in his mouth which forces him to scowl the famous Mussolini scowl." The poem Hemingway wrote after the conference and had published in *The Little Review* (Spring 1923) was even more caustic: "MUSSOLINI has nigger eyes and a bodyguard and has his / picture taken reading a book upside down."

It is not surprising, therefore, that when Hemingway was planning a trip to Italy in January 1923 he half-seriously asked Pound: "Can I . . . preserve my incognito among your fascist pals? Or are they liable to give Hadley castor oil? Mussolini told me at Lausanne, you know, that I couldn't ever live in Italy again."[8] Hemingway was outraged by the murder of the Socialist deputy Giacomo Matteotti in June 1924 and by the pardon of his murderers just one year after the crime. His insight into the character of Mussolini and the nature of Fascism, which now seems so obvious, was quite extraordinary in 1922. When the Duce took power—and long afterwards—he was widely praised and admired by such notable Italians as D'Annunzio, Pirandello, Marinetti, Puccini, Marconi and Croce (who later recanted), as well as by eminent Englishmen like Churchill and Shaw.

III

"In the fall I went out to Constantinople, Anatolia, Smyrna, Thrace etc. as war correspondent for The Toronto Star and the International News Service,"[9] Hemingway wrote with characteristic exaggeration, for the war was over before he arrived and he never reached either Anatolia or Smyrna. After a serious quarrel with Hadley, who did not want him to go, he sprained his ankle and broke his typewriter on the way to the station. He took the costliest train in Europe, the Orient Express, through the Simplon Pass and down to Sofia, and sent his first dispatch from Bulgaria. He reached Constantinople on September 30, 1922, stayed at the Hôtel de Londres and soon contracted malaria.

Hemingway arrived after the defeat, the retreat and the evacuation of the Greek army from Smyrna, after the fire and the massacre that followed the Turkish occupation of the city. But he described the physical squalor and political situation in "Constan" (still occupied by British, French and Italian troops); reported second hand (for journalists were excluded) the signing of the armistice treaty at Mudanya, on the Sea of Marmara, which halted the Turkish pursuit of the Greeks into Europe. He narrated, from Muratli in Eastern Thrace and from Madame Marie's lice-ridden hotel in Adrianople, near the Greek and Bulgarian frontier, the desperate flight of the Greek refugees toward Karagatch, on the Greek side of the Maritza River. He sent dispatches on the character of the Turkish general Mustafa Kemal and his involvement in Afghan politics. Hemingway was cynical about politicians, compassionate about civilian victims and sympathetic to the cruelly victorious Turks rather than the Greeks (both sides had committed atrocities). The Greeks were Christians, allies in the Great War and losers in the religious struggle against the Moslems that went back to the Crusades and, more recently, to the Greek War of Independence in the 1820s, which had stirred the soul of Byron. But Hemingway was furious about the murderous incompetence of the Greek officers.

Hemingway's brief involvement in the aftermath of the Greco-Turkish War produced fourteen articles for the *Toronto Star* and was immensely important in his development as a writer. The war inspired three superb vignettes from his first mature work, *in our time* (1924), which were as good, stylistically, as anything he ever wrote; a reference in the deleted conclusion to "Big Two-Hearted River" (1925); "On the Quai at Smyrna" (1930); two passages in *Death in the Afternoon* (1932); and two crucial flashbacks in his greatest story, "The Snows of Kilimanjaro" (1936). The retreat from Caporetto in *A Farewell to Arms* (1929) and the plight of the Spanish Civil War refugee in "The Old Man at the Bridge" (1938) also recall the Greek retreat through Eastern Thrace.

From the beginning of his career Hemingway sought to base his fiction on reality, but he tried to distill the essence of the experience so that what he made up was truer than what he remembered.[10] The vignettes from *in our time* illustrated his new aesthetic theory: "If a writer of prose knows enough about what he is writing about he may omit things that he knows and the reader, if the writer is writing truly enough, will have a feeling of those things as strongly as though the writer had stated them. The dignity of movement of an ice-berg is due to only one-eighth of it being above water."[11] He thus deliberately excluded all the political background of the Greco-Turkish War and objectively reported only the immediate events in order to achieve a concentration and intensity of focus—a spotlight rather than a stage.

He explained to Pound that in *in our time*, "The refugees leave Thrace, due to the Greek ministers, who are shot. The whole thing closes with the talk with the King of Greece and his Queen in their Garden."[12] Though Hemingway achieved the effect of immediate experience, he did not witness the executions of the Greek ministers nor talk to the king in his garden; and the historical links between these episodes are never made clear. But when we know what has been omitted—the history and geography of the Greco-Turkish War—we can see how these works evolved from his honestly acquired knowledge, understand as well as feel the powerful force of these episodes.

Smyrna (now Izmir) had been offered by the Allies to entice Greece into the war against the Central Powers. The occupation of the city by the Greeks in May 1919, followed by a massacre of the Turks, inspired the Turkish Nationalist Movement and was the immediate cause of the Greco-Turkish War. By the Treaty of Sèvres, signed in a suburb of Paris on August 10, 1920, "Greece obtained practically the whole of [Eastern] Thrace outside the conclave of Constantinople, and a mandate over Smyrna and its hinterland."[13] The six-hundred-year-old Ottoman Empire had been liquidated in Europe and in Asia, but the Turks still fought fiercely to retain the cities and plains of their Anatolian homeland.

There were three main campaigns in the Greco-Turkish War. During the first campaign, in 1920, the Greeks successfully advanced into Anatolia and Rumelia. In October 1920 King Alexander of Greece died from the bite of his pet monkey. The prime minister, Eleutherios Venizelos, was defeated in the elections; and Alexander's father, King Constantine, who had been deposed in 1917 by the pro-Allied Venizelists for his policy of neutrality during the war, was restored to the throne in November 1920. "When Constantine came into power," Hemingway explained from Muratli on November 3, 1922, "all the officers of the army in the field were suddenly scrapped, from the commander-in-chief down to platoon commanders. . . . Artillery officers who had no experience at all took over the command of batteries and massacred their own infantry."[14]

In March 1921 Russia signed a pact with Turkey that fixed the frontiers and established friendly relations. In the second campaign in 1921, the partially successful Greek offensives were terminated by major Turkish victories at Inonu and, under Kemal, at the Sakarya River. The political situation changed significantly after the domestic dissension that followed the fall of Venizelos and the first defeats in Anatolia. The Greeks, who had overextended themselves and proved incapable of ruling Turkish territory, began to lose the Allied diplomatic and military support they had enjoyed since the end of the Great War. At the same time, Turkish nationalism grew rapidly under the inspired military leadership of Kemal.

The third and final campaign, which began on August 18, 1922, was a series of Turkish victories that quickly drove the Greeks 350 miles westward from Ankara to Smyrna. They defeated the Greeks at Dumlupinar (north of Ankara) on August 20; and General Ismet Pasha broke the front at Afion Karahissar on August 26. The Turks advanced forty kilometers by the twenty-ninth; took Ushak and captured the Greek commander on September 2. Arnold Toynbee, who witnessed the war with the Red Crescent and became extremely pro-Turk, wrote:

> After this the Greek army crumpled up, their morale being completely shattered and their exhausted strength broken. . . . The rest of the drama is well known: the Greeks, defeated in the field, forsaken by their Allies, commanded by incompetent political appointees, demoralized by propaganda and discouraged by the rumoured evacuation of Smyrna, fell to pieces. . . . During the rout, the Greeks, abandoning everything but their rifles, and living off the country, stopped only long enough to set fire to village after village as they fled through them, leaving a trail of burning ruins behind.[15]

The Turks reoccupied Smyrna and completed the reconquest of Anatolia on September 9. Order prevailed for only a brief period, and arrests began immediately of vast numbers of Greeks and Armenians suspected of being implicated in the massacre of Turks in May 1919. According to the London *Morning Post*, on September 15 Turkish regular troops deliberately started a great fire, which totally destroyed the Greek, Armenian and European quarters of the city (the Turkish quarter was not burned) in order to conceal the massacre of 125,000 Christians.

The surviving population swarmed to the quay at the western extremity of the city while the fire raged behind them. The London *Times* of September 16 reported:

> A stream of refugees is still leaving Smyrna, and my informant describes the quay last night as packed with dense crowds herded together inside a cordon of Turkish regulars, while searchlights of foreign warships in the harbour played upon them. . . . The waters of the harbour were full of the dead bodies of persons drowned or shot by the Turks while trying to reach the ships, and some of the corpses were horribly mangled by the propellers.

Hemingway's "On the Quai at Smyrna" is not as horrifying as the English newspaper report, though he uses the same image of the searchlight scanning the crowds, who are screaming for survival. The

story is narrated by a British naval officer in the tone of voice Hemingway adopted from Chink Dorman-Smith and used in the two Mons
vignettes. The women who are having babies ("You just covered them
over with something and let them go to it") are logically and emotionally connected to those who would not give up their dead babies—even
after holding them for six days.

This story closes with a Goyesque image that haunted Hemingway
and recurred twice in *Death in the Afternoon*. When the Greeks "evacuated they had all their baggage animals they couldn't take off with
them so they just broke their forelegs and dumped them into the shallow water."[16] Here again, Hemingway does not explain why the Greeks
had to evacuate the city (their last chance to escape before the Turkish
onslaught) and why they had to prevent their valuable baggage animals
from falling into the hands of the enemy. Instead, he conveys two
powerful impressions: cruelty done to animals rather than to men;
cruelty done by Greeks (whose civilians were massacred as soon as the
Turks entered the city) rather than by Turks.

On September 27 King Constantine was deposed (for the second
time) for his support of the disastrous Greek policy in Anatolia. He was
succeeded by his eldest son, King George II, who had been excluded
from the throne in 1917 because of his pro-German sympathies.

Kemal marched north from Smyrna to Chanak in pursuit of the
remnant of the Greek army. At the end of September the British, whose
forces still occupied the Dardanelles, gave way to Kemal's demand to
cross the straits. But the armistice between Greece and Turkey, signed
at Mudanya on October 11, ended the war. "By its terms," writes
Bernard Lewis, "the [three] Allied governments agreed to a restoration
of Turkish sovereignty in Istanbul, the Straits, and eastern Thrace" up
to the Maritza River.[17] Hemingway, who explained far more in his
journalism than in his fiction, reported that Mudanya "marks the beginning of the end of European domination in Asia. . . . [The French]
supplied [Kemal] with arms, ammunition, and money. In return, it is
rumored, they received certain oil concessions in Asia Minor."[18]

As a result of the Greek defeat, a million broken-spirited refugees
from Anatolia, Smyrna and Eastern Thrace—who had not been rich or
fortunate enough to escape by boat or by train with the army and
government—had been driven on foot to seek safety across the Greek
frontier. But the Greek government had no food, accommodation or
employment for these hordes of exiles who had lost almost everything.

As winter approached, disease broke out in the overcrowded concentration camps.

Hemingway, in a final dispatch sent from Sofia, described a scene of gratuitous Greek cruelty on "the great stone road that runs from Adrianople across the Maritza valley to Karagatch": "A ragged, hungry-looking Turk farmer fell out of the cart on to his face, picked himself up in terror and ran down the road like a rabbit. A Greek cavalryman saw him running, kicked spurs into his horse and rode the Turk down. Two Greek soldiers and the cavalryman picked him up [and] smashed him in the face a couple of times."[19]

Hemingway's third vignette in *in our time* is derived from, but infinitely superior to, his article of October 20, 1922, "A Silent Ghastly Procession Wends Way from Thrace":

> Minarets stuck up in the rain out of Adrianople across the mud flats. The carts were jammed for thirty miles along the Karagatch road. Water buffalo and cattle were hauling carts through the mud. No end and no beginning. Just carts loaded with everything they owned. The old men and women, soaked through, walked along keeping the cattle moving. The Maritza was running yellow almost up to the bridge. Carts were jammed solid on the bridge with camels bobbing along through them. Greek cavalry herded along the procession. Women and kids were in the carts crouched with mattresses, mirrors, sewing machines, bundles. There was a woman having a kid with a young girl holding a blanket over her and crying. Scared sick looking at it. It rained all through the evacuation.[20]

The rain, emphasized in the first and last lines, brings the yellow river almost up to the bridge and turns the road to mud. The rain slows, then jams, the procession of bobbing Asian camels, buffalo, cattle and cattle-like men ("herded" by the mounted cavalry) that trudges toward and across the bridge from the Moslem minarets on the Turkish side of the river to the squalid Greek sanctuary of Karagatch. The motif of the woman giving birth *in extremis* on the open road, which recurs in many of the news reports, provides the only overt emotion ("scared sick") in the sketch. The six main components: rain, mud, carts, cattle, bridge, kids—are relentlessly repeated ("carts" five times) to achieve Hemingway's bare, direct, intense, elemental effect.

While in Constantinople Hemingway met the adventurer and soldier of fortune Charles Sweeny, who weaved in and out of his life for the next forty years. Sweeny was born in San Francisco in 1882, the son of a successful mining engineer who had made a fortune excavating silver in Idaho. His mother came from a Spanish-Catholic background and sent him at the age of thirteen to a seminary in Rome. He attended West Point, but became involved with a woman and did not graduate. He fought with Madero in the Mexican Revolution and against Gómez in Venezuela, where he was jailed for a time. He joined the French Foreign Legion before the Great War; was wounded in the Champagne offensive and became a lieutenant colonel in the American army during the war. He was a brigadier in the Polish army; colonel in the Moroccan air force during the Riff war in 1925; group captain in the RAF during 1940–41; founder of the Eagle Squadron in World War Two; and author of *Moment of Truth* (1943). Though Hemingway could not share Sweeny's right-wing politics and enthusiasm for imperialism, he "saw in Sweeny the kind of man he wished to be, a tough, battle-scarred man of action, a war hero and a romantic soldier of fortune following whichever side captured his imagination and sympathy, an extrovert who enjoyed life and could hold his own with women." He thought Sweeny had one of the most brilliant military minds he had ever known. Sweeny, who met Allen Tate in the late 1920s, told him that Hemingway "was a Mediterranean type, extroverted, suspicious, unloyal, and violent." With Sweeny, Tate said, "one talked about war, safaris, the rise of Hitler, women—the 'usual subjects of conversation,' in Pound's words in the *Cantos*, 'between intelligent men.' "[21]

Hemingway left Thrace on October 18, two days before his article on the refugees appeared in Toronto. He reached Paris exhausted, ill and so covered with bites and lice that he had to shave his head. He spent a month in Paris and arrived in Lausanne on November 22, two days after the opening of the conference that ratified the results of the Turkish victory. "The sessions of the conference itself were secret," Hemingway wrote, "and your official news came in hand-outs or press conferences with the spokesmen for each country and, since each country was anxious to present its version of what had happened before credence was given to any other country's account, these press conferences followed in rapid succession and you had to step very fast to get them all in."

The pressure on Hemingway was extreme, for he not only wrote feature stories about the Lausanne Conference for the *Star*, but also had a secret agreement (in violation of his exclusive contract) to cable news stories (under the pseudonym John Hadley) to Frank Mason of the International News Service and to Charles Bertelli of Hearst's Universal News Service. At Lausanne, he collected salary and expenses from three different organizations for the same job. When INS refused to refund certain expenses until they had received a more precise accounting, Hemingway was furious and sent the editor a terse telegram: "SUGGEST YOU UPSTICK BOOKS ASSWARDS." He found welcome relief in discussions with his much-admired colleague William Ryall Bolitho, who told Hemingway "many things that were the beginning of whatever education [he] received in international politics" and later became famous for his book *Twelve Against the Gods* (1930).[22]

The Lausanne Conference had representatives from England, France, Italy, Greece and Turkey. Hemingway left the conference on December 16, before anything significant had been decided. He again concentrated on the leading personalities and described Mussolini, Ismet Pasha (who had defeated the Greeks at Afion) and Chicherin, whom he had previously seen at Genoa.

The main issues at Lausanne were the new, de facto frontiers of Turkey; the redistribution of the Ottoman public debt; the much-needed protection of minorities; the exchange of populations; the Greek war reparations. The Turkish historian Salahi Sonyel summarized his country's substantial achievement: "The Treaty of Lausanne was generally acclaimed as the greatest diplomatic victory for Nationalist Turkey. It was the epilogue of a defeated and apparently shattered nation which rose from its ruins, faced the most powerful nations of the world on terms of absolute equality, and won from them all of its nationalist demands."[23]

"Scarcely had the Lausanne Conference begun," wrote the pro-Constantine Greek Royalist, Phocas-Cosmetatos, "when the Venizelist military clique . . . brought the political leaders who had been the Cretan's opponents before a military court . . . and had them executed out of hand. . . . It was for having continued M. Venizelos' war, this time with the consent of a properly elected National Assembly, that the opponents of that politician were put to death as traitors."[24] England, in protest, broke off diplomatic relations with the government of Venizelos, who was representing Greece at Lausanne.

The executions of the pro-Constantine, anti-Venizelist ex-ministers were described in detail in the London *Times* of November 29, 1922.

Though the former Prime Minister Gounaris was sick during the greater part of the trial and General Hadjinestis was mad, neither illness nor insanity saved them from death. Hemingway, who was in Lausanne when the ministers were executed in Athens, described the incident in the sixth and most powerful vignette of *in our time:*

> They shot the six cabinet ministers at half-past six in the morning against the wall of a hospital. There were pools of water in the courtyard. There were wet dead leaves on the paving of the courtyard. It rained hard. All the shutters of the hospital were nailed shut. One of the ministers was sick with typhoid. Two soldiers carried him downstairs and out into the rain. They tried to hold him up against the wall but he sat down in a puddle of water. The other five stood very quietly against the wall. Finally the officer told the soldiers it was no good trying to make him stand up. When they fired the first volley he was sitting down in the water with his head on his knees.[25]

Hemingway conveys sympathy for the victims while narrating their death with apparent objectivity, but never explains why the ministers are shot. Though they were actually killed at high noon, Hemingway shifts the execution to the traditional hour of dawn. Ironically, they are shot against the wall of a hospital whose shutters are conclusively nailed shut. The rain symbolically connects them to the refugees in Thrace (for whose plight they were responsible). The wet dead leaves in the court-yard, emphasized by the rhetorical parallels ("There were pools. . . . There were wet dead leaves"), foreshadow their inevitable fate. Gouna-ris, sick with typhoid, suffers a humiliating death. Carried downstairs and propped like a dummy against the wall, he slithers helplessly as his colleagues stand silently—and equally impotent—"against the wall" (repeated three times). The officer's remark, "it was no good," casts doubt on the ethics of the execution. During the first volley (there must always be a second to make certain of death) the sick man is "sitting down in the water with his head on his knees"—broken and crumpled up like the subject of Picasso's *Old Guitarist.*

The informal interview with King George II (1890–1947)—who suc-ceeded Constantine and ruled from September 1922 until December 1923—and Queen Elizabeth, his Rumanian consort, was conducted in Athens by the American cameraman Shorty Wornall in August 1923.[26] Wornall told the details of his royal interview to Hemingway, who used them in the last chapter of *in our time:*

The king was working in the garden. He seemed very glad to see me. We walked through the garden. This is the queen, he said. She was clipping a rose bush. Oh how do you do, she said. We sat down at a table under a big tree and the king ordered whiskey and soda. We have good whiskey anyway, he said. The revolutionary committee, he told me, would not allow him to go outside the palace grounds. Plastiras is a very good man I believe, he said, but frightfully difficult. I think he did right though shooting those chaps. If Kerensky had shot a few men things might have been altogether different. Of course the great thing in this sort of an affair is not to be shot oneself!

It was very jolly. We talked for a long time. Like all Greeks he wanted to go to America.[27]

Hemingway employs a playfully ironic tone and begins in the style of a nursery rhyme. The queen, clipping a rose bush like any suburban housewife, is utterly conventional; the king rather petulantly complains of his restriction to the grounds of the palace. He praises Nicholas Plastiras—the leader of the bloodless revolution of 1922, who deposed Constantine and put George on the throne, summoned the court-martial and was responsible for the execution of the five cabinet ministers and one general—as a "good man . . . but frightfully difficult." He justifies the executions as a political necessity and criticizes Alexander Kerensky (head of the Russian Provisional Government after the overthrow of the Czar), whose tolerance of political opponents led directly to the Bolshevik Revolution of October 1917. King George, who had less than four months left to rule, cynically believed survival was the most important thing. Despite his taste for whiskey and soda and British locutions (frightfully, chaps), the insecure and unhappy king is democratically reduced to the level of an immigrant. "Like all Greeks he wanted to go to America"—where men like the Hungarian crooks and Sam Cardinella met violent deaths in our time.

Hemingway also used his experience in Asia Minor in the brilliant italicized flashbacks of Harry's adventures in travel, love, violence and war in "The Snows of Kilimanjaro." The first flashback of the story takes place on October 18, 1922, the date Hemingway left the Greek frontier for Sofia and Paris:

He saw a railway station at Karagatch and he was standing with his pack and that was the headlight of the Simplon-Orient cutting the dark now and he was leaving Thrace then after the retreat . . . looking out the window and seeing snow on the mountains of Bulgaria. . . . It was the snow all right and he [Nansen] sent them on into it when he evolved exchange of populations. And it was the snow they tramped along in until they died that winter.[28]

Hemingway had to have a scapegoat for every mistake. In this passage, he unfairly blames the humane Fridtjof Nansen (the Norwegian Arctic explorer who helped repatriate prisoners of war in World War One and won the Nobel Peace Prize in 1922) for the death of the refugees in the Thracian winter, though the alternative to flight (as Smyrna proved) was massacre.

The second, more elaborate flashback refers to Hemingway's quarrel with Hadley before leaving for Constantinople; his memories of his first love, Agnes von Kurowsky (who he knew had been working for the Red Cross in nearby Rumania during 1920–21); and—more imaginatively—his attempt to assuage his guilt, longing and loneliness with a "hot Armenian slut" whom he stole from a tough British officer after a fist fight.

The breathless war episode in this flashback is based on Hemingway's newspaper interview with the British military observer in Anatolia, who saw the Greek *evzones,* in their traditional dress, mistakenly massacred by their own artillery and deliberately slaughtered (as the officers shot their own men) during their futile retreat from the superior Turkish forces in August 1922:

> They had made the attack with the newly arrived Constantine officers, that did not know a god-damned thing, and the artillery had fired into the troops and the British observer had cried like a child. That was the day he'd first seen dead men wearing white ballet skirts and upturned shoes with pompons on them. The Turks had come steadily and lumpily and he had seen the skirted men running and the officers shooting into them and running then themselves and he and the British observer had run too until his lungs ached and his mouth was full of the taste of pennies and they stopped behind some rocks and there were the Turks coming as lumpily as ever. Later he had seen the things that he could never think of and later still he had seen much worse.[29]

IV

Hemingway's poem "They All Made Peace—What Is Peace?," written just after the Lausanne Conference, satirizes the moral corruption of international diplomacy: "Lord Curzon likes young boys. / So does Chicherin. / So does Mustapha Kemal."[30] But Hemingway managed, for a time, to retain his admiration for the tough and tigerish leader of wartime France, Georges Clemenceau, who had lost office in 1919. In February 1922 he published an article on Clemenceau's position in postwar French politics and in September of that year first interviewed him on the Atlantic coast of France. He portrayed Clemenceau's striking physical appearance and penetrating eyes; but when Clemenceau insulted Canada, incorrectly insisted that Canadians had rejected compulsory military service and refused to help France in the war, Hemingway's editor John Bone refused to publish these views in the *Star.* William Ryall Bolitho shattered Hemingway's illusions in November 1922 by pointing out how Clemenceau had cruelly abused his political power. Bolitho's negative opinion, rather than Hemingway's positive impression, seems to have prevailed, for in an article of December 1934 Hemingway wrote that after the war Clemenceau had ordered the Garde Républicaine to ride down a parade of mutilated veterans.

One legacy of Clemenceau's punitive peace settlement at Versailles was the occupation of the industrial Ruhr in January 1923 by the government of Raymond Poincaré in order to exact the payment of impossible war reparations. The occupation of the Ruhr, the collapse of the Reichsbank and the severe economic crisis of 1923, which was marked by mass unemployment and uncontrollable currency inflation, wiped out a large part of the German middle class and made it receptive to the temptations of Nazism. Hemingway investigated conditions in the Ruhr for six weeks during April and May 1923; traveled northward from Offenburg to Frankfurt, Mainz, Cologne and Düsseldorf; and effectively exposed the official cant of Poincaré's government. His on-the-spot conclusions were similar to those expressed in John Maynard Keynes' brilliantly prophetic *Economic Consequences of the Peace* (1919): "From the start it was seen by the long-headed financiers that [the occupation] would only cripple Germany's ability to pay further reparations, unite her as a country and reflame her hatred against France—and cost more money than it would ever get out."[31]

Hemingway's direct and vivid involvement with statesmen and historical events during 1922–23 determined his mature political ideas. Wyndham Lewis, who was quite unaware of Hemingway's early journalistic experience, was mistaken when he maintained: "It is difficult to imagine a writer whose mind is more entirely closed to politics than is

Hemingway's." Archibald MacLeish was even more inaccurate in 1940 when he called Hemingway politically irresponsible. As a reporter in Kansas City, Hemingway consistently supported the underdogs and the oppressed: the persecuted Jew, the isolated smallpox case, the scorned prostitute. In Toronto in the fall of 1923, he described the plight of Japanese earthquake victims and advocated workers' rights. As a European reporter for the *Star,* he sympathized with exiled Russians, oppressed Greeks, mutilated Frenchmen, ruined Germans and victims of Italian Fascism. He was thinking of Mussolini's rule when he shrewdly observed that restrained intimidation was more effective than complete brutality: "Any government that uses machine guns once too often on its citizens will fall automatically. Régimes are kept in with the club and the blackjack, not the machine gun or bayonet."[32] The chapters of *in our time* also express sympathy for the victims of war and violence—German soldiers, executed ministers, wounded Americans, Hungarian revolutionaries, cowardly bullfighters, even convicted murderers like Sam Cardinella—and implicitly condemn generals, diplomats and kings.

Hemingway supported the Socialist Eugene Debs for President in 1932 and deepened his political awareness during the 1930s. His most courageous and humane article, the little-known "Who Murdered the Vets?" (September 1935), protested against the government's failure to protect 450 railroad workers who had been killed by a Florida hurricane. *To Have and Have Not* (1937) showed genuine compassion for the impoverished working class. His extraordinary effort on behalf of the Loyalists during the Spanish Civil War was the noblest moment of his life. He courageously attacked Joe McCarthy and his ally Cardinal Spellman during the Communist witch hunts in the early 1950s; and supported the first, idealistic stage of the Castro regime while living in Cuba during 1959–60. John Dos Passos, who knew him well, said the young Hemingway "had one of the shrewdest heads for unmasking political pretensions I've ever run into." And in 1941 Edmund Wilson, Hemingway's most penetrating critic, agreed with that judgment: "Going back over Hemingway's books today, we can see clearly what an error of the politicos it was to accuse him of an indifference to society. His whole work is a criticism of society: he has responded to every pressure of the moral atmosphere of the time, as it is felt at the roots of human relations, with a sensitiveness almost unrivalled."[33]

V

Hemingway's experience as a European reporter influenced but did not entirely account for the evolution of his distinctive style and values. To a large degree, his technique, tone, themes and code of honor came from his early reading of Rudyard Kipling. As Bill Smith recalled: "We tended to buy the English gents' code of gallantry as revealed in fiction. . . . It was the kind of thing we read in those days."[34] Kipling's works connect Hemingway, who was proud of his English heritage, to the traditional moral and military values of the Victorian age. Hemingway had a lifelong admiration for Kipling and continued to praise him long after it became fashionable to disparage the older writer. The impressive Chink Dorman-Smith was a Brushwood Boy of the trenches. A living embodiment of the Kipling code, tested by war and expressed in action, Chink reinforced Kipling's influence on Hemingway.[35]

The British military tone and diction in the two Mons vignettes of *in our time*—which portrayed war as a great game—derived from Kipling and the public school ethic and from the personal experience of Dorman-Smith. That good soldier also provided the Shakespearean quotation from *2 Henry IV* which Wilson quoted to teach Francis Macomber how to conquer fear and regain courage. In his Introduction to *Men at War,* Hemingway recalled "the feeling of having a permanent protecting talisman when a young British officer I met when in the hospital first wrote out for me . . . *'By my troth, I care not: a man can die but once; we owe God a death.'* "[36]

Edmund Wilson, who wrote essays on both Kipling and Hemingway in *The Wound and the Bow,* offers—in passing—a perceptive footnote on the similar portrayal of women in their fiction. Both tend to create a single woman in an all-male world, and believe men court disaster when they commit themselves to love:

> There would probably be a chapter to write on the relation between Hemingway and Kipling, and certain assumptions about society which they share. They have much the same split attitude toward women. Kipling anticipates Hemingway in his beliefs that "he travels the fastest that travels alone" and that "the female of the species is more deadly than the male"; and Hemingway seems to reflect Kipling in the submissive infra-Anglo-Saxon women that make his heroes such perfect mistresses. The most striking example of this is the amoeba-like little Span-

ish girl, Maria, in *For Whom the Bell Tolls*. Like the docile native "wives" of English officials in the early stories of Kipling, she lives only to serve her lord and to merge her identity with his; and this love affair with a woman in a sleeping-bag, lacking completely the kind of give and take that goes on between real men and women, has the all-too-perfect felicity of a youthful erotic dream. One suspects that *Without Benefit of Clergy* was read very early by Hemingway and that it made on him a lasting impression. The pathetic conclusion of this story of Kipling's seems unmistakably to be echoed at the end of *A Farewell to Arms*. [37]

Wilson's suggestion can be profitably extended to illustrate the similarities in the lives of Kipling and Hemingway, the extensive allusions and references to Kipling in Hemingway's work and the positive influence of Kipling. Hemingway, who was born in the Victorian era and learned its values from his father, was a contemporary of Kipling for thirty-seven years. He did not merely imitate the Master, but used him as an aesthetic model and learned from Kipling—more than from any American writer—how to master the art of the short story.

Hemingway had biographical as well as literary affinities with Kipling. Both suffered early trauma: Kipling by the sudden separation from his parents and his sadistic treatment at school (described in "Baa Baa Black Sheep"), Hemingway by his war wounds at Fossalta. Both left school early; both retained certain adolescent traits and never became completely mature. Both admired *Huckleberry Finn* and were influenced by Mark Twain's "use of vernacular dialect, his mixture of sentimentality and sadism, his lowbrow philistinism . . . his respect for expertise and excellence in work, his use of technical description, and reverence for men who are 'honest, trustworthy, faithful to promises and duty.' "[38]

Both authors were journalists as teenagers and later became distinguished war correspondents (Kipling reported the Anglo-Boer conflict). Both were excluded from the service by defective vision and later idealized army officers. Both were permanently shocked by the violent death of a loved one: Kipling's son was killed in 1915, Hemingway's father shot himself in 1928. Both were restless travelers, constantly crossing the ocean. Both were highly disciplined writers, dedicated to their craft. Both were phrase-makers and public figures who captured and expressed the mood of their time. Both moved from journalism to stories to novels. Both wrote about rites of initiation, in *The Jungle Books* and in the Nick Adams stories; about struggles against the ocean, in *Captains Courageous* and in *The Old Man and the Sea* (in Hemingway's novella, as in *Kim,* an old man instructs a young boy). The last completed books by Kipling and Hemingway were posthumously published autobiographies: *Something of Myself* and *A Moveable Feast.*

Hemingway's older sister and younger brother both emphasized that in boyhood "he particularly enjoyed reading Kipling."[39] His son Patrick recorded that Hemingway continued to read Kipling to his own children: "Papa loved Kipling. He would often quote, 'walk with Kings —nor lose the common touch.' His favorites among Kipling's short stories were *Without Benefit of Clergy* and *The Mark of the Beast.*"[40]

Hemingway owned twenty-two books by Kipling, continued to read them throughout his life and knew Kipling's works as well as those of any other writer. He particularly admired Kipling's effective titles. In a letter of 1927 to Scott Fitzgerald, Hemingway implied that *Men Without Women* expressed his affinity to Kipling's colonial soldiers and the assertion of his own virile values: "But the boys, principally Kipling, had been there before me and swiped all the good [titles] so I called the book Men Without Women hoping it would have a large sale among the fairies and old Vassar girls."[41]

When Hemingway moved from Paris to Key West in 1928 he gave Kipling's books to his unlettered fishing friends and reported: "Several of the boys I know have just been moved by first reading of Kipling." Writing in 1929 to Owen Wister, a friend of the master, Hemingway expressed his great respect for Kipling and said no one was ever born with more genius.[42]

Hemingway reiterated his praise of Kipling, not only in his letters of the 1920s but also in his published work of the 1930s, when Left-wing views were fashionable and Kipling fell from favor. In his essay "In Defense of Dirty Words" (1934) Hemingway distinguished the aesthetic from the political aspects of Kipling and stated that Maupassant "wrote more truly great stories than any other man but Rudyard Kipling whose work it is now fashionable to disparage because he was a fool about politics." In *Green Hills of Africa* (1935) he said that to write great prose, to achieve the fourth or fifth dimension, "there must be talent, much talent. Talent such as Kipling had."[43] When a young writer asked Hemingway which books to read, he declared in "Monologue to the Maestro" (1935): "all the good Kipling." In 1938 Hemingway borrowed from Kipling the unorthodox idea of publishing his play, *The Fifth Column,* with his collected short stories. As he told his editor Max

Perkins: "Remember the [Story of the] Gadsbys by Kipling [1889]. Was a vol of plays and stories. One of his best books of stories. Successful too."[44] He included Kipling's tale "The Taking of Lungtenpen" in his anthology, *Men at War* (1942).

Hemingway quoted Kipling's poem "The Virginity" in a letter of 1949 to Bernard Berenson. In his manic attack on *From Here to Eternity* (1951), he praised Kipling at the expense of James Jones, whose title came from the master's ballad "Gentlemen Rankers." Later that year Hemingway stated that he always had the greatest admiration for Kipling's wonderful stories.[45] And in a letter of advice to a young poet, he unconsciously echoed Gertrude Stein's phrase and once again told the novice to read the works of the master: "When I was your age I guess I wrote like Kipling. I thought he was the best short story writer that ever lived and I still know that some of the short stories are the best. . . . Why don't you start again at the beginning and read Kipling—i.e. 'The End of the Passage,' 'The Strange Ride of Maraby [Morrowbie] Jukes,' 'The Mark of the Beast.' " In 1954, the year he won the Nobel Prize, Hemingway paid a final tribute to Kipling, who had won the Prize in 1907, by calling him "a much better writer than I am."[46]

Hemingway had saturated himself in Kipling's works and inevitably absorbed the lesson of the master. His early poem "Kipling" (1922) parodied the opening lines of "Mandalay":

> There's a little monkey maiden looking eastward toward the sea,
> There's a new monkey soprano a'sobbing in the tree,
> And Harold's looking very fit the papers all agree.

Hemingway's new literary friends immediately saw the distinct influence of Kipling on his work. "Gertrude Stein rather liked the [early] poems, they were direct, Kiplingesque"; after meeting Hemingway, Anderson "compared his writing to that of Kipling."[47] Charles Fenton noted that in Hemingway's article "Wild Night Music of Paris" (March 5, 1922), "the syntax of the prose and the romanticism of the attitude point to his debt to Kipling"; that the first line of his article "Hamid Bey Wears Shirt Tucked In" (October 9, 1922) is a variation of the opening sentence of Kipling's "The Man Who Was." And Carlos Baker pointed out the "Kiplingesque mood" of his fourth dispatch from Europe, "Tuna Fishing in Spain" (February 18, 1922): "If you land a big tuna after a six-hour fight . . . you will be purified and be able to enter unabashed into the presence of the very elder gods."[48]

Hemingway learned more important lessons from Kipling about literary craftsmanship and technique, about cutting his work to achieve what Kipling called "economy of implication." The descriptions of literary creation in *Something of Myself* are remarkably close to the aesthetic theories expressed by Hemingway in *A Moveable Feast*. Both stress the importance of the subconscious mind to the imagination and the need for extreme compression:

> When your Daemon is in charge, do not try to think consciously. (Kipling)

> I learned not to think about anything I was writing . . . until I started again the next day. That way my subconscious would be working on it. (Hemingway)

> In an auspicious hour, read your final draft and consider faithfully every paragraph, sentence and word, blacking out where requisite. Let it lie by to drain as long as possible. At the end of that time, re-read and you should find that it will bear a second shortening. (Kipling)

> You could omit anything if you knew that you omitted and the omitted part would strengthen the story and make people feel something more than they understood. (Hemingway)[49]

Kipling's example helped Hemingway to achieve his characteristic close observation, precise detail and sensory immediacy. But in certain works, like "Mrs. Bathurst" and "Big Two-Hearted River," the radical omission of an essential element, which remained hidden beneath the surface of the story, left the meaning unclear.

Both authors have been accused of being simplistic. Henry James wrote that Kipling "has come steadily from the less simple in subject to the more simple."[50] Wyndham Lewis said that Hemingway's heroes were simpletons with few ideas. But Hemingway wisely avoided imitating Kipling's weakest stories: the whimsical, the supernatural, the sentimental, the brutal and the cruel.

Both men admired professional expertise. Kipling taught Hemingway how technical description could achieve verisimilitude and enhance the meaning of his fiction. Kipling employed legal, medical, military and mechanical terms just as Hemingway used the specialized vocabulary of hunting in *Green Hills of Africa* and of bullfighting (complete with glossary) in *Death in the Afternoon*. The operation of locomotives in ".007" is similar to the use of fishing gear in "Big Two-

Hearted River" and of explosives in *For Whom the Bell Tolls*. Hemingway adopted Kipling's laconic conversational tone, in which the self-assured expert instructs the unsophisticated novice. As C. S. Lewis observed of Kipling: "To belong, to be inside, to be in the know, to be snugly together against the outsiders—that is what really matters."[51]

Both writers deal mainly with foreign settings (the only Hemingway novel that takes place in America is *To Have and Have Not*) and both have an extraordinary ability to evoke what D. H. Lawrence called the "spirit of place." Kipling created the literary image of India just as Hemingway did of Spain. Both portray loyal retainers and primitive characters: Kipling's ferocious Afghans are reflected in Hemingway's fierce guerrillas. Both Kipling and Hemingway frequently use colloquial diction, foreign words and literal translations (rather than their English equivalents) to convey the flavor of unfamiliar languages.

There are also striking similarities in their themes and their portrayal of elemental emotions in extreme situations: action, violence, brutality as well as loneliness, insomnia, breakdown. Edmund Wilson's remark about Kipling applies with equal force to Hemingway: "The only authentic heroism to be found in the fiction of Kipling is the heroism of moral fortitude on the edge of nervous collapse." Kipling's description of insomnia in "At the End of the Passage" had a personal as well as literary meaning for Hemingway. Kipling's hero was one of those who descended into Dark Places and slept with a hunting spur to keep himself awake "when a spell was laid upon them to overtake them in their sleeping hours and they dared not sleep." Hemingway had also suffered from insomnia after his war wound and in "In Another Country" wrote: "I often lay in bed at night by myself, afraid to die and wondering how I would be when I went back to the front again."[52]

The closest thematic parallels appear in stories about the symptoms and cure of war neurosis and shell shock. In "In the Same Boat" the hero, "while he lay between sleep and wake, would be overtaken by a long shuddering sigh, which he learned to know was the sign that his brain had once more conceived its horror, and in time—in due time—would bring it forth."[53] Kipling was perhaps the first modern writer to describe the psychological effects of war, which Hemingway had personally experienced. His own war wound, which taught him to see a new emotional as well as literary dimension in Kipling, inspired some of his finest stories: "Big Two-Hearted River," "Soldier's Home," "Now I Lay Me" and "A Way You'll Never Be."

Kipling and Hemingway both oppose the cruelty, violence and darkness of the world with a moral touchstone: a steadfast, traditional code of honor. Kipling's concept of the Law, which includes discipline, generosity, bravery and fidelity, is expressed in the capable and responsible Kim and in "McAndrew's Hymn." Hemingway's code (which derives from Kipling) emphasizes dignity, solidarity, self-sacrifice and stoicism. In both writers there is a close correspondence between physical courage and moral strength. In Hemingway the code is compacted in the ritual of the bullfight, which specifies exactly what the matador must do and how he must act when confronted by danger, pain and death. Delmore Schwartz offered a useful synthesis of Hemingway's beliefs: "Courage, honesty, and skill are important rules of the code. . . . To be admirable, from the standpoint of this morality, is to admit defeat, to be a good sportsman, to accept pain without an outcry, to adhere strictly to the rules of the game and to play the game with great skill. . . . One must speak in clipped tones, avoid pretentious phrases, condense emotion into a few expletives or deliberately suppress it."[54]

Almost every major Hemingway story expresses this code by ironically rejecting the rational and conventional forms of behavior. In "The Undefeated" the old matador kills the bull, on the sixth attempt, after he is gored. In "Fifty Grand" the aging boxer endures pain from a low blow and survives to lose the fight and win his bet. In "The Killers" Andreson, who betrayed his pact with the gangsters, fatalistically accepts the dreadful consequences of his act. In "The Gambler, the Nun, and the Radio" the wounded Mexican refuses to denounce his assailant.

The ultimate response to suffering, loss and grief is precisely the same in both Kipling and Hemingway: proud stoicism. After his son's death in "Without Benefit of Clergy,"

> Holden realised his pain slowly, exactly as he had realised his happiness, and with the same imperious necessity for hiding all trace of it.

After his wife's death in "In Another Country" the Italian major,

> his head up looking at nothing, carrying himself straight and soldierly, with tears on both his cheeks and biting his lips, walked past the machines and out the door.[55]

Though the military code of honor may have moral, aesthetic and intellectual limitations (as noted by Henry James and Wyndham Lewis), it inspired the very best fiction of Kipling and of Hemingway.

VI

The stoical code was tested when Hemingway traveled to Spain with his first two publishers, Bill Bird and Robert McAlmon, in the summer of 1923—the first of eight trips to that country during the next decade. The festival of San Fermín at Pamplona, which included round-the-clock drinking and dancing, music and fireworks, processions and bullfights, allowed men to participate in the running and testing of the bulls. "Went down there about two months ago to study Bull fighting," he told Bill Horne, "and lived at a bullfighters' pension in the Calle San Jerónimo in Madrid and then travelled all over the country with a crew of toreros—Seville, Ronda, Granada, Toledo, Aranjuez seeing the stuff." He quickly overcame the Anglo-Saxon antipathy to the cruelty and "unfairness" of the bullfight, recognized the tragic and aesthetic aspects, and realized that the corrida provided the sensations that had excited him in war: "It isn't just brutal like they always told us. It's a great tragedy—and the most beautiful thing I've ever seen and takes more guts and skill and guts again than anything possibly could. It's just like having a ringside seat at the war with nothing going to happen to you."[56]

Hemingway's bible of bullfighting, *Death in the Afternoon,* helps to explain the complex reasons that attracted him to the mortuary playground and made him the leading exponent of the corrida outside the Spanish-speaking world. Its images and values were central to his work from *in our time* (1924) to "The Dangerous Summer" (1960). Hemingway—partly because he liked to kill animals and had nearly been killed himself—enjoyed the skillful evocation of violence and the "sweet smell" of blood that came from hunting, boxing, bulls, wounds, accidents. He observed that bulls were the only animals deliberately bred to kill humans, and was fascinated by the life-and-death contest between beast and man. The bullfight was analogous to his search for words that would express the essential aspects of existence: "The only place where you could see life and death, *i.e.,* violent death now that the wars were over, was in the bull ring, and I wanted very much to go to Spain where I could study it. I was trying to learn to write, commencing with the simplest things, and one of the simplest things of all and the most fundamental is violent death."[57] War had tested his courage and aroused his taste for killing.

Bullfighting satisfied his need to study the elemental quality of death.

The corrida aroused high tension when Hemingway saw "that sudden head-lowering, horn-reaching, quick cat-gallop that stopped your heart dead when it started." He wanted to witness both the thrill of perfection when the bull was properly killed and the sensation of disaster when things went wrong. Though pain and suffering fascinated him, he was quick to show compassion. He was not disgusted or excited by the prospect of the disemboweled horses, but merely curious about how he would respond to that bizarre spectacle. His description of Manuel Maera's death in the bullring, conveyed by a distortion of perspective and increase of apparent velocity, is one of the triumphs of *in our time:* "Maera felt everything getting larger and larger and then smaller and smaller. Then it got larger and larger and larger and then smaller and smaller. Then everything commenced to run faster and faster as when they speed up a cinematograph film. Then he was dead."[58]

Hemingway was naturally drawn to the ritual that emphasized strict rules, extreme compression, skillful technique, pagan drama and high courage. He identified with the risks and rewards of the bullfight, in which many matadors were wounded or killed and few achieved wealth and fame. He thought the writer, like the matador, must create and live his own style; that this style, expressed in art and action, *was* the man. He told Fitzgerald that bullfighters needed not only guts but also a more important, less tangible quality that he called (in one of his most famous phrases) "grace under pressure." He believed the matador (and, vicariously, the spectator) achieved a release from the fear of death by conquering fear and administering death: "bullfighting is the only art in which the artist is in danger of death and in which the degree of brilliance in the performance is left to the fighter's honor." Finally, he saw a close connection between killing and creating. The bullfighter, who mocks mortality and converts it to art, has the rare chance of overcoming death and becoming (for an instant) immortal: "When a man is still in rebellion against death he has pleasure in taking to himself one of the Godlike attributes; that of giving it."[59]

Hemingway showed his courage during several visits to the festival of San Fermín when the bulls ran two kilometers from the Puerta Rochapea to the plaza de toros. McAlmon, who went on the first two trips to Pamplona, wrote that in 1924, in the ring with the bulls (whose horns were padded), the powerful "Hemingway took a charge straight on face, and then, catching the steer's horns, attempted to throw it. He did break its strength and got cheered by the crowd." After Hemingway had rescued Don Stewart, who broke three ribs in the bullring, he minimized rather than exaggerated his exploits, saying that he wished he had saved Stewart's life, as the Chicago newspapers claimed. But Don was never in any real danger and the Spanish game was no rougher than boxing or football.[60] A good action photograph, taken in 1925 and sold as a postcard, shows Hemingway (wearing white trousers and a red Basque scarf) fighting the bull with an old sweater.

During Hemingway's third Pamplona festival in 1925, Niño de la Palma was awarded a bull's ear after a fine performance and gave the stiff piece of flesh to Hadley, who neatly wrapped it up in Don Stewart's handkerchief. Hemingway told her that she ought to throw it out, or cut it into pieces and send them to friends in St. Louis. But she refused to part with it.[61] In *The Sun Also Rises* Romero gives a bull's ear to Brett.

The *afición* for bullfights enabled Hemingway to establish close rapport—often through drinking—with ordinary Spanish people like the Guardia Civil, who escorted him through the gate when he lost his train ticket, and with Juanito Quintana, who owned a hotel in Pamplona. He liked and admired Spaniards, never felt like a foreigner in their country and did not think he was ever treated like one. He had some glorious fishing trips in the Irati River, near Burguete, northwest of Pamplona in the Pyrenees, which he immortalized in *The Sun Also Rises*. The context of the bullfights, the festival, the drinking and the peasants seemed to encourage Hemingway's tendency to appear uneducated and uncultured, to assume a persona and be a tough guy rather than an intellectual.

VII

It seemed as though Hemingway could continue to write and travel around Europe indefinitely. But he was forced to change his carefree way of life when Hadley became pregnant in January 1923. An intriguing, unfinished passage sheds some light on this important event. In a letter to Fitzgerald of December 1925, Hemingway denied that his story "Cat in the Rain" (1925) was about Hadley (though it certainly was about her) and wrote: "Hadley never made a speech in her life about wanting a baby because she had been told various things by her doctor and I'd—no use going into all that."[62] This passage could mean one of two opposite things. Either Hadley, who had been brought up as an invalid by her mother, was told by the doctor that she could not have a baby, took no precautions and had an accidental pregnancy; or she was told that she would have to abort a baby for her own good, took great precautions, became pregnant accidentally and decided to have the child. In any case, Hadley's pregnancy postponed, for about a year, Hemingway's abandonment of journalism for fiction.

The unwelcome pregnancy, which caused the second crisis of their marriage, led to significant changes in Hemingway's attitude toward Hadley. He came to see her, even before their child was born, as a woman who imposed restraints and limited his freedom. And he reverted, at times, to his adolescent belief: "Once a man's married he's absolutely bitched." Hadley told him about her pregnancy in February or March, when they were skiing in Cortina. He portrayed his sullen response in Nick's series of mechanical replies in "Cross-Country Snow," muttered as the two friends stare at the empty bottle that symbolizes his empty life:

> "Is Helen going to have a baby?" George said. . . .
> "Yes."
> "When?"
> "Late next summer."
> "Are you glad?"
> "Yes. Now."
> "Will you go back to the States?"
> "I guess so."
> "Do you want to?"
> "No."
> "Does Helen?"
> "No."
> George sat silent. He looked at the empty bottle and the empty glasses.
> "It's hell, isn't it?"[63]

In her *Autobiography* Gertrude Stein enjoyed exposing Hemingway's discomfort when he finally and bitterly announced the pregnancy and sought the maternal sympathy of the barren woman: "He came to the house about ten o'clock in the morning and he stayed, he stayed for lunch, he stayed all afternoon, he stayed for dinner and he stayed until about ten o'clock at night and all of a sudden he announced that his wife was enceinte and then with great bitterness, and I, I am too young to

be a father. We consoled him as best we could and sent him on his way."
He also revealed his immaturity and selfishness by blaming Hadley and
refusing to take responsibility when, in the summer of 1924, she apparently became pregnant for the second time, with a child who was never
born. McAlmon reported that "Hemingway was most unhappy because
he feared he was again to become a father. He told Hadley it would be
no fun at all any more if they had too many children at his age. She
wouldn't be a good playmate any more either. He was tragic about it,
and Hadley, too, became upset."[64]

In *A Farewell to Arms* Catherine Barkley expresses the guilt that
Hemingway imposed upon Hadley (who at the age of thirty may have
felt *she* was not too young to have children), and the insecurity of a
woman who is purely a sexual object and does not want to make trouble
or spoil the fun:

> "You aren't angry are you, darling?"
> "No."
> "And you don't feel trapped?"
> "Maybe a little. But not by you." . . .
> "She won't come between us, will she? The little brat. . . . I was afraid
> because I'm big now that maybe I was a bore to you. . . . I know I'm no
> fun for you, darling, I'm like a big flour barrel."

Hemingway also transformed his private accident and lack of loyalty
into a kind of malign retribution for romantic love: "This was the price
you [i.e., he] paid for sleeping together. This was the end of the trap.
This was what people got for loving each other." (Kafka's version of this
human dilemma is much more terrible, for he believed "Coitus is punishment for the happiness of being together.")[65]

The pregnancy forced Hemingway to leave Europe and return to
Toronto for what he thought would be a two-year stay. Hadley believed
that doctors, nurses and hospitals would be better there than in Paris.
During a sudden spurt of parental responsibility, Hemingway felt that
he should support his family with a steady job on the *Star*. On August
17, 1923, a month after returning from Pamplona, they sailed home on
the *Andania*. They arrived in Quebec ten days later, looked up Ralph
Connable and Gregory Clark, and took an apartment at 1599 Bathurst
Street. Hemingway began work on September 10 at $125 a week.

But going back to Toronto was like returning to Oak Park after the
war. He immediately sent letters to Pound, Stein and Sylvia Beach

complaining about Canada and saying how much he missed Paris. Wyndham Lewis, who was marooned in Toronto twenty years later, during World War Two, gave a brilliantly bitter description of the "sanctimonious icebox." The city reminded Lewis of Archangel or Murmansk, had barren bookstores whose "clients were practically Eskimos," seemed to contain the "dumbest English-speaking population anywhere" in the world, and needed at least two million Jews to bring it to life. He particularly despised the asphyxiating godliness of the Presbyterians and Methodists, who created "a reign of terror for the toper and the whoremaster" and forced him to grovel "before the ugly teetotal Baal set-up in these parts by the most parochial nationette on earth." As he told a cosmopolitan friend: "If New York is brutal and babylonian, in this place it is as if some one were sitting on your chest —having taken care to gag you first—and were croaking out [hymns by] Moody and Sankey from dawn to dayshut."[66]

Hemingway found the working conditions just as bad as the milieu. He had dealt with John Bone when he was a highly regarded European reporter; but was now assigned to the *Daily Star,* came under the immediate authority of the assistant managing editor, Harry Hindmarsh (who was married to the owner's daughter), and was deliberately persecuted and humiliated. During his first two weeks Hemingway was sent to cover the most trivial stories and did not even receive a by-line. J. H. Cranston, Hemingway's former editor on the *Star Weekly,* explained: "Hindmarsh hated prima donnas, and it was his regular practice to reduce men to size by giving them more or less common assignments after they had done an outstanding piece of work and were proud of themselves. . . . He was ambitious, cruel, and jealous of the success of others. . . . Hindmarsh was a driver, who expected implicit obedience from his men. He ruled by fear. . . . HCH is a sadist, or was, and he took delight in breaking or humbling men's spirits."[67]

Hemingway, who had very little tolerance for this kind of treatment, said "working under Hindmarsh was like being in the German army with a poor commander." Hadley confirmed that "Ernest felt if we did not get away from that atmosphere quickly, his soul, which means his own creative writing, would dry up within him." His frustration was increased because he was too exhausted after a long day's work to write his own stories. He told Edward O'Brien that he had to suppress the urge to write when his Kiplingesque Daemon took over: "a story starts in your head on the street car [and you] have to choke it off because it was coming so perfectly and easily and clear and right and you know that if you let it go on it will be finished and gone and you'd never be able to write it."

Hemingway was also sent on long journeys to cover his assignments. He went to Kingston, Ontario, to report on an escaped convict. He went up to Sudbury Basin, north of Lake Huron, to expose a fake coal company and consoled himself by reading Conrad's *The Rover* in the Nickel Range Hotel. He went to New York (just as Hadley was about to give birth) to report Lloyd George's tour of North America, failed (in his distracted, indifferent state) to cover an important speech and traveled with the "cantankerous, mean, temperamental and vicious" Prime Minister on a special train to Canada.[68]

Hemingway was upset that he could not get back in time to be with Hadley when their child was born, after an easy three-hour delivery, at 2 A.M. on October 10, 1923. He was called John Hadley Nicanor, which combined a conventional Oak Park name with that of a favorite Spanish bullfighter: Nicanor Villalta. But he was always called Bumby (a variation of baby), which suggested his bumpy, rambunctious behavior, even in the womb.[69]

It was only a matter of time before the longing for the friendship and stimulation of Paris; the dry, puritanical city; the exhausting, uninteresting assignments; the inability to do his own writing; and the demeaning persecution by the editor combined to cause a final break with the *Star*. Hemingway (with more passion than clarity) complained to John Bone, who failed to protect him from Hindmarsh and keep him on the newspaper, that

> work accomplished counts for nothing, nor results, and the only standard is to be at the mercy of any fit of temper or an outraged morbidity of dignity because of fancied slights. If it is a question of Mr. Hindmarsh or myself I of course must go. I was horrified while handling a big story, requiring speed and accuracy above all things, to be made the victim of an exhibition of wounded vanity from a man in a position of Assistant Managing editor on a newspaper of the caliber of the Star because he himself had made a mistake.

Hemingway finally resigned (as of December 31), according to J. H. Cranston, after "he had been assigned to an interview with Count Apponyi, Hungarian diplomat, and had breakfast with him. Apponyi gave him a number of documents relative to Hungarian aspirations which would help him get his facts straight, and extracted a promise they would be returned later in the day. Hemingway sent them to Assistant Managing Editor Hindmarsh with a note asking for their safe-keeping. When he reached the office they had been tossed in the W.P.B. [wastepaper basket] and sent to the furnace."[70]

Hadley loyally accepted financial insecurity when Hemingway resigned his $125 a week job in order to live in Paris on $50 a week and be free to write. After a quick visit to Oak Park to see his parents, the couple smuggled their possessions out of the flat, jumped their lease, sailed in the Cunarder *Antonia* on January 19, 1924, and reached Cherbourg ten days later.

As Charles Fenton has pointed out, Hemingway was exceptionally precocious in his personal and professional life. He was a reporter and a wounded war hero at nineteen; had an unhappy love affair at twenty; married at twenty-two; became a European correspondent at twenty-three; was a father at twenty-four. His first, thin book, *Three Stories and Ten Poems*—which included the "unprintable" "Up in Michigan," "My Old Man" and "Out of Season" (all of which had been sent out to editors when Hadley lost the manuscripts)—was dedicated to Hadley and published in August 1923, when he was twenty-four. When he left Toronto his apprenticeship was over, and he was now a professional if not a widely recognized author.

6

A Writer's Life
1924

We need a new prose to
handle our own time or
that part of it I've seen.

HEMINGWAY TO CHARLES POORE

I

"Hemingway had then and has always a very good instinct for finding apartments in strange but pleasing localities," wrote Gertrude Stein, "and good femmes de ménage and good food." They arrived in France on January 29, 1924, and soon found a flat above a noisy sawmill, near Pound's old studio, at 113 rue Notre Dame des Champs, where the street curves parallel to the Boulevard Montparnasse.

But the flat had more character than comfort. American friends, who were used to living well in France, were shocked by the squalor. Kitty Cannell said: "The Hemingways lived in a cold-water apartment that gave on[to] a lumber yard in the Montparnasse quarter. It had neither gas nor electric light." And the journalist Burton Rascoe wrote: "They lived, at the time, in an incredibly bare hovel, without toilet or running water, and with a mattress spread on the floor for a bed; it was in the court of a lumber yard, on the second floor, to which one climbed by a flight of rickety steps."[1]

When Hadley heated the water to give Bumby a bath in their cramped quarters, the wallpaper swelled out from the walls. When they went out at night, they would leave Bumby alone in the flat with their cat, Feather Puss, for company. William Carlos Williams, a poet and a hard-working obstetrician like Ed Hemingway, noted that when he circumcised Bumby in 1924 the redoubtable Hemingway "almost

125

fainted."[2] The infant had an ecumenical baptism in St. Luke's Episcopal Church on March 10, with the Jewish Gertrude Stein and the Catholic Chink Dorman-Smith as godparents. As the remarkably beautiful boy grew older, Hemingway taught him to put up his fists and assume a ferocious expression. Bumby acquired a devoted nursemaid, Marie Rohrbach, began to learn French as well as English and said, with more charm than grammar, *"la vie est beau avec Papa."* His mnemonic song about "Dix bis Avenue des Gobelins / That's where my Bumby lives" referred to Marie's house, not his own.

As soon as Hemingway's domestic life was settled, he followed Pound's suggestion to help Ford Madox Ford edit the *Transatlantic Review*. When Pound introduced him to Ford in January 1924 the older writer was well known for his literary friendships, his technical experiments, his fictional achievement and his editorial skill. Ford had close family connections with the Pre-Raphaelites; he was a good friend of several distinguished American writers: Henry James, Stephen Crane, Ezra Pound; he was a confidant and collaborator of Conrad, and in May 1924 offered to take Hemingway to England to meet the Master.

Ford was a stylistic innovator who introduced into English literature some of the Flaubertian techniques that were later adopted by Pound and Joyce. Pound defined Ford's lesson as "the limpidity of natural speech, driven toward the just word" and confessed that he "learned more from Ford than from anyone else."[3] Ford, who had published *The Good Soldier* in 1915, was working on the opening volume of the Tietjens tetralogy when Hemingway first knew him. He was also a brilliant editor and was the first to publish writers like D. H. Lawrence and Wyndham Lewis in the *English Review*.

Ford's personal qualities might also have appealed to Hemingway. Though Ford was over forty when the Great War broke out, he volunteered for service, had combat experience and was badly gassed in the summer of 1916. He had led a truly bohemian life before Left Bank expatriates made it fashionable. Despite his ungainly appearance, he conducted a number of sexual liaisons and had the reputation of a ladies' man. At the end of his life he was respected by John Crowe Ransom and Allen Tate, and revered as a teacher by Robert Lowell.

Ford published Hemingway's early stories—"Indian Camp," "The Doctor and the Doctor's Wife," "Cross Country Snow"—and several articles in the *Transatlantic Review*. Ford allowed him to edit the "American" issue of August 1924, which included work by Hemingway's friends John Dos Passos, Nathan Asch, Guy Hickok and Gertrude Stein. Ford consistently praised Hemingway in print and (on a fund-raising trip to America) even carried the good news to his family in Oak Park—who had strongly disapproved of their son's early fiction. In January 1927 Ed Hemingway told his son of "our very delightful dinner party this Noon with your great admirer present, Mr. Ford Madox Ford. I . . . was pleased that he spoke so kindly of you and your work."[4]

Ford maintained his admiration despite the hostility of the younger man. As he justly observed in *Provence:* "I never . . . wrote a contemptu-ous word of another living writer. . . . [And] I have never paid my tribute to greatness without being subsequently massacred." Ford first saw Hemingway shadow boxing in front of a Chinese portrait in Pound's studio. Pound told Ford: "He's an experienced journalist. He writes very good verse and he's the finest prose stylist in the world." When Ford objected that Pound had very recently called *him* the finest stylist, Pound exclaimed: "You! You're like all the English swine."[5] Heming-way, who liked to imitate the manner of the professional English sol-dier, reminded Ford of an "Eton-Oxford, husky-ish young captain of a midland regiment of His Britannic Majesty."[6]

When Hemingway's first trade book, *In Our Time,* was published in 1925, Ford's generous appreciation appeared on the dust jacket. Ford claimed, boldly yet accurately: "The best writer in America at this moment (though for the moment he happens to be in Paris), the most conscientious, the most master of his craft, the most consummate, is Ernest Hemingway." If Ford recognized himself and Stella Bowen as Mr. and Mrs. Henry Braddocks—foolish expatriates whose dance party makes Jake Barnes feel sick in *The Sun Also Rises* (1926)—he did not seem to mind. In his windy ramble on life in Paris in 1927, Ford good-naturedly confirmed what he had said about *In Our Time:* "Hemingway writes extremely delicate prose—perhaps the most delicate prose that is today being written."[7]

In his charming Introduction to the widely read Modern Library edition of *A Farewell to Arms,* Ford reminisced about the early days in Paris when Hemingway published his first, small-press books. Ford handsomely ranked Hemingway with Conrad and W. H. Hudson as one of "the three impeccable writers of English prose that I have come across in fifty years or so of reading" and—echoing the second sentence of the novel—said that Hemingway had the supreme gift of using words "so one of his pages has the effect of a brook-bottom into which you look down through the flowing water. The words form a tessellation, each in order beside the other."[8]

Yet everything about Ford—even his good qualities—seemed to irritate Hemingway. He refused to make allowances for Ford's eccentricities, and what might have been gratitude soon became wrath. Hemingway, who was extraordinarily handsome and fit in the early 1920s, found Ford, whom he called "the golden walrus," physically repellent. To Hemingway, Ford was slovenly, smelly and obese. The democratic Hemingway also thought Ford was a terrible snob, steeped in synthetic gentility and (he told Pound) too "goddam involved in being the dregs of an English country gentleman."[9] He failed to understand that Ford's fascination with the English gentry was not snobbery, but a rich source of his art.

Though Ford had indeed been an intimate of Conrad, Hemingway agreed with the author's widow that Ford had capitalized on their friendship and published a "disgusting," opportunistic book immediately after Conrad's death in 1924. Ford's pose as a great man of letters revealed, just beneath the surface, a vain, overbearing and self-deceiving personality. Ford bungled the role of teacher by patronizing his "pupils" and bragging about his disciples. Stein's remark (which may well have been false)—"It was Ford who once said of Hemingway, he comes and sits at my feet and praises me. It makes me nervous"—wounded Hemingway as it was meant to do. For Hemingway was not prepared to tolerate, and even justify, Ford's foibles as Stephen Crane had done: "You are wrong about [him]. I admit he is patronizing. He patronized his family. He patronizes Conrad. He will end up by patronizing God who will have to get used to it and they will be friends."[10]

More particularly, as Hadley confirmed, Ford would come to the out-of-the-way café where Hemingway worked and disturb him. Ford assumed that Hemingway would be delighted to benefit from the advice of an experienced writer and was entirely unaware of his intrusion. Burton Rascoe remembered Hemingway's rudeness in the fall of 1924. When Ford invited the Rascoes and Hadley to sit at his table, Hemingway shouted to his wife: "Pay for your own drinks, do you hear! Don't let [Ford] buy you anything!"[11] Hemingway, constrained by marriage but lusting after Duff Twysden, both envied and disapproved of Ford's liaison with Jean Rhys.

Jean Rhys' interesting roman à clef, Quartet (1929)—in which she is Marya, Ford is H. J. Heidler, Stella Bowen is Lois Heidler and Hemingway is Cairn—describes her love affair with Ford and throws some useful light on his character and his relations with Hemingway. Cairn advises Marya to break off her unhappy liaison with the treacherous Heidler, which had been encouraged by his wife. Heidler, who "made discoveries; he helped the young men, he had a flair,"[12] then forbade her to see Cairn. In the end Marya cannot break with Heidler, though she is hurt by her involvement with him, and is abandoned by her quite decent husband. Hemingway interfered in the sexual affairs of Ford and Jean Rhys, as he had done with Kenley Smith and Doodles, and offended the man who had been helping him.

Finally, Hemingway rightly thought Ford was mendacious and lived in a world of unreality. In a harsh passage, deleted from *A Moveable Feast*, Hemingway maintained that Ford would give his word about money and other practical matters, and would then tell lies that left scars. Ford's lies made Hemingway doubt Ford's truths, so that Hemingway (the Red Cross noncombatant) told Morley Callaghan: "Gassed in the war? Don't let him kid you. [Ford] was never gassed in the war."[13] Yet Hemingway lived his own lies just as Ford did, and was not always faithful to women, friends or truth. He could not bear to be helped, and fiercely judged his own faults—sexual adventures and telling lies—when he saw them manifested in others.

All Hemingway's criticisms became intensified when he agreed to assist Ford in editing the short-lived *Transatlantic Review*. Though Pound and most other writers admired the way Ford edited the magazine, Hemingway disliked both his policy and his taste. He felt the magazine was an unsatisfactory compromise between the traditional and the avant-garde, between conventional material that could be published in *Harper's* and surrealist "shit in French." Hemingway also claimed, not quite accurately and as an excuse for delays in his own fiction, that Ford had bitched his work for two months by begging Hemingway to bring out two issues so Ford could go to America and raise funds to continue the magazine. Hemingway, in fact, welcomed the opportunity to gain editorial experience and publish the kind of American work that *he* admired.

While Ford was away, Hemingway copied out and sent to the printer for serialization what seemed to be the complete works of Gertrude Stein but was merely *The Making of Americans*. Ford was naturally annoyed, for what he thought was a novella turned out to be an unreadable magnum opus that threatened to dominate the magazine indefinitely. Stein's work may have influenced his decision to cease publication.

Hemingway also gratuitously attacked T. S. Eliot in an obituary notice of Conrad (October 1924) and said that he would gladly grind Eliot into a fine powder if that would bring Conrad back to life. When Ford regained control of the magazine, he felt obliged to apologize— in his arch fashion—for Hemingway's literary bad manners: "We wish we could reconcile it with our conscience to excise the paragraphs in which our chronicler made attacks upon individuals. Thus two months or so ago one of these gentlemen made an attack on T. S. Eliot. . . . We had indicated no limits to his bloodthirstyness, our hands fell powerless to our sides."[14] Hemingway was naturally offended by Ford's recantation. But he also realized that his attack was misguided, and later apologized to Eliot for his insulting statement, his violence and his ignorance.

Hemingway attempted to save the magazine by introducing Ford to a bizarre couple: the shell-shocked Krebs Friend (whom he had known in Chicago) and his decrepit, moribund wife, who promised to give Ford $200 a month for half a year. But Ford objected to the financial arrangements Hemingway made with Friend and, as Hemingway told Stein: "ruined everything except of course himself, by selling the magazine to the Friends instead of taking money from them and keeping them outside as originally planned."[15]

In the end, the *Transatlantic Review* died in January 1925, after running just over a year, and closed off one of the few outlets Hemingway then had for his stories. Hemingway was thoroughly "sick of Ford and his megalomaniac blundering [and] the way he spoiled the chance he had with the review."[16] He felt that Ford spent all his time kissing the asses of wealthy people and then insulting those with less money to show he never kissed anyone's ass.

Hemingway's writings on Ford reveal his characteristic ingratitude toward a colleague who, for all his limitations, had given him very considerable assistance. In *The Torrents of Spring* (1926) Ford is portrayed as an old windbag and purveyor of stale anecdotes. Ford is credited with the rather pointless tale of the Marquess and the flamingo; and is probably the source of the stories about Henry James and the O.M., and about the beautiful woman in Paris. Hemingway's comment on Blaise Cendrars in *A Moveable Feast* applies with equal force to Ford and to himself: "when he was lying, he was more interesting than many men telling a story truly."[17]

In one passage on Ford deleted from *The Sun Also Rises*, Jake Barnes alludes to *The Good Soldier* and says that he dislikes Braddocks' fiction because the Jamesian passion in it is false and divorced from the realities of sexual life: "In [Braddocks' novels] there was always a great deal of passion but it took sometimes two and three volumes for anyone to sleep with anyone else. In actual life it seemed there was a great deal of sleeping about among good people, much more sleeping about than passion."[18] Hemingway's novel, by contrast, contains a great deal of sexual promiscuity.

In a second passage deleted from the novel Jake Barnes criticizes Braddocks for ignoring the work of younger writers: Braddocks "was very busy on something of his own and, as the years went on, found it increasingly difficult to read the works of writers other than himself." Ford, however, had been consistently generous about recognizing new literary talent—especially Hemingway's.

The chapter on Ford in *A Moveable Feast* (1964), substantially written in 1925 and originally a part of *The Sun Also Rises*, accurately reflects Hemingway's feelings toward Ford at the time the memoir takes place. In this respect, it is quite different from the chapters on Stein, Wyndham Lewis, Fitzgerald and Dos Passos, which were influenced by Hemingway's quarrels with these writers in the 1930s and reveal a hostile attitude that was formed long after his Paris years. Hemingway takes posthumous revenge on "the heavy, wheezing, ignoble" Ford. He compares the older writer to an "up-ended hogshead" and describes him as physically revolting, pedantic, rude, affected, snobbish and untruthful. Ford, in a discussion of English social nuance, tells Hemingway that he (Ford) is a gentleman and that James, Pound and Hemingway are not. Ford claims to have "cut" Hilaire Belloc (for his own good reasons), but Hemingway later discovers that the man he "cut" was in fact Aleister Crowley.

A third section of *The Sun Also Rises*, deleted from the original opening chapters, was an early version of the chapter on Ford in *A Moveable Feast*. In the novel the writer "cut" by Braddocks is carefully described; contemporary readers, who knew what Belloc and Crowley looked like, would realize that the man was actually Crowley: "Along the sidewalk came a tall, gray, lantern-jawed man, walking with a tall woman wearing a blue Italian infantry cape." But in the memoir, this precise description is omitted and the identity of Belloc-Crowley is left. in doubt until the end of the anecdote. This deleted section of the novel also states that Braddocks "cut" Belloc (not Crowley) because of Belloc's well-known religious bigotry (and anti-Semitism): "What did you row with him about?" Barnes asks Braddocks. "There was no row. Simply a matter of religious intolerance. Not a review in England will touch him."[19] But in the memoir, where Ford's justification is deliberately left vague, he seems muddled rather than high-principled, malicious rather than sympathetic. Hemingway's revisions from novel to memoir intensified his hatred of Ford.

Most critics think that this anecdote could not have happened as Hemingway relates it. Julian Maclaren-Ross maintains that Ford would not have mistaken Belloc for Crowley or glorified in "cutting" Belloc as a cad: "What seems more likely is that he got their names mixed up . . . or that he was simply sending himself up." Arthur Mizener agrees that the anecdote was "surely intended as a parody of what Ford knew to be Hemingway's idea of him."[20] It was probably a joke of Ford's that fell quite flat. A Moveable Feast, Hemingway's portrait of the artist as a young man, charts his movement from innocence to experience. It is actually a fictionalized memoir, loosely based on fact but not strictly true. His portrait of Ford—like those of Stein, Lewis, Fitzgerald and Dos Passos—was inspired by an intense personal animus which is never explained in the book. The motivation for the malice is like the iceberg in Hemingway's aesthetic theory: it lies almost entirely submerged but influences everything that appears above the surface. This theory works extremely well in Hemingway's fiction. But in A Moveable Feast, the reader who feels the effect of what is omitted also demands an explanation of why that particular effect was produced.

The treatment of Ford follows a recurrent vindictive pattern in Hemingway's life. He parodied Sherwood Anderson in The Torrents of Spring, satirized Harold Loeb in The Sun Also Rises, condemned Scott Fitzgerald in the first version of "The Snows of Kilimanjaro," pilloried John Dos Passos in To Have and Have Not, savaged Sinclair Lewis in Across the River and into the Trees, and attacked Stein and Ford in A Moveable Feast.

II

Though Hemingway was short of funds and had to support his family, he realized the dangers of commercialism and maintained his artistic integrity. "It is much more important for me to write in tranquility," he told his father, "trying to write as well as I can, with no eye on any market, nor any thought of what the stuff will bring, or even if it can ever be published—than to fall into the money making trap which [ruins] American writers." Like most authors, he found writing an extremely difficult and exhausting process, a perpetual challenge that could never be perfectly met. He did not believe writing could be taught; it could be learned only through long, laborious practice.

On rare occasions, however, he achieved an ecstatic breakthrough. On Sunday, May 16, 1926, in Madrid, when the San Isidro bullfights were snowed out and he was confined to the Pension Aguilar, Hemingway, in love with but separated from Pauline Pfeiffer (who became his second wife the following year), "had so much juice" that he completed three stories in one day: "The Killers," "Today is Friday" and "Ten Indians." The waiter in the pension "said the Señora wanted to know if I was going to write all night. I said no, I thought I would just lay off for a while. Why don't you just try to write just one more, the waiter asked. I'm only supposed to write one, I said. Nonsense, he said. You could write six. I'll try tomorrow, I said. Try it tonight, he said. What do you think the old woman sent the food up for?"[21]

Hemingway saw writing as a kind of fiercely competitive literary prizefight in which contemporaries pitted themselves against the established masters—as well as against each other—and tried to surpass what had already been achieved: "What a writer in our time has to do is write what hasn't been written before or beat dead men at what they have done."[22] To increase his skill and achieve superiority, he carefully studied and learned from his great predecessors. In 1925 he said his favorite authors were the sea-adventure novelist Frederick Marryat, Ivan Turgenev and Henry Fielding. Marryat's influence was negligible. Turgenev supplied the titles of "Fathers and Sons" and *The Torrents of Spring.* His *Sportsman's Sketches,* about hunting in the Russian countryside, seemed quite new to Hemingway and made the foreign landscape clear and vivid. Fielding's *Shamela* (an attack on Richardson's *Pamela*) was the model for a parody on a contemporary writer and Fielding's theories of satiric comedy were invoked in the chapter headings of *The Torrents of Spring.*

The literary influence of Tolstoy, Stephen Crane, Conrad and D. H. Lawrence (as well as of Kipling, Pound, Stein, Joyce and Ford) was more important than that of his early favorites. Tolstoy was Hemingway's literary hero, for both men had fought in battles and written about war. Hemingway's references to Tolstoy in four of his books and a major interview show that he used the Russian as an artistic standard, but retained sufficient critical judgment to avoid the dogmatism of his late works. He took Tolstoy's early accounts of combat in the Crimea and Caucasus on his first African safari, and in *Green Hills of Africa* admired his ability to evoke the Russian landscape: "I still had the Sevastopol book of Tolstoi and in the same volume I was reading a story called 'The Cossacks' that was very good. In it were the summer heat, the mosquitoes, the feel of the forest in the different seasons, and that river that the Tartars crossed, raiding, and I was living in that Russia again." In *A Moveable Feast* he tested Tolstoy's fiction against his own experience and praised the realistic portrayal of war: "the movement of troops, the terrain and the officers and the men and the fighting in Tolstoi. . . . Until I read the *Chartreuse de Parme* by Stendhal I had never read of war as it was except in Tolstoi."[23]

In a reminiscent *Esquire* article, "Old Newsman Writes," Hemingway made an important distinction between the didactic and imaginative passages in Tolstoy's greatest novel: "Read another book called *War and Peace* by Tolstoy and see how you will have to skip the big Political Thought passages, that he undoubtedly thought were the best things in the book when he wrote it, because they are no longer either true or important, if they ever were more than topical, and see how true and lasting and important the people and the action are." And in his Introduction to *Men at War,* his most substantial discussion of the master, he analyzed Tolstoy's account of Bagration's fighting and the battle of Borodino, his contempt for generals, his prolixity and the limitations of his thought. Hemingway learned an important lesson from the crucial weakness (accentuated in the late phase) of Tolstoy's art, and stated his own artistic credo: "There is no better writing on war than there is in Tolstoy. . . . I love *War and Peace* for the wonderful, penetrating and true descriptions of war and of people but I have never believed in the great Count's thinking. . . . He could invent more with more insight and truth than anyone who ever lived. But his ponderous and Messianic thinking was no better than many another evangelical professor of history and I learned from him to distrust my own Thinking with a capital T and to try to write as truly, as straightly, as objectively and as humbly as possible."[24]

Stephen Crane died at the age of twenty-eight in 1900, the year after Hemingway was born. Both Crane and Hemingway chose journalism instead of college; both were personally and professionally interested in the lives of prostitutes and criminals. Both covered a Greco-Turkish war (Crane in 1897, Hemingway in 1922); both spent significant time in Key West and Cuba; both became romantic and legendary figures; both had the unusual experience of reading their own obituaries. Crane was a friend of Ford, who very likely told Hemingway about the older writer. Both Crane and Hemingway were precocious authors who found their true voice in their early twenties. Both had simple, clear, succinct, intense yet detached prose styles. Both adopted an ironic, amoral tone. Crane's *Wounds in the Rain* (1899) suggests Hemingway's characteristic mood and contained a story whose title he borrowed: "God Rest Ye Merry, Gentlemen." Hemingway's "The Light of the World" resembled Crane's *Maggie: A Girl of the Streets;* his *Old Man and the Sea* was like Crane's *The Open Boat.* Finally, both writers were fascinated by violence. Hemingway, like Crane, spent "his life imaging, chasing, reporting, remembering War." Both novelists used historical sources rather than direct experience for *The Red Badge of Courage* and *A Farewell to Arms* (the retreat from Caporetto took place in 1917, when Hemingway was still in high school). And Hemingway's description of Crane's fictional technique characterized his own method: "He had read the contemporary accounts, had heard the old soldiers, they were not so old then, talk, and above all he had seen Mathew Brady's wonderful photographs. Creating his story out of this material he wrote that great boy's dream of war that was to be truer to how war is than any war the boy who wrote it would ever live to see. It is one of the finest books of our literature."[25]

Crane's friend Joseph Conrad was also a significant influence on Hemingway. In *The Sun Also Rises* he adopts Mr. Stein's phrase about Lord Jim, "one of us," to characterize Count Mippipopolous, who had been wounded by arrows in Abyssinia. And the description of Ricardo carefully shaving before meeting Lena in *Victory* may have influenced "all that barbering" that Robert Cohn does to prepare himself for Brett Ashley. Catherine Barkley is as completely self-effacing as Lena, who tells Heyst: "If you were to stop thinking of me I shouldn't be in the world at all. . . . I can only be what you think I am." "The Short Happy Life of Francis Macomber" recreates the great Conradian theme of moral failure and recovery of self-esteem just as *The Old Man and the*

Sea portrays Conrad's theme of victory in defeat. Both Hemingway and Fitzgerald learned from Conrad to use a more subtle and quiet conclusion in their fiction. As Fitzgerald told John Bishop: "It was EH who developed to me, in conversation, that the dying fall was preferable to the dramatic ending under certain conditions, and I think we both got the germ of the idea from Conrad." Conrad's belief in "scrupulous fidelity to the truth of my own sensations," expressed in his Author's Note to *Within the Tides,* is echoed in Hemingway's desire to portray "the actual things which produced the emotion you experienced." The most important lesson came from Conrad's famous Preface to *The Nigger of the 'Narcissus,'* which stressed the visual element in fiction: "My task which I am trying to achieve is, by the power of the written word to make you hear, to make you feel—it is, before all, to make you *see.*" Hemingway echoed this artistic credo when he insisted that the novelist must "find what gave you the emotion; what the action was that gave you the excitement. Then write it down making it clear so that the reader will see it too."[26]

The coy device of calling his wife and traveling companion P.O.M. (Poor Old Mama) in *Green Hills of Africa* was probably taken from D. H. Lawrence, who refers to his wife as Q.B. (Queen Bee) in *Sea and Sardinia.* "Francis Macomber" and several other stories express a Lawrencean hostility to castrating women and portray the struggle for domination in marriage. Like Lawrence, Hemingway exalted the primitive element in man in his Spanish and Cuban fiction; and he learned from Lawrence (as he did from Turgenev) how to express what he felt about a country, how to bring alive the landscape and convey the "spirit of place." Just as Lawrence believed in the therapeutic effect of "shedding one's sicknesses in books," so Hemingway maintained: "If he wrote it he could get rid of it. He had gotten rid of many things by writing them."[27]

Hemingway acknowledged his literary influences, but he misled readers about an artistic influence when he said, with deliberate vagueness, that he "was learning something from the painting of Cézanne." In the 1920s, when it was fashionable to claim a visual rather than a verbal master, Hemingway rather pretentiously maintained that he had learned to give more depth and dimension to his prose by using the pictorial techniques that Stein said *she* had learned from Cézanne. Though critics have invented ingenious explanations of Hemingway's claim, there is no convincing evidence of his debt to Cézanne.[28]

III

Hemingway discovered his genius as a very young man and took great pleasure in writing well. He knew a good deal about the craft of fiction and frequently expressed his sound and practical ideas in letters, interviews and introductions to his own works, in shrewd pieces like "On Writing," "Old Newsman Writes" and "Monologue to the Maestro"; and in tangential remarks in his nonfiction: *Death in the Afternoon, Green Hills of Africa* and *A Moveable Feast.* As a journalist Hemingway had always listened intently and trained himself to remember exactly what he heard. He took no notes after meeting Max Beerbohm in Rapallo in April 1922 and justly claimed, tapping his head, "I have every word of it in here." In order to increase his spontaneity and freshness, he did not keep a journal or take notes for his fiction; and he rarely made outlines for his stories or novels.

His basic principles of writing have been extremely influential:

Study the best literary models.
Master your subject through experience and reading.
Work in disciplined isolation.
Begin early in the morning and concentrate for several hours each day.
Begin by reading everything you have written from the start or, if engaged on a long book, from the last chapter.
Write slowly and deliberately.
Stop writing when things are going well and you know what will happen next so that you have sufficient momentum to continue the next day.
Do not discuss the material while writing about it.
Do not think about writing when you are finished for the day but allow your subconscious mind to ponder it.
Work continuously on a project once you start it.
Keep a record of your daily progress.
Make a list of titles after you have completed the work.

It often took Hemingway all morning to write a single perfect paragraph. But he said he could easily turn out five thousand words a day if, like Sinclair Lewis and Thomas Wolfe, he wrote "sloppily and shittily," "with all the ease of a man going to the toilet when he has amoebic [dysentery]." In Europe he wrote in cafés, in hotel rooms and at home; in Key West he wrote at a table in his separate studio. But after he moved to Havana in 1940 he began to write standing up at a lectern in his bedroom, beneath the horns of a huge water buffalo: "during the acquiring of them things went badly in the bush which ultimately turned out well. It cheers me up to look at them."[29]

In March 1925 Hemingway wrote a long letter to his father, who disliked his early work, explaining and defending the technique, aims and morality of his fiction:

> I'm trying in all my stories to get the feeling of the actual life across—not to just depict life—or criticize it—but to actually make it alive. So that when you have read something by me you actually experience the thing. You can't do this without putting in the bad and the ugly as well as what is beautiful. Because if it is all beautiful you can't believe in it. Things aren't that way. It is only by showing both sides—3 dimensions and if possible 4 that you can write the way I want to.
>
> So when you see anything of mine that you don't like remember that I'm sincere in doing it and that I'm working toward something. If I write an ugly story that might be hateful to you or to Mother the next one might be the one you would like exceedingly.[30]

Hemingway's aesthetic is based on two essential principles. The first —derived from newspaper experience which had trained him to report only what he had witnessed directly—was that fiction must be founded on real emotional and intellectual experience and be faithful to actuality, but must also be transformed and heightened by the imagination until it becomes truer than mere factual events. The knowledgeable writer, he felt, always begins with reality, but finally produces something that is much more interesting and significant than the original experience. Like Kipling and like his own fictional hero Robert Jordan, Hemingway "liked to know how it really was; not how it was supposed to be." When he first began to write, he explained in *Death in the Afternoon,* he forced himself to concentrate on real events and feelings: "I found the greatest difficulty, aside from knowing truly what you really felt, rather than what you were supposed to feel, and had been taught to feel, was to put down what really happened in action." And he told Bernard Berenson: "Fiction, prose rather, is possibly the roughest trade of all in writing. . . . You have the sheet of blank paper, the pencil, and the obligation to invent truer than things can be true. You have to take what is not palpable and make it completely palpable and also have it seem normal so that it can become a part of the experience of the person who reads it."[31]

The second principle was that fiction must be compressed to achieve intensity, that the underpinnings of structure and meaning that give a work solidity and strength must be concealed beneath the surface of the story. He believed a work of fiction could be judged by the quality of material the author *eliminated* and that "the most essential gift for a good writer is a built-in, shock-proof, shit detector. This is the writer's radar and all great writers have had it." The principle of elimination by shit detector led directly to the famous analogy of the iceberg: "I always try to write on the principle of the iceberg. There is seven-eighths of it underwater for every part that shows. Anything you know you can eliminate and it only strengthens your iceberg. It is the part that doesn't show."[32] The novelist H. E. Bates observed that Hemingway, whose sensitive characters become embittered, "was in reality so deeply susceptible to emotion that he strove constantly for the elimination of himself, his thoughts and feelings, from the surface of the work."

Though this technique functioned brilliantly for Hemingway, there were occasions when the omission was so radical that the meaning remained submerged in the mass of the iceberg. He said that in "Out of Season" he wanted to write one tragic story that did not contain violence and "omitted the real end of it which was that the old man hanged himself."[33] But this story, written before he had mastered the technique of omission, failed to provide sufficient justification for the suicide and even the most perceptive readers fail to see what is supposed to have happened. Hemingway's theories and techniques were formed in the early 1920s and remained consistent throughout his career. It was only when his shit detector began to fail in the 1950s that he diverged from his original principles and became self-indulgent, self-parodic and verbose.

Hemingway's technique was matched by his highly innovative style —the most influential prose in the twentieth century. The short words, limited vocabulary, declarative sentences and direct representation of the visible world appealed to the ordinary as well as to the intellectual reader. He prided himself on his purity of expression and suggestive simplicity. His Italian translator said that when she inadvertently used the expression "slang" in asking him to explain a vernacular word, "he yelled at me for quite a while: he had never used slang, all the words in his books were in the dictionary and could have been used by Shakespeare." When she described his prose as "metaphysical," he became enraged, would not speak to her for hours and then wrote a letter denying this aspect of his work.[34]

Hemingway's style was characterized by clarity and force. He stressed the function of the individual word, wrote five simple sentences for every complex one, used very few similes, repeated words and phrases, emphasized dialogue rather than narration. He expressed his violent themes in limpid, focused, perfectly controlled prose. He concentrated on sensations—the "exaltation of the instant"—and found physical details that produced the aesthetic effect. His style was precise and exact, yet highly connotative; sparse and bare, yet charged with poetic intensity.

IV

Hemingway's style and themes were so unusual that he had a great deal of difficulty publishing his poems and stories in the mid-1920s. The *Double Dealer* in New Orleans, the first American magazine (apart from the high school *Tabula*) to publish his poetry, printed his quatrain "Ultimately" on the same page as Faulkner's "Portrait" in June 1922. When the magazine did not pay him, Hemingway told the editor that its title reflected his morality. Pound helped him place in *Poetry* six of the ten poems that later appeared in his first book. But in 1926 Hemingway told Ernest Walsh that the editor of the magazine, Harriet Monroe, "is just a faintly sensitized, dried up old bitch who runs a long dead magazine. She never has written a line of poetry and never could." As late as the fall of 1926, "An Alpine Idyll" was rejected by the Communist *New Masses*, "the most puerile and shitty house organ I've ever seen." George Seldes recalled:

> In 1922 or 1923 in the Paris days Hemingway invented the myth about being rejected "by all the highbrow magazines" in the world. . . . [In Spain in 1937 he said that] when he was younger, and rejected, *The Dial* of New York had not only returned his short stories but sent him a letter suggesting he stick to newspaper reporting because he would never become a real writer. . . . Then, turning to me, he almost shouted "And the editor of the *Dial* who wrote me that was Gilbert Seldes, YOUR BROTHER," pointing at me. It was a sensation. When I got back to New York Gilbert said it was all false, and he went to the storage company and examined the record books of every contribution during his time as editor: there was no submission by Hemingway, no correspondence whatever.[35]

Though Gilbert Seldes did not turn down Hemingway's work, the rejections were not a myth. "The Undefeated" had been refused in the spring of 1925, when Scofield Thayer was editor of *The Dial.*

Hemingway did manage to publish some of his early work in Margaret Anderson's *Little Review,* Ford's *Transatlantic Review,* Alfred Flechtheim's *Querschnitt* (Cross-Section) in Frankfurt and Ernest Walsh's *This Quarter* during 1923–25. But he earned only fifty dollars in 1924. The few copies of *in our time* sold out fast, but the profits were used to balance the losses of other publications in the Three Mountains Press series. Hemingway did not have the sense to keep a number of copies (which now sell for as much as $10,000). He had one stroke of luck in January 1923 when he met the anthologist Edward O'Brien, "a gentle, shy man, pale, with pale blue eyes, and straight lanky hair he cut himself, who lived then as a boarder in a monastery up above Rapallo."[36] O'Brien read "My Old Man," the story of a boy's disenchantment with his crooked jockey-father. He accepted it for *The Best Stories of 1923* (published in January 1924) although it had not previously appeared in a magazine, and generously dedicated the volume "TO ERNEST HEMENWAY."

Hemingway wrote the first six vignettes of *in our time* in January–February 1923, between the Lausanne Conference and his tour of the Ruhr, and published them in the *Little Review* in the spring of 1923. He completed the remaining twelve sketches in a second concentrated spurt of creativity during late July and early August 1923, between his first trip to Pamplona and his departure for Toronto. He finished nine new stories, which formed the core of *In Our Time,* between January and July 1924, his first six months as a professional writer.

Three Stories and Ten Poems, a 58-page booklet published privately in August 1923 in a limited edition of 300 copies by McAlmon's Contact Publishing Company, was a youthful work. The stories had been fortuitously saved from inclusion in Hadley's lost suitcase and the poems were insignificant. But the eighteen short, untitled chapters of *in our time,* a 38-page booklet also privately printed, on hand-made paper, in March 1924, in an even more limited edition of 170 copies, by Bill Bird's Three Mountains Press, contained Hemingway's mature techniques, style and themes. Bill Bird—a slim, reserved and self-effacing young journalist— was born in Buffalo in 1889, graduated from Trinity College in Hartford and had been European manager of the Consolidated Press in Paris since 1920. He traveled with Hemingway to the Black Forest in 1922 and to Pamplona in 1923 and 1924, and later published *A Practical Guide to French Wines* (1924).

Hemingway explained the structure of *in our time*, which resembled a series of vivid cinematic flashbacks, in a letter to Ezra Pound:

> When they are read altogether they all hook up. . . . The bulls start, then reappear and then finish off. The war starts clear and noble just like it did, Mons etc., gets close and blurred and finished with the feller who goes home and gets clap ["A Very Short Story"]. The refugees leave Thrace, due to the Greek ministers, who are shot. The whole thing closes with the talk with the King of Greece and his Queen in their Garden. . . . The radicals start noble in the young Magyar story ["The Revolutionist"] and get bitched. America reappears in the cops shooting the guys who robbed the cigar store. It has form all right.[37]

The dust wrapper of *in our time* was a collage of a map and newspaper articles in English, French and Greek. All the sketches, except for the death of Maera, were based on actual events. But Hemingway witnessed only half of them directly: the retreat from Thrace, Nick's wounds, the last five bullfight vignettes (the first was published before he went to Spain). The other half he learned about indirectly from newspaper accounts and from Chink, Gertrude Stein and Shorty Wornall. For example, the description of potting the German soldiers at an "absolutely perfect barricade" was based on an incident that took place at Mariette Bridge in Quaregnon (five miles east of Mons) and was followed by the English retreat from Le Cateau on August 22–23, 1914. Chink told Hemingway this story, which was later recorded in his regimental history:

> The bridge-keeper's house on the north bank was placed in a state of defence and garrisoned by a party of twelve men under Sergeant Panter. The duty of the party was to report and delay the approach of the enemy; but they were to fall back south of the canal if in danger of being cut off. To cover the position the gates of the level crossing were jammed, and connected to the houses behind by a wire entanglement. In the rear of the post a further obstacle constructed from some iron railings was erected at the north end of the bridge, in which a small opening, easily closed, was left for the withdrawal of the sergeant's party.[38]

Hemingway's imagination transformed such bare accounts into prose that was as vivid as the descriptions of events he had actually seen.

These etchings of life and death between 1914 and 1923 were a bitterly ironic echo of the hope expressed in the *Book of Common Prayer:* "Give us peace in our time, O Lord." As the guerrilla Andrés reflects in *For Whom the Bell Tolls:* "I think that we are born into a time of great difficulty. I think any other time was probably easier. One suffers little because all of us have been formed to resist suffering."[39]

In Our Time, Hemingway's first commercially published book, was brought out by Boni and Liveright in October 1925 and dedicated once again to Hadley. The dust wrapper contained generous appreciations of Hemingway's work by Anderson, Ford, Dos Passos, Don Stewart, Edward O'Brien, Gilbert Seldes and Waldo Frank. This book was very different and much thicker than the earlier work with the same (but lower-case) title. *In Our Time* used the sixteen short sketches of its predecessor, *in our time,* as interchapters between fifteen short stories. Two of the stories came from his first book, two had been sketches in his second book, six (one of them now in two parts) had been published in little magazines, and four appeared for the first time. Horace Liveright aroused Hemingway's wrath by excluding "Up in Michigan" on the grounds of obscenity. "To hear him talk," Fitzgerald told Max Perkins, "you'd think Liveright had broken up his home and robbed him of millions—but that's because he knows nothing of publishing, except in the cuckoo magazines, is very young and feels helpless so far away. You won't be able to help liking him—he's one of the nicest fellows I ever knew."[40]

There are complex verbal (rain, blanket, soldiers, shot, blood) and thematic reverberations among the interchapters, which are rearranged in a quite different and now final order. They are independent yet related to each other, like a sequence of sonnets. The symmetrical structure emphasizes Hemingway's favorite analogy between war (chapters 1–7) and bullfighting (9–14): after the war in Europe, the two crooks are executed by the police in Kansas City (8); after the bulls in Spain, the murderer is executed by hanging in Chicago (15). In the first half, the drunken soldiers (1) mark the beginning of the war; the fearful Nick (7) marks the end of the war. The plight of the Greek refugees (2) leads to the political execution of the Greek ministers (5), which is justified by the Greek king (Envoi). There is a Greek retreat from Turkey (2) and an English retreat from Mons (4). In the second half, the mob responds to courage (9) and to cowardice (11) in the bullring. A bull kills a horse (10), a man kills a bull (12) and a bull kills a man (14). There are also important thematic connections between as well as within the two halves. There are drunken soldiers (1) and a drunken bullfighter (13); a garden in Mons (3) and a garden in Athens (Envoi); a wounded soldier (6) and a wounded bullfighter (9). Nick is terrified (7), a matador is terrified (11) and Sam Cardinella is terrified (15). The English shoot the Germans (3), the Greeks shoot the ministers (5), the Austrians shoot Nick (6), the police shoot the Hungarians (8). The traditional values—stoicism, endurance and courage—seem inadequate to deal with the dreadful loss of patriotism, justice and honor.

The stories between the interchapters are unified by the central character, Nick Adams (whose name may have come from Hemingway's favorite boyhood reading, the St. Nicholas Magazine), just as the trio of principal characters unifies Kipling's Soldiers Three (1888). Hemingway said that "every artist owes it to the place he knows best either to destroy it or perpetuate it."[41] He "destroyed" Oak Park by repudiating it and perpetuated Michigan by writing about it. The first five stories and the last one take place there. Like Joyce's Dubliners, the stories of In Our Time reflect the progressive stages of a man's life. The first five stories and "My Old Man" are about boyhood and youth; "A Very Short Story" and "Soldier's Home" are about readjustment after the war; "The Revolutionist" and "Mr. and Mrs. Elliot" are about expatriates in postwar Europe; "Cat in the Rain," "Out of Season" and "Cross-Country Snow" are about the disintegration of his marriage to Hadley; and in the final and most impressive story, "Big Two-Hearted River," Nick returns to his boyhood terrain to heal the trauma of war.

Hemingway's Paris acquaintance Chard Powers Smith (1894–1977), a contemporary of MacLeish at Yale and at Harvard Law School, was satirized in "Mr. and Mrs. Elliot." He had a private income, never practiced law, hung about the Latin Quarter, tried to write and talked a good deal about mysticism. He deeply resented the story, which suggested that he was impotent and his wife lesbian, and wrote Hemingway an abusive letter. Hemingway, skiing in Gstaad, threatened to punch him when he returned to Paris. Smith waited apprehensively in the Café Deux Magots and kept a pistol in his room, but there was no confrontation. In October 1924, when the unpleasant story first appeared in the Little Review, Smith's wife died while pregnant with twins.

"Big Two-Hearted River" clearly concerns much more than fishing in the Fox River, near Seney in the upper peninsula. Nick gets off the train and finds himself in a burnt, desolate, war-like landscape. He moves from there to the regenerative river, but cannot yet face the tragic swamp that symbolizes his unconscious fears. The lucid prose provides a brilliant contrast to the ambiguous tone and subtle allusiveness:

> It would not be possible to walk through a swamp like that. . . . You could not crash through the branches. . . . He did not feel like going on into the swamp. . . . The sun did not come through. . . . In the half light, the fishing would be tragic. In the swamp fishing was a tragic adventure. Nick did not want it. He did not want to go down the stream any further today. . . . There were plenty of days coming when he could fish the swamp.[42]

Nick encounters and identifies with a series of natural disasters: burnt timber and uprooted elms; blackened, sniped and pierced grasshoppers; trout killed by fungus, hooked in the jaw and disemboweled. He tries to keep himself steady, like the wavering trout in the stream, and solid, like the pegs he cuts for his tent. Though the source of Nick's anxiety is not specified in the story, a disturbing undercurrent swirls menacingly beneath the surface. Through the compulsive ritual of camping and fishing, Nick escapes from the psychological wounds of war, feels safe and experiences an unfamiliar happiness. This suggestive story expresses Hemingway's characteristic mixture of the primitive and the sophisticated, and conveys one of his great themes: the sense of loss. This is not simply grace under pressure—but under siege.

In an important letter to Edmund Wilson, written in October 1924 when *In Our Time* was completed, Hemingway explained the relation between the interchapters and the stories in terms of magnification and perspective, and emphasized the Conradian visual element. *In Our Time* meant "to give the picture of the whole between examining it in detail. Like looking with your eyes at something, say a passing coast line, and then looking at it with 15X binoculars. Or rather, maybe, looking at it and then going in and living in it—and then coming out and looking at it again."[43]

The first, hundred-word review of Hemingway's first book was written by Stein and appeared in the Paris edition of the *Chicago Tribune* on November 27, 1923. She graciously, if tautologically, acknowledged:

"*Three Stories and Ten Poems* is very pleasantly said. . . . As he sticks to poetry and intelligence it is both poetry and intelligent." But she advised Hemingway to "stick to poetry and intelligence and eschew the hotter emotions and more turgid vision."

When Hemingway heard that Edmund Wilson had read his six prose sketches in *The Little Review,* he sent Wilson copies of his first two books. Wilson's review in *The Dial* perceived the essence of Hemingway's talent and helped establish his serious literary reputation. Wilson stated "his prose is of the first distinction," linked him with Anderson and Stein, and noted that his colloquial diction conveyed "profound emotions and complex states of mind." He also saw that in *in our time* Hemingway was "remarkably successful in suggesting moral values by a series of simple statements," and that his "harrowing record of barbarities" had the sharpness and elegance of lithographs by Goya. When this review appeared, in October 1924, Hemingway wrote Wilson that he was glad that his early books had pleased so good a critic and praised the review as "cool and clear minded and decent and impersonal and sympathetic." Wilson's intelligence, he said, was an extremely rare commodity.[44]

In Our Time, which contained some of the best work Hemingway ever did, was immediately recognized by Allen Tate, Scott Fitzgerald and D. H. Lawrence as a work of astonishing originality. Lawrence said that Nick Adams was the thematic center of the "fragmentary novel": "It is a short book: and it does not pretend to be about one man. But it is. . . . The sketches are short, sharp, vivid, and most of them excellent. . . . These few sketches are enough to create the man and all his history: we need know no more."[45] In the brief, introductory reviews of Hemingway's early work, these distinguished writers focused on his unusual diction, style, technique and moral values, and saw him as an important new force in modern literature. By 1925 the young Hemingway had fulfilled his promise and launched his career.

By contrast, Hemingway's books received a fiercely hostile reception in the bosom of his puritanical family. Ed Hemingway, who was extremely prudish and conventional, insisted that he would rather see Ernest dead than writing about such sordid subjects: "The brutal you have surely shown the world. Look for the joyous, uplifting, and optimistic and spiritual in character." Later, when Hemingway became famous, his father would sadly exclaim: "Ernest's written another dirty book."[46]

Grace was even more horrified. She too was fond of telling Hemingway that she would rather see him in his grave than doing whatever he was doing at the time. While he was still a teenager, she told him "everything you write is morbid"; when *The Sun Also Rises* appeared, she denounced it as "one of the filthiest books of the year" and exhorted him: "surely you have other words in your vocabulary besides 'damn' and 'bitch'—every page fills me with a sick loathing." For many years afterwards, Grace would not tolerate such filth in her home. When his milder stories were serialized in *Scribner's Magazine,* his sister Carol had to read them secretly and replace them in the wrappers so Grace would not know she had seen them.[47]

Hemingway's parents were particularly shocked and outraged by his habit of placing and naming real people, well known to the family, in his scandalous fiction. The most egregious case occurred when he slyly compounded the first names of Jim and Liz Dilworth (the blacksmith and chicken-dinner cook of Horton Bay), and the surnames of Frances Coates (a high school girlfriend) and of Mr. Gilmore (a prominent Oak Parker who owned a department store), and used them for the animalistic lovers, Liz Coates and Jim Gilmore, in "Up in Michigan." All these people expressed their anger to Ed and Grace, who felt embarrassed and disgraced. Marcelline recorded the family's shame and revulsion as well as their need to affirm their respectability: "As I read on and realized that Ernest had put these kindly people into this vulgar, sordid tale . . . my stomach turned over. . . . Ernest's apparent lack of any decent consideration . . . horrified me. . . . Both [parents], very obviously, were shocked and horrified at some of the contents, especially ["A Very Short Story"]. . . . [Father] told him that no gentleman spoke of venereal disease outside a doctor's office." Grace, for her part, could not understand why her well-brought-up son had "to pick out words and thoughts from the gutter."[48]

When Ernest learned that someone named Hemingway in Oak Park had returned five (precious) copies of the limited edition of *in our time* to the publisher, he acidly asked his parents if the descriptions were too accurate and the attitude to life insufficiently sentimental to please them. Years later, however, when Hemingway was told that Mario Menocal, Jr., the son of a Cuban friend, had read "Up in Michigan" in his high school English class, "he made a face of amused astonishment, and said 'Really! All of it! There are some words in it. . . . I didn't think they'd read that!' "[49]

It is somewhat surprising—considering the rigidity of Ed and Grace's views, the moral gulf between parents and son, and the pleasure he derived from offending his family—that Hemingway cared enough about their feelings to justify himself after their attacks on *The Sun Also Rises*. Whenever he sent Grace one of his books, she would retaliate with a catalogue or review of her latest exhibition of painting. This prompted Hemingway to appeal to her as a fellow artist and to suggest the moral squalor beneath the unruffled surface of Oak Park:

> It is quite natural for you not to like the book and I regret your reading any book that causes you pain or disgust. . . . But it is not *all* unpleasant and I am sure is no more unpleasant than the real inner lives of some of our best Oak Park families. . . . Besides you, as an artist, know that a writer should not be forced to defend his choice of a subject but should be criticized on how he has treated that subject. The people I wrote of were certainly burned out, hollow and smashed—and that is the way I have attempted to show them.

Though Grace was pleased to be the mother of a famous son, she confirmed her judgment of his early work in a newspaper interview of 1951, the last year of her life: "Some critics and professors consider Ernest's books among the finest of our times, but I think the essays he wrote as a schoolboy were better."[50]

V

Hemingway continued to form friendships with writers in Paris—John Dos Passos, Archibald MacLeish, Ernest Walsh, Donald Ogden Stewart, Evan Shipman—after his return to the city in January 1924. His modest success as an author gave him a new artistic confidence and he no longer took the role of disciple as he had done with older masters like Pound, Stein and Joyce. He had now become a dangerous colleague; though his friendships began well, by 1937 he had quarreled with everyone but Shipman.

Hemingway had briefly met Dos Passos in Schio in 1918 and Paris in 1923, but they did not become close friends until 1924. Dos Passos was the grandson of an immigrant cobbler from Portuguese Madeira and the illegitimate son of a successful New York lawyer. Born in Chicago in 1896, he had been educated in Europe and at the Choate School before graduating from Harvard and driving ambulances in France and Italy. He had traveled widely in Spain and the Middle East and published his war novel, *Three Soldiers*, in 1921. Hemingway and Dos Passos drank in cafés and talked about writing; Dos Passos watched him bathe Bumby and helped him buy Miró's *The Farm*. The nearsighted and introspective Dos Passos did not engage in athletic competition with Hemingway, but Hemingway's enthusiasm had an invigorating effect and converted him to the current sporting mania. They went to bike races at the Vélodrome d'Hiver and horse races at Longchamps, saw bullfights in Pamplona and skied in Schruns. Dos Passos, who married Hemingway's childhood friend Katy Smith, spent a good deal of time with Hemingway in Key West. When Dos Passos was ill with rheumatic fever in 1933, Hemingway, always generous with money, sent him a thousand dollars.

Archibald MacLeish, born in 1892 in Glencoe, a Chicago suburb similar to Oak Park, was amused when Hemingway fabricated a tough background for himself and said he had grown up on the wrong side of the tracks. MacLeish had been educated at Yale and at Harvard Law School, but abandoned law in 1923 to write poetry. At the end of his life Hemingway, who thought of friendship in terms of places and experiences he had shared, recalled all the things they had done together in France and Spain: "Did you think I had forgotten Rue du Bac, Juan les Pins, Zaragoza, Chartres, that place of Peter Hamilton's you lived [in], our bicycles, Ada [MacLeish's wife] and the Six Jours [bike races], rue Froidevaux, and a million things, Gstaad,—don't ask me to name them all. Bassano and 'A Pursuit Race' [Hemingway's story]."

Hemingway could afford to praise MacLeish since his ceremonial poetry was so clearly mediocre. "This rhythm and vocabulary which my intelligence knows for second rate," MacLeish confessed to Amy Lowell, "are me, my 'style,' all that I have." In 1932 he sent his dull but unexceptionable long poem (which would win the Pulitzer Prize) to Ezra Pound, who bluntly told him that *Conquistador* was "damn bad." MacLeish worked for Henry Luce's *Fortune* magazine in the 1930s and then became a respected establishment figure: Librarian of Congress in 1939, Boylston Professor at Harvard a decade later. In 1945 Hemingway pronounced his final, witty judgment on the radical limitations of MacLeish's verse and character: "Does Archie still write anything except Patriotic? I read some awfully lifeless lines to a Dead Soldier by him in that Free World anthology. I thought good old Allen Tate could write the lifeless-est lines to Dead Soldiers ever read but Archie is going good. You know his bro[ther] Kenny was killed in last war flying and I always felt Archie felt that sort of gave him a controlling interest in all deads."[51]

Ernest Walsh was co-founder, with his middle-aged mistress, Ethel Moorhead, of the little magazine *This Quarter,* which published Hemingway's "Big Two-Hearted River" and "The Undefeated" in 1925. In *A Moveable Feast* Walsh—who resembled Stephen Crane—was portrayed as "dark, intense, faultlessly Irish, poetic and clearly marked for death." He promised a substantial literary prize to Hemingway, Joyce and Pound in order to get their contributions for his magazine, but none of the impoverished writers won it. In 1924, two years before Walsh died of tuberculosis, Hemingway cynically conceded: "now that he is dying [he] is getting to be a pretty nice guy. I wonder if it would have the same effect on the rest of us."[52]

Hemingway had more cordial relations with Donald Ogden Stewart and Evan Shipman. The witty and entertaining Stewart was born in Ohio in 1896, graduated from Yale and became an extremely successful writer of humorous and satiric fiction: *Parody Outline of History* (1921) and *Mr. and Mrs. Haddock Abroad* (1925). He ran with the bulls in Pamplona and went trout fishing in Burguete in 1924–25, was instrumental in getting *In Our Time* published in New York, and gave Hemingway a large check to help him during a difficult period in December 1924.

Matthew Josephson has provided a lively sketch of the shabby-genteel Evan Shipman: "The skinny, long-legged Shipman, descendant on his mother's side of a distinguished American family (the Biddles) and son of the once popular playwright whose name he bore, had two ruling passions: these were horse racing and poetry, leaving aside wine and women. . . . He looked somewhat moth-eaten at times because of his drinking habits, but even in worn clothes he had the casual elegance of an inveterate racetrack follower." The alcoholic Shipman was born in New Hampshire in 1904, briefly attended Groton and the University of Louvain, tutored Bumby in Key West in 1933, was wounded in Spain, became a sergeant in World War Two and published a volume of poetry and a book of racing stories, *Free For All* (1935). Hemingway admired the habitué of bar and track, dedicated *Men Without Women* (1927) to him and said: "He was a fine poet and he knew and cared about horses, writing and painting. . . . I saw him tall and pale and thin, his white shirt dirty and worn at the collar, his tie carefully knotted, his worn and wrinkled grey suit, his fingers stained darker than his hair, his nails dirty and his loving, deprecatory smile that he held tightly not to show his bad teeth."[53]

After his first meetings with MacLeish, Walsh and Shipman in the fall of 1924, Hemingway again took advantage of postwar inflation in the German-speaking countries and went skiing in the Austrian Alps from December 1924 to March 1925. The whole family could stay at Schruns, a sunny market town near Bludenz in northwest Austria (his old war enemy), for only eighteen dollars a week. During the winters of 1924 and 1925, the Hemingways borrowed a sack of books from Sylvia Beach and stayed in the stove-heated room 22 of the Hotel Taube, a whitewashed four-story building with a gabled Tyrolean roof. They ate exceptionally well, played poker and pool, and found a devoted nursemaid, Mathilde Braun, to take care of Bumby. Dos Passos, who joined them in 1925, wrote:

> Everything was fantastically cheap. We stayed at a lovely old inn with porcelain stoves called the Taube. We ate *forellen im blau* [poached trout] and drank hot kirsch. The kirsch was so plentiful they gave it to us to rub off with when we came in from skiing. . . .
>
> We used sealskins to climb. The great excursion was up to the Madlener Haus on a huge snowfield above the town. This was a sort of ski club with roaring fires and hot food. The people were as nice as they could be. Everyone cried "Grüss Gott" when they met you.[54]

In February 1925, while Hemingway was in Schruns, Boni and Liveright sent a telegram accepting *In Our Time* and offering an advance of two hundred dollars.

7

Duff Twysden and Scott Fitzgerald
1925

> I have found that a lot of people, after
> they have been given aid, pick a quarrel
> in order to get rid of the obligation.
>
> HEMINGWAY TO CHARLES FENTON

I

Hemingway's marriage began to deteriorate as his literary fame increased. Lack of money had been a serious problem since the beginning of 1924. Soon after Hemingway gave up his newspaper job, George Breaker (the husband of Hadley's St. Louis friend Helen), who managed Hadley's investments, reduced her capital by half and left her entirely without income for several months. Breaker sold $19,000 worth of Hadley's railway bonds for $11,000 and sent her, on account, a $2,500 check that bounced three times. After six months of tortuous negotiations by mail, they managed to recover a third of what they had lost. Meanwhile, Hadley could not afford to have her shoes repaired and felt that her worn, old-fashioned clothes provided a dismal contrast to the apparel of her chic American friends. The advance for *In Our Time* was especially welcome, for the tenants who had sublet their Paris flat for three months while they were in Schruns stayed only one month. Hemingway, however, could not be bought. John Peale Bishop was "with him on the day he turned down an offer from one of Mr. Hearst's editors which, had he accepted it, would have supported him handsomely for years."[1]

Hemingway, weary of poverty, was also becoming bored with Hadley. Their eight-year age difference became increasingly obvious after the birth of Bumby, when Hadley began to gain weight and look ma-

152

tronly. He had a stronger sexual drive. She wanted a quieter life, found it difficult to keep up with all his energetic activities and was not "fun" any more. She gradually exchanged the role of wife for that of mother, wrote that he must "be sure to eat well, sleep well, keep well and work well," and signed the letter "with Mummy's love." His youthful sweetheart was awfully nice, but he had now outgrown her. He was living among the bohemians and expatriates of Paris, and wanted someone more sophisticated and exciting. As Dorothy Hollis bitterly observes in *To Have and Have Not:* "They want some one new, or some one younger, or some one they shouldn't have, or some one that looks like some one else. . . . The better you treat a man and the more you show him you love him the quicker he gets tired of you."[2]

Hemingway wrote a number of stories about disintegrating relationships: "The End of Something" about Marjorie Bump, "Mr. and Mrs. Elliot" about Chard Powers Smith and four others, about the break-up of his marriage to Hadley: "Cat in the Rain," "Out of Season," "A Canary for One" and "Homage to Switzerland." The first three stories in this sequence are penetrating revelations of their marital problems, for Hemingway's ear was always more acute when he had been emotionally upset.

In "Cat in the Rain" (1925) the bored and restless wife is dissatisfied with her transient life and with her marriage to a self-absorbed, unresponsive husband. He is contrasted to the attentive hotelkeeper who gives her a "feeling of being of supreme importance." The parallel series of "She liked . . ." in respect to the *padrone* is contrasted to the series of "I want . . ." in respect to the husband. Her desire for long hair represents her quest for a femininity that will arouse her husband just as her passionate, almost manic desire for a compensatory cat (who, like the wife, is not having fun in the rain) symbolizes her wish for a baby. Her exasperated series of demands, which echo Eliot's "Game of Chess" section in *The Waste Land,* angers the husband, who tells her to shut up: "And I want to eat at a table with my own silver and I want candles. And I want it to be spring and I want to brush my hair out in front of a mirror and I want a kitty and I want some new clothes." All these demands—except the unspoken wish for a baby—could easily be satisfied. They express Hadley's quite reasonable desire, during a visit to Rapallo in January 1923, for domestic comfort, stability and security; her weariness of sacrificing her own needs to follow her husband through the journalistic, literary and sporting locales of Europe.

In "Out of Season" (1923) the wife feels rotten and acts sullen after a quarrel with her husband. He apologizes for the way he spoke to her at lunch and tries to effect a reconciliation. She remains indifferent, taunts him about breaking the fishing laws and says he has no guts. When he urges her to return home—"It's a rotten day and we aren't going to have any fun"—she follows his advice. In the end, he is unable to fish for trout because the drunken guide has forgotten to bring the lead sinkers. As the guide makes plans for the following day—"life was opening out" for him—the husband sceptically withdraws. There are parallels in the story between natural and emotional states, between breaking the law and breaking the bonds of marriage, between inability to fish and inability to love. In this "literal transcription" of an actual incident that took place in Cortina in about March 1923, the nature of the quarrel is not stated. But it is probably related to Hadley's first pregnancy and the title may be an oblique allusion to the unwanted baby.

Like "Cat in the Rain," "A Canary for One" (1927), based on the Hemingways' return from Antibes to Paris in August 1926, just before their separation, uses an animal to symbolize lost love and solitude. In this story, a deaf American lady is bringing the canary to her depressed daughter, whom she has forced to leave her Swiss lover because she believes "Americans make the best husbands." As the young American couple travel north, passing a burning house and a wrecked train, they mention their honeymoon in Switzerland. The end of the marriage parallels the end of the journey and the end of the daughter's love affair. But this story is less effective than the first two because the pattern is contrived and the meaning turns on the irony of the husband's concluding remark: "We were returning to Paris to set up separate residences."[3]

II

Hemingway's oldest friend, Bill Smith, who had recently recovered from a nervous breakdown, healed the 1920 quarrel about Doodles and announced his arrival in Paris in April 1925. Hemingway later explained Bill's problems in a letter to Buck Lanham: After serving in Marine Aviation during the Great War, Bill fell in love with a girl. She was married, he had no sexual experience. He naturally became very excited and was impotent during their first time in bed. Instead of performing a small kindness, the girl gave him the works, ruined him and sent him into manic depression. When he came out of the hospital, Hemingway invited him to Europe and tried to help him. In March 1925, when Bill asked him about conditions in Paris, Hemingway adopted a man-of-the-world attitude and satirized his friend's provinciality. He said you could buy toilet paper in Paris, Bible classes were offered all over town, everyone took turns cleaning the streets, a maternity hospital was just around the corner and it was impossible to buy shoes. Visitors should bring an extra pair with them.[4]

Hemingway had met another friend, Harold Loeb, through Ford in the spring of 1924. During the following year he frequently saw Loeb and his girlfriend Kitty Cannell. Loeb came from a wealthy Jewish family in New York, was co-editor of the little magazine *Broom* and author of *Doodab,* published by Boni and Liveright in 1925. Loeb was a good friend to Hemingway during these years. He bought him food and wine, boxed and played tennis with him, helped to get *In Our Time* published and defended him against charges of anti-Semitism. He could not understand why Hemingway later satirized him as Robert Cohn in *The Sun Also Rises.* Hadley thought Loeb was extremely good-looking and Hemingway may have resented this. Another source of conflict was that Loeb beat Hemingway on the courts. "He was no tennis player" Loeb wrote. "A bad eye, damaged in a street brawl [*sic*], and a weak leg injured by shrapnel, hampered his control. His back court drives were erratic and his net game non-existent. Nevertheless, he put so much gusto into the play and got so much pleasure out of his good shots and such misery from his misses, that the games in which he participated were never lackadaisical."[5]

Hemingway's marriage was threatened in the spring and summer of 1925 when he became infatuated with Loeb's friend Mary Duff Twysden, daughter of B. W. Smurthwaite of Richmond, Yorkshire. She was born in 1893 and (like Agnes, Hadley and Pauline Pfeiffer) was several years older than Hemingway. She had been educated in Paris and presented at Buckingham Palace. In 1917 she married her second husband, Sir Roger Twysden, tenth baronet and commander in the Royal Navy, who was an ugly drunkard. The following year they had a son, Anthony, who lived with her husband's family. When Hemingway met her she was attached to her cousin Pat Guthrie, who had been institutionalized for alcoholism.

Duff "was built with curves like the hull of a racing yacht," had gray eyes and short blond hair. According to Harold Loeb, "she was not strikingly beautiful, but her features had a special appeal for me. I particularly liked the expressive eyes and the fresh complexion, and there was a grace about the way she held herself. Her clothes were of the simplest: slouch hat worn askew, soft jersey, and tweed skirt." Hemingway, who called Lady Twysden an "alcoholic nymphomaniac," was attracted by her title and found her a lively drinking companion. He thought she was chic, witty, sexy, reckless and exciting. She greatly enjoyed enchanting and controlling Guthrie, Loeb and Hemingway, and making them compete for her favor. She was the model for Brett Ashley in *The Sun Also Rises* and was delighted by the literary notoriety.

Duff and Pat lived on remittances and were always short of cash. She once invited George Seldes to join her and some friends in a nightclub. They ordered champagne, drank it, said they were going to the ladies' room, left him with a $45 bill (a week's salary for him) and boasted about the escapade to everyone. In the fall of 1925, desperate for cash and aware that Hemingway was fascinated by her, she asked: "Can you possibly lend me some money? I am in a stinking fix but for once only temporary and can pay you back for *sure*. I want 3000 francs—but for God's sake lend me as much as you can. I hate asking you—but all my friends seem to be in the same boat—broke to the wide. Am living in the country on nothing—but owe the pub a packet and dare not return without it." Later on, even more desperate, Duff (like Brett at the end of the novel) sent out another plea for help: "Please come at once to Jimmie's bar—real trouble—just rang up Parnass and find no word from you. SOS Duff."[6]

In July the Hemingways left Bumby with his nursemaid Marie Rohrbach and—with Bill Smith, Don Stewart and Harold Loeb—went for the third time to the festival of San Fermín. During the 1925 fiesta, which directly inspired *The Sun Also Rises*, Hemingway first saw the bullfighter Cayetano Ordóñez, who fought under the name of Niño de la Palma. But the old masculine comradeship was now replaced by sexual rivalry. When Duff heard about the expedition she told Loeb: "I am coming on the Pamplona trip with Hem and your lot. Can you bear it? With Pat of course. If this appears impossible for you, let me know and I'll try to get out of it. But I'm dying to come and feel that even seeing you and being able to talk to you will be better than nothing."

Hemingway agreed to this and told Loeb it would ease her transition from the Latin Quarter if Loeb arranged "to have a band of local fairies meet her at the train carrying a daisy chain."[7] Loeb was justly worried that their friendship would be destroyed when Hemingway discovered he had secretly spent two weeks in June alone with Duff at St. Jean-de-Luz.

Hemingway usually disliked café life and irresponsible drunkards. But when Duff told Hemingway that his sexual magnetism tested her self-control, he could scarcely control himself in the wild atmosphere of Pamplona. Hadley stopped talking to Duff, and wept with jealousy and humiliation when Hemingway courted her rival. But Duff, despite her notorious promiscuity and her strong attraction to Hemingway, had her own standards of morality. "We can't do it," she told him. "You can't hurt people." She would not run off with him, even if she wanted to, because of Hadley and the baby. Hadley later stated: "I don't know if they had an affair. I think it's perfectly possible but I don't know it for a fact. That isn't the kind of thing a husband talks to his wife about."[8]

Hemingway arrived in Pamplona in a foul mood, for loggers had polluted the river and ruined the marvelous fishing at Burguete. He lusted after Duff, but he could not or would not sleep with her. He could never live permanently with her and did not want to ruin his marriage for a casual liaison. The residual Oak Park puritanism restrained him, but it also made him fiercely resentful of Loeb's temporary success with Duff. And he despised Loeb's Jewishness, wealth, vanity and self-abasement after Duff had jilted him. "What infuriated Hemingway," said Don Stewart, "was Harold's unpardonable crime of being bored with the bullfighting and of abandoning the brave company of men (at Burguete) to chase after Duff."

At the end of the fiesta the jealous, drunken Guthrie, who hated Loeb, bitterly attacked him and was supported by Hemingway. Loeb later recalled:

> "Why don't you get out?" Pat said. "I don't want you here. Hem doesn't want you here. Nobody wants you here." . . .
> "I will," I said, "the instant Duff wants it." . . .
> "You know . . . that I do *not* want you to go" [she said].
> "You lousy bastard," said Hemingway. "Running to a woman."

Provoked by these insults, Loeb finally lost his temper and challenged Hemingway to a fist fight:

I was scared—not shaken or panicky, but just plain scared. I had boxed enough with Hem to know that he could lick me easily; his forty-pound advantage was just too much. And the edge I sometimes had because of Hem's tendency to telegraph his punches would be lost in the dark. I could not hope to outbox him. My little jabs would miss their mark and Hem's swings would smash my face in. . . .

We reached the last café, the last illuminated shop front. We went down a few steps. Now there were only street lamps. The small street carried on in semi-darkness.

I took my glasses off and, after considering the safest place, put them in the side pocket of my jacket. Then I stopped, faced Hem, and took my jacket off.

"My glasses," I said, "are in the side pocket. If they're broken I couldn't get them fixed here."

Feeling ridiculous, I looked around for someplace to put my jacket.

"Shall I hold it for you?" he asked.

I smiled. There was just enough light for me to see that Hem was smiling too, the boyish, contagious, smile that made it so hard not to like him.

"If I may hold yours," I said.

We stood hesitantly looking at each other.

"I don't want to hit you," I said.

"Me either," said Hem.

We put on our jackets and started back.[9]

The pattern of losing and then suddenly regaining his temper during a fight was typical of Hemingway. The same thing happened in his fights with Arthur Moss in October 1927 and with Max Eastman in August 1937.[10]

But it was very rare for Hemingway to offer an abject apology, which he did (probably after being prompted by Hadley) in a letter to Loeb of July 13, 1925: "I was terribly tight and nasty to you last night and I don't want you to go away with that nasty insulting lousiness as the last thing of the fiestas. I wish I could wipe out all the mean-ness and I suppose I can't but this is to let you know that I'm thoroughly ashamed of the way I acted and the stinking, unjust uncalled for things I said." His contrition, however, was short-lived. In September, as he was completing the first draft of *The Sun Also Rises,* he savagely exclaimed to Kitty Cannell (whom Loeb had abandoned for Duff): "I'm tearing those bastards apart. I'm putting everyone in it and that kike Loeb is the villain."[11] Loeb later denied the rumor, started by Hemingway after the novel was published in 1926, that he got a gun and threatened to shoot the author.

III

Hemingway met Scott Fitzgerald in the Dingo Bar in late April 1925, two weeks after the publication of *The Great Gatsby* and six months before the appearance of *In Our Time*. Fitzgerald was writing for the three million readers of the *Saturday Evening Post* while Hemingway was publishing in little magazines. Though Fitzgerald was three years older, had gone to Princeton, achieved instant success with *This Side of Paradise* (1920), introduced Hemingway to Scribner's and helped him toward recognition, Hemingway became his artistic rival and heroic ideal. Hemingway had masculine strength, capacity for drink, athletic prowess and experience in battle which Fitzgerald, with his "noncombatant's shell shock," sadly lacked. Eighteen months after their first meeting he told Hemingway "how much your friendship has meant to me during this year and a half—it is the brightest thing in our trip to Europe for me." Nine years later he wrote to Max Perkins: "I always think of my friendship with him as being one of the high spots of life."[12] Fitzgerald respected his integrity, praised his fiction and used Hemingway as his artistic conscience.

Fitzgerald liked to tell admiring stories about Hemingway and invest his life with a special touch of glamour. The hero of his last, absurd "medieval" project, *Philippe, Count of Darkness,* was modeled on Hemingway as he might have existed in the Middle Ages. Fitzgerald said that he "had always longed to absorb into himself some of the qualities that made Ernest attractive, and to lean on him like a sturdy crutch in times of psychological distress." Glenway Wescott, who knew both writers, exaggerated Fitzgerald's irresponsibility and self-abasement when he claimed that Fitzgerald cared more about Hemingway's work than about his own—he wrote his greatest novel, *Tender is the Night,* after they met—but there is no doubt that Fitzgerald (like MacLeish) hero-worshiped Hemingway: "He honestly felt that Hemingway was inimitably, essentially superior. From the moment Hemingway began to appear in print, perhaps it did not matter what he himself produced or failed to produce. He felt free to write just for profit, and to live for fun, if possible. Hemingway could be entrusted with the graver responsibilities and higher rewards such as glory, immortality."[13]

Scott and Zelda had not yet begun their fatal decline—he into alcoholism, she into insanity—when Hemingway first met them, but he was sufficiently perceptive to see the signs of imminent disaster. Hemingway, vindictive to benefactors, felt superior to Fitzgerald and tended to bully him, "like a tough little boy sneering at a delicate but talented little boy." He said: "Scott was a man then who looked like a boy with a face between handsome and pretty. He had very fair wavy hair, a high forehead, excited and friendly eyes and a delicate long-lipped Irish mouth that, on a girl, would have been the mouth of beauty. His chin was well built and he had good ears and a handsome, almost beautiful, unmarked nose."

Hemingway despised Fitzgerald's worship of youth, his sexual naiveté, attraction to money, alcoholism, self-pity and lack of dedication to his art. He scorned Fitzgerald for saying, when they were walking down Fifth Avenue together: "If only I could play foot-ball again with everything I know about it now."[14] He felt Fitzgerald put so much value on youth that he confused growing up with growing old, never achieved maturity and "jumped straight from youth to senility" without going through manhood.[15] Fitzgerald also irritated Hemingway by asking if he had slept with Hadley before they were married. Hemingway must have envied and desired Fitzgerald's literary fame, material success and luxurious way of life, which provided a powerful contrast to his own obscurity and rather pinched existence. But he made a virtue of this, compared his own frugality to Fitzgerald's prodigality and ironically offered to send all his royalties to his friend's villa on the French Riviera.

Fitzgerald's worst qualities were his inability to hold his liquor and his compulsion to humiliate himself when he inevitably got drunk. Fitzgerald passed out on the very first evening they spent together and that memory remained rooted in Hemingways mind. Fitzgerald was particularly boorish in June 1926 when he deliberately broke up an elegant party given by Gerald and Sara Murphy to welcome the Hemingways to Antibes. He threw ashtrays at the other tables, laughed hilariously and drove the disgusted Gerald away from his own festivities. At times Fitzgerald seemed to welcome the opportunity to display the worst side of his character. After a disastrous drunken meeting with Hemingway and Edmund Wilson in March 1933, Fitzgerald apologized for his self-abasement: "I assume full responsibility for all unpleasant-ness—with Ernest I seem to have reached a state where when we drink together I half bait, half truckle to him." That same year he attempted to clarify his own self-destructive impulse when he told Max Perkins, who often received Fitzgerald's confidences and Hemingway's con-demnations: Ernest "has long convinced himself that I am an incurable alcoholic, due to the fact that we almost always meet at parties. I am *his* alcoholic just like Ring [Lardner] is mine and do not want to disillu-sion him." His alcoholism not only prevented him from writing, but also limited his understanding and choked off his lifeline to fictional mate-rial. "How could he know people," Hemingway (who prided himself on his memory) asked Malcolm Cowley, "except on the surface when he never fucked anybody, nobody told him anything except as an answer to a question and he was always too drunk late at night to remember what anybody really said."[16] He believed that Fitzgerald's troubles were self-inflicted, that he almost took pride in his shameless defeat and that if he *had* gone to war he would have been shot for cowardice.

Hemingway, ruthless with anyone who interfered with his work or his wishes, was appalled by Fitzgerald's sensitivity to criticism and lack of commitment to his art. He tried to encourage Fitzgerald during the long, difficult and discouraging nine years between *The Great Gatsby* and *Tender is the Night:* "You just have to *go on* when it is worst and most [hopeless]—there is only one thing to do with a novel and that is to go straight on through to the end of the damn thing." He felt Scott was uneducated, unaware of the immutable laws of fiction, "did every-thing wrong," but managed to succeed because of his great natural talent. When *Tender is the Night* finally appeared in 1934, Hemingway thought it was too autobiographical, too full of self-pity about Zelda's madness and Scott's own decline. Hemingway felt the confessional "Crack-Up" articles, which appeared in *Esquire* in 1936 and described Scott's alcoholism and mental breakdown, were a disgusting self-expo-sure and self-condemnation. And he thought the incomplete and post-humously published *Last Tycoon,* which had strong characterization in Monroe Stahr, suffered from a far-fetched plot, preposterous women and a surprising deadness, like "a slab of bacon on which mold had grown."[17]

The mixture of admiration and hostility in their friendship was re-vealed in the notorious boxing match, held at the American Club, be-tween Hemingway and Morley Callaghan (whom he had first met at the

Toronto Star in the fall of 1923), with Fitzgerald as timekeeper. There was no question of the delicate Fitzgerald actually getting into the ring with Hemingway, but in June 1929 he assumed the duties that had sometimes been entrusted to Joan Miró.

Hemingway was not troubled by his friends' fear that he would "hurt his brains" in boxing. He did not have good coordination of reflexes and always looked slow and clumsy against a lighter boxer. But his son Gregory recorded that "he must have been a good barroom fighter, especially if he could get in that first punch, because he was strong as an ox." Callaghan noted that Hemingway had thought a good deal about boxing, while Callaghan had actually worked out with fast college boxers. The judgment of Hemingway's boxing coach, George Brown—"He was like a spoiled child when he boxed, whose manners had to be corrected constantly"—was confirmed during the match. When Callaghan punched Hemingway's lip, he retaliated by spitting a mouthful of blood in Callaghan's face and exclaiming: "That's what the bullfighters do when they're wounded. It's a way of showing contempt."[18] Despite his limitations as a boxer, Hemingway took the sport seriously, was extremely aggressive and hated to lose.

As usual, there were several versions of the incident involving Fitzgerald, and Hemingway came out best in his own account. According to Callaghan, Fitzgerald, supposed to be keeping time, was thinking about something else and unintentionally allowed the round to go well past the prescribed period. After Callaghan knocked Hemingway down, Fitzgerald woke up and screamed: " 'Oh, my God! . . . I let the round go four minutes.' . . . 'All right, Scott,' Ernest said savagely, 'If you want to see me getting the shit knocked out of me, just say so. Only don't say you made a mistake.' . . . 'Oh my God [Fitzgerald said], he thinks I did it on purpose. Why would I do it on purpose?' "[19] Hemingway's answer would be that Fitzgerald was using Callaghan as a surrogate to punish him for his superiority in drinking, war and art, just as (according to Hemingway) Wyndham Lewis, "knowing nothing about what was going on, was waiting, hoping to see Ezra hurt" in his boxing match with Hemingway. It is unlikely that Fitzgerald, who genuinely admired Hemingway, wanted to see him hurt. He probably became absorbed in the fight and was distracted from his duties by seeing his hero beaten by Callaghan.

In Hemingway's version, which he related to his confidant Max

Perkins, he was drunk at the time, lost his wind, was beaten by Callaghan and prevented by pride from asking the time. He was convinced that Fitzgerald had been motivated by hidden animosity and had acted with deliberate malice:

> I couldn't see him hardly—had a couple of whiskeys en route. Scott was to keep time and we were to box 1 minute rounds with 2 minute rests on acct. of my condition. I knew I could go a minute at a time and went fast and used all my wind—then Morley commenced to pop me and cut my mouth, mushed up my face in general. I was pooped as could be and thought I had never known such a long round but couldn't ask about it or Morley would think I was quitting. Finally Scott called time. Said he was very sorry and ashamed and would I forgive him. He had let the round go three minutes and 45 seconds—so interested to see if I was going to hit the floor!

Three months later he also boasted to Perkins (who was no doubt alarmed at the battering of his literary properties) that he had won thirty-three out of thirty-five rounds against Callaghan, who was unable to do any real damage, even in the extra-long round. He said Callaghan was a fine boxer, but overweight, short-winded, a weak hitter and easily hurt.[20]

The matter would have ended with Callaghan victorious, Hemingway embittered and Fitzgerald guilty. But the Paris journalist Pierre Loving heard about the incident from either Callaghan or Fitzgerald and belatedly sent a distorted version of the story to the *Denver Post*. This "amusing" event was reported in the "Turns of a Bookworm" column of the *New York Herald Tribune* on November 24, 1929, by Isabel Paterson, who said that after an argument in the Café Dôme, "Callaghan knocked Hemingway out cold. The amateur timekeeper was so excited he forgot to count."

When Callaghan read this two days later, he sent a denial to Isabel Paterson. He then received an urgent cable from Fitzgerald (under considerable pressure from Hemingway, who was sensitive about his reputation as a boxer): "HAVE SEEN STORY IN HERALD TRIBUNE. ERNEST AND I AWAIT YOUR CORRECTION. SCOTT FITZGERALD." All was (more or less) forgiven when a correction appeared on December 8 and Hemingway, in a letter of January 4, 1930, blamed the story—though not the lapse in timekeeping—on Pierre Loving. Hemingway, who often (though not in this case) contributed to the controversy, was fated (especially as he grew older and more famous) to inspire many exaggerated or hostile newspaper stories about his war wounds, bullfights, boxing matches and plane crashes.

Hemingway selfishly discarded a sequence of sometimes rich and always devoted wives, and could not understand why Fitzgerald remained loyal to Zelda in her madness. Unlike Fitzgerald, Zelda instinctively disliked Hemingway and provoked his hostility (as she did with Scott) by calling his sexuality into question. She thought he was bogus, said he was too aggressively virile, told him "no one is as masculine as you pretend to be" and called him "a phony, 'a materialistic mystic,' 'a professional he-man,' 'a pansy with hair on his chest.' "[21] *The Sun Also Rises*, according to Zelda, was about "bullfighting, bullslinging and bullshitting."[22] She accused Scott of a homosexual liaison with Hemingway and reinforced McAlmon's charge that they were a couple of queers. Hemingway blamed Fitzgerald's troubles on Zelda and compared him to a guided missile without a guide. He agreed with H. L. Mencken that "Scott would never amount to anything until he got rid of his wife." And he told Fitzgerald, with brutal honesty: "Of all people on earth you needed discipline in your work and instead you marry someone who is jealous of your work, wants to compete with you and ruins you. It's not as simple as that and I thought Zelda was crazy the first time I met her and you complicated it even more by being in love with her and, of course you're a rummy."[23]

Edmund Wilson's diary of 1932 contained the earliest account of Fitzgerald's and Hemingway's response to Zelda's attempt at psychological castration: "Hemingway said, Scott thinks that his penis is too small. (John Bishop had told me this and said that Scott was in the habit of making this assertion to anybody he met—to the lady who sat next to him at dinner and who might be meeting him for the first time.) I explained to him, Hemingway continued, that it only seemed to him small because he looked at it from above. You have to look at it in a mirror." In a notorious passage of *A Moveable Feast*, Fitzgerald confesses: "You know I never slept with anyone except Zelda. . . . Zelda said that the way I was built I could never make any woman happy and that was what upset her." After a personal inspection in the toilet, the paternal, patronizing Hemingway reassures Scott about his physical equipment: " 'You're perfectly fine,' I said. 'You are O.K. There's nothing wrong with you.' " When Fitzgerald asks: "But why would she say it?" Hemingway justly responds: "To put you out of business. . . . Zelda just wants to destroy you."[24]

Fitzgerald may have felt the need to humiliate himself before the intimidating Hemingway, but it is doubtful that he would risk the possibility of a devastating confirmation of Zelda's accusations. His convincing statement in "The Crack-Up" that he slept with prostitutes as an undergraduate in 1917 ("that night was the first time that I hunted down the specter of womanhood that, for a little while, makes everything else seem unimportant") casts serious doubt on Hemingway's version of the incident.[25] Though Hemingway exaggerated Fitzgerald's innocence and naiveté, there is no doubt that Zelda, who was becoming increasingly frigid, had attacked Scott's sexual capacity.

Fitzgerald's flaws of character and limitations as a writer were not fully apparent in 1925, when Hemingway still trusted him as craftsman and critic. In *A Moveable Feast* Hemingway misleadingly states: "That fall of 1925 he was upset because I would not show him the manuscript of the first draft of *The Sun Also Rises.*" Fitzgerald, in fact, read and corrected the novel and Hemingway followed his advice about deleting the first two chapters before he sent it to the printer. He also took Fitzgerald's advice about cutting the opening anecdote of "Fifty Grand" (1927), though he later quoted it and regretted the deletion of "that lovely revelation of the metaphysics of boxing."[26] Hemingway himself cut the last few paragraphs of the original conclusion to *A Farewell to Arms* (1929), which hinted at the fate of the minor characters, but rejected Fitzgerald's admittedly ludicrous suggestions about how to improve the ending. Fitzgerald thought the novel would be more popular if Hemingway eliminated the scene where Bonello shoots the sergeant and if he brought in the U.S. Marines. He suggested Frederic read about their victory at Belleau Wood as Catherine is dying.[27]

IV

Hemingway probably met the Catalan painter Joan Miró through Gertrude Stein in the early 1920s. Miró sometimes acted as timekeeper during Hemingway's boxing matches and Hemingway visited him in Montroig, near Tarragona, in 1929. In October 1925, when *In Our Time* was published, Hemingway bought Miró's painting *The Farm* (now in the National Gallery, Washington) for $250 as a birthday present for Hadley. He described the details of the purchase in *Cahiers d'Art* in 1934:

> Finally everyone had to sell everything and if Miró was to have a dealer he had to let "The Farm" go with the other pictures. But [Evan] Shipman, who found him the dealer, made the dealer put a price on it and agree to sell it to him. This was probably the only good business move that Shipman ever did in his life. But doing a good business move must have made him uncomfortable because he came to me the same day and said, "Hem, you should have *The Farm*. I do not love anything as much as you care for that picture and you ought to have it." . . . So we rolled dice [to decide] and I won and made the first payment. We agreed to pay five thousand francs for *The Farm*.

Hemingway, Shipman and Dos Passos had to borrow the money for the final payment from various bars and restaurants, and as they took it home in an open taxi the wind caught the large 4-by-4½-foot canvas as though it were a sail.

The Farm (1923) is one of Miró's last realistic paintings. It portrays, in precise detail, the manifold activities of the farmyard at his house at Montroig, illuminated by the high-hanging sun and colored by the ochre and cobalt of the earth and sky. The painting is dominated by the stable and the barn, with their agricultural implements and domestic animals, and by a stylized, spiky-branched tree that shoots out small explosions of leaves. The footprinted path runs past a leaping dog to a woman washing clothes in a trough near the open pool and a mule drawing water at the well. In the background, luxuriant foliage erupts in front of sharp mountain peaks. The painting conveys an impression of stark vitality and, like *Death in the Afternoon,* captures the essence of Spain. Hemingway, who loved and lived with the picture for thirty years, said: "It has in it all that you feel about Spain when you are there and all that you feel when you are away and cannot go there." He moved the painting to Hadley's new flat when they separated in 1926. In 1934 he asked her if he could borrow the painting for five years and never returned it. Hemingway met other Parisian artists through Gertrude Stein and also owned works by Braque, Gris, Masson and Klee. André Masson thought he had good taste and a sound knowledge of modern painting.[28]

V

In Our Time was published on October 5, 1925, by Boni and Liveright. They had an option on Hemingway's next three books, which would lapse if they rejected any one of them. Six weeks later, between November 20 and 26, Hemingway wrote *The Torrents of Spring,* a satire on his friend Sherwood Anderson. Anderson, then at the height of his reputation, was Boni and Liveright's best-selling author. Almost all the reviewers of *In Our Time*—Edmund Wilson, Burton Rascoe, Hershel Brickell, Herbert Seligman, Paul Rosenfeld, Schuyler Ashley—made facile references to Anderson's influence on Hemingway, who resented being criticized as "much the same thing only not so good." He wrote *The Torrents of Spring* to dissociate himself from Anderson's influence and from his latest book, *Dark Laughter* (1925). "No I don't think 'My Old Man' derives from Anderson," Hemingway rightly insisted in a letter to Edmund Wilson. "It is about a boy and his father and race-horses. Sherwood has written about boys and horses. But very differently. It derives from boys and horses. Anderson derives from boys and horses. I don't think they're anything alike. I know I wasn't inspired by him."[29]

Hemingway's humorous writing for *The Trapeze* and for *Ciao* had been parodies of his boyhood hero Ring Lardner, and *Torrents* was a natural development of this tendency. His ability to parody Anderson shows how well he had learned and then rejected his lesson. Now that Anderson's reputation as a serious writer has virtually disappeared, it is rather difficult to realize how anyone could have admired the final paragraph of *Dark Laughter:* "Why couldn't Fred laugh? He kept trying but failed. In the road before the house one of the negro women now laughed. There was a shuffling sound. The older negro woman tried to quiet the younger, blacker woman, but she kept laughing the high shrill laughter of the negress. 'I knowed it, I knowed it, all the time I knowed it,' she cried, and the high shrill laughter ran through the garden and into the room where Fred sat upright and rigid in bed." Hemingway adopted the satirical practice of Fielding and wrote a devastating mockery of Anderson's sentimental primitivism: "His dark face shone. Sharply, without explanation, he broke into high-pitched uncontrollable laughter. The dark laughter of the negro."

The most interesting aspects of *Torrents*—as well as of *Death in the*

Afternoon, Green Hills of Africa and *A Moveable Feast*—are the digressions into literary reminiscence and the sharp criticism of other writers: James, Ford, Wells, Sinclair Lewis, Stein, Cather and H. L. Mencken. Mencken had written a negative notice of *in our time* and (Hemingway felt) was to blame for Knopf's rejection of *In Our Time.* *Torrents* was ironically dedicated "To H. L. Mencken and S. Stanwood Menken," a wealthy crusader against vice who stood for everything H. L. Mencken hated.

Hadley liked Anderson, felt that Hemingway was needlessly nasty to a friend who had been very kind to them, and thought the whole idea of the book was detestable. Dos Passos thought the book was funny, but tried to restrain Hemingway from publishing it. Fitzgerald, who was also loyal to Hemingway, thought the satire was a masterpiece and sent his opinion directly to Horace Liveright: "It seems about the best comic book ever written by an American. It is simply devastating to about seven-eighths of the work of imitation Andersons, to facile and 'correct' culture and to this eternal looking beyond appearances for the 'real,' on the part of people who have never even been conscious of appearances. The thing is like a nightmare of literary pretensions behind which a certain hilarious order establishes itself before the end."[30] At the time of *Porgy, All God's Chillun, The Emperor Jones, Nigger Heaven* and the cult of jazz, Hemingway rejected the fashionable assumption that the emotional and sensual life of the black race was superior to that of the white.

On Fitzgerald's recommendation, Max Perkins had expressed serious interest in *In Our Time* before he had even read the book, but his letter reached Schruns ten days after Hemingway had accepted Liveright's offer. Hemingway knew that if Liveright rejected *Torrents,* he would be free to follow Fitzgerald to Scribner's and obtain the benefits of a more commercially successful firm, a first-rate editor and an outlet for his stories in *Scribner's Magazine.* He probably expected Liveright to accept *Torrents,* as Fitzgerald had urged him to do, because both writers thought it was a funny and a salutary book. He was willing to break with Liveright, probably wanted to do so, but that was not his sole motive. He got pleasure from writing it and the book had an element of fun as well as of malice. If Liveright took it, he would have another advance and another book; if not, he would be free to go to Scribner's. Both publishers were well aware of his achievement and potential as a writer and knew that he had completed a draft of his first novel, which would go to the publisher of *The Torrents of Spring.*

Liveright had virtually no choice but to reject the book, and (when he recovered from the shock of reading it) gave different reasons when writing to Fitzgerald and to Hemingway. He told Scott that he actually liked the satire but was overruled by all his editors: "I am less violently opposed to Torrents of Spring than anyone else who has read it. I thought it was pretty funny and in spots extremely well done. . . . Everyone else around here thinks the book is just bad, and that it hasn't a chance." But he was less tactful to Hemingway and did nothing to soften the blow: "It would be in extremely rotten taste, to say nothing of being horribly cruel, should we want to publish it." Hemingway, who did not simply write *Torrents* in a week to break his contract as Johnson wrote *Rasselas* in a week to pay for his mother's funeral, explained his ambivalent motives in a letter to Fitzgerald: "I have known all along that they could not and would not be able to publish it as it makes a bum out of their present ace and best seller Anderson. Now in 10th printing. I did not, however, have that in mind in any way when I wrote it."[31] Critics like Allen Tate felt that Anderson's feeble fiction provoked and deserved Hemingway's witty and well-executed condemnation.

It was much easier for Hemingway to deal with Liveright than with Anderson, who was the first successful writer he had ever met and had used his influence with Liveright to get *In Our Time* published. *Torrents* was the first of many personal attacks that were intended to wound and to destroy the reputation of writers who had once been his close friends. The patronizing letter Hemingway wrote to Anderson when Scribner's published the book in May 1926 attempted to justify the composition, the sincerity and the high-minded motives. With Anderson, as with Fitzgerald in "The Snows of Kilimanjaro," Hemingway insisted that he was attacking the writer for his own good. He maintained that his satire was impersonal rather than *ad hominem*, that Anderson's thought and style would be significantly improved by reading the severe strictures of a novice:

> I had just loaned Dark Laughter to Dos. He'd read it and we talked about it. After lunch I went back to the house and started this Torrents of Spring and wrote it right straight through for seven days. . . . It is a joke and it isn't meant to be mean, but it is absolutely sincere. You see

I feel that if among ourselves we have to pull our punches, if when a man like yourself who can write very great things writes something that seems to me, (who have never written anything great but am anyway a fellow craftsman) rotten, I ought to tell you so. . . . It looks, of course, as though . . . because you had always been swell to me and helped like the devil on the In our time I felt an irresistible need to push you in the face with true writer's gratitude. . . . It goes sort of like this: 1. Because you are my friend I would not want to hurt you. 2. Because you are my friend has nothing to do with writing. 3. Because you are my friend I hurt you more. 4. Outside of personal feelings nothing that's any good can be hurt by satire.[32]

Though Anderson was hurt by the attack, he maintained a façade of friendship and was civil to Hemingway when asked to have a drink in Paris in January 1927.

Anderson recognized the real motives and told Stein, who was very angry when the book appeared, that the intensely competitive Hemingway attacked him because "he cannot bear the thought of any other men as Artists . . . wants to occupy the entire field." Hemingway was generous with young, unknown writers and with mediocrities, but he was extremely reluctant to praise serious rivals. Though he praised Faulkner publicly, he condemned him privately. The only contemporary books he disinterestedly praised were Cummings' *The Enormous Room* (published by Liveright in 1922), Dinesen's *Out of Africa* and Orwell's *Homage to Catalonia*. In 1959, in "The Art of the Short Story" (a notable contrast to his letter to Anderson of May 1926), Hemingway finally agreed with Hadley and Dos Passos and expressed regret for his youthful attack: "I did it because I was righteous, which is the worst thing you can be, and I thought he was going to pot the way he was writing and that I could kid him out of it by showing him how awful it was. So I wrote *The Torrents of Spring*. It was cruel to do, and it didn't do any good, and he just wrote worse and worse. . . . I'm sorry I threw at Anderson. It was cruel and I was a son of a bitch to do it."[33]

Hemingway's attack on Anderson followed the recurrent pattern of his literary quarrels with Ford, McAlmon, Stein, Loeb, Walsh, Stewart, Callaghan, MacLeish, Eastman, Fitzgerald and Dos Passos. His reaction to them changed from extreme enthusiasm to vengeful disillusionment. When he became bored with his friends, discovered their faults, found a real or imaginary grievance, or had no further use for them, he would ruthlessly, relentlessly and suddenly break off the friendship. Don Stewart, friend and victim, gave a perceptive analysis of this destructive syndrome and attributed it to Hemingway's fear of creating personal obligations that egoism made impossible to fulfill:

> The minute he began to love you, or the minute he began to have some sort of obligation to you of love or friendship or something, then is when he had to kill you. Then you were too close to something he was protecting. He, one-by-one, knocked off the best friendships he ever had. He did it with Scott; he did it with Dos Passos—with everybody. I think it was a psychological fear he had that you might ask something from him. He didn't want to be overdrawn at your bank.[34]

8

Pauline
1926

I have a theory that Ernest needs a new
woman for each big book. There was
one for the stories and *The Sun Also
Rises*. Now there's Pauline. *A Farewell
to Arms* is a big book. If there's another
big book I think we'll find Ernest has
another wife.

FITZGERALD TO CALLAGHAN

I

Hemingway and Hadley survived the first three crises of their marriage:
the lost manuscripts, the unwanted pregnancies, the flirtations with
Duff Twysden. Though Duff had resisted his advances, falling in love
with her had sapped Hemingway's moral strength and weakened his
emotional commitment to his wife. He was still susceptible to the temptations of love and began an affair with Pauline Pfeiffer in February
1926. He and Hadley separated, after considerable anguish, in August;
she divorced him in January 1927 and he married Pauline in May.

Pauline was more interesting-looking than attractive. McAlmon
called her "small-boned and lively as a partridge," with full lips, dark
bangs and long emerald earrings. Morley Callaghan—who disliked
Pauline and thought she was selfish, calculating and cold—said she
"wasn't a beauty, but she was pleasant-faced and steady-eyed. She had
firmness and quiet determination in her expression." Matthew Josephson, who knew Pauline in Key West in the mid-1930s, emphasized her
devotion to Hemingway and the powerful influence of his personality:
"Pauline was small and fine-boned with black hair and dark eyes, a

vivacious woman rather than a pretty one. One felt there were, or had been, strong bonds of affection between them; she, at any rate, often used Ernest's turns of speech and sometimes even the tone of characters in his books. She talked Hemingway."[1]

Her sister Jinny, a bright and witty woman, was much more attractive than Pauline. Laura Archera, the widow of Aldous Huxley, lived with Jinny for many years and called her "the most original and compassionate woman I have ever known. Her thinking was new and unpredictable. . . . She was known for her unique sense of humor which had a chameleon-like quality, made to fit the person it was directed to."[2]

Kitty Cannell introduced Pauline and Jinny to the Hemingways in March 1925, when they returned from their first winter in Schruns. Hemingway and Pauline were not immediately attracted to each other. She found him rather coarse and ill-kempt; he thought Jinny was better-looking than Pauline. Hemingway saw Pauline occasionally, perhaps secretly, during 1925; in the fall, after he had freed himself from the spell of Duff Twysden, he fell in love with her. Kitty Cannell was surprised to meet Pauline carrying skis through the streets of Paris en route to Schruns for a two-week Christmas holiday in 1925. There she began her campaign to win Hemingway from Hadley.

Pauline derived her confidence from a secure and prosperous background. Both her parents were born in Iowa. Her father, Paul Pfeiffer, was the son of a Lutheran immigrant and had spoken German as a boy. Her mother, Mary Downey, was the daughter of an Irish Catholic. Pauline was born in Parkersburg, Iowa, where Paul owned a drugstore, on July 22, 1895. The family lived in St. Louis, where Paul made a fortune as a commodity broker, from 1900 to 1912. Paul then moved to Cherry Street Hill in Piggott—a small, dull, hot southern town of 3,000 people—in 1913. He bought 60,000 acres in northeast Arkansas; cleared the timberland; planted wheat, cotton, clover, corn and soybeans; and became one of the richest landowners in the state. He owned the local bank, the land office, the cotton gin company, and ruled the region in a feudal fashion. Tall, well-organized, remote, Paul never actually worked on the soil. He sat in his office and "maneuvered," he went after other people's land and took whatever he could get. He was not religious; but his wife, a strict Catholic, built a chapel in her house and brought up Pauline and Jinny (born in 1902) in her faith.

Paul's brother Gus, an extremely wealthy man, owned Richard Hudnut Perfumes, Sloan's Liniment and William Warner Pharmaceuticals.

As Dos Passos noted, he was always very generous with Pauline and Hemingway: "Uncle Gus was a small nostalgic man, the big wheel in Hudnut's in New York. Stiff with money and having neither chick nor child as the saying was, he lavished attentions on his smart pretty nieces. Ernest fascinated him. Hunting, fishing, writing. He wanted to help Ernest do all the things he'd been too busy making money to do."[3]

Pauline graduated from the Academy of the Visitation in St. Louis and from the School of Journalism at the University of Missouri (where she was the roommate and close friend of Katy Smith) in 1918. She worked on the *Cleveland Star*, the *New York Daily Telegraph* and *Vanity Fair*, and had been engaged to her lawyer cousin in New York. She and Jinny came to Paris in the early 1920s and Pauline worked as assistant to Main Bocher, editor of the French *Vogue*, at 2 rue Edouard VII.[4] She attended fashion shows and sent in reports, but never actually published anything in *Vogue*.

Hadley and Pauline presented a striking contrast in 1926. Hadley was almost alone in the world; her parents were dead and she did not get on with her sister in St. Louis. She was tall and red-haired, with a full figure that was becoming matronly. Modest, kind, effacing and a good sport, married to Hemingway for more than four years, she had no reason to suspect his infidelity and had been secure until his infatuation with Duff. Hadley worried about the lack of money and her dowdy clothes, but she was deeply in love with her husband and absorbed with her two-year-old baby.

Pauline had the support of her family and a close friend in her sister in Paris. Small and dark, with a boyish figure, she was spoiled, self-assured, ambitious and (like all the Pfeiffers) used to getting her own way. She wore fashionable clothes, and pitied Hadley's humble flat and spartan existence. With no domestic or emotional ties, Pauline was free to do as she wished. Hemingway felt his lack of money seriously limited his freedom and was attracted to her fortune. In "The Snows of Kilimanjaro" he admitted it was strange "that when he fell in love with another woman, that woman should always have more money than the last one."[5] Pauline, like Duff, was sexually exciting and flattering. But Duff had been twice divorced, had a child, was poor, irresponsible and alcoholic, while Pauline was marriageable, stable and secure.

Hemingway associated Hadley with Chicago, bourgeois values, domestic bondage and the sawmill below their flat. He associated Pauline with *Vogue*, expatriates, freedom and the luxurious lives led by the

Fitzgeralds and the Murphys. He needed a new wife to match his new status as a highly respected author. Hemingway—who was handsome, self-confident, interesting and talented—always attracted both men and women. Pauline spoiled him with attention, threw herself at him and made it difficult for him to resist her. His sister Sunny (who disliked Pauline) claimed that when she later told Pauline that she herself had fallen in love with a married man and could do nothing about it, Pauline urged her "to go ahead and get him. She had found who she wanted, and had gotten him, and was glad she had."[6] Hemingway felt it exciting to have two attractive women in love with him and to sleep with both of them. The secrecy and danger of his affair intensified his pleasure.

In Schruns, Hadley took care of the baby while Hemingway taught Pauline how to ski. In early February 1926 he went to New York for ten days to change publishers. In Paris he saw Pauline, who offered to accompany him to New York, before he left and after he returned. They became lovers that month. On February 4, the day after Hemingway sailed on the *Mauretania,* Pauline disingenuously wrote Hadley: "your husband, Ernest, was a delight to me. I tried to see him as much as he would see me and was possible."

In the spring, when the Hemingways returned from Schruns, the Pfeiffer sisters invited Hadley on a car trip to the châteaux of the Loire. Pauline was short-tempered and in a bad mood. When Hadley asked Jinny how Pauline got on with Ernest, she replied, with an inflection that aroused Hadley's suspicion: "I think they're very fond of each other." In May, when Hadley frankly asked Hemingway if he loved Pauline, he replied—with classic Oak Park hypocrisy—that she was at fault for even mentioning the subject. He was not apologetic or contrite, and continued to see Pauline as if nothing had happened. "What he seemed to be saying to me," Hadley recalled, "was that it was my fault for forcing the issue. Now that I had broken the spell our love was no longer safe."[7] Though Hadley was aware of the affair and told Kitty Cannell that Pauline was stealing her husband, she held on for several more months. She believed in her marriage vows, hoped to protect Bumby and feared Hemingway would leave her if she forced a showdown with Pauline.

In May the Hemingways accepted the Murphys' invitation to stay at their villa at Cap d'Antibes. Fitzgerald, who later dedicated *Tender is the Night* "To Gerald and Sara: Many fêtes" and based the glamorous aspects of Dick and Nicole Diver on his friends, had introduced the

Murphys to Hemingway in October 1925. The Murphys lived in narcissistic luxury and provided lavish hospitality to American artists in France in the 1920s. All their energies were dissipated into the perfection of trivialities: raking a beach or furnishing a house. Their hedonistic existence became a monument to the nonessential. Gerald confessed: "we ourselves did nothing notable except enjoy ourselves"—until tragedy afflicted them.

The Murphys skied in Schruns in March 1926 and went to Pamplona in July. They encouraged Hemingway to leave Hadley for Pauline, gave him $400 when he was short of funds and lent him Gerald's sixth-floor studio at 69 rue Froidevaux after his separation from Hadley. Sara also criticized Hadley for telling Hemingway she thought he was in love with Pauline because "it put the idea in his head and made him feel guilty at the same time"—though he must have fallen in love with Pauline *before* Hadley suspected it.

Once the initial attraction wore off, the Murphys' vast wealth, genteel manners, exquisite taste and dabbling in the arts inevitably aroused Hemingway's wrath. In *A Moveable Feast* Hemingway—always in search of a scapegoat—bitterly but unjustly blamed Dos Passos and the Murphys for the destruction of his first marriage. He characterized Dos Passos as an unerring pilot fish who leads rich sharks (the Murphys) to their prey (Hadley and Hemingway) and then slips away while those who trusted him are destroyed: Dos Passos "has the irreplaceable early training of the bastard and a latent and long denied love of money." Hemingway's description of the Murphys, omitted from the published book, is even more savage:

> The rich never did anything for their own ends. They collected people then as some collect pictures and others breed horses and they only backed me in every ruthless and evil decision that I made. . . . It wasn't that the decisions were wrong although they all turned out badly finally from the same fault of character that made them. If you deceive and lie with one person against another you will eventually do it again. I had hated these rich because they had backed me and encouraged me when I was doing wrong. . . . They were bad luck for people but they were worse luck to themselves and they lived to have all of their bad luck finally; to the very worst end that all bad luck could go.[8]

In 1929, when the Murphys' son Boath contracted tuberculosis, Hemingway showed the generous, compassionate side of his character.

He wrote the boy many long letters, sent wonderful presents, often came to visit and was nearly reduced to tears by the suffering of the helpless child. When Boath died in 1935, Hemingway wrote a moving letter of condolence: "I can't be brave about it and in all my heart I am sick for you both. . . . Very few people ever really are alive and those that are never die, no matter if they are gone. No one you love is ever dead."

Hadley went down to the Murphys' villa in May 1926 and Hemingway joined her in June after spending three weeks alone in Spain. When Bumby caught whooping cough, the Murphys feared for the health of their delicate children and the Hemingways had to move to Fitzgerald's recently vacated villa at Juan-les-Pins. Pauline, immune to Bumby's illness, returned from a holiday in Italy and moved in with the Hemingways to cheer him up. When the lease expired on Fitzgerald's villa, they all went to the Hôtel de la Pineda. "Here it was," Hadley said, "that the three breakfast trays, three wet bathing suits on the line, three bicycles were to be found. Pauline tried to teach me to dive, but I was not a success. Ernest wanted us to play bridge but I found it hard to concentrate." In both Schruns and Antibes, Hadley took care of Bumby and left Hemingway and Pauline free to spend time with each other. Pauline learned from this experience always to put her husband's interests before those of her children. She left the infant Patrick with her parents and followed Hemingway to Wyoming in 1928, just as she left the baby Gregory at home and went to Africa with him in 1934.

The Hemingways, the Murphys and Pauline all went to Pamplona in early July and then returned to Antibes. A revealing photograph in Spain shows Hemingway balanced uneasily between his heavy wife and the svelte Pauline. Pauline idolized Hemingway and by mid-July was already "talking Hemingway." She either deliberately imitated or unconsciously absorbed his style and sounded exactly like the character based on Hadley in "Cat in the Rain": "I'm going to get a bicycle and ride in the bois. I am going to get a saddle, too. I am going to get everything I want."[9]

Pauline's Catholicism was a crucial factor in her character, in her affair with Hemingway, in their marriage and in their divorce. In *The Sun Also Rises*, Brett explains her reasons for renouncing Romero: "It makes one feel rather good deciding not to be a bitch. . . . It's sort of what we have instead of God." Pauline had God, and decided to be a bitch. She twisted her religion to suit herself, embraced or abandoned it according to her needs and risked her soul to get Hemingway. Pauline was an observant Catholic, yet she committed fornication and broke up the marriage of a couple with a small child. She felt guilty about contravening her religion while pursuing her love; but since the Church did not recognize his marriage (which made Bumby a bastard), she was able to marry him. She countenanced Hemingway's bogus conversion to the Catholic Church and encouraged him to attend Mass while committing adultery ("the outlet of confession would be very good for him").[10] Hemingway's insistence that he was perfectly willing to go to hell after death showed that he did not understand the concept of damnation and desperately needed instruction in the new faith. He did not mind being a Catholic as long as it was convenient, but was unhappy when Pauline reverted to the rules of the Church and refused to practice birth control.

Hadley accepted his affair and their humiliating *ménage à trois,* hid her pain and unhappiness, and hoped that his passion would subside—as it had done with Duff. When it persisted, they had an open confrontation and Hadley fought bitterly to save her marriage. "I have a good tongue for lashing back," she confessed, "and am ashamed at some of the things I said." Hemingway gave a vivid example of their quarrels about Pauline's sexual attraction and his greed for money in his unpublished fragment "James Allen lived in a studio." Allen's wife says she has seen his mistress and knows she is not better-looking. When he cannot explain why he is sexually aroused, the wife taunts him. She says his mistress must know special tricks and must have money, for he would only marry a woman who could keep him in comfort when his books did not sell. Hemingway also provided the key to his idealized portrayal of Hadley in *A Moveable Feast* when he wrote that he loved her much more after his infidelity.[11]

Hemingway was a romantic at heart. Every time he fell in love with a woman, he sincerely believed that he had to marry her and would remain married to her forever. Another unpublished fragment, "Philip Haines was a writer," reveals his ambivalent state of mind at the time. He blames and yet justifies himself, admits his desire for money and is torn between two women. The adulterous couple know they are guilty according to law, public opinion and their own morality. But they feel that something makes it all right as long as his wife, Harriet, does not know. They have to avoid scandal or Dorothy's family will stop her allowance, which they will need when they marry. He considers going back to his wife, but thinks that he's hurt Harriet, so why hurt Dorothy as well.[12]

Hemingway presented his simplistic moral standard in *Death in the Afternoon:* "I know only that what is moral is what you feel good after and what is immoral is what you feel bad after." If this test is applied to Pauline instead of to bullfighting, then Hemingway must have felt that he behaved immorally as he moved from a passive to an active role in his affair. Though committed to Pauline, he was guilt-ridden about his cruelty to Hadley. She tried to remain stoical and indifferent, but was deeply hurt by his betrayal. Don Stewart, who took Hadley home from a party after the separation, said she cried all the way back to the hotel. She recalled that when Hemingway "came to collect his things he sat down and cried. It was the end of something. I think he was very much in love with Pauline."[13]

"Our life is all gone to hell," Hemingway told Fitzgerald in September 1926, "which seems to be the one thing you can count on a good life to do. Needless to say Hadley has been grand and everything has been completely my fault in every way. That's the truth, not a polite gesture." He apologized to his parents for the great shame and suffering he had inflicted on the family by divorcing Hadley and accepted all the blame. But he also exaggerated his marital problems, did not admit he was adulterous, said Hadley had decided on the divorce and did not mention the enforced separation: "Our trouble had been going on for a long time. It was entirely my fault and it is no one's business. . . . For over a year I had been in love with two people and had been absolutely faithful to Hadley. When Hadley decided that we had better get a divorce the girl with whom I was in love was in America."[14] When Bill Bird asked the reason for his divorce he answered: "because I am a son of a bitch."

Hadley retrospectively realized that the best way to protect her marriage would have been to encourage Hemingway to burn out his passion for Pauline. Instead, she insisted on a hundred-day trial separation, which became more a penance than a test of their love. Hemingway, who grew up in a family of eight, was not used to—and could not cope with—solitude. Hadley knew that he was always lonely without the women who provided his inspiration and his audience. She may have hoped that Hemingway's guilt would overwhelm him and that his loneliness would drive him back to her; that Pauline's family would restrain her, that she would be disinherited, that she would change her mind. But none of these things happened. By keeping them apart she merely increased their desire for each other.

The correspondence between Hemingway and Pauline during their separation reveals their exhilaration and despair. Pauline began reassuringly as she sailed for America on September 24: "I am feeling very comfortable and warm and solid, and I love you more than ever. . . . Writing you everything, I can keep you very close to me and very much in my life until I see you again. . . . I'm cockeyed happy that I have you. . . . I look at all the people on this boat and wonder how they can get on without Ernest." But things became more difficult when she arrived in Piggott and faced her mother's cross-examination. Her egoism, however, was stronger than her feelings of remorse and she managed to survive the ordeal by presenting her family with a *fait accompli*. Her letter to Hemingway emphasized *her* suffering and *Hadley's* hatred, and urged him to assuage his guilt by paying off his wife:

> You got your terrible hell being day after day with Hadley and I think I'm getting mine with Mother. . . . In addition to feeling that her daughter has broken up a home and feeling so terrible about Hadley, she worries about me. . . . I can't comfort her because I don't seem to be able to find any comfort for her. . . . If there is anything Hadley wants you to do for her or Bumby, ever, no matter what, you gotta do it don't you. And any amount of money settlement. And I am not going to mention to you again about Hadley not liking me, because if she hates me it will be alright. . . . [You know] that I love you more than ever.

Some guilt about their treatment of Hadley emerged in late October, but it was immediately suppressed by the overriding demands of their love—the special "something that made it all right":

> Ernest and Pfeiffer, who tried to be so swell (and who were swell) didn't give Hadley a chance. We were so . . . scared we might lose each other —at least I was—that Hadley got locked out. Hadley was just locked out. I don't think you did this the way I did. . . . I think the times Hadley doesn't hate me she must know I was just blind dumb.
> Dearest, you and I have something that only about two persons in one or several centuries get. . . . And having it, when we say we can't face life without each other and then deliberately make some one else face life alone, it makes me very afraid about us.[15]

They both wondered if they could base their marriage on the betrayal of Hadley. Like Merton Densher and Kate Croy, the two scheming lovers in James' *The Wings of the Dove*, they were thrilled and appalled by what they had done. They were happy for several years, but when their marriage was threatened by another woman, guilt about the past helped to destroy their love.

Hemingway, who had a more tender conscience and was more sensitive to moral nuance, suffered much more than Pauline. In a cathartic letter of November 12, he feared that family pressure would destroy her resolution and spoke of suicide:

> I've felt absolutely done for and gone to pieces Pfife and I might as well write it out now and maybe get rid of it that way. It was certain that your mother would feel badly about your marrying some one who was divorced, about breaking up a home, about getting into a mess. . . .
>
> All I can think of is that you, that are all I have and that I love more than all that is and have given up everything for and betrayed everything for and killed off everything for, are being destroyed and your nerves and spirit broken all the time day and night and that I can't do anything about it because you won't let me. . . . But I'm not a saint, nor built like one, and I'd rather die now while there is still something left of the world than to go on and have every part of it flattened out and destroyed and made hollow before I die.

Hemingway saw Hadley when he visited Bumby and told her how much Pauline was suffering. After a thoughtful, solitary weekend in Chartres, Hadley cancelled the hundred-day separation and agreed to a French divorce on grounds of incompatibility. In a moving letter to Hadley, he expressed his genuine contrition, praised her generosity, offered to give her all the royalties of *The Sun Also Rises*, acknowledged her emotional and financial support during the composition of his first three books:

> Your reactions have always been right and I have always trusted them and believed in them as well as in your head.
>
> I think that perhaps when Pauline and I realized how cruel we had been to you in that way and that we could not expect to found any basis of happiness on such continued cruelty . . . it maybe [might] have helped remove your natural and right re-action against setting two people free to marry each other who did not seem to deserve each other or anything else. . . .
>
> In any event, no matter what you do, I am writing to Scribners that all royalties from The Sun Also Rises should be paid to you. . . . It is the only thing that I who have done so many things to hurt you can do to help you—and you must let me do it. . . .
>
> You supported me while they were being written and helped me

write them. I would never have written any of them In Our Time, Torrents or The Sun if I had not married you and had your loyal and self-sacrificing and always stimulating and loving—and actual cash support backing. . . . How I admire your straight thinking, your head, your heart and your very lovely hands and I pray God always that he will make up to you the very great hurt that I have done you—who are the best and truest and loveliest person that I have ever known.[16]

Hemingway was drawn to Pauline for many reasons. He had a very limited social and sexual life before marriage; he was too emotionally immature (despite his wide experience) to accept domestic and paternal responsibility; he was excited by bohemian life in Paris, travels in Spain and his flirtation with Duff; he was bored with Hadley and eager for new experience; he was attracted to Pauline's style and wealth; he was stimulated by their separation; he felt obliged, after the affair with Pauline, to respond to her demand for a Catholic marriage. Since Hemingway chose to leave Hadley, it was unfair of him, in A Moveable Feast, to shift the blame from himself to Pauline as well as to to blame Dos Passos and the Murphys and to hold them responsible for his own moral weakness.

In his autobiography, written long after his divorce from Pauline, he says he was the unwilling victim of an old trick: "an unmarried young woman becomes the temporary best friend of another young woman who is married, goes to live with the husband and wife and then unknowingly, innocently and unrelentingly sets out to marry the husband." Hemingway does not explain the contradiction between "innocently" and "unrelentingly," but admits that when he came back to Paris from New York he stayed there with Pauline instead of returning to Hadley in Schruns. A passage deleted from this chapter (and printed here in italics) stresses the mixture of joy and guilt in his love for Pauline: "When I got back to Paris I should have caught the first train from the Gare de l'Est that would take me down to Austria. But the girl I was in love with was in Paris then, *and where we went and what we did, and the unbelievable wrenching, killing happiness, selfishness and treachery of everything we did gave me such a terrible remorse,* I did not take the first train, or the second or the third. When I saw my wife again standing by the tracks as the train came in by the piled logs at the station, I wished I had died before I ever loved anyone but her."[17] In this crisis, as in all quarrels with wives, family and friends, he revised reality in his art, presented himself as a victim and projected guilt onto a convenient scapegoat in order to justify his own actions.

Once Hadley agreed to a divorce, she behaved with dignity and generosity. She found it difficult to accept the role of abandoned wife, but drew on her reserves of emotional strength, stopped loving Hemingway, found the end of the marriage a kind of relief and felt as if a great millstone had been lifted from her back. She also protected Bumby and made it easier for him to accept the divorce by explaining that Hemingway and Pauline were very much in love. She never criticized Hemingway nor expressed any bitterness about him.

Hadley had gained greatly from her marriage and was much better off—more self-assured and independent—when he left her than when he met her. He had rescued her from her oppressive sister, convinced her that she was not an invalid, taught her sporting skills, introduced her to life in Paris, taken her on travels in Europe, presented her to the leading writers and artists of the time, and fathered a beautiful child with her. She knew Hemingway during his best years, and did not have to endure and care for him during his steep decline.

Bumby attended the École Alsacienne, the École Montcel and the Denny School from 1928 to 1934. In 1933 Hadley married Paul Mowrer, chief editorial writer of the *Chicago Daily News*, and young Jack attended the Chicago Latin School. Paul was a sympathetic and loving parent; Jack felt fortunate to have two fathers who complemented each other perfectly and gave him everything he could possibly desire.[18]

For Hemingway, each marriage looked best in retrospect. He continued to write to Hadley, especially during periods of loneliness and emotional crisis, and to use their familiar nicknames. In 1939 (the year of their last meeting) he nostalgically recalled their early holidays together: "The more I see of all the members of your sex the more I admire you. . . . Maybe we have already had the hereafter and it was up in the Dolomites, and the Black Forest and the forest of the Irati." In 1942–43 he told Hadley that she was much nicer than the subsequent wives, who had parted from him with great bitterness, and that he still loved her:

> Good bye Miss Katherine Kat. I love you very much. It is all right to do
> so because it hasn't anything to do with you and that great Paul; it is just
> untransferable feeling for early and best Gods. But will never mention
> it if bad. Thought you might just be interested to know. . . . I never had
> so damned much time to think in my life, especially nights on the water

and here when I can't sleep from haveing lost the habit, and have thought about you with great pleasure and admiration and how wonderful you were and are.[19]

When Paul Mowrer objected to his wife's being cast in this romantic role, Hadley had to ask Hemingway to stop writing to her.

II

Hemingway's marriage to Pauline meant that he would have to become a Catholic and bring up his children in that faith. His mother was Episcopalian; he had been brought up as a Congregationalist, was married in a Methodist church and baptized his first son in an Episcopal church with Jewish and Catholic godparents. Hemingway married Pauline in a Catholic church, baptized his second and third sons as Catholics, but ceased to be a Catholic during the Spanish Civil War. Despite his suicide, he was given a Catholic burial. He had superficial connections with various Christian sects without having faith in any of them.

In order to avoid the trouble of religious instruction and a formal conversion, Hemingway claimed that he had been baptized by a priest from the Abruzzi—who had merely walked down the aisle anointing the men—after he was wounded at Fossalta. In January 1926, while skiing with Pauline at Schruns, Hemingway claimed to be a Catholic but expressed serious religious doubts: "If I am anything I am a Catholic. Had extreme unction administered to me as such in July 1918 and recovered. So I guess I'm a Super-Catholic. It is certainly the most comfortable religion for anyone soldiering. Am not what is called a 'good' Catholic. Think there is a lot of nonsense about the church. Holy Years, etc. What rot. But cannot imagine taking any other religion seriously." Agnes von Kurowsky, who knew him intimately in 1918, "could not remember his talking about religion at all. Her Catholic friends on the nursing staff in Milan would surely have said something if Ernie 'had been converted to Catholicism.' "[20]

Hemingway did not (and could not) produce baptismal papers to persuade the Church that he had become a Catholic. Instead, according to Giovanni Cecchin, Hemingway saw the Florentine priest, Giuseppe Bianchi, in Rapallo, while driving through Italy with Guy Hickok in

March 1927, asked Bianchi for a "sworn declaration of fact" and used this to convince the Church that he had been converted.[21] During his first years with Pauline he went to Mass, carried a religious medal and told Father Vincent Donavan that he always had more faith than knowledge. As a dumb Catholic, he hated to examine his belief. He did not want to be known as a Catholic writer because he had never been able to set a good example. He tried to live a good life and to write well, but found it easier to do the former than the latter.[22]

Hemingway's new faith soon turned to cynicism. He could not take religion seriously, stopped going to Mass, disliked martyrs and saints, hated the prohibition of birth control, which made many women, including Pauline, risk death to conform to Papal encyclicals. He was fond of transposing the French expression "I'm a believer but not practicing" into "I'm practicing but not a believer" *(praticant mais pas croyant).* [23] His Cuban friends thought "Ernest was no more a Catholic than he was a Moslem." He confirmed this by declaring: "Hell, any man could become a Catholic for a million bucks"; "Only suckers worry about saving their souls."[24]

Hemingway's works, during both the Protestant and the Catholic phases of his life, are consistently sceptical about religion and hostile to the Catholic Church. Two priests offer fatuous advice to Sam Cardinella in *in our time* (1924). The pagan swamps the religious element during the festival of San Fermín in *The Sun Also Rises* (1926). Brett Ashley becomes a Circean enchantress, turning the men who dance around her into swine. She wants to pray and to hear Jake Barnes confess, but is excluded from the church. Jake seems to express Hemingway's sentiments when he says: "[I] regretted that I was such a rotten Catholic, but realized there was nothing I could do about it, at least for a while, and maybe never, but that anyway it was a grand religion, and I only wished I felt religious and maybe I would the next time."[25]

There is no evidence of religious feeling in the playlet "Today is Friday" (1926), in which three Roman soldiers callously discuss the crucifixion in a modern idiom: "Why didn't he come off the cross? He didn't want to come down off the cross. That's not his play." Hemingway's self-reflective "Neothomist Poem" (1927), which criticized the "temporary embracing of the church by literary gents," parodied the Twenty-Third Psalm: "The Lord is my shepherd, I shall not / want him for long." In *A Farewell to Arms* (1929) the old Count Greffi says to Frederic Henry: "We none of us know about the soul. Are you *Croy-*

ant?" and he sceptically replies: "At night."[26] In *Death in the After-noon* (1932) Hemingway blasphemously imitates the format of a bullfight poster to announce the crucifixion: "A crucifixion of six carefully selected Christs will take place at five o'clock in the Monumental Golgotha of Madrid, government permission having been obtained. The following well-known, accredited and notable crucifiers will officiate, each accompanied by his cuadrilla of nailers, hammerers, cross-raisers and spade-men." He uses the same technique to parody the Lord's Prayer—"Our nada who art in nada, nada be thy name"—at the end of one of his finest stories, "A Clean, Well-Lighted Place" (1933). The titles "The Light of the World" (a metaphor for Christians in Matthew 5:14 and John 8:12) and "God Rest You Merry, Gentlemen" (the opening line of a Christmas carol), both published in 1933, are used for stories about the quarrel of two whores over a dead boxer and the attempted castration of a religious fanatic. In *The Fifth Column* Philip Rawlings blesses people with saliva from a cuspidor. He says, "God—er, oh you know, whatever it is, save us," and is warned by Dorothy Bridges: "Don't blaspheme. It's frightfully bad luck."[27]

Despite his antagonism to Catholicism in his work of the late twenties and the thirties, Hemingway maintained a pretense of affiliation until the Spanish Civil War, which coincided with his emotional break with Pauline. Hemingway passionately allied himself with the Loyalists and hated the Church for supporting Franco. As he explained to his mother-in-law Mary Pfeiffer, he missed the "Ghostly comfort" but felt it was egotistical and selfish to pray for oneself (it did not seem to occur to him to pray for others) during war. And he felt it was wrong to have faith in the Church when it supported the Fascists.[28]

Though Catholicism provided useful literary material, Hemingway was certainly not a sincere believer. Unlike Marcel Proust, he did not have an aesthetic attraction to the Catholic Church. His Catholicism was a way of distancing himself from and expressing his contempt for the Protestantism of his family and the moral values of Oak Park; it was a means of identifying himself with the Latin ritual, customs and culture of Italy, France and Spain; it provided a kind of insurance and satisfied the medieval superstition he nourished in place of religious belief; it was a convenient accommodation that pleased Pauline. It is ironic that she was not a practicing Catholic at the time of her death and that their two sons are not Catholics now.[29]

III

In February 1926, when Hemingway began his affair with Pauline, he could not decide whether or not to publish *The Torrents of Spring*. He was torn between Liveright and Scribner's, between his wife and his mistress. Hadley criticized his behavior, Pauline flattered him. His wife advised him to remain loyal to Anderson, to remain with Liveright and to suppress the satire. Pauline, who sensed that her own fate was involved in this decision and knew his feelings about the book, urged him to betray Anderson, to change publishers and to publish *Torrents* with Scribner's.

Hemingway followed Pauline's advice and sailed on February 3 to arrange matters in New York. He stayed at the Hotel Brevoort on Fifth Avenue, near Washington Square; saw the stage version of *The Great Gatsby* (he paid to get in and would gladly have paid to get out); and met Elinor Wylie, Marc Connelly, Robert Benchley and Dorothy Parker. He handled his own affairs without the intercession of an agent and later said: "I deal direct because I will not give ten percent to any son of a bitch to do what I can do better." He saw Horace Liveright, Alfred Harcourt and Max Perkins, and decided to sign contracts with Scribner's. He told Perkins that his literary experience did not yet include receiving money from publishers and was offered a generous $1,500 advance and fifteen percent royalties for *The Torrents of Spring* and *The Sun Also Rises*.

The staid family publishing house on Fifth Avenue had been founded by the grandfather of Charles Scribner. Charles graduated from Princeton and joined the firm in 1913, and ran the business from 1931 until his death in 1952. But the real attraction for Hemingway was Max Perkins, who had been highly recommended by Fitzgerald. Morley Callaghan, another Scribner's author, said: "Perkins had a talent for diplomacy in difficult human situations, and he had a kind of nobility of spirit and a fine sense of fairness."[30] Hemingway liked his kindness, modesty and tact, and the way he always kept his hat on in the office. But he criticized that "awful puritanical thing" which made Perkins give up experiences like duck hunting as soon as he found them enjoyable.

Perkins gave excellent literary advice to authors who needed it. He helped Thomas Wolfe—who portrayed him unsympathetically as Foxhall Edwards in *The Web and the Rock* (1939)—to stitch together his massive tomes from a pile of disordered fragments. Perkins wanted to retain the first two chapters of *The Sun Also Rises,* which Fitzgerald had advised Hemingway to cut, because they provided valuable background about the characters and afforded a more leisurely approach to the novel. But Perkins was overruled. He did not edit Hemingway, a careful author, beyond excising certain passages that were obscene and libelous. Hemingway was often irritated by these deletions, but understood that offensive passages would hurt the reception and sales of the book. Perkins accepted Hemingway's typescripts, published them and praised them. He provided moral support during difficult times and always got on perfectly with Hemingway.

The puritanical Perkins found it difficult to mention the obscenities he had to urge Hemingway to omit. He once noted "shit piss fuck bitch" on his things-to-do calendar to remind him to discuss these words with Hemingway during lunch. After Perkins left, Charles Scribner came into his office and was surprised to see these emphatic reminders. When Perkins returned, Scribner said, "You must be exhausted," and urged him to take the rest of the day off.

Hemingway did not establish such close personal relations with Jonathan Cape, who published *In Our Time* and his subsequent works in England. He disliked Cape, "a natural enemy," but felt it was better to fight with only one publisher than with many of them.

Hemingway had enjoyed seeing the witty and talented Dorothy Parker in New York and found her a lively companion as they sailed to France on the *Roosevelt* on February 19. Yet an unpleasant incident, sparked by Parker's failure to return his borrowed typewriter, took place at MacLeish's flat in Paris in October 1926 and caused a break with his old friend Don Stewart. Hemingway learned through gossip that Parker had become pregnant by the playwright Charles Mac-Arthur, had an abortion and tried to commit suicide. Instead of sympathizing with her suffering, he wrote a nasty poem about it, misjudged his audience and, according to Stewart, "read it to his [horrified] friends simply to be entertaining—to show how clever he was":

> [You] always vomited in time
> and bound your wrists up
> To tell how you could see his little hands

already formed
You'd waited months too long
that was the trouble. . . .
Spaniards pinched
the Jewish cheeks of your plump ass
in holy week in Seville.[31]

Fortunately, Parker's friends never mentioned this incident to her and she continued to praise Hemingway's work—from *Men Without Women* (1927) to *For Whom the Bell Tolls* (1940)—in enthusiastic reviews in *The New Yorker* (where she quoted his famous phrase "grace under pressure") and in the highbrow newspaper *PM*.

IV

Hemingway wrote *The Sun Also Rises* during a time of intense emotional turmoil. He began the novel on his birthday, July 21, 1925, in Valencia—just after going to San Fermín with Duff Twysden and Harold Loeb—continued it in Madrid and Hendaye, and completed the first draft in Paris two months later, on September 21. He revised slowly and extensively during the next six months, which coincided with his disenchantment with Duff and his love for Pauline. He completed it, after he had returned to Hadley in Schruns, at the end of March 1926. He corrected proofs in Gerald Murphy's studio after his separation from Hadley in August and dedicated it to his abandoned wife and son. Scribner's published the book in October 1926 while Hemingway was living an anguished life in Paris, during the separation from Pauline. He loved to create legends about himself and later told Bernard Berenson (a faithful octogenarian correspondent, whom he never met) that he sped through the novel in only six weeks, sent Hadley on a trip with Pauline and Jinny in September (rather than the following spring) and celebrated the conclusion of the book with a sexual escapade (which never took place):

Toward the last I was sprinting, like in a bicycle race, and I did not want to lose my speed making love or anything else and so had my wife go on a trip with two friends of hers down to the Loire. Then I finished and was hollow and lonely and needed a girl very badly. So I was in bed with a no good girl when my wife came home and had to get the girl out onto the roof of the saw mill (to cut lumber for picture frames) and change the sheets and come down to open the door of the court.

The origins of Jake Barnes' war wound derived from Hemingway's imaginative extension of his *own* wound at Fossalta and his convalescence at the hospital in Milan:

> It came from a personal experience in that when I had been wounded at one time there had been an infection from pieces of wool cloth being driven into the scrotum. Because of this I got to know other kids who had genito urinary wounds and I wondered what a man's life would have been like after that if his penis had been lost and his testicles and spermatic cord remained intact. . . . [So I] tried to find out what his problems would be when he was in love with someone who was in love with him and there was nothing that they could do about it.

His personal experience was reinforced by a story he heard in Schruns in December 1925 about an Austrian who was castrated after receiving war wounds: "Only scandal is that Herr Sten who was shot in the balls on Mount Grappa and who had one of his interstitial glands [cell groups in testes which secrete androgen] removed at the time and the other, after many operations, also removed last year. He in the meantime having married, but without children, is much plumper this year."[32] In the novel, Hemingway meant Jake, rather improbably, to have his penis rather than his testicles shot off—so there would be no humiliating hormonal changes and he would still be "capable of all normal feelings as a *man* but incapable of consummating them." Like the hero of Solzhenitsyn's *Cancer Ward,* whose sexual capacity is destroyed by radiation and chemotherapy, Jake's "libido remains, the libido but nothing else." Hemingway clarified this point, which remains unclear in the novel, when he added a comic subtitle and called it: "The sun also rises (like your cock if you have one)."[33]

Jake's sexual incapacity, revealed when he examines his absurd wound in front of a mirror, cries alone in the night and realizes Brett "only wanted what she couldn't have," is a projection of Hemingway's inability to consummate his love for Duff Twysden. In the novel, Brett, who pursues sex without love, is attached to Jake but sleeps with Mike, Cohn and Romero. Jake, who pursues love without sex, is hopelessly reunited with Brett when she renounces her hold on Romero. In Hemingway's later fiction—*A Farewell to Arms, To Have and Have Not, For*

Whom the Bell Tolls, Across the River—death replaces war wounds as the destroyer of love.

Though Hemingway, as Fitzgerald observed, needed a new woman for each new book, the heroines of *The Sun Also Rises* and *A Farewell to Arms* were inspired by the inaccessible Duff and Agnes rather than by Hadley and Pauline. After the novel based on Duff—who protested that she "never had slept with the bloody bull fighter"[34]—Hemingway's heroines tend to lose their ambiguity and to become either predatory or passive, bitchy or benign.

A major theme of *The Sun Also Rises* is expressed in the two epigraphs. Gertrude Stein's remark about postwar moral chaos—"You are all a lost generation"—is refuted by the long quotation from Ecclesiastes that emphasizes the cyclical structure of the novel, the eternal order of nature and the hope of a new generation. Hemingway explained that he meant to contrast the flawed characters with the fine country. He was fond of the earth, which "abideth forever," but not very fond of his own generation.

Two symbolic scenes express this theme perfectly. When Brett fails to meet Jake at the Hôtel Crillon, he takes a taxi to a café across the river: "Crossing the Seine I saw a string of barges being towed empty down the current, riding high, the bargemen at the sweeps as they came toward the bridge. The river looked nice. It was always pleasant crossing bridges in Paris." Jake is attracted to the barges—which are functional but empty, passive and drawn by the current of another will —because they represent his own character and situation. And he is attracted to the river because it flows out of the city and foreshadows the blissful fishing and swimming scenes in Spain.

Later in the novel, in a scene that recalls Brett's indifference, the empty barges and the sense of loss, Jake, against his better judgment and at the cost of his valued friendship with Montoya, helps Brett initiate her affair with the young bullfighter: "When I came back and looked in the café, twenty minutes later, Brett and Pedro Romero were gone. The coffee glasses and our three empty cognac-glasses were on the table. A waiter came with a cloth and picked up the glasses and mopped off the table."[35] Jake, caught in a masochistic trap, pimps for Brett and observes the debris while she makes love with Romero. His awkward role, however, allows him a certain measure of control over Brett and even a vicarious participation in her affair. It is a desperate yet poignant attempt to shore up the ruins of their disastrous lives.

Hemingway skillfully reports as well as imaginatively transforms the actual events that inspired the novel. His enthusiasm for blood sports and death—for the matador who holds "his purity of line through the maximum of exposure"—provides an illuminating contrast to Lawrence's expression of revulsion for "human cowardice and beastliness, a smell of blood, a nauseous whiff of bursten bowels!" in the opening bullfight chapter of his Mexican novel, *The Plumed Serpent* (also 1926). Hemingway, always the purist in sporting matters, regretted the reform of rules in 1928 that introduced protective pads for the horses of the picadors. Unlike Lawrence, he believed "nobody ever lives their life all the way up except bull-fighters." Hemingway created the literary image of Spain for American readers, and his descriptions of the Spanish landscape, the explosive festival, the running of the bulls and Romero's triumphant corrida reflect the movement from tension to release as the scene shifts from Paris to Pamplona, from moral corruption to regenerative ritual. Hemingway would agree with García Lorca that the bullring "is the only place where one can go in safety to contemplate Death surrounded by the most dazzling beauty."[36]

The style, action and theme of Hemingway's fifth book and first novel consolidated his reputation as a major American writer. The poet Conrad Aiken praised the brilliant dialogue, the profound revelation of character, the "extraordinary effect of honesty and reality," the dignity and detachment in telling a somewhat sordid yet intensely tragic story. Herbert Gorman, who wrote the first biography of Joyce, aroused interest in the novel by stating that it portrayed a "great spiritual debacle, a generation that has lost its guiding purpose and has been driven by time, fate or nerves . . . into the feverish atmosphere of strained passions."[37]

Though some critics disliked the immoral characters and wasted lives, Malcolm Cowley soon discovered that Hemingway's influence was spreading far beyond Paris and the literary reviews. College girls "were modelling themselves after Lady Brett. . . . Bright young men from the Middle West were trying to be Hemingway heroes, talking in tough understatements from the sides of their mouths."[38] The novel had an even greater influence on later generations (it put Pamplona on the tourist map and the town has never recovered), who identified with rather than rejected the sordid and nihilistic lives of the protagonists. *The Sun Also Rises* is now recognized as Hemingway's greatest work.

But the novel, which coincided with Hemingway's scandalous divorce and conversion to Catholicism, was not well received in Oak Park. His parents feared he had lost Hadley's valuable moral guidance and fallen into the clutches of a seductive Catholic who would encourage his vicious habits.

9

Accidents
1927–1928

The world breaks everyone and afterward
many are strong at the broken places.

A Farewell to Arms

I

Pauline sailed back to France on December 30. Hemingway met the
boat at Cherbourg and they spent the winter, with Jinny, skiing in
Switzerland. He often changed locales when he remarried and Gstaad,
a luxurious international resort, was a classy step upward from Schruns.
Pauline's wealth gave him all the comforts that the wife had demanded
in "Cat in the Rain." When they returned to Paris in March they found
an elegant flat in a high-windowed, four-story house with a courtyard
at 6 rue Férou, a quiet, narrow street off the Jardin du Luxembourg. It
had a large bedroom, living and dining room, a well-appointed kitchen,
two bathrooms, a child's room and a small study. Uncle Gus advanced
the money to pay for it just as he later helped them pay for their first
car, grand house, fishing boat and African safari. The outside toilet and
noisy sawmill were left far behind.

Hemingway took the ten-day bachelor tour through Italy with Guy
Hickok in March and obtained his Catholic credentials. He married
Pauline, who listed her birth date as 1897 to decrease their age difference, in the church of St. Honoré d'Eylan on May 10, 1927. They spent
their honeymoon in the Camargue at Grau-de-Roi, a colorful fishing
port with a long beach, and traveled through Spain in the summer. In
Grau, he experienced the first of several periods of impotence, which
were usually associated with new wives. In this case, as Hemingway

194

realized, the reasons were more psychological than physical. He still felt guilty about betraying Hadley and feared that he was now trapped in another marriage: "Don't know if it was autosuggestion from *Sun Also Rises* or maybe reaction to having just divorced Hadley, but . . . I couldn't make love. Had had very good bed with Pauline during all the time we were having our affair, and after Hadley left me, but after our marriage, suddenly I could no more make love than Jake Barnes. Pauline was very patient and understanding and we tried everything, but nothing worked."[1]

Hemingway soon made the sexual adjustment, for Pauline—like Hadley—was eager to please him and submit to his will. She tactfully said that she liked to be told what to do and was "really a muddle head alone." In "The Snows of Kilimanjaro" Harry's wife (who is based on Pauline) echoes Zelda's remark about Hadley and exclaims: "I left everything and I went wherever you wanted to go and I've done what you wanted to do." Bumby, who spent a good deal of time with Pauline and Hemingway in Paris and Gstaad, was at first a bit frightened by her strict discipline. But he soon felt as if she were a second mother: "She could not have been kinder or more loving to me than she was. She treated me as her own both before and after the breakup with Papa."[2] Pauline also arranged for Uncle Gus to set up a $10,000 trust fund for the boy.

II

"When he's going well he's awfully easy to get along with," Pauline declared. "But just before he gets going he's frightful. His temper has to go bad before he can write. When he talks about never writing again I know he's about to get started."[3] Hemingway wrote every other day in Gstaad and composed most of the fourteen stories that were published in October 1927 in the first book after his divorce, *Men Without Women*. Ten of the stories had appeared in national magazines—the *Atlantic Monthly*, *Scribner's Magazine* and the *New Republic*—as well as in *transition*, *The Little Review* and *This Quarter*. This uneven collection, which omitted "the softening feminine influence," concerned bullfights, war, abortion, gangsters, Fascism, boxing, homosexuality, infidelity, divorce, morbidity, drug addiction, blasphemy, wounds and death. The stories are less autobiographical, more objective than his early work. The book lacks the structure and unity of *In Our Time*, but contains three of his masterpieces in this genre: "The Killers," "Hills Like White Elephants" and "In Another Country" (all 1927).

"The Killers" is based on the comical-sinister gangsters of Al Capone's Chicago. The wisecracking dialogue, the sense of immediate experience and the sharp cinematic scenes influenced the portrayal of underworld stereotypes in the films of James Cagney, George Raft and Edward G. Robinson. Two screen versions were made of this tale. Hemingway thought the first one, filmed in 1946 with Burt Lancaster and Ava Gardner, was "the only good picture ever made of a story of mine"—because only the first ten minutes of the movie had anything to do with his work.

Max and Al—with derby hat, silk muffler, gloves and a sawed-off shotgun—turn up in a restaurant, which had been converted from a saloon during Prohibition, to murder a heavyweight boxer. He had agreed to throw a fight, but betrayed the gamblers. The suspense builds up as time passes, threats are made, motives are slowly revealed and Ole Andreson fails to appear for dinner at his customary time. The gangsters convey their indifferent, immoral but highly professional attitude—"We're killing him for a friend. Just to oblige a friend"—which astonishes young Nick Adams but is passively accepted by the victim.

The two main events of the story—the prizefight and the murder—are left out. And the theme, a boy's discovery of evil and death, is also conveyed obliquely when Nick goes to warn Ole. The boxer stoically, if not heroically, confronts his fate and rolls over toward the wall: "There isn't anything I can do about it. . . . I'm through with all that running around."[4] Nick moves from fear to compassion to disillusionment and realizes that things are not what they appear to be: the clock is fast, the gangsters look like a vaudeville team, the corrupt-honest fighter is strangely indifferent, Mrs. Hirsch is actually Mrs. Bell, and Ole's friends are much more frightened than he is. "The Killers" effectively portrays Hemingway's recurrent theme of The Undefeated and suggests that pity can be earned only by men who never demand it.

"Hills Like White Elephants" is Hemingway's most subtle story. (Anyone who thinks he does not understand women ought to read it carefully.) According to McAlmon, it originated in a discussion of birth control and "of the cruelty of the law which did not allow young unmarried women to avoid having an unwanted child." But this story, which originally began in the first person, may also portray Hemingway's response to Hadley's second pregnancy. The tone resembles the man's bitter reaction to the woman's pregnancy in "Cross-Country Snow" and *A Farewell to Arms*. It anticipates "Homage to Switzerland," one of the stories about Hadley, in which three unhappy men await their trains in Swiss railroad stations. And the title echoes Hemingway's description of Vigo—"Sun-baked brown mountains slump down to the sea like tired old dinosaurs"[5]—which he visited with Hadley on their first trip to Europe, in December 1921.

The comparison of hills with white elephants—imaginary animals that represent useless items, like the unwanted baby—is crucial to the meaning. The simile becomes a focus of contention and establishes an opposition between the imaginative woman, who is moved by the land-scape, and the literal-minded man, who refuses to sympathize with her point of view. As they wait between two destinations, Barcelona and Madrid, they are trapped between two lines of rails, between sun and shade, in the limbo of the Ebro valley. The theme of the story evolves from a series of polarities: natural v. unnatural, instinctive v. rational, reflective v. talkative, vital v. morbid. The egoistic man, unaware of the woman's feelings, tries to bully her into having an abortion (which is never actually mentioned) so they can be exactly as they were before: "It's not really anything. It's just to let the air in. . . . It's all perfectly natural." The woman, who finds it horribly unnatural, is frightened of killing the baby and hurting herself. Everything the man says is false; everything the woman says is ironic. He forces her to consent to this operation in order to regain his love, but the very fact that he can ask her to do such a thing means that she can never love him again. She agrees to this form of self-destruction after reaching the kind of dissocia-tion of self that was portrayed in Dostoyevsky's Underground Man and in Kafka's Joseph K., and that reflects his attitude toward her: "Then I'll do it. Because I don't care about me." She then walks away from him and, like Jake Barnes fishing the Irati or swimming in San Sebastian, finds comfort in nature: in the fields of grain, the trees, the river and the hills beyond. Her peaceful contemplation recalls Psalm 121 as she lifts up her eyes to the hills for help. But her mood is shattered by the man's persistent argument, which drives her to the edge of a break-down. Echoing King Lear's "Never, never, never, never, never," she frantically begs: "Would you please, please, please, please, please, please, please stop talking?"[6] Their anguished situation is another ex-pression of the end of something.

The title of "In Another Country," a miniature version of *A Farewell to Arms*, comes from Marlowe's *The Jew of Malta:* "But that was in another country / And besides the wench is dead." But "another country" has at least four other meanings: Italy, the hospital that separates the maimed from the healthy, the isolated world of the wounded and shell-shocked, the affectless condition in which one is "a little detached."

The first paragraph echoes Hemingway's article "Christmas on the Roof of the World," published in the *Toronto Star* in December 1923, and evokes through the repetition of fall, cold and wind the atmosphere of Milan during his convalescence in late 1918. The superb opening sentence—"In the fall the war was always there, but we did not go to it any more"—recalls the terrible repetition of five autumns of war; ironically assumes that the wounded, who can no longer participate in the war, are still capable of choice; and establishes the bitter mood of the story.

The therapeutic machines are supposed to restore the use of shattered and rebuilt limbs, but the officers lack confidence that they will ever do so. These hollow men are held together by nothing but their wounds and by the sense of nothingness that overwhelms them. Their disillusionment cannot be comprehended by the healthy masses who hate the officers for having led them into war. The noble words— fraternity, sacrifice—have become meaningless and the soldiers realize that medals have been awarded to those wounded accidentally rather than courageously. An Italian major with a shriveled hand had cautiously restrained himself and had not married until after he had been invalided out of the army. Yet his wife died of pneumonia after the war was over. He has not been able to resign himself to this loss and warns the young American not to marry: "He should not place himself in a position to lose. He should find things he cannot lose." The theme of "In Another Country," like that of "A Clean, Well-Lighted Place," is *nada*.

Men Without Women sold 19,000 copies in the first six months and —apart from a hostile review by Virginia Woolf, who was unlikely to be impressed by Hemingway's heroics—received a generally favorable press. Cyril Connolly acknowledged that Hemingway's immaturity, ferocious virility and silent sentimentality were "redeemed by humour, power over dialogue and an obvious knowledge of the people he describes." Dorothy Parker thought his "truly magnificent" stories were more effective and more moving than *The Sun Also Rises*. Even H. L.

Mencken, an old adversary, warmed to Hemingway, praised his technical virtuosity and suggested that increasing maturity should enable him to achieve his high promise. Edmund Wilson's perceptive review defended Hemingway's characters as "highly civilized persons of rather complex temperament and extreme sensibility." Wilson observed that "his drama usually turns on some principle of courage, of honor, of pity" that reveals his serious moral values.[7]

III

Two recurrent themes in Hemingway's works—venereal disease and homosexuality—are related to male fear of and rejection of women. Hemingway was both fascinated and repelled by venereal disease. He associated it with swaggering virility and with the kind of tough, lonely men he liked to write about: bullfighters, boxers, gangsters, soldiers. But he also thought of it as a scourge of sinful flesh: "His father had summed up the whole matter by stating that . . . a man who went with prostitutes would contract hideous veneral diseases." Hemingway absorbed and retained this belief, which was reinforced by the horrible color plates in Ed's medical books that showed chancres and venereal ulcers. In his poem "Oklahoma" he writes that the pounding wound "throbs in the night—(or is it the gonorrhea),"[8] and the rejected lover in "A Very Short Story" contracts gonorrhea from a Chicago salesgirl while having sex in a taxi. In *A Farewell to Arms* Frederic Henry wonders if his friend Rinaldi has syphilis and in "One Reader Writes" a woman asks a doctor what to do about a syphilitic husband. Though Hemingway boasted that he had had venereal disease and claimed it could inspire great writing, there is no evidence that he ever consorted with prostitutes or had this illness.

Hemingway was well known for his hostility to homosexuals. But he was not always unsympathetic and had a number of lesbian and homosexual friends: Gertrude Stein, Sylvia Beach, Janet Flanner, Jinny Pfeiffer, Robert McAlmon, Sidney Franklin and others. He may have rejected Jim Gamble's offer of a free year of travel in Europe because he suspected his friend was homosexual, and he had to discourage an Englishman who visited him in the hospital in Milan: "This Englishman used to bring me Marsala. That was fine. But then he got wet about wanting to see my wounds dressed. At that time I didn't know that well-brought-up people were like that. I thought it was only tramps. I explained to him that I was not that way."

In *A Moveable Feast* Hemingway exaggerates his violent experience with pederastic tramps: "I had certain prejudices against homosexuality since I knew its more primitive aspects. I knew it was why you carried a knife and would use it when you were in the company of tramps. . . . You had to be prepared to kill a man, know how to do it and really know that you would do it in order not to be interfered with."[9] In this memoir he makes a negative allusion to Jean Cocteau (who also takes drugs) and describes his anger when a homosexual disturbs his writing in a café. And he rejects the contrast between corrupt homosexuals and well-adjusted lesbians that was made by Gertrude Stein.

Brett Ashley makes her first appearance in *The Sun Also Rises* with a group of homosexuals who arouse Jake's irrational animosity: "I was very angry. Somehow they always made me angry. I know they are supposed to be amusing, and you should be tolerant, but I wanted to swing on one, any one, anything to shatter that superior, simpering composure."[10] In this scene, the inverts do not present the usual threat to masculinity since Jake's virility has already been destroyed. But their psychological wounds match his physical wound, and these men who are not men remind him of his own incapacity. Jake wants to reassert his male force against his mirror images rather than (like normal men) against his repressed fears.

Hemingway wrote four stories about lesbians and homosexuals. In "Mr. and Mrs. Elliot" the wife, unable to conceive a child, becomes a lesbian and sleeps with her woman friend instead of with her husband. This married couple, who are both repressed homosexuals, abandon their procreative function but retain the facade of a normal marriage. In a similar story, "The Sea Change," whose title comes from *The Tempest,* a woman who is unable to maintain this kind of facade tells her lover that she is leaving him for a lady friend. He calls her sexual taste a vice and a perversion and, though wounded, pretends he has benefited from the sea change that has affected both of them. In "The Mother of a Queen," a bullfighter whose homosexuality is manifested in stinginess refuses to pay for his mother's grave. His vice leads to vanity, self-deception, corruption, and to resentment against his mother for making him a queen.

The most interesting—and the most sympathetic—of the stories on this theme is "A Simple Enquiry" in *Men Without Women.* Like Lawrence's "The Prussian Officer," this tale concerns a military man's barely repressed attraction to his handsome young servant. In Lawrence's more fully developed story, homosexuality is expressed as sadism, and leads to the murder of the officer and the death of the orderly. In Hemingway's story this theme is portrayed in a series of subtle, half-spoken questions through which the Italian major tests the sexual response of his man: " 'And you don't really want—' the major paused. Pinin looked at the floor. 'That your great desire isn't really—.' . . . 'Don't be afraid,' the major said. His hands were folded on the blankets. 'I won't touch you.' " Though the major decides to leave the servant alone, he is not convinced by the man's passive rejection of his overtures or by his protestation of sexual innocence: "The little devil, he thought, I wonder if he lied to me." This unusually sensitive story is notable for its comprehension rather than condemnation of the major's moral and sexual dilemma.

Such sympathetic understanding is absent from Hemingway's later works. He satirizes the homosexual cook in "The Light of the World." In *Death in the Afternoon,* his most swaggering and opinionated book, he condemns Jean Cocteau and Raymond Radiguet. And on the dubious evidence of the "androgynous faces and forms that filled his imagination," he characterizes El Greco as homosexual and lumps him with Gide, Wilde and Whitman: "If he was one he should redeem, for the tribe, the prissy exhibitionistic, aunt-like, withered old maid moral arrogance of a Gide; the lazy, conceited debauchery of a Wilde who betrayed a generation; the nasty, sentimental pawing of humanity of a Whitman and all the mincing gentry. Viva El Greco El Rey de los Maricones."[11]

In *Islands in the Stream,* completed in 1951, Hemingway again attacks Gide (a rival who had won the Nobel Prize in 1947) as well as three fictional characters: the second houseboy, "with his faintly fairy, half Saint Sebastian, sly, crafty, and long-suffering look"; the "sad clerk with plucked eyebrows" at the reception desk of the American Embassy; and the worthless man who tried to justify homosexuality by high-minded references to classical and biblical lovers: "explaining to Tommy what it meant to be a fairy and all about the Greeks and Damon and Pythias and David and Jonathan."[12]

Though Hemingway's attacks may have seemed rather crude, he was actually quite acute in perceiving this aspect of Whitman long before scholars accepted it, in recognizing St. Sebastian as a homosexual icon and in criticizing the intellectual as well as the behavioral side of inversion. His notorious antagonism to homosexuals made Tennessee Williams quite nervous when Kenneth Tynan offered to introduce the playwright to Hemingway in 1959: " 'But won't he kick me?' said Tennessee, stricken with unease. 'They tell me that Mr. Hemingway usually kicks people like me in the crotch.' "[13] But his fears were ill-founded and their meeting was quite amiable.

Hemingway has been suspected and even accused of being a covert homosexual because of his aggressive masculinity, his preference for exclusively male company, his occasional impotence, his sexual boasts and his hostility to inverts. But this suspicion is as unconvincing as the theory that Don Juan is a homosexual because of his obsessive need to prove his virility. Despite all the theorizing, there is not a shred of real evidence to suggest that Hemingway ever had any covert homosexual desires or overt homosexual relations.

IV

Hemingway's adult life was characterized by emotional turmoil, constant travel, frequent illness and accidents. The timid and nearsighted Dos Passos, who often accompanied Hemingway on skiing and fishing trips, observed: "I never knew an athletic vigorous man who spent so much time in bed as Ernest did."[14] There were both physical and psychological reasons for Hemingway's numerous accidents. He was a huge, clumsy man with defective vision in one eye and very slow reflexes. He had a bad temper, behaved recklessly and irrationally, drank heavily and was frequently out of control. He deliberately placed himself in risky situations in driving, boxing, skiing, fishing, hunting and war.

He was also extremely strong and able to take punishment, felt that he was indestructible and had amazing recuperative powers. He willingly tested his body, to the point of self-destruction, in a self-hardening process that proved he was indifferent to wounds and pain. Eager for the extremes of experience, he was (like the Count in *The Sun Also Rises*) proud of the scars that authenticated his confrontation with violence and danger. He himself had been shot and knew what a man or an animal felt like when wounded by a bullet. In *Green Hills of Africa* he claimed: "I did nothing that had not been done to me. I had been shot and I had been crippled and gotten away. I expected, always, to be killed by one thing or another and I, truly, did not mind that any more." Joyce said of Hemingway: "He's a big, powerful peasant, as strong as a buffalo. A sportsman. And ready to live the life he writes about. He would never have written it if his body had not allowed him to live it." Hemingway had enjoyed his convalescence in Milan—where he was cared for, pampered, praised and loved—and after his experience with Agnes, usually found being in a hospital rather romantic. Finally, the accidents were also a therapeutic self-punishment for his feelings of guilt. "I wouldn't really be comfortable," he confessed to his parents, "unless I had some pain."[15]

Hemingway had three accidents, probably connected to his guilt, during the first year of marriage to Pauline. On their honeymoon he cut his foot; it became infected and swollen with anthrax, which kept him in bed for ten days. The second mishap occurred in Montreux in December 1927 while they were spending their second winter skiing in Switzerland. When he picked up Bumby to put him on the pot at night, the baby stuck his fingernail in Hemingway's good, right eye, cut a half-moon in the pupil and impaired his vision for several weeks.

Hemingway described the third accident, which took place in March 1928 in their flat on rue Férou, in a letter to Max Perkins:

> I was tired of recounting accidents so was not going to mention it. However it was the skylight in the toilet—a friend had pulled the cord that raised it instead of pulling the chain of the toilet and cracked the glass so that when I tried to hook up the cord (going into the bathroom at 2 A.M. and seeing it dangling) the whole thing fell. We stopped the hemorrhage with 30 thicknesses of toilet paper (a magnificent absorbent which I've now used twice for that purpose in pretty much emergencies) and a tourniquet of kitchen towel and a stick of kindling wood.

The heavy bleeding was caused by the severing of two small arteries in the head. Pauline phoned MacLeish, who took Hemingway to the American hospital at Neuilly. The wound was closed with nine stitches, but left a large welt above the right eyebrow. In *A Farewell to Arms* Catherine tenderly tells Frederic: " 'I want to feel the bump on your head. It's a big bump.' She ran her finger over it." Pound asked, in his backwoods dialect: "Haow the hellsufferin tomcats did you git drunk enough to fall upwards thru the blithering skylight!"[16]

When Pauline became pregnant and puffed up in late 1927, Hemingway thought Hadley looked much more attractive than his wife. But he was not upset about Pauline's child as he had been about Hadley's. Pauline also decided to have the baby in North America. Many of their friends had left Paris, which contained the memories and ghosts of his first marriage, and Pauline was eager to introduce her husband to her family. They heard enthusiastic reports about Key West from Dos Passos. In March 1928 they took an eighteen-day cruise on the *Orita* from La Rochelle to Havana and reached Florida in early April. After Hemingway left Paris, he never again lived in a big city.

10

Key West
1928–1929

The state with the prettiest name,
the state that floats in brackish water . . .
The state full of long S-shaped birds, blue and white . . .
who coast for fun on the strong tidal currents
in and out among the mangrove islands.

ELIZABETH BISHOP, "Florida"

I

Key West, the southernmost town in America, is the last in a string of small subtropical islands that stretches southwest from the tip of the Florida peninsula and divides the Gulf of Mexico from the Atlantic Ocean. The island is only 1½ miles wide and 4½ miles long; it is 90 miles from Havana, 120 from the American mainland, and in 1928 was accessible only by ferry. The weather is warm, the swimming and fishing superb. The maritime atmosphere of the seedy unpretentious town, with weathered clapboard houses and open balconies, was a mixture of Nantucket and New Orleans. The pace was slow-moving, with many bicycles and few cars. It was then an exotic, almost foreign locale. Spanish was spoken everywhere, the rollers of big cigars were prospering and there were many Cuban tourists. The place was far from urban distractions, but had two tennis courts at the Navy Yard, good cockfights, thriving whorehouses and an endless supply of smuggled Prohibition whiskey in several fine saloons. Hemingway was especially fond of Sloppy Joe's bar, on Green Street off Duval, which had high ceilings, rotating fans and a long front-to-rear bar. The owner, Joe

Russell, a former smuggler, became a fishing companion and model for Harry Morgan in *To Have and Have Not*.

Dos Passos described the people and the mood of the town:

> In those days Key West really was an island. It was a coaling station. There was shipping in the harbor. The air smelt of the Gulf Stream. . . . Cigarfactories attracted a part Cuban, part Spanish population. . . . The Englishspeaking population was made up of railroad men, old Florida settlers, a few descendents of New Englanders from the days when it was a whaling port, and fishermen from such allwhite settlements as Spanish Wells in the Bahamas. . . . There were a couple of drowsy hotels where train passengers on their way to Cuba or the Caribbean occasionally stopped over. Palms and pepper trees. The shady streets of unpainted frame houses had a faintly New England look.

Hemingway was equally enthusiastic and told Guy Hickok: "It's the best place I've ever been any time anywhere, flowers, tamarind trees, guava trees, coconut palms. . . . Got tight last night on absinthe and did knife tricks."[1] He found an apartment on Simonton Street, got up soon after sunrise, disciplined himself to write *A Farewell to Arms* for three or four hours in the morning, fished in the afternoon, and was exhilarated by the anticipation of pleasure and the reward after work. During his dozen years in Key West he produced a vast amount of writing: *A Farewell to Arms, Death in the Afternoon, Winner Take Nothing, Green Hills of Africa, To Have and Have Not*, "Francis Macomber," "The Snows of Kilimanjaro," *The Fifth Column, The Spanish Earth* and the beginning of *For Whom the Bell Tolls*.

In early April, soon after Hemingway reached Key West, his parents arrived and were introduced to Pauline. They had been in Florida to look after their real estate investments and were on the way to Cuba. Ed was thin, nervous and gray, deeply worried about failing health and financial problems. Grace, full of her usual energy, seemed to bloom as her husband wasted away.

Hemingway got on very well with ordinary people, liked strong, simple types, and made several new friends in Key West. He was perceptive, responsive and curious about everything; liked to test people and see how they would react; drank a lot but did not get drunk; had a certain panache and bravado that attracted sporting men. Down at the docks he met Captain Bra Saunders, who was born in the Bahamas in 1876, had a lean florid face, watery eyes and a long Roman nose, and taught Hemingway deep-sea fishing. He befriended Jim Sullivan, a bald, solidly built New Yorker in his forties, with many daughters. Sullivan ran a machine shop for boat repairs and later helped build the railroad on the Keys. Hemingway asked Sully to be godfather of his third son, Gregory, and dedicated *Green Hills of Africa* to him and to his closest Key West friend, Charles Thompson.

Thompson, born in Key West in 1898, was a tall, lean, broad-shouldered, soft-spoken man. He had been educated in New York City schools and Mt. Pleasant Military Academy, and served in the army of occupation after the war. Like Paul Pfeiffer, Thompson was a well-connected local aristocrat. His family owned the marine hardware store, pineapple factory, turtle cannery, icehouse and a fleet of fishing vessels, and he often took Hemingway out on his own boat. Pauline became friendly with Thompson's wife, Lorine, who was assistant principal of the high school and had a house full of books. Thompson, a crack shot, accompanied Hemingway on his first safari and was portrayed as Karl in *Green Hills of Africa*.

Hemingway was eager to share the pleasures of the island with his friends. Dos Passos, Bill Smith and Waldo Peirce, whom he had met in Paris in the spring of 1927, came down to Key West in 1928. Peirce—born in Maine in 1884—was a tall and heavy man, built like Hemingway. He graduated from Phillips Academy and Harvard, and was trained as an artist at the Académie Julian in Paris. He served in the ambulance corps during 1915–17, was married three times and had numerous children. Hemingway, always faithful to the burly and bearded Peirce, overrated his work and praised his character: "As a painter I think he is one of the very finest in America. As a friend he is loyal, understanding, generous and the best company anybody ever had."

The Hemingways went to Piggott, Arkansas, in late May to meet Pauline's parents. It was surrounded by cotton and soybean fields, and Hemingway disliked the dull, overfoliaged, closed-in country.[2] The small town had a weekly newspaper, a bank, two stores, some cotton gins and a strong evangelical atmosphere. It was rural and bigoted, had no black population and did not allow transient blacks to spend the night.

When Ernest inquired about coming to Walloon Lake and suggested that Pauline have the baby in Petoskey, he was discouraged by Dr.

Hemingway, who offered his obstetrical services in Oak Park. Pauline finally decided on a hospital in Kansas City and they spent the blazingly hot month of June with her friends Ruth and Malcolm Lowrey. Pauline gave birth on June 28. In contrast to Hadley's trouble-free delivery of Bumby, Pauline had a difficult seventeen-hour labor, a Caesarean section and a slow recovery. Hemingway vividly told Hickok: "They finally had to open Pauline up like a picador's horse to lift [him] out." The doctor, Don Carlos Guffey, told her that it would be unsafe to have another baby for three years. Hemingway believed fathers should not name children after themselves "because no son could live up to his name," and called the baby Patrick. Pauline described the baptism in August: "He didn't make a noise until the priest said, 'Patrick, do you renounce the Devil with all his works and pomps?' and he gave a little groan and a little whine of protest."[3]

Hemingway disliked infants, including his own, and kept away from them as much as possible. "If he keeps on yelling," he said of Patrick, "it is a cinch I won't be able to write and support him." He took Pauline and the baby back to Piggott in mid-July and then left for fishing country near Sheridan, Wyoming, with his old Red Cross friend Bill Horne. Pauline did not breast-feed Patrick, left him with her parents when he was six weeks old and joined Hemingway on August 18. His frequent trips from Florida and Cuba to the west, which reminded him of Spain, put him in touch with the quintessential American characteristics he had known as a boy in northern Michigan: virgin land, heroic origins, primitive Indians, pioneer solitude and individualistic triumph. He loved "the ranch and the silvered gray of the sage brush, the quick, clear water in the irrigation ditches, and the heavy green of the alfalfa. The trail went up into the hills and the cattle in summer were shy as deer."

The Hemingways left Wyoming in late September and continued to dash around the country. They spent a month in Piggott, visited Oak Park, had a week with MacLeish in Conway, Massachusetts, and saw the Princeton-Yale football game with the Fitzgeralds on November 17 before moving to 1100 South Street, on the Atlantic side of Key West, for the winter. In early December Hemingway traveled to New York to pick up Bumby, who had sailed from France with Jinny. On December 6, 1928, in Trenton, on the way back to Florida, he received the telegram that had been sent to Scribner's by Grace: "TRY TO LOCATE ERNEST HEMINGWAY IN NEW YORK ADVISE HIM OF DEATH OF HIS FA-

THER TODAY ASK HIM TO COMMUNICATE WITH HOME IMMEDIATELY."[4]
Hemingway wired Fitzgerald for money, left Bumby (on his first day in
America) with a reliable train porter and hurried west to Chicago.

II

Ed Hemingway killed himself, despite his religious beliefs, because he
had lost a good deal of money, was seriously ill and psychologically
depressed. He had always been a healer, but did not treat his own
disease. He was a strong and active man, and could not cope with
sickness. Marcelline wrote that her father irrationally exclaimed: "Do
you know what that means? I'm a diabetic! . . . I've never been sick. I
can't live that way. . . . I won't be an invalid. . . . I'm so ashamed.
. . . I think I've had it for years, but I never even made an analysis. I
didn't want to know. Gracie, I can't be sick!" He thought he had gangrene of the feet, which frequently accompanies neglected cases of
diabetes, and that he would be crippled by amputation. Ed's diabetes
led to hardening of the arteries and frequent attacks of angina pectoris,
a particularly painful form of heart disease. Carol recalled that her
father had terrible headaches at the end of his life, which he compared
to a steel band tightening around his head. According to Marcelline, he
became "an irritable, suspicious person. He was quick to take offense,
almost unable to let himself believe in the honesty of other people's
motives." Sunny said that when her father was exhausted and worried,
and spoke of killing himself during deep depressions, she would take
him for walks in the Botanical Gardens to get him into a better mood.
She knew he might commit suicide and was not completely surprised
when it happened.[5]

Though many patients owed Ed money, he could not find help for
his financial problems. In 1925, with Grace's enthusiastic support, he
had mortgaged his house and invested all his savings in Florida property. But its value had sharply decreased and left him with high mortgage payments and no income. Just before his death he went to his
wealthy brother George, who owned a real estate company and was a
bank director, to borrow the money to meet the payments due on
December 10. George refused to lend his brother money for what he
considered a hopeless investment and gave some sound if harsh advice:
" 'Unload, Ed,' Uncle George told us he advised my father. 'Don't try

to carry a burden too heavy for you. Sell now and get yourself out from under.' " But Ed planned to retire to Florida and had decided to keep his property. He rejected George's advice and refused to cut his losses. Sunny later said that everyone in the family deeply resented George's failure to help Ed during this financial crisis. Though George's refusal must have been on his conscience, he never expressed any regrets about it.[6]

The thirteen-year-old Leicester Hemingway was in bed with a cold that day. Ed came home for lunch, went up to his bedroom and shot himself just behind the right ear with his father's .32 Smith and Wesson revolver. In his autobiographical novel, *The Sound of the Trumpet,* Leicester gives a detailed account of the suicide and mentions that his father (though probably unconscious) did not die immediately:

> "It sounded like a shot."
> He knocked at the door. "Daddy!" He tried the door. It opened, and in the darkened room, all shades drawn except one, there on the bed lay his father, making hoarse breathing noises. His eyes were closed, and in that first instant as he saw him there in the half-dark, nothing looked wrong. He put his hand under his father's head. His hand slipped under easily and when he brought it out again, it was wet-warm with blood.

The *Chicago Tribune* printed Ed's photograph with his obituary and noted the fifty-seven-year-old doctor had been despondent about diabetes: "Dr. Clarence E. Hemingway, Oak Park physician, shot and killed himself yesterday in a bedroom at his home 600 North Kenilworth Avenue. The weapon he used was a .32 caliber pistol that his father, Anson T. Hemingway, had carried while commanding troops in the civil war."[7]

Grace had to be placed under sedation. Carol, called home from school to handle the emergency, suffered greatly. Sunny, typing *A Farewell to Arms* in Key West, also needed the care of a doctor when she heard the news. It was a tremendous shock for Hemingway, who was deeply attached to his father. He told Mary Pfeiffer that he had just written to Ed telling him to keep up his courage and not worry about money because Hemingway could always borrow from Scribner's and pay Ed's debts. This reassuring letter, Hemingway said, reached the house just twenty minutes after Ed had shot himself. He knew what Hadley must have felt after the suicide of her father in 1903 and warned: "I'll probably go the same way."[8] After his father's death he frequently considered the possibility of suicide.

Hemingway later wrote: "The handsome job the undertaker had done on his father's face had not blurred in his mind and all the rest of it was quite clear, including the responsibilities." Whenever he got the "real old melancholia" he felt more tolerant about his father's suicide. But in December 1928, after he had arranged for the funeral and settled the immediate financial problems, he drove the suicide out of his mind so he could concentrate all his powers on finishing his novel. He could not allow himself to feel *anything,* for fear of losing imaginative control of the book.[9] His first responsibility was to his art, but he felt guilty about suppressing his pity and sorrow.

Ed felt he was sacrificing his life for his family by providing the insurance money. But Hemingway told Perkins the financial situation for Grace—who had two teenage children, servants and a big house—was precarious:

There are my Mother and two kids Boy 12 girl 16 still at home—$25,000 insurance—a $15,000 mortgage on the house (house should bring 10 to 15 thousand over the mortgage but sale difficult). Various worthless land in Michigan, Florida, etc. with taxes to pay on all of it. No other capital —all gone—my father carried a 20–30 yr. Endowment insurance which was paid and lost in Florida. He had angina pectoris and diabetes preventing him from getting any more insurance.

Hemingway promised to send his mother $100 a month and settled the back taxes of $600. He urged her to get Uncle George to pay the mortgage or sell the house at a profit: "He did more than any one to kill Dad and he had better do something in reparation."[10] Grace followed his advice and moved to a smaller house in River Forest.

Hemingway also set up a substantial trust fund with $30,000 of his own money and $20,000 of Pauline's so that Grace would have an adequate income during her lifetime. He may have felt a certain satisfaction in gaining financial power over Grace, who had thrown him out of the Walloon Lake house for refusing to work, condemned his filthy books and criticized his disgraceful divorce. Now Grace wrote to him frequently about family and finances, expressed her gratitude and love, and retailed conventional pieties. Hemingway gave her a red terracotta bust of himself, which Grace kept on her grand piano. At Hemingway's request, she got the suicide weapon from the police, and sent it to him with a chocolate cake. He dropped the gun in a deep lake in Wyoming "and saw it go down making bubbles until it was just as big as a watch charm in that clear water, and then it was out of sight." In the spring of 1929 he sent Grace a sharp but witty reply to an irritating inquiry about her monthly checks. He quoted her statement: I don't know when or where it is coming from, and replied that it was coming each month from his bank account. She wanted the money sent to her in a lump sum so the interest would not be wasted. He said it was not being wasted because it remained in his own account and was paid to him.[11]

Orwell once "startled a contemporary at Eton by cynically criticizing his parents: 'He'd been the first person I had ever heard running down his own father and mother.'" Hemingway used to startle Dos Passos in the same way: "Hem was the only man I ever knew who really hated his mother."[12] Guilty about not helping his father in time and resentful about having to support his mother, Hemingway had to find a scapegoat for the suicide. Just as he had blamed Alice Toklas for his quarrel with Stein and Pauline for the break-up of his marriage to Hadley, so he now shifted the guilt from Uncle George and blamed his mother for his father's tragedy. He also revised the history of his own childhood to match his retrospective view of Ed as a castrated weakling, dominated by the monstrous Grace.

In "Poem, 1928," Hemingway included himself among the men "Who know our mothers for bitches." But he was always torn between his conventional duty and his hostile feelings: "Jesus, is it Mother's Day? Then I'll have to send the old bitch a wire." He made the classic statement of his revisionist feelings in a letter of 1948 to Malcolm Cowley, who had stirred up the old antagonism while interviewing Hemingway about his early life: "I hated my mother as soon as I knew the score and loved my father until he embarrassed me with his cowardice. . . . My mother is an all time all american bitch and she would make a pack mule shoot himself; let alone poor bloody father."[13] Friends of Hemingway who knew Grace in later life confirmed his view of her. His handyman, chauffeur and friend, Toby Bruce, met Grace in Key West and saw that Hemingway hated her. Bruce said she wore ankle-length dresses to cover varicose veins and fat legs, and behaved in a domineering manner. Martha Gellhorn, Hemingway's third wife, agreed that Grace was a "nightmare": superior, bossy, irritating. She did not dominate Hemingway, but he resented her domination of his father.[14]

Hemingway portrayed his father's weak character in "The Doctor and the Doctor's Wife" and "Fathers and Sons," and his suicide in several works of the 1930s. An unpublished fragment, closely related to

"Fathers and Sons" and written in about 1933, "In those days everyone was very fond of my father," describes a boy's recollection of his father's suicide. His father had chosen a lonely death, and had tried to help the family by making it seem accidental. He killed himself during a hunting trip to the Upper Peninsula of Michigan. The boy did not realize that his father was a suicide until he got into fights about it at school.

In a passage deleted from *Green Hills of Africa* (1935) Hemingway frankly calls Ed a coward in order to distance himself from his father's unjustified behavior and contrasts Ed's shameful act with his own mastery of fear while hunting big game:

> My father was a coward. He shot himself without necessity. At least I thought so. I had gone through it myself until I figured it in my head. I knew what it was to be a coward and what it was to cease being a coward. Now, truly, in actual danger I felt a clean feeling as in a shower. Of course it was easy now. That was because I no longer cared what happened. I knew it was better to live it so that if you died you had done everything that you could do about your work and your enjoyment of life up to that minute, reconciling the two, which is very difficult.[15]

The word "coward" recurs obsessively in Hemingway's works on bullfighting, hunting and war. He calls Cayetano Ordóñez a coward in *Death in the Afternoon* and accuses his father of cowardice in *Green Hills of Africa* and *For Whom the Bell Tolls*. In the Spanish novel, Robert Jordan, worried about his own courage the night before the climactic attack on the bridge, contrasts his grandfather's heroic record with his father's cowardice and wonders which strain will prevail when he is tested in battle. He calls the suicide egoistic, describes the effect it had on him and blames his mother for his father's weakness:

> Both he and his grandfather would be acutely embarrassed by the presence of his father. Any one has a right to do it, he thought. But it isn't a good thing to do. I understand it, but I do not approve of it. *Lache* was the word. . . . You have to be awfully occupied with yourself to do a thing like that. . . .
> I'll never forget how sick it made me the first time I knew he was a *cobarde*. Go on, say it in English. Coward. It's easier when you have it said and there is never any point in referring to a son of a bitch by some foreign term. He wasn't any son of a bitch, though. He was just a coward and that was the worst luck any man could have. Because if he wasn't a coward he would have stood up to that woman and not let her bully

him. I wonder what I would have been like if he had married a different woman? That's something you'll never know, he thought, and grinned. Maybe the bully in her helped to supply what was missing in the other. . . . He understood his father and he forgave him everything and he pitied him but he was ashamed of him.

Hemingway wrote "Indian Camp," in which a baby is born and a father dies, a few months after the birth of Bumby. In that prescient story, which reveals Hemingway's early fascination with suicide, Nick asks his doctor-father:

"Why did he kill himself, Daddy?"
"I don't know, Nick. He couldn't stand things, I guess." . . .
"Is dying hard, Daddy?"
"No, I think it's pretty easy."[16]

Four years later, when Patrick was born by Caesarean birth a few months before Ed died by his own hand, Hemingway, like Joyce in "Ecce Puer," felt joy, sorrow and guilt when confronted by the natural cycle of birth and death:

A child is sleeping:
An old man gone.
O, father forsaken,
Forgive your son!

III

Hemingway returned to Key West in mid-December, spent five hard weeks revising A Farewell to Arms, finished it on January 22, 1929, and gave the manuscript to Sunny and Pauline to type. The sister and the wife did not get on very well, for Sunny remained loyal to Hadley, resented Hemingway's love for Pauline and felt that Pauline treated her like a servant. In late May 1929 Hemingway, who made puritanically harsh judgments on all his sisters except Ursula, told his mother that Sunny was a great disappointment and called her dirty, slovenly, sullen, selfish and interested only in running after boys.[17]

Hemingway's activities in 1929 typified the pattern of his life with Pauline in the early 1930s. After completing A Farewell to Arms, he craved release in the outdoors and sent urgent invitations to friends to come down to Key West to fish and shoot. Perkins and Dos Passos responded. Dos Passos met Katy Smith, the childhood friend of Hemingway and roommate of Pauline, in Key West early in 1929 and married her in August. The Hemingways sailed from Havana to France on April 5 and returned to their flat on rue Férou. Hemingway went to the horse races, bicycle races and boxing matches. In June he was beaten in the famous bout with Callaghan that was prolonged by a puzzled and paralyzed Fitzgerald.

Hemingway was planning to write a book on bullfighting. In 1928 he had missed San Fermín for the first time in five years; but in July 1929 he drove down to Pamplona in the new Ford roadster provided by the munificent Uncle Gus and spent a week there with Jinny and the Hickoks. The Hemingways then visited Joan Miró in Montroig and went on to Valencia, Madrid and the old pilgrimage town of Santiago de Compostela in the northwest corner of Spain. In September they followed the fortunes of the Jewish-American bullfighter from Brooklyn, Sidney Franklin. They returned to Paris on September 20, met Allen Tate, the southern poet who had written favorable reviews of Hemingway's books, and spent some time with Gertrude Stein and Charles Sweeny. *A Farewell to Arms* was published on September 27 and the Wall Street stock market crashed a month later. Hemingway followed the bike races to Berlin (which he had visited in November 1927) and, with the money from his new novel, bought Paul Klee's painting *Monument in Arbeit* from the publisher of *Querschnitt:* "He loved to look at it and he remembered how corrupt it had seemed when he first bought it in Berlin. . . . He knew no more about it now than when he first saw it in Flechtheim's Gallery in the house by the [Spree] river that wonderful cold fall in Berlin." After a short skiing trip in Montana-Vermala, Switzerland, where Hemingway and Dos Passos visited the Murphys, the Hemingways sailed back to Havana on January 3 on the *Bourdonnais* for their third winter in Key West.

In his Introduction to the crudely illustrated 1948 edition of *A Farewell to Arms,* Hemingway described the travels and emotional events that took place during the composition of the novel and suggested that he could write while on the move:

> This book was written in Paris, France, Key West, Florida, Piggott, Arkansas, Kansas City, Missouri, Sheridan, Wyoming, and the first draft of it was finished near Big Horn in Wyoming. It was begun in the last

winter months of 1928 and the first draft was finished in September of that year. It was rewritten in the fall and winter of 1928 in Key West and the final writing was finished in Paris in the spring of 1929.

During the time I was writing the first draft my second son Patrick was delivered in Kansas City by Caesarean section and while I was rewriting my father killed himself in Oak Park, Illinois. I was not quite thirty years old when I finished the book and the day it was published was the day [sic] the stock market crashed.[18]

The novel exemplifies Hemingway's theory of inventing from knowledge, his belief that an author must have some actual experience though not necessarily the precise experience of what he writes about. To illustrate this idea, he contrasted Tolstoy's memoir of the Crimean War with his fictional description of Napoleonic battles in *War and Peace:* "Dr. Tolstoi was at Sevastopol. But not at Borodino. He wasn't in business in those days. But he could invent from knowledge. We were all at some damned Sevastopol." And in a letter to his French translator, Maurice Coindreau, he emphasized the imaginative rather than the autobiographical elements of the novel, discounted his service in Italy and did not even mention his war wound. He refused to furnish biographical or military material because the publishers used it to make his novel seem a "document." And he forbade Scribner's to use personal publicity because he wanted his work to be judged purely as fiction.[19]

Hemingway was defensive about documentation because he employed the methods of Tolstoy and Stephen Crane to recreate the realistic battle scenes. In *A Farewell to Arms,* the only novel set on terrain which Hemingway did not actually visit, he used military histories and newspaper accounts to provide the factual basis of the Austro-Italian campaigns that took place when the novelist was still in high school in Oak Park. His account of the disastrous defeat in October 1917, when the Austrians, with the help of German troops released from the Russian front after the Revolution, launched an attack on Caporetto, broke the Italian line and hurled it back to the Piave, was so painfully convincing that Mussolini's government banned the novel, which was not published in Italy until after World War Two. Frederic Henry's military failure "is the epitome of the general performance of the Italian Second Army during the retreat" and the book accurately reflects the principal causes of the defeat: the Socialist revolt in Turin, the severe shortage of food, the effective enemy propaganda and the poor Italian leadership.

Hemingway's novels concern one woman in a male world and portray his fictional heroines as he wanted them to be in real life. In the
early but posthumously published story "Summer People," Hemingway's alter ego Nick Adams sleeps with Katy (Smith). In a similar fashion, both *A Farewell to Arms* and *Across the River and into the Trees*
portray his unconsummated love affairs with Agnes von Kurowsky and
Adriana Ivancich as if they had actually taken place. (He did this so
realistically that both Agnes and Adriana were embarrassed and angered by the novels.) Sylvia Beach, for one, disliked Hemingway's
fictional wish-fulfillment and anticipated critics of his passive heroines
by unfairly remarking: "Hem just thinks that women are something to
fuck."[20] But Beach missed the main point of Hemingway's novels of
love and war: the characters must pay for sex with death.

Catherine Barkley, like Maria in *For Whom the Bell Tolls* and
Renata in *Across the River,* is revealed and reflected in the man she
loves. Hemingway idealizes the romantic and tragic Catherine, emphasizes her fine background, her flawless physical attributes, her military
virtues of loyalty and self-sacrifice, and her touching mental derangement—caused by the death of her fiancé in war—which explains her
impulsive involvement with Frederic Henry. (Brett Ashley also lost her
lover in the war, but she is portrayed as an aggressive nymphomaniac
rather than as a submissive virgin.) Like Hadley and Pauline (but unlike
Agnes), the self-effacing Catherine is desperately eager to please her
lover and tells Frederic: "I'll say just what you wish and I'll do what you
wish. . . . I'll do what you want and I'll say what you want. . . . I want
what you want. There isn't any me any more."

The essence of Catherine's tragedy is her unwanted baby, and for
this aspect of the novel Hemingway transposes to Agnes his resentment
about Hadley's accidental pregnancies and his fear about Pauline's Caesarean delivery. (The surnames of the heroes, Henry and Barkley, suggest Hadley; and Catherine awaits the birth of her baby in a village
above Montreux that is based on Chamby, where Hemingway and
Hadley stayed in January and May 1922.) In the novel, Frederic compares the newborn baby to a freshly skinned rabbit in order to dissociate
himself from the realities of paternity. Frederic (who, like Hemingway,
had a son instead of the expected daughter) confesses: "I had no feeling
for him. He did not seem to have anything to do with me. I felt no
feeling of fatherhood."[21] And Catherine has a series of uncontrollable
hemorrhages that lead to her death. In *A Farewell to Arms,* as in "In

Another Country," the woman dies after the man escapes from the war. Though Catherine "leaves" Frederic, the punitive death of the mother and child suggest Hemingway's rejection of Hadley and desertion of Bumby. His heroines are modeled on the women in his life and bear the tragedy he felt was inherent in sexual love.

Hemingway told Sinclair Lewis that he could not write about anything until a long time after the event. During the decade between his war experience and the composition of the book, he moved from the youthful idealism expressed in the letters sent from the Milan hospital to the bitter disillusionment portrayed in the great scenes of the novel: the wounding of Frederic, the retreat from Caporetto, the escape into the river, the rowing up Lake Maggiore into Switzerland,[22] the account of ants swarming toward destruction on a burning log and the death of Catherine in childbirth.

Harold Loeb's observation that Hemingway "distrusted abstractions and intangibles" and put his faith in concrete reality is confirmed in *A Farewell to Arms* when Frederic states: "I was always embarrassed by the words sacred, glorious, and sacrifice and the expression in vain. . . . Abstract words such as glory, honor, courage, or hallow were obscene beside the concrete names of villages, the numbers of roads, the names of rivers, the numbers of regiments and the dates." The abstractions were lies; only the actual places where men had fought and died had any dignity and meaning. Another thematic passage—which foreshadows Catherine's fate—expresses Hemingway's pessimistic but stoic response to a malign universe: "If people bring so much courage to this world the world has to kill them to break them, so of course it kills them. The world breaks every one and afterward many are strong at the broken places. But those that will not break it kills. It kills the very good and the very gentle and the very brave impartially. If you are none of these you can be sure it will kill you too but there will be no special hurry."[23]

Frederic Henry participates in the retreat from Caporetto rather than in the redemptive battle of Vittorio Veneto, which occurred exactly one year later and led to the surrender of Austria, in order to represent—like the autobiographical heroes of Robert Graves' *Goodbye to All That,* Richard Aldington's *Death of a Hero* and Erich Remarque's *All Quiet on the Western Front* (all published in 1929)—the destruction of idealism in the war.[24]

The manuscript revisions of *A Farewell to Arms* show that Hemingway was a good self-critic and nearly always improved his early drafts. He drew up a list of thirty-four possible titles, mainly from the Bible and the *Oxford Book of English Verse*, and finally chose one from the Renaissance poet George Peele. He wrote thirty-two versions of the end of the novel, which clearly gave him the most trouble, and wisely omitted a conclusion that sourly and ponderously surveyed the fate of the surviving characters:

> It seems she had one hemorrhage after another. They couldn't stop it.
>
> I went into the room and stayed with Catherine until she died. She was unconscious all the time, and it did not take her very long to die.
>
> There are a great many more details, starting with my first meeting with an undertaker, and all the business of burial in a foreign country and going on with the rest of my life—which has gone on and seems likely to go on for a long time.
>
> I could tell you how Rinaldi was cured of the syphilis and lived to find that the technic learned in wartime surgery is not of much practical use in peace. I could tell how the priest in our mess lived to be a priest in Italy under Fascism. I could tell how Ettore became a Fascist and the part he took in that organization. I could tell how Piani got to be a taxi-driver in New York and what sort of singer Simmons became. Many things have happened. Everything blunts and the world keeps on. It never stops. It only stops for you. Some of it stops while you are still alive. The rest goes on and you go on with it.
>
> I can tell you what I have done since March, nineteen hundred and eighteen, when I walked that night in the rain back to the hotel where Catherine and I had lived and went upstairs to our room and undressed and slept finally, because I was so tired—to wake in the morning with the sun shining in the window; then suddenly to realize what had happened. I could tell what has happened since then, but that is the end of the story.[25]

Scribner's Magazine paid Hemingway an unprecedented $16,000 for the serial rights of *A Farewell to Arms*, which he dedicated to Gus Pfeiffer. The June issue was banned in Boston because of immoral episodes and objectionable language, but the unsavory publicity merely intensified the public's interest in the book and increased the substantial sales. Critics felt that Hemingway had achieved a new maturity and depth. The novel received even more praise than his earlier works and in 1929 brought him to the pinnacle of his reputation.

Malcolm Cowley, one of Hemingway's greatest admirers, discussed the extra-literary reasons for his sudden fame: his distance from the jealousies of the New York literary world, his personal legend, his artistic pride, his use of sensational material, his ability to express the viewpoint of his postwar contemporaries. And he saw a new tenderness and seriousness in Hemingway's second novel: "The emotions as a whole are more colored by thought; perhaps they are weaker and certainly they are becoming more complicated. They seem to demand expression in a subtler and richer prose." In *The Criterion* of April 1933 T. S. Eliot refuted the criticism that Hemingway was both hard-boiled and sentimental, and defended him as a writer who expressed his truest feelings: "The illusion which pervades the whole various-climated American continent is the illusion of the hard-boiled. Even Mr. Ernest Hemingway—the writer of tender sentiment, and true sentiment, as in 'The Killers' and *A Farewell to Arms* . . . has been taken as the representative of the hard-boiled. . . . Mr. Hemingway is a writer for whom I have considerable respect; he seems to me to tell the truth about his own feelings at the moment when they exist." J. B. Priestley, in his literary puff for Jonathan Cape's house magazine, noticed that the characteristically modern lovers "seem to be curiously lonely, without backgrounds, unsustained by any beliefs," and that this somehow adds to the "terrible poignancy and force" of the concluding scene.[26]

One dissenting opinion was expressed by Aldous Huxley, the supreme example of a detached, intellectual writer, who in "Foreheads Villainous Low" sharply observed: "In *A Farewell to Arms,* Mr. Ernest Hemingway ventures, once, to name an Old Master. There is a phrase, quite admirably expressive (for Mr. Ernest Hemingway is a most subtle and sensitive writer), a single phrase, no more, about 'the bitter nail-holes' of Mantegna's Christs; then quickly, quickly, appalled by his own temerity, the author passes on . . . passes on, shamefacedly, to speak once more of lower things. . . . It is not at all uncommon now to find intelligent and cultured people doing their best to feign stupidity and to conceal the fact that they have received an education." Hemingway (who did not attend a university) was clearly disturbed by this comment, for he took the trouble to answer Huxley's attack. In his next book, *Death in the Afternoon,* he avoided the essence of the criticism —that he posed as a lowbrow writer—and stated that the allusion to Mantegna was a consistent and effective way to reveal an aspect of the character: "If the people the writer is making talk of old masters; of

music; of modern painting; of letters; or of science, then they should talk
of those subjects in the novel. If they do not talk of those subjects and
the writer makes them talk of them he is a faker."[27]

Hemingway had less success with the stage and film versions of the
novel. It was adapted by Laurence Stallings, opened at the National
Theater in New York on September 22, 1930, and ran for only twenty-
four performances. In December 1931 the play was produced at the
Deutsches Theater in Berlin. Hemingway received $24,000 for the film
rights, but thought "The movies ruined everything. Like talking about
something good." He hated the screen version of *A Farewell to Arms*,
made in 1932 with Gary Cooper and Helen Hayes, and condemned the
fake morality, lack of plausibility and the happy ending as well as the
absurdity of the phony marriage ceremony, Rinaldi's incredible with-
holding of letters and Frederic Henry's inexplicable desertion from the
army.[28] He sent a violent but futile protest in a cablegram to Hollywood
and wondered if anyone, after seeing such a terrible film, would ever
want to read his book. But the first printing of 31,000 copies had doubled by January 1929, and the novel had sold 1,400,000 copies by 1961.

11

The Public Image
1930–1932

> I want them to teach me a lament like a river
> that has gentle mists, and deep, deep banks,
> to bear the body of Ignacio, that it may be lost
> without hearing the double panting of the bulls.
>
> LORCA, "Lament for Sánchez Mejías"

I

Hemingway's literary achievement is all the more remarkable in view of the numerous illnesses and accidents—as well as the heavy drinking—that sapped his vitality, forced him to spend so much time in bed and interrupted his work. He suffered kidney pain from fishing in a cold Spanish stream in October 1929; was troubled by eye problems and began to wear glasses in the summer of 1931; caught bronchial pneumonia in April 1932; and had a throat operation in October 1933.

The annual moves from Key West to Wyoming, when the humidity and hurricanes coincided with the hunting and fishing season, repeated the childhood pattern of trips from Oak Park to the wilderness around Walloon Lake. At Lawrence Nordquist's ranch, twelve miles south of Cooke City, Montana, at the northeast corner of Yellowstone Park, Hemingway found the most beautiful country he had seen in the American West. He hunted deer, elk, bighorn sheep and grizzly bear—the only dangerous animal in North America—and had two serious accidents in 1930. (He had torn a muscle in his groin in October 1929 and slashed his right index finger on a punching bag in May 1930.) At the Nordquist ranch on August 22, his horse bolted while he was riding through thick woods and his arms, legs and face were lacerated by the branches. Two months later, on November 1, while driving to Billings,

Montana, with Dos Passos in the Ford roadster he had used in Spain, he badly fractured his right arm. Hemingway's weak eyes were blinded by the headlights of an oncoming car and the Ford swerved, lurched off the road and flipped over. Dos Passos climbed out and extracted Hemingway, who was pinned behind the wheel; he stopped a passing car and took Hemingway the twenty-two miles to Billings. Hemingway remained in St. Vincent's Hospital for seven weeks. In a letter to the sympathetic Perkins, he enumerated the recent disasters that had interfered with the composition of *Death in the Afternoon:* "Since I started this book have had compound fracture of index finger—bad general smash up in that bear hunt—14 stitches in face inside and out—hole in leg—then that right arm—muscular spiral paralysis—3 fingers in right hand broken—16 stitches in left wrist and hand. Eyes went haywire in Spain—with glasses now. Can't do more than about 4 hours before they go bad."

During a two-hour operation on his right arm, the surgeon bored holes through the bone and tied it together with kangaroo tendons. In *Green Hills of Africa* Hemingway emphasized the grisly details of his convalescence and remembered "one time in a hospital with my right arm broken off short between the elbow and the shoulder, the back of the hand having hung down against my back, the points of the bone having cut up the flesh of the biceps until it finally rotted, swelled, burst, and sloughed off in pus. Alone with the pain in the night of the fifth week of not sleeping."[1] MacLeish, worried about his ailing friend, took considerable trouble to visit him in Billings. But Hemingway, whose nerves were exacerbated by pain and insomnia, responded irrationally to the visit and accused MacLeish of coming west to see him die.

Hemingway grew a full beard, wore a smock and looked like a Russian peasant. Some shady fellow patients provided the direct inspiration for his story "The Gambler, the Nun, and the Radio," in which a Mexican crook, like Ole Andreson in "The Killers," follows his own stoical code and refuses to denounce his assailants: "There is a Russian across the hall who was shot through the thigh at the same time that a Mexican across the hall was shot through the stomach. The Russian groaned a good deal at first but is now very quiet. The Mexican, on the other hand, has three tubes in him, and drains a good quality of high-grade pus. Two Mexicans came to visit him today—one of whom was a lousy crook if I ever saw one, and they also visited me" and drank his bootleg whiskey.[2]

II

The Hemingways spent Christmas in Piggott and in January 1931 returned for their fourth winter in Key West. Pauline became pregnant again in February (three years having passed since the birth of Patrick). In February, Hemingway—with Perkins, Strater and another friend, John Hermann—was pleasantly marooned on the Dry Tortugas (seventy miles from Key West) for seventeen days. In April, Uncle Gus bought Pauline a rather grand but run-down house and they began extensive repairs of the leaking roof, broken windows, rotting sills and flaking plaster. The Hemingways sailed from Havana to Vigo on May 4, met the painter Luis Quintanilla in Madrid, traveled through Spain in the summer, spent September in Paris and returned to America at the end of the month. On November 12, 1931, Pauline, using the same doctor who had delivered Patrick, had her second, even more difficult Caesarean birth. Dr. Guffey told her the operation had endangered her life and that she should not have any more children. Since she still refused to practice birth control, the Hemingways began to have serious sexual and marital problems.

Pauline had hoped to give birth to a daughter to please Hemingway. But she had a son whom they named Gregory Hancock, after Gregory Clark of the *Toronto Star* and Hemingway's maternal grandmother, Caroline Hancock. Both parents may have felt some unconscious resentment against the infant whose birth had threatened Pauline's life and who turned out to be the wrong sex. Pauline did not breast-feed the baby; despite his screams, he was given the bottle on a rigid schedule. Gregory was cared for by a nurse from the time he was two weeks old and rarely saw his mother. Indeed, Pauline did not have much to do with her sons until they started school. She sacrificed her children to care for her husband and devoted herself to renovating the house, creating the perfect environment for Hemingway's work, and accompanying him on trips to Europe and the West. Gregory later remembered that Pauline shared Hemingway's hostility to infants and admitted: "Gig, I just don't have much of what's called a maternal instinct, I guess. I can't *stand* horrid little children until they are five or six." Gregory felt Pauline had not given him the care he needed as a small child and had made it clear that she loved Patrick (who looked like her) much more than she loved him.[3]

Gregory was brought up by Ada Stern, a silent, blue-eyed, Germanic spinster from Syracuse. He took baths and slept with his nurse rather than his mother, and became unnaturally dependent upon her. Jack and Patrick hated Ada and were allied against Gregory. When they went with their father on hunting trips to Wyoming or voyages to Europe, Gregory always accompanied Ada to Syracuse. In *Islands in the Stream* Hemingway wrote of Andy (Gregory): "Rochester . . . was where he used to be left with his nurse when she stayed with her family in the summer months when the other boys went west." Gregory has described the severity, rage and emotional blackmail that inspired the love-hate relation with his nurse:

> Mother left my rearing entirely to Ada, an odd sort of Prussian gover-
> ness, who had never married in her youth, which by the time we met
> was far behind her. . . . My parents would often go off on long jaunts
> somewhere, leaving me with Ada. I was about three and a half when
> they took the nine-month safari that produced *Green Hills of Africa*.
> . . . Any infraction of her innumerable rules would cause her to fly into
> a screaming fit. . . . She would pack her bags and go hobbling down the
> stairs with me clinging to her skirts, screaming, "Ada, don't leave me,
> please don't leave me!"

Neither Patrick nor Gregory seemed to mind their parents' trip to Africa during 1933–34, but both were clearly aware of their father's absence during the Spanish Civil War. Patrick later realized what his parents failed to notice at the time: that Ada had serious emotional problems and was a secret drinker, a lesbian and a "pretty monstrous woman."[4]

The three-year-old Patrick, who was also hostile to the new baby, had not entirely renounced the devil and his works. When Gregory was six weeks old, Hemingway told Perkins, Patrick filled a jar with mosquito, tooth and talcum powder "and sprayed his little brother thoroughly—he woke up and cried loud enough to attract attention before it killed him—Patrick spraying manfully, the harder he cried the more spray he received. 'Did you want to hurt your little brother?' 'Y e s,' said Patrick, very scared." Ten days later, during another family crisis, Hemingway stayed up all night with Patrick, who had eaten some arsenic ant poison and vomited for hours.

Despite disclaimers, Hemingway was a devoted and often tender father. When Louis Cohn (who published the first bibliography of Hemingway in 1931) and his wife visited the Hemingways at the Hotel Brevoort in New York in September 1931, they watched Hemingway put Patrick on the toilet and sing him a French lullaby. He was a lenient parent who never spanked his sons and often spoiled them. They once had a black maid in Key West who carried a land crab in the fold of her hat to threaten the children and make them obey. When Jack spat at her for frightening his brothers, she was furious and insisted that Hemingway punish the boy. He took Jack into the next room, slapped his own leg and pretended to beat his son.[5] Like all fathers, Hemingway also fought with and punished his children, especially when Gregory squirted glue during the house repairs or painted a pair of cats green or stabbed one of the pets with a dagger.

Hemingway wrote of David (Patrick) in *Islands in the Stream:* "He was affectionate and he had a sense of justice and was good company"; and in the novel Tom (Jack) generously admits: "I know you love [David] the most and that's right because he's the best of us." Patrick later recalled his father's judicious response to his behavior: "Our relationship was reasonably good. Not perfect, mind you. In adolescence I was hot under the collar. We quarreled, but my father was tolerant. He didn't lose his temper. He never allowed himself to be pushed over the edge by me."[6]

III

The house at 907 Whitehead Street, one of the few substantial mansions in Key West, cost Uncle Gus $12,500. The two-story Spanish colonial house had been built in 1851 by Asa Tift, a wealthy architect and shipping magnate. It had high ceilings and arched French windows that opened onto the wide, shaded, ironwork balconies around the first and second floors. The house was decorated with Venetian chandeliers and Spanish antiques (sent home from the Paris flat); and the twin beds in the master bedroom were joined by a headboard made from an old wooden gate. There were two fireplaces in the house; the outdoor kitchen was moved inside; and the indoor toilets, a rarity on the island, were serviced by septic tanks. The mansion was situated across the street from the lighthouse, which could be seen from the front porch, and had banyan, fig and lime trees growing in the lush tropical garden.

Hemingway was fully occupied with the roofer, carpenter, electrician and plumber who were restoring the house when they moved in on December 19, 1931, five weeks after the birth of Gregory. They converted the second floor of the carriage house and servants' quarters into a study that was connected to the main house by a narrow iron catwalk. The cool and quiet study was a wonderful place to work. It had a bathroom, and was furnished simply, with shuttered windows, red-tiled floor, bookcases, rattan chairs and a round Spanish writing table. In November 1932 Hemingway wrote: "Have been working until my eyes haywire every day. Gone back to the old system of starting in bed when I wake and working through until toward noon. That way they can't bring things to your attention the way they do if you are up."[7] Just as Ed Hemingway's collection of stuffed owls, raccoons, squirrels and chipmunks were arranged on top of the bookcases that lined his medical library, so Ernest decorated his study in Key West and in Cuba with animal trophies from hunting trips in Wyoming and Africa. The final, extremely expensive addition to the house was made in 1938, when their marriage was deteriorating. Pauline built a 65 × 20-foot salt-water swimming pool, surrounded by swaying date palms, which was the first in the Keys and the only one (she boasted) between Miami and Panama. A large pet turtle had the run of the pool.

IV

The first book finished on Whitehead Street was *Death in the Afternoon*. Hemingway wanted to interpret Spanish culture for American readers, to reflect on his personal experience and to fulfill a long-standing ambition. As early as April 1925 he had told Perkins: "I hope some day to have a sort of Doughty's Arabia Deserta of the Bull Ring, a very big book with some wonderful pictures"—which is precisely what he produced in the well-named *Death in the Afternoon*. Following Doughty's encyclopedic use of ethnology and Melville's of cetology in factually based works of literature, Hemingway did first what no one else has ever done better. "It is intended as an introduction to the modern Spanish bullfight," he wrote at the very end of the book, "and attempts to explain that spectacle both emotionally and practically. It was written because there was no book which did this in Spanish or in English."[8] The heroes of this technical tract, which covers every aspect of the corrida from the breeding of the bull to the moment of truth, are Juan Belmonte, Nicanor Villalta and Manuel Maera.

Attitudes toward the bullfight—the last pagan spectacle of the modern world—have been sharply divided along racial lines. The Mithraic combat, based on a ritual that is as formal as the Mass, has been celebrated by Latin writers: García Lorca, Rafael Alberti, Henri de Montherlant; and condemned by Anglo-Saxons: D. H. Lawrence in *The Plumed Serpent* and Wyndham Lewis in *Snooty Baronet*. Lewis, who had fought at Passchendaele, found the corrida tedious (as Hemingway found it exciting) because it provided vicarious participation in violence and death. In Lewis' novel, when Rob MacPhail (based on the bullfight enthusiast Roy Campbell) jumps into the bullring in the south of France and is badly gored, Snooty remarks: "I am simply bored at bull-fighting —at street accidents and trench warfare. . . . The War accustomed me to death too much. . . . I had seen too many bodies lying in that strange and rather irritating repose—mutilated but peaceful—the debris of attacks."

Hemingway rejected the humane Anglo-Saxon attitude and found the corrida a source of inspiration for his fiction. It aroused the intense emotion that he channeled into interchapters IX–XIV of *In Our Time*, "The Undefeated," "Banal Story," "The Mother of a Queen," "The Capital of the World," *The Sun Also Rises* and parts of *For Whom the Bell Tolls*. *Death in the Afternoon* provides the technical background that is needed to understand these works.[9]

Hemingway adopted a defensive tone to counter the cultural hostility of his audience. His difficult task was to arouse interest and convey information about a subject that was both unfamiliar and repulsive. To achieve this end he was at once propagandistic and pedagogic, digressive and discursive. He gave an insider's view based on extensive experience, mingled memory and desire, and provided essential reading for anyone interested in the subject or the author.

Death in the Afternoon—a loose, baggy monster—contains a color frontispiece of *The Torero* by Juan Gris; 278 pages of text; 64 pages of black-and-white photographs, some with long, illuminating captions; an elaborate and amusing glossary of bullfighting terms, including entries on heel vendors, pickpockets, homosexuals, whores, beer, sherry, wine, appetizers and shellfish. It also includes a compilation of his friends' first reactions to the bullfight;[10] an inflated estimate of Sidney Franklin as bullfighter; a calendar of corridas in Spain and South America; and an inadequate bibliographical note which obscures rather than reveals his sources. There is, unfortunately, no index.

Hemingway varied the factual account with intermittent dialogue. His innocent interlocutor, the Old Lady, is an unfortunately arch invention: "Madame, does all this writing of the bullfights bore you?" . . . "It does not flag. It is only that I get tired sometimes." Flat rather than funny, she is introduced on page 64 and quietly dropped on page 190. Hemingway followed Dos Passos' sound criticism (as he had followed Fitzgerald's about *The Sun Also Rises*), and deleted some long-winded philosophizing. Perkins may also have had some reservations about the book, but did not suggest deletions. He confined himself, as always, to praise and encouragement.

The last half of Chapter 12, subtitled "A Natural History of the Dead," appeared separately in *Winner Take Nothing* (1933), without the gratuitous interruptions of the Old Lady. The horrible and shocking description of the *un*naturally dead and wounded in battle illustrates Hemingway's analogy between bullfighting and war. The ironic tone parodies the close observation and dogmatic optimism of Gilbert White and more far-flung natural historians of Patagonia and Africa, and describes a brutal world without God. Hemingway draws on his experience in Italy and Turkey, and provides the verbal equivalent of Goya's etchings *Disasters of War*. He reports a corpse-filled landscape similar to the one described in the opening pages of "A Way You'll Never Be" —"The color change in Caucasian races is from white to yellow, to yellow-green, to black"—in which men have died like animals from bullets, shells, gas and disease. Hemingway compares, through allusive paraphrase, the worms in Marvell's "To His Coy Mistress" to "a half-pint of maggots working where [men's] mouths have been."[11] The powerful story ends with the confrontation between a humanistic artillery officer who wants to shoot a hopelessly wounded soldier and a realistic military doctor who must try to save his life. The doctor, cursed by the officer, becomes enraged and throws iodine in his eyes. The dead have thus brutalized the living.

Death in the Afternoon is about bullfighting, but it is also about much more than bullfighting. The most interesting aspect of the book is the subtle infiltration of the ostensible subject matter with a wide range of tangential yet fascinating observations. Hemingway arrived in Spain, on his seventh and last trip before writing the book, in May 1931, just after King Alfonso had been deposed and the Republic declared under Alcalá Zamora. This was the beginning of the chaotic and critical five-year period of transition from monarchy to Civil War. Hemingway, who had been carefully studying the country since 1923, was well qualified to discuss Spanish character, culture, customs, history, politics, literature, art, climate, landscape, cities, gypsies, beggars, wine, food and fishing. He is able to distill the essence of a northern province into one vivid passage: if you could "make clouds come fast in shadows moving over wheat and the small, careful stepping horses; the smell of olive oil; the feel of leather; rope soled shoes; the loops of twisted garlics; earthen pots; saddle bags carried across the shoulder; wine skins; the pitchforks made of natural wood (the tines were branches); the early morning smells; the cold mountain heights and long hot days of summer, with always trees and shade under the trees, then you would have a little of Navarra."[12] Anyone who knows Spain well will immediately see how these intensely visual images capture the contours of the country.

Death in the Afternoon is at once a personal memoir, a history of culture and a dissertation on tauromachy. Hemingway discusses his family and friends (Hadley, Bumby, Stein, Shipman, Juanito Quintana and Luis Quintanilla); his life in Michigan, Italy and Constantinople; *The Sun Also Rises* and his long, unfinished bullfight story, "A Lack of Passion"; his ideas on psychoanalysis, homosexuality, syphilis, work, sport, courage, war, suicide and death. He is perceptive about Velázquez, El Greco, Goya and about literary characterization, style and technique. The most unattractive aspect of the book, he admits, is the mean criticism of fighters and writers. He condemns potential rivals: Waldo Frank and William Faulkner; recent critics of his work: Virginia Woolf and Aldous Huxley; and inverts, who are contrasted to the virile matadors: Whitman, Wilde, Gide, Cocteau and Radiguet.

A minor hero of the book is Sidney Franklin (né Frumpkin), the son of a Jewish policeman and a cousin of the critic Clifton Fadiman. Franklin, who had never heard of Hemingway when they first met in 1929, had given him a great deal of help with *Death in the Afternoon* and had been badly gored in March 1930. Hemingway loyally overrated Franklin's talent, just as he faithfully puffed the stillborn daubs of Waldo Peirce and Henry Strater, the turf tales of Evan Shipman, and the leaden verse of Archie MacLeish: "[Franklin] has the ability in languages, the cold courage and the ability to command of the typical soldier of fortune, he is a charming companion, one of the best story tellers I have ever heard. . . . Franklin is brave with a cold, serene, and intelligent valor but instead of being awkward and ignorant he is one of the most skillful, graceful, and slow manipulators of a cape fighting to-day."[13]

It is ironic that Hemingway chose to glorify Franklin, for the American phenomenon "had absolutely no standing as a matador in Spain" and (though Hemingway did not know it at the time) was a secret "homosexual, despite his rugged appearance and bravura, and a child molester."[14] Franklin was so politically naive that when the Civil War broke out he asked Hemingway: "which side are we on, Papa?" Yet his knowledge of the language and country was invaluable during the war. "[He] bought us all our food," Hemingway wrote, "cooked breakfasts, typed articles, wangled petrol, wangled cars, wangled chauffeurs, and covered Madrid and all its gossip like a human dictaphone."[15] Franklin became jealous of Hemingway's attachment to Martha Gellhorn, and spent less time with him as the war progressed.

Hemingway became more superstitious as he grew older. Alarmed by the abbreviated title on the proofs of his book, he expressed his rage to Perkins: "raise hell with the son of a bitch who slugged all these galleys Hemingway's Death. You know I am superstitious and it is a hell of a damn dirty business to stare at that a thousand times." He dedicated the book to Pauline and later inscribed a copy for his Ketchum friend Tillie Arnold: "Such a Big Book for Hemingstein to have written day and night for such a long, long time."[16] A surprisingly large first printing of 10,300 copies, published on September 23, 1932, reflected Hemingway's current stature. The book did well at first, but sales soon declined because of the Depression and the morbid subject matter. He complained to Gregory that *Ferdinand the Bull* made ten times more money than *Death in the Afternoon.*

Hemingway's work is the classic study of bullfighting in English and has influenced everything written on the subject since it first appeared. But his first work of nonfiction was also the first of his books to be badly received by the critics. They attacked his swaggering public persona, which measured men by their machismo and *cojones,* gibed at his fellow writers and arrogantly pontificated to the Old Lady. As H. L. Mencken wrote in a review called "The Spanish Idea of a Good Time," the book is "an extraordinarily fine piece of expository writing, but . . . often descends to a gross and irritating cheapness."

Robert Coates admitted that like most American readers he knew nothing and cared less about bullfighting, and was bored by the exhaustive treatise. He called Hemingway a romanticist "in his inability to accept the idea of death as the end and complement of life." Hemingway, increasingly aggressive about his critics, called this review "a condescendentious piece of phony intellectuality . . . in the New Yorker."[17]

In a more balanced review, Malcolm Cowley saw the wider ramifications of the book and described it as "a Baedeker of bulls." It concerns "the art of living, of drinking, of dying, of loving the Spanish land," for bullfighting symbolizes "a whole nation and a culture extending for centuries into the past." He stated that for Hemingway bullfighting is "an emotional substitute for war" and called his work an "elegy to Spain and vanished youth."[18]

The first truly damaging critique was Max Eastman's "Bull in the Afternoon," published in the *New Republic* seven months after Cowley's review. Eastman, who had known Hemingway in Genoa in 1922, disliked his ecstatic adulation of the corrida and attempted some literary psychoanalysis. Eastman argued that Hemingway's "bull" is "juvenile romantic gushing and sentimentalizing of simple facts" about the brutal, shocking and ignoble aspects of a bullfight. He defined this, in opposition to Hemingway, as "men tormenting and killing a bull." After exposing Hemingway's posturings, Eastman moved—more menacingly —from his literary to his personal faults and seemed to question his sexual capacity: "It is of course a commonplace that Hemingway lacks the serene confidence that he *is* a full-sized man. . . . [he has] a continual sense of the obligation to put forth evidences of red-blooded masculinity." Eastman lifted Hemingway's satiric phrase about Sánchez Mejías ("It was as though he were constantly showing you the quantity of hair on his chest or the way in which he was built in his more private parts"), bitingly turned it against him and said he had developed "a literary style, you might say, of wearing false hair on the chest."[19]

This review provoked Hemingway's rage. He told Perkins that he was tempted to stop publishing because swine like Eastman were not worth writing for, that he found the whole reviewing racket as disgusting as vomit. MacLeish stoked the fires by telling Hemingway that Eastman had attacked his sexual capacity. Hemingway told MacLeish, just after the review appeared, that he was discouraged by Eastman's notice. It was not a criticism of the book but an assertion (false hair on the chest) that meant Hemingway was either impotent or queer. He also drew a telling analogy between Eastman and the treacherous Middleton Murry, who had envied his friend D. H. Lawrence and tried to destroy him in the name of holiness.[20]

Four years later, in August 1937, Hemingway accidentally discovered Max Eastman in his editor's office, and had one of the best-documented and most-publicized fights since the championship bouts of Jack Sharkey and Primo Carnera. Max Perkins described the comic dénouement in a letter to Fitzgerald:

> Ernest ripped open his shirt and exposed a chest which was certainly hairy enough for anybody. Max laughed, and then Ernest, quite good-naturedly, reached over and opened Max's shirt, revealing a chest which was as bare as a bald man's head. . . . Then suddenly Ernest became truculent and said, "What do you mean accusing me of impotence?" Eastman denied that he had. . . . [Then Ernest] hit Eastman with an open book. Instantly, of course, Eastman rushed at him. I thought Ernest would begin fighting and would kill him, and ran round my desk to try to catch him from behind, with never any fear for anything that might happen to Ernest. At the same time, as they grappled, all the books and everything went off my desk to the floor, and by the time I got around, both men were on the ground. . . . I looked down and there Ernest was on his back, with a broad smile on his face.— Apparently he regained his temper instantly after striking Eastman, and offered no resistance whatever.[21]

Hemingway changed from anger to amiability with Eastman just as he did in the fight with Harold Loeb.

Eastman gave himself the heroic role in his version of the fight. According to Eastman, Hemingway opened his shirt, bared his thick chest hair and asked: "what did you say I was sexually impotent for?" He accused Eastman of trying to kiss Hadley in a Paris taxi, read the offensive passage from a book on Perkins' desk and "pushed the open book into my face—insultingly, though not hard enough to hurt." Eastman then grappled with Hemingway, "threw him on his back across Perkins' desk" and grabbed his throat. Hemingway smiled up at him and said: "You're not as soft as I thought you were." As Perkins pleaded: "Max, please! Please don't do this," they disengaged.[22] Hemingway seemed more interested in testing his opponent than in fighting him.

Like the Hemingway-Callaghan bout in 1929, this literary combat was reported in the newspapers. Eastman told a friend about the wrestling match and the friend told the *Post* and the *World-Telegram*, which printed Eastman's account of the fracas. Hemingway countered with his own version in the *Times* and the *Herald Tribune* and stated that he had slapped Eastman in the face with such force that he "tottered backwards and collapsed on the window seat."[23] After *Death in the Afternoon* he became as sensitive as Virginia Woolf to all personal and literary criticism. The dust jacket of *For Whom the Bell Tolls* (1940) carried a photograph of Hemingway, unshaven at the typewriter, with his sleeves rolled up to expose an unusually hairy forearm.

V

Hemingway continued his habitual round of work, sport and travel in 1932. He discovered Cuban marlin fishing in April, stopped in Piggott en route to Wyoming in July, spent the late summer and early fall hunting in the West, returned to Florida in October, and drove with Jack from Key West to Piggott for Thanksgiving (a journey that inspired "Fathers and Sons"). Perkins was lured down to Arkansas for duck shooting in December. A fire broke out that month in the studio Toby Bruce had built for Jinny in the upper part of the Pfeiffers' barn. The studio, where Hemingway worked and slept, had a pot-bellied stove that was insulated with inflammable Cellotex. The Hemingways went to breakfast at the main house on a cold morning while a hired boy overloaded the stove with kindling and caused it to flame up. Hemingway's traveling and shooting clothes, guns, typewriter, first editions, manuscripts and unanswered letters were burned, though some papers were later salvaged and dried out. Hemingway was upset, but took it well and never blamed anyone for the accident.

Toby Bruce, born in Piggott in 1910, became Hemingway's valet, chauffeur, handyman, traveling companion and friend. Bruce was a small, thin, shrewd and precise young man who used colorful back-country expressions and had many useful skills. He was a carpenter, knew about fishing and shooting, could fix guns and cars, built the garden wall and did many of the renovations on the Key West house, and later helped repair the Finca Vigía near Havana. Unlike the reckless Hemingway, Bruce was a careful and defensive driver and went on many of the cross-country trips in the 1930s. They usually shared a room when they traveled together, and ate country ham and egg sandwiches with raw onion for breakfast. Hemingway, worried about keeping his weight down, did exercises on the bed in the morning and ran along the road for about three miles. Bruce would give him a head start and then pick him up on the way out of town. They had no car radio and did not talk much on the long trips, remaining silent for three or four hours at a time. Hemingway carefully observed the landscape, watched the weather and the wildlife, and sometimes noted down his thoughts. He enjoyed the respite from writing and felt comfortable with Bruce, who followed orders and made no demands. Hemingway gave Bruce many inscribed copies of his books, including a bound set of corrected galley proofs of *For Whom the Bell Tolls.* [24]

VI

Hemingway's youngest sister, Carol, had scarcely known him when she was a child. But during 1930–32 she spent several Christmas and spring vacations in Key West. She had disliked following her sisters in school, had broken with the family tradition of going to Oberlin and attended Rollins College in Winter Park, Florida. Hemingway encouraged Carol's writing and sent her reading lists of French and Russian authors. During her visits Hemingway and Pauline got on very well, for his wife always submitted to his wishes and tried to please him. She welcomed Carol, who never felt (as Sunny did) that she was being treated as a servant.

Carol deepened her understanding of Hemingway when in July 1932 they drove alone from Key West to Piggott, an uncomfortable journey that may have made her more critical of and less willing to obey him. He did most of the driving, went for very long periods without rest and insisted that she run into cheap restaurants to buy them fried egg sandwiches because "he didn't want to be recognized." She took this to be egoistic posturing since no one in the small southern towns would have known who he was. She pleaded with Hemingway to stop for a decent interval at a good restaurant with a clean bathroom, but he pushed on relentlessly—testing his endurance and driving up to 650 miles a day. Carol thought his driving accidents usually occurred when he was drunk.

After his father's suicide Hemingway supported the family and considered himself the head of the household. He liked to play the Papa figure and expected everyone to obey him. In 1932 Carol told Hemingway she had met a young man at Rollins, John Gardner, and was very fond of him. Hemingway took an instant dislike to Gardner, considered him priggish and domineering, and told Carol: "That sounds like the name in a musical comedy. I don't want to hear about it again."[25] In March 1933 Carol announced that she was going to marry Gardner, who had been seeing her during her junior year abroad in Vienna. Hemingway called Carol a damned fool, forbade her to marry and threatened to beat the hell out of Gardner. Angered by the threat, Gardner called him "an inverted boy scout." Hemingway swore he would never see Carol again if she married Gardner and, when she disobeyed, cut her completely out of his life. She later made many overtures to him—sent him Christmas cards and photographs of her children—but he kept his oath and never saw her again. He was bored with his family and eager for an excuse to sever relations. He needed adulation and was annoyed when the Gardners refused to be impressed by his literary reputation. And he was outraged at being criticized and contradicted.

Hemingway never explained the reason for his irrational opposition to Carol's marriage, but he expected his friends to endorse his decision. He thought Jinny had helped to bring Carol and Gardner together, and complained to his mother-in-law that Jinny supported Gardner partly because she liked him, partly to be difficult and irritate Hemingway. He felt Gardner was as bad as they come, though the inexperienced Carol thought he was wonderful. He disliked taking the ungrateful role of parent, which was thrust upon him after his father's death, and said he would never mention Carol or Gardner again. In a letter to MacLeish, Hemingway linked Gerald Murphy (who had supported Carol as he had supported Pauline) to Max Eastman, though the only thing they had in common was their criticism of Hemingway, and said that Gerald took pleasure in Gardner's opposition to him.[26]

If anyone ever asked Hemingway about Carol, he would say she was divorced or dead. Even more bizarre was his fantasy that Carol had been "assaulted, knocked out and raped when she was 12 by a sexual pervert." Carol's willful opposition continued to rankle, for in 1950 he savagely told a former instructor at Rollins (in a letter that may not have been sent) that the main cause of Carol's unhappiness, apart from being raped as a child, was attending a college where she was taught by incompetents and met awful people like John Gardner.[27] Hemingway's attitude toward Carol resembled that of the infatuated father in his favorite story by Thomas Mann, "Disorder and Early Sorrow," who is deeply wounded when his daughter first expresses interest in a young man. Hemingway behaved as if he had been rejected by his long-desired daughter rather than his younger sister, and transformed Carol's sexual life with her husband into rape by a sexual pervert.

By the mid-1930s Hemingway was on bad terms with most of his family. He had blamed his mother for his father's death, publicly called his father a coward, quarreled with Marcelline (a bitch "complete with handles") for criticizing his divorce, condemned Sunny's behavior in Key West and rejected Carol for marrying Gardner. Leicester tried desperately to imitate and to please Hemingway during the 1930s, but he was also repudiated during World War Two. Hemingway was critical of Jack after the war and quarreled bitterly with Gregory in 1952. Only the quiet Ursula, in far-off Hawaii, remained in favor till the end. He never saw any of his nieces and nephews, apart from one visit from Sunny's boy. When he heard that one of Marcelline's children had lost an eye in an accident while cutting metal straps around an orange crate, he deliberately gave it an evil twist (as he had done with Carol) and declared: "Marcelline has the kind of boys who put each other's eyes out."[28]

VII

The negative side of Hemingway's character became more prominent in the early 1930s after his break with Hadley, his marriage to Pauline, his conversion to Catholicism, his father's suicide, his move to the big house in Key West, the success of *A Farewell to Arms* and the publicity surrounding the film. Wealth and fame led to accidents, quarrels and the belligerent literary persona that first emerged in *Death in the Afternoon*. Leaving Paris and dividing his time between Key West and Wyoming cut Hemingway off from cosmopolitan culture and educated friends, and shifted his interest to marlin fishing and bear hunting. He had no intellectual equals in Florida and dominated friends who deferred to him as the local hero. He was a great listener before he moved to Key West and a great talker afterwards. The new atmosphere encouraged him to adopt coarse language, to indulge in heroics, to boast, to swagger, to suppress the sensitive side of his nature and to cultivate the public image. In Key West Hemingway was (and is) not only a living legend, but also the main tourist attraction.

Hemingway tried to merge art with action, the sensitivity and perception of a writer with physical courage and sporting skill, personal solitude with public fame. He did not subjugate his life to his work—like Henry James, Flaubert and Joyce, but enhanced his art with his life—like D'Annunzio, T. E. Lawrence and Malraux. Hemingway tried to balance the varied and often contradictory aspects of his life, and wrote of himself, with unusual optimism: "I am naturally a happy guy so I have a good time and I love my wife and the ocean and my kids and writing and reading and all good painting along with bar life and whores and responsibility and paying my bills and other mixed pleasures." He believed that he could—but feared that he could not—have money and remain pure, enjoy luxury and write well.

Like Mark Twain in the nineteenth century, Hemingway, the most famous example of the great writer and the commercial success, was the Hero as Man of Letters. The public image, which he helped to create, sold his books, attracted the interest of Hollywood and made his private life a subject for public consumption. But Dwight Macdonald, influenced by the publicity that surrounded Hemingway, was quite mistaken when he claimed that his "life, his writing, his public personality, and his private thoughts were all of a piece."[29] The public wanted to believe in the existence of a phenomenal human being who fought, hunted, loved and *wrote* so perfectly. The heroic image satisfied the needs of the public, but was irrelevant to the real Hemingway. It tempted, corrupted and finally helped to destroy him.

Hemingway always embroidered the events of his life. His exaggerations, lies and heroic image were related to the traditions and myths of frontier humor that had inspired his youthful works. But he not only helped to create myths about himself, he also seemed to believe them. He felt he could write only about what he had actually experienced and his literary credo was to tell it as it was. But he combined scrupulous honesty in his fiction with a tendency to distort and rewrite the story of his life. Given his predisposition to mythomania, his reluctance to disappoint either his own expectations or those of his audience, and the difficulty of refuting and verifying certain facts of his life, he felt virtually forced to invent an exciting and imaginative alternative to commonplace reality.

Hemingway turned his lies into legends and was able to live out his private fantasies. Like Vincent Berger, the hero of Malraux's *The Walnut Trees of Altenburg*, "he could perhaps have found some means of destroying the mythical person he was growing into, had he been compelled. But he had no wish to do so. His reputation was flattering. What was more important, he enjoyed it." As early as 1925 Ernest Walsh had celebrated Hemingway in verse as

> Papa soldier pugilist bullfighter
> Writer gourmet lionhead aesthete
> He's a big guy from near Chicago.[30]

In May 1926, *Town and Country* magazine said he was a matador in Spain. The tough image took hold in the 1930s—the decade of *Green Hills of Africa,* fishing articles for *Esquire* and the criminal adventures of *To Have and Have Not*—and was wittily portrayed in Raymond Chandler's *Farewell, My Lovely* (1940):

> He looked at the one with the moustache again. "This guy is very tough," he told him. "He wants to shoot an Indian."
> "Listen, Hemingway, don't repeat everything I say." . . .
> "I can't think of any reason why he should call me Hemingway," the big one said. "My name ain't Hemingway." . . .
> "Who is this Hemingway person at all?"
> "A guy that keeps saying the same thing over and over till you begin to believe it must be good."[31]

Mario Menocal, Jr., has written perceptively about the split between the inner man and the public hero: "Ernest engaged in creating and perpetuating the Hemingway *persona,* and engaged in promoting and selling his works, was a part of the first personality while Ernest engaged in the creation of his works belonged to the second. . . . No one was more conscious than Ernest of the figure and image he possessed in the minds of the American press and reading public. He felt (I am sure) that this was an important matter to him in terms of dollars and cents on book sales or fees for articles. He deliberately set out to keep the legend and image alive in the form he wanted it."[32]

Two of Hemingway's most successful public images were the soldier and the sage. He was a natural leader and claimed that he had "fought in all the wars," though he had actually fought in none of them. When the journalist Vincent Sheean denied that Hemingway was a combatant in Spain, Pauline insisted that he had merely pretended to be a newsman "while in fact holding a high combat command with the Loyalists. 'This legendary, mythogenic quality,' adds Sheean, 'was not Ernest's fault; it was intrinsic to his character; he created such stories as unthinkingly as others breathe.' "[33]

It was sometimes difficult for him to be a writer, lover, sportsman and warrior, to fulfill everyone's high expectations, to be Ernest Hemingway every day. He may have created the Papa persona because he felt more comfortable in a role than as himself. The name Papa kept people at a distance and was used by courtiers. Walsh called him Papa in the poem, but not in life. Sidney Franklin and Robert Capa started to call him Papa during the Spanish War; Winston Guest imitated Hemingway's sons and used it in the early 1940s. One of the earliest appearances of the name, invented of course by Hemingway, was in a letter to MacLeish of March 1931 when he apologetically wrote: "Papa bragging again."[34] He refers to himself as Papa in "Notes on Dangerous Game" (July 1934) and Pauline appears as (the variant) Poor Old Mama (P.O.M.) in *Green Hills of Africa* (1935).

Two obsessive habits began about the time Hemingway became Papa. The first was the compulsive counting of words written, birds shot, fish caught and animals killed. (Later on it would include the daily annotation of his blood pressure and weight.) The second was the frequent repetition of words and expressions that he considered witty, suggestive or direct. From Captain Bra Saunders he picked up: "men are dying this year who have never died before"; from a Restoration play (undoubtedly quoted in a modern book) he fixed on "How do you like it now, gentlemen?"; and after the war he was fond of two tedious epithets: "phony" and "chickenshit."

During his lifetime, the Hemingway legends took hold and replaced reality. Matthew Bruccoli has noted "how difficult it is to establish the truth about virtually everything involving Hemingway," how "difficult to differentiate the public Papa from the private writer." As Joyce observed: "the unfacts, did we possess them, are too imprecisely few to warrant our certitude."[35] Everyone believed that Hemingway had Indian blood, was kept out of school for a year to play the cello, ran away from home, injured his eye while boxing, associated with gangsters, had affairs with the actress Mae Marsh and the spy Mata Hari, fought with the Italian *Arditi,* was fitted with an aluminum kneecap, kept a mistress in Sicily, reported the battles of the Greco-Turkish War in the wilds of Anatolia. Yet virtually all the drinking, boxing, hunting, fishing and fornicating stories are exaggerations or fantasies. Edmund Wilson, who turned against Hemingway in *The Wound and the Bow,* observed that by 1939 he had already passed "into a phase where he is occupied with building up his public personality. . . . Hemingway has created a Hemingway who is not only incredible but obnoxious. He is certainly his own worst-invented character."[36]

As Hemingway began to experience the vulgarity and betrayal of publicity, he realized that success could be as humiliating as failure. He was well aware of the dangers of corruption, but could not always avoid them. He had already asked his French translator not to mention his war service. He had warned Scribner's to disclaim the publicity about his military career and personal life that was disseminated with the film of *A Farewell to Arms.* In a letter of June 1930 to his bibliographer Louis Cohn, Hemingway said he always tried to keep his life separate from his work, to avoid publicity and critics so that subjective feelings would not affect literary judgments. "I want to run as a writer," he told Robert Cantwell, listing his public personae, "not as a man who had been to the wars; nor a bar room fighter; nor a shooter; nor a horse-player; nor a drinker. I would like to be a straight writer and be judged as such."[37]

A man is essentially what he hides. The real and most important of the many Hemingways was the reflective man who wrote the books and concealed his innate sensitivity under the mask of a man of action. Though he liked to rage against aesthetic posturing—"Artist, art, artistic! Can't we ever hear the last of that stuff!"—he was, as James Thurber remarked, "gentle, understanding, sympathetic, compassionate."[38] Yet Hemingway rejected this side of his character. Max Eastman said that in *Death in the Afternoon* Hemingway deliberately turned "himself into a blustering roughneck crying for more killing and largely dedicated to demonstrating his ability to take any quantity of carnage in his powerful stride." Gertrude Stein, who knew his strengths and weaknesses, agreed that: "He had compensated for his incredibly acute shyness and sensitivity by adopting a shield of brutality. When this happened he lost touch with his true genius."[39] The transformation from private to public man, spurred by wealth and fame, began to take place in the early 1930s. It helped to explain the gradual decline of his work after *A Farewell to Arms* and the sharp descent after *For Whom the Bell Tolls.* Unlike George Orwell, whose persona strengthened and confirmed his image of the upright man, Hemingway's legend swamped and destroyed the real artist. Unlike Robert Lowell, who could skillfully manipulate his public image, Hemingway could not attract publicity without damaging his integrity.

12

Jane Mason

1932–1936

> What could have made her peaceful with a mind
> That nobleness made simple as a fire,
> With beauty like a tightened bow, a kind
> That is not natural in an age like this.
>
> YEATS, "No Second Troy"

I

During their voyage to New York on the *Île de France* in September 1931, when Pauline was seven months pregnant with Gregory, the Hemingways met Jane and Grant Mason. At twenty-two, Jane was as stunning as Grace Kelly, as sexy as Duff Twysden and as wild as Zelda Fitzgerald. A tall woman with an athletic figure, she wore her smooth, strawberry-blond hair parted in the middle, drawn back from her forehead and gathered in a knot on her neck. She had classic and delicate features, large blue eyes, fresh complexion, a perfect oval face, and a bearing that suggested refinement and distinction. President Coolidge had called her the most beautiful woman ever to visit the White House.

Vivacious and amusing, Jane was a good drinker, a daring driver and a crack pigeon shot at the Club de Cazadores in Havana. She loved sports, fished for marlin in Cuba and hunted big game in Africa. Mario Menocal, Jr., "had never known a woman so perfectly at home in the almost exclusive company of men and who insisted on being treated by them as 'one of the boys.'" Jane had artistic talent, was accomplished in songwriting, needlework and sculpture; she did a bust of Hemingway in Key West and wrote imitation-Hemingway stories. In letters to the Hemingways (keeping up the pretense that she was writing to both of

242

them), Jane adopted the same bright, joking tone that had once been used by Pauline: "Darlings. . . . There is something about this place which forces even the most robust and gutsy to dash about in whispers. . . . I have taken the gun of my sister-in-law, as a French grammar might put it, and have tried to shoot skeet. . . . As for the writing I have done one piece which may, or may not, turn into something which could double for a portion of tepid hash with an underdone egg."[1] But Jane was also high-strung, temperamental, moody and emotionally unstable. Her son said that she was accident-prone and often unwell, that in the course of her life "she broke every bone in her body and had every conceivable illness." The ironic inscription she wrote for her own tombstone read: "Talents too many, not enough of any."

Jane's mother, Betty Lee, was a singer from Syracuse. Jane Mason was born Jane Welsh in 1909, grew up on an estate in Tuxedo Park, a wealthy suburb north of New York City, and adopted the name Kendall when her mother remarried. Educated at Briarcliff School and in Europe, she had two debuts in Washington in 1926. The following year she married Grant Mason, a tall, good-looking, well-born but unassertive graduate of St. Paul's School and Yale.[2] Grant was a founder and Caribbean manager of Pan American Airways, owned a half-interest in Cubana Airlines and was heir to a great fortune. The Masons lived in splendor at Jaimanitas, thirty minutes west of Havana, had nine servants, including an English governess, owned a large boat and gave lavish parties—sometimes with white pigeons dyed various colors—that lasted twenty-four hours. Jane and Grant adopted two young English boys in the early 1930s and Hemingway became godfather of the older son, Antony. An erratic and irresponsible mother, Jane let the servants take care of her children, who felt resentful about her neglect.[3]

Though Jane had apparently amiable relations with Grant, she was bored with his stolid personality and looked for adventures. Grant worked very hard and traveled frequently; he neglected Jane, could not control her and left her free to behave as she wished. She could keep up with Hemingway, downing straight gin with champagne chasers (Toby Bruce "never saw her fried"), but the heavy drinking hurt her marriage. In 1935 she told Hemingway that she had (at least temporarily) given up the bottle. No love was lost between Hemingway and Grant, a complaisant but hostile husband who epitomized the inherited wealth of the yachting set that was satirized in *To Have and Have Not.*

Hemingway did not have the means to satisfy Jane's luxurious tastes, disliked her emotional parabolas and never seriously thought of marrying her.

Hemingway liked his wives to be talented and accomplished. But he also hated competition and wanted them to abandon their professional work when they married him. (He resented Martha Gellhorn for continuing her career in journalism.) When his wife had become thoroughly domesticated and devoted herself to husband, children and house, he was drawn to livelier women who were still free to pursue their own interests—though not at his expense. Most of Hemingway's mistresses were women he later married. But Gregory Hemingway's statement: "During the late 1930s he used to cuckold Mother unmercifully in Havana with an American lady friend," refers to Jane Mason. Despite Hemingway's boasts about a series of love affairs beginning with Prudy Boulton, he disliked casual sex. There is no evidence that he had affairs with anyone (apart from his wives) but Jane Mason in the 1930s and perhaps two other women in the 1950s.

Hemingway blamed the failure of his marriage to Pauline on their sexual problems. He said that after her second Caesarean birth, her doctor thought it would be dangerous to have another child and he was forced to practice coitus interruptus with Pauline. (Hemingway always desired a daughter, but Martha Gellhorn did not want children and his fourth wife, Mary Welsh, had a miscarriage and could not conceive again.) Pauline referred to their sexual problem (after she had lost her faith) when she told Mary Welsh: " 'If I hadn't been such a bloody fool practicing Catholic, I wouldn't have lost my husband.' . . . Coitus interruptus? I wondered but never asked."[4] With Jane Mason, who was unable to conceive and had adopted two children, there was no need for birth control or fear of pregnancy.

Jane was like Marjorie in "The End of Something": "She loved to fish. She loved to fish with Nick."[5] Hemingway's love for Jane coincided with his discovery of marlin fishing in Cuba in April 1932. He taught Jane to fish as he had taught Pauline to ski, and Pauline stayed with the children in Key West as Hadley had stayed with Bumby in Schruns. Pauline must have felt extremely threatened by Jane, who was fourteen years younger, came from a socially prominent family and was far more beautiful, exciting, talented, athletic and wealthy than she. Pauline's sons and Leicester Hemingway were all overwhelmed by Jane's charm and praised her when they returned from fishing trips in Cuba. Pauline, tolerant to the point of self-abnegation, patiently waited four years for the affair to end and never forced the issue to a crisis as Hadley had done by insisting on the hundred-day separation. The trip to Africa, the fishing boat, the swimming pool—as well as the attempt to transform herself with a new hair style and color (blond, like Jane)—were partly rewards and bribes to keep her husband.

Jane was aboard Captain Joe Russell's boat, the *Anita,* in May 1932 and must have been the one who teasingly but childishly wrote in the log: "Ernest loves Jane." When Jane went to New York for an operation in May, Hemingway tendentiously linked her to the shell-shocked Nick Adams in "A Way You'll Never Be" and claimed that he had been watching her go crazy out of love for him. He asked MacLeish to visit her in hospital and called her a hell of a fine girl.

Hemingway and Jane were fond of drinking a jar or two of frozen daiquiris and then taking off for a daredevil, teenage driving game in her fast sports car. According to Leicester: "The object was to see how long whoever was passenger could ride without saying 'slow down' or 'watch out.' The driver was free to cut away from the road and actually head out cross-country. . . . Jane and Ernest would each take a turn driving. The game lasted until one called a halt. It was a primitive game of 'chicken' played on some of the most rugged terrain imaginable."[6]

On May 27, 1933, Jane—with Bumby, Patrick and her son Antony in her large Packard—was forced off the road near Havana airport by an old Ford bus that was coming from the opposite direction. As the soft shoulder gave way, the car tumbled down a forty-foot embankment, rolled over once and landed on its wheels at the bottom of a gulley. Jane, though severely bruised, remained cool, reacted quickly and turned off the ignition. The boys were unhurt and Bumby said: "Don't worry Mrs. Mason. I'll get you right out." This accident, and a minor one involving Patrick and Gregory in April 1947, inspired the telegram that Thomas Hudson receives from his Paris bank manager in *Islands in the Stream:* "YOUR SONS DAVID AND ANDREW KILLED WITH THEIR MOTHER IN MOTOR ACCIDENT NEAR BIARRITZ ATTENDING TO EVERYTHING PENDING YOUR ARRIVAL DEEPEST SYMPATHY."[7]

A few days after the car accident, in early June, Jane became desperately depressed. In an apparent suicide attempt, she jumped from the second-story balcony of her house at Jaimanitas and broke her back. Grant Mason callously described the tragic incident as a stunt for sympathy. The injury occurred as a result of

jumping out of our home in Jaimanitas at an altitude, all her friends
agreed, which would be reasonably impressive as an effort at suicide but
not high enough to cause death or serious injury. As I remember it, she
went off a second story balcony. . . . I do not think the accident was
directly related to anything currently happening with Ernest or me or
with anyone else but just one of her changeable fits of elation and
depression. In case she tried another such stunt, I arranged for constant
nurse attendance and then shipped her to New York on a Ward Line
vessel with special bars on the portholes.

Hemingway, with somewhat more sympathy, said Jane was a damned
beautiful woman and it was no fun to break one's back at the age of
twenty-four. But he also called her "the girl who fell for him literally."[8]
Jane spent five months in Doctors Hospital in New York, had to wear
a back brace for a year (which must have impeded her sexual and
sporting activities with Hemingway) and began extended psychoanalytic treatment with Dr. Lawrence Kubie. Her children spent
that winter with their grandfather on Park Avenue.

From August 1933 to March 1934 the Hemingways were away in
Europe and Africa. It is possible that Jane may have jumped because
Hemingway told her he was leaving, that Pauline may have taken him
to Africa to get him away from Jane, and that Hemingway may have
agreed to go to Africa because Jane was now incapacitated. In any case,
their love affair resumed in May 1934, soon after Hemingway acquired
his fishing boat, the *Pilar*, and sailed alone to Cuba to spend July
through October with Jane.

"The rooms on the northeast corner of the Ambos Mundos Hotel in
Havana," Hemingway wrote, "look out, to the north, over the old cathedral, the entrance to the harbor, and the sea, and to the east to Casablanca peninsula, the roofs of all houses in between and the width of the
harbor." Hemingway later bragged to Jack that Jane liked to climb
through his hotel room window for their rendezvous. Jane's date book
for the summer of 1934 records that when Grant went on a business trip
to Venezuela, she spent the week swimming, fishing, lunching and
dining with Hemingway.[9] Pauline would write jolly or desperate letters
pleading for his return to Key West, would come to Cuba for a few
weeks and then go back (or be sent back) to the house, children, eighteen goldfish, four raccoons, three peacocks and a possum.

During the winter of 1934–35 Jane, inspired by Hemingway's trip
to Africa the previous year, went lion hunting with Bror von Blixen. The

husband of the novelist Isak Dinesen was a friend of Hemingway and the partial model for the white hunter Wilson in "The Short Happy Life of Francis Macomber." Jane shot leopard, rhino, antelope and a baby zebra, which she had made into a rocking horse for Antony. While in Africa, Jane also had an affair with Colonel Richard Cooper, who had been Hemingway's host during the safari of 1934. Cooper, a handsome Englishman who had been decorated for bravery in the Great War, owned a coffee plantation in Tanganyika and hunted extensively in East Africa. He later married an American, discovered oil on their land in Wyoming and drowned—while drunk—in three inches of water in Lake Manyara.[10]

II

Just after she returned from Africa, Jane became unwittingly embroiled in a quarrel between her psychiatrist and her lover. In 1934 Lawrence Kubie, who had been analyzing Jane, was commissioned by Henry Canby, the editor of the *Saturday Review of Literature,* to write psychoanalytic interpretations of Erskine Caldwell's *God's Little Acre,* of William Faulkner's *Sanctuary* and of the books published by Hemingway between 1924 and 1933. Kubie's first two essays appeared in the fall of 1934, but the last one was suppressed by Hemingway and not published until 1984.[11] Kubie, who corresponded with Perkins, Charles Scribner, Jr., and Hemingway about the essay, was both naive and imperceptive in thinking that Hemingway would tolerantly submit to a public analysis. "I had always run as an adjusted person," Hemingway said, "though various tinhorn biographers had attempted to prove otherwise."[12] While writing to his lawyer in 1963, Kubie admitted what he had previously denied and Hemingway had always known: that Kubie was more interested in analyzing Hemingway's neuroses than in discussing his work.

Though Hemingway's public persona began to emerge after the publication of *Death in the Afternoon* in 1932, there was very little biographical information available in 1934. Kubie probably did not know about—and certainly did not mention—one of the most traumatic events in Hemingway's life: the suicide of his father. In the essay, Kubie promises—but does not deliver—an investigation of "universal human problems" rather than the psychology of an individual writer. He convincingly identifies Hemingway's dominant theme as the triumph over fear; women often die in Hemingway's works, but men either survive danger or meet a glorious defeat. Kubie, echoing Aldous Huxley's criticism in "Foreheads Villainous Low" (1931), attacks Hemingway's belief that a man not concerned with violence and death is a "sissy. "

In Kubie's rather awkward title, "Cyrano and the Matador," the matador symbolizes fear of death (or, more accurately, overcoming the fear of death by a ritualistic test of courage) and Edmond Rostand's dramatic recreation of Cyrano de Bergerac represents the fear of women. Kubie links the fear of death, the fear of genital injury and the fear of sex, and says the bullfight represents "the struggle between two fighting males [father and son] for genital mastery." It is unlikely that Kubie ever saw a bullfight, and when analyzing the meaning of the corrida he makes some fundamental errors that weaken the force of his argument. The bullfight is not a struggle between two fighting males, each of whom is trying "to acquire the sexual powers of the other," for the bull (insofar as we can determine his motives) neither needs nor wants the sexual power of the man.

Kubie next identifies two types of males in Hemingway's work: the kind, individual father figures and the destructive, collective males. Yet even the father figure, who represents the threat of (passive) homosexuality, inspires in the son a conflict of love and hate. The main struggle in Hemingway, then, is a struggle against both the seductive and the terrifying older man: against fear of the father. The cultured "sissy" succumbs to the father; the killer defies the father. "In such a [neurotic] turmoil," Kubie's essay concludes, echoing the title of Hemingway's latest book, "frustration is the only possible outcome, and it is not to be wondered at that in the end, 'Winner Takes Nothing.' "

Kubie's rather restrained essay on the conflicts manifested in the first decade of Hemingway's work was convincing and, for its time, perceptive. Hemingway—like many ordinary men—had been engaged in an Oedipal struggle against his father for the possession of his mother. If the bullfight symbolizes sexual intercourse, as it clearly does in *The Sun Also Rises* ("the sword went in, and for just an instant he and the bull were one"), then the matador's triumphant domination of the bull at the moment of orgasmic death represents a virile defense against the threat of homosexuality.

There are, however, significant limitations in Kubie's analysis. First, it is surprising that Kubie does not extract more evidence from the cornerstone of his argument, "Fathers and Sons," which Hemingway overtly treats as a cathartic release from parental conflicts: "If he wrote it he could get rid of it. He had gotten rid of many things by writing them."[13] In this story, the heroic father fiercely represses the son's awakening sexual desires by threatening him with the horrors of venereal disease. The only outlet for the son's resentment, impotence and anger at paternal domination is a retributive fantasy about shooting his father with the very weapon his father had given him.

Second, it is not at all surprising that Hemingway's impressive father had a great influence on him and that Hemingway had strong, and often ambivalent, feelings about his father—who was both a friend and a rival. Third, Kubie does not mention that the Oedipal struggle is a necessary stage in the developmental process of every boy. Finally, Kubie states that his analysis of Hemingway's fiction reveals neurotic conflicts, but he does not explain how, in Hemingway's particular case, these conflicts were sublimated and transformed by his genius into art.

In November 1934 Canby belatedly sent his lawyers the page proofs of what Kubie privately admitted to be "speculative personal analysis"; Canby was told the essay was libelous and at the very last moment substituted the Caldwell for the Hemingway article. When Kubie protested, Canby responded that Hemingway would surely sue if he published the article. Kubie thought the whole idea of a libel suit was preposterous and rashly offered to eat his manuscript "if Hemingway finds a word in it to object to." In December Canby said he would publish the article only if Kubie obtained a signed release from Hemingway. Kubie displaced his aggression toward the editor and expressed his hostility to the author when he facetiously suggested: "How would it be if we simply killed Hemingway and then published?"

Kubie then came up with the unrealistic idea of submitting a softened version of the essay to *Scribner's Magazine*, which would, he imagined, intercede with the novelist and smooth the way to publication. Kubie offered the article to Max Perkins, who said that Hemingway wished to keep his life entirely private and predicted that Hemingway would object to the essay. Perkins discussed the matter with Hemingway during a Cuban fishing trip in February 1935. He then told Kubie that Hemingway wanted his books to remain independent of his life and was unalterably opposed to publication.

Perkins' sound advice, far from dissuading Kubie, convinced him that Hemingway's objection to his interpretation merely confirmed its accuracy. In April 1935, driven by an egoistic desire to publish his findings, Kubie sent the essay with an extraordinarily naive letter to Hemingway. Kubie appealed to Hemingway's sporting instincts and (assuming a tough-guy manner) disingenuously wrote: "I don't know a damned thing about you as an individual, and I have made an effort not to find out anything, because I have had no impulse to analyze you." He asked Hemingway to state his objections, suggestions and feelings about publication.

Hemingway's works from *in our time* (1924) to *A Farewell to Arms* (1929) enjoyed an enthusiastic reception from the critics, but there was a strong shift in opinion after he adopted a swaggering pose in *Death in the Afternoon.* In 1933 Gertrude Stein called Hemingway a coward in *The Autobiography of Alice B. Toklas* and Max Eastman claimed Hemingway had false hair on his chest in "Bull in the Afternoon." These savage but witty attacks, both by former friends of Hemingway, were followed in 1934 by the massive onslaught of Wyndham Lewis' damaging essay, "The Dumb Ox."

If Kubie had reflected for a moment, he would have realized that Hemingway—the lover of Kubie's patient Jane Mason—would be outraged by Jane's revelations of their intimate conversations and sexual life, and extremely hostile to her doctor's public analysis of his sexual conflicts. On May 1, 1935, in a brief but ferocious note, Hemingway told Kubie that he had sent the letter and article to his attorney for appropriate action and warned Kubie that he would have to wait until Hemingway's death to libel him with impunity.

In July 1935 Canby got wind of Hemingway's wrath and tried to exculpate himself with an awkwardly expressed and quite gratuitous lie: "I am writing you this because I want you to understand that our relation to the article was simply that, on receipt of the manuscript and after attempts to revise it, we decided not to publish it" because it might be misunderstood. In August, Kubie, after reading a copy of the letter, sent Canby a furious outburst. He asked Canby to compare his letter to Kubie of December 14, which said he could not publish for fear of a libel suit, with his letter to Hemingway of July 29, which said he feared the article would be misunderstood: "If you can do this without blushing, you have an amazingly easy conscience. . . . It seems to me that you could have stood by me more loyally and without going out of your way to write Hemingway an unnecessary untruth." Finally, Kubie justly accused Canby of stealing the ideas in Kubie's essay and publishing them under his own name in Canby's article "Fiction Tells All," which appeared in *Harper's* in August 1935. Canby, caught with his pants down, tried to wriggle out of the sticky situation by explaining that he had twice mentioned Kubie in his *Harper's* article. But Kubie ruthlessly replied: "It remains very odd that you can feel yourself free to use material which you yourself have not the courage to publish."

Twenty-eight years later, in 1963, Kubie's chance meeting with Charles Scribner, Jr., reminded him of the painful episode. He frankly admitted, in a letter to Scribner, that he had used Hemingway to express his major concern: the relation of neurosis to the creative process. "Nobody could read [the essay]," Kubie said, "without thinking that I was making a kind of public exposure, stripping down Hemingway in the flesh." Kubie conceded that he had been wrong in writing the article and that Hemingway had been right in suppressing it. He also explained, not quite accurately, that he had been "seduced," compelled almost against his will, into writing about Hemingway and that he did not, at the time, care whether or not his essay was published. In a letter of June 1963 to his lawyer, Kubie also stated that he had completely changed his mind about the practice of analyzing living artists: "This is too much like undressing a man in public; and in this sense it is a violation of his right to privacy."

The controversy surrounding Kubie's essay reveals a great deal about the character of the people involved in the dispute. Jane Mason, who confessed that she was the only one of Kubie's patients he could not help, was caught in an emotional crossfire.[14] She was terrified that she had revealed intimate secrets that would be indiscreetly and unprofessionally used in Kubie's analysis of Hemingway. Kubie, fascinated by his own ideas and obsessed by a desire to publish, deceived himself about his motives and methods. When his own interests were involved, he lost his analytic objectivity and insight, and was surprisingly insensitive about Hemingway's feelings. He was the first critic to take an interest in the personality behind Hemingway's haunting stories. His analysis of the works led to statements about the psychology of the author and to moral judgments about his inner conflicts. Yet, as Kubie admitted, he actually knew very little about the man he had never met and was attempting to analyze him through his works.

Hemingway, a notoriously touchy writer, was clearly disturbed by Kubie's conclusions, which were confirmed in the autobiographical passages of *For Whom the Bell Tolls* (1940). Though his works were public revelations of his conscious and unconscious feelings, he tried to keep his life private. He thought he was psychologically healthy, did not feel the conflicts expressed in his art were neurotic and quite naturally rejected the implication of personal inadequacy. He knew his legal rights and, though a public figure, was prepared to enforce them. He remained above the fracas until the appropriate moment and then delivered the crushing blow that ended all hope of publication.

III

Jane's affair with Richard Cooper and her involvement in the dispute with Kubie must have angered Hemingway, who had not seen Jane since she left for Africa at the end of 1934. But he invited her to fish with him in Bimini during the summer of 1935. He found it difficult to break with her completely and their separations made him all the more keen to see her again. Hemingway became severely depressed in January 1936: "Thought was facing impotence, inability to write, insomnia and was going to blow my lousy head off." In the spring of 1936, while writing "Francis Macomber," he saw Jane frequently. When he spoke of sailing the *Pilar* to Cuba, Jane volunteered to come over to Key West and accompany him. He mentioned Jane's boredom, freedom and lack of sex in marriage in a wry letter to Dos Passos: "Mrs. Mason, I believe is also crossing with us. Mrs. Mason is almost as apt at going places without her husband as Mr. Josie [Russell] is without his wife. But then Mrs. Mason has also had her husband for a long time too although Mr. Josie I believe there is no doubt has had his much much oftener as well as longer than Mr. Mason." In June Jane chartered her own boat to vie with Hemingway in a deep-sea fishing competition.

Hemingway apparently had a violent and bitter break with Jane in April 1936. This led directly to his satiric portrayal of Jane as Margot Macomber, a beautiful but bitchy woman who sleeps with the white hunter and shoots her husband. The reasons for their quarrel are not known. She may have said or done something to antagonize Hemingway; they may have had an awkward sexual encounter; she may have rejected him for Richard Cooper, who was fishing with her in Bimini in June; Pauline may have put some pressure on him to return to married life. Leicester's friend Jake Klimo said that sometime after Hemingway acquired the *Pilar* (May 1934): "The air's all charged up because he's been caught playing hanky-panky and [Pauline] comes rushing over here [Havana] to protect her interests. They probably had a terrible fight already over that woman."[15]

Hemingway's first literary allusion to Jane, who is called by her fictional name, occurs during a conversation with Pauline in *Green Hills of Africa* (1935). Hemingway asks: "Who's a beautiful woman?" and answers his own question by stating: "Margot is." When Pauline agrees with him and admits: "I know I'm not," he reassures her by saying: "You're lovely." In "Francis Macomber" (September 1936) Hemingway describes Margot (Jane) as "an extremely handsome and well-kept woman of the beauty and social position which had, five years before, commanded five thousand dollars as the price of endorsing, with photographs, a beauty product which she had never used. She had been married to Francis Macomber for eleven years [in 1936 Jane had been married to Grant for ten years]. . . . She had a very perfect oval face, so perfect that you expected her to be stupid. But she wasn't stupid." When Margot torments her husband after he has run away from a charging lion, Wilson thinks that wealthy American women like Margot are "the hardest in the world; the hardest, the cruelest, the most predatory and the most attractive and their men have softened or gone to pieces nervously as they have hardened."[16] While discussing Margot Macomber in a late essay, Hemingway bitterly said, with his familiar revision of reality, that he had hated Jane and she had loved him: "I invented her complete with handles from the worst bitch I knew (then) and when I first knew her she'd been lovely. Not my dish, not my pigeon, not my cup of tea, but lovely for what she was and I was her all of the above." It is worth noting that Jane showed no signs of bitchiness before Hemingway quarreled with her in April 1936. She evidently preferred literary fame to an accurate portrayal of her character and was, according to Hemingway, "flattered when people took her for Mrs. Macomber."[17]

The more intense Hemingway's passion was in life, the greater the expression of hatred in his fiction. His portrayal of Jane and Grant Mason as Helène and Tommy Bradley in *To Have and Have Not* (1937) is even more hostile than in "Francis Macomber." In the novel Jane is once again predatory, Hemingway innocent: "Mrs. Bradley collected writers as well as their books but Richard Gordon did not know this yet." In "Fathers and Sons" Nick makes love with Trudy as her brother Billy watches them; in *To Have and Have Not* Bradley opens the door of the bedroom and observes Hélène and Gordon making love in his house. When the distracted Gordon turns around to look at Bradley, Hélène, with a desperate sexual urgency, exclaims: "Don't mind him. Don't mind anything. Don't you see you can't stop now? . . . He knows all about these things. Don't mind him. Come on, darling. Please do." And when Gordon is unable to continue after this coitus interruptus, she says: "My God, don't you know anything? Haven't you any regard for a woman?" and slaps him twice across the face. That is the end of the affair.

Later in the book, two homosexual yachtsmen discuss the Bradleys. One of them calls Hélène a whore; the other asks if Tommy is impotent and is told that he is simply broad-minded. The first homosexual then conclusively condemns the couple: "She represents everything I hate in a woman, and Tommy Bradley epitomizes everything I hate in a man." Finally, the mistress of a Hollywood director calls Hélène a "stupid and well-intentioned and really selfish" bitch. An obscure but libelous passage, deleted from the published book, appears to describe an emotional confrontation between Hélène and Tommy Bradley. Like Margot Macomber, she seizes the upper hand and pushes her weak and fearful husband toward psychiatric treatment (Francis Macomber had "gone to pieces nervously"). The wife, faintly red-eyed, her make-up running in her tears, smiles brightly and stares at the husband with a determined look, intent on sending him to a clinic in Zurich. He is a tanned, handsome yachtsman, notoriously fearful of the sea, who gets his weatherbeaten color by lying on the deck and anointing his face with Elizabeth Arden suntan lotion.[18]

The last, nostalgic allusion to Jane appeared the following year in *The Fifth Column* when Philip Rawlings remembers staying up all night, dancing and gambling in a Havana casino, and then driving "in to Jaimanitas for breakfast in the daylight. And everybody knows everyone else and it's very pleasant and gay."[19] Like many novelists, Hemingway used his art to compensate for the disappointments in life. But his portrayal of Hélène weakens the novel because the negative side of her character is never convincingly shown and (like Ford and Lewis in *A Moveable Feast*) she is condemned for reasons that are external to the book.

IV

In the summer of 1937, shortly before the publication of *To Have and Have Not*, Jane Mason and Jinny Pfeiffer, who had become great friends, traveled to Mexico with Richard Cooper. Jinny tried to seduce Jane. And Toby Bruce, who had driven Jinny's car from Piggott to Acapulco and had the imported car noted on his passport, was jailed for three days when he tried to return to America without the vehicle.[20]

The Masons moved from Havana to Washington in 1938, when Grant joined the Civil Aeronautics Board, and they were divorced the following year. Grant served as a Colonel under Hap Arnold during the war and later became consultant to the Secretary of the Air Force. He remarried, had several children, was divorced for the second time and nearly married Jane again. Jane had more husbands than any of Hemingway's women: Pauline was married once; Agnes, Hadley, Martha Gellhorn and Adriana Ivancich twice; Duff and Mary Welsh thrice; and Jane four times. She married John Hamilton, a lawyer and Republican National Chairman, in 1940; George Abel, a *Herald Tribune* columnist and European chief of Time-Life, in 1947; and Arnold Gingrich, a friend of Hemingway and editor of *Esquire*, in 1955.

Hemingway had met Gingrich through his bibliographer Louis Cohn in January 1933. Hemingway frequently contributed hunting and fishing articles and helped to build the reputation of *Esquire*—which was meant to be the masculine equivalent of *Vogue*—from the first issue in the fall of 1933 to August 1936, when *Esquire* published "The Snows of Kilimanjaro." Dos Passos provides an amusing description of how Hemingway charmed and controlled Gingrich on a fishing trip:

> The man was in a trance. It was a world he'd never dreamed of. He was mosquitobitten, half seasick, scorched with sunburn, astonished, half scared, half pleased. It was as much fun to see Ernest play an editor as to see him play a marlin. Gingrich never took his fascinated eyes off Old Hem. Hem would reel in gently letting his prey have plenty of line. The editor was hooked. Sure he would print anything Hemingway cared to let him have at a thousand dollars a whack.[21]

Pauline (perhaps to distract Jane from Hemingway) introduced her to Gingrich in Bimini in June 1936. He began to see her secretly in New York that year, but did not marry her until two wives and two husbands later. Gingrich, like Lawrence Kubie, was involved both in Jane's emotional life and in Hemingway's literary affairs. It is ironic that Hemingway sought Gingrich's advice about libelous passages in *To Have and Have Not* and that he advised Hemingway to cut passages about Jane and Grant Mason. In an unpublished essay, "The Home Front," Hemingway wrote that when his sons asked why he always used to write for *Esquire* and no longer did, he would say it was because he and Gingrich disagreed about a blonde. When in 1958 Antony Mason told Hemingway that Gingrich had married Jane, Hemingway absolutely exploded: "That shit! I can't get over it."[22] After the death of Hemingway, who had introduced Gingrich to deep-sea fishing, Gingrich got even for having been played like a marlin by criticizing Hemingway's lack of finesse as an angler: "Ernest was a meat fisherman. He cared more about the quantity than about the quality, and was more concerned with the capture of the quarry than with the means employed to do it. He was also—and this is what no true angler is—intensely competitive about his fishing, and a very poor sport."[23]

Gingrich's marriage to Jane was predictably stormy. He moved out of their house a few times, was extremely possessive and would not allow Jane's children or grandchildren to visit her. At the end of her life, she suffered from hypoglycemia and had a crippling stroke that suddenly transformed her into an old lady. When she died in 1981 she had four photographs at her bedside: Grant Mason and Arnold Gingrich, Richard Cooper and Ernest Hemingway.

Hemingway's frustrated love for one woman often triggered his consummated love for another. His bitter break with Jane in April 1936 made him all the more receptive to Martha Gellhorn, whom he met in December, just as the rejection by Agnes made him responsive to Hadley and the temptation of Duff prepared him for Pauline.

13

Africa
1933–1934

> Kilimanjaro is a snow covered
> mountain 19,710 feet high. . . .
> Close to the western summit
> there is the dried and frozen
> carcass of a leopard. No one
> has explained what the leopard
> was seeking at that altitude.
>
> "The Snows of Kilimanjaro"

I

While Hemingway was seeing Jane Mason in Cuba, between April 1932 and her suicide attempt in June 1933, he was writing the stories that were published in *Winner Take Nothing* in October 1933. Eleven thousand copies, more than half the first printing of 20,300, were sold the first month. The critics felt this volume was the weakest of Hemingway's three collections because of the intellectual limitations of his characters—soldiers, criminals, prostitutes, bullfighters—and the monotonous repetition of his subjects: divorce, despair, fever, syphilis, castration, shell shock, corpses, death. The novelist William Plomer, however, perceptively justified the negativism implicit in Hemingway's title and violent subject matter: "This is partly the nihilism of our time, the time of the War and of our permanent Crisis and of our spiritual dislocation, but it is also the nihilism that so often goes with vitality."[1]

This book exposed the widening fissure between Hemingway's actual life and the substance of his art. While leading a healthy, leisurely and luxurious existence in his fishing boat and his seigneurial residence, drinking and sporting with his mistress, he continued to draw on the

257

radically different past experience of childhood, war and low life in Michigan, Kansas City, Paris and Madrid. He portrayed authentic lower-class characters, but did not (like most writers of the thirties) treat them from a Left-wing, social-realist point of view. Though Hemingway frequently repeated violent themes, he also developed his concern with the emotional and psychological conflicts of the family, the trauma and despair of wounds and the problem of men's relation to women.

The fourteen stories in this uneven collection range from thin sketches like "One Reader Writes" and "A Day's Wait" to three of his finest works in this genre: "A Way You'll Never Be," "A Clean, Well-Lighted Place" and "Fathers and Sons." "A Way You'll Never Be" concerns the delusions and horrors of war that were also portrayed in the poetry of Wilfred Owen and Siegfried Sassoon. It describes Nick Adams' shell shock and psychological breakdown after receiving a wound in battle; it is closely connected to two earlier stories about the war in Italy: "In Another Country" and "Now I Lay Me"; and it continues the theme of war trauma that runs from the earliest sketches in *in our time* (1924) to Colonel Cantwell's memories of the Piave in *Across the River and into the Trees* (1950).

Hemingway said the story shows the damage war does "to a man, a village and a countryside." The title refers both to the shattered character and to the safe noncombatants who can never truly understand Nick's condition. The story opens with the unheroic aftermath of a successful Allied attack, which contrasts the ideal hopes with the ugly reality of war. Nick, still emotionally unstable, is sent on an absurd propaganda mission: "I am supposed to move around and let them see the . . . American uniform that is supposed to make them believe others are coming." Nick's voice is unnatural, he cannot sleep without a light, he is terrified, he has nightmares, he has been certified as "nutty." His rambling lecture on locusts—an attempt to prevent a crack-up and a sure sign that he is about to have one—parodies a military briefing and turns into a recurrent nightmare of the moment he was shot in the head. The story ends with a deceptive vision of military glory: "It was on that stretch that, marching, they had once passed the Terza Savoia cavalry regiment riding in the snow with their lances. The horses' breath made plumes in the cold air."[2] For these troops are merely riding to their slaughter.

"A Clean, Well-Lighted Place" is an intensely concentrated, highly charged and deeply moving story, expressed in compassionate but ironic understatement. The illuminated café represents a kind of peace, order, security and refuge that stands in opposition to the old client's deafness, isolation, loneliness and despair. The war, the destruction of idealism and the loss of God have led inevitably to the concept of *nada:* no tangible thing, but a palpable and overwhelming sensation of nothingness. The theme is subtly expressed through a series of suggestive polarities: light and shadow, sleep and insomnia, confidence and despair, courage and fear, dignity and degradation, faith and scepticism, life and death. The passing soldier has a girl, the intolerant young waiter is eager to return to his wife; but the old client has lost his wife and tried to hang himself and failed. The older waiter sympathizes with the insomniac client and shares his fear of the night: "I am of those who like to stay late at the café. . . . With all those who do not want to go to bed. With all those who need a light for the night." His savage parody of the Lord's Prayer ("Our nada who art in nada") expresses a desperate but illusory hope for comfort in this world—if not in the next. James Joyce admired and praised this story: "He has reduced the veil between literature and life, which is what every writer strives to do. Have you read 'A Clean, Well-Lighted Place'? . . . It is masterly. Indeed, it is one of the best short stories ever written; there is bite there."[3]

"Fathers and Sons" is one of Hemingway's most personal and revealing stories. The title from Turgenev suggests the conflict of generations. Nick, both a father and a son, attempts to form a communion with his son by describing his own impressive and threatening father. The story opens as he drives through the cotton country around Piggott, Arkansas; his son is sleeping on the front seat and Nick is thinking about his father. A keen-eyed hunter with vision but no insight, his father taught Nick fishing and shooting, but warned him about illicit sex. As a boy, Nick had threatened to kill the Indian who wanted to sleep with his sister as well as the father who tried to prevent him from sleeping with the Indian girl. The adverbial description of orgasmic sex with Trudy —"uncomfortably, tightly, sweetly, moistly, lovely, tightly, achingly, fully, finally, unendingly, never-endingly, never-to-endingly, suddenly ended, the great bird flown like an owl in the twilight"[4]—anticipates the account of Robert Jordan and Maria in the sleeping bag in *For Whom the Bell Tolls* and the metaphorical bird that flutters above Cantwell and Renata, symbolizing the transitory nature of their affair, when they make love in a gondola in *Across the River.* The warning and the threat by Nick's father establish the connection between hunting

4. *East Africa*

and sex, for both can be seen as predatory conquests of a passive victim, achieved through the exertion of power. Nick hints at but does not specifically mention the suicide of his father, who acted out Nick's fantasy and killed himself with a gun. Nick wants to compensate for his father's weakness with his own son, whose desire to pray at the tomb of his grandfather emphasizes Nick's guilt about his lack of reverence and respect.

II

After Hemingway completed *Winner Take Nothing* he fulfilled his ambition, expressed in *The Sun Also Rises*, of "going to British East Africa to shoot." In 1933 Uncle Gus gave him $25,000 to pay for the African safari, and Hemingway asked MacLeish and Strater to be his guests. Both refused the invitation, fearing that Hemingway's fierce competitiveness would turn the holiday into a daily struggle for superiority. They agreed with Damon Runyon's remark about Hemingway: "Few men can stand the strain of relaxing with him over an extended period." Charles Thompson, his Key West friend, accepted the invitation and accompanied him to Africa.

On August 7, while Jane Mason was in hospital, the Hemingways sailed from Havana to Santander on the *Reina de la Pacífica*. They spent August to October in Spain, arrived in Paris in late fall, read the hostile reviews of *Winner Take Nothing* and had a farewell dinner with Joyce: "The last night Joyce and his wife came to dinner and we had a pheasant and a quarter of the chevreuil [kid] with the saddle and Joyce and I got drunk because we were off for Africa the next day."[5] On November 22 they sailed on the *General Metzinger* from Marseilles, passed through the Suez Canal and into the Indian Ocean, stopped at Port Said, Djibouti and Aden, and arrived in Mombasa on December 8.

The Hemingways were fortunate with their white hunter. Philip Percival was born in Somerset, the youngest of three sons. He went to Reading School, worked on a newspaper and served in the militia before going to Kenya at the age of twenty in 1905. He had hunted with Winston Churchill and with Teddy Roosevelt, and charged a thousand dollars a month. In *African Game Trails* (1910) Roosevelt wrote: "At Bondoni was Percival, a tall sinewy man, a fine rider and shot. . . . He wore merely a helmet, a flannel shirt, short breeches or trunks, and puttees and boots, leaving the knee entirely bare. I shall not forget seeing him one day, as he walked beside his twelve-ox team, cracking his long whip, while in the big wagon sat pretty Mrs. Percival with a puppy, and a little cheetah cub." In Kenya, Percival had farmed ostriches and organized lion drives for hunters, been allocated 5,000 acres at Potha Hill and worked for British Intelligence under Colonel Richard Meinertzhagen during the Great War. Denis Zaphiro, who hunted with Hemingway and Percival on the second African safari, in 1953–54, described Percival as "perhaps the greatest hunter living when I first met him in 1950. Out past his prime. Lovely sense of humour. Head of the Professional Hunters Association for many years. Unspoiled reputation. Always chosen when the best hunter was needed. Father to us all."[6]

Percival (who was called Pop in *Green Hills of Africa*) had the British military virtues and reminded Hemingway of a thick, heavy version of Chink Dorman-Smith. Pauline adored him and Hemingway portrayed him as a nobler version of himself: "Pop was her ideal of how a man should be, brave, gentle, comic, never losing his temper, never bragging, never complaining except in a joke, tolerant, understanding, intelligent, drinking a little too much as a good man should, and, to her eyes, very handsome." Percival returned this admiration; he praised Hemingway's character, shooting skill and memory, and told Zaphiro that he was "good fun to be with. A bull-shit merchant of the first class though. Amusing, friendly and quite a good shot. I liked him. Fantastic recall. He quoted what I said word for word years later in his letters and in *Green Hills of Africa*. You'll get on well with him."[7]

The Hemingways traveled inland from Mombasa to Nairobi, spent a few days hunting near Percival's farm at Machakos (twenty miles from Nairobi), and on December 20 started south to the Serengeti plain in Tanganyika. It was near the cone-shaped, snow-covered Mount Kilimanjaro and filled with thousands of wild animals. As MacLeish and Strater had feared, the hunting trip soon turned into a competitive struggle between Hemingway and Thompson for the finest trophies. Pauline did a great deal of watching, formed the cheering section and was credited with one lion that Hemingway actually shot. Though Pauline prayed for her husband's success, the Deity favored Thompson, who bagged better trophies of every animal they killed.

Thompson (called Karl in *Green Hills of Africa*) was described as "quiet, friendly, gentle and understandingly delicate." But his luck and skill aroused Hemingway's hostility. When Thompson killed a rhino whose small horn was longer than the large horn of Hemingway's rhino, Ernest felt positively queasy, but could still be ironic about himself: "We all spoke like people who were about to become seasick on a boat, or people who had suffered some heavy financial loss." Pauline diplomatically but vainly tried to restrain her husband: " 'Papa, please try to act like a human being,' she said. 'Poor Karl. You're making him feel dreadfully.' " Hemingway lamely explained: "We had tried, in all the shoot, never to be competitive. . . . I knew I could outshoot him and I could always outwalk him and, steadily, he got trophies that made mine dwarfs in comparison." When Hemingway was poisoned with envy after discovering that Thompson's greater kudu horns were even greater than *his* greater kudu horns, Percival regretfully remarked that hunting often aroused atavistic feelings: "We have very primitive emotions. . . . It's impossible not to be competitive. Spoils everything, though."[8]

The safari was interrupted in mid-January 1934 when Hemingway suffered a serious attack of amoebic dysentery, which he had contracted on the voyage to Africa. His large intestine became infected and swollen, and three inches of it dropped out of his body. According to Pauline, he "was passing nearly a quart of blood daily." In an unpublished essay, "Africa," he recalled that he had amoebic dysentery on his first trip there. After visiting the Ngorongoro crater he began to bleed and at first thought it was piles. He soon had 150 bowel movements a day and a prolapsed intestine that he had to wash with soap and water, and put back into his body. Finally, when he could no longer get out of bed, he was carried outside the camp while Percival's assistant ordered a private plane.[9] Hemingway was flown back to Nairobi. He was successfully treated with emetine (an amoebacide and purge) while staying at the New Stanley Hotel, recovered rapidly and returned to Tanganyika a week later. The plane that rescued him when he was seriously ill and flew past the highest mountain in Africa on the way to Nairobi, would reappear in Harry's dream at the end of "The Snows of Kilimanjaro."

Hemingway shot three lions, a buffalo and twenty-seven other beasts until hunting stopped, after seventy-two days in Africa, when the rains came. In mid-February they returned to the coast at Malindi, north of Mombasa, for a week of fishing. They sailed back to France on the *Gripsholm* with Bror von Blixen and Alfred Vanderbilt; stopped in

Haifa, where they met Lorine Thompson, and visited the Sea of Galilee; and arrived in Villefranche on March 18. Hemingway punched the vase of tulips across Sylvia Beach's bookshop after reading Wyndham Lewis' "The Dumb Ox" on March 24, sailed for New York three days later, and met Marlene Dietrich on the voyage home.

III

Hemingway began to write *Green Hills of Africa* as soon as he returned to Key West. He had read extensively about big game hunting, but the book tried to capture the initial enthusiasm rather than synthesize his expertise on the subject. In the Foreword he somewhat defensively states: "The writer has attempted to write an absolutely true book to see whether the shape of a country and the pattern of a month's action can, if truly presented, compete with a work of the imagination." But his competitive attempt does not match either novels like Conrad's *Heart of Darkness* (1899) or nonfiction like Greene's *Journey Without Maps* (1936).

As in *Death in the Afternoon,* the focus is on Hemingway's literary persona, autobiographical reflections and incidental opinions as well as on the ostensible subject matter. But the African book is not nearly as good as the Spanish one. Hemingway was interested in the African landscape and animals, but not in the customs and the people; his account of hunting in Africa conveys the excitement of getting close to wild beasts in their natural element, but lacks the artistic and cultural context of bullfighting in Spain. *Death in the Afternoon* explores the technical, tragic, aesthetic, stylistic, dramatic and sexual aspects of bullfighting, and relates them to the character and courage of the Spaniards. It is an art and a sport which appeals to a great range of people and allows the poorest men to achieve the greatest success. The highly bred fighting bulls are killed with a sword, an extension of the matador's body, in an orgasmic climax that exposes him to maximum danger. Big-game hunting, by contrast, is a rich man's sport, which also requires courage but is far less dangerous, for the wild animals are killed from a distance by purely mechanical means. Hemingway was not successful in depicting domestic life on safari, for his true *métier* was the portrayal of romantic and tragic love. When Hemingway glorified hunting and himself, he produced a poor book; but when he was severely critical of both hunters and himself, he was able to write two brilliant stories about Africa.

In *Green Hills of Africa* he seems to have exaggerated his egoism in a perverse response to the critics' harsh judgment of his last two books. He recounts his own exploits, patronizes the Africans but is greatly admired by them (" 'Shut up, you,' M'Cola told him. 'The Bwana can shoot after you cannot see.' "), criticizes many classic and contemporary writers,[10] and denies any feelings of guilt about killing the beautiful animals. He behaves boorishly with Karl, transfers his own negative qualities to his friend and characterizes him as competitive, edgy, nasty and bitter. Thompson may well have resented this harsh portrait, for he seems to have drifted out of Hemingway's life after 1935 and sided with Pauline (a close friend of Lorine) after the divorce.

Hemingway saved the best of his experience for his fiction, as he later did while serving as a war correspondent in Spain and Europe. The italicized flashbacks foreshadow the memories of Paris in "The Snows of Kilimanjaro" and *A Moveable Feast;* but they are—like the recollections of sport, war and travel in Michigan, Italy, Switzerland, Spain, Montana and Cuba—surprisingly flat. The belligerent tone of the book signals, as it always does in Hemingway, the failure of his literary skill.

Green Hills of Africa expresses themes that began to haunt Hemingway as he became successful and figure prominently in his work from "The Snows of Kilimanjaro" and *To Have and Have Not* to *A Moveable Feast:* the betrayal of talent and the fear of corruption. Hemingway was well aware of the dangers of corruption at the very moment he abandoned the ethics and morals of the midwestern middle class and adopted those of the eastern leisured class; but he seemed powerless to see what was happening to *himself* or to do anything about it. He acutely states that America destroys its authors, economically and critically:

> Our writers when they have made some money increase their standard of living and they are caught. They have to write to keep up their establishments, their wives, and so on, and they write slop. . . . Or else they read the critics. . . . At present we have two good writers [Fitzgerald and Anderson] who cannot write because they have lost confidence through reading critics

—and, he might have added, through being attacked by Hemingway. When he is asked by Kandinsky, the Austrian interlocutor who replaces the Old Lady of *Death in the Afternoon,* to name "the actual, concrete things that harm a writer," he fatalistically responds: "Politics, women, drink, money, ambition. And the lack of politics, women, drink, money and ambition."[11]

Green Hills of Africa was serialized in *Scribner's Magazine,* which paid $5,000, was published in October 1935 and had a first printing of 10,550 copies. The book was dedicated to Philip Percival, Charles Thompson and Jim Sullivan (who stayed behind in Key West). The critics, whom Hemingway had provocatively characterized as "lice who crawl on literature," attacked him for his escapist theme and for avoiding the economic and political issues of the Depression. Most reviewers felt that his obsession with blood sports and death, though technically accurate, could *not* compete with a work of the imagination.

Bernard De Voto noted that Hemingway's nasty asides about critics meant "Either the reviewers have been getting under his skin or he is uneasy about this book." He said that much of this unimportant work —a curious mixture of description, straight fictional technique, literary discussion and exhibitionism—was dull, and he regretted the new experience of being bored by Hemingway. Carl Van Doren was more tolerant of Hemingway's exhibitionism and admired the richer and more complex prose. Although Hemingway was at times superficial and tiresome, Van Doren thought, "he is mature as an artist, expounding his own art and exhibiting it in prose that sings like poetry without ever ceasing to be prose, easy, intricate and magical."[12]

Writing in the Communist journal *New Masses,* Granville Hicks (who had disliked *Death in the Afternoon*) stated: "I have always felt that Hemingway was by all odds the clearest and strongest non-revolutionary writer of his generation." But he was seriously disappointed that Hemingway concerned himself with dull and unworthy subjects on the margins of life and refused to "let himself look squarely at the contemporary American scene." He concluded that in the six years since *A Farewell to Arms,* "Hemingway has not produced a book even remotely worthy of his talents."[13]

Edmund Wilson, who had been an enthusiastic partisan of Hemingway's work until *Green Hills of Africa,* made the most damaging appraisal of the book in his major revaluation of 1939: "He has produced what must be one of the only books ever written which make Africa and

its animals seem dull. Almost the only thing we learn about the animals
is that Hemingway wants to kill them. And as for the natives . . . the
principal impression we get of them is that they were simple and inferior people who enormously admired Hemingway."[14]

Though Hemingway felt "he had made the mistake of daring the
critics to attack and they had taken up the dare, 'ganging up' on his
book and refusing to judge it on its merits," he heeded their advice.[15]
The Spanish Civil War intensified his political convictions and led to a
gesture of social commitment in *To Have and Have Not*. In that novel,
the individualistic hero is placed in a corrupt society and shares the fate
of oppressed men.

IV

Hemingway had returned to America to claim the audience he had won
in Paris, for he would not have been satisfied with the coterie success
of Joyce and Pound. He had a genuine need to engage in blood sports
as a release from the daily tension of creative work; he loved to write
about boxing, bullfighting, fishing and hunting; but he knew they were
not generally accepted as the subjects of serious literature. His fiction
had attracted a vast audience without succumbing to the fashionable
mode of proletarian literature, but he sometimes confused literary
greatness with good reviews, large sales and huge royalties. He was
aware, from Fitzgerald's experience and his own, of the conflict between the loneliness of his vocation and the seductive influence of slick
magazines, high fees and a luxurious life. He had a psychological need
to write well and truly, and maintained his artistic integrity. But when
he wrote directly about himself in *Green Hills of Africa* he pretended
to—though he did not—confront the writer's problem of drink, women,
ambition for money and fame. He had composed "an absolutely true
book" in the first person immediately after the safari, but failed to
capture and recreate the essence of his African experience. By 1936,
however, he had achieved the necessary objectivity, irony and self-
scrutiny, and transmuted his hunting expedition into two undisputed
masterpieces: "The Short Happy Life of Francis Macomber" and "The
Snows of Kilimanjaro."

Hemingway based "Francis Macomber" on a scandalous case of
adultery and suicide that had been suppressed in the newspapers and

whitewashed by the British government. Like everyone else in Kenya, he was fascinated by the story of a beautiful wife who had a love affair with a hunter and was involved in the death of her husband. He heard this story from Philip Percival while drinking around the evening campfire (Percival told Patrick the same story in the 1950s).

The details of the case, buried in the Colonial Office papers, concern an eccentric and reckless colonel who was himself the author of a best-selling book. John Henry Patterson (1867–1947) was born in Dublin of a Protestant family, went to Sandhurst, joined the Essex Yeomanry, was an engineer in the British army in Africa and India. When plague broke out in Nairobi in 1899, Patterson outraged the traders by burning down the bazaar without consulting his superiors. In 1898 he became the engineer responsible for the initial survey of the railway from the Kenya coast to Uganda. His Parsee coolies, following the traditions of the Towers of Silence in Bombay, left the bodies of their dead out in the open to be picked clean by the vultures. But the lions of Tsavo ate them first, developed a keen taste for human flesh and devoured twenty-eight railway workers before being shot by Patterson. These experiences, and the mutiny of the coolies who nearly murdered him during the crisis, inspired his book *Man-Eaters of Tsavo* (1907).[16]

In March 1908 Patterson left Nairobi on safari with a Mr. and Mrs. Audley James Blyth. Son of the first Baron Blyth and late lieutenant of the Essex Yeomanry, he was born in 1874 and married Ethel Jane Brunner in 1903. The first official word of the tragedy was sent in a dispatch of May 7, 1908, from Lieutenant Colonel Sir J. Hayes Sadler, governor of the East Africa Protectorate: "Patterson informs me that Blyth died on the morning of the 21st March at Laisamis [225 miles north of Nairobi], 35 miles [south] from Marsabit, where he accidentally shot himself in the head with a revolver. Death immediate. He had been ill for two days. Patterson had been with him all night. Accident occurred early in the morning whilst temporarily alone. Patterson returned very ill. . . . Mrs. Blyth comes today. Leaves for England on *Herzog*."

The following day, in a long letter to the governor, Patterson gave his version of the events. He stated that Blyth—"an old friend of mine, brother officer and our wives were intimate"—accidentally shot himself while suffering from fever and sunstroke, that Mrs. Blyth did not see the body, that he returned to Nairobi as quickly as possible and that Mrs. Blyth, who was devoted to her husband, "was quite heart broken by the sad occurrence."[17]

Patterson, with considerable cheek, gave substantially the same account of the safari in his book *In the Grip of the Nyika,* published in November 1909. He maintained in the Preface that three Europeans set out on the expedition, "but, alas! only two got back, the *nyika* [African wilderness] having claimed the third," and that he himself suffered from fever and dysentery while writing the volume. Patterson described how "Mr. and Mrs. B." came to accompany him on the journey into the unknown country in northern Kenya; how B. fell ill and developed an abscess on his instep; how the natives were impressed by Mrs. B.'s very long hair, "which she wore in a single plait down her back"; how Mrs. B. shot lion, elephant, rhino, buffalo, oryx, antelope, gazelle, impala and wart hog; how Mr. B. shot himself and was buried, while Mrs. B., "with her usual pluck, tried to bear up under the terrible blow with what fortitude she could command"; how Patterson, after burning B.'s tent ("I did not wish painful memories to be recalled"), quelled the native mutiny and pressed north to continue the government survey; how Mrs. B. moved into his discreetly partitioned tent and nursed him through his illness. Patterson prints photographs of Mr. B. carried uneasily by African bearers and of Mrs. B. triumphant upon a dead rhino. He also mentions that she has a small son in England.[18]

The provincial commissioner, in a letter to the governor of July 8, 1908, soon began to pick holes in Patterson's testimony: "The fact of his being able to go after buffalo appeared to me to contradict his statement that he was suffering acutely from diarrhoea. . . . I was convinced that Colonel Patterson was not so seriously ill as he would have us suppose. . . . It was remarked that Colonel Patterson told [friends] that he was going to take Mrs. Blyth to England."[19] Since his letter no longer seemed credible, the governor asked Patterson to furnish a full explanation of his conduct.

The governor, determined to reach the bottom of this "ugly business," received some startling revelations from his zealous subordinate. On February 5, 1909, nearly a year after Blyth's death, the provincial commissioner finally managed to track down the Africans on the ill-fated expedition. The native witnesses revealed that there were only three Europeans on the safari; that Mrs. Blyth had also shot big game; that Patterson and Blyth had quarreled about an elephant they both had killed; that Mrs. Blyth was in the tent with her husband when the shot was fired; that after the suicide shot "Colonel Patterson was crying out, my friend, my friend, so I went away quickly"; that Patterson told the Africans to bury Blyth deep in the ground; that he had burned all

Blyth's clothes and papers; that after the suicide Patterson and Mrs. Blyth had continued north to Marsabit instead of immediately turning south to Nairobi.

Most significantly, the Africans contradicted Patterson's account of Blyth's death and revealed that the white hunter had sexual relations with the disaffected wife:

> Colonel Patterson and the other European had a big quarrel but eventually made it up by shaking hands. . . . When [Blyth] returned he was taken ill and was like one who was mad. We poured cold water on his head and he gradually got better. We think the lady must have been afraid of him because she went and slept in Colonel Patterson's tent. . . .
>
> We saw the lady leave the sick man's tent and go to Colonel Patterson's tent and she stayed there all night. In the morning . . . [she] went back to her husband's tent and directly she entered we heard a shot and the lady came running out and we ran to the tent and found that the European had shot himself in the mouth and the bullet had come out near his ear. . . . After the death of the European, Colonel Patterson and the lady occupied one tent.[20]

The Africans' testimony was forwarded by the governor to the colonial secretary, Lord Crewe. Though it conclusively proved that Patterson was deeply implicated in Blyth's death, Crewe decided to exonerate rather than condemn him, in return for his resignation. Crewe wanted to protect the family of one of the members of the House of Lords and to prevent a scandal in East Africa. He was unable to bring criminal charges against Patterson (who was morally but not legally responsible for Blyth's death) and was unwilling to use the testimony of Africans to expose Mrs. Blyth's adultery. Patterson resigned on March 30, two days before Crewe's speech in the House of Lords, which was a perfect manifestation of sexual hypocrisy and class interest.

In his speech—reported in the London *Times* of April 2, 1909, and the *East African Standard* (Mombasa) of May 8, 1909—Lord Crewe provided details of the tragic expedition that provoked the cruel behavior of the colonel toward the husband who killed himself, but he was mendacious about Patterson's relations with the Blyths and deliberately vague about the cause of the gunshot:

> Last summer Colonel Patterson returned invalided from his post, and since that time rumours of a damaging and even of a sinister character

have been prevalent regarding him, not merely in East Africa, but, as I have been told, they have reached England. . . . The rumours to which I have alluded arose to a certain extent out of the unfortunate death of Mr. Blyth, the son of a member of [the House of Lords]. . . . Colonel Patterson was going on duty with a safari of porters to the northern game reserve, and he was permitted by his superior officer to take with him Mr. Blyth and his safari also. Mr. Blyth died in the course of this expedition, died by a revolver-shot wound, undoubtedly inflicted by himself, either by accident or in a fit of delirium consequent upon a severe attack of fever from which he suffered throughout the journey. . . . Rumours concerning Colonel Patterson arose, in some cases absolutely taking the form that he had responsibility for Mr. Blyth's death, owing to some disputes which were supposed to have taken place. At any rate he was accused of having shown distinct inhumanity toward Mr. Blyth.

Well, my lords, I have examined all the documents relating to the case and I can assure your lordships that for these reports there is no foundation whatever. There was no tinge of evidence—quite the contrary indeed—to connect Colonel Patterson in any way with the cause of Mr. Blyth's death. . . . Colonel Patterson throughout treated Mr. Blyth with nothing but kindness and humanity during the journey. . . . The best proof I can give to the House that we did not consider Colonel Patterson unworthy of continuing in His Majesty's service is that I sanctioned his return to East Africa. But his health is broken down to a very great extent and this has prevented his return.

Sadler's note of March 11, 1909, in contrast to Crewe's misrepresentations, expressed the real sentiments of the government and settlers in Kenya: "Would it not be better to conclude the whole matter by telling Colonel Patterson that his services are no longer required. His return to East Africa would, I am assured, result in an outburst in the Press and elsewhere causing a scandal of the most acute description. On his own show his conduct was unbecoming an official in our service."[21]

Hemingway was interested in Colonel Patterson—hunter, hero, author, lover—and in the unsolved mystery of Blyth's death, for the African setting, the predatory woman and the test of male courage were closely related to his personal life and artistic themes. Blyth's violent death inevitably reminded Hemingway of his father's suicide; and like Blyth, he would later attempt to punish his wife by blowing his brains out.

Hemingway believed that fiction must be based on actual experience. The knowledgeable writer, he felt, always begins with reality but produces something more significant than the original facts. In "Monologue to the Maestro" (1935) he told a disciple: "Good writing is true writing. If a man is making a story up it will be true in proportion to the amount of knowledge of life that he has and how conscientious he is; so that when he makes something up it is as it would truly be." In his Introduction to *Men at War* (1942) he emphasized: "A writer's job is to tell the truth. His standard of fidelity to the truth should be so high that his invention, out of his experience, should produce a truer account than anything factual can be."[22] And in a letter of 1957 he defined literature as inventing truly from honestly acquired experience so that what you invent is truer than what you remember.[23]

The Patterson case, which had a great many suggestive details but few firm conclusions, was a Jamesian "germ" that inspired Hemingway's imagination but left him free to delineate the traits of his characters. It had great intrinsic interest, was just as good a story as "Francis Macomber" and is significant not only for the way it influenced Hemingway but also for the way he changed it. Hemingway kept the African setting, the love triangle, the tough characters of the wife and the hunter, and their callousness toward the husband. In both stories the wife goes to the tent of the hunter, who wonders if the husband will shoot him. The tone of Macomber's conversation with Margot when she comes back from Wilson's bed is perfectly appropriate to Mrs. Blyth's situation:

> "You think that I'll take anything."
> "I know you will, sweet."
> "Well, I won't."
> "Please, darling, let's not talk. I'm so very sleepy."
> "There wasn't going to be any of that. You promised there wouldn't be."
> "Well, there is now," she said sweetly.

Hemingway changed the originals into Americans, though his first two fictional heroines—Brett Ashley and Catherine Barkley—were British. He turned the hunter into a hero; for Wilson's only vice is sleeping with the wife—a prerogative of his job: "What does he think I am, a bloody plaster saint? Let him keep her where she belongs. It's his own fault."[24] The victim of the story does not shoot himself, he is murdered. Cuckoldry, which makes Blyth lose courage, helps Macomber to regain it. His wife's infidelity leads directly to his short happy life—between shooting the charging buffalo and being shot by Margot —after he violates and then redeems the unwritten but omnipotent hunting code. Hemingway's comment in a little-known interview conclusively resolves the ambiguous ending of the story: "Francis' wife hates him because he's a coward. But when he gets his guts back, she fears him so much she has to kill him—shoots him in the back of the head."[25]

The real villain in Hemingway's story is Margot Macomber. He transforms the Patterson affair into a more modern and bitter tale of a predatory (rather than a passive) female who is both betrayer and murderer, and emphasizes (as in "Fathers and Sons") the connection between shooting and sex. When Macomber refuses to follow the wounded lion into the bush, Wilson "suddenly felt as though he had opened the wrong door in a hotel and seen something shameful."[26] A reconstruction of the betrayal, cowardice and corruption in the Patterson case shows how Hemingway used these motifs to recreate the great Conradian theme of moral failure and recovery of self-esteem.

While Hemingway was writing "Francis Macomber" an incident in his own life provided additional material for the story. Hemingway, thin-skinned and quick-tempered, was famous for brawling. His most notorious fight took place with Wallace Stevens, who weighed 225 pounds but was twenty years older than Hemingway. The poet, while drunk, made Ursula Hemingway cry at a Key West cocktail party by insulting her brother and "telling her forcefully what a sap [he] was, no man." According to Matthew Josephson, who spoke to several eyewitnesses, Stevens was the belligerent one. When they met, he exclaimed: " 'You think you're Ernest Hemingway?' then challenged him to put up his hands. Stevens was of good height and he had been an amateur boxer, but he was nearly sixty and very tight. Ernest, usually pugnacious, this time urged the older man to go away and sober up. But Stevens threw a punch at him; and there followed a bare-knuckled fight on the dock in which Stevens put up a good show of resistance, but was badly battered."[27] Hemingway pursued the poet, "knocked all of him down several times and gave him a good beating,"[28] before Stevens broke his hand in two places by hitting the novelist on the jaw. Stevens, who had disturbed the idea of order at Key West, emerged from the fray with a black eye and bruised face, and was seen the next day wearing dark glasses to conceal the damage.

Though Hemingway gleefully revealed the story to Sara Murphy, he warned her that Stevens was anxious to protect his reputation as a Hartford business executive: "you mustn't tell this to anybody . . . because he is very worried about his respectable insurance standing and I have promised not to tell anybody and the official story is that Mr. Stevens fell down a stairs."[29] Hemingway added that Pauline, who usually hated his fights, was delighted; that he eventually shook hands and made it up with the poet. Stevens apparently held no grudge and later praised Hemingway's art in his letters: "Some one told me the other day that Ernest Hemingway was writing poetry. I think it likely he will write the kind of poetry in which the consciousness of reality will produce an extraordinary effect. It may be that he will limit himself to the mere sensation. No one seems to be more addicted to épatant [shocking] (but not in any meretricious sense)."[30]

The fight took place on February 19, 1936, and "Francis Macomber" was completed on April 19. Macomber compounds his cowardly flight from the lion by breaking the code of gentlemanly behavior and asking the hunter Wilson:

> "It doesn't have to go any further, does it? I mean no one will hear about it, will they?"
> "You mean will I tell it at the Mathaiga Club?" Wilson looked at him now coldly. He had not expected this. So he's a bloody four-letter man as well as a bloody coward, he thought. . . . "It's supposed to be bad form to ask us not to talk."

Macomber's lapse from the code of courage brings out the predatory nature of his wife, Margot, who is delighted by the revelation that her husband is "no man" and by the opportunity to humiliate him by sleeping with Wilson. When Macomber redeems his honor by killing the charging buffalo, he wrests the sexual power from Margot and makes it up with Wilson. But Margot exacts revenge on both men. When she sarcastically remarks: "I didn't know you were allowed to shoot [animals] from cars. . . . I mean chase them from cars," Wilson responds:

> "Wouldn't mention it to anyone though. It's illegal if that's what you mean." . . .
> "What would happen if they heard about it in Nairobi?"
> "I'd lose my licence for one thing. Other unpleasantnesses. . . . I'd be out of business."[31]

When the elated and sexually restored Macomber goes after the wounded buffalo, Margot fears he will leave her and shoots him in the skull from the car. At the end of the story, the balance of power shifts finally to Wilson, who repeats: " 'There will be a certain amount of unpleasantness [in Nairobi],' " and now "has something on her" as she once had on Macomber.

Hemingway's use of the Stevens incident—another transformation of reality into fiction—reaffirms his belief that exposing oneself to violence tests one's moral code. It also shows the close correspondence of physical courage and moral strength in both his life and his art. Hemingway beat Stevens because the poet had insulted his manhood (as Margot did Macomber's). And he despised the poet, who exhibited bad form by worrying more about his reputation than his physical prowess and by asking Hemingway not to tell anyone about his shameful behavior (as Macomber did by asking Wilson to keep silent about his cowardice). Though Hemingway kept his promise to say nothing publicly about the fight, he retained his moral stranglehold on Stevens by telling the story to Sara Murphy and hinting at it to Dos Passos. In a similar fashion, Margot threatened to expose the moral faults of Macomber and Wilson, and Wilson revenged himself by threatening to expose her murder of Macomber. Stevens' request "not to tell anybody" becomes a dominant motif in the story and binds all three characters in a net of corruption.

V

"The Snows of Kilimanjaro," like "Francis Macomber," successfully blends historical and literary material with personal experience to produce fictional characters that are much more subtle and substantial than the complacent, one-dimensional self-portrait of *Green Hills of Africa*. Tolstoy and Scott Fitzgerald contributed to the genesis of "The Snows of Kilimanjaro" as Patterson and Wallace Stevens did to "Francis Macomber."

Hemingway matched his own short story against Tolstoy's finest work in that genre when he consciously imitated and transformed "The Death of Ivan Ilych" (1886) in "The Snows of Kilimanjaro" (1936). In both stories the heroes are dying in early middle age of a smelly disease, which has trivial origins (a knock on the side, a scratch from a thorn) and symbolizes the corruption of their personal and professional lives.

Both stories employ a suffocating symbol (the black sack and the hyena) to represent encroaching death. Both Ivan and Harry betrayed themselves for security, comfort and material success. Both never loved and now hate their wives, who encouraged their corruption and remain attached to the values their husbands have renounced. Both vacillate between self-loathing and self-pity. Both temporarily escape from their present torments by recalling happy memories (of childhood and early manhood) when they still possessed innocence and a sense of morality. As disease sharpens their insight both heroes reject the familiar lies and comforting deceptions about their recovery, suddenly accept the awful fact that they are going to die and by doing so lose their fear of death. The dreadful confrontation with mortality forces them to repudiate their past—which has been nothing more than a living death—and allows them to gain, in their final moments, spiritual conversion and self-redemption. In Tolstoy's tale Hemingway recognized a similar temperament and a literary form that enabled him to recreate in the modern tradition his own story of revelation and redemption.

Both Tolstoy and Hemingway use disease and dying realistically and symbolically. Both heroes feel responsible for and guilty about their sickness and try to blame their wives, who resent the hostility of the dying. Both heroes connect their decay and destruction to their spiritual states. But disease and morality are not scientifically related: bacteria and virus are impartial, good and evil men equally subject to death. Hemingway adapts the subject of Tolstoy's moral fable—the death of the central character, his reflections on the past, his insights while dying—to the poignant situation of his typical hero, who betrayed his own stoical code and is condemned by his own moral weakness. The tragedy expressed in Tolstoy's morbid imagery and claustrophobic interiors is relieved by Ivan's joyful encounter with God. Hemingway's natural imagery and vital description of the Masai country—"This was a pleasant camp under big trees against a hill, with good water, and close by, a nearly dry water hole where sand grouse flighted in the mornings"[32]—intensify Harry's tragic sense of waste and final loss of life. Hemingway removes Tolstoy's story from the Christian context, stresses self-fulfillment rather than faith in God, emphasizes the individual rather than the social background, and gives it a bitter modern tone, but he retains the same redemptive pattern and the same exemplary mode.

Hemingway said the idea for "The Snows of Kilimanjaro"—for the theme of corruption by drink, women and money—came after a rich woman (possibly Jane Mason) had offered to pay for another safari to Africa. Hemingway refused the offer—as he had refused Jim Gamble's invitation to live in Italy for a year after the war—and started "to think what would happen to a character like me whose defects I know, if I had accepted that offer." The story (like *A Moveable Feast*) is full of nostalgia for the past, when he was poor and beginning to establish his reputation as a writer. Though written at the height of his worldly success, it reveals that the process of moral corruption (symbolized by the smelly gangrene) had already begun. And it predicts his failure as a writer and his spiritual death: "Each day of not writing, of comfort, of being that which he despised, dulled his ability and softened his will to work."[33]

Though Hemingway wrote directly about himself in "The Snows of Kilimanjaro," he also made a cruel attack, in the *Esquire* version of the story, on Scott Fitzgerald. He was, for Hemingway, a frightening example of a good writer who had betrayed his talent and been destroyed by literary success. The hostile reference to Fitzgerald originated in a sharp exchange between Hemingway and the Irish writer Mary Colum when they were dining in New York with Max Perkins in 1936. After Hemingway declared: "I am getting to know the rich," Mary Colum wittily replied: "The only difference between the rich and other people is that the rich have more money." Hemingway avenged himself by appropriating the remark and victimizing Fitzgerald when he was particularly vulnerable: "He remembered poor Scott Fitzgerald and his romantic awe of [the rich] and how he had started a story once that began, 'The very rich are different from you and me.' And how some one had said to Scott, Yes, they have more money. But that was not humorous to Scott. He thought they were a special glamorous race and when he found they weren't it wrecked him just as much as any other thing that wrecked him."[34] (Scott's name was later changed to Julian.)

Though Hemingway had a luxurious house, a boat and his wife's private fortune which paid for his African safari, he felt he could define himself in opposition to the very rich who lived on unearned income because he wrote for a living and made enough money to support himself. He justified the passage in his story by stating that Fitzgerald's revelation of his disastrous personal life in "The Crack-Up" articles (which had also appeared in *Esquire* in 1936) left him open to the kind of public lesson that Hemingway had previously given to Sherwood

Anderson. Though Hemingway made a similar but more subtle personal confession in "The Snows of Kilimanjaro," he convinced himself that the brutal truth of the story would give Fitzgerald a salutary jolt and shake him out of his disgraceful self-pity. Scott was so disturbed by this story that he attempted suicide, but vomited from an overdose of morphine.

A passage mercifully deleted from *To Have and Have Not,* which also deals with the corruption of the rich, summarizes Hemingway's view of Fitzgerald's weaknesses and anticipates the more extensive critique of Scott's character in *A Moveable Feast.* Hemingway said that Scott wrote too much when he was very young, lacked good sense and had a great deal of bad luck that was not his fault. He had charm and talent, but no brains, was romantic about money and youth, and went directly from youth to senility without passing through manhood. He thought old age came right after youth—and for him it did. If he gave up self-pity, he still might pull himself together.[35]

Hemingway's indictment in *A Moveable Feast* is even more crushing, despite his almost affectionate description of their ludicrous car trip from Lyon to Paris. In that posthumous time bomb he portrays Fitzgerald as hostile to the French, naive and gauche, sexually and psychologically inexperienced, unreliable and irresponsible, troublesome and irritating, hypochondriac and insecure, dependent upon and dominated by Zelda, a complacent and self-confessed cuckold, an alcoholic, an artistic whore and a destroyer of his own talent. Hemingway's emphasis on the weak, girlish, feminine aspects of Scott's character subtly yet cruelly confirms Zelda's accusations of sexual inadequacy.

In 1940, when Hemingway was at the height of his reputation and Fitzgerald at the nadir of his, he sent a copy of *For Whom the Bell Tolls* inscribed: "To Scott with affection and esteem," which expressed his feelings at the time they first met. Though Fitzgerald was always embarrassed by the contrast between Hemingway's success and his own "authoritative" failure, his analysis of his friend was both perceptive and prophetic: "He is quite as nervously broken down as I am but it manifests itself in different ways. His inclination is toward megalomania and mine toward melancholy."[36]

Pauline was also attacked in Hemingway's story and transformed from the sympathetic companion of *Green Hills of Africa* to the repulsive woman of "The Snows of Kilimanjaro." Harry thinks Helen is the instrument of his corruption and self-betrayal, and connects her to

Fitzgerald's infatuation with the very rich, whom Scott describes as soft and cynical. But it is actually the gangrenous Harry—not the hard-boiled Helen—who manifests these traits. His excessive comfort has "softened his will" and he becomes defensively cynical when confronted with the truth about his life.

The ironic theme of "The Snows of Kilimanjaro" is that the dying Harry "would never write the things that he had saved to write until he knew enough to write them well."[37] Harry's mental flashbacks contrast his potential with his tragic failure, connect the image of snow with the theme of death, portray a truthful natural life and the enjoyment of pleasures that were not bought by money but earned by war. The flashbacks also reveal that the threat of death has concentrated Harry's mind, that he had a great and genuine talent, and that he could have fulfilled his promise and ensured his salvation (for Hemingway equates artistic with moral effort) if he had only been able to record the vivid memories that show him at the very height of his powers.

14

In the Caribbean
1934–1936

> The lights in the fishing boats at anchor there,
> As the night descended, tilting in the air,
> Mastered the night and portioned out the sea.
>
> STEVENS, "The Idea of Order at Key West"

I

Hemingway, passionate for fishing and outdoor life, soon acquired his own boat in Key West. It was a visible sign of his wealth and success—functional rather than glamorous—which gave him pleasure and made him independent. It provided an almost daily diversion from writing and allowed him to compete with other big-game fishermen in the Gulf Stream.

The *Pilar,* named after the patron saint of Zaragoza, was custom built and delivered to Miami in May 1934. It was thirty-eight feet long, had a twelve-foot beam, drew three and a half feet of water; had a black hull, green roof and varnished mahogany cockpit. The two engines, of seventy-five and forty horsepower, could do sixteen knots. The boat held three hundred gallons of gas, had a cruising range of five hundred miles and slept six in the cabin. It cost $7,500, of which $3,000 was advanced by Arnold Gingrich as payment for articles that Hemingway promised to write for *Esquire* during the next few years. The first mate was a fisherman, Carlos Gutiérrez, born in Cuba in 1883, whom Hemingway had met in the Dry Tortugas (off Key West) and who first told him about the great marlin of the Gulf Stream.

Carlos was hired away while Hemingway was reporting the Spanish War and replaced in 1938 by Gregorio Fuentes, a maritime version of Toby Bruce and a model for Santiago in *The Old Man and the Sea.*

280

Hemingway met Gregorio, who was born in Lanzarote in the Canary Islands in 1888, when they were storm-bound in the Dry Tortugas in 1930, and was impressed by his clean ship as well as by his seamanship. Mario Menocal, Jr., described Gregorio as "a supremely capable fishing-boat captain, and, incidentally, a marvellous cook. A strong character who was perfectly capable of chewing Ernest out when the latter misbehaved [by issuing drunken orders while at sea]. Ernest respected and paid attention to him. . . . He was always complaining that Ernest worked him too hard and paid him too little (we considered that both complaints were justified). . . . Ernest required him to hand back half the proceeds from catches of the *Pilar.*"[1]

Hemingway immediately invited all his friends to go fishing on the new boat. MacLeish came down to Key West in May and they had the sort of serious quarrel that Archie had feared would take place if he went on the African safari. Hemingway had dedicated his last book, *Winner Take Nothing* (1933), to MacLeish. But he also criticized his friend for involving himself in political and economic affairs (Hemingway was criticized for his *lack* of involvement in contemporary issues) and for "whoring" at *Fortune* magazine (MacLeish could not support his family by his poetry and had to seek employment in journalism). Like Fitzgerald and Dos Passos, MacLeish disliked Hemingway's deliberate insensitivity and belligerent egoism, which made him a difficult companion.

MacLeish tended to minimize their hostility. He later explained that the adolescent but bitter quarrel began on the *Pilar*—where Hemingway tended to be domineering rather than relaxed—when Hemingway expressed his aggression toward MacLeish by pointlessly killing some birds:

> It was a childish business. It was simply that we'd been together too long out in the Gulf Stream, fishing, and anything we said to each other infuriated us. . . . Ernest took to shooting terns, taking one with one barrel and the grieving mate with the other. He was fed up with the world and I was fed up with him. It was a simple conflict of overexposure. . . .
>
>   When we got to his house—Ernest and me—we began taking it out on each other. Sample: I told him somebody ought to prick his balloon. He told me my prick wasn't big enough. Result—no dinner—and he drove me home and we had a rather anguishing conversation.[2]

Writing to the more mature and manly Waldo Peirce at the end of May, Hemingway condemned MacLeish, with the same terms he had used to describe Fitzgerald, as "righteous, fussy, and a bloody bore. Strange mixture of puerility and senility."[3] But once his anger had subsided, Hemingway usually became conciliatory. He valued Mac-Leish's friendship and sensed he had behaved badly. In the mid-thirties and again in the early forties, he sent Archie a series of apologetic letters which condemned, with astonishing frankness and insight, his own boastful, lying, obscene, boring, overbearing, ill-tempered, touchy, vindictive and self-righteous character. He was aware that he had talked too much, had retailed dubious recollections and dull obscenities. He admitted that when he was in a bad mood, he could be a bossy and irritating son of a bitch; that he quickly, frequently and unjustly took offense:

> I will promise absolutely not to be self righteous, no-good and bastardly as in my great 37–38 epoch when [I] alienated all my friends (who I miss like hell) (not to mention my sonofabitching epoch of 1934 when was even worse). . . . I was *awful* for a whole period of years. Too awful for anybody to stand. . . . That's one reason why I would like you to come down to see how good, non-righteous, non-bragging, non-boasting, almost non-chicken-shit I have become.[4]

MacLeish (who did not hold grudges as Hemingway did) was appeased, and they resumed their correspondence and collaborated on the Loyalist film *The Spanish Earth*. But MacLeish became permanently wary of him and never felt the same warmth for Hemingway after May 1934.

Leicester Hemingway, only two years old when Ernest left Oak Park for the *Kansas City Star* in the fall of 1917, had built a small boat in Alabama and wrecked it on the way to Key West in the spring of 1934. Leicester had the same square-jawed good looks as his brother, but inherited Grace's blond hair and blue eyes. Hemingway said he disliked Leicester, who always reminded him of his mother; he was embarrassed by his brother's odd mixture of enthusiasm and ineptitude and by the consistent failure of all his endeavors. Leicester was a kind and ineffectual youth who spent his entire life attempting to imitate Hemingway as tough guy, sportsman, myth-maker and writer. He would constantly try to impress his older brother, pathetically fail to do so and be crushed by Hemingway's caustic comments. Forgetting his own youthful fantasies about his engagement to Mae Marsh, which his parents had taken literally, Ernest was contemptuous about Leicester's legends and wrote: "Will you, for Christ's sake, stop writing those wild letters to your mother? You want to scare her to death with a bunch of wild exaggerations? . . . Here's something about a fucking boa constrictor you supposedly fought with. Will you please stop this kind of crap before you give the woman a heart attack." Leicester's first wife, Patricia, believed that his childish need to be the center of attention led him into unwise competition with his older brother and that Ernest's mesmeric hold

> was as much Les' fault as his. I wanted Les to be his own person. Les idolized him and tried to emulate him. Unfortunately never quite achieving the same results as Ernest. As far as I could see Ernest liked being the "top" Hemingway and tried to keep Les from joining him. Les hung on his every word, and felt a glow of happiness whenever Ernest acknowledged that he even existed, or wrote to, talked to or helped him financially. Ernest was "The Greatest" in Les' eyes. He never got over that.[5]

From July to October Hemingway worked on *Green Hills of Africa*, fished in Cuba and saw Jane Mason. He also acquired an undistinguished disciple when young Arnold Samuelson hitchhiked from Minnesota to sit at his feet and was taken on as cabin boy. Samuelson, supposedly a skilled violinist, was nicknamed Maestro; but when Hemingway heard him play he shortened his name to Mice. Since Samuelson was also hopeless on the *Pilar*, Hemingway thought he might have a future as an author; and he immortalized him in his essay on the techniques of writing, "Monologue to the Maestro," published in *Esquire* in October 1935.

Hemingway had first met the Spanish revolutionary and painter Luis Quintanilla in Montparnasse in 1922. Quintanilla said: "from the first moment he showed a great curiosity to know about Spain and a desire to learn Spanish by ear." Hemingway kept in touch with him, seeing him in Madrid in 1931 and 1933. In November 1934 Quintanilla was arrested, jailed and charged with serving on the revolutionary committee in Madrid and inspiring the October riots that protested against the inclusion of the Spanish Catholic Party in the Republican government. When Hemingway heard that his friend was threatened with a sixteen-year sentence, he tried to get him out of prison by writing to the President of Spain, protesting his incarceration and organizing, in December, an exhibition of his work at the Pierre Matisse Gallery in New York. Hemingway paid for the pulling of the prints and the expenses of the show, bought a number of the etchings and wrote an Introduction to the catalogue. The Introduction drew on his experience with political violence and warfare, contained one of the finest passages in his works, and ended with a short sketch that recalled the atrocities in the stark vignettes of *in our time*. Hemingway contrasted Quintanilla, an artist in action, to

> all those who write the word and never have been shot nor shot at; who never have stored arms nor filled a bomb, nor have discovered arms nor had a bomb burst among them; who never have gone hungry in a general strike, nor have manned streetcars when the tracks are dynamited; who never have sought cover in a street trying to get their heads behind a gutter; who never have seen a woman shot in the head, in the breast or in the buttocks; who never have seen an old man with the top of his head off; who never have walked with their hands up; who never have shot a horse or seen hooves smash a head; who never have sat [on] a horse and been shot at or stoned; who never have been cracked on the head with a club nor have thrown a brick; who never have seen a scab's forearms broken with a crow-bar, or an agitator filled up with compressed air with an air hose; who . . . have never moved a load of arms at night in a big city; nor standing, seeing it moved, knowing what it was and afraid to denounce it because they did not want to die later; nor (let's end it, it could go on too long) stood on a roof trying to urinate on their hands to wash off the black in the fork between finger and thumb from the back-spit of a Thompson gun, the gun thrown in a cistern and the troops coming up the stairs.[6]

Hemingway and Dos Passos eventually secured the release of Quintanilla, who became a Loyalist general during the Spanish War.

II

The *Pilar* enabled Hemingway to extend the range of his fishing from Key West to the milieu of wealthy yachtsmen. In April 1935 he discovered the narrow tropical island of Bimini, 220 miles northeast of Key West and 45 east of Miami, in the British West Indies. Coconut trees, clapboard houses and a few half-empty hotels lined the white beach, beyond which stretched the green of the South Island. Two-thirds of the people were black and worked as sponge fishermen on the Great Bahama Bank or in the straw market. Dos Passos, who came along for the ride if not for the action, emphasized the natural shabbiness that appealed to Hemingway: "There was a wharf and some native shacks under the coconut palms and a store that had some kind of barroom attached, where we drank rum in the evenings, and a magnificent broad beach on the Gulf Stream side. There was an official residency and a couple of sunbeaten bungalows screened against the sandflies up on the dunes."[7] In 1935 Hemingway met Mike Lerner, who owned a chain of clothing shops in New York, was a keen sportsman and lent Hemingway his house on top of Bimini hill to use while fishing off the island.

In Bimini that season Hemingway also met the wealthy sportsman and playboy Tommy Shevlin, whose family's great lumber interests in the Pacific Northwest obviated his need to work. Shevlin was born in 1914 and went to the Hill School; but he resisted family pressure to attend Yale, where his father had been an All-American football player and a coach. Tall, thin, athletic, handsome, charming, urbane, Tommy built the first house on Cat Cay; he was a good fisherman and shot, a golfer, polo player and big-game hunter. Hemingway liked socialite athletes (like Shevlin, Winston Guest and George Plimpton) who combined wealth and sporting skill, and in September 1936 lured Tommy away from summer idleness in Southampton to hunt grizzly bears in Wyoming. Hemingway, who demanded praise and hated criticism, gave Tommy the manuscript of *To Have and Have Not* to read and became angry when he dared to express a negative opinion. Tommy was stationed in Havana with the Coast Guard during World War Two, spent his second honeymoon aboard the *Pilar* and in 1947 went hunting in Africa with Philip Percival.[8]

Hemingway's sporting activities led to a regular recurrence of spectacular accidents and illness. He had an infection and blood poisoning in his right index finger when writing *Green Hills of Africa* in 1934; an attack of amoebic dysentery in January 1935; and self-inflicted but unintentional bullet wounds while sailing to Bimini with John and Katy Dos Passos on April 7, 1935 (the month he quarreled with Lawrence Kubie). Dos Passos described the freak yet entirely characteristic accident (Hemingway was terribly fond of shooting sharks) in a letter to Patrick, the invalid son of Gerald and Sara Murphy:

Ernest had out his small colt automatic (.22) and was just going to finish the shark off with a final shot to get his hooks and leaders back when the shark went into a tremendous spiral convulsion and broke the pole of the gaff. The broken piece hit the pistol which went off. We didn't hear the shot on account of the great snapping noise the gaff made breaking. The bullet (a softnosed lead bullet) hit the brass edging of the boat's rail and splattered into both calves of Ernest's legs. Fortunately the wounds were not very bad.

They poured iodine into the wounds and, with Katy in a rage over Hemingway's buccaneering carelessness, turned back to find a doctor in Key West. Hemingway made literary use of this mishap in his essay "On Being Shot Again" (*Esquire,* June 1935), where he stoically wrote: "There was no pain and no discomfort; only a small hole about three inches below the knee-cap, another ragged hole bigger than your thumb, and a number of small lacerations on the calves of both legs."[9]

About a year later, in February 1936, Hemingway kicked a locked gate at his Key West house and broke his right toe. Though he was not hurt during four trips to the Spanish War, he sustained a few more injuries on the home front. He stuck his foot through a mirror while trying to show a friend's son how to dropkick at the Waldorf in the late thirties. He scratched the pupil of his bad left eye in August 1938, and had the first of many severe liver complaints that December.

In order to keep what was left of him in shape, get plenty of sparring partners, arouse some sporting interest and give the local men a chance to earn money, Hemingway offered to take on all boxing challengers in Bimini and pay a prize to anyone who could stand against him for three rounds. Harry Sylvester, a Notre Dame athlete who met Hemingway in 1936 and often sparred with him in friendly fights, agreed with Gregory's estimate: "Even allowing for his war wounds, Hemingway was slow on his feet. But he was tremendously strong, one of the strongest men I ever knew, and could maul you if you let him get too close and hit you. You had to move very fast with him and stay well out of his way."

The crowd supported him against contenders from other islands and screamed: "Kill him, Mr. Ernest, kill him. Send that nigger back to Nassau on ice."[10] But Hemingway talked tougher than he actually was. Mario Menocal, Sr., doubted Carlos Baker's account (based on an unreliable letter from Hemingway to Buck Lanham) of Hemingway "cooling" a "big Negro named Willard Saunders, who . . . was reputed to be able to carry a piano on his head." According to Menocal: "Willie was over 60 years old. He was not very tall. I would say about 5′8″.... He couldn't carry this television set. He was an old man."[11]

Hemingway, who considered himself the greatest contemporary American writer, became increasingly boastful and belligerent—emphasizing his toughness and sporting skills—during the sustained critical attack on his books from *Death in the Afternoon* (1932) to *The Fifth Column* (1938). He admitted he was afraid of slithery snakes in Africa and slippery mountain ledges in Wyoming, but anyone foolish enough to challenge or provoke him—as Wallace Stevens did—was brutally punished. In May 1935 he knocked out a magazine publisher, Joe Knapp; and in January 1939 beat up a lawyer in the Stork Club.

Hemingway begged his literary friends to visit him and often complained that he had no one to talk to while living between the fashionable sporting set and the proletarian "four-letter folk." Marjorie Rawlings, author of *The Yearling*, lived in Florida and observed Hemingway's response to his fame, his audience and his critics. She also noted the deleterious effect of the very rich:

> Hemingway is among these people a great deal, and they like and admire him—his personality, his sporting prowess, and his literary prestige. It seems to be that unconsciously he must value their opinion. He must be afraid of laying bare before them the agony that tears the artist. ... They are the only people who would be pleased by the things in his work that distress all the rest of us.[12]

III

In *Green Hills of Africa* Hemingway made some caustic remarks about the idealism of the New Deal and the effect of the Depression in Key West: "Some sort of Y.M.C.A. show. Starry eyed bastards spending money that somebody will have to pay. Everybody in our town quit work to go on relief. Fishermen all turned carpenters. Reverse of the Bible."[13] But in September 1935 a natural disaster that struck the Keys deepened his social and political awareness, and inspired his great (but little-known) polemical work.

Though Key West seemed an idyllic place to live and work, it was particularly vulnerable to economic troubles and tropical storms. In

1934 Monroe County went bankrupt. The navy yard had been closed, the Mallory Steamship Line no longer serviced the island, the sea freight business had gone to New Orleans, the cigar rollers had left for Tampa, the sponge divers had moved up the coast and the local fishing industry was crippled. During the Depression, unemployment was even higher than in the rest of the country. Eighty percent of the population of 11,600 were on relief and the jobless war veterans who had built the Florida East Coast Railway across the Keys idled about in the shady streets.

On September 2, 1935, a tremendous hurricane, bringing two-hundred-mile-an-hour winds and seventeen-foot tidal waves, struck the war veterans of the Civilian Conservation Corps. They were living on Upper and Lower Matecumbe Keys, fifty miles northeast of Key West, and building the highway that linked the Keys to the Florida mainland. Hemingway rushed to the disaster in Bra Saunders' boat, brought in emergency medical supplies, helped volunteers collect the bloated and mutilated bodies of the drowned men. He knew the terrain, got there first, brought aid and took grisly photographs. He then presented an indictment of responsibility that was filled with savage indignation. Though officials in Washington had been warned that the violent storm was headed for the Keys, they did not attempt to evacuate the seven hundred veterans who were living in flimsy huts with their families, and hundreds of them were killed. On September 7 he wrote to Max Perkins:

> The veterans in those camps were practically murdered. The Florida East Coast had a train ready for nearly twenty-four hours to take them off the Keys. The people in charge are said to have wired Washington for orders. Washington wired Miami Weather Bureau which is said to have replied there was no danger and it would be a useless expense. The train did not start until the storm started. It [was blown off the tracks and] never got within thirty miles of the two lower camps. The people in charge of the veterans and the weather bureau can split the responsibility between them.

Hemingway, who had not seen so many bodies since the fighting on the Piave in July 1918, reported the disaster for the Communist *New Masses* on September 17, 1935. He vividly narrates his own elaborate preparations against the powerful force of the hurricane, which *missed* Key West, and then states: "The veterans had been sent there; they had no opportunity to leave, nor any protection against hurricanes; and they never had a chance for their lives. . . . Who sent nearly a thousand war veterans . . . to live in frame shacks on the Florida Keys in hurricane months? . . . Why were the men not evacuated . . . when it was known there was a possibility of a hurricane striking the Keys *and evacuation was their only possible protection?*"

Finally, he describes the deadly effects of the hurricane, in a passage which resembles "The Natural History of the Dead" and the battle carnage in the opening pages of "A Way You'll Never Be":

> The wind makes a noise like a locomotive passing, with a shriek on top of that, because the wind has a scream exactly as it has in books, and then the fill goes and the high water rolls you over and over and then, whatever it is, you get it and we find you, now of no importance, stinking in the mangroves. . . .
>
> You could find them face down and face up in the mangroves. The biggest bunch of the dead were in the tangled, always green but now brown, mangroves behind the tank cars and the water towers. They hung on there, in shelter, until the wind and the rising water carried them away. They didn't all let go at once but only when they could hold on no longer. Then further on you found them high in the trees where the water had swept them. You found them everywhere and in the sun all of them were beginning to be too big for their blue jeans and jackets that they could never fill when they were on the bum and hungry.[14]

The only consolation was that there were no buzzards to pick at the corpses, for the high wind had also killed the big-winged birds.

The Matecumbe hurricane, coming after the bankruptcy of Monroe County and the exhortations of Left-wing critics for him to interest himself in public issues, brought out one of Hemingway's most admirable characteristics: his generosity with money. Hemingway—who was soft-hearted and made an easy touch—justly claimed: "The only thing in life I've ever had any luck being decent about is money so am very splendid and punctilious about that." Even when poor in Paris, he was the only one who ever repaid his debts to Don Stewart. After his marriage to Pauline, he usually insisted on picking up everyone's check. He supported his mother and younger siblings after his father's death; often gave substantial sums to friends (Pound, Dos Passos, Margaret Anderson, Gustavo Durán, Solita Solano, Gustav Regler, Ned Calmer and many others); helped Leontes Valladares to open a bookstore in Key West in the early thirties; made generous contributions to the Loyalist cause during the Civil War; supported a number of Spanish refugees and Cuban hard-timers after he moved to Havana in 1940. He was also scrupulous (and rather nervous) about the payment of income tax and instructed his lawyer: "I do not want you ever to initiate any action for any refunds of taxes without first consulting me and presenting the matter fully to me so that I may judge whether it is an honorable and ethical action to take, not simply legally, but according to my own personal standards."[15] Though well-off, Hemingway was not materialistic; apart from his house, boat, paintings and guns, he owned little of value.

Though Hemingway was generous with money, he was critical of the Pfeiffers' fortune. At a time when gasoline was nine cents a gallon, a good meal could be had for a quarter and a double room with bath at the best hotel in Havana cost $2.50, Hemingway lived in much grander style than anyone else on the increasingly impoverished island of Key West. As conditions visibly deteriorated, he became more and more guilty about the luxurious life that was sustained by his royalties, Pauline's income and Uncle Gus' contributions. Pauline's father had held all his cotton in 1931 and made a great deal of money by selling it the following year. In December 1935, Uncle Gus offered to put up $800,000 to build a bullring in Cuba and introduce Spanish bullfighting —with large bulls that would be properly fought and killed. In the mid-1930s Hemingway ironically and irrationally began to blame Pauline, as Harry blamed Helen in "The Snows of Kilimanjaro," for the corrupting influence of her wealth.

IV

As Hemingway's sons grew older—in 1936 Jack was thirteen, Patrick eight and Gregory five—he became more aware of them and began to spend more time with them. In January 1936 he admitted to Mary Pfeiffer that he had been remote from his boys: "It is only this last year that I have gotten any sort of understanding or feeling about how anyone can feel about their children or what they can mean to them. . . . I was never a great child lover but these kids are really good company and are very funny and I think (though may be prejudiced) very smart." He took the boys out (separately) on fishing trips, taught them the skills he had learned from his father, and felt proud of their courage and sporting achievements. During the Cuban revolution of 1933, Hemingway seemed pleased when "the children said, 'Mother, can we go out in the afternoon to see the shooting?' They got so worked up about revolution we had to stop mentioning it. Bumby got so blood thirsty about Mr. M[achado] he had terrible dreams." And in *Islands in the Stream,* when Hudson asks his oldest son: " 'What are you thinking about, Schatz?' 'Fly-tying,' the boy would say, his face lighting instantly."[16] During a rare visit in 1939, Grace gave Patrick a new pocket knife and tried to instill some feeling of family tradition by saying it had belonged to his grandfather, but he immediately saw through the ruse and knew she had bought it in the local dime store.

The boys naturally craved their father's affection. Jack lived with Hadley and did not see him very often; Patrick, and especially Gregory, felt that Pauline had not given them sufficient attention and love during their early years. Both Harry Sylvester, who knew Hemingway in Key West in the late thirties, and Bill Davis, who first saw him with the boys in Sun Valley in the fall of 1941, thought he was an ideal father and had good relations with his sons. But as they became adolescents and then adults, their relations with him deteriorated. He wanted to dominate their lives (as he dominated everyone's), and would not allow them to find their own way and make their own mistakes. All three sons suffered from the Hemingway code—Jack the least, Gregory the most—as he put pressure on them to live up to his own standards and criticized them when they did not fulfill his expectations. As he acquired increasingly younger wives, he also entered into a dangerous (and perhaps not entirely conscious) sexual rivalry with his maturing sons.

An incident that occurred when Gregory was at the Canterbury School in Connecticut in the mid-1940s casts some interesting light on father and son. In an attempt to please his father, Gregory plagiarized a tale from Turgenev and won first prize in the school competition. (In a roughly analogous situation, the ten-year-old Ernest had lied to his father and claimed as his own prize a quail that had actually been shot by Ed Hemingway.) Gregory confessed to his father, who had known the story was plagiarized and was furious that the teachers failed to recognize the source.

This incident inspired his fine unpublished story "I guess everything reminds you of something," probably written after his irreparable quarrel with Gregory in 1952. Hemingway praises Gregory's brilliant pigeon shooting, for the boy had tied for the Cuban championship, and then lost in the tie break, at the age of ten in July 1942. Hemingway wrote that the boy shot as if he were guided by radar. He never took a shot out of range or let a driven bird come too near. He shot pheasants and ducks with beautiful style and perfect timing. But seven years later, when reading a book in the boy's room, the fictional father discovers that his son had plagiarized a story and is overwhelmed by an irrational revulsion against him. Hemingway wrote that the boy had behaved in a hateful and stupid way, and that his vileness came from his sickness.[17]

V

To Have and Have Not is the only full-length novel Hemingway set in America and the only one he published in the 1930s. The book, written intermittently and with considerable difficulty between 1933 and 1937, reflected his life in Key West and Cuba. It was a half-hearted attempt to meet the contemporary demand for political awareness but reflected only a token commitment to the class struggle. Unlike *The Sun Also Rises* and *A Farewell to Arms,* which came from the depths of Hemingway's psyche, expressed his great theme of romantic love and poured out of him, *To Have and Have Not* seemed forced and took a long time to write. In contrast to the Spanish and Italian landscapes of his earlier novels, the Caribbean setting of boats and bars is thinly sketched and fails to come alive.

To Have and Have Not began as a short story about bootlegging, "One Trip Across," which was sold for the enormous sum of $5,500 and published in *Cosmopolitan* in April 1934. The second part appeared as "The Tradesman's Return" in *Esquire* in February 1936—when Hemingway was completing his two perfectly realized African stories. After the Spanish War broke out in July 1936, he attempted to combine these two mediocre tales of adventure with the third and longest section, which introduced many new characters and had very little connection to the first two parts. Despite some recurrent motifs—three offers, two betrayals, three bursts of machine gun fire, three shipmates and three soliloquies—the novel lacks unity and structure. Part One is written in the first person; Part Two in the third person; and Part Three in the first and the third person. The weak structure of the novel reflects the two poorly integrated aspects of his life: tough and hedonistic.

The style of the book is also uneven. It ranges from tough-guy passages that influenced Dashiell Hammett, Raymond Chandler and a whole hard-nosed school of American writers ("Touching the head, the gun made a noise like hitting a pumpkin with a club. Harry put down the gun and lay on his side on the cockpit floor. 'I'm a son of a bitch,' he said.") to lyrical-sexual interior monologues of the ex-whore Marie Morgan and the masturbating mistress Dorothy Hollis that imitated Joyce's Molly Bloom ("I didn't want to, but I am, now I am really, he *is* sweet, no he's not, he's not even here, I'm here, I'm always here and I'm the one that cannot go away, no never").[18]

The main character, Harry Morgan, is named after a seventeenth-century Welsh pirate who also had sailed and fought in these waters. He is a brute parody of a Hemingway hero and tries to stand alone in a world of overwhelming violence. Though resourceful, courageous and loyal, the ex-policeman is also a pathological criminal who uses economic problems and domestic necessity to justify smuggling and murder. Harry loses his clients, fishing equipment, contraband liquor, charter boat, right arm, shipmates and, finally, his life. (Hemingway's fictional decline becomes immediately apparent when the death of Catherine Barkley is compared to the death of Harry Morgan.) Before he dies, Harry achieves a moment of insight and expresses the simplistic and baldly stated theme of brotherhood: "No matter how a man alone ain't got no bloody fucking chance."[19] But Harry's rejection of the individualist's "separate peace" is not convincing and his death does not result from being alone, but from breaking the law.

There are several other inconsistencies in the portrayal of the political theme. Hemingway supports the revolution that overthrows the tyrannical Machado regime in Cuba, but also condemns the bloodthirsty revolutionaries. And his provincial prejudice toward Jews, Irish, Chinese and Negroes—who replaced the Anglo-Saxon immigrants to America at the turn of the century—jars incongruously with his apparent sympathy for the unemployed fishermen and demoralized veterans.

The heavy-handed satire on successful, *individualistic* capitalists at the end of the novel—which links financial manipulation with sexual perversion—is flawed because Hemingway condemns his own economic class from the "have-not" point of view while continuing to enjoy his comfortable life. In the 1930s, and especially after World War Two, Hemingway was friendly with Cuban and American millionaires (Alfred Vanderbilt, Tommy Shevlin, Winston Guest, Gus Pfeiffer) and with the Spanish and Italian nobility. As the Marqués de Valparaíso y Mérito said: "Ernest always 'puts rich people down' in his books, in spite of the fact that in real life theirs was the only company which interested him."[20]

Our interest in *The Sun Also Rises, A Farewell to Arms* and *For Whom the Bell Tolls* is primarily aesthetic while our interest in *To Have and Have Not, Across the River* and *Islands in the Stream*, which must be read and interpreted quite differently, is mainly autobiographical. In Hemingway's artistic failures, his personal feelings are openly expressed rather than imaginatively transformed. When *To Have and Have Not* is seen from an autobiographical viewpoint, the commonplace adventure story becomes a fascinating revelation of his emotional and sexual life.

Hemingway put part of himself into Harry Morgan and portrayed his affair with Jane Mason in Richard Gordon's liaison with Helène Bradley. All the other characters in the novel are based on his friends and enemies. Joe Lowe (killed in the Matecumbe hurricane) was the model for the rummy mate Eddy; Captain Bra Saunders for Captain Willie Adams; Joe Russell (a Prohibition rum-runner and proprietor of Sloppy Joe's bar) for Freddy Wallace; George Brooks (a Key West lawyer) for "Bee-lips," Richard Simmons; Jack Coles (a friend of Dos Passos) for James Laughton; Professor Harry Burns (of the University of Washington) and Arnold Gingrich for Professor John MacWalsey; Grant Mason for Tommy Bradley. Dos Passos was the model for aspects of Harry Carpenter and the pathetic radical author Richard Gordon, who is writing a novel about a strike in a textile factory and is savagely condemned by his wife, Helen: "I've seen you bitter, jealous, changing your politics to suit the fashion, sucking up to people's faces and talking about them behind their backs. I've seen you until I'm sick of you."

Most interestingly, Helen Gordon is clearly based on Pauline, a fervent Catholic who is deceived by her husband. (Hemingway's wife and mistress, closely connected in his life and mind, were named Helen and Helène in the novel. Pauline is also called Helen—and Hemingway called Harry—in "The Snows of Kilimanjaro"; and Hadley is named Helen in "Wedding Day.") Pauline's money, like that of the wealthy yachtsman, came (via Uncle Gus) "from selling something everybody uses by the millions of bottles [Sloan's Liniment], which costs three cents a quart to make, for a dollar a bottle in the large (pint) size." Gordon still loves "her curly black hair, her small firm breasts under the sweater forward against the edge of the table." But Helen, in the most revealing passage in the novel, bitterly exposes his selfishness, their sexual problems, her tortured Irish-Catholic conscience and her abortions:

> Love is that dirty aborting horror that you took me to. Love is my insides all messed up. It's half catheters and half whirling douches. I know about love. Love always hangs up behind the bathroom door. It smells like lysol. To hell with love. Love is you making me happy and then going off to sleep with your mouth open while I lie awake all night afraid to say my prayers even because I know I have no right to any more. Love is all the dirty little tricks you taught me that you probably got out of some book. All right. I'm through with you and I'm through with love. Your kind of picknose love. You writer.[21]

This is Pauline's version of "Hills Like White Elephants"; not as subtle and sophisticated, but more personal and powerful.

The book Hemingway intended as his comeback in fiction received mostly negative reviews, but the public (after waiting eight years) was eager to read it. The novel appeared while he was reporting the Spanish War, was on the best-seller list from October to December 1937, and sold 36,000 copies in the first five months.

Cyril Connolly found the novel "morally odious" and listed the reasons for the decline in Hemingway's reputation: "His book on big-game hunting, his flashy he-man articles in *Esquire* and his attitude to criticism have alienated a great many people." But he still admired Hemingway and correctly predicted "he is obviously the person who can write the great book about the Spanish War."

Alfred Kazin found moral significance in the unusual hero of the novel: "The hero of the book is not, like most of Hemingway's heroes, an elaborately self-conscious man against society; he is rather a mass man. . . . Harry Morgan's vice is his excessive self-reliance, the pride in his own tough loneliness. . . . Harry is unique because he is capable of struggle and casual about annihilation." Kazin ended positively by stating that Hemingway "is rather less sure of himself than usual, but a good deal more intense. . . . [He] is a genuine artist who has worked his way out of a cult of tiresome defeatism."

Malcolm Cowley, one of Hemingway's best critics, believed he had a beneficial effect, had encouraged authors to abandon affectation and "to write as simply as possible about the things they really feel." Cowley was, however, disappointed by the novel, which was defective in both plot and characterization, and called it "the weakest of Hemingway's books—except perhaps *Green Hills of Africa.*"[22]

Philip Rahv, writing in the *Partisan Review*, stated that Hemingway's "favorite theme of human endurance and valor in the face of physical annihilation [is now] enacted on the stage of world events." He thought the novel may have begun a new phase of Hemingway's work, for Morgan "represents Hemingway's review of his own past. . . . Morgan's death may presage Hemingway's social birth." But Rahv, like most other critics, felt that the novelist had still not reached political maturity: "In transcending his political indifference, he has not, however, at the same time transcended his political ignorance."

The long retrospective consideration by the poet Delmore Schwartz in the *Southern Review* was the most complex analysis of the novel and one of the best essays on Hemingway. He began by defining the pattern in Hemingway's work: "There is an extraordinary interest in sensation; there is an extraordinary interest in conduct and the attitudes toward conduct; and there is always the background of war." But Schwartz found no "clear link between the interest in sensation and the interest in conduct." After suggesting Hemingway's strengths, Schwartz harshly concluded: "[It] is a stupid and foolish book, a disgrace to a good writer, a book which should never have been printed."[23] Though none of the reviewers really liked the book, many of them felt or hoped that it contained a promising new social awareness.

In 1944 William Faulkner wrote a screenplay of the novel. In the film, starring Humphrey Bogart and Lauren Bacall, she spoke the famous lines: "You know how to whistle, don't you, Steve? You just put your lips together and blow."

To Have and Have Not was Hemingway's misguided response to the critics' demand for political commitment. He was not particularly interested in social theories, and generally adhered to bourgeois values about family and home, marriage and children, money and success. He responded emotionally and practically to human suffering, took sides on public issues when he was deeply moved, but was basically bored by politics. Like most artists, his main interest was in turning inward and developing his own creative genius. *To Have and Have Not* was, on a superficial level, about economic injustice and the need for solidarity: "Most everybody goes in boats calls each other brother."[24] But Hemingway's greatness lay in stories like "Big Two-Hearted River," where the style is clear and the meaning obscure, rather than in novels like *To Have and Have Not,* where the prose is turgid and the theme overt. After several unsuccessful works in the 1930s, the war in Spain turned him toward a truer source of inspiration.

15

Martha and the Spanish War
1936–1938

On that table-land scored by rivers
Our fever's menacing shapes are precise and alive.

AUDEN, "Spain"

I

Hemingway's love for Martha Gellhorn was inextricably connected to his participation in the Spanish Civil War, just as his love for Agnes von Kurowsky was to the Great War and his love for Mary Welsh to World War Two. He was in hospital when he fell in love with Agnes, and in London, far from the front, when he met Mary; but his affair with Martha was conducted in the midst of the war, which made it much more exciting. Just as Hadley had tried to prevent him from reporting the Turkish War, so Pauline attempted to keep him from going to Spain. He was with Martha during his four visits to Spain and separated from her when he returned to Pauline; and these separations intensified his passion, as they had done during his courtship of his first two wives.

Hemingway's affair with Martha had an uncanny resemblance to his affair with Pauline. Like Pauline, Martha was a youthful, attractive, glamorous and fashionably dressed woman. She too insinuated herself into the household, courted the passive Hemingway, who became her athletic instructor while his wife was preoccupied with domestic responsibilities, and wrote endearing letters thanking the wife for her kind hospitality. In both cases, the affair was conducted secretly and at a safe distance. When Pauline discovered it, she (like Hadley) remained tolerant, struggled to hold her husband and tried to maintain the marriage. But the mistress eventually displaced the wife. When Heming-

way married Martha, he felt guilty about abandoning his wife, revised
the true history of the latest marriage and found a suitable scapegoat
to bear the responsibility for his own unpalatable behavior. After his
divorce from Pauline, and from Martha, he turned for consolation to
Hadley and recalled the sentimental memories of their marriage.

Martha's father, like Hemingway's, was a doctor who specialized in
obstetrics. Dr. George Gellhorn, like Hadley's mother, died shortly
before the daughter met Hemingway; and he compensated, in part, for
the loss of the parent. Martha, like Hadley and Pauline, came from an
upper-middle-class family in St. Louis and had been educated at private
schools in that city. Like Hadley, Martha attended but did not graduate
from Bryn Mawr; like Pauline, she was trained as a journalist and
worked for a time on the Paris edition of *Vogue*. Martha had recently
ended her liaison with the French journalist Baron Bertrand de Jouve-
nel, whom she had lived with for several years. Hemingway had recently parted from Jane Mason, who had been his mistress for four
years. Though not as exquisitely attractive as Jane, Martha was much
more of a threat to Pauline (whose tolerance, in any case, was wearing
thin after years of infidelity); for she was not, like Jane, married, a heavy
drinker and emotionally unstable. Just as Hadley was associated with
Chicago and Paris, Pauline with Key West and Africa, so Martha was
connected to the war in Spain and the move to Cuba.

Martha, born in St. Louis in 1908, was nine years younger than
Hemingway and thirteen years younger than Pauline. Her Austrian-
born father was a professor at Washington University Medical School;
her mother, who had graduated from Bryn Mawr, was a leading social
reformer and suffragist. Martha had worked as a journalist in America
and Europe in the early 1930s and published two books: *What Mad
Pursuit* (1934), a novel with an epigraph from *A Farewell to Arms*
("nothing ever happens to the brave"), and *The Trouble I've Seen*
(1936), a collection of stories based on her experience as an investigator
for Roosevelt's advisor Harry Hopkins in the Federal Emergency Relief
Administration. (Hemingway makes a satiric crack about the F.E.R.A.
in *To Have and Have Not.*) Martha's second book had a preface by
H. G. Wells, was praised in Eleanor Roosevelt's syndicated newspaper
column and admired by Graham Greene, who noted in the *Spectator:*
"her masculine characters are presented as convincingly as her female,
and her writing is hard and clear."[1]

Martha was a physical contrast to Pauline. If Pauline, as Hemingway wrote in *Green Hills of Africa,* was like a little terrier, then Martha could be compared to a wolfhound: "lean, racy, long-legged and ornamental." Martha was tall and shapely, with long blond hair, blue eyes, fine skin, sensual yet girlish features. She could be quite charming, and was intelligent, capable, ambitious. Hemingway met her in Sloppy Joe's bar in December 1936 when she was on holiday with her family; they were immediately attracted to each other and established a sympathetic rapport. Martha naively confessed to Pauline that she had spent so much time in the Key West house, she felt like a fixture there. Most observers agreed that Martha courted Hemingway.[2] After her family had left, he spent a great deal of time going swimming with his "mermaid" and showing her around the island. When they were alone, Pauline would say, with weary irony: "I suppose Ernest is busy again helping Miss Gellhorn with her writing." Martha insisted that Hemingway never taught her how to write, since she had published two books before she met him. But he claimed to have tutored her, and many reviewers commented on Hemingway's strong influence on her work.

Martha admitted that he enriched her experience by teaching her about boats, bulls, fishing and shooting.[3] When she left by car in January, he flew north to meet her in Miami and took the train with her as far as Jacksonville. On January 5, 1937, Martha gave her friend Eleanor Roosevelt (whom she had met through Harry Hopkins) her first impressions of Hemingway as man and writer:

> [He is] an odd bird, very lovable and full of fire and a marvelous story teller. (In a writer this is imagination, in anyone else it's lying. That's where genius comes in.) So I sit about and have just read the mss of his new book [*To Have and Have Not*] and been very smart about it; it's easy to know about other books but such misery to know about one's own. So Hemingway tells me fine stories about the Cuban revolution and the hurricane and then I come home and . . . try to make a solid plan for a book. . . . If there is a war then all the things most of us do won't matter any more.

Hemingway and Martha (who was a more politically committed anti-Fascist) shared an interest in Loyalist Spain and planned to go to the war together. In February Martha wrote him, in the jocular style much favored by Pauline and Jane Mason: "This is very private. We are conspirators [a reference to their effort to get into Spain] and I have personally already gotten myself a beard and a pair of dark glasses. We will both say nothing and look strong. . . . Angel, I have so much to tell you, but suddenly I find that there is no time even to think straight. . . . Please, please leave word in Paris [in case she missed him in New York]."[4]

Hemingway and Martha tried to be discreet, corresponded covertly, traveled separately, behaved tactfully in public and attempted to keep their love secret from Pauline. He set up a separate bank account with funds from Scribner's to pay for his affair.[5] They used pet names as he had done with Hadley and Pauline: he was the phallic Scrooby, she was the mawkish Mooky. When Joseph Losey met her in the Connecticut country house of Fred Field, a Vanderbilt grandson, Martha, clad in black silk and pearls, abandoned discretion. She said that Hemingway was an extraordinary man and praised his barrel chest, his enormous potency and his skill as a lover.[6] Hemingway's attraction to Martha—strengthened by the commitment to Spain, the physical hardship and the danger of war—must have been extremely powerful to overcome both his love for and his guilt about Pauline. MacLeish, close to Hemingway during the Spanish War, shrewdly wrote of his passion for Pauline: "how he ever broke through so strong a feeling, I have never understood. . . . I have always suspected that his subsequent detestation for [Martha] was in part the consequence of his own sense of disloyalty." Pauline—who lacked Hadley's kindness and equanimity, could not bear the role of rejected wife, and was both bitter and vindictive after their divorce—told Hemingway that Martha was egoistic, selfish, stupid, childish, phony and almost without talent.[7] The "*almost* without talent" was the limit of her generosity.

II

Hemingway, nourished on the history and traditions of the American War Between the States, believed: "Civil war is the best war for a writer, the most complete."[8] He made four separate trips to Spain as a war correspondent and spent about eight months there during 1937–1938. During the first and most significant tour, from March to May 1937, he reported the siege of Madrid and worked on the film *The Spanish Earth;* in the spring he returned to America to complete *To*

Have and Have Not, made a political speech at Carnegie Hall, showed the film at the White House and went on a fund-raising trip to Hollywood. From September to December 1937 he sent dispatches from Madrid and wrote his play, *The Fifth Column;* in January he was brought home by a hysterical Pauline for a brief, unwilling stay. From March to May 1938 he reported the battle of the Ebro delta; in the summer he returned to write articles and stories about Spain, to revise his play and to publish *The Fifth Column and the First Forty-Nine Stories.* In November 1938, after his war correspondent's contract had lapsed, he witnessed the events that led to the fall of Barcelona; and finally returned to write his most ambitious novel, *For Whom the Bell Tolls.*

Hemingway felt corrupted, bored and restless in Florida and had an intense personal attachment to the country, culture and people of Spain. On July 19, 1936, Franco's Fascists rose against the Republican government in a revolution from the *Right* that was clearly a prelude to World War Two. Hemingway, inspired by Martha, was desperately eager to go to his third war and devote himself to the cause of the Loyalists (those loyal to the democratically elected Republican government). As he told Matthew Josephson: "I've got this nice boat and house in Key West—but they're both really Pauline's. I could stay on here forever, but it's a soft life. Nothing's really happening to me here and I've got to get out. . . . In Spain maybe it's the big parade starting again."[9]

Pauline disliked the idea and tried to restrain him. She quite naturally felt he had already risked his life in war and feared he would be wounded or killed. As a Catholic, she supported Franco and had no sympathy for the Loyalists, who were extremely hostile to the Church. She was worried about their troubled marriage and thought his love for Martha would intensify if he went with her to Spain. But Martha was determined to go and Hemingway had to follow her—and compete against her—if he wished to win her. Pauline was slightly mollified when Sidney Franklin, a useful man in Spain, agreed to accompany Hemingway. Franklin had no political understanding, though his heart was in the right place. He was devoted to Hemingway and was "on Hemingway's side"—whatever that side happened to be.

Hemingway's journalistic experience in Spain (as in World War Two) released him from literary stagnation and inspired his fiction. It also marked his transition from Key West to Cuba, from Montana to Idaho, and from his relations with older women to younger wives and mistresses.

Early in 1937 John Wheeler, manager of the North American Newspaper Alliance, which supplied material for sixty newspapers including the *Kansas City Star* and the *New York Times,* heard that Hemingway was going to Spain. Wheeler offered him a contract that paid $500 for each cabled story and $1,000 for each mailed story (up to 1,200 words), with no limit on the number of dispatches he could send. Hemingway, having shed his blood for Italy, was now being paid to expose himself to danger and write about the war in Spain. Before leaving, he paid the passage of two Loyalist volunteers and sent $1,500 to buy ambulances.

Hemingway knew from the very beginning that the war was a fight against Fascism, that Germany and Italy were testing their men and weapons for the next war, and that the Republic could not win unless England, France and America abandoned their policy of neutrality and supported the Left as actively as Germany and Italy supported the Right. Though many of his friends among the wealthy matadors and bull breeders sided with Franco, he understood perfectly that "Fascism is always made by disappointed people." In July 1933 he had expressed his individualistic-anarchic beliefs to the irredeemable Pound, who actively supported Mussolini. He said he hated the entire idea of the State, felt no obligation to it and did not want anything from it—except to be left alone. An organized state bred bureaucrats, injustice and oppression.[10]

During the war he explained to the pro-Franco Harry Sylvester (whom he called "a plainclothes Jesuit") why he supported the working class against the Church, the Communists against the Fascists, and defended himself against the charge that he was politically naive: "Why was the church in politics on the side of the oppressors instead of for the people? . . . My sympathies are always for exploited working people against absentee landlords even if I drink around with the landlords and shoot pigeons with them. . . . I think that's a dirty outfit in Russia now but I don't like any governments." He also told Sylvester that he believed discipline and a united front were essential in wartime. He liked and respected the Spanish Communists and thought they were the best people in the war.[11]

5. *Spain*

III

Hemingway spent January and February 1937 in New York, writing the commentary for a Loyalist propaganda film, *Spain in Flames,* a weak compilation made from pro-Franco newsreels. He sailed to France with Sidney Franklin and Evan Shipman in late February; saw Solita Solano and her friend Janet Flanner, the *New Yorker* correspondent, in Paris; flew from Toulouse to Valencia on March 16 and drove to Madrid. On March 22 he met Martha, who was accredited to *Collier's* magazine, and told her: "I knew you'd get here, daughter, because I fixed it so you could"—though he knew perfectly well that he had done nothing at all to help her.

He praised Martha's courage and endurance in war and was furious when Frederick Voigt, the Berlin representative of the *Manchester Guardian,* gave Martha a sealed envelope with an uncensored cable about the "terror" which he claimed existed in Madrid: "The only ugly thing was that the girl to whom he had entrusted it could, under the rules of war, have been shot as a spy if it had been found among her papers when she was leaving the country. The dispatch was a lie and he had given it to a girl who trusted him to take it out of the country."[12] Hemingway warned Martha about this danger. She was impressed by his prestige, devoted friends, connections, resourcefulness, strength, understanding of war, knowledge of Spain and endlessly amusing stories. They stayed at the Hotel Florida on the Gran Vía and became lovers in the spring.

There is a remarkable unanimity in the accounts of Hemingway in Spain. Almost everyone who knew him there agreed that he showed the best side of his character, was courageous and generous, and did everything he could for the Loyalists. His fame gave him privileged status as a correspondent; the authorities allowed him a car, driver and gasoline; and he had complete freedom of movement. He always shared his quantities of superior food (bought or gathered by Franklin) with his colleagues. He enjoyed the test of nerve under conditions of warfare, seemed to thrive during bombardments at the front and contrasted his youthful reaction on the Piave to his mature response in Madrid: "in the war in Italy when I was a boy I had much fear. In Spain I had no fear after a couple of weeks and was very happy."[13] His German friend Gustav Regler, who was seriously wounded while fighting with the Twelfth Brigade, said: "For him we had the scent of death, like the bullfighters, and because of this he was invigorated in our company." Arturo Barea, a Spanish novelist working in the office of censorship, described Hemingway's rough charm: "big and lumbering, with the look of a worried boy on his round face, diffident and yet consciously using his diffidence as an attraction, a good fellow to drink with, fond of dirty jokes 'pour épater l'Espagnol,' questioning, sceptical and intelligent in his curiosity, skilfully stressing his political ignorance, easy and friendly, yet remote and somewhat sad." Jason Gurney, however, saw the noncombatant in a reckless moment and sourly noted: "The most controversial visit of them all was Ernest Hemingway, full of hearty and bogus *bonhomie.* He sat himself down behind the bullet-proof shield of a machine-gun and loosed off a whole belt of ammunition in the general direction of the enemy. This provoked a mortar bombardment for which he did not stay."[14]

During April 1937 Madrid was besieged by Franco's forces; they shelled the capital from University City but could not capture the town. The front was only a short tram ride from the Hotel Florida, which was hit by shells intended for the nearby telephone exchange. Martha observed: "No matter how often you do it, it is surprising just to walk to war, easily, from your own bedroom where you have been reading a detective story or a life of Byron."

Hemingway's first reports celebrated the Loyalist victories over Italian troops at Guadalajara and Brihuega. His dispatches were entirely different from those he sent to the *Toronto Star* from Turkey in 1922, which concentrated on the specific event and did not attempt to illuminate the background. In Spain, he described the landscape, military action, strategic significance, political importance, effect on the civilian population, and gave many personal details. His cowardly chauffeur, for example, "looked like a particularly unattractive, very mature dwarf out of Velasquez."[15] He exaggerated the significance of the "major," "decisive" victories (gained after eight months of defensive fighting), scarcely mentioned the defeats and conveyed the impression that the Loyalists were winning the war.

Hemingway met and made a great many friends in Spain. The Florida, headquarters for most foreign writers, had a special atmosphere of excitement and commitment. He saw the dashing French novelists André Malraux and Antoine de Saint-Exupéry; the poets Pablo Neruda and Rafael Alberti; the Russian correspondents Mikhail Koltzov and Ilya Ehrenburg (both lived separately and luxuriously in the Hotel Gaylord and spoke to him in French); his much-admired journalistic colleagues Herbert Matthews of the *New York Times* and Sefton (Tom) Delmer of the London *Express;* the courageous photographer Robert Capa and Ring Lardner's son John (later killed in action); the Spanish generals Luis Quintanilla and Gustavo Durán; the Hungarian general Lukács and Dr. Werner Heilbrun of Regler's Twelfth Brigade; Milton Wolff and Alvah Bessie of the Abraham Lincoln Brigade.

He also met a heroic but little-known figure, Major Robert Merriman, who led the final assault on Belchite and was a model for Robert Jordan in *For Whom the Bell Tolls:*

A native of Eureka, California, he had worked at various manual jobs, the last of which had been logging, before going to the University of Nevada in 1929. Following graduation three years later, he received a fellowship in economics at Berkeley. When war broke out in Spain, he was studying in the Soviet Union on a travelling fellowship and was gathering materials for a book about collective farming. In January, 1937, he was among the first Americans to reach Spain, and because of his ROTC experience and his political rapport with the Communist leaders of the International Brigades, he was appointed adjutant of the original Abraham Lincoln Battalion. When the Lincolns went into action at Jarama a month later, Merriman was acting commander until wounded on the twelfth day of fighting. When he returned to duty after the Brunete offensive in July, he was promoted to chief of staff, [and was later killed in action].[16]

IV

Though Hemingway made many new acquaintances in Spain, he also had an irreparable political quarrel with his closest literary friend, John Dos Passos, soon after he arrived. Dos Passos' character was the opposite of Hemingway's. He was gentle, quiet, scholarly and introspective; more political and less emotional; not at all a man of action. Though Dos Passos was not competitive, Hemingway saw him as a rival who married the girl Ernest had a crush on in boyhood (and claimed to have slept with in "Summer People").

Their dispute concerned Dos Passos' close friend and translator, José Robles, who taught Spanish at Johns Hopkins and joined the Loyalists as a colonel after the war broke out. When Robles was arrested by the Communists who controlled the Madrid front in December 1936, Dos Passos was told the charges were not serious and that he would be released. But Hemingway heard that Robles had been accused of espionage and secretly executed. He assumed that Robles was guilty and the sentence was just, and broke the news to Dos Passos in April 1937. Dos Passos was deeply shocked, refused to believe his friend was treacherous and was furious when Hemingway suggested he was politically naive. His biographer stated: "Dos could no longer tolerate what he saw as a Communist subversion of left-wing movements. Hemingway, only recently politicized and much absorbed in the courageous fight of the Loyalists, could not believe Dos Passos's charges, nor could he accept the challenge to what he considered his superior knowledge of the subject."

After Robles' death, Dos Passos defected from the Loyalists and attacked the Communists. Hemingway had no personal feelings about Robles and was callous about his death. (He would have behaved very differently if Robles had been *his* friend.) He did not particularly care if a few doubtful men were shot during the War and thought the cause was more important than the individual. He was angry at Dos Passos' de facto support of the Fascists and told him: "A war is still being fought in Spain between the people whose side you used to be on and the fascists. If with your hatred of the communists you feel justified in attacking, for money, the people who are still fighting that war I think you should at least try to get your facts right." Though Dos Passos was probably right and Hemingway wrong about Robles, Dos Passos—more honest about Communist atrocities—hurt the Loyalist cause while Hemingway helped it. During a personal confrontation at Gerald Murphy's New York flat in the summer of 1937, Hemingway made nasty remarks about Dos Passos' Portuguese blood and called his wife a thief.[17]

Both novelists prolonged the conflict in their books. While completing *To Have and Have Not* that summer, Hemingway included hostile passages about Dos Passos' refusal to repay loans (to the Murphys and others) and about Katy's habit of stealing from stores. But they were clearly libelous and had to be omitted from the published novel. Hemingway wrote that because the novelist is supposed to be incorruptible, all his rich friends lend him money. But he never repays his debts when his books come out and does not have to because of his sterling reputation. His wife also steals like a monkey. When they were children, she would steal from groceries, drugstores and newsstands. She was finally arrested in Wanamaker's department store and taken to court, but was acquitted through family influence.

After Dos Passos published his virulently anti-Communist novel of the Spanish War, *The Adventures of a Young Man* (1939), Hemingway returned to the attack in his Introduction to *Men at War* (1942) and condemned one of Dos Passos' best books: "I would have liked to include something from 'Three Soldiers' by John Dos Passos which, written under the influence of Barbusse, was the first attempt at a realistic book about the war written by an American. But in spite of its great merit, like Barbusse, as a pioneering book, on rereading it did not stand up. . . . The dialogue rings false and the actual combat is completely unconvincing."[18] For good measure, he told Faulkner in July 1947 that Dos Passos was a "terrible snob (on acct. of being a bastard)." The following month, in a nightmarish repetition of the car crash in Billings in November 1930, Dos Passos, driving through Wareham, Massachusetts, "was blinded by the afternoon sun and did not see a truck which had pulled off to the side of the road. They crashed into it, shearing off the top of the car and practically decapitating Katy. She died immediately; Dos was hospitalized by the loss of his right eye."[19]

Hemingway satirized Dos Passos as Richard Gordon in *To Have and Have Not,* but was furious when Dos Passos returned the compliment, used Katy's stories about their Michigan childhood, and portrayed Hemingway as the ludicrous and loathsome George Elbert Warner in *Chosen Country* (1951). Dos Passos makes Hemingway into a difficult adolescent, bullying his friends and battling all authority. In one scene Warner is knocked overboard by the boom of a boat. When he is pulled out of the water, dripping like a wet dog and with fishhooks in his trousers, he claims that his friends tried to drown him. Hemingway somehow failed to appreciate the satire. After reading *Chosen Country* he told Bill Smith that "in Cuba he kept a pack of fierce dogs and cats trained to attack one-eyed Portuguese bastards who wrote lies about their friends." In a letter to Charles Fenton, written the year after the novel appeared, Hemingway explained that Dos Passos said he had exploited a scandal when, in fact, he had nothing to do with it:

> He takes the incident when Bill's brother Y.K., his wife and that toothsome morsel you met or corresponded with named Donald Wright got involved in some sort of a killing out at a place called Palos Park south of Chicago. Some woman who was in love with Y.K. shot a gardener by mistake I believe [in 1924]. . . . Dos makes the loathsome character who is supposed to be me in the book then betray Kate, Y.K. et al by publishing a photograph and writing a feature story in some Chicago newspaper accusing them of weird sex cult rites. . . . [But] I was in Europe and knew nothing about the case.

Dos Passos outlived him by ten years, but Hemingway had the last word in *A Moveable Feast,* where he characterizes his old friend as a fish who leads the rich Murphy-sharks to their prey and helps to destroy his marriage to Hadley: "The rich have a sort of pilot fish who goes ahead of them, sometimes a little deaf, sometimes a little blind, but always smelling affable and hesitant ahead of them. . . . These rich loved and trusted him because he was shy, comic, elusive, already in production, and because he was an unerring pilot fish."[20]

The break with Dos Passos was an important turning point in Hemingway's life. He had quarreled with Anderson, Stein, Ford, Lewis, Fitzgerald, MacLeish; with Robert McAlmon, Ernest Walsh, Harold Loeb, Don Stewart, Dorothy Parker, Morley Callaghan and Max Eastman. He was still on good terms with Pound and Joyce, but they lived in Europe and had taken different paths, into the *Cantos* and *Finnegans Wake*. After 1937, Hemingway had no close writer-friends: jealousy, bitterness, arrogance, ambition, pride and politics had knocked them all out of his life. In the 1940s and 1950s he knew soldiers, sportsmen, cronies, millionaires, hangers-on, actors and parasites—but he had no friends who were artists. Their absence coincided with the emergence of Papa Hemingway, his last public persona.

V

Hemingway made *The Spanish Earth* (1937) with Joris Ivens, the Dutch film director. Ivens maintained that he had been a member of the Communist Party in the Netherlands from 1928 to 1930 and had remained sympathetic to their aims after he left the Party, but that he had not been recruited to influence Hemingway's politics and had not tried to do so. In 1935 Ivens toured American cities and colleges, and showed his pioneering documentaries. In New York he met Dos Passos, MacLeish and Lillian Hellman, who were concerned about the first military offensive of Fascism and eager to alert Americans to the Loyalist point of view. They formed a company, Contemporary Historians, to fund and distribute *The Spanish Earth* and an earlier film, *Spain in Flames*, which Ivens had made with the Cuban novelist Prudencio de Pereda. The company raised $2,000 to send Ivens—and his tall, blond, young, Dutch cameraman, John Fernhout (called Ferno)—to Spain. *The Spanish Earth* would portray the war and show how it affected the lives of poor peasants. Early in 1937, Ivens, with Dos Passos as Spanish translator, filmed the first sequences in a wine-growing village, Fuentidueña, forty miles east of Madrid, where the Tagus River crosses the road to Valencia. When Dos Passos left to investigate the death of Robles, he suggested that Hemingway take his place.

Ivens first met Hemingway, just before the novelist entered Spain, at the Café Deux Magots in Paris in March 1937. He had heard about *Death in the Afternoon* and had read *A Farewell to Arms* in a French translation; he knew that Hemingway was an experienced newspaper-man and an internationally known novelist. Hemingway brought more money from America, was eager to find the truth and help the cause, and established an immediate rapport with Ivens. He mentioned the trench mortar wound he had suffered in the Great War and seemed moved by the horrors of battle. Ivens thought he was a humane man, though he valued bodily perfection and physical force.[21] In his memoirs Ivens wrote:

> Hemingway seemed to me that day like a simple and direct man, a kind of big boy scout who imposed himself by his physique and his manner of expressing himself. I knew he had been seriously wounded during the 1914–1918 war. It was not a sufficient reason to accept his odd charac-ter, but I did not want to clash with him. Hemingway knew Spain in peace, but not in war. In Paris he could see things from a distance, but I knew that once we were there things would be different. . . . He was a very physical man who knew how to control himself and never showed his fear.[22]

In Paris, Hemingway also told Ivens: "My beautiful girl friend is coming. She has legs that begin at her shoulders." He and Martha were not affectionate in public and did not become the subject of gossip; during the war no one was particularly concerned with his private life. Martha made a good impression on Ivens and he joked a good deal with her. She had good rapport with the men in the Lincoln Brigade and was a very professional reporter.

In his Afternote to *The Spanish Earth,* Hemingway stressed the physical hardship: "The first thing you remember is how cold it was; how early you got up in the morning; how you were always so tired you could go to sleep at any time; how hard it was to get gasoline; and how we were always hungry." His silver flask of whiskey was useful in this weather. Just as his father liked to eat onion sandwiches and his hero Nick Adams "cut one half into slices and made onion sandwiches," so Hemingway risked Martha's displeasure and Ivens' disgust and "always carried raw onions in the pockets of my lumberman's jacket and would eat them whenever I was really hungry." In his undistinguished Spanish War story "Night Before Battle," Hemingway wrote of the filming with unusual awkwardness: "The big camera was the most expensive thing we had and if it was smashed we were through. We were making the film on almost nothing and all the money was in the cans of film and the cameras. We could not afford to waste film and you had to be awfully careful of the cameras."[23]

Hemingway spoke Spanish with shaky grammar and a poor accent,[24] but he was fluent and quickly established contact with the Spaniards. He dealt with practical rather than artistic matters; he kept up morale, advised about locations and, because he was strong, often carried the heavy equipment. Most important, he gave military advice about how to film the battles on the Madrid front, as they ran and sweated with the cameras, took cover in the folds of the hills. In a war dispatch from Spain he wrote: "The first [attack] was in the grey, olive-studded broken hills in the Morata de Tajuna sector where I had gone with a friend [Ivens] in order to take film pictures of infantry and tanks in action. We moved behind the infantry and filmed the tanks as they moved like ships up the steep hills and deployed into action."

Ivens, who called him "Hem" and got to know him well in these difficult conditions, thought he had no false bravura or romanticism, was serious and responsible about his duties, made a good impression on the Spanish military leaders. Ivens found him intelligent, courageous, a good comrade and extremely knowledgeable about the conditions of war. He could be witty, but also made fierce, cutting remarks. He wanted to be exceptional, to be admired, to be first in everything. "He showed a quick comprehension and understanding of the documentary film and a very helpful humility towards this new profession."[25]

The Spanish Earth was filmed hurriedly in three months and completed in April 1937, when they left Spain. The cost came to $13,000 and Hemingway paid a quarter of the expenses. As Hemingway began to write the narration in New York in May, Ivens warned him: "don't write about what you see, don't repeat the image. You must reinforce the image by writing about related things." At first, Hemingway made the same mistake as everyone else: his script was too long and too elaborate. Though Hemingway was a proud and sensitive man, Ivens audaciously criticized his work. When Hemingway saw the red marks on the script, he shouted, half-seriously: "You God-damned Dutchman. How dare you correct my text?" But when Ivens showed him that the spoken words lasted five minutes longer than the fifty-minute film, Hemingway realized there was too much talk.

Hemingway then remarked: "Now I see. I'll write you another one." He learned fast, avoided the usual faults of explaining everything and assuming a God-like authority. He understood Ivens' style perfectly, and created a unity of text and film. When the frame showed the German word *drucken* (press) on the parachute, Hemingway wrote: "I can't read German either." In the morgue scene, he stated: "Three Junkers did this." His short, lapidary sentences and characteristic understatement had an enormous influence on documentaries. The simplistic but effective theme of the compassionate film was the desire to reclaim the Spanish earth in the Spanish War: "We gained the right to cultivate our land by democratic elections. Now the military cliques and absentee landlords attack to take our land from us again. But we fight for the right to irrigate and cultivate this Spanish Earth which the nobles kept idle for their own amusement."[26]

Virgil Thomson and Marc Blitzstein compiled the sound track from forty records of Spanish folk music. In June, MacLeish gave Orson Welles the script and asked him to record it. Welles later provided a lively but quite fanciful account of how he bear-baited Hemingway:

> There were lines as pompous and complicated as this: "Here are the faces of men who are close to death," and this was to be read at a moment when one saw faces on the screen that were so much more eloquent. I said to him, "Mr. Hemingway, it would be better if one saw the faces all alone, without commentary."
>
> This didn't please him at all and, since I had, a short time before, just directed the Mercury Theatre, which was a sort of avant-garde theatre, he thought I was some kind of faggot and said, "You ——— effeminate boys of the theatre, what do you know about real war?"
>
> Taking the bull by the horns, I began to make effeminate gestures and I said to him, "Mr. Hemingway, how strong you are and how big you are!" That enraged him and he picked up a chair; I picked up another and, right there, in front of the images of the Spanish Civil War, as they marched across the screen, we had a terrible scuffle. It was something marvellous: two guys like us in front of these images representing people in the act of struggling and dying. . . . We ended by toasting each other over a bottle of whiskey.

Prudencio de Pereda doubted that anything like this ever happened. He recalled that they had a quiet and serious discussion during which Welles (like Ivens) criticized the script.[27]

MacLeish and Ivens (whose English was not very good at that time) were pleased with Welles' reading. But Lillian Hellman and Fredric March disliked it; they thought his polished, theatrical voice clashed with the stark, realistic script. When Ivens suggested that Hemingway read his own words, Hemingway (perhaps remembering his mother's musical experience) said: "No, no, I can't do it. I don't have the proper training in breathing." He was finally persuaded to speak the commentary without watching the film and did it extremely well. Though the poor sound recording of that time made his thin midwestern voice sound rather flat, his natural tone made the intense experiences on the screen more believable. As Ivens recalled: "While recording, Hemingway found the emotions that he had felt at the front. From his first sentences, his commentary acquired a sensibility that no other voice would have been able to communicate. It was achieved, we had succeeded in giving the film its true dimension."[28] Ivens asked MacLeish to explain to Welles that he had become the voice on the recording room floor, but MacLeish was too embarrassed to do this. Welles, who had worked without a fee, was naturally furious, and took mild revenge in his account of the recording session.

VI

Hemingway arrived in Paris on May 9. Three days later he gave a reading of "Fathers and Sons" to an audience that included James Joyce, at Sylvia Beach's Shakespeare and Company:

> He stammered through a few comments on writing and war and the difficulty of writing in a fascist country. Then he gulped down some beer and began reading "Fathers and Sons" from *Winner Take Nothing* (1933). He was whispering, and a woman asked him to speak louder. He then began to read, according to a French news reporter, "with the air of an innocent child and a strong American accent. This shyness could only make him seem more likeable." Growing gradually more assured, according to the reporter for the Paris *Herald Tribune*, "he began to put expression in his clean, terse phrases. He was beginning to show grace under pressure." Pausing, he downed more of the foamy beer.[29]

The Paris reading was useful preparation for the stirring anti-Fascist speech on "The Writer and War" that Hemingway made to an audience of 3,500 at the League of American Authors Congress on June 4, 1937. Martha, MacLeish and Don Stewart were on the platform of Carnegie Hall in New York when Hemingway said: "Really good writers are always rewarded under almost any existing system of government that they can tolerate. There is only one form of government that cannot produce good writers, and that system is fascism. For fascism is a lie told by bullies. A writer who will not lie cannot live or work under fascism."[30]

On July 8 Hemingway interrupted work on *To Have and Have Not*, flew from Key West to Washington, and showed *The Spanish Earth* to Franklin and Eleanor Roosevelt at the White House. Hemingway told Mary Pfeiffer: "Martha Gellhorn, the girl who fixed it up for Joris Ivens and I to go there [as Hemingway claimed he had "fixed up" Martha's entry into Spain], ate three sandwiches in the Newark airport before we flew to Washington. We thought she was crazy at the time but she said the food was always uneatable."[31] The dinner, in fact, matched Martha's prediction: rainwater soup, rubber squab, wilted salad and tasteless cake. The Roosevelts were moved by the film, which was meant to encourage their active support of the Loyalists, but thought it should have had more propaganda. One alarming newspaper headline announced: "COMMUNIST DIRECTOR INVADES WHITE HOUSE."

On July 10 Hemingway and Ivens flew to Los Angeles to show the film at the house of Fredric March and raise money to buy ambulances for Spain. The evening was a great success and Hemingway's speech inspired the seventeen guests, including Scott Fitzgerald, to contribute $17,000. They added $2,000 more from a showing at the Ambassador Hotel, and collected enough to buy the chassis of twenty ambulances, which had been ordered from the Ford factory in Detroit.

The text of *The Spanish Earth* was privately printed in Cleveland in a limited edition of a thousand copies in June 1938, and contained an apologetic end note by the high school student and publisher, Jasper Wood:

> Ernest Hemingway had nothing to do with the preparation of this book, never saw the proof, furnished no material for the introduction, and has just wired me protesting that he considers the introduction inaccurate and in bad taste since it gives him credit for a film the credit for which should go to Joris Ivens and John Ferno. He also protests against the F.A.I. [*Federación Anarquista Ibérica*] banner in front and back of the book and has requested that all money to be paid to him from the book be paid directly to Almuth Heilbrun, widow of Dr. Werner Heilbrun of the Twelfth International Brigade, who was killed in action at Huesca in June, 1937.[32]

The film was well received and has since become a classic. In an enthusiastic review in the Left-wing *New Republic*, the distinguished young film critic Otis Ferguson stated the two simple themes were "the suffering and dogged purposefulness of war for the cause; and . . . the earth and its rightful function." (This was also a theme of *The Sun Also Rises*.) He also agreed with Ivens and praised Hemingway's script and narration: "Much of the carrying power in understatement should be credited to Ernest Hemingway's commentary. . . . [With his] feeling for the people of Spain which comes from the heart, the combination of experience and intuition directing your attention quietly to the mortal truth you might well have missed in the frame, there could hardly be a better choice."[33] But *The Spanish Earth* failed to find a commercial distributor and was confined to limited audiences in film societies.

The last meeting of the two comrades and colleagues took place accidentally in about March 1950 in a provincial French town, where Ivens had agreed to speak at a showing of *The Spanish Earth*. While Ivens was waiting in a café for the performance to begin, Hemingway (who had been driving from Italy to Paris) suddenly appeared in a big car, greeted Ivens with a bear hug and asked: "Are you still at it?"

VII

Hemingway completed *To Have and Have Not* in June 1937 (between the Carnegie Hall speech and the White House preview), fought with Max Eastman in Perkins' office on August 11, sailed for France three days later and arrived in Spain for his second tour in early September. The war was going badly. Franco had taken the north coast and held two-thirds of the country. With Herbert Matthews and Tom Delmer, Hemingway toured the Aragon front, southeast of Zaragoza, where the Loyalist offensive had captured Belchite. He saw them take Teruel, between Madrid and the east coast, and entered the city with the victorious troops in December. Matthews recalled the difficult conditions: "In the first twelve days [of December], Hemingway, Delmer, and I drove nearly 3,000 miles. On four occasions we drove, worked, and wrote for more than twenty-four hours (once for forty-four) at a stretch. I have never in my life experienced such cold. We rarely got a square meal."[34]

Hemingway wrote his only play, *The Fifth Column*, while the Hotel

Florida was under bombardment in the fall of 1937. The title, a translation of the phrase *la quinta columna,* spoken by the Fascist General Mola in 1936, alludes to the secret sympathizers within Madrid who were prepared to help the four Fascist columns that were besieging the city. The hero of this improbable melodrama, a counterespionage agent of the Stalinist underground in Madrid, renounces his girl and prophetically states: "We're in for fifty years of undeclared wars and I've signed up for the duration." But the real interest of the play is Hemingway's characterization of himself and Martha as Philip Rawlings and Dorothy Bridges.

Hemingway and Martha had a symbiotic literary relationship and portrayed each other in their work—though Martha wisely left him the subject of the Spanish War. In *The Fifth Column* Rawlings is described as very large and hearty, with big shoulders and the walk of a gorilla. Dorothy admiringly says: "He's so full of life and good spirits. . . . He's so lovely and so sort of *vital* and so gay." But when angered, she exposes his faults and calls him a "conceited, *conceited* drunkard. [A] ridiculous, puffed-up, posing braggart."[35]

Dorothy is a tall, handsome blonde with a cultivated voice and hair like a wheat field. She has the "longest, smoothest, straightest legs . . . [and] the loveliest damn body in the world." She wears a silver fox cape as gracefully and elegantly as a model, but Rawlings disapproves of her luxurious tastes and his friend warns her: "Don't be a bored Vassar bitch."[36] Rawlings is infatuated with Dorothy, but (like Pauline) is presciently aware of her radical flaws: "Granted she's lazy and spoiled, and rather stupid, and enormously on the make. Still she's very beautiful, very friendly, and very charming and rather innocent—and quite brave"—and absolutely straight. He tells her she is an uneducated, useless, lazy fool; and Hemingway, with astonishing clairvoyance, has Rawlings tell the whore, Anita: "I'm afraid that's the whole trouble. I want to make an absolutely colossal mistake" with Dorothy. Hemingway, furious when Martha left him to go on an American lecture tour in December 1937, stresses the theme of personal loyalty in the play. Echoing Helen in "The Snows of Kilimanjaro," Rawlings asks Dorothy: "Would you like to marry me or stay with me all the time or go wherever I go, and be my girl?" It would seem that this program would not be particularly appealing to the fiery and independent Martha. Yet Martha herself echoed these very words and sounded like all the other submissive Hemingway wives when she wrote on December 4, 1939:

"I'll never leave you and you can go everywhere you want and do anything you like, only please, I'll come too."[37]

Hemingway—a strong, protective man—felt emotionally drawn to women when they were passive, silent and asleep; judged the beauty and character of women by the way they looked while sleeping. In *The Fifth Column* Dorothy-Martha is virtually narcoleptic. She sleeps soundly; stirs in bed, wakes and yawns; and then announces: "I'll go back to sleep for just a little while longer. I feel so sleepy." In a note on Martha in *Collier's* of March 1944, written when their marriage had all but disintegrated, he told his readers that she "hates to get up in the morning. She needs twelve hours sleep, can use twelve and has to have ten. But when she is at the front," he conceded, she was capable of sustained periods of consciousness: "she will get up earlier, travel longer and faster and go where no other woman can get and where few could stick it out if they did."[38]

In "The Last Good Country," Littless (Sunny) "looks like a small wild animal . . . and she sleeps like one." In *Green Hills of Africa,* Pauline "was always lovely to look at asleep, sleeping quietly, close curled like an animal." And in *Across the River,* he contrasts the way his past wife (Martha) and present love (Adriana Ivancich) look while dormant: "He did not like to remember how the career girl slept, yes he did. But he wanted to forget it. She did not sleep pretty, he thought. Not like this girl who slept as though she were awake and alive; except she was asleep. . . . [She] was soundly sleepy [i.e., sleeping] now the way a cat is when it sleeps within itself." Hemingway told Bernard Berenson, three years after the novel appeared, that he loved to look at Martha except when she was sleeping, for no ambitious woman looks lovely when asleep.[39] The career girl did not "sleep pretty" because she was restless and uneasy. The ideal, for Hemingway, was a sleep that seemed as natural as an animal's and as lively as a woman when awake.

Though Pauline satisfied his aesthetic of sleep and Martha did not, he had not yet fully realized that Martha (who had refused to relinquish her successful career as a war correspondent) was ambitious and that Pauline (who had given up her career, had children and devoted herself to her husband) was not. He originally dedicated *The Fifth Column* "To Marty and Herbert [Matthews] with love," but discreetly dropped these words from the book, which was published while he was still married to Pauline.

A minor but irritating point of contention between Hemingway and Martha concerned personal hygiene. She thought he was too dirty (she fondly, then less fondly, called him The Pig), he thought she was too clinically clean. Martha urged him to bathe more frequently and defended her own immaculate habits: "I am really not abnormally clean. . . . I've lived in places and been in places where to keep even faintly clean was a sinister thing. But Ernest was extremely dirty, one of the most unfastidious men I've ever known." He caustically countered: "She liked everything sanitary. Her father was a doctor, so she made our house look as much like a hospital as possible." This conflict inspired Dorothy's first words in the play: "clean your boots before you come in here," and the maid's comment on Rawlings' habits (a private joke between Martha and Hemingway): "He is very clean. He takes baths all the time even with cold water. Even in the coldest weather he washes his feet."[40]

This minor theme recurs in *For Whom the Bell Tolls*, published three weeks before his marriage to Martha, when Maria asks Jordan: "Dost ever wash thy shirt?" and he reluctantly replies: "Sometimes." Though Maria's character is quite different from Martha's, the Spanish girl has some of the Nordic attributes that so excited Hemingway when he first met Martha in Sloppy Joe's bar: "Her skin and her eyes were the same golden tawny brown. She had high cheekbones, merry eyes and a straight mouth with full lips. Her hair was the golden brown of a grain field." And Jordan tells her, with some trepidation: "Thou hast a lovely face and a beautiful body, long and light, and thy skin is smooth and the color of burnt gold and every one will try to take thee from me." Maria is a portrait of Martha as Hemingway would have liked her to be. Though beautiful, Maria is subservient and submissive, docile and devoted. And like a domestic pet, she is grateful for Jordan's attention: "Jordan reached his hand out and patted her head. She stroked under his hand like a kitten."[41]

VIII

While Hemingway was writing about Martha in *The Fifth Column*, Pauline became weary of waiting for him to break with Martha as he had done with Jane Mason. She knew that every minute he spent in

Spain strengthened his commitment to her young rival. During his first visit to the war Pauline wrote patiently, cheerfully and drearily of her longing for him: "I am going to say right now that I am sick and tired of all this. . . . I wish you were here sleeping in my bed and using my bathroom and drinking my whiskey. . . . Dear Papa, please come home as soon as you can." But all her virtues: money, style, wit, taste, tact, critical judgment, desire to please, self-effacement—even the new swimming pool she built for him—meant nothing when he was in love with Martha.

Just as Martha left for her lecture tour, Pauline arrived without warning in Paris in a desperate attempt to preserve her marriage. But it did not work. Gregory noted Hemingway's "ability for destroying people with words, and had even seen him use it on Mother. Once he had written her a letter entitled, 'How Green Was My Valet,' with Mother portrayed as Hettie Green, the eccentric Wall Street millionairess, and the 'valet' referring to the nature of their former relationship."[42] As he confessed in "The Snows of Kilimanjaro," the intensity of their old love made their quarrels more bitter: "With the women that he loved he had quarrelled so much they had finally, always, with the corrosion of the quarrelling, killed what they had together. He had loved too much, demanded too much, and he wore it all out." Pauline simply said, using Hemingway's turn of phrase: "We made too many cruelties on each other. We couldn't erase them."[43] In Paris she threatened to jump out of the hotel window—as Jane Mason had done. Though their Christmas meeting was a disaster, Pauline managed to drag him back to Key West, more or less against his will, for three months.

In 1938 Hemingway returned to Spain and to Martha from late March until mid-May. That spring he covered the battle of the Ebro delta as the Fascists lunged toward the Mediterranean, captured Tortosa on the coastal road and cut communications between Madrid and Barcelona—the last major cities in Loyalist hands. In a dispatch written for *Pravda* in July 1938 but not discovered until 1982, he attacked the base motives of the Fascist victors: "They murder for two reasons: to destroy the morale of the Spanish people and to try the effect of their various bombs in preparation for the war that Italy and Germany expect to make."[44]

Hemingway returned to America for the third time on May 31,

1938, to write stories about Spain and revise his play. Perkins told Fitzgerald, with considerable understatement: "I think Ernest is having a bad time, by the way, in getting re-acclimated to domestic life, and I only hope he can succeed."[45] In July, coming back in a bad mood after an unsuccessful fishing trip, he found Pauline preparing for a costume party and discovered the key to his locked studio had been lost. He remedied matters by seizing his .38 revolver, firing it into the ceiling and shooting the lock off the door. Things were no better when they left for Montana in August, for he and Pauline quarreled all the way to the Nordquist ranch and had a miserable time once they got there.

In mid-August Hemingway told Mary Pfeiffer that he had accomplished a great deal since the beginning of 1937. He had revised and published *To Have and Have Not,* helped film *The Spanish Earth,* written *The Fifth Column,* completed thirteen articles (mainly on Spain) for Arnold Gingrich's magazine *Ken* and earned $15,000 for twenty-eight newspaper dispatches for the North American Newspaper Alliance, which were reprinted in *Fact* and the *New Republic.* He had also become completely alienated from the Catholic Church, which supported the Fascist enemy, and had wrecked his second marriage. He returned to Europe for the fourth time in late August 1938, spent two months in Paris with Martha and witnessed the events that led to the fall of Barcelona and Madrid, and the loss of the war.

Herbert Matthews described how Hemingway saved his life in November with a rowing feat that equaled Frederic Henry's in *A Farewell to Arms:*

> It was during the Ebro battle in 1938; we had to take a rowboat to get over from the west to the east bank because the bridges had been bombed down. The current was swift and there were some nasty rapids a few hundred yards down the river, so the boat was being partly pulled across by a rope, which snapped. We started drifting swiftly toward the rapids. Hemingway quickly took the oars; [Henry] Buckley acted as coxswain to pace his strokes with shouts, and by an extraordinary exhibition of strength, Ernest got us safely across. He was a good man in a pinch.[46]

In October 1938, while Hemingway was with Martha in Paris, *The Fifth Column and the First Forty-Nine Stories* was published. This composite volume contained the play, all of *In Our Time, Men Without*

Women and *Winner Take Nothing,* and four uncollected stories: his two African masterpieces; "The Old Man at the Bridge," about a refugee in the Spanish War; and "The Capital of the World," his best story about bullfighting.

"The Capital of the World" (June 1936) concerns the theme of illusion, the attempt to make dreams a reality. Hemingway carefully places Paco's minor tragedy in the social context of Madrid and shows the Anarchists' hatred of the Church on the eve of the Civil War. All the inhabitants of the pension on the Calle San Jerónimo deceive themselves. The maids escape into the fantasy world of a Garbo movie; the priests imagine their request will be met by the bishop. The novelty bullfighter thinks he will come back into fashion, the cowardly bullfighter thinks he still has courage, the tubercular bullfighter thinks he will recover.

The provincial waiter Paco executes elaborate passes with an apron in the kitchen and insists he would not be afraid in the bullring. His friend Enrique first challenges Paco by tying sharp knives on the legs of a chair and charging like a bull, then warns him that their game is very dangerous. When his warning is ignored, the fantasy is suddenly shattered. The knife goes into Paco, "in him, in him," as the horn had penetrated the cowardly bullfighter. Paco's blood drains out like dirty bath water and he dies (lying face down like the tubercular matador) full of illusions in the illusory Capital of the World.

Like most critics, Alfred Kazin liked the stories much better than the play, which failed to do justice to the important theme of commitment and to the complex politics of the war. Malcolm Cowley believed the heroine negates the tragic implications of the play, for she is unintentionally presented "as a chattering, superficial fool, a perfect specimen of the Junior Leaguer pitching woo [starting a courtship] on the fringes of the radical movement." He also noted that Hemingway's violence, which once appeared excessive, now "seems a simple and accurate description of the world in which we live."

Edmund Wilson's severe review asserted that the play was almost as bad as *To Have and Have Not,* did not do "very much either for Hemingway or for the revolution": "the action is rather lacking in suspense and the final sacrifice rather weak in moral value." Wilson shrewdly observed that the power of Hemingway's early stories, in contrast to the play, was his ability to identify himself with both the injurer and the injured. At their best, Hemingway's stories represented "one of the most considerable achievements of the American writing of our time."

Lionel Trilling's persuasive and salutary essay opposed the critical trend of the entire decade and argued that literary works did not have to provide solutions to contemporary political problems. Trilling began with Edmund Wilson's distinction between Hemingway the "man" and the "artist," and attributed his failures to the intrusion of the former into his literary work. He then analyzed the enormous critical pressure —and misinterpretation—placed on Hemingway, and suggested that a detached perspective was necessary for reading his work. Trilling concluded that we must not expect a political effect from a work of art: "In removing from art a burden of messianic responsibility . . . we may leave it free to do whatever it can actually do."[47]

Hemingway could not solve the intractable problems of staging *The Fifth Column*. In November 1939 he agreed to let the screenwriter Benjamin Glazer rewrite and adapt it, and to divide the royalties with him. But he was, inevitably, dissatisfied with the results. He felt it would hurt his reputation and ironically commented that the original play was about a very attractive girl. If it had a moral, it was that agents employed by the Comintern have little time for domestic life.[48] Martha did not think Dorothy was a believable character and wryly agreed that the adaptation embarrassed both of them.

In the spring of 1940, after the defeat of the Spanish Loyalists and the beginning of World War Two, *The Fifth Column* opened in New York. Produced by the Theatre Guild and directed by Lee Strasberg, it starred Franchot Tone and Lee J. Cobb, who were praised for their remarkably fine acting, and ran for eighty-seven performances. Joseph Wood Krutch, who disagreed with most critics, did not like the play. He thought the theme of "reconciling the aims of a holy war with the methods which it must inevitably use" was not well-developed: "what had begun as a complex picture of life in a war-torn city ends stagily as the love story of a hard-boiled hero whose grandiose gestures" were familiar and unconvincing. Stark Young, who observed that Glazer gave more space to the love story and added a drunken rape scene, also found the style uneven and the ending unconvincing. But he called the acting and direction excellent. Wolcott Gibbs wrote that though the character of Dorothy had been weakened and "Mr. Glazer has unquestionably cheapened the play here and there, I think it is emphatically worth seeing."[49]

IX

Hemingway's dispatches from Spain were not nearly as good as those he had sent from Turkey in 1922. There were several reasons for this. He was deeply involved with Martha and distracted by his many friends; he was not trying to establish his reputation and could afford to coast on his past achievements; he put a good deal of his energy and concentration into writing *The Fifth Column;* he was saving the best material about the war for *For Whom the Bell Tolls;* he found it difficult and demoralizing to describe the Loyalist defeats; and he felt obliged to write propaganda rather than facts. He believed the Loyalists had a chance to win the war if they could gain the support of the western democracies—who would never commit themselves if they felt the cause was lost. As he wrote in his Preface to Gustav Regler's *The Great Crusade:* "The Spanish Civil War was really lost, of course, when the Fascists took Irun [near the Atlantic border with France] in the late summer of 1936. But in a war you can never admit, even to yourself, that it is lost."[50]

Hemingway's portrayal of the French political commissar, André Marty, in *For Whom the Bell Tolls* shows that he was well aware of the Communist horrors in Spain. He and Orwell were among the very few writers who were honest enough to criticize the Communists from the Left point of view (though Hemingway did not criticize them until after the war) and both writers were reviled by the Communist press. Hemingway condemned Max Eastman, James Farrell and Edmund Wilson for remaining in New York and attacking everyone who went to Spain as a tool of Stalin. Like all correspondents sympathetic to the Loyalists, he minimized the Russian support and emphasized the assistance that Germany and Italy gave to the Fascists. Hemingway cared more about the Spanish cause than about himself or what he could get out of it. His very presence in Spain helped morale and influenced world opinion. As Martha said: "I think it was the only time in his life when he was not the most important thing there was."[51]

Yet some of Hemingway's emotional and political limitations become apparent when he is compared to Orwell, who thought telling the truth was more important than winning the war. Orwell narrates his memoir, *Homage to Catalonia* (1938), from the point of view of the victim of war. His belief in comradeship allows him to be exploited and this victimization ironically reaffirms his idealistic belief in the brother-hood of man. His achievement was to create a meaningful work of art out of his immediate involvement in contemporary events, despite his limited perspective and ignorance about what was actually happening, and his book still stands as the most valuable account in English of the war in Spain. According to Orwell: "The sin of nearly all left-wingers from 1933 onwards is that they have wanted to be anti-Fascist without being anti-totalitarian."[52] They tolerated and even endorsed Stalin be-cause he fought against the enemy, though both sides used the same brutal methods, and (Orwell shows) the internecine strife among the Loyalists in Catalonia was even more horrible than the war against the Fascists.

Hemingway was a newsman rather than a soldier, a spectator rather than a participant in the war. He went to Spain to gather material for a novel, exposed himself to personal risk and privation for limited peri-ods of time, and considered his experience a great adventure—rather like a hunting expedition with political overtones. He became a victim of his own facile reporting and his novelist's self-absorption, which was heightened by his love affair with Martha. He was not capable of Or-well's political insight and abandoned interest in politics after his side lost the war in Spain. But his acute sensitivity and passionate response to the cause enabled him to transmute his experience into the greatest novel about the Spanish War.

16

The End of Something
1939–1940

> Every damn thing is your own
> fault if you're any good.
>
> *Green Hills of Africa*

I

Hemingway's separation from Pauline was hesitant, protracted, guilt-ridden and bitter—rather than sharp and clean, as he would have liked it to be. But he worked well in times of emotional turmoil. In *The Sun Also Rises, A Farewell to Arms* and "The Snows of Kilimanjaro" he had confronted his personal guilt and transformed it into art. He wrote most of *For Whom the Bell Tolls* in the Caribbean and the Rockies during 1939. He also traveled a great deal, as he had while composing his earlier novels. He left Pauline in mid-February 1939 to spend a month in room 511 of the Ambos Mundos Hotel in Havana. It had a roof garden overlooking the bay, was owned by his friend Manuel Asper, and had often been the scene of his meetings with Jane Mason. He returned to Key West in mid-March to see Jack, who had come down to Florida for his spring vacation. He met Martha in Havana on April 10 and they rented the Finca Vigía. Pauline went to Europe with friends in July and August. He drove Martha to visit her family in St. Louis and reached Wyoming alone on September 1. Pauline joined him at the Nordquist ranch early that month, but she caught a terrible cold and they were unhappy together. (Her minor illness precipitated their break-up just as Bumby's whooping cough had helped terminate his marriage to Hadley in 1926.) He met Martha in Sun Valley later in September and spent the autumn there with her. In November, two months after the war broke out, Martha went to Finland to report that country's struggle against Russia. He drove back to Florida with Toby Bruce in mid-December and moved from Key West to Cuba.

Hemingway had been taking the four-hour voyage across to Cuba to write and fish ever since he arrived in Key West in 1928 (he used both locales in *To Have and Have Not*) and was thoroughly familiar with the island when he moved there in 1939. In Havana, his home for the next twenty years, he found a place that was the exact opposite of Oak Park: Latin, Catholic, tropical, leisurely, unstable, sinful and corrupt. Graham Greene also enjoyed the *louche* atmosphere of Havana, "where every vice was permissible and every trade possible," in the early 1950s. He went there "for the brothel life, the roulette in every hotel, the fruit-machines spilling out jackpots of silver dollars, the Shanghai Theatre where for one dollar twenty-five cents one could see a nude cabaret of extreme obscenity with the bluest of blue films in the intervals." Hemingway was familiar with these places, but there is no indication that he ever participated, as Greene did, in the low life of the city.

When Hemingway lived in Cuba the country was ruled by Fulgencio Batista, whose regime was at first benign and then repressive. In September 1933 Batista led the sergeants' revolt that toppled the twenty-four-day government of Carlos Manuel de Céspedes, who had overthrown the dictator, Gerardo Machado. The provisional president, Ramón Grau, promoted Batista to colonel and four months later he overthrew Grau. Batista ruled by patronage rather than by terror from 1934 to 1940, when he resigned from the army and was elected president. Four years later he stepped down and was succeeded by Grau, moved to Florida and invested his huge fortune there. He was elected president in 1952 and again in 1954. He promised to restore normal conditions but became a brutal dictator, repressed the universities and provoked the Castro revolt in 1956. On December 31, 1958, Batista fled to the Dominican Republic (and then to Portugal), and Castro seized control of the country the following day.

The character of the lizard-shaped island leavened Hemingway's midwestern Protestantism and satisfied his needs. In "The Great Blue River," published in *Holiday* in 1959, he praised the virtues of Cuba and explained why he lived there. He liked the cool hills above Havana, the flower and vegetable gardens, the migratory and local birds, the mangoes, the baseball team, the shooting club, the informality, the solitude and privacy that allowed him to work in peace (his Key West house was in the center of town and could be seen from the street), and the deep-sea fishing in the Gulf Stream, which was only half an hour away from the Finca. The duck, dove, quail and pheasant could be killed, not merely admired, and he especially enjoyed shooting them when the tail wind increased their speed of flight. The large number of Loyalist refugees also made the town attractive and enhanced the Spanish ambience. In his evocative novel *Our Man in Havana*, Graham Greene described the shoddy city, which had scarcely changed in the past twenty years, just before Castro took over:

> The long city lay spread along the open Atlantic; waves broke over the Avenida de Maceo and misted the windscreens of cars. The pink, grey, yellow pillars of what had once been the aristocratic quarter were eroded like rocks; an ancient coat of arms, smudged and featureless, was set over the doorway of a shabby hotel, and the shutters of a night-club were varnished in bright crude colours to protect them from the wet and salt of the sea. In the west the steel skyscrapers of the new town rose higher than lighthouses into the clear sky.[1]

There was very little intellectual life and nobody treated Hemingway like a writer. He could be one of the boys in boat and bar, and thrived in the place that had helped to destroy his exact contemporary, Hart Crane. In a passage deleted from *To Have and Have Not* he described the disastrous decline of the homosexual poet who had jumped off a ship and drowned near Cuba in 1932. Hart Crane was an unlucky bugger who always solicited the wrong sailors and was beaten up. He had gone to Mexico on a fellowship to write a great poem and had not been able to do it. He came back broke and mentally bankrupt, and was given a dreadful beating in Havana the night before his boat sailed. That beating finished him off.[2]

Hemingway's favorite bar and restaurant (which he made famous) was the Floridita, where Calle Obispo crossed Monserrate, in the old part of town near Morro Castle. The comfortable, old-fashioned place with ceiling fans and a three-piece band was the regular hangout for his old friend, the prostitute Leopoldina Aroste, who could always count on a handout from Papa. In a letter of 1952, Hemingway described his Cuban house, routine and habitual diversions:

> It is a good place to work because it is out of town and on a hill so that it is cool at night. I wake up when the sun rises and go to work and when I finish I get a swim and have a drink and read the New York and Miami

papers. After work you can fish or go shooting and in the evening [my wife] and I read and listen to music and go to bed. Sometimes we go into town or go to a concert. Sometimes we go to a fight and see a picture and go to La Floridita afterwards. Winter we can go to the Jai Alai. . . . When I hit New York it is like somebody coming off a long cattle drive hitting Dodge City in the old days.[3]

In the spring of 1939 Martha found the Finca Vigía (Lookout Farm) in the village of San Francisco de Paula, twelve miles southeast of Havana. The one-story, run-down Spanish colonial house had high ceilings, tile floors, a sixty-foot living room, swimming pool and tennis court. It was surrounded by fifteen shambling acres and stood on a 468-foot hill that caught the breezes and had a fine view of the lights of the capital. Gregory Hemingway described the luxuriant setting: "Mango trees lined the driveway leading up to the house, and tall royal palms grew beside the path leading down to the swimming pool in back. Flowers and bougainvillea vines bloomed all over. Hummingbirds made their tiny neat square nests in the tropical foliage." Hemingway came out to look at it, told Martha it was fine if she liked it, and took off for a long fishing trip. When she had done it up, he was well pleased with the house. He proudly exhibited his hunting trophies and his fine collection of modern paintings: Miró's *The Farm,* Klee's *Monument in Arbeit,* Juan Gris' *The Guitarist* and *The Torero* (frontispiece to *Death in the Afternoon*), five works by André Masson and a Braque that was stolen when he was in Idaho in 1961. Martha wanted to maintain her financial independence, always paid half their expenses and had to accept journalistic assignments when she needed the money.[4]

They first rented the house for $100 a month from Roger D'Orn, who came from New Orleans and owned the Fibrocemento factory; in December 1940 Hemingway bought it for $12,500 with the first earnings of *For Whom the Bell Tolls.* Under the regimes of Martha and Mary (who inherited the Finca from Martha and kept many of the furnishings) they gradually acquired a cadre of servants. The butler, René Villareal, was "energetic, *simpático,* with a perfect sense of his own worth, devoted to his employers (who were equally devoted to him, and trusted him implicitly)." The Chinese cook, Ramón, who was assisted by his apprentice, Fico, sometimes threatened the other servants with a carving knife and, in calmer moments, prepared lunch at 1:30 and dinner at 8:30. There were also three gardeners, two maids (including

Clara, who had emotional problems), the chauffeur, the carpenter and the trainer of the fighting cocks for local combats. In *Islands in the Stream* a disenchanted Hemingway described the scenery and the squalor that he passed on the drive from the Finca into town:

> The highway ran downhill for three miles with big old trees on either side. There were nurseries, small farms, large farms with their decrepit Spanish colonial houses that were being cut up into subdivisions, their old hilly pastures being cut by streets that ended at grassy hillsides, the grass brown from the drought. . . . [There was] poverty, dirt, four-hundred-year-old dust, the nose-snot of children, cracked palm fronds, roofs made from hammered tins, the shuffle of untreated syphilis, sewage in the old beds of brooks, lice on the bare necks of infested poultry, scale on the backs of old men's necks, the smell of old women, and the full-blast radio.[5]

II

After he moved to Havana, Hemingway's friends were not writers and rivals but soldiers and sportsmen: men of action with integrity and technical skill. He had two tiers of friends in Cuba: wealthy, cultivated aristocrats who shared his interest in fishing and shooting, and usually spoke to him in English; and quite ordinary men, his dependents and cronies, who spoke to him in Spanish. His closest friends in Cuba were Mario (Mayito) Menocal, Elicio Arguelles and Thorwald Sánchez, who enjoyed their leisure, participated in exclusively male activities and valued Hemingway's passion for sport.

Menocal, a big man who was a year younger than Hemingway and had met him in Bimini in 1935, came from a distinguished family. His father, a Cornell-trained engineer, had been a general in the war of independence against Spain and president of Cuba from 1913 to 1921. He opposed Machado, was jailed in 1932, went into exile and returned to Cuba, after the revolution, in 1935. He built the first sugar mills on the island, at Santa Marta in Camagüey province; and his son Mayito, who was educated in America, managed them. Hemingway and Menocal would discuss sport, fishing, shooting, current books, local gossip, Cuban and world politics while drinking gin with champagne chasers. Once, dressed as boxers—with helmets and shorts over their trousers—they crashed a party given by Hemingway's neighbor, Frankie Stein-hart, whose father had built the Havana tramways. Hemingway's Cuban friends often visited the Finca, but were almost never able to return his invitations. Menocal had marriage problems; the wives of Menocal and Sánchez thought Hemingway had a bad influence on their husbands and discouraged his visits. Mayito's son said:

> When Hemingway had a drop too much he began to tell stories that were, quite simply, lies. They were not lies from which he would ever derive any benefit; and he knew that my father and Elicio knew they were lies. . . . He never lied when he was sober. . . . His capacity for recuperation was incredible. He would be drinking quite heavily; one day he would stop drinking heavily, and drink normally. The next day he was just as well, just as strong, just as normal as he could be. . . .
> He was a man who enhanced life, in the Arab sense, for all his friends. Things became more enjoyable when done with him or looked at through his eyes. . . . He managed to imbue the most trivial sporting activity with his own sense of the challenging and dramatic.

Arguelles agreed about this and said: "I have never known a man who enjoyed life more. He did everything to the fullest."[6]

In 1948 Hemingway told his army friend Buck Lanham that Mayito was one of the finest and straightest men he had ever met. He loved him like a brother. Mayito had grown up in the presidential palace, gone to Lawrenceville School and fought in his father's revolutions. When they failed, he had worked as a bouncer and croupier in Miami. As soon as Mayito could return to Cuba, he had set up a dairy farm on the family estate.[7] Hemingway gave Menocal proofs of *The Fifth Column* and *For Whom the Bell Tolls,* and invited him as a guest on the 1953 safari (Mayito left Africa earlier than Hemingway and avoided the plane crashes). Menocal was forced to leave the proofs and his hunting trophies behind, with all his other possessions, when he left Cuba after the Castro revolution.

Elicio Arguelles met Hemingway through his cousin, Mayito, in about 1945. He was born in 1910, trained as a lawyer, owned a cattle ranch and sugar farm on the far side of the island. Elicio, "a much better shot and fisherman than Hemingway," was a top Cuban skeet and pigeon shooter, won the fishing championship four times and broke the record for tuna caught in one day in Nova Scotia in the early 1950s. Elicio owned the jai alai fronton in Havana, and Hemingway often went there to watch his Basque friends play and bet on the game. Though their politics were diametrically opposed—Elicio's father was the chief Cuban fund-raiser for Franco—they remained good friends. Hemingway had a wonderful library and would often lend Elicio books to read. He would remain secluded for two or three months while writing; then call up his friends when he had finished a book and go fishing in the Bahamas on Mayito's big yacht, *Delicias.* Hemingway hated to lose any competition and liked to take dangerous shots at sharks as Gregorio pulled them into the boat. Elicio thought Hemingway was one of the strongest men he had ever known; he could steer the *Pilar* for ten straight hours, and fought his huge fish standing up instead of using a bucket seat and a harness. Arguelles' world was destroyed by the Castro revolution, and he did not see Hemingway again after leaving Cuba for Florida in April 1960.[8]

Thorwald Sánchez, like Hemingway, was a big, handsome man with a tremendous personality. Born in 1902, he was the grandson of the Danish consul in Havana, a relative of Anaïs Nin, a member of one of the wealthiest families in Cuba and heir to a great sugar fortune. He had extensive real estate interests, owned a shrimp business and ran Guarina, the largest ice cream factory in Cuba. He met Hemingway in Key West in the late 1930s, and hunted, shot and fished with him in Havana. He smoked expensive cigars, owned a yacht, invented a daiquiri popsicle and, according to a well-informed bartender, could "drink more martinis than any man I've ever seen and never slur a word." During his high-spirited fortieth birthday party at Sánchez' house, Hemingway got completely drunk, threw Thorwald's clothes out the window and began to break the Baccarat crystal glasses while Tina Sánchez screamed for the butler to lock them up. Thorwald, who adored Hemingway, was amused by these pranks—but his wife was furious. Though she felt Hemingway influenced Thorwald's heavy drinking and aggressive behavior (he once grabbed the microphone at a formal dinner and insulted the American ambassador), Thorwald's friends thought he did not need much encouragement to drink.[9]

Leicester Hemingway observed, with rare insight: "Ernest was never very content with life unless he had a spiritual kid brother nearby. He needed someone he could show off to as well as teach. He needed uncritical admiration. If the kid brother could show a little worshipful awe, that was a distinct aid in the relationship." Hemingway's need for admiration increased as his literary powers declined after 1940. When Leicester failed in the role of junior crony, obliging confidant and trusted playmate, he was replaced by Winston Guest, Aaron Hotchner and Gianfranco Ivancich. Hemingway's instructional impulse was strong. He learned fast, and expertly taught his older and younger wives, his mistresses, his sons and anyone else who came into his orbit.

His need for a kid brother gradually expanded to include a substantial group of followers and dependents. As early as 1934, Katy Dos Passos cast a critical eye on Hemingway and told the Murphys that he was "followed around all the time by a crowd of Cuban zombies who think he is Hernan Cortez.—He was sweet but has a tendency to be an Oracle." One friend put it more bluntly: "Hemingway loved to have a stooge, some person who would take care of 'the details.' "[10]

The pals in this category, all suitably nicknamed, included Father Andrés Untzaín (the Black Priest), Roberto Herrera (El Monstro) and Juan Dunabeitia (Sinsky)—with assorted Basque jai alai players as a kind of athletic chorus. Mario Menocal, Jr., wrote: "Father Andrés was a Basque priest, about the same age or a little older than Ernest, who had apparently blotted his copybook in Spain, through too much sympathy with the Loyalist cause, and had been sent by his superior to rusticate in a Cuban parish [Guira de Melena]. . . . Don Andrés was 100% Basque in his appetite for good and plentiful food and wine." Father Andrés was a character who drank, cursed and did not behave like a priest (it was extremely rare for anyone in the Spanish Church to support the Loyalists in the Civil War). He would arrive at the Finca smelling like a billy goat, and the maid would have to launder his habit and hang it out on the line to remove what Hemingway called his "odor of sanctity."

Roberto Herrera—younger brother of José Luis, who had been a surgeon in the International Brigade—was a bald, wiry man with a high-pitched voice. He worked for Sears in Havana and later became caretaker of the Finca. He was called El Monstro because he had once been bitten by a shark and lost a great deal of blood: only a monster could have survived that ordeal.[11] Juan Dunabeitia was a Basque sea captain from Bilbao who ran a freighter from Cuba to America and was called Sinbad the Sailor, or Sinsky. He would arrive at the Finca unannounced, release his unhousebroken dog, get drunk and begin to break valuable champagne glasses. All these cronies were rough, unconventional types who loved to drink and were completely devoted to Hemingway.

Another member of the cadre, who cared for Hemingway's body as Toby Bruce looked after his car, was George Brown, a tall ex-boxer who owned a gymnasium on West Fifty-seventh Street in New York. He would come down to Cuba for a month to spar with, exercise and massage the master. Brown once felled a strong jai alai player—who boasted he could not be knocked down by one blow—with a single punch to the stomach.

III

Hemingway composed *For Whom the Bell Tolls* between March 1939 and July 1940 in a Latin ambience that may well have made it easier for him to recreate the war in Spain. He wrote a poor book and two great stories about Africa, five poor stories and a great novel about the Spanish War. It seems that he could no longer use the same experience to achieve perfection in both genres, as he had done with the Great War. *A Farewell to Arms* was written ten years after the war; *For Whom the Bell Tolls* was begun while the war was still being fought. The young Hemingway delayed writing his earlier novel because he needed time to recover from the physical and psychological effects of his wound, to absorb and understand his experience, to learn how to write fiction. The older Hemingway was familiar with war, had observed the battles as a spectator rather than as a participant, and was writing for American readers who had not fought in the war and were eager to read about it. He knew another war was coming soon and felt he could not wait to write about Spain.

He planned to dedicate the book to Martha (who had shared his experiences in Spain and inspired the physical aspects of Maria) and wanted to create a work that was better than anything he had written while married to Pauline. He believed that "great writing comes out of a sense of injustice"[12] and wished to celebrate the ideals of the Loyalists even in their hour of defeat. There was a tremendous change in Hemingway from *A Farewell to Arms* to *For Whom the Bell Tolls*: from the portrayal of a personal to a national war, from the disillusionment and pessimism of a "separate peace" to the creation of a hero "involved in *Mankinde.*" The epigraph from John Donne's *Meditations* expressed this theme and foreshadowed the death of Robert Jordan.

The novel was also inspired by the noble example of *War and Peace*,

1. Young Ed and Grace Hemingway, a handsome Victorian couple, in 1897, a year after their marriage. Ed had a "big frame, quick movements, wide shoulders, hooked, hawk nose and beard that covered the weak chin" ("Fathers and Sons"). *(Hemingway Collection, John F. Kennedy Library)*

2. Anson Hemingway proudly poses in his Civil War uniform and medals in Oak Park on Memorial Day 1907, with his six grandchildren: Sunny, Ursula, Ernest, Marcelline and two of their cousins. Ernest is also martial and well armed with an oversized pistol and holster. *(Hemingway Collection, John F. Kennedy Library)*

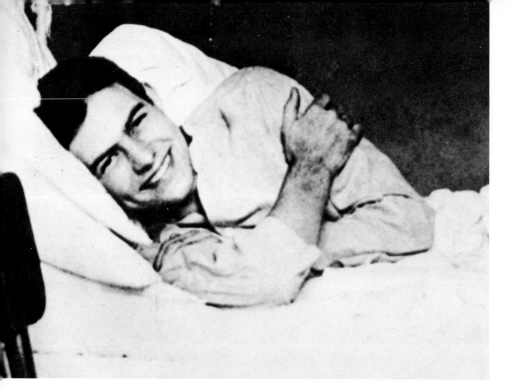

3. Ernest seems well on his way to recovery from his war wound in the Red Cross Hospital in Milan, July 1918. His leg is healing, he is in love with his nurse and he appears more joyous than traumatized. *(Hemingway Collection, John F. Kennedy Library)*

4. Agnes von Kurowsky, Milan, 1920. Agnes "was quite tall. She wore . . . a nurse's uniform, was blonde and had a tawny skin and gray eyes. I thought she was very beautiful" *(A Farewell to Arms). (Hemingway Collection, John F. Kennedy Library)*

5. Major General Chink Dorman-Smith, early 1940s. Chink, Hemingway's "best friend" after the Great War, had "the game cock walk of the professional British soldier" ("The Spanish War"). *(Christopher Dorman-O'Gowan)*

6. Hemingway and Hadley in Alpine gear in Chamby, Switzerland, January 1922, four months after their wedding. Hadley looks lovely and their eight-year age difference is not yet apparent. "She was smiling, the sun on her lovely face tanned by the snow and sun, beautifully built, her hair red-gold in the sun" *(A Moveable Feast)*. *(Patrick Hemingway)*

7. A rather dreamy and poetic John Dos Passos, New Orleans, winter 1924. After their quarrel Hemingway called him "a one-eyed Portuguese bastard." *(Elizabeth Dos Passos)*

8. Gertrude Stein, Paris, 1920s. "She had beautiful eyes and a strong German-Jewish face that also could have been Friulano and she reminded me of a northern Italian peasant woman with her clothes, her mobile face and her lovely, thick, alive immigrant hair" *(A Moveable Feast). (Harlingue-Viollet)*

9. Ford Madox Ford, James Joyce and Ezra Pound, Paris, 1923.

10. Scott, Zelda and Scottie Fitzgerald (looking a bit anxious), December 1925. They are elegantly dressed and doing a music hall turn in their luxurious Paris apartment—a strong contrast to the Hemingways' humble flat. *(Frances Fitzgerald Smith)*

11. Maxwell Perkins, 1920s. "I liked the way he wore his hat and the strange way his lips moved" ("The Art of Fiction").

12. Charles Scribner, early 1930s. "I loved Charlie very much and I understood him and appreciated him" *(Letters)*. *(Charles Scribner, Jr.)*

13.   Hemingway is balanced uneasily between the chic Pauline Pfeiffer (center) and the matronly Hadley while Gerald and Sara Murphy, who encouraged Pauline to pursue Hemingway, look on. Three Spanish shoeshine boys attend Gerald in Pamplona, July 1926. *(Hemingway Collection, John F. Kennedy Library)*

14.   Hemingway, warmly clothed and heavily bandaged after pulling a skylight down on his skull, has a look of sardonic resignation. Sylvia Beach gazes at him with girlish adoration in front of her Paris bookshop, Shakespeare and Company, March 1928. *(Patrick Hemingway)*

15.   A Herculean Hemingway, smartly dressed in a double-breasted wool suit, glowers at the camera for an unusually good snapshot, Princeton, October 1931. *(Hemingway Collection, John F. Kennedy Library)*

16. Hemingway, who lost many pounds during a bout of amoebic dysentery, triumphantly grips two kudu horns, Tanganyika, early 1934. *(By permission of Charles Scribner, Jr., courtesy of the Hemingway Collection, John F. Kennedy Library)*

17. Jane Mason, an outdoor Grace Kelly who had a love affair with Hemingway during his Key West period, with her husband Grant and two sons in their luxuriant garden at Jaimanitas, outside Havana, in the 1930s. *(By permission of Antony Mason, courtesy of the Hemingway Collection, John F. Kennedy Library)*

18. Gustavo Durán, 1936, in Loyalist uniform: "a damned good general
commanding a brigade" *(For Whom
the Bell Tolls). (Bonte Durán)*

19. Hemingway, showing real hair at the wrist, seems pleased with himself in
New York in the late 1930s. Martha Gellhorn wears a fox jacket. "She's very
beautiful, very friendly, and very charming and rather innocent—and quite
brave" *(The Fifth Column). (Hemingway Collection, John F. Kennedy Library)*

20. Hemingway and Martha with his three sons—Gregory, Patrick (seated), Jack (standing with crossed arms)—and his chauffeur Toby Bruce, enjoying life in Sun Valley, Idaho, fall 1940, as guests of the management. *(Tillie Arnold)*

21. Hemingway and Colonel Buck Lanham (who looks like Dashiell Hammett) standing near a captured German 88, on the Siegfried Line, September 1944, while a soldier readies a projectile to blast the Krauts. *(By permission of Jane Lanham, courtesy of the Hemingway Collection, John F. Kennedy Library)*

22.   Hemingway (canteen no doubt filled with gin) is being drawn by the war artist John Groth and photographed near the Siegfried Line, September 1944. *(John Groth)*

23.   Hemingway feeds Boise, one of his innumerable cats, while Mary, a "pocket Rubens," looks on. On the wall are Joan Miró's *The Farm* and a stuffed, silky-maned kudu. Finca Vigía, Havana, late 1940s. *(Hemingway Collection, John F. Kennedy Library)*

24. Hemingway, unusually attired in a tuxedo (but with short socks) talks to his beloved Adriana Ivancich during her visit to the Finca Vigía in October 1950. "She had pale, almost olive colored skin, a profile that could break your, or any one else's heart, and her dark hair, of an alive texture, hung down over her shoulders" *(Across the River). (Hemingway Collection, John F. Kennedy Library)*

25. The white-bearded Papa rests with a magnificent leopard, shot on his second safari to Kenya in the fall of 1953, just before the two air crashes destroyed his health. *(Earl Theisen)*

26. Hemingway, in a Basque beret, leather vest and Abercrombie hunting shirt, with Luis Miguel Dominguín and Ava Gardner, at El Escorial, May 1954.

27. A robust Hemingway, with flat checkered cap, stands between the bullfighters Cayetano Ordóñez, the model for Pedro Romero in *The Sun Also Rises,* and his son, Antonio, hero of "The Dangerous Summer," Spain, 1959. "Watching Antonio with the bull I saw that he had everything his father had in his great days" ("The Dangerous Summer"). *(Arjona)*

28.   Hemingway, despite his heroic persona, was a bookish man who owned a library of 7,400 volumes. He usually wore baggy shorts and loafers with no socks at the Finca Vigía, late 1950s. *(Hemingway Collection, John F. Kennedy Library)*

29. Hemingway's dazed and vacant stare reveals that the shock treatments at the Mayo Clinic have damaged his memory. He has become a frail old man. Ketchum, Idaho, April 1961. *(Hemingway Collection, John F. Kennedy Library)*

by his literary rivalry with André Malraux, and by the life and work of T. E. Lawrence. The ambitious scope, the epic quality, the vivid portrayal of a people and culture, the ideal of peasant wisdom, the interaction of war and love, the alternation of battle scenes with peaceful recollections—in flashbacks to Montana, Paris and Valencia before the war—all derive from Tolstoy. His letters to Perkins suggest how Hemingway was both stimulated by the military scenes and wary of the didactic passages of *War and Peace:* "Have the Bagration piece in [*Men at War*] and it is certainly the most compact account of an action in which the whole is visible through the part that is shown, that you can get. . . . I can write it like Tolstoi and make the book seem larger, wiser, and all the rest of it. But then I remember that was what I always skipped in Tolstoi."

Hemingway thought Malraux's *Man's Fate* (1933), a novel about the betrayal of the Communist revolution in Shanghai, was the best book he had read in ten years. But he was angry when Malraux, who had achieved a fine record in Spain, left the war to write a novel and published *Man's Hope* as early as 1937: "When finished am going to settle down and write and the pricks and fakers like Malraux who pulled out in Feb 37 to write gigantic masterpisses before it really started will have a good lesson when write ordinary sized book with the old stuff unfaked in it."[13] He was delighted when his novel, frequently compared to Malraux's, outsold Malraux's in France. Their personal and military rivalry would intensify in the next war.

Hemingway greatly admired T. E. Lawrence, whose guerrilla warfare defeated the Turks in the Arabian peninsula in World War One. He was thoroughly familiar with the numerous biographies of Lawrence, owned a copy of *Seven Pillars of Wisdom* (1935) and shared many of Lawrence's attitudes toward suffering and war.[14] Both Lawrence and Hemingway tested themselves by exposing their bodies to great pain. The explorer St. John Philby recorded that on a freezing train ride through Jordan in 1921, "we travelled ourselves on the engine, cowering as near the boiler as possible against the icy wind and driving sleet. Lawrence stood out on the dashboard the whole journey of three or four hours." Bill Smith recalled that the young Hemingway walked over broken glass with bare feet, cut his foot to show how tough he was and "set great store by it."

Both men believed endurance and pain led to self-knowledge. In the Arabian campaign Lawrence suffered stings and bites, boils and bruises, thirst and starvation, dysentery and delirium, broken bones and bullet wounds, torture and degradation. He wrote: "My body so dreaded further pain that now I had to force myself under fire. Generally, I had been hungry, lately always cold: frost and dirt had poisoned my hurts into a festering mass of sores."[15] Hemingway also suffered a long series of injuries and illnesses; and stressed the intense cold, hunger and fatigue in the Spanish War. Like Lawrence in *Seven Pillars of Wisdom*, he took morbid pleasure in emphasizing the grisly details of war wounds in "The Natural History of the Dead." And like Lawrence, he was fascinated by gruesome photographs of mutilated bodies; he took and collected pictures of bloated corpses after the Matecumbe hurricane and reproduced some astonishing horrors in "Dying, Well or Badly" (*Ken,* April 1938).

Both Lawrence and Robert Jordan are technical experts who, though foreign, assume the leadership of a guerrilla group operating behind enemy lines. Both have a scholarly background, have spent a long time in the country before the war, and have a sound knowledge of the language and culture of the people they lead. Neither feels like a foreigner nor is treated like one. Both adopt an alien cause for their own idealistic reasons. Both destroy bridges by detonating explosives. Both are forced to kill their own wounded men.

Tolstoy, T. E. Lawrence and Hemingway all wrote from personal experience in combat. Like *War and Peace* and *Seven Pillars of Wisdom, For Whom the Bell Tolls* includes elements of autobiography, history, ethnology and topography. All three books express heroic idealism and epic grandeur, combine chaotic scenes of warfare with minute observation of detail, and mingle intervals of meditation with a yearning for primitivistic and patriarchal simplicity.

There are three kinds of characters in *For Whom the Bell Tolls:* the purely fictional (the Spanish guerrilla band); the ones based on real people (Maria on Martha, Robert Jordan on Hemingway and Robert Merriman, Karkov on the Russian correspondent Mikhail Koltzov, General Golz on the Polish soldier Karol Swierczewski); and real military and political figures who appear under their own names to give a sense of historical immediacy (Gustavo Durán, Enrique Lister, La Pasionaria, Queipo de Llano and the murderous French commissar, André Marty).[16]

The novel criticizes religion ("If there were God, never would He have permitted what I have seen with my eyes. Let *them* [the Fascists] have God.") and supports the Reds ("Here in Spain the Communists offered the best discipline and the soundest and sanest for the prosecution of the war."). But it also describes Communist atrocities, for the Reds in Pilar's village beat the Fascists to death with flails and throw them off the top of the cliff into the river. The physical setting of this scene was inspired by the deep El Tajo gorge that cuts through the Andalusian town of Ronda. In *Death in the Afternoon* Hemingway wrote that in Ronda "they drag the dead horses over the edge of the cliff and the buzzards that have circled over the town and high in the air over the ring all day, drop down to feed on the rocks below the town." His description of how Marty (who "kills more than the bubonic plague")[17] prevents Andrés and Major Gomez from delivering Jordan's message asking General Golz to cancel the hopeless attack explains how the factionalism of the Left led to their defeat in the war.

The action takes place during three days in late May 1937 (a month after Hemingway arrived in Spain) in the magnificent Sierra de Guadarrama, northwest of Madrid, between El Escorial and Segovia. Jordan must blow up the bridge as soon as the Loyalist attack starts, and not before, so that Fascist reinforcements cannot use the road. The strategy of the novel is to create a number of elements that increase the difficulties and intensify the suspense. In addition to the precise timing of the mission, there is Pilar's fatal prophecy, Pablo's treacherous opposition, Maria's love (which arouses the men's hostility toward Jordan), the snow, the Fascist planes, the difficulty of escaping afterwards, the massacre of Sordo's band, the loss of the detonators, the enemy's awareness of their plans, the cavalry patrols, the defense of the bridge and Andrés' inability to deliver the message to Golz.

The taut structure perfectly enhances the meaning. The words of the last sentence repeat those of the first one ("He lay flat on the brown, pine-needled floor of the forest") and—as in Joyce's *Finnegans Wake* (1939)—link with each other to complete the circular unity of the book. The sexual encounters with Maria mark the passage of the nights. And there is a fine counterpoint in the last ten chapters, which alternate between Andrés' difficulties en route to Golz and Jordan's preparations to blow up the bridge—if the attack cannot be cancelled.

Pilar, the domineering, operatic leader of the guerrilla group, has more than a touch of Grace Hemingway's forceful personality. Her peroration on the odor of death (which recalls the hyena in "The Snows of Kilimanjaro" just as the final sentence of the novel echoes the last sentence of that story) is one of the most moving passages in the book. Pilar expresses Hemingway's favorite analogy between bullfighting and battle just as Jordan compares the American and the Spanish civil wars, the behavior of his brave grandfather and his cowardly father. Pilar's coarse encouragement of the lovers has been criticized as unconvincing (like Rinaldi in *A Farewell to Arms,* she questions the lovers about their sexual relations). But Pilar reveals her complex motives when she declares her love for Maria, says she does "not make perversions" and suggests she is satisfying her sexual attraction to both Jordan and Maria by a vicarious participation in their love life.

The relation of Jordan and Maria has some interesting similarities to that of Frederic Henry and Catherine in the earlier novel of love and war. Both romances are speeded up and intensified by the stress of psychological wounds and the pressures of combat: "You had better love her very hard," Jordan says, "and make up in intensity what the relation will lack in duration and in continuity." Catherine has been traumatized by the death of her fiancé, Maria by the political execution of her father and her brutal rape by the Fascists. Love helps to heal and obliterate both tragedies. Despite Maria's violation, which makes her more sexually exciting, she retains her essential innocence without losing her sexual desire. Frederic replaces Catherine's lost fiancé; Jordan imaginatively cancels the rape, restores Maria's virginity and triumphs over his sexual rivals: "And no one has done anything to thee. Thee, they cannot touch. No one has touched thee." Maria instantly responds to *his* touch, which embarrasses even Pilar, takes the initiative and asks where he is sleeping so she can come to him at night. The second description of Jordan and Maria in the sleeping bag, with the metaphor of the earth moving during orgasm (probably inspired by experiencing a bombardment in bed), is the most famous scene in Hemingway's work. When his fishing friend Ben Finney got an erection while reading this passage in typescript, Hemingway cynically said: "It will sell."[18]

He wrote and then cut one scene where Jordan masturbates on the night before battle because Maria has "great soreness and much pain," but left in the references to Onan in Chapter 31. He also deleted a 1,500-word epilogue, in two short chapters, as he had done in *A Farewell to Arms:*

In the first of these Karkov and Golz meet after the failure of the attack, and in driving back from the front they talk together about it, and about

Robert's message and his success in blowing up the bridge. In the second, Andrés and Gomez motorcycle back to the outpost and then Andrés makes his way over the ground he covered before, and eventually reaches the abandoned camp, sees the ruined bridge, and knows all that has happened there.[19]

Two bizarre incidents occurred after the novel was published, in October 1940. In April 1941 the book was unanimously voted the best American novel of the year by the Pulitzer Prize committee, but the nomination was vetoed by the extreme Right-wing president of Columbia University, Nicholas Murray Butler, and no prize was awarded that year. In June 1941 Hemingway was accused of plagiarizing his novel from the work of a screenwriter, John De Montijo. He alleged Hemingway had attended a party in Hollywood in February 1939 at which De Montijo read aloud his script *Viva Madero.* Hemingway made a sworn statement that he was living in Havana at the time of the party, won the suit and was awarded the $4,500 costs. But De Montijo was unable to pay them and Scribner's aroused Hemingway's fury by deducting $1,000 from his royalties for his share of the legal fees.[20]

For Whom the Bell Tolls was a Book-of-the-Month Club choice and sold half a million copies in the first five months. The critical equaled the commercial success. Most reviewers received the book enthusiastically and thought it fulfilled the promise, in *To Have and Have Not,* of a new social and political awareness. They felt it compensated for the disappointing works of the 1930s and triumphantly re-established Hemingway's literary reputation.

Despite Hemingway's clear sympathy with the Loyalists, the novel was attacked by Communist critics for portraying the atrocities of the Left. Alvah Bessie, a veteran of the Lincoln Brigade, claimed in an open letter to the *Daily Worker* that Hemingway had maligned the popular leader La Pasionaria, slandered the political commissar André Marty and misrepresented Russia's attitude toward Spain. As Bessie lamented in *New Masses:* "He is found in bad company; in the company of his enemies, and the people's enemies who will fawn upon him and use him, his great talents and his passion for the people's cause, to traduce and betray those talents and those people."[21]

Though Edmund Wilson had serious reservations about the merits of the novel, his review in the *New Republic* in October 1940 (quoted here) was more favorable than his judgment in *The Wound and the Bow*

(1941): "There is in *For Whom the Bell Tolls* an imagination for social and political phenomena such as he has hardly given evidence of before. . . . What Hemingway presents us with in this study of the Spanish war is not so much a social analysis as a criticism of moral qualities." Dorothy Parker, who had admired Hemingway's stories in 1927, was ecstatic about the novel: "It is written with a wisdom that washes the mind and cools it. It is written with an understanding that rips the heart with compassion." Howard Mumford Jones, who began with an interesting comparison with *A Farewell to Arms,* also praised the characters, style, theme and (unlike the Communist critics) the honesty: "He has not omitted the drunkenness, the disorder, the cruelty, the selfishness, the confusion. The hero dies because of stupidity and treachery on his own side." And the playwright Robert Sherwood agreed that Hemingway's degree of delicacy proved that he "is capable of self-criticism and self-development" and has achieved a rare "sense of permanence and nobility of spirit."[22]

Lionel Trilling, in a positive review, stated Hemingway "is wholly aware of the moral and political tensions which existed in actual fact." He said the book revealed "a restored Hemingway writing to the top of his bent" and that the episodes of El Sordo and Andrés "are equal to Tolstoy in his best battle manner." He then proceeded to delineate the weaknesses: the astonishing melodrama in place of tragedy, the devastating meaninglessness of the death of Robert Jordan, the "rather dull convention in which the men are all dominance and knowledge, the women all essential innocence and responsive passion." After unfavorably contrasting Hemingway's attitude toward death with that of John Donne, Trilling concluded: "he is wholly at the service of the cult of experience and the result is a novel which, undertaking to celebrate the community of men, actually glorifies the isolation of the individual ego."

Mark Schorer was primarily concerned with the change and development in Hemingway's subject and style, "from violent experience itself to the expressed evaluation of violence. . . . If the early books plead for sporting conduct on violent occasions, this book pleads for the moral necessity of political violence." Schorer disagreed with Edmund Wilson's argument that Hemingway had no political persuasion, for in this work the individual "vanishes in the political whole, but vanishes precisely to defend his dignity, his freedom, his virtue." Schorer's statement that Hemingway presented a "poetic realization of man's *collec-*

tive virtues" is more convincing than Trilling's view that he "glorifies the isolation of the individual ego."[23]

The English critics were, as usual, less keen than the Americans. In a lively review in the *Spectator,* Graham Greene criticized the love story, "told with Mr. Hemingway's usual romantic carnality," but acknowledged that "he has brought out of the Spanish war a subtlety and sympathy which were not there before." V. S. Pritchett, author of *The Spanish Temper* (1954), repeated Wyndham Lewis' idea that Hemingway had been an unreflective and unself-critical writer, felt that Malraux was immeasurably superior, and agreed with Greene that the novel was marred by the love affair, which was "fatal to the austerity of the narrative." But he praised the dignity and pathos of the characters, the "astonishingly real Spanish conversation" and the "studied and intense" action. He concluded that the Spanish War has "restored to Hemingway his seriousness as a writer."

E. M. Forster, writing a short moralistic paragraph in the *Listener,* called Hemingway a combatant and saw a penitential theme in the novel: "It is full of courage and brutality and foul language. It is also full of tenderness and decent values, and the idea running through it is that, though there must be a war in which we must all take part, there will have to be some sort of penance after the war if the human race is to get straight again."[24]

The most unusual and provocative response to the novel was a discussion of Spanish culture and mores by the novelist Arturo Barea, who had known Hemingway during the Civil War. Barea argued that Hemingway understood very little of Spain beyond the bullring, failed to render the reality of the Spanish War, and produced an unreal and untruthful picture of the people and the period. Barea's five main criticisms were that the peasants of Old Castile could never have accepted as their leaders "the old gypsy whore from Andalusia with her lover, the horse-dealer"; that the community of a Castilian village would never have followed Pablo in his organized butchery of the Fascists; that in the rape scene, it would be "impossible for a Spaniard to want the union of his body with that of a woman still warm and moist from another male"; that Maria could not ask "a foreigner to let her come into his bed the very first night after they had met . . . and keep the respectful adoration of the members of her guerilla group"; and that he "invents an artificial and pompous English" to convey the original Spanish.[25]

Though Barea is a Spaniard, his generalizations about the Spanish people are less convincing than Hemingway's. The villagers might have accepted Pilar and Pablo as their leaders, during the unusual conditions of guerrilla war, if they were the most effective military commanders; and the violence and hatred of wartime might well have led to the kind of brutal massacre that would otherwise have been impossible. The violent emotions aroused during rape would be sufficient to dispel fastidious feelings about moist females. It is unlikely that Maria would make sexual overtures to Jordan; but she has been deranged by the rape and then encouraged by Pilar to sleep with Jordan, and her behavior arouses the hostility rather than the adoration of the group. Moreover, Hemingway is clearly writing a highly romanticized rather than a strictly realistic love story. Finally, he does not attempt to translate the Spanish, but provides an English version that will sound archaic, poetic and noble. In this novel, as well as in *The Sun Also Rises,* he often achieves his effects by rendering stilted latinate equivalents instead of colloquial translations.

Hemingway named Donald Friede agent for the film rights of *For Whom the Bell Tolls* to compensate him for the "loss" of *The Sun Also Rises,* which he had advised Horace Liveright to publish in 1925. Friede sold the rights to Paramount for $100,000 (Arguelles remembered Hemingway's excited phone call announcing this sale), and after this novel more income came from movies than from books.

IV

When Hemingway finally left Pauline in September 1939, he made the transition from Wyoming to Idaho just as he did from Key West to Cuba —he had to change his residence when he changed his wives—and spent the rest of his life in Havana and in the old mining town of Ketchum. Sun Valley (a new town built just east of Ketchum) is situated amidst the marvelous scenery of the Sawtooth Mountains of south-central Idaho, twelve miles north of Hailey, where Pound was born in 1885. It had been opened as a ski resort in 1936 by Averell Harriman and the Union Pacific Railroad. The company, eager for publicity and well aware of Hemingway's reputation as a sportsman, paid all his expenses there, beginning in 1939, in return for using his name in their advertisements. Like Wyoming, Idaho had excellent shooting and fishing, and offered a stimulating change from the humid hurricane weather in the Cuban autumn. A number of Basques—who had a reputation for being tough and anarchic, and had opposed Franco during and after the war—farmed the land around Sun Valley and provided another attraction. Hemingway spent part of the fall and winter in Sun Valley during 1939–41 and 1946–47, and in Ketchum (where he bought a house) during 1958–61.

Hemingway immediately made a number of new friends in Idaho —Clara Spiegel, Taylor Williams, Lloyd and Tillie Arnold—who shared his interest in outdoor life. In this society, as in Cuba, the most highly valued trait was sporting skill. Clara was the wife of Frederick Spiegel, who had served with Hemingway as a Red Cross ambulance driver in Italy and was a successful businessman in Chicago. She met Hemingway in 1939 and became a close friend of both Martha and Mary Welsh. Clara was very fond of Hemingway; she thought he was witty and great fun, extremely sensitive and a good father. He gave her excellent advice about writing (she later published several novels) and invited her to watch the televised prizefights on Friday nights.[26]

"Beartracks" Williams (twelve years older than Hemingway) came to Idaho from Kentucky with his three children in about 1910, opened a hardware and sporting goods store, and became the chief guide of Sun Valley. He liked bourbon, chased the ladies till his death in 1959, and used his free Union Pacific rail pass to spend some winters in Key West and enjoy the whorehouses of Havana. Hemingway admired his skill as pathfinder and deerslayer; and Beartracks paid him a handsome compliment in 1941: "I saw Ernest jump from his horse, cover a hundred-yard dash on foot, and drop a running antelope at two hundred and seventy five yards with a single shot."[27]

Lloyd Arnold—whom Toby Bruce called a fun-loving fellow, "full of piss and vinegar"—was born in 1906 in Council Bluffs, Iowa. He found his job as an undertaker's apprentice rather confining, joined the Union Pacific as a photographer, came to Sun Valley in 1937, worked with Gene Van Guilder (the head of public relations, who was killed in a hunting accident in 1939) and became head photographer two years later. In 1968 Arnold wrote a homespun picture book, *High on the Wild with Hemingway*, which had cameo appearances by Ingrid Bergman and Gary Cooper, and portrayed his hero in field and stream, bar and barbecue.

Tillie Arnold, Lloyd's petite and pretty wife, worked in the Sun

Valley camera shop and met Hemingway soon after he arrived in September 1939. When she asked about his strange breakfast of marinated herring and beer, he explained: "Daughter, it's good for the kidneys." She heard him tell many richly embellished stories, and (like most of his listeners) found them fascinating. She almost never saw him drunk, though he once said: "Daughter, will you take me home?" In 1940, when she saw him shaving and mentioned that he and the boys would be late for church, he seemed in no hurry and replied: "We'll get there for the seventh inning."[28]

V

All the events of 1939—the commitment to Martha, the moves to Cuba and Idaho, and the writing of *For Whom the Bell Tolls*—were overshadowed by the storm and stress of his separation from Pauline. This was, in many ways, a repetition of his break with Hadley and aroused powerful feelings of remorse. He felt guilty about not having loved Hadley and Bumby enough to resist the attractions of Pauline. (Though the big money would not come until after the publication of *For Whom the Bell Tolls* in 1940, he was much wealthier than when he first met Pauline in 1925 and confident of his ability to earn as much as he needed.) When he finally left Pauline in September, he blamed her for making him betray Hadley and thought she was getting exactly what she deserved. He was fond of quoting Matthew 26:52 (as Robert Cohn had done in *The Sun Also Rises*) and telling Pauline: those that "live by the sword shall perish by the sword."[29]

When Hemingway reached Key West in late December 1939, he told Toby Bruce to take from the house everything that Pauline did not want. He stored his trunks, suitcases, books and animal heads in Sloppy Joe's bar; and they remained there for more than twenty years until rescued by Mary, after his death, in the fall of 1961. On December 26 he drove onto the Key West–Havana ferry. Harry Sylvester, who was at the dock with Hemingway's sons (Pauline had gone to New York to avoid her husband), recalled:

> The two children had brought little firecrackers, but we had no matches, so I borrowed a cigarette from a lady at the dock and the boys lit and threw the firecrackers toward the boat, which was not very big so

that the two boys could get as close as 15 or 20 feet to their father. Some fat, professional liberal, whom I have not seen before or since, managed to introduce himself to EH and this distracted him during the farewell.[30]

The boys took the break-up of the marriage very well. They were used to the prolonged absences of their father in Cuba, Wyoming, Africa and Spain during the 1930s. Jack seemed very happy to live with his mother and spend holidays (when Hemingway was at his best) with his father. Patrick felt he was treated better by both parents after the divorce. Pauline, though much more hostile than Hadley had ever been, helped Hemingway during Patrick's serious illness in 1947.

It must have been unpleasant for Pauline when the boys returned from Cuba ecstatically praising the young, adventurous Martha, as they had once praised Jane Mason. Though Pauline was bitter, it took quite a while for her to get over her passion for Hemingway. Gregory remembers that after the divorce, Pauline looked at photographs of Hemingway and exclaimed: "God, he was handsome then, look at those *eyes*, so alive and interested." Hemingway, who always needed someone to blame, told Hotchner, after Pauline's death and his quarrel with Gregory, that he always had good relations with Jack and had been fine with his other sons for a long time. But Pauline had deliberately turned the younger boys against him and created hostility between them.[31]

One significant and recurrent pattern of behavior in Hemingway's life was the revision, in his own mind, of what had actually occurred and the selection of a scapegoat to relieve himself of any guilt. He blamed his mother for his "unhappy childhood," for preventing him from going to college and for his father's suicide. He blamed Pauline, Dos Passos and the Murphys for breaking up his marriage to Hadley; and Jinny Pfeiffer for destroying his marriage to Pauline. As early as December 1939, he complained to Mary Pfeiffer: "Virginia's version of my life and conduct is a very fantastic one. But she spread it sufficiently and at the right time to break up my home." He later claimed that Martha cuckolded him and accused Gregory of causing Pauline's death. He could perceive this revisionist tendency in others and criticized Charles Thompson for the same weakness in *Green Hills of Africa:* "As always when he was confused, it was someone [else's] fault,"[32] but he could not see it in himself. Gregory attributed this characteristic to Hemingway's puritan conscience and told the Murphys' daughter: "My father had a terribly powerful remorseful conscience. It would give him no rest when he made a mistake so he constantly had to find scapegoats." Hemingway even called Pauline a whore (which was certainly not true) to justify his behavior.[33]

Hemingway had been fascinated by lesbianism since the early 1920s. Hadley had admitted her sexual attraction to Mrs. Rapallo; he had observed this aspect of Gertrude Stein and Sylvia Beach; and he had satirically portrayed lesbianism in "Mr. and Mrs. Elliot" (1924) and "The Sea Change" (1931). Robert McAlmon, who was an invert, started the rumor in the late 1920s that Hemingway was homosexual and Pauline lesbian, and was socked in the jaw for his malice. Hemingway believed that Jinny had always been jealous of his marriage and told Toby Bruce: "Jinny is a lesbian—and trying to get Pauline into the business."[34]

There was only a particle of truth in this fundamental distortion. Though Jinny was a lesbian, she did not try to influence Pauline's sexual tastes or turn her against Hemingway until *after* the marriage broke up. Pauline tolerated his infidelity from 1933 to 1939 and clung to him, amidst the ruins, throughout their final year. The separation had a much more powerful effect on her than on Hemingway or the boys; and she was shocked to be abandoned when she was forty-four. After the divorce, she tried to rebuild her life and opened a fabric shop in Key West with Lorine Thompson. She had a few liaisons with naval officers during World War Two and once asked Gregory if he thought she should marry one of her suitors. In about 1946, disillusioned with men, she turned to her own sex, had love affairs with the poet Elizabeth Bishop and several other women. After his divorce from Martha, Hemingway radically revised his view of his second and third marriages, and wrote more sympathetically of Pauline (whom Martha had now replaced as the villain) in an awkward, unpublished passage in "The Monument." He said that he did not like Martha and never wrote to her. But he sometimes wrote to Pauline, who was busy with naval officers in Key West, with business ventures, with the upkeep of her estate and with the land of Gomorrah. Pauline hated him and thought him a fool for marrying Martha, and he entirely agreed with her judgment.[35]

Jinny later adopted two children and in the 1950s lived next door to Aldous and Laura Huxley on Deronda Drive in Los Angeles. The Huxleys moved into Jinny's rented house after a fire destroyed both the Huxley and Pfeiffer homes in 1961, and Aldous died there two years later. Laura lived in Jinny's house for many years and helped bring up her children. Huxley's biographer described Jinny as "a quiet woman; observant, intelligent; of precarious health herself, good with the ill, the depressed; helpful and self-forgetting in a crisis. Aldous liked her. 'She has no Bovaristic [self-deceiving romantic] angle,' he would say."[36]

When the crisis in Pauline's marriage occurred, Jinny felt Hemingway was behaving cruelly and naturally sided with her sister. She was prone to judge others in an Olympian way and certainly stiffened Pauline's resolve to inflict economic penalties on Hemingway—tangible retribution for his guilt—after the divorce. When things went badly, Jinny told Pauline: "you can't stand for this."[37] When he asked Pauline for a divorce, she said: " 'Ernest, if you divorce me I'll take everything you've got.' Ernest replied, 'Pauline, if you let me have a divorce, you can have everything I've got.' " But he bitterly regretted this concession after paying Pauline $500 a month child support for ten years and criticized her in a letter to his latest love, Adriana Ivancich. Pauline, wrote Hemingway ironically, after inheriting half a million dollars from her mother, felt very poor and demanded more money from him.[38]

In 1943, when his guilt about Pauline was compacted with his disillusionment about Martha, he compared suffering from women to an incurable disease that even penicillin could not cure, and told Max Perkins, with a flash of insight that suggested he knew his own behavior might have had something to do with his three failed marriages: "take as good a woman as Pauline—a hell of a wonderful woman—and once she turns mean. Although, of course, it is your own actions that turn her mean. Mine I mean."[39]

17

Finca Vigía and China
1940–1942

> Anyone who marries three girls from
> St. Louis hasn't learned much.
>
> GERTRUDE STEIN

I

Toward the end of 1940 Hemingway had a new wife and a new novel, just as he had Pauline and *A Farewell to Arms* in 1929. *For Whom the Bell Tolls* was his most ambitious and successful book, Martha his most beautiful and talented wife. But he could not maintain his marriage or his literary achievement and both began to decline that year. The Spanish novel would be his last book for a decade and the best times with Martha were nearly over by the time they actually married.

When Hemingway fell in love with a woman he usually tried to convince himself, despite all previous failures, that he would be able to love her for the rest of his life. Suited to serial if not permanent matrimony, he confessed: "I'm a fool with women—I always feel I have to marry 'em." But he also boasted: "I always marry good wives."[1] Hadley was eight years older than Hemingway, Pauline four years older; but Martha, nine years younger, was young enough to be Hadley's daughter. He could no longer be sure that Martha (like his previous wives) was physically attracted to him: his literary reputation was also an important factor for the ambitious lady writer. When they had sexual problems, his doubts about their relationship increased and were expressed in aggressive behavior. The older wives seemed to have the advantage in the struggle for power in marriage, but Martha stood up to him much more than any woman since Grace Hemingway. Though Martha could

348

not dominate him, she would not submit to his will—and the clash of two competitive egos eventually destroyed their marriage.

On September 1, 1940, as they were leaving for Sun Valley, Martha told Clara Spiegel why they had to maintain discretion and travel separately: "We had hoped to be married (for the convenience of it) by the time we came west. . . . It would seem that wherever we travel, citizens want E's autograph, and absolutely lamentable females from St. Louis recognize me. This is only troublesome because of repercussions where they will do most harm [at home]. Myself, I think living in sin is wonderful (we are now on our fourth contented year), but matrimony is probably simpler." When they married in Cheyenne on November 21, shortly after his divorce became final, Martha increased their age difference (Pauline had decreased it) and said she was twenty-eight, though she was actually thirty-two.

As they continued east to Kansas City, he was interviewed and photographed by his old newspaper, the *Star*. He recalled Italy's modern military defeats at Adowa, Caporetto and Guadalajara, and predicted that country would suffer disasters in Albania and Greece. He also had a warm reunion with Luis Quintanilla, who had commanded the Loyalist forces at the siege of the Alcázar in 1936 and was then artist-in-residence at the University of Kansas City. Hemingway praised his friend's splendid record in the war: "Luis went up fast in the Spanish Loyalist army. He was one of the leaders who seized the Montana barracks in Madrid when the war began. He became a general. Later, he was in charge of the counterespionage against the fifth column in Madrid."[2]

Martha was very good with Hemingway's sons (as Pauline had been with Jack), partly because she could have fun with them on holidays without the tedium and responsibility of daily life. Jack found her glamorous and exciting, and was fascinated by her stories of war; Patrick thought of her more as a friend than as a stepmother; Gregory, who had the greatest need for maternal love and was most attached to her, later took a more cynical view: he felt that she tried hard to be a good mother because it was expected of her, but had more primness than natural spontaneity. Hemingway praised her relations with the boys, said that she tried very hard to please them and had won their love.

Hadley and Pauline had considered Hemingway's life and work more important than their own and had devoted themselves to caring for him, his children and his house. Martha got along very well with him until their marriage and reasonably well until 1944, but she did not want to be merely the wife of a famous writer. Though she refused to publish under the name of Martha Hemingway, she appeared on the dust jacket of her novel *A Stricken Field* (1940) as "Martha Gellhorn (now Mrs. Ernest Hemingway)." She had spent two months (November 1939–January 1940) covering the war in Finland—which provoked Hemingway's homespun query: "What old Indian likes to lose his squaw with a hard winter coming on?"—and spent the rest of their marriage traveling and reporting for *Collier's* in the Caribbean (1942) and in Europe (1943–45). Fitzgerald, whose prediction about a new wife for each new novel had come true, foresaw problems and thought it odd to see "Ernest married to a really attractive woman. I think the pattern will be somewhat different than with his Pygmalion-like creations."[3]

Hemingway, not used to solitude, became gloomy when left alone and resented Martha's frequent absence. When she was with her mother in St. Louis and Florida and when he was sub hunting on the *Pilar*, she wrote him loving letters to cheer him up and mollify his anger. In May 1942 she told him: "I'm counting every day until I come. I guess I love you very much or something." In December 1942 she said she was grateful for their marvelous life and would kill herself if anything happened to him. In July 1943 she promised, with oriental obsequiousness, to spoil him with too much attention when he returned and scatter rose petals wherever he walked. And as late as October 1943, when she left for London without him, she apologetically confessed: "Please know how much I love you. . . . You are a much better man than me, but I hope I am not too bad a wife even if I have gone away when I thought you would be away too."[4]

Hemingway missed her when she was away and criticized her when she returned. On Christmas day 1943, two months after Martha had left for England, he sent a pitiful lament to MacLeish that showed how deeply he loved her. He said he was sick with loneliness for Marty and felt his heart had been cut out. He loved her so completely and exclusively that he had been abandoned by everyone who used to love him. He now had Marty and no one else. If anything happened to her, he would be destroyed. A year and a half later, when the marriage was over, he told Sara Murphy, with more sarcasm than sentiment: "I need a wife in bed and not in the most widely circulated magazines."[5] Though lonely, he was not seriously tempted by other women and remained faithful to Martha while living in Cuba.

Though they longed for each other when separated, they found it difficult to live together; and their frequent quarrels provoked Martha to take more trips. His rough but obsequious gang of Cuban cronies— the Black Priest, El Monstro, Sinsky and all the rest—disturbed her household and got on her nerves. When Hemingway's income from the royalties and film rights of *For Whom the Bell Tolls* shot up in 1941 and 1942, he began to pay enormous income tax: over $100,000 a year or eighty percent of his earnings. Though still well off, he became anxious about alimony, taxes and the lack of cash, and felt he might go broke. Martha resented the fact that he never bought her anything; he complained that she was mean about pennies and extravagant with large sums of money. Martha, who had a critical temperament and a sharp tongue, did not hesitate to express exasperation and anger about his dirtiness, his lies, his drinking, his rudeness and his smelly cats. Hemingway, used to adoration and absolute freedom, became savagely abusive.

Martha admittedly had a mania for keeping clean; Hemingway, while sailing, habitually wore shirt and shorts stained with fish blood. Even friends like Thorwald Sánchez noticed that his clothes did not fit him and were not clean. Martha, who always dressed well, wanted him to bathe more often, be well-groomed and wear smart apparel—but this was a hopeless cause. His Cuban and Sun Valley friends enjoyed his drunken, exaggerated stories (for they did not have to listen to them every day), but Martha was more censorious and expressed scorn for the man who talked a good deal about telling the truth in his work yet was an inveterate liar.

One of the most serious problems in their marriage was Hemingway's heavy drinking. Like many modern American writers—Jack London, Sinclair Lewis, Ring Lardner, O'Neill, Chandler, Hammett, Fitzgerald, Faulkner, Hart Crane, Steinbeck, Wolfe, O'Hara and Agee—he suffered from alcoholism. Like the others, he found liquor an instant relief from the oppressive strain of writing as well as an anodyne for the even greater torments of creative sterility. It was always easier to drink than to work. His drinking noticeably increased after 1940, after the hardships of Spain and the exhausting effort on his novel. Toward the end of his life, when his alcoholism became dangerous and he was forced to revert to ancestral teetotalism, he regretfully told MacLeish: "Trouble was all my life when things were really bad I could always take a drink and right away they were much better. When you can't take a drink is different. Wine I never thought anybody could take away from you. But they can."

Leicester said that during the late 1930s in Key West, his brother was drinking about seventeen Scotch and sodas a day. Hemingway always made the adolescent association between heavy drinking and masculinity, and boasted in February 1940: "Started out on absinthe, drank a bottle of good red wine with dinner, shifted to vodka in town before the pelota game and then battened it down with whiskeys and sodas until 3 a.m." While fishing in Cuba, he would take a bottle of champagne to bed and empty it by morning. During World War Two, according to Buck Lanham, he was a "massive drinker. Bottle at bedside, drank all day." In 1953 Mayito Menocal saw him sneaking out of his African tent for a drink at five in the morning. But Lanham "never saw him stagger, lose balance, get overly thick-tongued."[6] Clara Spiegel, who was impressed when he drank wine from a goatskin and sang at the same time, saw him affected by drink but never actually drunk. In the 1940s, his tremendously strong constitution seemed able to absorb unlimited quantities of alcohol without adverse effects. But it would eventually take its toll. The escape into heavy drinking certainly made him more aggressive, unpleasant and difficult to live with. Martha noted that his drinking was directly related to his anxiety; that he drank very little, for example, during the critical acclamation of *For Whom the Bell Tolls*. Hemingway was well aware of the danger, but thought he could control it and did not try to limit his drinking. In "The Snows of Kilimanjaro," the autobiographical hero wasted his talents as a writer "by drinking so much that he blunted the edge of his perceptions"; in October 1940 Hemingway admitted to Perkins that he was "not nearly as good with a rifle [as he had been] due I guess to drinking too much for too many years."[7]

Many friends witnessed the Hemingways' explosive arguments. In July 1940, four months before their marriage, Martha, furious that he had failed to keep an appointment for lunch, found him with friends in the Floridita and screamed: "You can stand me up, but you can't do that to my mother."[8] Carlos Baker reported two extremely unpleasant incidents that occurred at the end of 1942: "One night in Havana he scolded her publicly for lack of generosity in Christmas gifts to the Finca servants, and then drove the Lincoln home alone, leaving her to fend for herself. On another evening, when she insisted on driving because he had been drinking, he slapped her with the back of his hand.

She braked his well-loved Lincoln to a safe ten miles an hour and deliberately drove it through a ditch and into a tree, leaving him there and walking back home."[9] This was a degrading contrast to his joy rides with Jane Mason.

Hemingway trusted Pauline's literary judgment—possibly because she praised inferior works like *Green Hills of Africa* and *To Have and Have Not*—and when she refused to read *For Whom the Bell Tolls,* he solicited Martha's opinion. She genuinely admired the book, praised his hard work and called the novel funny, wonderful, live and exciting. Many years later, however, Martha claimed that she had always been terribly critical of Hemingway and had deliberately wounded him: "I hurt his feelings early on in the Bell by failing to be approving. I don't like the book at all actually. Same with articles [on Spain]. So, hurt and furious, he sought better audiences like his hunting and fishing chums. Very funny sweet scene in Cuba, E. reading aloud from The Bell to a bunch of grown-up well-off semi-literate pigeon shooting and fishing pals, they sitting on the floor spellbound."[10] Martha apparently resented his Cuban friends, who were not semi-literate but quite intelligent. In 1940, during their honeymoon period, Martha (even if she had not admired the book) would not have been foolish enough to express her disapproval of his magnum opus. She knew very well that he was highly sensitive and easily hurt, that he needed encouragement to continue his work, that her adverse opinion would arouse his hostility and have a disastrous effect on their marriage.

During a dinner in Paris with the novelist Louis Bromfield in March 1927, Hemingway was disgusted when Bromfield's "cats kept jumping on the table and running off with what little fish there was and then shitting on the floor." But in Cuba he too developed a passion for cats, kept dozens of them and was more tolerant of their habits than Bromfield ever was. The cats walked all over the dinner table and had a terrible smell. In about 1943, when he was away from the Finca, Martha sterilized all the males. His Cuban friends—Thorwald and Tina Sánchez, Elicio Arguelles and Mario Menocal, Jr.—believed this was a petty act of revenge and a symbolic castration of her husband. Martha maintained that she castrated the cats to prevent them from inbreeding with siblings and producing great numbers of blind and deformed offspring. Hemingway was deeply hurt and angry. He often exclaimed: "she cut my cats!" and never forgave Martha for mutilating them without his knowledge or consent. Years later, he said of his favorite cat, Boise:

"Strange. He hates wimnies, really. It was a wommy who sent him to have his balls cut off."[11]

Toby Bruce and Leicester Hemingway, observing his frequent quarrels with Martha and her flirtations with other men, believed that she was having an adulterous affair. Leicester, interviewed in 1970, accused Martha of malice as well as infidelity, but did not name her lover: "She deliberately set out to cuckold Hemingway—not for the fun of it for herself, but for the pain of it for Mr. Poppa. She had then written a non-fiction story about the experience and sold it to a magazine. . . . All the characters in her story were easily identifiable."

The prime suspect was a Basque jai alai player named Felix Areitio, who adopted the name of his native village (between Bilbao and San Sebastián) and played as Felix Ermua. Felix was a handsome, rugged young man with dark wavy hair, who often played tennis at the Finca and was a crew member during the sub-hunting expeditions. Hemingway seemed to confirm the suspicions about Martha when he humorously referred to Felix as "my rival." He accused Martha of betraying him—as he had accused Pauline—and blamed her for the break-up of their marriage. He later told his friend Bernard Berenson (who took vicarious pleasure in sexual gossip) that Martha was a rabbit and he was well deceived.

Martha denied having an affair with Felix. Friends who observed them agreed that her behavior was provocative, but there was no affair. Mario Menocal, Jr., who was eighteen in 1941 and frequently visited the Finca, clarified their ambiguous relations:

> If you have ever seen a picture of a Spanish movie actor named Jorge Mistral, that is more or less what Ermua looked like. It may or may not have been true that Martha was misbehaving, but even allowing for the freer manners of an emancipated American woman of her age and time, it certainly looked that way. She may have been doing it to tease or annoy Ernest. . . .
>
> I don't think it was ever an affair, but it was certainly taken past the point to which a flirtation should have been taken. . . . If I had been Ernest I would have objected to the physical familiarities Martha and Felix allowed themselves—yet it was precisely those physical familiarities which convinced me then and continue to convince me now that there was never an affair between them. . . . For example, Martha jumping into Felix's arms at the tennis-court so he would have to carry her up the hill to the house instead of her having to walk.[12]

Another perceptive observer, the American diplomat Robert Joyce, emphasized the impossibility of conducting an affair in Havana without Hemingway's knowledge:

> Ernesto and Martha argued bitterly all the time about politics, but she was also a published writer so they also fought about literary values. I think it is absurd even to think that Martha had an affair with a Basque pelota player. She is not a promiscuous lady . . . *Where* in Cuba could she have had a secret affair? They lived in a village twelve miles from Havana. And when either of them came into town they were immediately recognized as distinguished *Americans*, which they were in Cuba.

Jack Hemingway put the same argument more succinctly: "Felix never could have gotten away with it. Papa would have killed him."[13]

Martha's ambivalent attitude toward Felix is most clearly revealed in her story "Night Before Easter," a brief account of an evening of sensual dancing in Havana nightclubs with a Basque jai alai player. The heroine is clearly attracted to the handsome young man and aroused by their dancing, but she is also condescending and has no trouble restraining herself:

> They come to my house to play tennis on the days they are not going to play pelota and we have the war in Spain between us, the memory and the understanding of the war, and that makes me their friend. . . .
>
> I wanted to . . . talk to Félix, who is not very clever but always tells me things that are interesting and that I am glad to learn. Besides that, Félix's face moves me and it is a pleasure to talk to him, to watch his mouth and to watch his smile. . . .
>
> Félix dances as if he were afraid of what he would do if he really danced. It is all there but checked, so that he holds you loosely and you know how it would be if he held you close against him.[14]

Martha was faithful, but had sexual problems with Hemingway. Robert Joyce suggested that her interest in sex was more literary than personal, that she was more excited by Hemingway the writer than by Hemingway the man, that ambition rather than passion had inspired her marriage. After discussing this point with Martha (who had lived with a French baron for several years before she met Hemingway), Bernice Kert wrote in *The Hemingway Women* that Martha was not sexually responsive and could not bring herself to tell Hemingway about their problems: "They were not sexually compatible. . . . 'With my body I thee worship' was always lacking in Martha, who, through ignorance and self-doubt, never discussed it with Ernest. Though his physical ardor was constant, he was totally insensitive to Martha's feelings. In such a one-sided situation, love-making could not provide the balm that softens so many marital quarrels."[15] Gregory Hemingway hinted at the reason for their sexual incompatibility without actually defining it: "According to papa there was also a basic sexual problem that explained a lot of their arguments. It could have been easily corrected by a visit to a doctor."[16] The problem was medically corrected and their sex life improved.

Hemingway, who had three sons with his first two wives, wanted to have a daughter with Martha. But she was completely committed to her career as a novelist and war correspondent, was vain about her figure and her looks, may have feared childbirth, probably realized that their marriage would not last, disliked sex with Hemingway and did not want to bear his child. She seemed to value literature more than life and in 1941 said of For Whom the Bell Tolls: "His brand new book is something wonderful. Probably better than looking at a brand new child." Martha adopted a baby just after the war and said: "There's no need to have a child when you can buy one. That's what I did."[17] It is ironic that both Hadley and Pauline seem to have had abortions (if we accept the evidence of McAlmon and of Helen Gordon's intensely personal tirade in To Have and Have Not) when Hemingway did not want to have another child, and that Martha did not have a child when he apparently wished to have one.

II

All their marital problems were temporarily solved when they went to their second war in January 1941, two months after their wedding, and recaptured in China the excitement of Spain. As Martha, who longed for travel and adventure, wrote of their first winter in Madrid: "There is a sort of blindness and fervor and recklessness about that sort of feeling which one must always want. I hate being so wise and so careful, so reliable, so denatured, so able to get on."[18] Her idea of fun, Hemingway complained, was a honeymoon on the Burma Road.

When Martha accepted an assignment from Collier's, Hemingway (whose uncle Willoughby had been a medical missionary in the north-

ern province of Shansi) arranged to write for *PM*. The newspaper was
a tabloid-sized highbrow journal of current affairs, which did not have
advertising, was supported by Marshall Field, the department store
millionaire, and edited by Ralph Ingersoll, the publisher of *Fortune*
magazine. Hemingway's mission was to study the strategic, economic
and political situation, see how Chiang Kai-shek's war against Japan was
progressing and (less than a year before the Japanese attacked Pearl
Harbor) decide how the war affected American commercial and military interests in the Orient. The war in China was four years old and
three-quarters of the country was occupied by the Japanese. According
to Auden and Isherwood, whose much jollier trip to China was recounted in *Journey to a War* (1939), the combination of civil war and
foreign intervention in China seemed to repeat the conditions that
characterized the struggle in Spain.

The Hemingways' 30,000-mile journey was arduous and exhausting.
They left San Francisco on the *Matsonia* on February 1, 1941, and had
a rough crossing to Honolulu. They dined there with Ed Hemingway's
sister Grace, noted the vulnerability of Pearl Harbor and visited the
volcanic island of Hawaii. They flew from Honolulu via Guam to Hong
Kong, arrived in late February and spent a month in the Peninsular
Hotel in Kowloon and in a country hotel on the far side of the island
at Repulse Bay. Hemingway soon acquired a familiar entourage in
Hong Kong and greatly enjoyed the food, drink, shooting and racetrack.
Martha wrote in *Travels with Myself and Another* (i.e., Hemingway),
which was based on her articles in *Collier's* in 1941 and is the main
source of information about the trip:

> He had learned to speak coolie English, a language related to West
> African pidgin and Caribbean English, and was seen laughing with
> waiters and rickshaw coolies and street vendors, all parties evidently
> enjoying each other. He loved Chinese food and would return from
> feasts with his Chinese crook-type friends swearing they'd been served
> by geisha girls, and describe the menu until I begged him to stop, due
> to queasiness. He was ready to try anything, including snake wine, the
> snakes presumably coiled and pickled in the bottom of the jug. . . . He
> felt that the Hongkong Chinese, given to gambling, rice wine and fire-
> crackers, had great savoir vivre.[19]

On the island Hemingway met the colorful General Morris (Two-
Gun) Cohen, a Jewish mercenary soldier from the East End of London,

6. *China and Burma, 1941*

who had commanded the troops of Chinese warlords and had been chief of police in Canton. Hemingway told Jonathan Cape that they had been good friends in Hong Kong and that Cohen would have a marvelous story if he told it truthfully.

Another friend, Emily Hahn, the sister-in-law of Kenley Smith, recalled Hemingway's gallant gesture:

> When the Hemingways were in Hong Kong I was very pregnant indeed with Charles' [Hahn's] daughter. We were not married, as he had a wife sitting out the war in Singapore. . . . I was pretty much of a scandal in the community, walking down Des Voeux Road, and Ernest was sitting in front of the Hong Kong Hotel, now deceased, drinking a Bloody Mary (which he introduced to the colony). He asked me to join him. They had been at my place the evening before. I joined him, and in the middle of a sentence he suddenly said, "What's going to happen to Charles about this baby? Won't they kick him out of the army?"
>
> "No," I said. "They daren't, because he's the only man they have who can speak Japanese."
>
> He looked doubtful. "Tell you what," he said. "You can tell 'em it's mine."

Emily Hahn was surprised when Dr. H. H. Kung, minister of finance and brother-in-law of Chiang Kai-shek, referred to Hemingway as "Ernie" and explained that he had known the whole family while an undergraduate at Oberlin.[20]

Their month in the interior of China began on March 25, when they flew one and a half hours north from Hong Kong, over the mountains and the Japanese lines, to Namyung. There they met their incompetent interpreter, Mr. Ma, and spent seven horrible days traveling south in conditions that were an "agony to watch and horror to share." They journeyed by land and water, with car, boat and horse, to the Canton front, just next to Hong Kong, which was the nearest sector held by Chiang's Kuomintang. After driving all day from Namyung to Shaokwan on roads that were "rivers of mud, rutted, gouged, strewn with boulders," they spent three days visiting the monastery and dining with the provincial governor and the commanding general of the Seventh War Zone.

They traveled for three hours on an old truck to cover thirty-five miles to the North River; spent twenty-four hours on an antique Chris-Craft that passed through a cholera epidemic; and completed the final stage to Wongshek, where there were no roads at all, on horseback. At the Canton front, headquarters of the Twelfth Army Sector, the Chinese and Japanese machine guns were only three kilometers apart, but an undeclared truce was in effect. After visiting a cadet training camp, Hemingway outdrank fourteen Chinese officers who gradually collapsed and slithered under the table. Martha found the squalor unbearable: "The pond water was rotting garbage and mud rather than water, pigs rooted in the muck, flies swarmed, and over all villages hung the smell of China: night soil, the deadly national manure." She told a friend that "China was a hell of a thing, absolutely exhausting and appalling and discouraging and dreary (because there are four hundred million people who live worse than animals and in a state of filth and disease to break your heart)."[21]

After spending forty-three hours on the boat back to Shaokwan and twenty-five hours on a 400-mile train trip to a filthy hotel in the beautiful city of Kweilin, they flew northwest to remote Chungking (in Szechwan province, about 770 miles from Hong Kong), which was the wartime capital of China. The town stood on a high bluff above the airstrip in the riverbed: "Grey, shapeless, muddy, a collection of drab cement buildings and poverty shacks, the best feature a lively market. The Japanese bombed when they wished though not while we were there." While staying for two weeks in the run-down house of a friend, they had lunch with Chiang and his Wellesley-educated wife. The Generalissimo —who was "thin, straight-backed, impeccable in a plain grey uniform and looked embalmed"—discussed the Chinese Communists, whom he feared more than the Japanese. The high point of the trip to the interior was a secret meeting with Chou En-lai, a friend of Joris Ivens, who was living underground and in constant danger in Chungking. Martha called him "the one really good man we'd met in China."[22] During their debriefing in Washington, the Hemingways predicted that the Communists would take over China after the war.

While Martha remained in the capital, Hemingway flew north to Cheng-tu. He visited a Chinese military academy, established by the Germans, and watched 100,000 workers build an airfield. After his return to Chungking, they flew southwest to Kunming and over the Burma Road to Lashio. They continued by car to Mandalay and by train to Rangoon, where they spent a sweltering week in late April, just before the monsoons. Hemingway called the saffron-robed Buddhist priests "religious bums." After leaving Rangoon, Martha visited Singapore and Djakarta; Hemingway flew back to Hong Kong, spent another week there and invented a wonderful story about spending the night with three beautiful Chinese girls. He flew to Manila on May 6 and nine days later left for New York by way of Guam, Wake, Midway, Honolulu and Los Angeles. After his departure from Asia, Hong Kong and Rangoon fell to the Japanese.

Hemingway was always at his best in adversity. Martha praised his calm, flexibility, patience and courtesy—not "his most familiar qualities." During the "unsurpassable horror journey" she constantly complained while he remained stoic; she had to endure the nightmare of China, he had to put up with both Chinese discomfort and Martha's complaints. Despite Martha's admission that "he saw the Chinese as people while I saw them as a mass of downtrodden valiant doomed humanity," he praised her war dispatches—if not her temperament: "Her pieces are always about people. The things that happen to her people really happen, and you feel it as though it were you and you were there. . . . She gets to the place, gets the story, writes it and comes home. That last is the best part."[23]

Hemingway wrote seven flat dispatches for *PM* and cautiously concluded that Japan might well go to war with America. His best story about the trip concerned the farmers' dissatisfaction with the quality of watery night soil during a cholera epidemic. When the buyers complained, the vendors allowed them to test the thickness of the product by sucking it up through straws. China remained a rather repulsive memory and he was fond of comparing Faulkner's *A Fable* to "the night soil from Chungking."[24]

The uncomfortable, exhausting and often boring trip to China was a disappointing experience for Hemingway. He had no real interest in the country (which was Malraux's literary territory) and went only to accompany Martha. He had a good time in Hong Kong, did his duty at the tedious official functions and tried to ignore the horrors that made Martha writhe with discomfort. He never actually saw the war—or anything else of extraordinary interest—during this quiescent period in China. He disliked Rangoon and was indifferent to Manila. Neither his imagination nor his emotions were deeply stirred by this experience and he did not feel he knew enough to write fiction about China.

III

The trip to the Orient suspended but did not eliminate the problems in Hemingway's marriage. Instead of being stimulated, as he normally was, by travel, new experiences, change of residence, a new wife and literary success, he lapsed into his longest period of literary sterility. The loss of literary friends, remoteness from cultural life and lack of intellectual stimulation were increased by the move to Cuba, which put him out of touch with social and political reality in America. At the same time, his estrangement from his family and separation from his children increased his sense of isolation. The *dolce far niente* life in the tropics made it more difficult to discipline himself. When Martha was away, he missed his immediate audience, became lonely, and lacked the orderly household and attention to his needs that he had become accustomed to with Hadley and Pauline. When Martha was at home, their domestic quarrels upset him. As his third marriage headed toward disaster, he found it more and more difficult to concentrate on his fiction.

The great fame he had achieved with *For Whom the Bell Tolls* also brought new problems. He was exhausted by work on the novel and feared he would never be able to equal it. He enjoyed his great reputation and did not want to risk it by failing to meet, in his next novel, the high expectations of his audience. The attendant publicity and establishment of his public persona led to a suppression of his innate sensitivity and intelligence, and a desperate attempt to live up to the myth he himself had helped to create. The large amount of money he made from the book and the film eliminated, in two ways, the financial incentive to write: he no longer needed the money and felt that most of what he earned was taken away in taxes.

As he had feared and predicted, he gradually became corrupted by the yachting friends in the Caribbean, the gossip columnists and restaurateurs in New York, the film stars in Sun Valley. At the same time, he gathered an expanding entourage of adoring toadies and parasites. He was no longer subject to salutary criticism of intellectual equals like Pound, Stein, Fitzgerald, Dos Passos and MacLeish. (Scribner and Perkins had too much invested in Hemingway to risk serious criticism.) He began to drink heavily, not as a relief after writing, but as a substitute for it. The drinking increased his dangerous accidents and steadily undermined his health. As he took refuge in the distraction of war and involved himself in the spy network and sub hunting, his leisure activities became more important than his writing.

After his enormous output in the 1930s, culminating in *For Whom the Bell Tolls,* Hemingway published only a few minor works during the next decade: war dispatches from China and Europe, and an Introduction to *Men at War* (dedicated to his three sons). In August 1943 he told MacLeish: "Would like to take two months somewhere away from tropics and write something that would like to write."[25] He virtually stopped writing compressed stories—his most perfect genre—after 1939, and his novels became undisciplined and long-winded.

His frustration and anger about not writing exacerbated his difficulties with Martha. He was egoistic and domineering at home, and his abortive sub-hunting expeditions were usually followed by compensatory drinking sprees and fights at the Finca. Martha longed to return to journalism, but Hemingway felt threatened by her career. Her refusal to submit to his will puzzled and hurt him, and he did not understand why she did not follow his wishes as Hadley and Pauline had done.

Some thought that Martha's ambition was greater than her talent. But she cultivated powerful friends, and H. G. Wells and Eleanor Roosevelt publicized her works. Her beauty and her marriage to Hemingway made her a public figure and helped to establish her literary reputation. Though her novels were distinctly inferior to Hemingway's, he was intensely irritated by her competition. In letters to Clara Spiegel in 1940, Martha described the problems of writing about the experience of war and remaining loyal to her artistic vision. She worked hard, set high standards for herself and was frustrated when she failed to achieve them. She alone of Hemingway's wives understood the difficulty and challenge of artistic expression. In contrast to Hemingway, who had an eager audience, Martha (like most novelists) had a limited readership and felt, when her fiction appeared, that months of work had dropped into the void. She had a much more enthusiastic audience in *Collier's,* which was a great incentive to follow her restless instinct and go to war.[26]

At the very time that Hemingway's creative urge dried up, he appeared in one novel and three stories by Martha. *A Stricken Field* (1940), dedicated to Hemingway and bearing a pseudo-medieval epigraph written by him, is a fictionalized account of her visit to Prague at the end of 1938, shortly after the Nazis occupied the Sudetenland.

Two scenes with Mary Douglas' lover, John, are clearly based on holidays with Hemingway. In Switzerland, John is characteristically messy, Mary terribly tidy, but they have a good time together and she is grateful for his love:

> It had been very cold at night and the feather bed was a perpetual problem and one morning John spilled his entire cup of coffee with whipped cream on it, and she worked for hours trying to tidy up the mess. . . . They ate at least five meals a day and laughed all the time because that was almost the beginning of their life together and I anyhow, she thought, was probably laughing with wonder that anything so fine should happen to me.

The second scene, which recalls the idyllic Paris days, recaptured in *A Moveable Feast*, expresses her love for Hemingway with unusual tenderness:

> Drinking coffee with John on the terrace of Weber's, and watching him read *L'Auto*, and he'll stop reading and see you watching him and smile, and you'll hold hands probably for a moment in the sun, and then he'll go on reading about the boxing at the Salle Wagram. . . . After breakfast you'll take his arm and walk down the rue Royale, stopping at all the expensive shop windows.[27]

In 1941 Martha moved to Scribner's (which she left when she left Hemingway) and published a collection of stories, *The Heart of Another*. This book contained the tale Leicester referred to when he said that Martha cuckolded Hemingway and then wrote about it. In "Portrait of a Lady" (a title used by James, Pound, Eliot and Hemingway) the narcissistic autobiographical heroine, Ann Maynard, is similar to Mary Douglas in *A Stricken Field*: a beautiful, luxury-loving, expensively dressed war correspondent, who worries about her appearance ("I'll never get over this trip, my skin is practically ruined"), emphasizes the importance of her own work and charms the officers to get the information she needs.

Ann Maynard has a brief affair with a Finnish aviator, who is shot down and burned to death, but this episode is not convincing evidence that Martha had actually betrayed Hemingway. Indeed, it is unlikely that she would write so boldly if she had committed adultery. The most revealing aspect of the story is Ann's thoughts about her older husband, their freedom to behave as they wished and the crass nature of their

mutually exploitative relationship, which is based (like that of the Ma-
combers) on his name and wealth and her great beauty:

> Charles was charming, good-looking, and fifteen years older than she.
> Charles did not go in for worry. They agreed, four years ago when they
> married, not to be like other people. They would not bore and ham-
> per each other the way most married people did; they would go on
> with their two lives and be quite free. He provided her with his val-
> uable name and the solidness of his money. In return, she was the
> great ornament of his life. They had never discussed the terms of
> their bargain and it worked very well. I'll cable Charles tomorrow,
> she thought, he wouldn't like people to think he didn't hear from
> me.[28]

"November Afternoon" seems to be based on Martha's affair with
Hemingway in Paris in November 1938, just after their first trip to
Spain and before her journey to Czechoslovakia. The couple drive into
the countryside for a weekend, but the man decides it is too dreary and
they return to the city. (Hemingway's driving is described in Hemingway's style: "He drove well and fast through the cramped paved village
streets"—with a superfluous adjective.) There is a strong suggestion that
the man is entangled with the heart of another and that the woman is
sick of his complicated emotional life. This story portrays Hemingway,
torn between Pauline and Martha, struggling to assert his own selfish
needs above those of his family:

> He had been trying to see a clean way out of their trouble. . . . He had
> a feeling that every one was pulling at him. . . . He had also begun to
> think that he would like a few things for himself, that it would be good
> at last not always to consider his actions as they affected others. He
> thought it would be fine just to do something he wanted to do and the
> hell with all the people who could be hurt or disappointed.[29]

Martha's last, bitter and prophetic story about Hemingway, written
after their marriage had ended, is "A Psychiatrist of One's Own." It
concerns a handsome and successful American novelist, Matthew Hendricks, who is in his forties and has lived on a Caribbean island and in
Montana. No longer able to write, he becomes depressed and begins to
lose his mind. Martha also reveals unpleasant aspects of her own character when Hendricks' friend, the self-absorbed Madge Jarvis, contem-
plates a sexual liaison and then wonders if it is worth the trouble: "It
did mean you could not look after your skin properly at night, was it

worth it? . . . O, damn, she thought; it meant rushing to dress for dinner, afterwards, when one wanted to rest."[30]

If Hemingway resented Martha's "competitive and ambitious" writing, Martha must have resented her inability to escape from the influence of his style—which critics were quick to point out. In "A Psychiatrist of One's Own," a woman uses one of Hemingway's favorite military words and says: "I'll get all the gen [correct information] about it for you." And a Hemingwayesque locale and passage appears in "Zoo in Madrid": "Just a little way down from Chicote's on the Gran Vía we saw a wide new hole, the granite cobblestones lying smashed and dusty around it, and leading to the nearest doorway was a neat straight fresh trail of blood. Chicote's was crowded with soldiers and civilians and handsome Spanish girls with peroxided hair. The beer was cold and good."[31]

Martha had convinced Hemingway to cover the wars in Spain and China, had gone alone to Finland and was a reporter in England between October 1943 and March 1944. She criticized his idleness and lack of contribution to the war effort, felt he was wasting his time with his amateur spy network and was jealous of the sub hunting in Cuba—though she helped procure weapons by using her influence with President Roosevelt. Martha nagged and needled him to follow her example and become an official correspondent at the European front.

In the fall the war was always there, but he did not want to go to it any more. He had risked his life in Spain and still suffered from the emotional effects of his break with Pauline, was exhausted by the strain of completing *For Whom the Bell Tolls* and discouraged by the extreme discomfort of his trip to China. After his experience in Spain and China, he believed that the lies, propaganda and censorship necessary in wartime made it almost impossible to be an honorable correspondent. Patrick Hemingway provided a less idealistic reason: "He felt that he was entitled to stay behind, living in a place that he liked, and enjoying himself."[32] Well aware of his literary stature, Hemingway felt he was a kind of national monument that ought to be preserved.

18

Our Man in Havana
1942–1944

> We must have our man in Havana, you
> know. Submarines need fuel. Dictators
> drift together. Big ones draw in the lit-
> tle ones.
>
> GRAHAM GREENE

I

In the early years of the war Hemingway spent his time in Cuba in
sporting and social activities: fishing, shooting, drinking with his numerous friends. He was resting on his achievement, writing nothing, uncer-
tain about what to do. When offered the opportunity to join the war
effort without leaving Cuba, he organized a private spy network and
gathered information about Nazi sympathizers on the island. His references to this activity were usually self-deprecating; he stressed the fun
they had and called it the Crook Factory. Martha and most of his Cuban
friends assumed that it was little more than a diverting racket.

The 124-page FBI file on Hemingway cast quite a different and
more menacing light on this episode. It showed that the Bureau resented his amateur but alarming intrusion into their territory; that it
unsuccessfully attempted to control, mock and vilify him; that it feared
his personal prestige and political power. The file was extremely repetitive, and became unintentionally funny when the solemn bureaucrats
reported the bizarre behavior of the author. Their stilted letters seem
written on a typewriter by a typewriter. Though there were ludicrous
elements in this story, the file revealed that Hemingway, the American
Embassy in Havana, the State Department in Washington and the FBI
all took the Crook Factory quite seriously.

Hemingway's venture into espionage introduced him to a new set of friends and contacts. The cast of characters in this tragicomedy included Spruille Braden, the American ambassador to Cuba; Robert Joyce, the second secretary, coordinator of intelligence activities and liaison with the FBI agents; and Gustavo Durán, who had skillfully commanded Loyalist divisions in the Spanish Civil War. The stage villains were Raymond Leddy, the Legal Attaché (i.e., FBI agent) in Havana, a colorless chap who helped train men for the Cuban FBI; and General Manuel Benítez, chief of the Cuban police, who had once played Latin lovers in grade-B Hollywood films.

Braden was born in Elkhorn, Montana (Hemingway hunting country), graduated from Yale, married a beautiful but arrogant Chilean, had a successful career as mining engineer and capitalist entrepreneur in South America.[1] He was ambassador to Colombia before assuming the sensitive post in Cuba in the spring of 1942, just after America had entered the war. Though pompous and self-righteous, a bit of a blowhard and blusterer, he was an independent and effective diplomat. Hostile to Communists, he was praised by Robert Joyce as "a huge man and a tough number" and characterized by the historian Hugh Thomas as "an intelligent man, with considerable Latin American experience . . . a distinctly Radical diplomat, with strong views of social reform. He was regarded by many Cubans as the best ambassador the U.S. ever sent to Havana."

In his memoirs, *Diplomats and Demogogues,* Braden stated that there were 300,000 Spaniards in wartime Cuba, of whom 15,000 to 30,000 were "violent Falangists." Braden claimed that *he* asked Hemingway "to organize an intelligence service that will do a job for a few months until I can get the [additional] FBI men down. These Spaniards have got to be watched." Beginning in August 1942, Hemingway "built up an excellent organization and did an A-One job."[2] His temporary work ended with the arrival of the FBI operatives in April 1943.

Both Hemingway and the FBI stated, more accurately, that Hemingway first approached Braden and volunteered to investigate the Spanish Falange with the aid of his Loyalist refugee friends. (The hero of *The Fifth Column* was secretly engaged in espionage.) Supported by the ambassador, who admired the novelist and loved to have him in the embassy, Hemingway discreetly established an amateur but extensive information service with his own confidential agents: priests, waiters, fishermen, whores, pimps, and bums. He had twenty-six informants, composed of six full-time operatives and twenty undercover men. His expenses came to a thousand dollars a month and he had 122 gallons of scarce gasoline given to him from the embassy's private allotment in April 1943.

Hemingway and Martha were close friends of Robert and Jane Joyce, who arrived in Havana in January 1941. Joyce was a wealthy, handsome, sophisticated and intelligent man. He had grown up in Pasadena, gone to prep school in California, graduated (like Braden) from Yale and attended the École des Sciences Politiques in Paris. After joining the Foreign Service in 1929, he served in China, Latin America and Yugoslavia. Hemingway would make weekly visits to Joyce's office, using the back door, and present the intelligence reports with his written comments.[3] After the war Hemingway told Buck Lanham that Joyce, a high-class character, was objective, intelligent and patriotic. He and Joyce had worked together for Braden, and Joyce knew all about the seaborne comic strip they had conducted in Cuban waters from 1942 to 1944.[4]

In October 1942 Hemingway achieved a great administrative coup by recruiting Durán to assist him. A man of complex character and extraordinary experience, Durán was significant both in Hemingway's life and in his art. Yet their association in Cuba destroyed their friendship and was, for Durán, a subsequent cause for regret. The son of an engineer, Durán was born in Barcelona but soon moved to Madrid. His parents' marriage was unhappy, for his father chased after women and wanted to get rid of his emotionally unstable wife. When Durán was ten years old, his father told his mother to dress for the opera and placed her in a mental hospital. The following week, his mistress moved into his home. Durán hated his father and visited his mother every week until her death. From this shattering emotional experience, he developed a cool, detached manner, a hatred of illness and an inability to deal with emotional displays.

Durán attended a Jesuit school (though he was not religious), a business college (1920–23) and a conservatory of music (1923–27). After his compulsory military service, he lived in Paris from 1928 to 1934, studied with Paul Dukas and Nadia Boulanger, and tutored the children of Yehudi Menuhin. He worked as a pianist, composed ballet scores and dubbed Paramount films into Spanish. Blond, blue-eyed and extremely handsome, he was also elegant, cultivated and worldly. A precious señorito and man about town, he was a well-known figure before the

Civil War and a friend of the very best Spanish artists: the poets Lorca
and Alberti, the musicians de Falla and Segovia, the artist Dali and the
director Buñuel. As his brother-in-law, Michael Straight, observed: "His
taste was impeccable, his knowledge formidable, his talent overwhelming."⁵

Like Hemingway and Malraux, Durán was an artist and a man of
action. Malraux had asked Durán to compose the music for his film
L'Espoir, which was based on his Spanish novel. And Durán's appearance, mannerisms, speech and actions had inspired the character of
Manuel in *Man's Hope*:

> Manuel rarely had with him his Communist party card. He earned his
> living in the film industry as a sound-man. A vaguely Montparnassian
> style of dressing enabled him to fancy that he had escaped, anyhow
> sartorially speaking, from the influence of the bourgeoisie. In his dark,
> rather thick-set features, only the bushy eyebrows struck a proletarian
> note. . . .
>
> Since Ramos' propaganda campaign in the Sierras, the peasants had
> come to feel a certain, if somewhat diffident, regard for Manuel. It had
> steadily intensified as he grew more and more ill-shaven, and the pale
> green eyes under the jet-black lashes, which brought to mind that of a
> rather heavy-jowled Roman emperor, became more and more like a
> Mediterranean fisherman's.⁶

Durán returned to Madrid in 1934 to manage a cinema and took
part in the October riots which led to the imprisonment of another
artist-soldier, Luis Quintanilla. Durán had a reserve commission in the
Spanish army and was called up at the beginning of the Civil War. Great
demands were made on him and he used his abilities to the fullest. He
made an astonishingly rapid transformation from playboy and dandy to
exceptional soldier and strategist, and was more brilliant in battle than
in music. Asked to explain his military career, he drew parallels between war and art that would have pleased Hemingway: "Modern war
also demands intelligence, it is an intellectual's job. . . . War is also
poetry—tragic poetry."

Durán was a confident and charismatic leader who inspired loyalty
in his men. When his soldiers had to shave their heads to remove lice,
he shaved his own head as an example. He was the fighting commander
of a battalion in August 1936, a brigade in January 1937, a division in
July and (as a colonel) of the XX Army Corps in November. "Wounded

twice, he fought in Madrid, the retreat from Toledo, the front at Casa del Campo, the counteroffensive of Jarama," Brunete, Teruel and Valencia.[7] He quarreled with the popular but brutal guerrilla leader El Campesino, and hated the control of the Soviet political commissars. At the end of the war, he sided with the moderate Socialist General Miaja against the Communist commanders, Lister and Modesto, who wanted to prolong the hopeless conflict.

As the Loyalist cause collapsed, Durán escaped to Valencia, just ahead of the Fascist army, with the chief of staff, General Rojo. When Franco's troops entered the city, the Loyalist army dispersed and tried to escape. Durán asked for asylum at the American Consulate, but was told he would have to take the consequences of defeat. He then gave himself up, preferring a clean shot to a lynching by the mob that was pulling people out of houses and killing them in the streets. Interrogated by an old school friend who said he was mad to surrender, Durán was given civilian clothes and a pass to the house of his sergeant's parents, who took him in. Granted asylum by the British consul, he was taken by car to the port of Gandía (south of Valencia), by the warship *Galatea* to Marseilles and by train to London. After the war, Durán's father was arrested. When told that his son had been captured and shot, he cut his throat. Durán felt that his life was essentially over in 1939. He had not been able to follow his musical career; and had lost his political struggle, his war, his country, his language and his culture. But he tried to live in the present, never talked about the Civil War and never returned to Spain.

At Dartington Hall in Devon, the home of Michael Straight's mother, the military historian B. H. Liddell Hart (a close friend of Dorman-Smith) introduced Durán to his future wife, Bonte Crompton. Bonte found Durán charming, scintillating, witty, and married him three months later. After a honeymoon in Cornwall, they moved to America in May 1940 and stayed at her family's summer house in New Hampshire. Durán worked with Luis Buñuel at the film division of the Museum of Modern Art in 1941; in the music division of the Pan American Union in Washington during 1941–42; and for Nelson Rockefeller, Coordinator of Inter-American Affairs at the State Department, during 1942.

Hemingway first met Durán in Paris in 1929 and saw him soon after arriving in Spain in April 1937, during the siege of Madrid. Durán was the Dorman-Smith of Spain: Hemingway saw him in action, and admired his courage and skill. In his story "Night Before Battle" (1939) he wrote that after fierce fighting around Madrid, "Durán took the new race track. The *hipódromo*. We've narrowed down the corridor that runs up into University City." Durán did what Hemingway would have liked to do in the war, and fought with General Walter in the attack on Segovia that inspired *For Whom the Bell Tolls.*

Hemingway—jealous of Durán's friendship with Malraux—asked for Durán's criticism while writing the novel in 1939, thanked him for correcting the Spanish and was pleased to earn his praise. He said the Spaniards in his novel would not be like the phony characters in *Man's Hope.* But he was always insecure when corresponding with professional soldiers and felt the need to invent his own exploits. He told Durán that when he was only nineteen he had commanded a company and then a battalion, which had suffered many losses, but had been demoted to platoon leader because he could not write.[8]

During an interview conducted in August 1940 when Hemingway and Durán were going over the proofs of his book, Hemingway said that "Durán was a character in the new novel, which is set in Spain during the civil war, and that while he was writing the book he badly wanted to see Durán, 'to straighten things out, to get information.' "[9] In the novel, on the night before the attack, Robert Jordan is inspired by thoughts of Durán's achievement: "Just remember Durán, who never had any military training and who was a composer and lad about town before the movement and is now a damned good general commanding a brigade. It was all as simple and easy to learn and understand to Durán as chess to a child chess prodigy."[10] This was Hemingway's most enthusiastic tribute to a friend.

Hemingway sent £50 to Durán in London, tried to get him hired as technical advisor to the film of *For Whom the Bell Tolls* and enclosed a check for $1,000 (which Durán returned) when this job fell through. The Duráns met Hemingway three times in New York during 1940–41. He gave a fascinating account of gangsters he had known in Chicago and Kansas City, praised the crime novels of Raymond Chandler and Dashiell Hammett, competently shuffled around the dance floor of "21" with Bonte and exclaimed: "Gustavo was my hero in Spain." Martha told Bonte that in 1941 Hemingway looked at a photograph of their baby daughter with joy and pride (as if *he* had given birth to Gustavo), and said: "He's done everything and now he's made a fine baby."

According to Agent Leddy, writing directly to J. Edgar Hoover on

August 13, 1943, Hemingway had described Durán to Braden "as the ideal man to conduct this work, 'an intelligence and military genius that comes along once in a hundred years.' " Durán became a naturalized American citizen, was appointed Auxiliary Foreign Service Officer and in October 1942 was sent from Washington for the special purpose of assisting Hemingway in the Crook Factory. Durán was a popular man, a born diplomat, spoke excellent English (with a strong accent) and was valued by Braden. But he did not understand the Foreign Service mentality; his special position aroused hostility among the regular officers and made him feel uncomfortable in Cuba.

In December 1942, according to Hoover's Bureau colleague D. M. Ladd, he was getting out of hand and had already become a potential enemy of the FBI: "Durán's operations and attitude . . . assume proportions of domination and direction rather than assistance to the agencies properly engaged in investigating subversive activities." By August 1943 Leddy, though completely ignorant of the labyrinthine politics of the Spanish Left, was zealously conducting an investigation to determine if Durán was an active member of the Communist Party and political infiltrator into the American Embassy.

Braden, a fierce crusader against corruption in Cuba, had also directed Hemingway to look into the involvement of Cuban officials in the all-pervasive local graft. But Ladd, who called Braden "a very impulsive individual," warned Hoover on December 17, 1942, that the Augean stable could not be cleaned. If we get involved in investigating Cuban corruption, he said, "it is going to mean that all of us will be thrown out of Cuba 'bag and baggage.' . . . [Hemingway, like Durán,] is actually branching out into an investigative organization of his own which is not subject to any control whatsoever. . . . Hemingway's activities are undoubtedly going to be very embarrassing unless something is done to put a stop to them." Patrick Hemingway was involved in one investigation when the Crook Factory explored the caves of German sisal planters to see if they contained supplies for German submarines. Patrick, the only one small enough to crawl inside, found nothing there except the caps of beer bottles—which were not even German.[11]

The FBI attempted to thwart Hemingway in two ways: by discrediting the information that was supplied to Braden and passed on to Leddy; and by claiming that Hemingway, like Durán, was a Communist. A week before President Batista's visit to Washington in 1943, Hemingway warned that General Benítez was proposing to seize power when Batista was out of the country. Leddy looked into the matter and pointed out that no such preparations were observed by FBI agents working "in daily contact" at police headquarters. But Braden reported in June 1944 that General Benítez, a habitual plotter, "was meeting in a house in the outskirts of Havana, making plans to throw out Batista."[12]

On December 9, 1942, Hemingway reported sighting a contact between a German submarine and a Spanish steamer, *Marqués de Comillas,* off the Cuban coast while "he was ostensibly fishing with [the millionaire playboy] Winston Guest and four Spaniards as crew members, but was actually on a confidential mission for the Naval Attaché." The FBI duly investigated the incident and reported "negative results."

According to a Bureau memo from C. H. Carson to Ladd on June 13, 1943, Hemingway, after reading about a new type of oxygen-powered German submarine, investigated the supply and distribution of oxygen and oxygen tanks in Cuba. Hemingway enthusiastically claimed (in the FBI's version of his words): "at last with this development we have come to the point after months of work where we are about to crack the submarine refueling problem." The FBI doggedly checked the supply and distribution of the island's oxygen and found everything properly accounted for. They gleefully announced: "Nothing further was heard from Hemingway about the subject" and noted the inevitable change in his attitude: "Hemingway's investigations began to show a marked hostility to the Cuban Police and in a lesser degree to the FBI."

Another ludicrous confrontation between Leddy and Hemingway has all the characteristics of a Graham Greene entertainment:

In January, 1943, Mr. Joyce of the Embassy asked the assistance of the Legal Attaché in ascertaining the contents of a tightly wrapped box left by a suspect at the Bar Basque under conditions suggesting that the box contained espionage information. The box had been recovered from the Bar Basque by an operative of Hemingway. The Legal Attaché made private arrangements for opening the box and returned the contents to Hemingway through Mr. Joyce. The box contained only a cheap edition of the "Life of St. Teresa." Hemingway was present and appeared irritated that nothing more was produced and later told an Assistant Legal Attaché that he was sure we had withdrawn the vital material and had shown him something worthless. When this statement was challenged by the Assistant Legal Attaché, Hemingway jocularly said he was only joking and that he thought there was something funny about the whole business of the box.

After this incident the Bureau was forced to conclude: "The 'intelligence coverage' of Hemingway consisted of vague and unfounded reports of a sensational character. . . . His data were almost without fail valueless." Though both Braden and the State Department praised the quality of Hemingway's reports, it seems clear that this information, however well-intentioned, was (like that of Graham Greene's agent Wormold) based more on fantasy than on fact. The entire Crook Factory, which Martha refused to take seriously, seemed to be little more than a charitable scheme to support a few dozen indigent Cubans and Loyalists. Leddy noted, with considerable relief, that Hemingway's organization was disbanded and its work terminated as of April 1, 1943, because of a "general dissatisfaction over the reports submitted."

Robert Joyce explained why the reports of the Crook Factory were so fantastic and why they were tolerated at the embassy and in Washington:

> Of course their intelligence was completely fabricated. If their reports were sensational they were paid more—$20 instead of $10. And most of their reports were contradictory—less than useful, as they caused confusion in Washington headquarters at the Pentagon—not to speak of the FBI at home and in Havana.

But a major general who headed G-2 in the Pentagon in 1942 "said Army intelligence was interested in and welcomed reports from military attachés on *all* matters, including educational policy, sports, etc., *everything* in short."[13] The general was a very powerful man at the time and personally overruled Hoover's attempt to close down the Crook Factory.

The best that can be said for the Crook Factory is that it placed a certain limitation on the activities of the pro-Nazi Falangists in Cuba by keeping them under surveillance and did more good than harm at very little cost to the nation. Only the force of Hemingway's legend and overpowering personality could have convinced the ambassador, despite overwhelming evidence from the FBI, that his spy games had any real value.

Hemingway had replaced writing with spying; he had to justify its worth to Martha, Braden, and the FBI, and wanted Durán to praise the

Crook Factory as he had praised the novel. But Durán soon became as disillusioned as the FBI about Hemingway's activities. He had commanded 55,000 troops in battle and felt he was now wasting his time on a foolish enterprise that produced unreliable reports. As Hemingway's rivalry with the FBI intensified, he demanded absolute loyalty and became hostile when he failed to receive it. Durán was the only man in Cuba on an equal plane with Hemingway and his defection was a serious blow. Robert Joyce closely observed the disintegration of the friendship:

> When Durán took over the Crook Factory from Ernesto, he quickly saw that its production of "intelligence information" was adding nothing of value. He started spending more and more time at the Embassy as cultural attaché. . . . He made it clear to Hemingway that he thought little or nothing of the efforts of the Crook Factory. E.H. considered this a breach of friendship and was furious. He came to my apartment one night in Havana and said: "Gustavo is a bastard and I have fired him as head of the Crook Factory." From then on E.H. treated Durán and his attractive wife with cold contempt.[14]

It was characteristic of Hemingway to veer violently from hero worship to hostility if his idol proved unsatisfactory. The two men had been good friends during the Spanish War, when Hemingway admired Durán. After the war, Hemingway was helpful and generous. But in Cuba, the men changed and their relations deteriorated. Both of them had overwhelming personalities and were bound to clash. Durán had been reduced to a subordinate position; Hemingway, surrounded by cronies, expected gratitude. When they came into daily contact each became disillusioned with the other.

Hemingway had many attractive qualities. He was handsome, tough, skilled at sports, witty and tremendous fun. Almost everyone he met adored him. In Cuba, however, his capacity for fun changed to a reckless disregard of common decency and he began to resemble his own description of the bullfighter Maera: "proud, bitter, foul-mouthed and a great drinker."[15]

Hemingway wanted to keep the spy network an all-male operation and was annoyed when Bonte Durán came to Cuba in November 1942 to join her husband. When she arrived at the Finca guest house, above the office of the Crook Factory, she immediately noticed a change in the Hemingways' behavior. So kind and charming in New York, Hemingway now seemed critical and domineering. He insisted Durán carry a pistol, disliked his trips to Havana and wanted him to control the agents from the secret isolation of the Finca.

Durán disapproved of Hemingway's Cuban life, his values and his rich friends who had supported the Fascist cause. A refined and cultivated man, he disliked Hemingway's macho affectation, his obscene language (more extreme in Spanish than in English), his feudal attitude toward his servants, and his shooting live pigeons at the Club de Cazadores. Though grateful to Hemingway, he was unable to return "Ernesto's" enthusiastic affection.

The Duráns, living at the Finca, often saw the ugly side of Hemingway when he got drunk, became angry and went out of control. He fed beef to his cats when meat was rationed in wartime; and boasted to Bonte that after some dogs had killed his cats, he shot them in the guts so they would die in agony. After Bonte (who liked to proselytize) accused him of cruelty and wanted to leave the house, he said: "I'm sorry I told you but not sorry I did it"—which made things even worse. Durán was upset by this incident and told her: "Ernesto has been like a father to me and helped me in every way."

Yet even Durán could not tolerate the boorish behavior that tested the limits of their friendship. When a dog jumped on Bonte, Hemingway shouted: "Don't bother the bitch." Bonte at first thought he referred to the dog, then realized he was talking to the dog about her. He said Spanish Commander Fernando Gerassi, who had been at the front for two years, was "yellow." At Durán's birthday party in Havana, he behaved as Fitzgerald had done at the Murphys' party in 1926. He got drunk, pushed salad down the back of an embassy nonentity and threw steak across the table (which inspired friends to follow his example). When Durán left to walk home (as Gerald Murphy had done), Hemingway yelled: "You can't take it any more."

Martha was having her own problems with Hemingway. In public she was affectionate rather than critical, and she cut her hair short in the style of the fictional Maria. She asked Hemingway (using Stein's pet name for Toklas!): "But Pussy darling, you like it, don't you?" and got the curt reply: "I've said it's all right." Martha complained that the Crook Factory interfered with her work, and at times vented her irritation on Bonte. When Bonte gave Martha a manicure set in a pigskin case, she disparaged the gift and said: "Now I don't have to go into Havana for my toenails." When Bonte asked if she could borrow *Moll*

Flanders, Martha said: "Don't you think it's a bit heavy for you?" And when Bonte wore a flower on her dress, Martha exclaimed: "Darling, I didn't tell you it was a costume party. You really do dress like a Cuban." Durán, placed in an extremely awkward position, complained to Hemingway about Martha's rudeness and was told: "Martha doesn't like any woman except her mother."

The inevitable rupture came three weeks after Bonte's arrival when the Duráns were driven back to the guest house from a music festival at 5 A.M. by a friend who thoughtlessly blew the car horn under Martha's window. The next morning Hemingway shouted: "I don't know who your friends were last night, but I would have shot them if I could. If Martha is awakened, she has to take a sleeping pill and can't work the next day." Martha added, with heavy sarcasm: "I hear your husband has ulcers. Don't you think you ought to get him to bed earlier? I think Gustavo is able to pay for his own hotel." After they moved to the Ambos Mundos, Hemingway sent an apologetic bouquet of long-stem red roses with a message saying: "Sorry there was no longer room at the house."

During a lunch at the embassy with Robert Joyce, Hemingway savagely attacked Durán and ended the friendship. They met for the last time, after Hemingway returned from the war in May 1945, at a farewell party for Braden; he had been appointed ambassador to Argentina and had asked Durán to serve on his staff. When Durán mentioned the birth of his second daughter and asked about Jack Hemingway, who had been captured by the Germans, Ernest caustically remarked: "You managed quite well to keep out of the war, didn't you?" In view of his military record in Spain and the fact that he had volunteered for both the British and the American army, these last words (which echoed *The Fifth Column*[16]) made Durán more angry than hurt.

II

Agent Leddy was both disdainful of Hemingway's operations and fearful of his power. Trained to see everything in black and white, with no subtle gradations of meaning, he was puzzled by the Communist attacks on Hemingway, who had supported the Left in the Civil War. The novelist clearly troubled the FBI, just as they would later worry him; and Leddy wrote directly to Hoover about his difficulties with Hemingway. Like everyone the FBI disliked, Hemingway was immediately suspected—and privately accused—of being a Communist, though no proof was—or ever could be—offered. "To hell with the Church when it becomes a State and the hell with the State when it becomes a church," he told Dos Passos in 1932. "I can't be a Communist because I hate tyranny and, I suppose, government."[17] The mood, tone, phrases and technique of the FBI during the hot war in the early 1940s clearly foreshadowed those employed by Joe McCarthy during the Cold War in the early 1950s.

Leddy's first letter to Hoover, which opened the file on October 8, 1942, made two charges against Hemingway. First, "when the Bureau was attacked early in 1940 as a result of the arrests in Detroit of certain individuals charged with Neutrality Act violations for fostering enlistments in the Spanish Republican forces, Mr. HEMINGWAY was among the signers of a declaration which severely criticized the Bureau."[18] (Ladd called this attack on the FBI a "general smear campaign.") Second, "in attendance at a Jai Alai match with HEMINGWAY, the writer [Leddy] was introduced by him to a friend as a member of the Gestapo. On that occasion, I told HEMINGWAY that I did not appreciate the introduction." Hemingway clearly enjoyed mocking the FBI agent, who unwillingly became his straight man. Though this was not a particularly funny joke in 1942, Leddy's response was intolerably priggish.

Hoover dug into his files and answered in person on December 17 to enlighten and encourage his local agent: "Any information which you may have relating to the unreliability of Ernest Hemingway as an informant may be discreetly brought to the attention of Ambassador Braden. In this respect it will be recalled that recently Hemingway gave information concerning the refueling of submarines in Caribbean waters which has proved unreliable." Two days later Hoover added, with considerable restraint: "[Hemingway's] judgment is not of the best, and if his sobriety is the same as it was some years ago, that is certainly questionable."

On the same day that Hoover first wrote to Leddy, Ladd told Hoover that "Hemingway has been accused of being of Communist sympathy, although we are advised that he has denied and does vigorously deny any Communist affiliation." This was followed on April 27, 1943, by eleven typed pages of "Hemingway's Activities on Behalf of Loyalist Spain," which made his humanitarian efforts to provide ambulances for the wounded, medical aid for the sick and asylum for the refugees seem like unconscionable acts. In the same report, under "Possible Connections with Communist Party," the Bureau vaguely but accusingly stated: "In the fall of 1940 Hemingway's name was included in a group of names of individuals who were said to be engaged in Communist activities."

Other FBI letters noted Hemingway's first and only political speech, at the American Writers Congress at Carnegie Hall on June 4, 1937, attended by shady and suspicious types like Archibald MacLeish, U.S. Senator Gerald Nye and Congressman John Barnard; Hemingway's threat to expose "Fascist influences" in the State Department and the Vatican, which he claimed were responsible for the political "castration" of the film version of For Whom the Bell Tolls (1943); and his statement in Look on May 4, 1954: there is nothing "wrong with Sen. Joseph McCarthy (Republican) of Wisconsin which a .577 solid would not cure."[19] This was a brave and even reckless assertion to make when McCarthy was at the height of his power.

Such was the FBI's own "smear campaign"—but they dared not carry it out in public. For the "Communist" Hemingway, Leddy reported to Hoover, was himself attacked by Communist newspapers in New York and Havana. In June 1943 Hoy (Today) quoted Hemingway advocating "the sterilization of all Germans as a means of preserving peace" and claimed For Whom the Bell Tolls was "directed against the Communist Party and against the Spanish people."[20]

Moreover, as Carson explained to Ladd in an FBI memo of June 13, 1943, Hemingway's close friendship with Braden, his immense popularity in Cuba (where he was greeted like a popular monarch as he drove through the streets), his fame in America and prestige abroad, made it imperative to keep a safe distance from the rogue elephant. If molested, he was capable of inflicting serious wounds on the Bureau-crats:

> Regarding Hemingway's position in Cuba, the Legal Attaché advises that his prestige and following are very great. He enjoys the complete personal confidence of the American Ambassador and the Legal Attaché has witnessed conferences where the Ambassador observed Hemingway's opinions as gospel and followed enthusiastically Hemingway's warning of the probable [i.e., unlikely] seizure of Cuba by a force of 30,000 Germans transported to the island in 1,000 submarines. A clique of celebrity-minded hero worshippers surround Hemingway wherever he goes, numbering such persons as Winston Guest, Lt. Tommy Shevlin (wealthy son of a famous Yale football player), Mrs. Kathleen Vanderbilt

Arostegui and several Embassy officials. To them, Hemingway is a man of genius whose fame will be remembered with Tolstoy. . . .

It is known that Hemingway and his assistant, Gustavo Durán, have a low esteem for the work of the FBI which they consider to be methodical, unimaginative and performed by persons of comparative youth without experience in foreign countries and knowledge of international intrigue and politics. Both Hemingway and Durán, it is also known, have personal hostility to the FBI on an ideological basis, especially Hemingway, as he considers the FBI anti-Liberal, pro-Fascist and dangerous as developing into an American Gestapo.

In *To Have and Have Not,* Hemingway wrote that "Edgar Hoover exaggerates the publicity" he received for capturing famous gangsters in the thirties. And in *Islands in the Stream,* the grubby old salt calls the Agents "draft-dodgers" and satirizes the obtrusive, ineffectual, "inescapable FBI men, pleasant and all trying to look so average, clean-cut-young-American that they stood out as clearly as though they had worn a bureau shoulder patch on their white linen or seersucker suits."[21]

Robert Joyce confirmed that Hemingway's intense hostility to Leddy and the other agents was based on his belief that they were all pro-Franco, and lacked the proper training and technical skill for their work:

These young [FBI] men were mainly of Irish descent. E.H. hated them as, according to him, all were Roman Catholics who were probably sympathetic to Franco's cause in Spain. None of them spoke Spanish nor had any experience in Latin America. E.H. referred to them as *F*ranco's *B*astard *I*rish—FBI. . . . Ernest considered Leddy's special agents to be real naive innocents. Leddy and his staff, as virtuous young Catholics, considered that E.H.'s agents were unreliable—many of them were free-thinking bad Catholics and some were retired whores or operators of brothels.[22]

On December 19, 1942, Hoover agreed with Carson's advice about avoiding conflict with Hemingway and cautiously commented on the "impulsive" Braden: "The Ambassador is somewhat hot-headed and I haven't the slightest doubt he would immediately tell Hemingway of the objections being raised by the FBI. Hemingway ["one of the real danger spots in Cuba"] has no particular love for the FBI and would no doubt embark upon a campaign of vilification."

Finally, the FBI realized that Martha's friendship with Eleanor Roosevelt carried Hemingway's influence directly to the President. On October 9, 1942, Leddy told Hoover, with considerable awe: "During the week commencing October 12, 1942 Mrs. HEMINGWAY is to be the personal guest of Mrs. ROOSEVELT during her stay in Washington." Braden took advantage of this visit to ask Martha to brief Roosevelt and Harry Hopkins about urgently needed funds to combat "the periodically reappearing enemy agents" in Cuba.[23] In view of all this, Carson concluded, it was best to prevent a direct confrontation with their formidable adversary: "The Legal Attaché at Havana expresses his belief that Hemingway is fundamentally hostile to the FBI and might readily endeavor at any time to cause trouble for us. . . . It is the recommendation of the Legal Attaché at Havana that great discretion be exercised in avoiding an incident with Ernest Hemingway."

Hemingway, who had come a long way since his Catholic "conversion" in 1927, told Buck Lanham that he had enjoyed irritating and competing with the FBI. But he also saw them as a menacing and authoritarian threat to freedom. He said there was more double-crossing in the FBI than in the army, for they were determined to put everyone else out of business. The FBI was essentially a Catholic organization. The agents were educated by the Jesuits and taught to be loyal only to the Bureau. They could be teased, but never trusted.[24]

Hemingway was strong enough to resist the persecution of the FBI and other government agencies that conducted witch hunts of suspected Communists, but Gustavo Durán was not. It was not as dangerous to be accused of being a Communist in the early 1940s, when America was fighting a war with a Russian ally, as it was in the early 1950s, when America was fighting the Communists in Korea. In the early forties the FBI was under the control of Braden in Cuba and of President Roosevelt in America, but as Hoover and McCarthy gained overwhelming strength during the Truman and Eisenhower administrations, the FBI—as Hemingway had predicted in the 1940s—became virtually autonomous and had almost absolute power.

Durán worked on Braden's staff in Havana and Buenos Aires, and in Washington when Braden was Assistant Secretary of State for Latin American Affairs. Durán was first investigated by the State Department and resigned immediately after he was cleared in August 1946. He joined the United Nations that year and worked on education and population studies in the Department of Economic and Social Affairs. In May 1947 Congressman Ed Gossett wrote to George Marshall, the Secretary of State: "There is no doubt but that [Durán] has been an ardent Communist all of his life. Authentic records of the FBI and of the House Committee on Un-American Activities clearly prove this. . . . I insist that he ought to be immediately discharged, and am confident that you will take such action when you look into the matter."[25] Durán's association with Hemingway displeased the FBI. He was persecuted as a Communist for the next ten years, during the Cold War and the McCarthy regime, and was specifically attacked by the senator in 1951.[26] He was denied a passport that year, despite his diplomatic status, and appeared before a grand jury in New York in 1952.

While Durán was still working for Braden, he was accused of being a Soviet secret agent by formidable political enemies who resented his influence in the State Department: Francisco Franco and Juan Perón. The germ of truth in this false charge, first made by the Falangist newspaper *Arriba* (Arise), was that in October 1937 Indalecio Prieto, the minister of defense, put Durán in charge of the Madrid zone of the Servicio de Investigación Militar. Before leaving to fight at Teruel, he had worked for the Russians for three weeks. According to his family, Durán (like thousands of other Spanish Loyalists) was a card-carrying Communist for a short period (not more than a year) at the beginning of the war, but lost his commitment when he realized what the Party represented.

In May 1954 (the first of five final hearings) Durán appeared in Foley Square before the Loyalty Board, who were all so polite that he felt he was being killed by angels. He denied he was a Communist or a sympathizer (he was not and knew he would be ruined if they discovered the truth about his Communist connections in 1936) and was successfully defended by Hiram Todd. Braden, meanwhile, "had become prey to paranoic fears of Communist infiltration and influence in Washington, fears that he had fully expressed to Congressional committees in December 1953 and March 1954."[27] Threatened by his association with Durán, he acted out of fear and self-interest, and testified against his former colleague and friend in May 1954. (Durán mistakenly thought Braden would be a witness *for* him.) Hemingway wrote Patrick, with considerable shock and anger, that Braden had told Joe McCarthy

Hemingway had set up the Crook Factory. According to the Cuban newspapers, the outfit was made up of monarchists, aristocrats, priests, bartenders, criminals and whores.[28]

Trygve Lie, the Norwegian secretary-general of the U.N.—who was afraid of antagonizing America, the main source of U.N. funds—did not support Durán or demand the return of his passport. Durán had lost most of his resilience after defeat in the Spanish War and was devastated by this nightmarish decade of persecutions. He was scornful about his adopted country (with which he had no strong connections), commented bitterly on the lack of freedom in America and suffered even more from McCarthy than he had from the Civil War.[29]

Though Hemingway won the first round with the FBI and shifted to sub hunting after the Crook Factory was (as planned) dismantled after eight months, the FBI kept watch on him for the rest of his life. They maintained surveillance, collected information and waited for the moment to strike. The FBI continued to swell Hemingway's file with reports on General Benítez' film career (1944), Hemingway's responsibility for placing Durán on Braden's staff (1947), his political activities and intelligence work (1949), his criticism of Senator McCarthy in *Look* (1955), and even the quarrel of his fourth wife, Mary, with a Havana gossip columnist about whether or not lion steak was, as she claimed, a delectable dish (1954).

Hemingway's spy activities and conflict with the FBI reveal a great deal about his restless and reckless character in the early 1940s. Courageous, faithful to the Loyalists and intrigued by espionage, he was willing to try a wild scheme to help his country during war. He persuaded the embassy and the State Department that he was both serious in his endeavors and able to conduct the spy network. The FBI could not differentiate between anti-Fascist and pro-Communist, and had no evidence to support their accusations against him, but they saw the Crook Factory as a rival company and wanted to put it out of business. Hoover, who did not seem to have anything better to do when America was at war, answered Leddy personally during 1942–43. Hemingway was then at the height of his reputation: just after the publication of his most widely acclaimed novel and before his decline became apparent. But the more famous he was, the more dangerous he seemed to the FBI. Almost any other American citizen would have been ruined and destroyed, but Hemingway was one of the very few people strong enough to resist the hostility of the FBI.

III

On October 8, 1942, Leddy told Hoover that Braden "has acceded to HEMINGWAY'S request for authorization to patrol certain areas where submarine activity has been reported . . . and an allotment of gasoline is now being obtained for his use." His sub-hunting expeditions, which coincided with and then replaced his spy network, were inspired by the heroics of Gabriele D'Annunzio and Count Luckner in the Great War, and—oddly enough—by Leicester's activities in the western Caribbean at the beginning of World War Two. In February 1918 D'Annunzio was aboard one of the three torpedo boats that penetrated heavy marine defenses, entered a sound near Fiume (on the Adriatic coast), sank an Austrian ship and returned safely. This expedition was celebrated by the poet in the *Beffa di Buccari* (Jest of Buccari), where he boasted: "In spite of the cowardice of the Austrian fleet, the sailors have advanced with fire and sword to scare caution into its lurking-place." Hemingway, who had been wounded in that war against Austria, praised D'Annunzio's military achievements and condemned his political faults in *Across the River,* and called him: "writer, poet, national hero, phraser of the dialectic of Fascism, macabre egotist, aviator, commander, or rider, in the first of the fast torpedo attack boats, Lieutenant Colonel of Infantry without knowing how to command a company, nor a platoon properly, the great, lovely writer of *Notturno* whom we respect, and jerk."[30]

Ellis Briggs, who served in the Havana embassy at the time, recalled: "Ernest's project started with a discussion of how Count Luckner of the Imperial German Navy foxed the Allies in World War I by disguising a sailing ship as a Norwegian fishing boat. We spoke also of the British Q-boats that looked like tramp freighters until the false bulwarks fell away and the guns started firing." In February 1940 Leicester, financed and accompanied by Sir Anthony Jenkinson, fitted out a small boat for a "snoop cruise" to discover Nazi sub-refueling stations in Central America. According to Toby Bruce (who repeated Leicester's version of his exploits), Leicester found eight stations and reported them to the Navy, who used his intelligence to bomb the stations after America had entered the war. According to Leicester's first wife, his snoop cruise had blundered into and spoiled the Navy's plan to attack the German bases. Though Hemingway may have imitated Leicester, it is unlikely that he ever admitted: "I worked it out like you and Tony did."[31]

Hemingway's idea was that the *Pilar,* fully manned and heavily armed, but disguised as a fishing boat, would attract the attention of a German submarine. The sub would signal the *Pilar* to come alongside (as they frequently did in 1942) in order to requisition supplies of fresh water and food. As the sub approached, Hemingway's men would machine-gun the crew on deck while a jai alai player threw a small bomb into the conning tower. The Marine colonel John Thomason, who had advised Hemingway on his *Men at War* anthology and was Chief of Naval Intelligence for Central America, realistically objected: " 'Suppose he stands off and blows you and the *Pilar* out of the water?' . . . 'If he does that,' replied Ernest, 'then we've had it. But there's a good chance he won't shoot. Why should a submarine risk attracting attention when the skipper can send sailors aboard and scuttle us by opening the seacocks? He'll be curious about fishermen in wartime. He'll want to know what kind of profiteers are trying to tag a marlin in the Gulf Stream with a war on."[32]

Hemingway managed to convince Thomason and Braden that this was a serious project and they gave him what he wanted: a radio, a collapsible rubber boat, machine guns, grenades, bombs and Don Saxon, a volunteer Marine master sergeant. The sub hunting began in June 1942 (two months after he started the Crook Factory) and continued sporadically until he left for New York and London in April 1944. The crew changed over the years, but the permanent members were the *Pilar*'s mate Gregorio Fuentes, Sinsky the sailor, the Basque jai alai player Paxtchi Ibarlucia and Hemingway's friend Winston Guest. All epitomized the unquestioning devotion that was notably absent in the more critical Gustavo Durán.

Hemingway first met Guest—handsome, charming, sweet and silly —in East Africa in late 1933. Born in England in 1906, Guest was the godson and second cousin of Winston Churchill. His father had been aide-de-camp to General Sir John French; his mother, the daughter of Henry Phipps—philanthropist and partner of Andrew Carnegie—had left him one of the great American fortunes. Hemingway once told Bill Davis that Guest had become depressed and lost sleep when he realized he was down to only fifteen million dollars. Guest—who was six feet six inches tall, weighed 235 pounds and had a square red face—was called Wolfie because he reminded young Gregory of Lon Chaney, Jr., in a horror film, *The Wolf Man.* Guest graduated from Yale and from Columbia Law School, and became an international champion polo player in the thirties. He practiced law in New York, founded an airline in Mexico, ran unsuccessfully for the U.S. Senate and became a captain in the Marines in World War Two. Hemingway portrayed Guest as Henry Wood in the "At Sea" section of *Islands in the Stream,* which describes hunting down and killing the crew of a sunken German submarine: "The biggest man that Thomas Hudson knew, and the most cheerful and with the widest shoulders and the best manners came in. . . . He was so big he made everyone at the bar look stunted and he had a lovely smile . . . [and a] handsome face."

Despite his education and senatorial aspirations, Guest was apparently rather dim (often a great advantage with Hemingway). Mario Menocal, Jr., completed Hemingway's fictional portrait with a description of Guest's winning temperament as well as his epic achievements in athletics, alcohol and sex:

> Guest was one of the least intelligent and most scatterbrained people I have ever known. . . . [He had] indisputable ability at every sort of sport, and [I admired] his unfailing, instinctive good manners and cheerful disposition. . . .
>
> It is impossible not to like this huge, kind, strong, good, gifted man, the best of good companions. . . . His consumption [of drink] was *astounding.* . . . One evening at Casa Marina, the world-famed Havana house of ill fame, he took four women upstairs, one after the other, *in the course of a single hour*—and later curious research proved that he achieved his purpose with each of them and was still going strong at the end.[33]

Hemingway disliked Guest's second wife, Ceci—a well-dressed debutante who had appeared in the Ziegfeld Follies of 1944—and banned her from his house and boat.

All of Hemingway's Cuban friends believed the sub-hunting expeditions were little more than boyish escapades (though mature in youth, Hemingway often seemed adolescent in middle age); an excuse to get strictly rationed gasoline so he could fish and drink with comrades on the *Pilar,* tell friends he was engaged in secret war activity and prove to Martha that he was courageously committed to victory at sea. Elicio Arguelles said: "The Embassy asked Hemingway during World War II to go out in his boat, the *Pilar,* to watch for German submarines. He would go out, but all he did was fish." And Mayito Menocal agreed:

"That was a stunt. Of course I went there with him. They didn't do a goddamn thing—nothing. Just cruise around and have a good time. He went with Winston Guest and a few Basque friends. . . . He built that up into a war act. But it was really nothing. We used to kid him about that."[34]

However, Braden and Robert Joyce, who knew more about the sub hunting than his Cuban friends, believed that Hemingway performed a useful function. Though he never got close enough to destroy a submarine, he risked his boat and his life when "wolf-packs" of German U-boats were able to cut off Cuba from the American mainland for months at a time. Braden told Malcolm Cowley (with perhaps some justification of his support for Hemingway): "He obtained valuable information on the location of German subs on various occasions. So worthwhile was Ernest's contribution that I have strongly recommended him for a decoration."[35] And Robert Joyce, the embassy's intelligence officer, explained why Hemingway (whose apparent frivolity maintained his secrecy and misled his Cuban friends) was supported by the diplomatic and military authorities:

A specially prepared bomb thrown down the hatchway of the sub would disable the navigation controls. A small U.S. coastguard vessel would be radioed to rush to the disabled sub and capture it. The U.S. Navy at Guantanamo bought the entire concept and supplied E.H. with the weapons necessary for the operation. It *was* "a serious military venture" which might very well have succeeded.[36]

19

To the Siegfried Line
1944–1945

> Intellectuals are like women. . .
> soldiers make them dream.
>
> ANDRÉ MALRAUX

I

When the Navy eliminated the threat of German U-boats in Cuban waters, Hemingway's sub hunting came to an end. He then looked for another way to serve the war effort, responded to Martha's suggestion and became a correspondent. In World War Two, as in the Spanish War, Hemingway fought his domestic battles in the midst of a European conflict. Competing professionally with Martha and eager to impress his mistress, he behaved recklessly in war and outrageously in London and Paris. His reporting was weak; he did not take it seriously and put all his effort into action rather than into work. He used his status to obtain weapons and engage in battle, and enhanced his flamboyant public image. During his ten months in Europe, he severed his ties with Martha and developed his relationship with Mary Welsh, while participating in the triumphal entry into Paris and the Allied invasion of Germany.

All Hemingway's friends agreed that he could be fiercely caustic when crossed and angered. Toby Bruce said he "could be as mean as a striped-assed ape"; Robert Capa stated: "Papa can be more severe than God on a rough day when the whole human race is misbehaving"; and Buck Lanham insisted: " 'When Hem was nasty' he qualified as 'The King of All Nasties.' "[1] Martha gave an example of his savagery, which erupted when she returned to the Finca in March 1944. As she was

389

escaping into sleep (which he always resented), he attacked her with the same arguments that Pauline must have used to dissuade him from going to Spain:

> Ernest began at once to rave at me, the word is not too strong. He woke me when I was trying to sleep to bully, snarl, mock—my crime really was to have been at war when he had not, but that was not how he put it. I was supposedly insane, I only wanted excitement and danger, I had no responsibility to anyone, I was selfish beyond belief. It never stopped and believe me, it was fierce and ugly.

In New York, en route to London in April 1944, Martha had to endure his "hideous and insane reviling" and told him he was making it impossible for her to go on loving him. Gregory summarized the end of their marriage—and Hemingway's characteristic revision of actuality —when he wrote that Martha "was driven from that house in Cuba . . . by the return in greater force of papa's megalomania. . . . He just tortured Marty and when he had finally destroyed all her love for him and she had left him, he claimed she deserted him."[2]

Hemingway seemed to have learned very little from his marital mistakes. As he grew older, he became increasingly difficult to live with. He was selfish and always put his books before his wives. But he was a good husband to Hadley until Pauline appeared, and he retained Pauline's love—despite Jane and Martha—till the very end of their marriage. His marriage to Martha was an ill-fated battle of two domineering personalities, and they parted in December 1944 with intense bitterness and mutual hatred. Mary surpassed all the wives in her ability to stand the abuse and punishment. She remained with him until the end, endured a great deal to remain Mrs. Ernest Hemingway and she suffered far more difficult times than any of the previous wives.

Martha felt that Hemingway had deliberately betrayed her and blocked her career by offering to write for *Collier's*, which had been her magazine since 1937. Since each magazine was permitted to have only one correspondent at the front, Hemingway—who became Martha's chief in Europe—automatically destroyed her chances of covering the fighting war in an official capacity. Martha had arranged with Roald Dahl, who was then air attaché at the British Embassy in Washington, to get Hemingway a priority seat on a flight to London on May 17, 1944. She naturally thought Hemingway would arrange a place for her on the same plane. When he refused to help her ("I couldn't do that. They only fly men."), she was forced to take an extremely dangerous two-week passage on a freighter filled with dynamite.

Before leaving for London the Hemingways spent an evening at Tim Costello's bar on Third Avenue with Vincent Sheean and Paul de Kruif. John O'Hara mistakenly felt he had not been invited to the informal gathering and sulked in the corner. After a few drinks, O'Hara claimed that he had the best Irish walking stick in New York. Hemingway bet fifty dollars that he could break it, snapped the blackthorn over his own head, and demolished a rival and his weapon with one blow.[3]

Hemingway's first and only trip to London brought out his ambivalent feelings about the English. As a boy, he had been close to his English grandfather, Ernest Hall, and proud of his English heritage. He hero-worshipped Dorman-Smith; he admired his Kiplingesque ethic, adopted his military bearing and employed his laconic speech in the early vignettes of *in our time*. Attracted by Duff Twysden's beauty, title and sophistication, he fell in love with her and transformed her into the heroine of *The Sun Also Rises*. The novel also contained a sympathetic portrait of the Englishman Harris, whom Jake meets while fishing at Burguete. Catherine Barkley, the heroine of his second novel, was Scottish; and Robert Wilson, the hunter in "Francis Macomber," was based on his English friend Philip Percival. Though the English disapproved of bullfighting, they loved to kill animals in sport.

After his quarrels with Ford Madox Ford and Wyndham Lewis, Hemingway began to associate the English with snobbery and affectation, while to them he epitomized the brashness, brutality and violence of America. His works had been praised by Ford, D. H. Lawrence and Greene, but had also been lashed by Woolf, Huxley and Lewis. He never had the same critical recognition, book sales and literary influence in England as he had in America. He found his publisher Jonathan Cape unsympathetic and had a number of serious arguments with him.

Hemingway believed that the English volunteers had fought badly in Spain and deserted in large numbers from the International Brigade after the battle of Jarama; that the British government had been cowardly and even suicidal by refusing to oppose Hitler and Mussolini in the Spanish War. He was fond of C. S. Forester's critique of the British military mentality in *The General* (1936) and claimed that it had inspired Hitler to attack England. Finally, he hated Churchill for destroying Dorman-Smith in 1942 and would portray his friend's career in

Across the River. He arrived in England in May 1944 with a rather hostile attitude.

Hemingway's first contacts in London were with the American press corps in the Dorchester Hotel. During the weeks before D-Day, everyone seemed to have free time for parties and plenty of money to spend on drinks. Hemingway once brought a piece of a buzz bomb to a party, announced that it might explode and convinced some of the guests that it actually would. His fame, charm and charisma made him lionized wherever he went. He enjoyed playing the role of Papa, and found it a comfortable way to distance and deal with people who treated him as a great man.

Hemingway had known Irwin Shaw, author of *Bury the Dead* (1936), in the late thirties; when he returned from the Spanish War, he told him: "we make the dead and you bury them." In London, Shaw (like Leicester Hemingway) was a private in the combat camera unit of the Army Signal Corps and had been sent from the Mediterranean to prepare for the filming of D-Day.[4] Shaw was then having an affair with Mary Welsh. In late May, he introduced Hemingway to Mary during lunch at the White Tower restaurant on Percy Street. (Under its former name, Tour Eiffel, it had been a gathering place of Wyndham Lewis and the Vorticists before the Great War.) In *The Young Lions* (1949) Shaw described his liaison with Mary, who shared many traits with the fictional Louise M'Kimber: "small, dark and clever-looking . . . warm and undemanding." The hero, Michael Whitacre, "never could decide whether he loved Louise or was annoyed with her. She had a husband somewhere in the Pacific of whom she rarely spoke, and did some sort of semi-secret job for the O.W.I. [Office of War Information] and she seemed to know every big-wig in the British Isles. She had a deft, tricky way with men, and was always being invited to weekends at famous country houses where garrulous military men of high rank seemed to spill a great many dangerous secrets to her."

Hemingway and Leicester also appear in the novel as Ahearn and Keane. The former, a short, fat war correspondent for *Collier's* with "a very serious round face, mottled heavily with much drinking," is rather pompously doing research on the "pure state" of fear in war. Ahearn reappears after the liberation of Paris and makes some absurd pronouncements about war while the other characters are facing death in combat. Leroy Keane is a garrulous scrounger with a reputation for being unlucky, a "constipated, brother-and-hero-haunted man with a frigid wife" and three unwanted children. Keane's much older brother won the Congressional Medal of Honor (a symbol of Hemingway's literary prestige) for killing eleven Germans in one morning, but Whitacre comments on the hero's lack of caution and good sense, and wonders if he won the Medal "out of sheer stupidity."[5]

Hemingway thought that Shaw portrayed him as a buffoon and Mary as a whore, and was furious. He called Shaw a conceited and despicable jerk who liked to publish his fantasies about Jews killing Germans. He hated Shaw for sleeping with Mary, portraying her in *The Young Lions,* publishing a novel on World War Two (which he considered his private subject), writing on war without knowing much about it, impressing the critics and getting good reviews. When they met at "21" in March 1950, he threatened to punch Shaw and made an ironic reference to his Jewish background by calling him "a Brooklyn Tolstoy."

Mary Welsh's background, quite different from the genteel St. Louis origins of Hemingway's first three wives, appealed to his imagination. She grew up in a small town in northern Minnesota. Her father was a logger who supplemented his income by running a Mississippi riverboat that was linked to the romantic and literary tradition of Mark Twain. In contrast to Martha's aristocratic dress and manner, Mary's style was hopelessly unchic and middle class. Like his previous wives, Mary had been to college (Northwestern); like all the wives but Hadley, she was a journalist. Hemingway had told Hadley, just after their first meeting: "There's the girl I'm going to marry"; and he also told Mary, just after they met, that he wanted to marry her.[6] She resembled the actress Mary Martin; and had a sharp little face, a good figure, short curly blond hair (and heavy calves). Though not beautiful or even pretty, she was a cute and attractive woman who combined Pauline's petite figure and athletic ability with Martha's fair complexion and professional background. Hemingway was the first husband of his first three wives; but Mary had been married twice before: to Lawrence Cook, a student at Northwestern, from 1929 to 1931 and to Noel Monks, an Australian journalist, from 1938 to 1946. Hadley had lasted six years, Pauline fourteen, Martha seven; but Mary endured for seventeen years.

Mary was society reporter on the *Chicago Daily News* when Leicester was on the staff and Hadley's husband Paul Mowrer was managing editor. She worked for Beaverbrook's *Daily Express* in London and joined the *Time* bureau there in 1940. Her colleague Lael Wertenbaker said she had "absolute guts" and was always cool during bombing raids.

Michael Foot, who then worked on the *Evening Standard,* thought Mary was a good journalist who conveyed a lively sense of the war in England. Mary's colleague Bill Walton noted, more acutely, that she was a pedestrian, hard-working, uninspired journalist who could discover and present the facts in a straightforward way, but was not able to convey or interpret the deeper meanings of a story. During the heightened sexual atmosphere of wartime London, when women reporters were rare, Mary openly used her attractions to obtain information from high-ranking officers. Hemingway later made a contemptuous accusation and exclaimed: "I haven't fucked generals in order to get a story for *Time* magazine."[7]

When they met in 1944 Mary (who loved celebrities) gave Hemingway almost everything he wanted and had failed to get from Martha. Martha, as their marriage disintegrated, was critical, competitive, unsympathetic and sexually cold to him; Mary, lively and uninhibited, "full of laughs and full of lovers," adored him, was sexually responsive and "treated him as the hotshot warrior, macho man, great in bed." An unpublished description of sexual relations, "Make you stop flying," written after he met Mary, recalls the satisfying sleeping bag scenes in *For Whom the Bell Tolls.* In contrast to the willful and independent Martha, Mary understood his emotional needs and made a conscious effort to please him. As she later said: "I wanted him to be the master, to be stronger and cleverer than I, to remember constantly how big he was and how small I was."[8]

When Martha rejected him, Mary ministered to his ego and his libido. She was praised in two intolerably sentimental poems (the worst things he ever wrote) for "Coming small-voiced and lovely to the / hand and eye to bring your heart back that was gone; to cure / all loneliness." Four months after meeting Mary, he told his son Patrick (who had politely listened to his complaints about Martha): "I saw [Mary] again in Paris and we had fine time. Think you would like. Have nicknamed [her] Papa's Pocket Rubens. If [she] gets any thinner will promote to pocket Tintoretto. . . . Very fine girl. Looked after me in worst time ever had."[9]

On May 25, a week after he arrived in England, Hemingway met the *Time* reporter Bill Walton at a party given by Robert Capa. Walton had spent his summers near Charlevoix in northern Michigan, came from a similar midwestern and newspaper background, and was a friend of Mary Welsh. Born in Jacksonville, Illinois, in 1909, he graduated from the University of Wisconsin, worked on his family paper and on *PM* in New York (with the ubiquitous Leicester) before joining *Time* in Europe. Walton, trained to parachute into Normandy with General Ridgway on D-Day, was closely questioned by Hemingway about his experience. He brought Walton's mail to the press camp in Cherbourg in mid-July; they met in Paris, shared a double bed during the Hürtgen-wald campaign (when Hemingway would take a cold sponge bath and then put his smelly clothes back on) and spent New Year's Eve 1944 together.

Walton found Hemingway extremely alert. Because of his war experience in Italy and Spain, he was an excellent soldier—better adjusted in war than in peace. He could recognize the distinctive sound of a German plane and once saved Walton's life (as he had saved Herbert Matthews' life in Spain) by ordering him to jump from a jeep and landing on top of him just before they were strafed by a plane. He criticized Walton's dispatches from the Hürtgenwald and suggested illuminating parallels with the Spanish Civil War. During the war in Germany, "Ernest talked a good deal about Oak Park, high school and Michigan, scurrilously about Martha, adoringly of Mary. Contemptu-ously of psychiatry, romantically of the Spanish War. He detested all Krauts except Marlene [Dietrich] and dreamed of Cuba. . . . [In Cuba] he read compulsively every day and loved discussing it in the evening and could be very, very funny. My Finca memories are more of laughter than of anger though there was both."[10]

As Hemingway was being driven home, during the London black-out, from Capa's party in Belgrave Square to the Dorchester Hotel on Park Lane, the car struck a water tank in Lowndes Square. He was thrown into the windshield, suffered a severe concussion, needed fifty-seven stitches and was reported dead by some newspapers.

As with Bumby's whooping cough on the Riviera and Pauline's se-vere cold in Wyoming, physical illness led to the breakdown of Heming-way's marriage. A few days after the accident, Martha, still nursing her resentment about his cruel accusations, his preemptive job with *Col-lier's* and her dangerous sea voyage, arrived in England and visited him in St. George's Hospital. Instead of expressing concern and compassion, as he had expected, she merely laughed at the huge bandage covering his head. Later on, forgetting his description of Frederic Henry's hoard of bottles in the Milan hospital, she illogically explained: "If he really had a concussion he could hardly have been drinking with his pals or even receiving them. He did not look the least ill anyway." He was, in fact, seriously injured. He had forgotten his own hostile behavior, was deeply hurt by Martha's callous indifference and told Patrick (using a favorite racetrack metaphor):

> I am sick of her Prima-Donna-ism. When head was all smashed and terrible headaches etc. she would not do anything for a man that we would do for a dog. I made a very great mistake on her—or else she changed very much—I think probably both—But mostly the latter. I hate to lose anyone who can look so lovely and who we taught to shoot and write so well. But have torn up my tickets on her and would be glad to never see her again.[11]

Dr. José Luis Herrera, brother of El Monstro and former surgeon of the Twelfth International Brigade in Spain, thought Hemingway should have had his head opened and his hemorrhage drained, and convalesced for at least three months. Instead, he left the hospital on May 29 in order to fly with the RAF, observe the landings at Normandy on June 6, 1944, return to the sympathetic comfort of Mary, and take immediate and long-term revenge on Martha. He made a dinner appointment with Martha, stripped off his clothes and, when she entered his room, pretended to attack her and reduced her to tears. She thought his behavior in London was "shameful, arrogant, boastful, embarrassing" and that he behaved irresponsibly with the American army in France and Germany.[12]

His happiest times with Mary, as with Martha, took place when he was courting her and on his best behavior—before their marriage in 1946. But when Hemingway lost his temper (as he frequently did) they had some ugly moments, which gave her a vivid idea of what to expect in marriage. (Everyone bet it would not last more than six months.) He told one friend that he wanted to give Mary the clap; told Mary, when she was sick, that she looked like a spider; and after she had called his army pals—who vomited all over her bathroom—drunken slobs, he slapped her on the jaw. Mary retaliated by telling Hemingway that Shaw had a bigger penis.[13]

Roald Dahl, who knew Hemingway in both America and England, saw the sensitive side of his character: "I got no impression of swagger or bullying in my relations with him. I found him to be a shy and rather jumpy fellow and I only saw him thoroughly at ease in [George Brown's] boxing gymnasium in New York." But other British officers felt he acted boorishly with the tight-lipped, stoical fliers of the RAF. General Sir John Hackett thought he was a "war snob" who favored certain services, regiments and jobs. The poet and public relations officer John Pudney, who saw him in shaggy and ill-fitting battle dress in June 1944, felt his Papa persona was extremely awkward: "To me, he was a fellow obsessed with playing the part of Ernest Hemingway and 'hamming' it to boot: a sentimental nineteenth-century actor called upon to act the part of a twentieth-century tough guy. Set beside . . . a crowd of young men who walked so modestly and stylishly with Death, he seemed a bizarre cardboard figure."[14]

More precise details of Hemingway's insensitive behavior with the pilots were supplied by Nigel Hamilton, the biographer of Field Marshal Montgomery:

> There is a story I was told of Hemingway by an old friend, the R.A.F. war poet, John Pudney (died in 1977). Apparently Hemingway visited John's aerodrome before D-Day—and to John's disgust Hemingway held court at the bar, pontificating before three junior pilots and claiming that their senior officers were "cowards" because they were not at that time flying over enemy territory. Now as it happened, all senior officers who had been let in on the D-Day plans, were "grounded"—i.e. once told, they were not allowed to take the risk of being shot down over enemy-held territory. John—who thought very highly of Hemingway's writing—was absolutely furious over his buffoon-like performance at the airfield. "I was *ashamed* of him," he told me. . . . That Hemingway should boast and brag at the bar about his own bravery and exploits, in front of innocent but brave pilots, and condemn the senior officer (who was much decorated and certainly the most courageous flier John knew in the R.A.F.: he is still alive—an Air Marshal): it was to John a *typical* case of the egoism, vanity and shameful bragging of a certain kind of writer.

The Air Marshal, whom Hemingway flew with in pursuit of V-1 rockets and greatly admired, was Peter Wykeham, who recorded in the London *Times* his indulgent impression of Hemingway's blustering and madcap behavior:

> He impressed me as the sort of man who spends his whole life proving that he is not scared. . . . I met Hemingway through a life-long friend of mine, the poet John Pudney. I think he was in charge of Hemingway, being in the R.A.F. public relations department. . . . [He was] like a gentle man who's accidentally found himself leading a rampaging bull.

He got into more and more drunken parties, fights and wrangles, being thrown into fountains, ejected from hotels and locked in people's rooms.[15]

Hemingway shared some of the arrogance of the American troops who had come from a prosperous nation to a war-ravaged country and felt they were saving the English from the Germans. It is ironic that Hemingway, the creator of the stoic, laconic hero, was not well attuned to the way Englishmen hid or expressed their feelings. His lack of sensitivity derived from his drinking, his egoism, his failure with Martha and his civilian uneasiness with combatants.

II

Hemingway had what he called "a good war": short, irregular, exciting, comradely and lucky. His seven months' participation in the conflict (June–December 1944) were, he said, the happiest of his life. As in the Great War, Turkey and Spain—but to a much greater degree—he tried to prolong his military experience for as long as possible after the war was over by keeping in touch with friends who had shared his adventures, adopting a tough front-line diction, exaggerating his exploits in conversations and letters. As the spelling and syntax broke down, the sentimentality and boastfulness increased. He planned a great war trilogy, but incorporated only a fraction of his experience in six thin dispatches and part of *Across the River*.

Hemingway participated in combat as if he were an infantry officer and then reported what he had actually experienced. He made a clear distinction between journalism and serious writing, and depended on his reputation—rather than his content—to justify the dispatches that he typed out at top speed. Roald Dahl stated:

As a war correspondent in the Hitler war I would rate him as very poor, but he didn't try to be good then. I remember him telling me about a wonderful episode concerning a man jumping out of a burning tank after his return from the invasion and when I said, "But you have to put that in your *Collier's* piece," he answered, "You don't think I'd give them that, do you? I'm keeping it for a book."[16]

Hemingway liked combat, enjoyed killing and thought war was the greatest outdoor sport. World War Two released in him a blood lust that

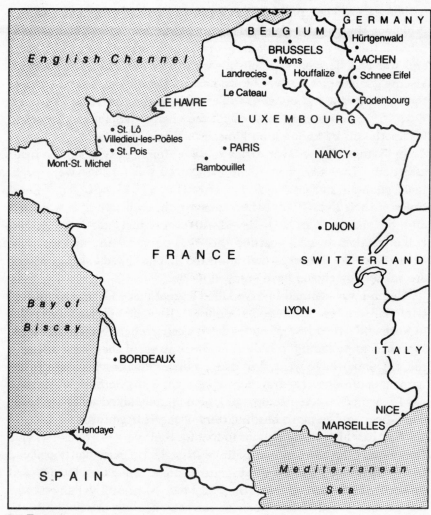

7. *France*

earlier wars had not, perhaps because he was too old to fight as a soldier. A lifelong student of the natural history of the dead, he had slaughtered fish and animals since boyhood. He drew analogies between bullfighting and war and derived vicarious pleasure from watching the matador assume godlike powers over life and death. He killed half-ton marlin in the Gulf Stream and dangerous big game in the American West and East Africa; he watched soldiers kill the enemy in Spain; and reached his apotheosis by killing men himself in World War Two.

In "Wings Always Over Africa" (1936), Hemingway made the pious assertion: "The only people who ever loved war for long were profiteers, generals, staff officers and whores. They all had the best and finest times of their lives."[17] But there was a radical change in his feelings after the Spanish War. He believed with Camus that "absolute freedom is the freedom to kill," learned the "fear-purged, purging ecstasy of battle" and (like Robert Jordan) admitted that he "liked to kill as all who are soldiers by choice have enjoyed it."[18]

Hemingway claimed to have killed a great many Germans and certainly killed a few of them. On August 3, 1944, at Villedieu-les-Poêles in Normandy, he threw grenades down a cellar where Nazi troops were supposed to be hiding, but did not check to see if they were actually there. He may have wanted to take credit for this doubtful enterprise without confronting the fragmented remains of his victims. On November 22, armed with a machine gun, he definitely killed some Germans who attacked Lanham's headquarters in the Hürtgenwald.

War, in which entire nations fought for their very existence, was for Hemingway the ultimate competitive struggle. He particularly enjoyed the exhilarating pleasure of absolute victory: "re-taking France and especially Paris made me feel the best I had ever felt. Ever since I had been a boy [1918] I had been in retreats, holding attacks, retreats, victories with no reserves to follow them up, etc., and I had never known how winning can make you feel." He also achieved tremendous satisfaction after overcoming obstacles by heroic will, a transfiguring exaltation after passing through a dangerous storm of steel:

> I think there is a steady renewal of immortality through storms, attacks, landings on beaches where landing is opposed, flying, when there are problems and many other things which are all awful and horrible and hateful to those who are not suited to them. . . . These things make a katharsis which is not a pathological thing, nor a seeking after thrills, but

it is an ennobling thing to those who are suited for them and have the luck so that they survive them.[19]

Things began badly when Hemingway, considered a precious cargo by the military authorities, observed the D-Day invasion from a landing craft but was not allowed ashore. Martha, stowed away on a hospital ship, managed to land in Normandy—and he never forgave her. He reported the war in France from mid-July; and on July 26, after the breakout from St. Lô, he met the fourth of his military heroes, Colonel Charles Trueman (Buck) Lanham. He was—like Dorman-Smith, Charles Sweeny and Gustavo Durán—an intellectual and a writer. Born in Washington, D.C., in 1902 and graduated from West Point in 1924, Lanham had a distinguished military record and a wide range of interests. Hemingway accompanied Lanham as "he led the 22nd Infantry Regiment of the fourth Infantry Division, which spearheaded the Normandy breakout, entered Paris, attacked the Siegfried Line and held a key salient in the Battle of the Bulge." Later, he was promoted to general in the field, attacked Cologne and met the Soviet army at the Moldau River; immediately after the war he commanded the occupation forces in Austria and Czechoslovakia and was chief spokesman for Eisenhower at SHAEF. Lanham's obituary stated that he was "an amateur poet and writer as well as a combat infantryman. He was also a leading military instructor, something of a diplomat, and, after his retirement from service, an industrial executive" with the Xerox Corporation. In his unpublished story "The Monument," Hemingway emphasized Lanham's ability to fight well under pressure and the combat experience that bound them together in friendship.[20]

Bill Walton described Lanham as "small, delicate and very neurotic." With his lean, gray look, he bore a striking similarity to Dashiell Hammett. Though a gallant soldier, he was also old-fashioned, straitlaced, thoroughly conventional, personally unimpressive and surprisingly dull. Gregory Hemingway characterized him—in a far-fetched but perfectly appropriate word—as a *nebbish*.[21] It would not be an exaggeration to say that Lanham, Hemingway's alter ego, was one of his greatest fictional creations. He was idealized to heroic proportions to match Hemingway's urgent need for a wartime comrade who would reflect, confirm, exalt and perpetuate his own martial expertise and daring adventures.

Durán, like Martha, adopted a critical attitude toward Hemingway.

Lanham, like Mary, accepted his faults and adored him. Lanham, with some exaggeration (Hemingway never carried a canteen of vermouth and did not drink heavily in war), told the *New York Times* correspondent C. L. Sulzberger:

> Hemingway has the heart of a lion and is first class in war, but horrible in peace. Hemingway used to wander around with two canteens strapped to his belt. One was filled with gin and the other with vermouth. Whenever there was a quiet moment, he would haul out a battered tin cup and suggest: "Let's have a Martini." He was a good fighter with all weapons, although, strictly speaking, he was not permitted to bear arms. . . . He is entirely fearless.[22]

Under fire, Hemingway lost all fear of risking himself in war and all the tact and restraint that had characterized his behavior in Spain. His deliberate exposure to danger was inspired by a number of complex factors: a fatalistic attitude, an ability to dismiss the possibility of death, a belief that he was lucky and therefore invulnerable, and a desire to make an impressive if adolescent gesture—even at the risk of his life—which would prove his courage. In Spain he wrote of artillery shells that "came with that authentic personal final rush of splitting air that you flatten to without choice or pride," yet felt secure during the bombardment of the Hotel Florida because his room had "a safe angle" and could not be harmed.

One incident, which took place inside Germany in September 1944 and was witnessed by both Lanham and the artist John Groth, epitomized Hemingway's combination of bravery and bravado. When their farmhouse headquarters, named Schloss Hemingstein, was suddenly hit by German artillery, everyone ducked under the table or into the cellar. Hemingway alone continued to eat and drink as if nothing had happened. He maintained, against all reason, that if you could hear a shell coming, it could not harm you. Groth could not determine if Hemingway's behavior was valiant or stupid, fatalistic or operatic, intuitive or calculated to astonish his more cautious comrades. It was both impressive and insane.[23]

Lanham maintained that Hemingway did not affect his hard-boiled pose until after the war and was deeply moved by the death of soldiers in battle: "Things of this sort always hit him deep down where he lived." It was impossible to think of Hemingway as hard and cynical, for he was "one of the most compassionate, sensitive, gentle people." Yet Lanham also mentioned that Hemingway condemned a liaison officer who (he thought) tried to fake battle fatigue and felt "someone should shoot the bastard."[24]

In St. Pois on August 5, between the landings in Normandy and the liberation of Paris, Hemingway had a second serious accident. While riding on a motorcycle with Robert Capa, he was forced to leap into a ditch to avoid a German anti-tank gun, was fired on by a machine gun, banged his head on a boulder and suffered another concussion. Charles Collingwood, the CBS reporter, who saw him a few days later, noticed that he had abrasions on his face and was still woozy. Hemingway told Mary that his double vision, "slowness [of thought and speech], loss of verbal memory, tendency to write backhand and backwards and the headaches, condition Mr. S[crooby] was in and the inertia, headaches and ringing in the ears were all symptoms of what had been done to head."

Mr. Scrooby was a suggestive euphemism (which he had used with Martha) for his penis. The impotence he suffered from August to November as a result of this accident was caused by physical rather than by the psychological factors that had affected him just after his marriage to Pauline in May 1927 and during a crisis with Jane Mason in January 1936. But it must have led to considerable embarrassment during his courtship of Mary in the Ritz Hotel in Paris during September and October 1944. "Mr. S." became their code word and Hemingway sometimes mentioned it—with regret or anticipation—when he was separated from Mary during the early years of their marriage. He wrote that he loved her face and body and lovely place. When they were unkind to each other it was unnatural, like when her lovely place closed or Mr. S. was hurt. But Mr. S. was alert at the moment, and made a tent when Hemingway wrote about Mary. Mr. S. may do an Old Faithful before Mary returns, but he will *be* an Old Faithful when she comes back.[25] His sexual boasting was directly related to his fear of impotence and his declining sexual powers in middle age.

Shortly after this accident Hemingway, Capa and six other war correspondents had a brief holiday at the Hôtel de la Mère Poularde in Mont-St. Michel. The peninsula has a glorious church that inspired the classic book by Henry Adams and is cut off by tides from the mainland twice a day. The journalist Helen Kirkpatrick found Hemingway "good company, amusing, dogmatic and holding forth always on strategy and interpreting the next moves." His fascination with military matters was not objective and analytical; it was the obsession of a writer who wanted to be a field officer.

Charles Collingwood provided a fascinating description of Hemingway's character, conversation, love of teaching, leadership, attitude toward criticism, preferential treatment and military expertise:

> He certainly looked the part, powerful in physique and presence. When the mood was on him, as it usually was, he exuded good humor and charm. The mood was not always on him and he would lapse into periods of silence, or abruptness, when he did not speak. In those periods he seemed to belie the complete assurance and self-confidence he usually sought to convey. From time to time one sensed a certain vulnerability about him.
>
> He could be a marvellous talker and raconteur and a boon companion. He was often very indulgent to those younger than he, as I was, but not always—sometimes, especially if one had said something out of line, he would cut you off. . . . There was a didactic streak in him and he loved to instruct younger writers in the techniques and mechanics of the craft. His advice was not high-faluting but extremely practical. . . .
>
> He did often dominate the conversation, out of sheer force of character and exuberance. But he was always willing to listen to others and to discuss and even argue with them. He was not a conversational monopolist. And when his dark mood was on him, he said little.
>
> He was, whenever there was a group, the leader of the band. For instance, when a group of us were staying at Mont-St. Michel at the Hôtel de la Mère Poularde, he was the principal organizer, having completely won over la patronne, Mme. Chevalier. He chose the wine, decided on menus, etc. He had great force of personality and a gift for organization. He was and wanted to be seen as the principal character in any situation. . . .
>
> At Mont-St. Michel he showed me the piece he had written and asked me for my comments. . . . So, being a brash youngster, I blurted out, "Well, Papa, it sounds like a parody of Ernest Hemingway." His face froze, and I forget whether he actually ushered me out or made it very clear I was to leave, which, of course, I did—feeling like the most insensitive clown after so flattering a gesture on his part. He cut me dead for weeks. . . . [But after the war, in Cuba,] he asked me if I remembered a time in France when he had asked my opinion of a piece he had written for COLLIER'S and I said it sounded like a parody of Ernest Hemingway. "You were right, of course," he said. . . . Did he receive preferential treatment as a war correspondent? Yes, I am sure

he did. So did a good many others, Ed Murrow, Ernie Pyle, Quentin Reynolds and several others. This accrues to fame and wide circulation. But Hemingway's special privileges by no means depended on his literary renown. He had covered wars before and was, moreover, very much a military buff. He was an expert on strategy, tactics and military history. He spoke the same language as senior officers and many of them sought his company and conceived a great respect and personal affection for him.[26]

Hemingway's most controversial campaign in the war, the week of fighting around Rambouillet (twenty-three miles southwest of Paris), took place just after he left Mont-St. Michel, and ended with the liberation of the capital on August 25. In early August he acquired a devoted chauffeur, Archie (Red) Pelkey. A martial version of Toby Bruce, he had "bright red hair, six years of regular Army, four words of French, [and] a missing front tooth." Bill Walton sympathetically described him as an uneducated redneck, a natural shot and experienced woodsman who worshipped Hemingway and waited on him hand and foot.[27]

At Rambouillet, Hemingway, accompanied by Pelkey, patrolled ahead of the regular army, led a private group of Free French partisans into the town and held the place for a day after it had been evacuated by the retreating Germans. He acted like a military governor, established headquarters, raised the American flag, took prisoners and stacked his room with weapons. Most important, he secured valuable information about enemy defenses on the road to Paris that facilitated General Leclerc's triumphant march to the capital.

Near Rambouillet, Hemingway met Lieutenant Irving Krieger: "short, stocky, exceedingly tough and very cheerful." In England, the reckless Hemingway had encouraged the RAF pilot Peter Wykeham to act against his better judgment and attempt to destroy enemy flying bombs; in France, his aggressive drive and wild attempt to be the first American into Paris provoked Irving Krieger to rush ahead of the army:

His jeep driver asked me if I knew about mines. I told him I was the regimental mine platoon leader and that it was my job to know about mines. It seemed to me that Ernest Hemingway was glad to hear this and invited me . . . to come along with him in his jeep. I thought he was going to show me some mines a few hundred yards ahead. . . . Instead we drove ahead about 10 miles to Rambouillet. I was sent ahead to check on mines, but to drive ahead 10 miles seemed ridiculous especially since I was not sure that [the road] was reasonably secured by our own troops.

At Rambouillet we found American trucks from the Engineers Corps out there that had been ambushed and seven soldiers killed. Mr. Hemingway spoke French to the few ladies there who gave him the dog tags of the dead soldiers. . . .

He wanted to keep on going to Paris. I told him what I had done could be explained but to go farther and jeopardize my soldiers more would require further interrogation. . . . The only reason I got out there 10 miles in front of our own troops was due to Ernest Hemingway's aggressiveness in his desire to get a story and get to Paris first. I was too concerned for the safety of my men to wander out 10 miles in front of our troops, but through a series of happenings, there I was, 10 miles out with my platoon and the Battalion Commander & higher authority knew that there were no Germans at least 10 miles out.

When Hemingway met Irwin Shaw at Rambouillet, he said: "I have a motorcycle. Let's look for Germans and draw fire." Since the Germans were retreating, Shaw thought it foolish to make daring gestures and take risks.[28]

David Bruce, then a colonel in the O.S.S. and later American ambassador to Germany, gave a detailed and reliable account of Hemingway's intelligence work, leadership of partisans, judicial decisions, counterespionage activities and rivalry with other correspondents when he settled into the Hôtel du Grand Veneur in Rambouillet on August 20:

Ernest Hemingway was with the G-2 [intelligence officer] of that division, exchanging information. He had just returned from Rambouillet, which he said had been evacuated by its German garrison, and he thought if we went there we might obtain some useful details about the disposition of the enemy forces in the country between Rambouillet and Paris. . . .

"Red" [Pelkey] was a courageous fellow, and carried an arsenal of weapons on his person. There was a truckload of French Resistance men also in attendance on Ernest. They were devoted to him, accepted his leadership without question, and called him "Le Grand Capitaine," or sometimes "Le Chef."

Ernest, as a war correspondent, did not carry arms, but he had as workmanlike a lot of partisans under his informal command as one could wish for. These F.F.I. [French Forces of the Interior] were dressed in motley, their principal adornment being strings of hand grenades festooned about their waists or over their shoulders. A few of them had Sten guns, carbines, and revolvers. They lived on the country, and on captured German stores. . . .

Ernest's bedroom was the nerve center of these [intelligence] operations. There, in his shirt sleeves, he gave audience to intelligence couriers, to refugees from Paris, to deserters from the German Army, to local officials, and to all comers. A fierce-looking F.F.I. with a machine gun at the ready stood guard at the door. Within, Ernest, looking like a jolly, dark Bacchus, dispensed the high, low and middle justice in English, French and broken German. His language was strong, salty, and emphatic. . . .

Two fancy ladies accused of commerce with the Germans were brought in from the Versailles road, were submitted to Ernest for interrogation, but, instead of having their heads shaved as their persecutors desired, he read them a severe moral homily, and added them to his kitchen staff. . . .

We had established an imperfect, but functioning, counter-espionage system, and had interrogated with good effect some suspected German agents and sympathizers. It was evident from these and other reports that it would be difficult for a strong allied force to penetrate as far as Paris. . . .

Suddenly, there was an influx of American and Canadian newspaper correspondents. . . . There was considerable feeling displayed by a few of them against Ernest, apparently for having been first on this particular scene. He was obliged, quite gently for such a Hercules of a man, to push a couple of them around with the back of his hand, which, in addition to broken noses, resulted eventually in the lodging of jealous charges against him that he had actively borne arms against the Germans, thereby violating his war correspondent status. . . . Ernest, Mouthard [a French secret service agent] and myself gave the General's [Leclerc's] intelligence officer a detailed summary, with sketches, of the German strength between Rambouillet and Paris, along all routes, of the obstacles to be expected, etc. I believe this information had a determining effect upon the successful accomplishment of Leclerc's march to Paris. It was an admirable example of excellent intelligence reporting. . . .

I entertain a great admiration for [Ernest], not only as an artist and friend, but as a cool, resourceful, imaginative, military tactician and strategist. He unites, from what I saw of him, that rare combination of advised recklessness and caution that knows how properly to seize upon a favorable opportunity which, once lost, is gone forever. He was a born leader of men, and, in spite of his strong independence of character, impressed me as a highly disciplined individual.[29]

Hemingway's contribution to the war effort was significant but illegal; under the Geneva Convention war correspondents were not allowed to bear arms. But this regulation was not strictly enforced; some reporters had guns in their jeeps, and it was easy for Hemingway to obtain weapons once he made contact with the F.F.I. When the other American journalists reached Rambouillet, they were angry about his preferential treatment, swaggering manner and journalistic scoop. They rightly felt that by flagrantly defying the rules he had risked the noncombatant status of the other correspondents, who would be in danger if they were captured by the enemy. According to one account: "Bruce Grant, the veteran Chicago newsman, was in the dining room of the hotel [in Rambouillet] complaining loud and clear that he couldn't get a room because Hemingway had them all tied up. Hemingway strode to where Grant was standing and knocked him to the floor." According to Irwin Shaw, Grant provoked the blow by mocking "General Hemingway and his maquis."[30]

Hemingway's personal liberation of the Ritz, the Travellers Club and other notable drinking spots in Paris later became the basis of self-aggrandizing legends. But his claim to be the first into the city was absurd in an operation of that size. Sylvia Beach, still hero-worshipping him after twenty years, enhanced the myth by describing how he dispatched snipers on the rooftops of the rue de l'Odéon. And Hemingway later amused Berenson with the unlikely story of how he got the better of Malraux during a witty exchange in French about who "took Paris." It was ludicrous for Hemingway—rarely more than a journalistic observer—to compare himself with Malraux, who had flown combat missions in Spain and who had been captured by the Germans, escaped from a POW camp at Sens, led 1,500 maquis in the Dordogne region of southwest France, "commanded the Alsace-Lorraine Brigade under General Leclerc from September 1944 to February 1945, took part in the capture of Dannemarie in November, the defense of Strasbourg against von Runstedt's offensive in December, the march on Colmar and Sainte-Odilie, and the triumphant entry into Stuttgart."

David Bruce was closer to the truth when he told Hemingway that the Germans holding Paris "were a rather tired and frightened lot hiding behind closed blinds and prepared, like nuns in the path of warfare, for the worst."[31] Even Hemingway admitted, in *Across the River*: "The taking of Paris was nothing. . . . It was only an emotional experience. Not a military operation." The main thing he achieved in

Paris, apart from a good time at the Ritz (which encouraged his public enthronement), was abundant hospitality for his friends and all-too-willing girls for the troops. As he confessed to Lanham: "I'm on the verge of losing my standing as an amateur pimp."[32]

Lanham tolerated and even encouraged some of Hemingway's worst *miles gloriosus* tendencies. Like most people who were drawn by Hemingway's magnetic personality and valued him more as a companion than as a writer, Lanham found it amusing and exciting to be with him and to be known to have been with him. (The general is remembered today not for his military career but for his friendship with Hemingway.) While Hemingway was at the Ritz during the first week of September with Mary, Lanham, echoing Henry IV's taunt to the Duke of Crillon after a victory at Arques, sent him a provocative message. "Go hang yourself, brave Hemingstein. We have fought at Landrecies and you were not there."

This was (as Lanham knew) an irresistible challenge, and Hemingway immediately hastened northeast from Paris to Landrecies and Le Cateau (where Dorman-Smith and the British army had retreated after the bad show at Mons in the Great War). "The countryside through which Hemingway travelled in order to reach my command post," wrote Lanham, who had summoned him there, "was alive with Germans who had been by-passed. All of these people were trying frantically to get back to Germany proper and the Siegfried Line. He was very lucky indeed to have made this trip without being killed."[33] He remained with Lanham's 22nd Infantry Regiment for four weeks, entered Germany with the first American tanks on September 12 and covered the heavy fighting around the fortified Siegfried Line near Schnee Eifel.

In mid-September Hemingway met John Groth, who had illustrated his work in *Esquire,* was a correspondent for the *Chicago Sun-Times* and later did the drawings for the 1946 reprint of *Men Without Women.* At Schloss Hemingstein near Bleiauf, a farmhouse with no electricity and a French woman as cook, Hemingway rolled live grenades toward Groth to "show him what war was all about." He informed Groth that the American soldiers in the forward trenches went rear at night and left the farmhouse to face the front alone. He had to put the Schloss in a defensive position and ordered Groth to drop grenades from the second-floor window if a German patrol came through the garden. Groth could not tell if he was serious, but Hemingway kept his turn at the watch and avidly read the *Reader's Digest* when nothing else was available. In his Introduction to Groth's *Studio Europe* (1945) Hemingway praised the author and wrote: "All of us liked him. All of us respected him"—though he gave a less favorable opinion in a private letter to Lanham.[34]

Several correspondents, including perhaps Bruce Grant, whom Hemingway had punched, complained about his adventures at Rambouillet. He was summoned by the Inspector General of the U.S. Third Army to a judicial investigation at Nancy on October 6, 1944. The unpublished war diary of the free-lance South African war correspondent Barbara Loxton reveals that Hemingway had carried arms, that the American military authorities were aware of his unorthodox behavior and (though they could not control him) unofficially attempted to dissociate themselves from his illegal activities. Barbara Loxton records that on February 2, 1945, at the Hôtel Scribe in Paris, a Lieutenant Leary told her:

> He doesn't like Ernest Hemingway. When EH was with the FFI, Lieutenant Leary was sent by SHAEF to make it clear [to Hemingway] that EH was acting entirely on his own; SHAEF took no responsibility. This made Hemingway mad, very mad. Little Brazilian correspondent [Nemo Canaberro Lucas] kept saying, well Mr. Hemingway, what are you going to do now? Hemingway whisked out gun and shot at him, missing his head by a couple of inches. Brazilian looked at hole in the wall and walked out and hasn't spoken to Hemingway since. (This is apropos of correspondents carrying guns.)[35]

The allegations were that "Mr. Hemingway stripped off correspondent's insignia and acted as a colonel, French Resistance Troops; that he had a room with mines, grenades and war maps; that he directed Resistance patrols, which action is believed to violate credential rights of the correspondents." This was all true, as SHAEF well knew. But since he had clearly helped the Allied armies, they had no desire to create adverse publicity, after the liberation of Paris, by making an example of Hemingway, taking away his accreditation and repatriating him.

He was defended in testimonials by three officers, including Colonel David Bruce, who had given him written permission to bear arms and command partisans during the extraordinary conditions at Rambouillet. Lanham vouched for his bravery: "I met Ernest Hemingway for the first time on 26 July 1944 at my Command Post in the vicinity of Le

Mesnil, France. . . . He is without question one of the most courageous men I have ever known. Fear is a stranger to him. His calmness and casual air under fire has always had a beneficial effect upon both officers and men." Major James Thornton stated: "It was apparent that we should require the assistance and cooperation of all allied personnel on the spot, and the services of War Correspondent Ernest Hemingway were welcomed." Bruce, with some diplomatic stretching of the truth, asserted: "I witnessed no instance of Mr. Hemingway having conducted himself in any manner other than appropriate for a loyal American acting efficiently during a period of emergency. I never saw him armed nor did I hear of any instance of his having personally engaged in combat with the enemy."[36]

To justify these depositions and ensure exoneration, Hemingway was ordered by two officers on General Patton's staff to commit perjury: to swear that he was not armed in Rambouillet (he did not state that he had been armed *outside* the town) and to deny under oath actions he was proud of. Since all the witnesses swore they had never seen Hemingway with weapons (the angry correspondents, who perhaps arrived too late to see him in action, were apparently not summoned), the Inspector General rather disingenuously found "no violation by him of the existing regulations for war correspondents."[37] Hemingway was licensed to do as he pleased and famous enough to get away with anything.

Determined to prove himself once more, after the investigation at Nancy, Hemingway participated in the ferocious fighting in the Hürtgenwald, between Aachen and Bonn, from November 15 to December 4. One of the most costly attacks of the war took place as the Germans made a last stand on the frontier in "freezing rain, sleet, snow, flood, mud, pillboxes, and dense, dank woods straight out of German folk tales." An army historian wrote that in three days in mid-November, the 22nd Infantry Regiment, weakened by mines, enemy infiltration and shelling, "had incurred more than 300 battle casualties, including all three battalion commanders, several key staff officers, about half the company commanders, and many key company officers and noncommissioned officers." Despite this sacrifice, they managed to penetrate only a mile and a half after a five-day attack. When the battle ended in mid-December, 24,000 Americans were killed, wounded, captured or missing. Colonel Jim Luckett, who fought in this battle, which resembled the pointless slaughter of the Great War, "believed the entire

Hürtgen operation was stupidly conceived, 'since it would have been relatively easy to bypass this dank, dark, muddy mass of mines, prepared positions, and prepared fireplans for mortars and artillery.' "[38] This fierce fighting inspired some of Cantwell's most horrific memories in *Across the River*.

III

On October 28, 1944, three weeks after the proceedings at Nancy, Jack Hemingway parachuted into Occupied France with the O.S.S. He was wounded and captured by the Germans; and was not released until May 1945. There was more family trouble when Hemingway met Martha in Paris in October, and alternated between submissive and scurrilous behavior. John Groth was astonished when he observed them at lunch with Hemingway's friends. In the restaurant, Martha irritated him by correcting his imperfect French and barked out a series of trivial commands: "Ernest, get a waiter. . . . Ernest, get the wine list. . . . Ernest, give me the wine list; you don't know anything about wine. . . . Ernest, give someone else a chance to speak."[39]

Hemingway's meek tolerance soon gave way to vitriolic public quarrels. Lael Wertenbaker heard him read to a group of friends his tender if mawkish "Poem to Mary." This was followed by a crude but funny pornographic poem (which recalled his tasteless verse on Dorothy Parker in October 1926) "To Martha Gellhorn's Vagina," which he was pleased to compare to the wrinkled neck of an old hot-water bag.[40]

Martha asked for a divorce on November 3. Hemingway (as usual) revised the facts and claimed he had rejected her. He reviewed the reasons for the breakdown of their marriage—her career, her competition, her absences, his loneliness and his inability to write without an appreciative woman at his side—and also noted that his love and loss of Martha were closely connected to the wars they had seen:

> Once I was gone she wanted back very much. But we want some straight work, not to be alone and not have to go to war to see one's wife and then have wife want to be in different war theatre in order that stories not compete. Going to get me somebody who wants to stick around with me and let me be the writer of the family. Since childies

have to be in school am not going to be lonely to die and not able [to] work. . . .

I got sort of cured of Marty [by] flying [with the RAF]. Everything sort of took on its proper proportion. Then after we were on the ground I never thought of her at all. Funny how it should take one war [Spanish Civil War] to start a woman in your damn heart and another to finish her. Bad luck.[41]

Hemingway caught pneumonia during the fighting in Germany in December and coughed blood into the toilet of the Ritz. He was still in poor health when his military friends, unaware of the parlous state of his marriage, brought the couple together for Christmas in Rodenbourg (ten miles northeast of Luxembourg City). They spent their last night together in Lanham's bedroom. Jealous of Martha and angry at the way she criticized Hemingway, Lanham disliked her snobbery, her "arrogance, her general snottiness."

Bill Walton met Martha in Luxembourg City on December 31, spent a day with her driving around in a jeep and invited her to New Year's Eve dinner. Hemingway suddenly turned up, insisted on joining them, became drunk and abusive. When Walton tried to restrain him, he insisted: "You can't hurt an elephant with a bow and arrow." Seven months later, when living in Cuba with Mary, he wrote one of his few honest and perceptive letters about Martha. He said he did not like Marty (citing *The Fifth Column* as evidence), but that he had loved her very much. His marriage to Marty was the biggest mistake in his life, though he could not blame her for his own stupidity. She was brave in Spain, where there was no Geneva Convention to protect her, did a fine job in Finland, and was very good in Singapore and the Dutch East Indies. But she failed badly in China and was ruined for him by her behavior in the last war.[42]

Martha later said that Hemingway could always make her laugh when she wanted to murder him, but lost that knack when their marriage deteriorated and could never forgive her for leaving him. He made difficulties about the divorce, which would have been easy since they were both Cuban residents, until he decided to marry Mary. Martha also remained bitter about their marriage—though not as bitter as Hemingway. She wrote: "I spent seven years in Hemingway's orbit. . . . I am goddamned if I am going to be hounded by those seven years." She could not understand why Mary stayed with him to endure "a slave's life with a brute for a slave owner" and caustically observed that he "was progressively more insane every year. And the biggest liar since Munchausen."[43]

Hemingway's break with Martha was the most traumatic of all his separations and the most wounding emotional experience since Agnes had jilted him in 1919. He probably loved the high-spirited, romantic and enchanting Martha more than any of his wives. She was the only woman who was his equal in will and intellect and the only woman in his life, apart from his mother, who had defied and even dominated him. Pauline had also been competitive and ambitious, but she competed against Hadley and was ambitious for him. Hadley and Pauline had been hurt by Hemingway; but *he* was hurt by Martha. He blamed himself for the break-up of his first two marriages—but not for his third.

The recurrence and passionate intensity of his comments about Martha betrayed the strength of his attachment to her. During the decade from 1944 to 1953 he rehearsed the familiar accusations: that she talked too much, had different interests and tastes, made more money than he did as a correspondent, did not love him enough, produced no children; that she was silly, pretentious, worthless, ambitious, war crazy and (as he also said of Mary) conducted her campaigns in the generals' beds. After years of struggling to dominate her, he took pleasure in acquiring a housemaid named Martha and giving orders that she instantly obeyed. Relying on his trusty racetrack metaphor, and reviving the charges of desertion and somnolence, he said that his ex-wife "had but three gaits, running away, over-work, and sleep." He feared, when Martha and Pauline met in Venice in 1949, that they were spreading lurid inventions and queering his Italian pitch.

His longest and most virulent blast—a strange mixture of truth and falsehood—was reserved for her friend Bernard Berenson, and revealed as much about Hemingway as about Martha. He unfairly complained to the ancient art critic about Martha's philistinism, vanity, love of politics and enthusiasm for war. But he also admitted his own guilt about deserting Pauline, his excessive drinking and his need to escape from the responsibility of writing. He praised Martha's knowledge of French, her generosity and devotion to the causes she believed in. He liked her mother, Martha's affection for his children, and her astonishing beauty, which moved him whenever he saw her. Yet her nose, he thought, was badly drawn and, like all ambitious women, she had a wrinkled, crepe-like neck. He also criticized her lack of interest in painting, music and literature, and her collection of well-tailored uniforms. He claimed that Martha had never seen a man killed in battle, but had made more money writing about atrocities than any woman since Harriet Beecher Stowe. She liked the spurious glamour of war and the attention she received from thousands of lonely men.[44]

Like many ex-husbands, Hemingway remained in love with his wife after their marriage was over and was jealous of his "rivals." When Martha sent a letter to Walton, then a guest at the Finca, Hemingway suspected they were lovers and got into a black rage. Just as Pauline had admired photographs of Hemingway after their divorce, so—during an interview with Robert Manning in 1954—he took a pile of photographs from a drawer and proudly exclaimed: "There's my beautiful Martha. Isn't she beautiful?" When Manning told this story to Martha, thinking she would be moved by it, she merely said: "That son of a bitch!"[45]

Just as Martha had portrayed him in her fiction, so Hemingway— after *The Fifth Column* and *For Whom the Bell Tolls*—continued to recreate her in his own work. In an unpublished postwar story, "It was very cold in England," he critically but lovingly described Martha, with a characteristic emphasis on her hair, and gave a relatively mild sample of their combative conversation. The Martha character walks with an insolent swagger, has fine shoulders, a good back and a small behind she's proud of. Her natural blond hair, streaked with lovely shades of lightness, swings heavily as she walks. The man says she reminds him of badly laid mines in the war, washed up on the coast years later after big storms. She mocks his labored literary comparison and says that she has been well laid. She notes that he doesn't like the way she talks, and he tells her she's changed since they first met.

His final fictional comment on Martha appeared in *Across the River*, when Cantwell explains his ex-wife's character to his young Italian mistress and makes a rare admission—in the very last word—of his own responsibility for the destruction of the marriage:

> "She was an ambitious woman and I was away too much. . . . She had more ambition than Napoleon and about the talent of the average High School Valedictorian. . . . She is too conceited ever to be sad, and she married me to advance herself in Army circles, and have better contacts for what she considered her profession, or her art. She was a journalist." . . .

"But you couldn't have married a woman journalist that kept on being that?"

"I told you I made mistakes." . . .

You lose [women] the same way you lose a battalion; by errors of judgment; orders that are impossible to fulfill, and through impossible conditions. Also through brutality.[46]

IV

Not quite purged of his love for Martha, Hemingway returned to Paris and to Mary in early January 1945. Mary had real doubts about marrying him and certainly knew what to expect after February when he placed a photograph of her Australian husband in the toilet bowl, blasted it with a machine pistol and flooded their room at the Ritz. (The management tried to be understanding.)

Hemingway claimed to have met Orwell, who was reporting the war for the *Observer* (both men were in Paris between February 15 and March 6), and offered rare praise of a contemporary writer. He called *Homage to Catalonia* a first-rate book and Orwell a first-rate man, and regretted he had not been able to spend more time with him. He thought his own politics were quite close to Orwell's, and was sorry that Orwell had fought for the POUM Anarchists. Orwell, who had published *Animal Farm* in 1945, told Hemingway he was afraid of being killed by the Communists and asked to borrow a pistol.[47] Orwell never mentioned their meeting and there is no other record of their conversation.

Hemingway left for America on March 6 and saw Martha for the last time while passing through London. He was photographed in the Stork Club wearing his correspondent's uniform, and reached Cuba in the middle of the month. He had recurrent nightmares and serious difficulties in readjustment after World War Two just as he did after World War One. But he impressed Mary—as he had once impressed Hadley—with his military exploits. At the beginning of April he told Mary that in his nightmares he was surrounded by Germans, pinned down or killed by a direct hit.[48]

The nightmares and the persistent symptoms of the two concussions delayed his projected epic trilogy on the sub hunting at sea, the RAF in the air and the 22nd Infantry on land. He began to brag more as writing became increasingly difficult; changed from listing the number of fish caught and game shot to the number of Krauts killed; said his current command consisted of maid, butler, cook, houseboys and gardeners. When in New York, he would invite John Groth to dinner at "21" or Toots Shor's to listen to and confirm his war exploits. His letters to Lanham revealed the worst side of his postwar character: the crude language, the obsessive replay of military adventures, the compensatory bragging. To Scribner and Perkins, he emphasized his desire to write a novel about the war he had followed and survived for seven months: from the landings and breakthrough at Normandy to the penetration of the Siegfried Line and the empty victory at Hürtgenwald. To Lanham, he confided that he was bored with civilian life (an inevitable letdown after the excitement of battle), did not give a damn about writing and hoped Mary's arrival would rouse him from his lethargy.

20

Mary
1945–1948

> Hemingway's mistake was that
> he thought he had to marry
> all of them.
>
> WILLIAM FAULKNER

I

Hemingway's three marital failures did not affect his belief in women
or in himself, and he returned to Cuba in mid-March to prepare for his
fourth marriage. He wanted to be a good husband to Mary in 1945 as
he had been to Hadley in 1921: sober, well-behaved, devoted and faithful. While recovering from his injuries and making the adjustment from
war to peace, he got the house and boat ready for Mary's arrival. (She
awaited passage home and then visited her aged Christian Scientist
parents in Chicago.) He was eager to show her the places that had
inspired his work, to teach her sporting skills and to introduce her to
his friends. The Crook Factory and sub-hunting mob was still intact;
Gregorio, Father Andrés and Paxtchi were in attendance. But he was
always lonely without a woman, found the six-week wait passed very
slowly and was desperate for Mary to arrive. She would confirm his
capacity to conquer and to love, help him readjust to civilian life and
re-establish himself as a writer.

Mary was Hemingway's wife during the years of his greatest fame
and most radical deterioration, of the Nobel Prize as well as the Mayo
Clinic. She felt she had been an entity, and feared she would become
an appendage. At the age of thirty-six, she gave up her independence
and professional career, adopted his sporting passions, entertained his

418

coarse cronies, matched his numerous accidents with her own falls and fractures, and even tolerated his infatuation with two teenage girls: the "vestal virgin," Adriana Ivancich, and the flirtatious Valerie Danby-Smith. Mary had been brought up on boats and loved the Gulf Stream. Hemingway noted with pleasure that she fished, swam and cooked well; she liked the cats, the sea and the Cuban climate. He told Lanham that she was beautifully tanned, adaptable, unselfish, kind and brave; in other words, decorative and amenable to his wishes. He thought Mary was forty times more woman than Martha.

Hemingway's sons agreed with his judgment. Jack was impressed, at their first meeting in June 1945, when Mary came out of the pool naked to greet him. He found her well-built, well-informed, bright and interesting. She interrupted Hemingway's conversation, but he was tolerant, witty and affectionate with her. On this postwar trip to Havana, Jack got drunk with his father, watched *Casablanca* on his private screen at the Finca and shot buzzards (which had defecated in the water tank) as they fed on the goat bait left on the roof.

Jack had started college at Dartmouth before the war and did a postwar year at the University of Montana. In 1949 he married the young widow of an air force colonel who had been shot down in Germany; he was a professional soldier in Berlin and at Fort Bragg, North Carolina, from 1948 to 1954. Hemingway was proud of Jack's war record and army career, but was displeased when Jack married, left the army and did not make money as a stockbroker with Merrill Lynch in Havana and San Francisco. Hemingway did not go to his sons' weddings, disapproved of and tried to dominate his sons' wives—but sought their approval of his own marriages. His daughters-in-law found it difficult to deal with his overbearing manner and tended to keep their distance. Jack and Puck had three daughters between 1950 and 1961, but they lost a son five hours after a Caesarean birth in 1951.

Gregory, who had a crush on Mary, was impressed by her willingness to "go fishing day after day on the *Pilar*, before and after their marriage, exposing her fair Nordic skin to the tropical sun without complaint. Mary also learned Spanish quickly and well. . . . And she brought order to the domestic chaos that Marty had left behind." Like Jack, Gregory realized how uninhibited Mary was when he used the word "cocksucker." When she asked: "what's wrong with that?" he mollified her by saying: "I meant between men."[1]

Toby Bruce rarely saw Hemingway quarrel with Mary and thought they were happy together. When Hemingway refused to take her home, she waited patiently, if angrily, in the car. When he became too friendly with Cuban whores, she threw "a slight fit"—nothing serious. George Plimpton described her as a jolly governess-manager who ran the house well, made life pleasant and was a generous hostess. Elicio Arguelles thought "Mary loved him much more than Martha did. She took much better care of him" and showed her affection for him in everything she did.[2]

Hemingway was kinder to his wives in print than in person. Though Mary (as her book on Hemingway later revealed) lacked psychological insight and showed little understanding of his complex inner self, he exaggerated her talents and boasted about his own good choice when presenting his ideal wife to the public in his "Situation Report" of 1956: "Miss Mary is durable. She is also brave, charming, witty, exciting to look at, a pleasure to be with and a good wife. She is also an excellent fisherwoman, a fair wing shot, a strong swimmer, a really good cook, a good judge of wine, an excellent gardener, an amateur astronomer, a student of art, political economy, Swahili, French and Italian and can run a boat or a household in Spanish."[3]

On June 20, 1945, Hemingway had his third serious road accident in thirteen months. While he was driving slowly and soberly in Havana, his car skidded on a muddy road, jumped a ditch and crashed into a tree. He suffered a smashed knee and a deep wound on his forehead, which banged into the rearview mirror. Mary had a deep and bloody cut on her left cheek, which required plastic surgery. Soon after she met Hemingway, their sporting life led to a long sequence of accidents and illnesses. She fractured her right ankle in a skiing accident in Cortina in January 1949 and her left ankle in February 1950. (Hemingway told Jonathan Cape, with his usual lack of sympathy, that Mary had broken her "near hind leg.") She had a blood clot in her right leg in September 1950, cracked her ribs in a plane crash in January 1954, broke her toe in July 1959, shattered her left elbow after falling on the ice in November 1959 and fell down the stairs in April 1961. When Mary groaned in the car after the accident on the ice, he said:

"You could keep it quiet."
"I'm trying."

"Soldiers don't do that."

"I'm not a soldier."

He also complained that her fracture had ruined his plans for a hunting trip, just as he had condemned Hadley's pregnancy for spoiling his skiing in 1923. There were a few other bizarre accidents at the Finca. In September 1947 the Chinese cook, Ramón, had a heart attack while preparing dinner and silently fell onto the stove. No one noticed anything odd until the smell of roasting human flesh wafted in from the kitchen.[4] In June 1951 another cook aimed Hemingway's rifle at a bothersome buzzard and accidentally shot himself in the shoulder.

The gravest crisis occurred in Casper, Wyoming, on August 19, 1946, five months after their marriage on March 14. Mary awoke at seven in the morning with intense pain and a severe internal hemorrhage. She had a tubular pregnancy—a fertilized egg in the Fallopian tube instead of in the uterus—and the tube suddenly ruptured. Hemingway, as usual, responded brilliantly in the emergency and saved her life: "While Dr. was administering the spinal anaesthetic preparatory to operating, M.'s veins collapsed, there was no pulse and he could not get a needle in to give plasma. Dr. told me was hopeless; impossible operate; she couldn't stand shock; to tell her good-bye (useless maneuver since she unconscious). I got asst. to cut for a vein and got plasma going. . . . It was closest one I've ever seen. Dr. had given her up—and taken off his gloves. Certainly shows never pays to quit."[5] He was impressed by Mary's courage and she was always grateful that he had rescued her. When Mary (an only child who had no children from her previous marriages) discovered that she could never give him the daughter he desperately desired—for one Fallopian tube had been removed and the other occluded—she felt inadequate and guilty. He tried to comfort her, but was bitterly disappointed and later held her sterility against her.

While visiting Pauline in Key West in April 1947, Patrick and Gregory had a car accident, which was followed by a serious illness. The car was wrecked and Patrick bumped his head; he complained of headaches, but did not seem injured. He returned to Cuba and on April 14 suddenly became feverish, raving and violent. "I saw Mousie [Patrick] when he was delirious," Hemingway said, "defying Satan and all fiends and all local devils"—which Patrick had promised to renounce when he was baptized. Hemingway (and later on, Mary) called the illness an undiagnosed concussion and blamed it on long sets of tennis after the car accident. But it was actually a complete mental breakdown. Hemingway also responded to this crisis with energy and devotion. He slept outside Patrick's room, faithfully nursed and fed him for three months, and was helped by Pauline, his servants and Basque friends. (Mary had flown to Chicago to care for her sick father.) By late June, Patrick was lucid for a few hours each day. He was eventually diagnosed as "paranoid-schizophrenic" and treated by Dr. Frank Stetmeyer, a German Communist in Havana. He gave Patrick electro-convulsive therapy three times a week for about six weeks during July and August, destroyed his immediate memory (including all recollection of the shock treatments) and "cured him."[6]

When Mary returned from Chicago, she helped Pauline nurse Patrick and became her friend. They continued to meet for the next four years and liked to discuss techniques of managing "the old monster." Hemingway must have felt some guilt about Patrick's breakdown, which he assuaged by caring for his son. In *Islands in the Stream* he conflated memories of Jack and Patrick's more serious car accident with Jane Mason in 1933, Patrick and Gregory's car accident in April 1947 and fears about Jack in the war, in the scene where the lonely Thomas Hudson "had lain in the night thinking about how he had lost the three boys [two die in a car accident, one is shot down in war] and the fool he had been. . . . [He] had moved from one disastrous error of judgment to another that was worse."[7] Most significantly, by postponing the discovery and then concealing the real cause of Patrick's breakdown, he revealed his inability to face the reality of mental illness, which had led to his father's suicide and would lead to his own.

Leicester was also a problem and an embarrassment. During the war in Europe, according to Irwin Shaw and Bill Walton, his noisy enthusiasm, lack of ability and boring attempts to trade on his brother's name made him an irritating and unpopular companion. In 1936 he married a girl who had been adopted by his uncle Tyler Hemingway in Kansas City and brought up as his cousin, and they had two sons. After the war, he continued to fail at various enterprises. He built boats, worked for U.S.I.S. in Bogotá, went into the shrimp business, declared himself king of a tiny Caribbean island, was a bookmaker and a publicity man for a jai alai fronton in Miami, ran a charter boat in Montego Bay (but had an unfortunate tendency to cut the lines of his fishing clients) and wrote adventure stories for trashy magazines in New York.

Leicester published a war novel, *The Sound of the Trumpet,* in 1953, which opens with the autobiographical hero attached to a film unit on D-Day. His older brother Rando Granham (sometimes called Granham-stein) appears after the liberation of Paris, frees the Crillon Hôtel and has a historic encounter with Malraux. The novel, much closer to the reality of Leicester's war than of Ernest's, continues with the fighting in Germany and the freeing of the concentration camps. Hemingway had a predictably low opinion of Leicester's effort and told Lanham that his book was a chickenshit abortion filled with the worst crap he had ever read. The few good parts were like ripe plums in vomit. When Peter Viertel asked Hemingway why he blamed Irwin Shaw for attacking Leicester, since he had attacked Leicester himself, Hemingway replied: "He's a shit, but he's also my brother."[8]

II

Despite Mary's admirable qualities and his own hopes, promises and intentions, Hemingway was not a good husband. He usually woke up in the morning happy, but could not sustain that mood throughout the day. He sometimes distrusted his wife. He once showed Bill Walton his family albums and said: "Don't tell Mary. She'll sell them to *Life* right away." If Mary said or did something to irritate him, he would burn slowly, erupt into fireworks and become an absolute devil. When she failed to get his pocket knife repaired, for example, he called her a "thief."

In April 1950 (repeating his rude behavior with Martha and her mother in July 1940), he kept Mary and her cousin waiting at lunch for an hour and then turned up with an attractive young whore whom he called Xenophobia. Mary, weary of his bad manners, steel-bound ego, petulant irritability and deliberate nastiness, announced she would leave him—but did not carry out her threat. But she was not always self-effacing. Like all his wives, she would sometimes compete with him for attention, tell his stories, criticize him. This would inevitably lead to high tension, cutting remarks and terrible quarrels. Still sensitive about Martha's comments on his personal cleanliness, he wrote to Mary, in a wounded tone, that he was hurt not only by her comment that his fingernails were dirty but also by her insistence, after he had apologized, that his fingernails were always dirty. When Mary called him a son of a bitch, he replied: "Most people would be running if they called me that." But he would often apologize and say: "I'm sorry, kitten. I was too rough,"[9] and did not sulk after their explosive fights.

The most serious problem in their marriage was Hemingway's attraction to other women: Nancy (Slim) Hawks and Virginia (Jigee) Viertel in the late 1940s as well as Adriana and Valerie later on. The tall, blond, intelligent Slim, a former model and a socialite, was born in California in 1918. Hemingway had known her in Key West before she married two powerful Hollywood figures: Howard Hawks (who directed the film of *To Have and Have Not*) and then Leland Hayward (who produced the film of *The Old Man and the Sea*). Slim thrived on men's admiration: she needed it, wanted it, noticed it and was pleased by it. The Hawkses visited the Hemingways in Cuba early in 1946 and they were on holiday together in Sun Valley that fall. On October 31, 1946, Slim mistakenly fired her rifle next to Hemingway's head and singed the hair at the base of his skull. Martha had recommended Slim as her successor and Hemingway told Bill Davis that Slim was one of his "true loves." Mary, who called her "one of his admired and admiring girl friends," felt that Slim threatened her marriage. Many friends believed that Hemingway was in love with Slim; but his letters to her, "of a very personal nature,"[10] are not available.

Jigee—small, vivacious, sexy, vibrant—was a contrast to Slim. She had been the wife of Budd Schulberg and was married to the novelist and screenwriter Peter Viertel. When they were staying with the Hemingways at the Ritz Hotel in Paris in December 1949, Mary recorded: "It is now one hour and a half since I left Jigee Viertel's room, # 94, and Ernest said, 'I'll come in a minute.' . . . About a month later my husband described to me in devastating detail Jigee's campaign to snare him. '[Mary] obviously doesn't appreciate you. We'll have a ranch with horses in California and you can give up the heat of Cuba. I understand your wonderful sensibilities.' " Peter Viertel believed that Mary attributed Hemingway's seduction attempt to Jigee, who was not independently wealthy and could not have supported him in Californian luxury. Viertel was as curious as Mary about Jigee's relations with Hemingway. When he asked her about it, she answered that it was nothing more than a "deep flirtation" with an older man. Jigee also loved adoration and had to feel needed; she took many lovers during their marriage and would have admitted an affair with Hemingway if there had been one.[11]

In 1947 the millionaire Tommy Shevlin, who had met Hemingway in Bimini in 1935 and hunted with him in Montana, spent five days of his honeymoon aboard the *Pilar*. Hemingway made quite a different impression on the sophisticated wife than on the athletic husband; and the recollections of Tommy's young bride, Durie, vividly convey Hemingway's marine milieu as well as the difficulties that Mary had to face. Durie was used to outdoor sports and had hunted in Africa with Philip Percival in the late 1940s; but she was not particularly interested in fishing and found life on the *Pilar* a "perfectly awful" ordeal. Slim Hawks Hayward, who left the boat as the Shevlins arrived, warned Durie: "watch out, kid." Durie expected a rich and famous writer to have a fine boat, but the *Pilar* was tiny, crowded, uncomfortable—and they ran out of ice and fresh water. Gregorio, Hemingway and Mary, who was keen on fishing and helped run the boat, slept on deck; Tommy and Durie slept below in the cabin with Beartracks Williams, who occupied the opposite bunk and hawked and spat throughout the night. Durie found it impossible to eat peanut butter sandwiches for breakfast, but was determined not to complain. There was no bathroom on the boat and she was eager to have a hot shower, but the hot-water heater had been turned off at the Finca and the house was filled with filthy cats.

After Tommy's enthusiastic praise, Durie found Hemingway a great disappointment. A man's man, he was not an attentive host and did not seem at all interested in Durie. He had a scrubby beard, wore a long visor cap with a sweaty handkerchief hanging behind his neck, drank heavily and spoke in rapid pidgin English, with "chickenshit" (an unfamiliar term to her) inserted after every few words. When they saw two turtles mating on the beach, Durie said: "Look, how sweet." Hemingway immediately rowed ashore in a dinghy, disturbed their congress, captured one for cat food and carried it aboard. He turned the turtle on its back; and it became pink, then purple, smelled horrible and died slowly. Tommy, who adored Hemingway and was flattered by his friendship, was surprised that Durie did not find him sexually attractive.

When their daughter, Shirley, was born in 1948, the Shevlins took her on a visit to Hemingway. He wrote a charming poem for the child about a lion of Venice who ate only shrimp, and a lion of Africa. He first offered to give it to them, but placed it instead in a safe. When Tommy asked Mary for the poem after Hemingway's death, she did not respond.[12] This "poem" seemed to be an early version of his short prose fable "The Good Lion," published in *Holiday* in March 1951.

In August 1947, overweight at 256 pounds, Hemingway felt the first signs of the high blood pressure that would plague him for the rest of his life. Two years later Lanham, who found him much worse in peace than in war, told C. L. Sulzberger about his heavy drinking, persistent head wounds, skin diseases and insomnia:

> In battle [Hemingway] is quiet and modest. Yet, when Lanham visited Hemingway in Cuba, he was loud and boastful, surrounded by toadies. He insisted on dominating everyone.
>
> Lanham claims that Hemingway drinks gallons of hard liquor—mostly Martinis mixed at the rate of fifteen-to-one. He had a head injury in an automobile accident in England some years ago and every now and then the wound breaks open. He has a bad skin disease on his face, and cannot shave. Although he takes handfuls of sleeping pills, he always wakes up around four-thirty o'clock in the morning. He usually starts drinking right away and writes standing up, with a pencil in one hand and a drink in the other.[13]

Despite his decline in health, Hemingway still had an overwhelming personality. Lanham and other friends felt that all his physical and mental characteristics—strength, courage, daring, skill, intellect, wit, conversation, capacity for drink—were much greater than those of ordinary men. George Plimpton found Mary a welcome relief from the cyclone force of his character. Hemingway, noticing that Walton also felt the need to practice "survival techniques" and flee to Mary for rest and recuperation, would slyly say: "I see you slipping out of the room." Aaron Hotchner conveyed their sense of uneasiness when he remarked: "You were never safe when Ernest was in the room. You watched yourself."[14]

To compensate for sexual inhibitions and inadequacies as he approached his climacteric, Hemingway boasted in a startling and embarrassing manner of his sexual, sporting, alcoholic and physical exploits. Ignoring (at the very least) his past relations with Agnes and with Duff, he told Malcolm Cowley, who was collecting information for his "Portrait of Mister Papa": "I have fucked every woman I wanted to fuck and many I did not, and fucked them all well I hope." To Charles Scribner (a captive audience who had to listen patiently to whatever Hemingway said) he announced that spilling sperm no longer interfered with spilling ink: "To celebrate my fiftieth birthday . . . I fucked three times, shot ten straight at pigeons (very fast ones) at the club, drank with five friends a case of Piper Heidsieck Brut and looked the ocean for big fish all afternoon."[15] His description of drinking and fishing was probably more accurate than that of sex and shooting.

Hemingway, imitating his violent exploits in youth and war, sometimes went out of control during physical confrontations. Gene Tunney provided an amusing description of sparring with him at the beginning of 1946:

> All of a sudden Ernest came at me and started swinging. He came and cut me across the lips, and there was blood, and then he jabbed me in the left elbow. I said to Ernest, "Do stop it please, Ernest," but he kept right on punching. . . . I thought to myself: what Ernest needs is a good little liver punch. There's a little liver punch, and it has to be timed exactly, and when I saw the moment I let him have it. I was a little alarmed, if I do say so! His knees buckled, his face went gray, and I thought he was going to go down. But he didn't, and for the next few hours Ernest was perfectly charming.

The following year, he compensated for this setback while boxing in Havana with the Brooklyn Dodgers pitcher Hugh Casey. As Casey was putting on his gloves, Hemingway threw the first punch and knocked him down—exactly as he had done to Lewis Galantière in 1922. In September 1949 he played with circus lions in their cage and was raked by their claws. And in July 1952, while describing an apocryphal fight with a Great Dane that had seized his dog Blackie, he claimed to have torn open the dog's mouth, gouged out his eyes and killed him with his bare hands.[16]

Hemingway's postwar boastfulness and physical violence (lifelong but now intensified characteristics) coincided with his advertising endorsements and increasing involvement with the movies. In "The Snows of Kilimanjaro" he had condemned Fitzgerald for his infatuation with the rich and expressed his own fears of corruption and spiritual death. In 1946, when he had virtually abandoned self-scrutiny, he adopted the attitude of his own fictional hero. Using the metaphor of an uncorrupted explorer, he said he was not attracted to the very rich but went into their country as he would enter any country.[17]

Hemingway made a good deal of money from the film rights of his books; but he was not a shrewd dealer and did not earn as much as he should have. In May 1939 he sold the film, radio and television rights of *To Have and Have Not* for $10,000 to the Hughes Tool Company (with which Howard Hawks had connections). In October 1943 Hawks bought these rights from Hughes Tool for $92,500 and sold them to Warner Brothers for that sum plus a quarter interest in the picture. In December 1945 Hemingway sold Mark Hellinger the rights of "The Killers" for $37,500 and of "The Snows of Kilimanjaro" for $75,000. *The Killers* made $3 million, but Hemingway got only $50,000.

Hemingway allowed himself to be photographed in his home for glossy magazines; endured foolish interviews when his books appeared; encouraged Walter Winchell, Earl Wilson and Leonard Lyons to gossip about him in their columns; let *Esquire* subsidize his sports and holidays in return for inferior articles; lived without expense in Sun Valley while lending glamour to the new resort; appeared at the Stork Club and in "21"; became friendly with movie stars and helped choose the actors for his films; endorsed Parker pens and Ballantine beer; spent months fishing in Cuba and Peru to get proper pictures for the cinematic version of *The Old Man and the Sea*. In all these activities he was imitating a mythical image. Like a film star, he was handsome, glamorous, wealthy, well traveled and much married. In later life he enjoyed the adoration of young women, stayed in luxurious hotels, and made various attempts to return to earlier pastimes and settings he (and the public) associated with his dashing youth—poverty in Paris, bullfights in Spain, safaris in Africa. He was ravaged by ailments, age and alcohol, and his slow destruction and final death traced the pattern of a movie idol's career. But with Hemingway the debunking began almost as soon as the hero worship. For the exciting aura that surrounds the stars of public life also has its destructive side: the public discovers and learns to despise the weaknesses of eminent people. His pugnacious character helped to spread stories of a bullying, boastful loudmouth; unwashed, apparently uneducated and more at home with a gun than a pen.

III

Hemingway had several kinds of relationships that recurred throughout his life. He had a deep-rooted emotional need for a certain type of friend and constantly sought replacements when he lost the original. (His locales were also interchangeable: Havana replaced Key West as the Caribbean port, Idaho replaced Wyoming as the mountain wilderness, Venice replaced Paris as the sophisticated city.) His series of wives fit a general pattern: midwestern, Protestant, college-educated, professional journalists. His father-mentors were Ed Hemingway, Bra Saunders, Philip Percival; his soldier-heroes were Dorman-Smith, Gustavo Durán, Buck Lanham; his kid brothers were Leicester and Aaron Hotchner; his surrogate sons were Gianfranco Ivancich and Antonio Ordóñez; his trusty drivers were Toby Bruce and Archie Pelkey; his teenage idols were Adriana Ivancich and Valerie Danby-Smith.

In a letter to Mary in September 1945, Hemingway made a distinction between his intelligent, "head" friends and his drinking and sporting cronies. In the first category he placed Sweeny, Shipman, Perkins, Lanham, Janet Flanner, John Peale Bishop and Mikhail Koltzov. The last two were not close friends and he rarely saw any of the others— thought he frequently corresponded with and was occasionally visited by Perkins and Lanham. Only two of these intelligent friends (Perkins and Lanham) appeared on Hotchner's suggestive, if not definitive, list of Hemingway's closest friends in 1954. Of the remaining twelve, two were friends of the 1920s (Beach and Peirce), three were sporting friends (Percival, Guest, Ordóñez), three were friends from the war, Spain and Ketchum (Walton, Bill Davis and Bud Purdy), and four were celebrities (Marlene Dietrich, Gary Cooper, Leonard Lyons and Toots Shor). In "The Christmas Gift" he paid tribute to Lyons, Shor, Sherman Billingsley, Earl Wilson and Walter Winchell. Though Walton and Davis would qualify as "head" friends, there is no doubt that the cerebral quality of Hemingway's friendships declined sharply after the war.

He occasionally had stimulating encounters when famous intellectuals passed through Havana. In January 1947 Trygve Lie, Secretary-General of the United Nations, came to dinner at the Finca. In August 1949, when Jean-Paul Sartre (whom Hemingway had met in Paris in December 1944) appeared for a meal, the two writers talked like businessmen of royalties. From 1949 to 1957 he corresponded with (though never met) Bernard Berenson—who resembled an old play that had been running for eighty years. In June 1928 he had condemned Berenson as an empty asshole and kike patron of the arts. By August 1949, he had shed his anti-Semitism and told Berenson: "you are one of the liveing people that I respect most."[18] In the 1920s he was a friend of the finest writers of the time: Joyce, Pound, Stein, Fitzgerald, Dos Passos; after the war—while married to Mary, who was not as intellectual as Martha—he preferred to spend time with Charles Ritz, Sherman Billingsley, Earl Wilson, Ingrid Bergman, Ava Gardner.

Hemingway quarreled with his family, wives and friends, but he was faithful to his publishers, lawyers and doctors. The fatal heart attack of Max Perkins on June 17, 1947—in the midst of Patrick's illness—was the first in a series of deaths of family and close friends that occurred during the next five years. Perkins' death removed a solid pillar that had supported Hemingway since 1926. Fitzgerald had died in 1940, Joyce in 1941, Stein in 1946, and Pound had been confined to a mental hospital. Between 1947 and 1952 Hemingway was stunned by the premature and unexpected deaths of his boyhood friend Katy Dos Passos, his lawyer Maurice Speiser, his former wife Pauline, his publisher Charles Scribner, and of his aged mother.

In June 1947 Hemingway eulogized Perkins and (perhaps to warn Scribner) exaggerated his editorial *laissez faire:* "while Max was my best and oldest friend at Scribners and a great, great editor he never cut a paragraph of my stuff nor asked me to change one. One of my best and most loyal friends and wisest counsellors in life as well as in writing is dead." But he was much more critical when writing to Scribner in 1951, and wittily expressed his hostility to Perkins' wife (whom he disliked almost as much as he did Ceci Guest and Mary Lanham) as well as to his literary rivals:

> Please bury Max's ghost for keeps and cut out this about he, Tom Wolfe and Scott being gods and you etc. It makes me ashamed. Max was Max with five daughters and an idiot wife. Tom Wolfe was a one book boy and a glandular giant with the brains and the guts of three mice. Scott was a rummy and a liar and dishonest about money with the in-bred talent of a dishonest and easily frightened angel.[19]

Perkins' death brought Hemingway closer to Charles Scribner—"a dignified, solemn, slow-speaking gentleman with silvery hair" (and a complete contrast to Hemingway)—who became his primary contact in the firm. (Scribner's apparently did not pay interest on the money they kept for Hemingway in a separate account, but charged him interest when they lent him funds.) Perkins was replaced by Wallace Meyer, who was born in Minnesota, graduated from Northwestern and worked for Scribner's from 1921 to 1958. Following Perkins' suggestion, Meyer had called on Hemingway in Paris in 1926, before the publication of *The Sun Also Rises,* and Hemingway—"a considerate host and gentleman when in the right mood"—had taken him out to a convivial lunch with Waldo Peirce. Though Meyer recognized the weaknesses of *Across the River,* he did not dare point out its defects to the firm's most valued and sensitive author.[20]

The emotional strain of Patrick's illness, Perkins' death and his own high blood pressure, combined with a competitive rivalry with and increasing estrangement from fellow novelists, inspired Hemingway's extreme reaction to an innocuous statement made by William Faulkner in the spring of 1947. The Hemingway-Faulkner connection (the latter was two years older) went back to the appearance of their early poems on the same page of the New Orleans *Double Dealer* in June 1922. Hemingway owned fourteen books by Faulkner and was thoroughly familiar with his work.

In 1932 he told Louis Cohn that his own *Double Dealer* poem, "Ultimately," was sufficiently poor to go perfectly into a collection of Faulkner's "early shit." In *Death in the Afternoon,* published that year, he took a swipe at Faulkner, along with everyone else, and made the same charge against him as he had made against the outpourings of Thomas Wolfe and Sinclair Lewis: "You can't go wrong on Faulkner. He's prolific too. By the time you get them ordered there'll be new ones out." In an *Esquire* article of June 1935, he said that he had been reading and admiring *Pylon.* The following year he conceded to James Farrell that Faulkner was a far better writer than he himself was. In 1945, writing to Malcolm Cowley, who helped to establish Faulkner's reputation, he criticized Faulkner in the same terms as he had once criticized Fitzgerald: "He has the most talent of anybody and he just needs a sort of conscience that isn't there." He repeated this charge, with more generosity, to Gregory: "You'd think no man could write half whore and half straight. But Faulkner can. God, I'd love to have his talent."[21] Borrowing Wyndham Lewis' witty allusion to *Sanctuary* in an incisive essay on Faulkner, Hemingway privately referred to his rival as "Corncob." In 1947, then, as Faulkner loomed as his chief competitor, Hemingway rightly believed that Faulkner had more talent but he had more art; that he had recognized Faulkner's ability before the critics did and praised him publicly when he himself enjoyed a far greater reputation.

Hemingway did not know, at that time or later, that Faulkner had acknowledged his influence and praised his work. Robert Linscott, Faulkner's editor at Random House, told William Styron that when writing "Red Leaves," Faulkner had no idea how to render imaginary Indian talk into English and solved the problem by reading *Death in the Afternoon.* Hemingway's book "seemed to Faulkner's ear to have just the right eccentric intonation for his Indians, and so his dialogue became a grateful though individualized borrowing—as anyone who compares the two works will readily see." The trouble with this tribute is that "Red Leaves," very different in style from *Death in the Afternoon*, appeared in *These 13* (1931), a year before Hemingway's work. If there is any truth in this story, then Faulkner, or his editor, meant to say that he was influenced by the way Spaniards and Italians spoke English in *The Sun Also Rises* and *A Farewell to Arms.* However, in his original but unproduced Warner Brothers screenplay of 1942, "The De Gaulle Story," "one of his characters praises *For Whom the Bell Tolls* as a source of political and personal inspiration."[22]

Faulkner's criticism of Hemingway in 1947, made during an informal interview at the University of Mississippi, sparked the memory of Stein's charge of cowardice in 1933. Faulkner listed Hemingway fourth among five contemporary novelists—after Wolfe, himself and Dos Passos but (mercifully) before Steinbeck—because Hemingway "has no courage, has never climbed out on a limb. He has never used a word where the reader might check his usage by a dictionary." He clarified this statement in a 1955 interview with Harvey Breit: "I rated Hemingway last [i.e., fourth] because he stayed within what he knew. He did it fine, but he didn't try for the impossible."[23] Coming after the publication of his most ambitious work, *For Whom the Bell Tolls,* this judgment seemed unduly harsh. Hemingway deliberately chose to interpret moral courage to mean physical courage—just as he had taken Eastman's "false hair" to mean that he was impotent. Rather absurdly, Hemingway persuaded Lanham to send Faulkner a testimonial of his courage under fire. Though this document must have puzzled "Corncob," it induced an uneasy squirm of apology.

From then on, and especially after his rival had won the Nobel Prize in 1950, Hemingway felt threatened by Faulkner. His comments became increasingly severe as Faulkner's work declined and his fame increased. In 1948 he told Cowley that Faulkner had no moral fiber and was as much of a prick as Edgar Poe. Four years later he sent Breit a letter that ironically and transparently revealed his envy: "You see what happens with Bill Faulkner is that as long as I am alive he has to drink to feel good about haveing the Nobel prize. He does not realize that I have no respect for that institution and was truly happy for him when he got it." In 1955, after Hemingway had won the Nobel Prize, he condemned Faulkner for alcoholism and for taking money from Hollywood to rewrite *To Have and Have Not*. The following year he returned to his original comparison between Faulkner's work and shit when he likened *A Fable* to the night soil of Chungking. And in 1959, when he himself was an alcoholic, he took credit for praising Faulkner in Europe and showed that the criticism Faulkner had made twelve years before still rankled in his breast: "[I] built him up about as high as he could go because he never had a break then [when he was not known in Europe] and he was good then. So now whenever he has a few shots, he'll tell students what's wrong with me. . . . He cons himself sometimes pretty bad. That may just be the sauce. But for quite a while when he hits the sauce toward the end of a book, it shows bad."[24]

Aaron Hotchner provided the kind of uncritical admiration that Hemingway required during his postwar rivalry with Faulkner. Born in 1920 in St. Louis and trained as a lawyer, he met Hemingway in May 1948 when Hotchner was sent to Cuba to convince him to write an absurd article for *Cosmopolitan*. Hemingway seemed to like and trust him. Hotchner was good fun, knowledgeable about New York literary and sporting gossip, and willing to assume the role of pupil and factotum. Hotchner accepted the nickname "Freckles" and even joined Ordóñez's *cuadrilla* during a bullfight. He wrote successful television adaptations of several stories, a play and a novel by Hemingway—and usually split the profits with the Master. Hemingway spent a long time between books and needed the money from subsidiary rights to live in comfort. They formed the Hemhotch betting syndicate and he helped Hemingway cut the "Dangerous Summer" articles for *Life*. Castillo-Puche, who loathed the "crafty gypsy" Hotchner, quoted Hemingway's judgment: "He's a smart cookie. . . . He has lots of connections in television and the movies and knows his way around. . . . He's as faithful as a bird dog. . . . He's done a fine job of looking after my interests. . . . Hotchner's a good friend of mine, but he's a sharp customer. . . . He's also out for number one."

Hotchner was genuinely interested in Hemingway as writer, friend and biographical subject. He was always ready to respond to his summons, listen to his exaggerated exploits and tolerate his behavior (drunk or sober). Hotchner never lost his reverential attitude, never ceased to marvel at Hemingway's superb skill and infinite patience. He was a close observer and recorder of Hemingway's physical and mental deterioration during the last year of his life. Though Hotchner provided some valuable services, he was disliked by many of Hemingway's friends. They noted that he was treated more like a servant than an equal, believed he brought out the worst in Hemingway and felt he was clearly on the make.[25]

On August 7, 1948, between Hotchner's visit and the first postwar trip to Europe, Hemingway's lawyer Maurice Speiser died of cancer. He had met Speiser in a barbershop in Hendaye in about 1928. After Speiser stopped the unauthorized filming of *The Sun Also Rises* without charge, he became Hemingway's lawyer and earned a ten percent commission for negotiating film rights. Speiser was a collector of paintings and owned a Tintoretto. When he became ill, Alfred Rice, who had a separate practice specializing in trusts and estates, took over the work Speiser had been doing on Hemingway's contracts, royalty collection and tax returns. He succeeded Speiser as Hemingway's lawyer and still handles the legal aspects of the estate.[26]

IV

Hemingway was more aroused by women's hair than by any other feature; he considered it the distinguishing erotic mark and emphasized hair in many of his stories and all his major novels. He enjoyed watching women comb their long hair; he liked his wives to let their hair grow long and then cut it short, to change their hair styles and hair color—often in competition with one another. In "The Last Good Country," *A Farewell to Arms, For Whom the Bell Tolls, Islands in the Stream* and the unpublished *The Garden of Eden,* the lovers experiment in dyeing their hair the same color and cutting it the same length in order to exchange sexual roles and merge their identities.

Hemingway's fascination with hair probably began in childhood. His mother had long thick hair and Marcelline remembered, from her girlhood, "the light tickling wisps of the curls of her hair touching my face. . . . [We] grew up admiring red hair because Mother always pointed it out to us as the most beautiful hair in the world. Ernest's first wife, Hadley, had hair that color." Hemingway described the hair of most of the women he loved. In "Cat in the Rain"—written when women's long hair symbolized tradition and short hair represented revolt—the hair of the Hadley-heroine becomes a point of contention. She is tired of looking like a boy and wants to let her short fair hair grow long, but her husband likes it the way it is. At the end of *A Moveable Feast*, when Hemingway returns to Schruns after a trip to New York, Hadley's hair is "red gold in the sun, grown out all winter awkwardly and beautifully." In *A Farewell to Arms*, Agnes-Catherine's hair is compared to shining water "just before it is really daylight."[27] In *The Sun Also Rises*, Jake first sees Duff-Brett with her hair brushed back like a boy's; in the last scene, she tells him that Romero wanted her to let her hair grow long.

In July 1929 Pauline dyed her hair blond to surprise Hemingway, and she frequently changed her hair color and style during her rivalry with Jane Mason in the 1930s. In *To Have and Have Not*, Marie Morgan (like Pauline) cuts her hair short and dyes it blond to please her husband, and provides a tawdry contrast to Jane-Hélène's "bright hair spread over the pillow." In *The Fifth Column* and *For Whom the Bell Tolls*, he compares Martha-Dorothy's and Martha-Maria's hair to fertile nature: blond like a wheat field and rippling like a field of grain. Maria's long braids are crudely cut with a razor blade before her rape and Jordan is aroused by feeling "the thick but silky roughness of the cropped head rippling between his fingers." Martha cut her hair to resemble the fictional Maria and sought Hemingway's approval. In the summer of 1945 Hemingway asked Mary to bleach her hair blond. But he was much more excited by the "dark hair, of an alive texture," that hung down over the shoulders of Adriana-Renata in *Across the River*. He used "alive" with the same syntactical eccentricity to describe Gertrude Stein's "lovely, thick, alive immigrant hair."[28]

Hemingway said he liked Stein better before she cut her hair, and believed that it marked a turning point in her life and their relations. Similarly, Hemingway (like Pope in "The Rape of the Lock") employed hair in a thematic as well as descriptive fashion to reveal a significant change in character. In the early story "Up in Michigan" (1923), Jim notices that Liz's hair is always pinned up neatly; after their awkward sexual encounter and her loss of virginity, "she worked out from under him and sat up and straightened her skirt and coat and tried to do something with her hair." In "The Last Good Country," Sunny-Littless always wanted to be a boy, thinks she can disguise her sex by clipping her hair, and (like his later heroines) expresses her symbolic sex change and close bond with Ernest-Nick by cutting it off: "Do I look like a boy? . . . Now I'm your sister but I'm a boy, too. Do you think it will change me into a boy?"[29]

The exchange—as well as the disguise—of sexual roles frequently occurs in Hemingway's novels. In *A Farewell to Arms*, Catherine expresses her love for Frederic by a surrender of selfhood and personal identity (which Hemingway desired in women) and by suggesting they have the same length but different color hair: "Let it grow a little longer and I could cut mine and we'd be just alike only one of us blonde and one of us dark. . . . It might be nice short. Then we'd both be alike. Oh, darling, I want you so much I want to be you too." For the same reason, Jordan tells the cropped Maria that after the battle of the bridge he will have her hair properly cut in Madrid: "They would cut it neatly . . . as they cut mine," and she enthusiastically agrees: "I would look like thee. . . . And then I would never want to change it." In *Islands in the Stream*, as Thomas Hudson dreams of sleeping with his first wife, she asks: "Should I be you or you be me?," he answers: "You have first choice," she decides: "I'll be you"—and swings her hair across his face.[30]

This complex, recurrent theme reaches its apotheosis in *The Garden of Eden*. Hemingway began to write the novel at the beginning of 1946 and completed eight hundred pages by June. (Mary built a three-story work tower in September 1947, but he preferred to write where he could hear the familiar sounds of the house. He found the tower too lonely and turned it over to the cats.) *The Garden of Eden*—unpublished and unavailable for examination—has been described as

> Filled with astonishing ineptitudes and based in part upon memories of his marriages to Hadley and Pauline, with some excursions behind the scenes of his current life with Mary. . . . The [characters'] nights were given to experiments with the transfer of sexual identities. . . . Nick had allowed his Indian-black hair to grow for five full months. . . . [Barbara] trimmed it to look like hers in all but color. . . . Catherine surprised her husband by having her hair shaped to the contours and colors of his own.

The journalist Aaron Latham mentioned another aspect of the novel: "They make love in some new, unusual way, which is never clearly explained. They talk about what they are doing as being 'shameless.' " Mary provided a clue about the mysterious love-making in *The Garden of Eden* when she recorded an imaginary interview in December 1953:

> Reporter: "Mr. Hemingway, is it true that your wife is a lesbian?"
> Papa: "Of course not. Mrs. Hemingway is a boy."
> Reporter: "What are your favorite sports, sir?"
> Papa: "Shooting, fishing, reading and sodomy."

Reporter: "Does Mrs. Hemingway participate in these sports?"
Papa: "She participates in all of them."[31]

In the hair fetishism, reversal of sexual roles and merging of the lovers into an indistinguishable unity, the Hemingway women become Conradian doubles: secret sharers of his forbidden erotic dreams.

Hemingway's increasing obsession with women's hair and sexual fantasies coincided with the distressing loss of his own hair. In *Death in the Afternoon* he criticized Cayetano Ordóñez as "prematurely bald from using hair fixatives" and condemned a young homosexual who "had had his hair hennaed." But at the Dorchester Hotel in May 1944, while using an eyedropper to apply hair-growing lotion, he told Roald Dahl that he needed the implement "to get the stuff through the hair and onto the scalp." When Dahl observed: "But you don't have much hair to get through," he irritably replied: "I have enough."[32] In May 1947, while writing *The Garden of Eden*, Hemingway dyed his own hair a bright copper color and then claimed he had mistaken the bottle for Martha's old shampoo.

21

Adriana
1948–1950

> When we two parted
> In silence and tears,
> Half brokenhearted,
> To sever for years.
>
> BYRON

I

In September 1948 the Hemingways made their first postwar trip to Europe, on the Polish ship *Jagiello,* which sailed from Havana to Genoa. It was his first journey to Italy since the ten-day car tour with Guy Hickok in March 1927. After the Great War, during his early years in Paris, Hemingway had been impressed by the vitality of European culture and participated in the artistic life of the city. Now he was a famous American tourist, returning to the ruins of a recently defeated country.

As a young man, interviewing Mussolini in January 1923, Hemingway wrote: "Really brave men do not have to fight duels, and many cowards duel constantly to make themselves believe they are brave." But as a well-known author he was forced to succumb to the situation, to accept the challenge and to prove himself. Because of his fame as hero and writer, strangers sometimes came up to him and threw a punch without any explanation. If *he* hit anyone, he risked bad publicity and a lawsuit, and now felt he was too rich to take part in fights.

But on the ship he was insulted in front of Mary by the drunken Polish engineer, who criticized the big Buick he was transporting to Europe and called him a "capitalist, bourgeois pig." Hemingway challenged him to a duel with pistols on deck the next morning, but the

438

engineer failed to appear. The ship's blacksmith loyally volunteered to push the engineer overboard (just as a maquis had reputedly offered to knock off Malraux for him after a sharp exchange of words in Paris in 1945), but Hemingway declined the generous offer.

In the summer of 1954 Edward Scott, a New Zealand columnist on the *Havana Post,* got into a heated dispute when Mary maintained that lion steaks were good to eat. Hemingway objected to Scott's public criticism of Mary, and Scott challenged him to a duel. Hemingway magisterially refused to apologize or to fight, said he did not consider Scott a worthy opponent and explained to his second: "Aside from other considerations my obligation at this time is to continue my writing and regain my health [after the African plane crashes]. . . . If any friends of Mr. Scott consider that to be an act of cowardice they are at liberty to think so."[1] In 1948 Hemingway tried to act like a young man and treated the drunken engineer as an equal in combat. By 1954 he was too ill to fight and recognized the absurdity of the provocation. Acting with unusual restraint, he refused to participate in the dueling tradition that ran from Pushkin to Proust.

Hemingway did not fight duels, but his illness and accidents persisted. In March 1949 in Cortina d'Ampezzo (a ski resort north of Venice in the Dolomites), an infection from a dust particle or scratch in his left eye turned into erysipelas, a contagious and febrile skin disease, and disfigured his face. He later claimed, more romantically, that the disease was caused by a knock from an oar in a duck blind or by the wadding of a shotgun shell. In any case, the doctors feared the infection might cause meningitis. On April 1 they placed him in a hospital in Padua and he recovered after treatment with penicillin. His fears about losing his vision during this disease led to two minor stories about blindness: "Get a Seeing-Eyed Dog" and "A Man of the World," both published in the *Atlantic* in November 1957.

Hemingway's bad luck continued throughout 1950. In February he had another skin infection, from gunpowder, and in May developed benign skin cancer from his long exposure to the tropical sun at sea. In July (possibly while drunk) he fell heavily on the slippery deck when Gregorio sharply turned the *Pilar* to avoid a wave, and gashed his head. As he told Dorman-Smith: "[I] drew a five inch cut (incised) that reached into the bone and severed some artery whose name I never caught. (I fell among the big gaffs and the clamps that hold them.) Also a concussion of about force 5."[2] In September he had severe leg pains from encysted shell fragments of the Great War. Hemingway continued to abuse his body in middle age, as his strength diminished and his drinking increased.

II

In November 1948, soon after he first arrived in Italy, Hemingway returned to a source of his creative life and revisited Fossalta, on the Piave River, where he had been wounded, when he was nearly nineteen, in July 1918. In Cortina he met some aristocratic Italian sportsmen —Conte Carlo Kechler and Barone Nanyuki Franchetti—who invited him to shoot birds on their feudal estates. In December, while duck hunting with Kechler, he met Adriana Ivancich, who was nearly nineteen, in Latisana on the Tagliamento River, twenty-five miles northeast of Fossalta. She was waiting for Kechler and standing alone in the rain —always an ominous sign for Hemingway, and for Catherine Barkley —when they picked her up in the luxurious Buick. As he watched Adriana drying her long black hair near the kitchen fire of the hunting lodge, she asked for a comb. Instead of giving her the entire comb, he broke his in two and gave her half: this was their first talismanic bond. He later told her that their dramatic encounter "was just something that struck me like lightning at the cross roads in Latisana in the rain."

Hemingway met Adriana for lunch at the Gritti Palace Hotel when he returned to Venice in April, after leaving the hospital in Padua. He frequently corresponded with her in the summer and fall of 1949, while writing *Across the River,* and met her (with perfect decorum) in Cortina, Venice, Paris and Le Havre (where she saw him off at the pier) during January–March 1950. Adriana and her mother, Dora, visited the Hemingways in Cuba from late October 1950 to early February 1951. They had a final reunion in Venice after his return from Africa in April 1954. He wrote at least sixty-five long letters to Adriana, who inspired both the heroine of *Across the River* and the composition of *The Old Man and the Sea.* Though she disliked his Venetian novel, she was proud of the fact that she had helped him write it: "And then I arrived. I had so much life, so much enthusiasm that I transmitted it to him. He had begun writing again and suddenly everything seemed easy. He had finished the book and then had written another one—for me—even better. Now he could write again, and well, and he thanked me."[3]

Adriana designed the dust jackets for both novels and did the drawings for "The Good Lion" in *Holiday*. He supposedly wrote this little fable for Adriana's nephew, Gherrardo Scapinelli, but (like most writers) he never wasted anything and actually recycled the poem or story he had originally composed for Shirley Shevlin.

The family of Adriana Ivancich, as her name suggests, originated on the Dalmatian island of Losinj, which had once been part of the Venetian empire. Educated in a Catholic girls' school and for six months in Switzerland, she came from a good family. They still retained their charming house on the Calle de Rimedio in Venice, which was said to have been an underground headquarters and arms depot for partisans fighting with British and French troops in Italy. The villa on their estate at San Michele al Tagliamento had been destroyed by American bombs and her father, Carlo (who planned to run for mayor of Venice after the war), was called out of his house during the postwar chaos and murdered by his political enemies on June 12, 1945.

Hemingway, exactly Adriana's age when he was wounded, associated the girl with the locales and battles of his heroic youth. Both of them, he felt, shared many hidden wounds. She was born in 1930, a year before Gregory, and was therefore the age that Hemingway's daughter would have been if (as both he and Pauline desired) Gregory had been a girl. Adriana was his lost daughter—he called her "daughter"—Hemingway was her lost father. She became especially important to him in 1951: the year of their estrangement and of his quarrel with Gregory after the death of Pauline. The father-daughter relationship helped to prevent sexual consummation.

As Hemingway became older, he desired younger women. He fell in love with older women (Agnes, Hadley, Duff, Pauline) when he was in his teens and twenties; with younger women (Jane, Martha, Mary and Slim) in his thirties and forties; and with teenage girls (Adriana and Valerie) in his fifties. He had often been in love with two women at the same time (Hadley and Duff, Hadley and Pauline, Pauline and Jane, Pauline and Martha, Martha and Mary, Mary and Slim) and was now torn between Adriana and Mary. His romantic ideal was to be on good terms with his past wives, have a devoted present wife and enjoy dalliance with a young girl who might become his future wife. Hemingway's love affairs with young girls sparked the jerky graph of his heart, inspired fantasies of rejuvenation and rebirth, and led to a desperate need to have his wife and his maiden competing for his favors.

Adriana—beautiful, sexy, aristocratic, intelligent, innocent, tragic—connected Hemingway to the country and the culture he had loved as a young man and seemed an appropriate reward for the personal sacrifice he had made for Italy. She bound him to the aesthetic splendor and the literary associations of Venice, one of the two cities he loved. He had been called, and was conscious of being, an American Byron. He also associated the Veneto with the flamboyant hero, lover and myth-maker Gabriele D'Annunzio, whom he praised in his 1922 interview with Mussolini as "that old, bald-headed, perhaps a little insane but thoroughly sincere, divinely brave swashbuckler."

His relations with Adriana also have a curious Jamesian resonance (he told her that Venice had been a haunt of James): the story of a highly bred, poetic and sheltered girl, the last hope of a cold, grasping and aging widow, offered as a sacrificial lamb on the altar of art. In Hemingway's case the Jamesian theme was ironically reversed; for the older, more experienced man, manipulated by the young Italian gentlewoman, became the innocent abroad. As Cantwell observes of Renata: "She'd out-maneuver you the best day you were ever born."[4]

Adriana's older brother, Gianfranco, who was born in 1920 (three years before Jack Hemingway) and resembled his sister, was for Hemingway the complement and mirror image of Adriana. He also had a fascinating background. Gianfranco had fought as a cavalry officer in World War Two, first with the Gruppo Corazzuto Esplorante in Rommel's rear guard in the North African desert, where he was wounded by a British Spitfire, and then with the partisans of the Friuli in northeast Italy. He was part of the American O.S.S. intelligence mission that played an important part in the liberation of Venice, and was a translation officer during the German surrender at Trieste. He took part in a postwar vendetta against his father's killers and had his own life threatened. After graduating in law from the University of Padua in 1947, Gianfranco took a job with Sidarma, an Italian shipping company in Havana, and lived there from November 1949 to January 1953. Hemingway called Gianfranco "a classy soldier,"[5] which was a high compliment, and saw him as a victim of war—as he himself had been in 1918. Hemingway, therefore, had a physical, psychological, emotional, historical and cultural attraction to both Adriana and Gianfranco.

The Hemingways returned to Cuba on the *Jagiello* and arrived in late May 1949. A week before they left on their second postwar trip to Italy, Gianfranco arrived in Havana without a visa. Hemingway helped him get off the ship, allowed him to live in the tower of the Finca for three years and became his paternal friend. Gianfranco was small, compact, good-looking, quiet, unassuming and withdrawn—something of a misfit in the boisterous Hemingway entourage. He was also rather artistic and bohemian. He drove a beat-up convertible with a hole in the floor and no top, and during the tropical rainstorms his girlfriend would get soaked while attempting to cover herself with an open umbrella. During Gianfranco's second visit to Cuba, from 1954 to 1956, Hemingway gave him his Lancia.

According to Pedro Menocal, Gianfranco did not do well in business ventures because he trusted everyone and lacked the will to succeed. He invested all his money in an eggplant crop and lost it all. In 1956 he married a Cuban girl, Cristina Sandoval, whom Hemingway disliked. But after they returned to Italy, she fell in love with the more glamorous Nanyuki Franchetti and left Gianfranco. Mario Menocal, Jr., concluded that Gianfranco was "a nice fellow and a thoroughgoing gentleman, but silent and colorless."

Hemingway, however, saw Gianfranco in an entirely different light: as a male version of and vicarious substitute for Adriana. Hemingway told Adriana that he was not lonely when he was with Gianfranco, who treated him well and cheered him up when he longed for her.[6] He revealed the incestuous overtones of his emotions when he said that both he and Gianfranco loved Adriana, but could not marry her. He defended Gianfranco when he lost his job at the shipping company, praised his unpublished novel, worried about his health, looked after his finances, lent him money to buy a farm, presented him with the manuscript of *The Old Man and the Sea* and tried to get him a job with the company that was filming the novel.

Gianfranco, more approachable and available than Adriana, provided an excuse both for Hemingway to write to her and for her to visit Cuba as his guest. The letters that he wrote to her between 1949 and 1955 were unrestrained and passionate expressions of his love. He again stressed the themes of exchanging identities and merging into a unity when he addressed her as "Hemingstein" and signed his letters "A. Ivancich." He missed her "rapier wit and [her] lovely mind, body and spirit";[7] he wanted to hold her in his arms, though he knew he was not permitted to do so; he wished only to serve her well, like a chivalric knight; he urged her to forget about him and marry a fine husband, but added that he would need a major operation to cure him of his love.[8]

When she earned $500 for the *Holiday* illustrations, he advised her about how to deal with art editors, reassured her that she had incurred no obligation to him, and tried to convince both her and himself that her work had been accepted on its own merit.

Adriana wrote about twenty-five letters to Hemingway, mostly in Italian, from 1950 to 1954 (though none were written during 1951–52). She was charming, and appealed for help with her writing and in understanding herself. She called him Papa and appreciated his generous assistance with Gianfranco. Her brother did not write home very often, and her mother worried that he was not doing well in his job. Adriana claimed to be hurt by gossip about her romantic interest in Hemingway and emphasized their friendship. Her family was in financial difficulty and she was grateful for the opportunity to earn money as an illustrator.

While he was corresponding with Adriana during 1949 and 1950, Hemingway was also writing his Venetian novel, *Across the River*. The physical characteristics of Renata were precisely modeled on Adriana, while her sexual behavior with the aging colonel was a fictional compensation for Hemingway's platonic relationship: "She came into the room, shining in her youth and tall striding beauty, and the carelessness the wind had made of her hair. She had pale, almost olive colored skin, a profile that could break your, or any one else's heart, and her dark hair, of an alive texture, hung down over her shoulders. . . . Her voice was low and delicate and she spoke English with caution. . . . [He] kissed her and felt her wonderful, long, young, lithe and properly built body against his own body."[9] Cantwell and Renata dream of taking a trip together in America; and in the dull, unpublished "Miami" section of *Islands in the Stream,* Hemingway describes Roger and Helena's long drive through Florida to New Orleans (based on a journey Mary made with Adriana and Dora), which ends with the story of how his first wife lost a suitcase with all his manuscripts.

In his postwar fiction, Hemingway drew on his past work as well as on his past experience. Like *A Farewell to Arms, Across the River* portrays a sexual consummation in fiction that never took place in real life. Like *For Whom the Bell Tolls,* the Venetian novel of love and war is compressed into a few days and includes references to many real people in a fictional context. Like *To Have and Have Not, Islands in the Stream* is a tripartite novel of maritime violence that fails to achieve artistic unity. Like "On the Blue Water" (1936), *The Old Man and the Sea* recounts the story of a giant marlin that is caught by an old fisherman and then devoured by sharks. Like *Green Hills of Africa* and "The Snows of Kilimanjaro," *A Moveable Feast* describes Hemingway's personal life and friendships in the 1920s.

All of Hemingway's major heroines have suffered a traumatic shock. Brett and Catherine have lost their lovers in the war, Maria has been raped by the Fascists, and Renata (according to the iceberg theory) is also meant to be a tragic victim—though the destruction of Adriana's house and the murder of her father are only briefly mentioned in the book. In his best novel, *The Sun Also Rises,* his most attractive, vivid and convincing heroine, Brett Ashley, dominates and controls all the men. But in his later works, he does not permit his fictional women (any more than his actual wives) to live a life of their own. Apart from castrating bitches like Margot Macomber, they are all subservient to the heroes of the books. When Hemingway asked Adriana what she thought of the Venetian novel, she said the girl could not exist. She could not come from a noble family and attend Mass at the same time that she drinks heavily and goes to bed with the foreign colonel in hotel rooms. "Sincerely," she told him, "I think the dialogues are a bit boring; that the colonel and the girl sit too much in Harry's and the Gritti."[10]

According to Adriana, Charles Scribner chose her anonymous dust jackets for *Across the River* and *The Old Man and the Sea* as the best of the numerous designs that had been submitted. Charles Scribner, Jr., agreed that Adriana's were indeed selected as the best ones for both novels. But authoritative evidence suggests that Hemingway (impelled by love and generosity) persuaded Scribner to accept Adriana's drawings and rigged the contest so that she would win. Julien Dedman, irritated at being forced to use her inferior illustrations, stated:

From 1949 through 1956 I was advertising and promotion director of Charles Scribner's Sons. As such, I was right in the middle of the many controversies attendant on the publication of ACROSS THE RIVER AND INTO THE TREES and THE OLD MAN AND THE SEA. The jacket drawings for both of these books as executed by "A" were so bad that we had to have them skillfully re-drawn. So what was on the jacket was not actually her original art, which was pretty abominable.[11]

III

The three-month visit of Adriana and Dora to Cuba in the fall of 1950 allowed Hemingway's friends to form their own opinion of his Italian love. Gregory Hemingway found her beautiful but boring: "Adriana was an attractive girl with dark hair and eyes, high cheekbones, a thin but not too angular face, and a lovely smile that betrayed no conceit or over-awareness of her lineage. . . . [But] she was dull, and had a hook-nosed mother in constant attendance." Tina Sánchez did not find her especially attractive, but thought she was bright, artistic and talented. Hemingway liked to touch Adriana and stroke her hand; he took her to philharmonic concerts and gave a grand ball in her honor on New Year's Eve. He wanted to introduce Adriana to Cuban society and asked Tina to invite them to the country club. Tina agreed but said that Hemingway had to wear a jacket and tie, and was surprised when he appeared in a tuxedo.[12]

Mario Menocal, Jr., and his brother Pedro—who were a few years older than Adriana—found her more impressive. Mario praised Adriana's looks, intelligence and sophistication. He noted how she controlled Hemingway, described her effect on his marriage, and criticized both Hemingway's infatuation and Adriana's selfishness:

> Adriana [was] so full of life and beauty, so bright and clever and witty! . . . [She was] a charming, intelligent, gifted member of the Venetian establishment. Supremely worldly and sophisticated, even at the age of 19 or 20 as she was in the Hemingway period. Very good-looking, super-sexy in a very Italian way. . . .
>
> Adriana could easily give Ernest the probable 28-to-30 years' difference in age and experience, and run rings around him. . . . She managed to make it quite clear that she knew exactly what was going on, and that it seemed as ludicrous to her as it did to the rest of us. . . .
>
> What an unmitigated disaster Ernest's falling in love with Adriana was for all concerned, Ernest included. . . .
>
> It [must have] damaged his marriage to Mary—and above all, it made him look such a fool! . . .
>
> I find it hard to condone both Ernest's fawning, self-deceiving attitude, and Adriana's acceptance of attentions. . . . Perhaps if Adriana had had the slightest spark of feeling for him as a man, they would have had an affair. . . . She accepted his hospitality, kindness, generosity towards herself and her family—and gave nothing in return.[13]

In the Latin ambience of Cuba, Hemingway cut an absurd figure, for he spent a great deal of time and money on a girl but never slept with her.

Adriana inspired not only *Across the River* but also *The Old Man and the Sea,* which he wrote during her visit. He told Gregory: "Adriana is so lovely to dream of, and when I wake I'm stronger than the day before and the words pour out of me"; and he thanked Adriana for coming by every morning and helping him to write it. Nevertheless, the visit went badly, led to disappointment and ended abruptly. For neither Hemingway nor Adriana and Dora—who all pursued their own selfish desires—showed much insight about each other or gave the slightest consideration to Mary's feelings. Adriana merely dismissed her as "tiny and springy, with short blonde hair; when she laughed she wrinkled up her blue ferret eyes."[14]

A week before Adriana's arrival, Hemingway attempted to reassure Mary's father that he was a loyal husband. He wrote that he knew a number of girls in Venice and could not help being fond of them. But he could control his emotions and had never been unfaithful to Mary.[15] Despite his good intentions and confident assertions, the worst phase of his marriage to Mary took place during Adriana's visit. His heavy drinking, his lies, his self-delusion, his foolish behavior and his cruel treatment of Mary at that time were caused by the harsh reception of *Across the River,* the inability to recapture his lost youth through Adriana, his feeling that Adriana was superior to Mary in beauty, breeding, sophistication, intelligence and culture, and his intense frustration at being unwilling or unable to sleep with or marry Adriana. He preferred to keep their relationship on an imaginative rather than a realistic plane. He loved her too much to seduce and abandon her (he never did this with women), and realized that he was too old to marry her. Despite his longing for romance, he knew that Mary would be a better wife in his declining years.

Martha Gellhorn and some of his friends correctly believed that Adriana wanted to marry Hemingway—the first man who took her seriously and fell in love with her—and that her mother, whose motives and behavior were confused and irresponsible, wanted her daughter to restore the family fortunes by marrying a rich and famous writer. Adriana enjoyed Hemingway's generosity and love, for he knew how to please her, but she was not attracted to him and could see, by reading his novel, that he had an unrealistic idea of the kind of woman she was.

She rather crassly believed that "Mary owed her a great debt because she had not walked away with Ernest. 'I could have, you know,' she said some years later."[16]

The sacrificial self-effacement of Mary, who was twenty-two years older than Adriana, turned her into Hemingway's scapegoat and victim. Patrick felt that his father took "advantage of her determination to take whatever he dished out." Like Robert Lowell's wife, Elizabeth Hardwick, Mary had an infinite capacity for suffering. When the disastrous reviews of *Across the River* coincided with the visit of the real-life heroine of the book, Hemingway contrasted Mary's lack of culture to Adriana's "fast brain," while Mary hoped he would consult the psychiatrist who had helped Patrick. A few days before Adriana's arrival, Hemingway, depressed and nervous, caustically called Mary a "camp-follower and a scavenger" and said, without provocation: "You have the face of a Torquemada." She humbly thought: "I guess my pride is expendable. A luxury I can't afford."[17]

Shortly after Adriana and Dora arrived to stay in the guest house, and in their presence, Hemingway hurled Mary's typewriter onto the floor and threw wine in her face. She forgave his excesses and bravely told him: "I'm going to stay here and run your house and your Finca until ... you tell me truthfully and straight that you want me to leave." Soon after this, he called her a slut and broke her Venetian ashtray. Mary abased herself yet failed to please him. But, as Mario Menocal, Jr., observed: "She was still a good and big enough person to be sorry *for him* and respected him enough to deplore the entire mess perhaps even more for his sake (as we, his friends, deplored it) than for her own." Mary tolerated his "neglect, rudeness, thoughtlessness, abusive language, unjust criticism, false accusations"[18] not only because she liked being the wife of a great writer and enjoyed playing the role of Sophia Tolstoy, but also because she admired him, loved him and was loyal. Mary's surpassing love, her devotion merging into martyrdom, her humiliating masochism, her unlimited capacity for suffering and endurance, made her the most tragic heroine of Hemingway's life.

When Adriana and Dora were in Cuba, rumors began to circulate in Venice that connected the sexual relations of Cantwell and Renata to those of Hemingway and Adriana. When the news reached the Finca in February 1951, Dora, who had permitted and then encouraged her daughter's friendship with Hemingway and accepted his invitation to Havana, said they had to return to Venice and stop the scandal. "It was as if a cyclone had descended on us," Adriana wrote. "Mother more and more stayed in the guest house, lying on her bed. Gianfranco said nervously that one should not give weight to gossip. Mary said she had predicted it and it was a shame Papa hadn't followed her advice and given the girl red hair and blue eyes and had her born in Trieste." But Adriana's friend Afdera Franchetti maintained that there was no scandal in Venice, that Adriana's reputation was not harmed, and that both Dora and Adriana adored every minute of their glamorous friendship with Hemingway.[19]

In *La Torre Bianca*, Adriana explained that *she* was the one who had started the gossip in order to impress and attract Guido Brandolin, a handsome young friend of Gianfranco. In the spring of 1949 she met Guido in the street, told him she had just lunched with Hemingway and had agreed to his request to use her physical appearance for a character in his novel. She tried to explain that she was not the heroine, that she merely looked like her, but Guido ignored that distinction and spread the news through the tightly knit society of the island.

Hemingway explained, in a letter of March 18, that Adriana was not the girl in his novel and was not responsible for Renata's sins and mistakes. He bound himself to Adriana (as he had tried to do from the moment he gave her the comb) by connecting Dora's disapproval of his fictional methods with Grace Hemingway's disapproval of him after "the scandal I made in our village" with the sexual scenes in *Three Stories and Ten Poems* and the divorce from Hadley. While disclaiming all connection between Adriana and Renata, he did everything he could to make amends for the trouble he had caused. He forbade the book's publication in Italy and it did not appear until after his death, in 1965. He inscribed her copy of the novel: "For Adriana who inspired everything that is good in this book and nothing that is not."[20] The final irony was that Mary, the only one of his women from Agnes to Martha who did not achieve literary immortality in his fiction, received the dedication of his love tribute to Adriana.

To make matters even more complicated, and arouse the jealousy of Hemingway, Adriana fell in love with a young Cuban, Juan Veranes, who came from a good but equally impoverished family. (Both Hemingway and Mary disliked him.) To avoid further gossip, Hemingway remained behind at the Finca when Mary accompanied Dora, Adriana and Juan on a curtailed version of the trip Hemingway had planned to take with them. With Hemingway *hors de combat*, the car trip (to New

Orleans instead of to Sun Valley) brought Adriana and Juan closer together. Juan planned to fly to Paris and to marry her, and Gianfranco used the little money he had to travel from Venice in 1953 to meet Juan at the airport. But they continued to suffer the bad luck that had pursued the Ivancich family since the war and were cruelly disappointed and humiliated when Juan failed to show up. After Adriana had left Cuba, Juan met and fell in love with Angelita Osborne, an heiress of the sherry family. Though Juan jilted Adriana, he did not, in the end, marry Angelita. Adriana provided a brief history of her disastrous suitors: "I loved Juan but when I returned to Italy I gave him up [sic] for Enrico, who left me for a Venezuelan. I thought I loved Nikki and he was killed in an auto accident."[21]

Adriana's book, *La Torre Bianca* (named after the tower on the Finca), partly reveals her feelings about Hemingway and presents a romantic, self-pitying and condescending portrait of their friendship. But it does not explain Adriana and Dora's attitude and conduct in this potentially dangerous affair. The book never takes into account the feelings of other people, but treats every event from her own point of view. Even the photograph on the dust jacket of the memoir is deceptive, for it shows Adriana and Hemingway but neatly cuts off Mary—the third party in the triangle. Written in middle age, the book was meant to exorcise but actually revives her romance.

Adriana's focus is on herself: her relationship with Hemingway, her link to the character of Renata and the trouble that followed the publication of the novel. The narcissistic, impressionistic memoir is an expanded and much-padded version of her article, published in *Epoca* in July 1965, with the less ambiguous title: "La Renata di Hemingway sono io" (I am Hemingway's Renata). The tone of the book is bitter and proud: she has pride in her family background and her artistic achievements, in Hemingway's love and her inspiration of his art; bitterness about the effect of this friendship on her life.

The book establishes her physical resemblance to Renata, but it denies any similarities in behavior and emphasizes that Adriana was always chaperoned. She clings to reflected glory, yet needs to vindicate herself. The letters and conversations reported in the book suggest a friendship both flirtatious and paternal. Hemingway maintains the role of passive suitor and their relationship does not develop. Yet he goes out of his way to please Adriana and she willingly accepts his devotion. Throughout the book she describes herself at the center of his life: "What tenderness he had, my massive irascible friend!"

Despite her assertions of affection, her portrait of Hemingway is negative. In Venice he is a tired, jaded, hard-drinking sentimentalist; in Havana, rude, dominating, obsessive; in their final meeting, shattered and tearful. Adriana's attitude to Hemingway remains ambivalent. She affirms her loyalty to him, but describes herself as a victim of his love, burdened by the sheer number of his letters. She is tempted to burn them and be rid of "that Hemingway who covered me with mud."[22] But she sold them, instead, to a New York dealer for $17,000.

Though Hemingway continued to write to Adriana until 1955, her unhappy departure from Cuba put an end to their relationship—if not to his love. Her new fiancé, jealous of her friendship with the famous novelist, insisted that she stop writing to him—and Hemingway withdrew for the sake of her happiness. Though Adriana saw Hemingway for a compassionate visit after his African plane crashes, he felt he could not return to Venice while she was still living there. During his last journeys to Europe he abandoned Italy and returned to Spain and to bullfighting.

All the people involved in the Hemingway-Adriana relationship behaved rather badly. Dora, who should have known better, though she had suffered a great shock from her husband's death, seemed to act in a cold-blooded and exploitive manner by encouraging a friendship that could lead only to sexual rumors, an adulterous liaison or a disastrous marriage. Adriana, by her own admission, gave Hemingway little more than the pleasure of her company and the joy of her conversation. Their few furtive kisses were called, more appropriately than ironically, "mistakes." Knowing Hemingway gave her status, encouraged her artistic pretensions (her drawings and her poetry were equally poor) and allowed her to earn some money as an illustrator by producing inferior designs for his dust jackets. Her book reveals her greatest faults: vanity, snobbery, superficiality and selfishness. Mary chose to tolerate Hemingway's emotional infidelity (as Hadley and Pauline had done), but may have lost his respect by accepting his abusive behavior.

By inviting Adriana to stay with him in Cuba, Hemingway was certainly insensitive to Mary. He was selfish as well as artistically inept in the way he used Adriana as a fictional model. If the love idyll really existed, then it was a mistake (as Mary noted) to describe Adriana in precise detail and make it easy to recognize her. If her behavior had no factual basis, then it was foolish and irresponsible to portray her realistically.

Hemingway, smitten like a schoolboy, fell in love with Adriana as soon as they met. As with Agnes and with Hadley before their marriage, he spent very little time with her. She was his fictional creation—in life as well as in art. She combined, in the most intriguing and absorbing way, his personal and artistic fascination with hair and with rain, with his past, his wound, his attachment to the Veneto. She was his lost youth and his lost daughter; his muse and his inspiration. She was connected, through literary traditions and memories, to Byron, D'Annunzio and Henry James. Adriana inspired, when Hemingway was having difficulty writing, "The Good Lion," a deleted section of *Islands in the Stream* and two late novels: *Across the River* and *The Old Man and the Sea.* But the personal, as opposed to the literary, results were negative. It caused embarrassment to Dora and Adriana, grief for Mary and frustration for Hemingway. He behaved like a tame bear and looked like a fool.

After being jilted by Juan Veranes and breaking off her engagement to the second *fidanzato* who objected to her correspondence with Hemingway, Adriana had an unhappy three-year marriage to an older Greek, Dimitri Monas (whose name is an obscene word in Venetian dialect), who was intensely jealous and kept her locked up in the house. In 1963 she married a German count, Rudolf von Rex, had two sons and lived on a farm at Orbetello, on the coast northwest of Rome. Her second marriage was also a disaster. She became obsessed by Hemingway, fantasized about the past and was deeply disappointed by the failure of her book. She became hostile to her husband and alienated from her sons, drank heavily, suffered from nervous ailments and twice attempted suicide. In March 1983, attempting to punish her family, she hanged herself from a tree on her farm, was cut down while still alive and died in the hospital.[23]

22

The Lost Hero:
Across the River and into the Trees
1950

> Seems like when they get
> started they don't leave
> a guy nothing.
>
> "My Old Man"

I

The critical battering of *Across the River*—the most personal and revealing of all Hemingway's novels—reminded him, in the most painful way, of the devastating judgments that Max Eastman, Gertrude Stein and Wyndham Lewis had made in 1933–34. The critics, both early and late, did not stop at the literary text, but related the work to the supposed defects of the writer. By 1950 Hemingway was much more than a novelist: he was a cultural presence, a larger-than-life public figure, an object of admiration and envy. The incongruity between the heroic ideals of his early work and the unpleasant details of his private life was well known. Hemingway had deliberately projected a Cantwell-like persona in Lillian Ross' 1949 *New Yorker* profile, which depicted an arrogant, anti-intellectual, free-spending celebrity. When the novel appeared, the critics were quick to identify Hemingway with his central character, and blamed him for Cantwell's self-pity, sentimentality, sexual and military boasting. The reviewers, expecting a great Hemingway novel, were disappointed and puzzled by what seemed to be an embarrassing self-exposure.

Hemingway never developed a detached, Olympian response to criticism and was deeply wounded by the negative reviews. They intensified his long-standing hostility to critics and his extreme sensitivity to attacks on his books; they made him feel undervalued and were serious blows to his confidence as a writer; they reinforced his doubts about his creative capacity and, as he reached middle age, his despair about the future of his work.

Hemingway responded to the provocative judgments in an aggressive way and lashed out at those who had hurt him. He felt the sterile reviewers were malicious and had conspired against him to pay off old debts. He believed critics resented imaginative writers: wanted to undermine their confidence, impair their creative mechanism and destroy their work. His hostility to criticism had a significant effect on the reception of his novel and on his personal relations with those who wrote about him in the late forties and early fifties.

Hemingway's aggressive attitude went back to the very beginning of his literary career, when he was writing articles for Ford's *Transatlantic Review,* and remained consistent throughout his life. In 1924 he loftily declared: "I have always regarded critics as the eunuchs of art," and compared them to subterranean scavengers, feeding on the corpses of true writers: "The critics will dive into their vocabularies and come up with articles on the death of Conrad. They are diving now, like prairie dogs." The following year, in a letter to Sherwood Anderson, he said he was sickened by the critics' attempt to explain what only the author knows about his work, exaggerated his indifference to critical opinion and succinctly stated: "All criticism is shit."[1]

Hemingway had worked very hard to achieve his remarkable style and thought he was his own severest critic. He felt that through his writing he was in touch with the deepest psychological truths, that any judgment on them was a violation of his inner self. He believed in his art above all else and thought he knew infinitely more than a critic who was neither devoted to nor disciplined by creative work. He claimed that praise was meaningless and that even a favorable review was enough to turn his stomach; but he was easily hurt and angered by adverse opinions.

In his poetic squib "Valentine" (1927), Hemingway ironically noted that envious critics were always "the first to hail / any happy weakening or sign of quick decay." That year he told Scribner's to stop sending him the distracting and dispiriting reviews. He forgave the mistakes of his unfortunately named German translator (she may have made errors but was always Horschitz), but was bitter about Virginia Woolf's barbed review of *Men Without Women.* He attacked Woolf (and other hostile critics) in *Death in the Afternoon* and condemned her exclusive attitude in a perceptive letter to Perkins in November 1927: "The Virginia Woolf review was damned irritating—She belongs to a group of Bloomsbury people who are all over 40 and have taken on themselves the burden of being modern and all very promising and saviours of letters. When they are all busy at it they dislike what they consider the intrusion of anybody much under 40 into the business."[2]

After a sharp dispute with *Hound and Horn* in 1932, Hemingway referred to that journal as "Bitch and Bugle." In *Green Hills of Africa* he categorized incestuous New York writers, cut off from physical experience and the natural world, as "angleworms in a bottle, trying to derive knowledge and nourishment from their own contact." He savagely called critics "the lice who crawl on literature" and maintained that two unnamed writers (Anderson and Fitzgerald) had been rendered impotent by bad reviews. In July 1936 he told Perkins that the New York critics were antagonistic to his work and would try to kill his stories if Scribner's brought out a collection in the fall. His fears were justified by the negative reviews of *To Have and Have Not,* which he attributed to their enmity and his own aggression:

> You want to remember, Max, there was about the biggest gang-up in the reviews on that last novel, which was not a bad novel, that you would almost ever see. . . .
>
> I don't think it is persecution mania or egotism if I say that there are a lot of critics who really seem to hate me very much and would like to put me out of business. And don't think I mean it conceitedly when I say that a lot of it is jealousy. . . .
>
> I know some of the critic thing too is my fault. I have been very snotty and they hate you for that too.[3]

Edmund Wilson, the most distinguished critic in America, wrote the most influential study of Hemingway. Wilson's 1939 essay, "Hemingway: Gauge of Morale," marked a turning point in the history of Hemingway's critical reputation. Though Wilson had been a great admirer of Hemingway's early work, he now contrasted the successful art of the 1920s with the radical decline in the following decade and emphasized his exhibitionism, his public personality, his lack of objectivity, craftsmanship, taste, style and sense. Wilson's essay was included in his book *The Wound and the Bow,* which originally had been commissioned by

Scribner's; but Perkins, quite reasonably, refused to publish an attack on their leading author (just as Liveright had refused to publish Hemingway's attack on Anderson). As Wilson wrote in a letter of March 1941: "When they laid eyes on my essay on Hemingway, they protested that they could not print it, and as I refused to withdraw it, broke their contract (though on terms pretty favorable to me). . . . Hemingway has been getting worse (crazier) of late years, and they are scared to death that he may leave them."

Hemingway delayed publication of Wilson's work by filing an injunction against Houghton Mifflin, which eventually brought out the damaging book in 1941. Three years later, Hemingway attacked Wilson, who also married several times, in a letter to Perkins: "You can trace the moral decay of [Wilson's] criticism on a parallel line with the decline in Dos Passos's writing through their increasing dishonesty about money and other things [politics], mostly their being dominated by women."[4] Despite the excellent notices of *For Whom the Bell Tolls*, Hemingway was still disgusted by the criticism and told Maxwell Geismar that the best things in his review were the quotations.

Hemingway repaid the universal praise of his Spanish novel with gratuitous attacks on literary parasites in his Introduction to Elio Vittorini's *In Sicily* (1949), where he squeezed the last drop from the image of the critical wasteland: "New York literary reviews grow dry and sad, inexistent without the watering of their benefactors, feeding on the dried manure of schism and the dusty taste of disputed dialectics, their only flowering a desiccated criticism as alive as stuffed birds, and their steady mulch the dehydrated cuds of fellow critics."

Hemingway believed the artist must satisfy his own standards and rejected all criticism. Though it would have been foolish and indeed impossible to trim his sails to suit the prevailing winds, he revealed his limitations by refusing to recognize the defects in his work and by blaming the critics for pointing them out. He knew that some of his books were better than others, but felt that if he accepted the current view that his powers were failing and his work declining, he would lose self-confidence—for he had his own doubts about his creative ability—and be unable to write. He therefore protested his indifference or launched a counterattack. Both responses were self-protective, suggested profound insecurity and showed how frightened he was by the revelation of his literary defects.

II

Hemingway's wife, editor and friends, who saw the weaknesses of *Across the River,* did not dare to mention them, for he depended on his inner circle for emotional support. Mary disliked the novel (for personal as well as artistic reasons), but said: "I kept my mouth shut. Nobody had appointed me my husband's editor or the bombardier of his self-confidence."[5] So the harsh reaction to the book took Hemingway by surprise.

Across the River was condemned by all serious critics when it first appeared, in September 1950, and is still considered Hemingway's worst novel. A few writers, like John O'Hara, praised the book out of loyalty to Hemingway or his past reputation; but Cyril Connolly, Morton Dauwen Zabel, Northrop Frye, Joseph Warren Beach, Alfred Kazin, Evelyn Waugh and Isaac Rosenfeld all agreed with Maxwell Geismar's critique of Hemingway's ideas and his negative evaluation in the *Saturday Review of Literature:*

> This is an unfortunate novel and unpleasant to review for anyone who respects Hemingway's talent and achievement. It is not only Hemingway's worst novel; it is a synthesis of everything that is bad in his previous work and throws a doubtful light on the future. It is so dreadful, in fact, that it begins to have its own morbid fascination. . . . The ideological background of the novel is a mixture of *True Romances,* Superman, and the Last Frontier.[6]

John O'Hara, a disciple of Hemingway and one of the few contemporary admirers of the novel, wildly overstated his case, on the front page of the *New York Times Book Review,* by describing Hemingway as "the most important author living today, the outstanding author since the death of Shakespeare." His surprisingly simple-minded review combined adulation with wisecracks and called Renata "practically all that a middle-aged man with a cardiac condition could ask for."[7]

Many critics felt they had overrated Hemingway's earlier work, expressed dissatisfaction by sharpening their knives on his abrasive novel and protected themselves by attacking him. They criticized the technical flaws of the novel and the limitations of its values. But the two main criticisms, as expressed by Philip Rahv in a *Commentary* review, were that Hemingway was "indulging himself in blatant self-pity and equally blatant conceit" and that "there is hardly any aesthetic distance between the author and Colonel Richard Cantwell. . . . They have so much in common, in their private history and war experience no less than in their opinions, tastes, attitudes and prejudices, that there is no telling them apart."[8]

Cyril Connolly observed: "It is not uncommon for a famous writer to produce one thoroughly bad book." He wryly remarked that though Hemingway's "adventurous life has been an inspiration to writers who don't want to be publishers or Government officials," his novel suffers from two unreal and unsympathetic characters. The Colonel is a "drink-sodden and maundering old bore. . . . His ladylove is a whimsical wax-work." Connolly concluded with the shrewd prediction that Hemingway could still produce a valuable "bestiary or a truthful autobiography"—which is almost exactly what he did in his next two books. Hemingway tried to retaliate by telling the porcine Connolly that he was an afterbirth, a well-fed or overstuffed abortion.[9]

In a review entitled "A Good Day for Mr. Tolstoy," Morton Dauwen Zabel noted the flat dialogue and the static plot, emphasized the decline from Hemingway's previous work and asserted "this new novel is the poorest thing its author has ever done." The novel reveals "the impasse of routine mechanism and contrivance a talent arrives at when an inflexibly formulated conception of experience or humanity is pushed to the limits of its utility." Northrop Frye focused on the disparity between the potential and the actual novel. The hero meets his fate "with a compelling dignity," "his approaching death gives a bitter intensity to the ordinary events of his life" and "his story is intended to be a study in isolation, of how the standards of a decent soldier are betrayed by modern war." But Hemingway fails, in an egoistic and embarrassing way, because he has not achieved the necessary technical detachment from the hero.[10]

Joseph Warren Beach, who had written a novel about Hemingway, *The Glass Mountain* (1930), read *Across the River* as largely autobiographical. He remarked that "the hero of Hemingway's novels is always much the same person" and that "Colonel Cantwell is the oldest of all these avatars of Nick Adams." He thought it was too thin a subject for a long book and, because of sentimentality, did not do full justice to the theme of love. Alfred Kazin, as severe as Connolly, Zabel, Frye and Beach, called the book a distressing vulgar travesty. But he partially excused it by noting that in 1949 Hemingway thought he would die of an eye infection and "turned aside from the more ambitious novel he had been working over for some years to do this little book in the short time he felt was left."[11]

Evelyn Waugh, writing from a different cultural background, explained the complex reasons for the critics' hostility to "one of the most original and powerful of living writers." Waugh mentioned Ross' blitz in the *New Yorker,* Hemingway's deliberately cultivated philistine image, his "delight in the technicalities of every trade but his own," his bitterness and frustration. But the most important reason was his unfashionable, "quite unforgivable Decent Feeling [and] . . . sense of chivalry—respect for women, pity for the weak, love of honour—which keeps breaking in."

The psychoanalytically oriented review-essay by Isaac Rosenfeld came closer than most critics to perceiving what Hemingway was trying to do. Rosenfeld saw a new humanity in Hemingway and concluded that the power of the novel derived from the "courage to confess, even if it be only through self-betrayal, the sickness and fear and sad wreck of his life behind the myth." Hemingway, at work on *The Old Man and the Sea,* remarked: "It will be nice to win after the shit I had to eat about the last book."[12]

III

Across the River is not as good as Hemingway's best fiction, but it has been misinterpreted and maligned for purely external reasons. When we separate Hemingway's hero from his public persona and recognize the confessional mode, we can see that the work has considerable interest and would have been hailed as impressive if it had been written by anyone but Hemingway. There are four reasons why the novel received an intensely hostile reception: Hemingway's alienation of the critics, the novel's place in his literary career, the autobiographical aspects of Colonel Cantwell and the decline of Hemingway's personal legend. These factors led to a simplistic identification of the hero with the author and a misinterpretation of the book.

In 1950, Hemingway had not published a novel for ten years. Scribner's advance publicity had led readers to believe that *Across the River* was a major work and would present Hemingway's experience in World War Two in the same way that *A Farewell to Arms* and *For Whom the Bell Tolls* had done for the Great War and the war in Spain.

The undignified serialization in the low-brow but high-paying ladies' magazine *Cosmopolitan* (February–June 1950) was the first disappointment. For the publication of the novel followed Malcolm Cowley's glorification of the Papa legend in *Life* magazine (January 10, 1949) and coincided with John McCaffery's admiring collection of essays (September 1950).

The critics inevitably compared Hemingway's latest novel with his finest works. Those who had staked—and in some cases established—their reputations on praising the greatness of his earlier novels were intensely disappointed and irritated when their star failed to perform. But it was impossible for him (or anyone else writing in 1950) to maintain the standard of *The Sun Also Rises* and *A Farewell to Arms*.

Jake Barnes—a modern Abelard—is wounded and impotent yet stoic and admirable. Disciplined, restrained and laconic, he is honest about himself, aware of the limitations of his friendship with Brett and morally perceptive in a decadent milieu. Jake nobly accepts his tragic condition, but Richard Cantwell feels forced to justify himself. Bitter, boastful, self-indulgent and long-winded, he defies sickness and death with the selfish pleasures of the table and the bed. Hemingway's descriptions of duck hunting and of the light, wind and water of Venice are impressive, but there is no dramatic conflict in his story and the *ex cathedra* conversation merely rambles on. The difference between his early and late work is immediately apparent in passages from the end of each novel:

> "Oh, Jake," Brett said, "we could have had such a damned good time together." . . .
> "Yes," I said. "Isn't it pretty to think so?"

By contrast, Cantwell clumsily tells Renata:

> "There are some things that a person cannot do. You know about that. You cannot marry me and I understand that, although I do not approve it."

Across the River is a derivative version of *A Farewell to Arms*. Both books are set in Italy; both bitterly portray Hemingway's war experience; both criticize heroic values; in both novels the soldiers escape to a romantic milieu; in both love is a compensation for war; both have a tragic idealized heroine; both have one doomed lover.

Across the River also includes some of the notable faults of Hemingway's earlier works. The tone of the novel is similar to the exhibitionistic hunting and fishing articles that appeared in *Esquire* in the mid-1930s, and to those manuals of expertise—*Death in the Afternoon* and *Green Hills of Africa*—in which he attempted to refute Gertrude Stein's admonition: "Hemingway, remarks are not literature."[13] Renata's persistent questions, like those of the tedious Old Lady in *Death in the Afternoon,* provide an excuse for a series of smug disquisitions. Cantwell's self-justification and the adoration he receives from underlings—he treats the servants at the Gritti like the Africans on safari—recall the unpleasant posturings of *Green Hills of Africa.* Renata, like Maria in *For Whom the Bell Tolls,* is a Latin child-mistress. The Venetian novel, like *Islands in the Stream,* describes what Hemingway would normally omit. Cantwell and Renata have nothing significant to say to each other, and the themes of the novel—which becomes diverted from a war to a love story—are repeated rather than developed.

Certain superficial details recalled Hemingway's marriages and war experience, and reinforced the biographical interpretation of *Across the River.* The book expressed his adoration of Adriana, contained a tasteless and transparent attack on Martha, and was dedicated to Mary. Cantwell, as Hemingway planned to do at Fossalta, ritualistically "relieved himself in the exact place where he had determined, by triangulation, that he had been badly wounded thirty years before." And the absurd Order of Brusadelli, created by Cantwell and the maître d'hôtel, was based on the award—Cavaliere di Gran Croce al Merito in the Knights of Malta—that Hemingway received in Venice in October 1948.

Critics were also encouraged to connect Cantwell's illness to Hemingway's. On October 13, 1949, the *New York Times* (using information that Hemingway gave Scribner's) disclosed that during the previous winter in Italy, "a tiny fragment of shotgun wadding fell into his eye and its presence was not discovered for several days; by this time, blood poisoning had set in, and it spread so rapidly and so virulently that Mr. Hemingway's doctors despaired of his recovery. He was given only a short time to live." In fact, Hemingway had erysipelas, not blood poisoning; his unglamorous disease was caused by a dust particle or scratch, not by shotgun wadding; his admission to the hospital was a precautionary measure, not a sign of imminent death. This misleading, sensational account of his illness seemed intended to evoke sympathy and provide an excuse for the defects of the novel. Though Hemingway "was taking nitroglycerin at that time, due to a real or fancied heart disorder,"[14] Cantwell's heart disease was based not on Hemingway but on Sinsky, who had several serious heart attacks in the late 1940s.

Though Hemingway liked publicity, he had always been as hostile to biography as to criticism. Soon after he joined Scribner's he told Perkins:

> I hate all that [biography] so that I thought if I didn't furnish it there would not be any. So it would be a great favor to me if we could lay off the Biography—or if the first paragraph on this sheet could go out in the publicity sheets so it would correct the other. . . .
>
> Would like to see you spread this statement around: . . . "While Mr. H[emingway] appreciates the publicity attempt to build him into a glamorous personality like [the journalist] Floyd Gibbons or Tom Mix's horse Tony he deprecates it and asks the motion picture people to leave his private life alone."[15]

Despite these disclaimers, Hemingway did not maintain a consistent attitude and cooperated with the writing of biographical articles by Malcolm Cowley and Lillian Ross. He loved to be admired and wanted to profit from his fame. He was naturally kind, and had a tendency to delude himself. He assumed that his friendship with these critics meant that they would give him unqualified praise and failed to foresee how their articles would damage his reputation.

Cowley, who was a year older than Hemingway and had been a writer in Paris in the 1920s, won his respect with a number of favorable reviews and a perceptive introduction to the *Portable Hemingway* (1944). Cowley's "A Portrait of Mister Papa" was published in *Life* and reprinted in McCaffery's critical anthology. It appeared at the end of Hemingway's fallow decade and prepared the basis of the legend. Cowley's epigraph resembled the transparent disclaimer that novelists customarily place in their books to avoid libel suits: "he asked me to state that he is not responsible for any inaccuracies or legendary accomplishments of any sort which may have been attributed to him."

Cowley's postwar piece took the sub hunting too seriously, and stressed Hemingway's war service as roving correspondent and commando. But even Hemingway could not swallow the stories that Cowley (and C. L. Sulzberger) had heard from Lanham. He asked Buck if anyone would ever carry canteens of gin and vermouth at Hürtgen. Good vermouth could not be found and no one would give it canteen space in a war. That story was just another old chestnut from Cowley's essay in *Life.* [16]

Cowley also emphasized Hemingway's physical prowess and patriarchal life in Cuba, the risks and scars of shooting and fishing on the *Pilar* with a cadre of faithful followers. According to Cowley, Hemingway broke his nose in a teenage boxing match with a professional but returned to fight again the next day. He no longer had fought with the *Arditi* (as Cowley had said in the *Portable Hemingway*), but still had an aluminum kneecap. Though *For Whom the Bell Tolls* was ideologically repugnant to the Communists because it criticized Soviet policy in Spain, and was not translated into Russian until 1968 (and then with heavy cuts), Cowley dubiously claimed it was used by Stalin's armies in World War Two as a "textbook of guerrilla fighting." Though Cowley tried for accuracy and obtained information from Hemingway's friends as well as from his subject, his heroic view of Hemingway is very close to the way the writer chose to present himself to the public: he-man at the typewriter, experiencing and recording violent action.

Despite his tough image, Hemingway was a soft-hearted man. He was apparently persuaded to grant Cowley interviews in Cuba after the critic pleaded that his son's education was at stake; and later reminded him that Cowley had written, when Hemingway was reluctant to let him do the *Life* article, that it would allow the boy to go to Exeter. Hemingway regretfully told Dos Passos that he had a private life until Cowley intruded on it, and wrote to an editor: "there has been too damned much written about my personal life and I am sick of it. It was a very bad thing for me that Malcolm Cowley's article was published in LIFE."[17]

As early as 1927 Edmund Wilson wrote: "The reputation of Ernest Hemingway has, in a very short time, reached such proportions that it has already become fashionable to disparage him."[18] Lillian Ross' *New Yorker* profile, which appeared on May 13, 1950, as an antidote to Cowley's sympathetic portrait, struck a devastating blow to the Hemingway legend. Ross met Hemingway in 1947 when she was working on her first *New Yorker* profile, on his bullfighter friend Sidney Franklin. Hemingway invited her to Ketchum the day before Christmas and gave her generous help. In a letter of July 1948 he adopted the pidgin-English persona that disguised his respectable background: "I talk bad on account where and how brought up. Can talk properly. But I remember I asked you if you minded and you said no and so I talked naturally."[19] He was pleased to maintain a pugnacious stance and refused to speak and act like an intellectual—even if he thought and felt like one.

Ross spent November 16–18, 1949, with Hemingway and tried to set down exactly what she had seen and heard. In her profile, the celebrity flies into New York from Havana, sees Marlene Dietrich, drinks great quantities of champagne, buys a coat and slippers at Abercrombie's, meets Winston Guest, goes to the Metropolitan Museum with Patrick and signs a contract with Scribner. The title and leitmotif of the piece comes from Hemingway's compulsive repetition of the meaningless phrase "How do you like it now, gentlemen?" Hemingway put on a performance for Ross, expected her to see through his act and show the highbrow readers of her magazine the man behind the rather transparent mask. Instead, she accepted the façade, repaid his generosity with meanness and established her reputation at his expense.

Though Hemingway treated the interview as a joke, assumed the role of dumb ox, and constantly spoke with wisecracks and sporting metaphors, he was not as stupid and boorish as Ross' account suggested. She never recorded or revealed the serious and sensitive side of his character, and chose to portray him as a boring braggart who keeps punching himself in the stomach. She did demonstrate, however, that he had followed a descending path—characteristic of successful American novelists—from the charm and discomfort of the Paris flat above the sawmill in the early 1920s to the luxury and snobbery of the grand hotels of Venice in the late 1940s.

The American emphasis on immediate success, the idea of art as a competitive business and the gladiatorial concept of the writer encouraged Hemingway to view literature as a kind of boxing match: an aggressive struggle in which writers were pitted against each other to see who came out on top. He first expressed this idea as early as "Monologue to the Maestro" (October 1935), where he stressed the importance of originality and the need for modern writers to match their work against the finest literature of the past: "What a writer in our time has to do is to write what hasn't been written before or beat dead men at what they have done. The only way he can tell how he is going is to compete with dead men." This quite reasonable idea became more vulgar and debased with each repetition. In a combative letter to Faulkner in July 1947, he foreshadowed his interview with Ross and exclaimed: "You should always write your best against dead writers

. . . and beat them one by one. Why do you want to fight Dostoyevsky in your first fight? Beat Turgenieff—which we both did soundly. . . . Then nail yourself DeMaupassant. . . . Then try and take Stendhal. . . . You and I can both beat Flaubert who is our most respected, honored master." And he confessed to Charles Scribner, two years later (and two months before he met Ross in New York): "Am a man without any ambition, except to be champion of the world, [but] I wouldn't fight Dr. Tolstoi in a 20 round bout because I know he would knock my ears off."[20]

Hemingway's vainglorious boast, recorded by Ross, began with a handsome compliment to the Slavic slugger, but provoked disastrous retaliation from reviewers and seriously damaged his own reputation:

> Book start slow, then increase in pace till becomes impossible to stand. . . . I started out very quiet and I beat Mr. Turgenev. Then I trained hard and I beat Mr. de Maupassant. I've fought two draws with Mr. Stendhal, and I think I had the edge in the last one. But nobody's going to get me in any ring with Mr. Tolstoy unless I'm crazy or I keep getting better.[21]

The statement seemed even more absurd since Hemingway was clearly getting worse. In October 1950, a few months after the self-parodic interview and a month after the publication of the novel, *The New Yorker* also published E. B. White's witty send-up, "Across the Street and into the Grill." Most critics, who seemed convinced that Hemingway had become too simple-minded to write a good book, accepted his pugilistic challenge and compared his work unfavorably with that of the nineteenth-century masters.

The defensive, disingenuous tone of Ross' Preface to her profile, which she hastily published as a book just after Hemingway's death in 1961, presented a notable contrast to the text. She claimed "it was a sympathetic piece" and affected surprise when some readers "thought that in describing that personality accurately I was ridiculing or attacking it." When Irving Howe condemned her book in the *New Republic,* she unconvincingly replied: "It was a loving portrait of a great and lovable man." She had sent the Hemingways proof before publication and assumed, when they returned it with corrections, that they approved of her work. But Hotchner said that when Hemingway received Ross' proofs on the Monday of the week the essay appeared, it was too late to change anything.[22]

Hemingway was apparently taken by, but not taken in by, Lillian

Ross. Since he could not punch her in the nose, he chose—shrewdly if uncharacteristically—to ignore and forgive her attack on Mary and on Marlene Dietrich as well as on himself. Privately, however, he was "shocked and felt awful." He told a publisher: "Lillian Ross wrote a profile of me which I read, in proof, with some horror. But since she was a friend of mine and I knew that she was not writing in malice she had a right to make me seem that way if she wished."[23] But he remarked, more caustically, to Hotchner: "As for Lillian, Christ, she didn't understand anything, did she? She's a good girl who should have been practicing 'deadman's float' in the shallow water and had no business on the high dive." In distant Paris, even the waspish Alice Toklas, who had always been jealous of Hemingway's friendship with Stein, disliked Ross' "Shooting an Elephant" and expressed compassion for her old adversary: "It has strange revelations and exposures by himself and his wife—which were partially explained by Janet Flanner's telling me that he was mortally ill. . . . It is painful to know the present situation and the horror it must hold for him."[24]

IV

Hemingway also got into the ring with contemporary writers and in *Across the River* continued his running battle with Sinclair Lewis. He began the quarrel with an unpleasant article, in the *Toronto Star Weekly* of August 5, 1922, on the equestrian ineptitudes of Lewis. Lewis responded by praising Hemingway's "superb" *A Farewell to Arms* in his Nobel Prize speech of 1930. Hemingway continued to taunt the older, well-established writer—whom he clearly saw as a threatening rival—in *Green Hills of Africa*, where he flatly stated: "Sinclair Lewis is nothing." Lewis' review of that book in the *Yale Literary Magazine* was understandably testy. He suggested that Hemingway enjoyed cruelty and said the volume "tells how extremely amusing it is to shoot lots and lots of wild animals, to hear their quite-human moaning, and see them lurch off with their guts dragging." He also included a little squib on Hemingway's obscene language:

> Speak up, man! Be bravely heard
> Bawling the four-letter word!
> And wear your mind décolleté
> Like Mr. Ernest Hemingway.

Hemingway's attack on fellow writers in the African book also inspired Lewis' short parody "Literary Felonies: Obtaining Game Under False Pretensions," in the *Saturday Review of Literature* in October 1936. The battle went on with Lewis' attack in *Newsweek* on *To Have and Have Not*, "this thin screaming little book" about "boresome and cowardly degenerates."[25]

Lewis redeemed himself, however, by presenting Hemingway with the Limited Editions Club gold medal on November 26, 1941, and allowing his speech to be used as an Introduction to a handsome edition of *For Whom the Bell Tolls* the following year. Hemingway did not attend the presentation ceremony, but was desperate for praise and became furious when Scribner's failed to send a stenographer to record Lewis' speech:

> Scribner's not haveing taken it down as I requested as a favour was the most careless, shiftless and callous action I have ever met in civil life. . . .
>
> It is over and I'm fucked on that. Had driven all the way from Idaho to Arizona looking forward, like a dope, to reading it and then from Arizona here [San Antonio]. Now know I never will and that something that could have had will never have. It was the only thing connected with writing I ever wanted to keep.

The literary provocation for the vitriolic attack in *Across the River* was an ineffectual passage in Lewis' "Mr. Eglantine" (1948), which mildly satirized Hemingway's drinking, fishing, beard and preference for continental life:

> [After the first Strega] Verny and Mitzy sighed and smiled and felt good —like a Hemingway hero after the seventh beer—and they knew that in Europe there would never be a time when Americans too sensitive to cope with high schools and tarpon fishing and gum and airconditioning will not be able to find somewhere an asylum where the less-hairy Whitmans will sit together from 22:30 to 2 and tell one another how superior they are to all the Babbitts in Iowa.[26]

While Hemingway was in hospital in Padua in April 1949, Lewis subjected Mary to a three-hour diatribe in the Gritti bar and criticized Hemingway for his snobbery, meager literary production and lack of gratitude for Lewis' praise of *For Whom the Bell Tolls*. He pitied Mary for having to put up with Hemingway and left her to pay for the drinks. Hemingway, who had not said a word in print about Lewis since 1935, now took revenge.

He felt Lewis was guilty on several counts. Lewis had won the Nobel Prize, Lewis had helped him, Lewis had foreshadowed his own alcoholic and literary decline, Lewis had a bad complexion which recalled his own unsightly skin disease. George Seldes, who admired Lewis, described him as the ugliest man he ever knew. Lewis suffered from skin cancer, which had to be burned off every few months by cobalt treatments and his raw, red skin had horrible pockmarks coated with white pus. Hemingway focused on Lewis' ugliness, as he would later do with Ford and Wyndham Lewis in *A Moveable Feast.* In the novel, Cantwell spots the unnamed Lewis in the Gritti bar and describes his thin ferret features and ghastly skin craters as looking "like Goebbels' face, if Herr Goebbels had ever been in a plane that burned, and not been able to bail out before the fire reached him."[27] Lewis, bitterly hurt and angered by Hemingway's cruelest passage, died three months after the novel was published.

Hemingway's manic reaction to James Jones' *From Here to Eternity* (1951) was also inspired by profound insecurity about his own literary stature and revealed how deeply wounded he had been by the critical judgments of *Across the River.* His fear of younger literary rivals who challenged him by writing about World War Two was deep-rooted. He was furious because Jones used his name in the novel without permission, received more publicity from Scribner's and had better reviews from the critics. He felt—rather unfairly—that Jones complained too much about conditions in the army, lacked real combat experience, was a psychological weakling and a physical coward. He despised Jones' admission that "he went over the hill" in 1944 when others, like Hemingway, were fighting and dying, and believed the "book will do great damage to our country" by encouraging weakness and lowering moral standards. Hemingway's letter to Scribner employed his most pathological imagery and was even more vituperative than his attack on Sinclair Lewis:

> Probably I should re-read it again to give you a truer answer. But I do not have to eat an entire bowl of scabs to know they are scabs; nor suck a boil to know it is a boil; nor swim through a river of snot to know it is snot. I hope he kills himself as soon as it does not damage his or your sales. If you give him a literary tea you might ask him to drain a bucket of snot and then suck the pus out of a dead nigger's ear.[28]

V

The biographical details revealed by Cowley and Ross encouraged critics to abolish the subtle distinction between hero and author. They equated Cantwell with the popular image of Hemingway, and felt emboldened to expose his personal and artistic weaknesses by exposing his hero. But he was well aware of the radical defects of his fictional character. Though Hemingway revealed more of himself than he perhaps intended, he deliberately created and controlled a negative but essentially sympathetic hero who repeatedly confesses his own failure. The novel presents a partial self-portrait and a scathing analysis of his own character, rather than a pitiful expression of self-indulgent egoism. As Edmund Wilson later wrote of *Islands in the Stream:* "here is Hemingway making an effort to deal candidly with the discords of his own personality—his fears, which he has tried to suppress, his mistakes, which he has tried to justify, the pangs of bad conscience, which he has brazened out."[29]

Cantwell shares many characteristics of Hemingway's heroes. He moves on familiar terrain and recalls his past life to purge his bitterness. Wounded and defensive, he tries to control every aspect of his existence and walks with a slightly exaggerated confidence. Like the much-admired Santiago in *The Old Man and the Sea,* he exudes expertise and conveys to a devoted novice inside knowledge about everything from opening wine to cutting clams. His pride in trivial expertise is a feeble compensation for his overwhelming sense of professional failure. He has a desperate and rather pathetic desire to be liked and admired, and to be constantly reassured that he is liked and admired.

The relationship of Othello and Desdemona (specifically mentioned in the novel) is vital to an understanding of Cantwell and Renata:

> She loved me for the dangers I had pass'd,
> And I loved her that she did pity them.

The allusion to Othello—an unsuitable soldier-husband for a Venetian noblewoman—suggests that Cantwell was also meant to be seen and judged from the less critical, more sympathetic viewpoint of the innocent, hero-worshipping Renata, that his mode of speech in the novel is confessional. Renata allows and encourages Cantwell to explore himself and to teach her during the last days of his life, functioning as an interlocutor and extension of her lover rather than as an independent and substantial being. Cantwell frequently admits that his conversation about military matters is boring—to himself as well as others—but he cannot stop confessing to such a sensitive and compassionate listener: a countess who serves as a priest. Cantwell's recital of his faults continues throughout the novel. Like Hemingway, he blames others for his own failure and seems more concerned about his demotion than about his slain soldiers. He is a shit, a mean son of a bitch, a brusque and brutal bastard; he exhibits a wild-boar truculence and loves his enemies more than his friends. Like all Hemingway's later heroes, Cantwell is doomed to defeat and death. But his relations with Renata suggest the possibility of a romantic and rejuvenating love. The portrayal of the way Cantwell defies despair and chooses to spend the last days of his life, of his progress toward and preparation for death, is a significant if hedonistic contribution to the *ars moriendi* tradition.

Across the River presents a montage of Hemingway's experiences in both wars, a mixture of recent memories and distant recollections of the same locale. Hemingway liked to draw parallels between the life of the novelist and that of the soldier. Cantwell's confession of failure, his revelation of a certain hollowness at the core, his demotion from the highest rank, was perhaps Hemingway's admission of disappointment with his own novel and of his declining powers after an impressive career. Hemingway's failure is manifest in the contrast between his objective and finely controlled presentation of dramatic scenes that revealed the thoughts and feelings of the characters in his early fiction, and his subjective and self-indulgent statement of personal opinion and sentimental desires in his late work. In his art, as opposed to his life, he conceded defeat and could no longer take on Mr. Turgenev, Mr. de Maupassant and Mr. Stendhal.

VI

Across the River alludes to Hemingway's experience in war, expresses his own sense of failure and his confrontation with death, but it is much more than a long autobiographical reverie. For the veteran soldier embittered by the betrayal of his superiors is carefully modeled on the military experience of his close friend Chink Dorman-Smith. Though they had been out of touch for fifteen years, Hemingway (well read in military history) kept an eye on his friend's progress and proudly told Hadley in 1939: "Old Chink is one of the biggest big shots on the British General Staff now and is the author of The Future of Infantry."[30] In 1947, Hemingway promoted Chink (who retired as a major general in 1944) and told Lanham that he had been reading *Operation Victory* by Major General Sir Francis de Guingand. He had just discovered that his best friend in the Great War, Lieutenant General Eric Edward Dorman-Smith, had been busted by de Guingand when he was Auchinleck's chief of staff, just before Montgomery took over. Chink was the most intelligent soldier he had ever known until he met Lanham.[31] Though de Guingand did not actually "bust" Dorman-Smith, it is significant that Hemingway knew what had happened to Chink two years before he began the novel.

In April 1950—just before Hemingway read proofs of *Across the River*—Chink, while on a visit to New York, went to Scribner's, got Hemingway's address and met him at the Sherry Netherland hotel. Chink wryly recalled that Hemingway "was large, grey bearded, husky voiced, successful. There was not much left of the boy I'd known. Also, replacing beer, were two bottles of champagne on ice." Hemingway then heard the full story of his friend's tragic career. He wrote to Chink for the next five years, invited him to visit Cuba and urged him to take up residence on the island. Hemingway's letter to Lanham of April 15, 1950, expressed his view that Chink would have had Montgomery's job if there were any justice in the world; it correctly shifted the blame from de Guingand to Churchill (but retained Chink's elevated rank) and provided a useful gloss on his own fictional references to Monty:

> He went on to be a Lieut. Gen. (British) and Auchinleck's chief of staff in the desert. He was to have the 8th Army but Churchill put in Monty (that Prince among Men). This boy, Chink, now Lieut. Gen. Retired, told me the whole story, not the whole but the basic, of what happened and it was clear, anyway to me, that they had Rommel beaten when he could not take Alexandria and they were just recuperating and getting ready to run him out on a cheap basis when in comes Monty with his 14/1 or I won't move concept of war.[32]

In the Hotel Gritti bar, Cantwell orders "Two very dry martinis. . . . Montgomerys. Fifteen to one" (the ratio is raised from the letter to the novel). This punning request alludes not only to the extreme proportions of gin to vermouth and to Monty's campaigns in the desert, but also to the General's need for overwhelming superiority before he would risk confrontation with the enemy. Cantwell then tells Renata:

> "Monty was a character who needed fifteen to one to move, and then moved tardily."
> "I always supposed he was a great General."
> "He was not," the Colonel said. "The worst part was he knew it. I have seen him come into a hotel and change from his proper uniform into a crowd-catching kit to go out in the evening to animate the populace." . . .
> "But he beat General Rommel."
> "Yes. And you don't think any one else had softened him up?"[33]

Cantwell admits that he criticizes the universally admired heroes of the war, Generals Patton, Montgomery and Leclerc, because "I have failed and I speak badly of all who have succeeded." Hemingway deleted a passage that severely criticized the great distance between Eisenhower's headquarters and the fighting at the front, but told Jonathan Cape that if Cantwell ever called Monty a shit, he could alter it to a complete shit.[34]

The apparently gratuitous references to Monty are actually central to the meaning of the novel. For the fascinating story of how Chink "softened up" Rommel explains why Hemingway denigrated Monty's achievement, attacked him in the novel for sartorial showmanship and criticized him for delaying the capture of Paris by his inability to close the gap at Falaise during the reconquest of Normandy in the summer of 1944.[35] Chink's story also makes clear why Cantwell was demoted from major general to brigadier to colonel.

Correlli Barnett gave a detailed appraisal of Chink's career in *The Desert Generals*:

> His is a strange story: up to 1942 regarded as among the most brilliant and erudite staff officers in the British Army, he sank after the Cairo Purge into professional obscurity [because he forgot to conceal his brilliance or tolerate the mediocrity around him]. . . .
> While there was no question about Dorman-Smith's able mind and profound military knowledge, there was a darker side to his career, adumbrating professional extinction should he ever once fall from grace. He had had an astonishing run of quick promotion [from captain to brigadier in ten years]. He wore his brilliance openly on his sleeve. He was a theoretician and a perfectionist; he did not always understand

how to handle the common clay of mankind. He could not and would not compromise in the comfortable British way. In his career he created much admiration, many special friendships, but also a general fund of ill-will among the hidebound, the slow and the "Establishment."[36]

B. H. Liddell Hart, the leading British military theoretician and historian of the century, clarified (in his obituary of Chink) why Hemingway —who admired courage, intellect and imagination—was so impressed by this "forceful, outspoken and quick-witted personality" when they first met in 1918 and why he so eagerly renewed their friendship in 1950. Chink "was one of the most brilliant soldiers that the British Army has produced in modern times. . . . He had such a flow of ideas, combined with a caustic tongue, that it was often imagined that he was essentially a staff officer and theorist rather than a commander. That widely held view was mistaken."[37]

Chink's downfall came just after he had conceived the plan that met Rommel's final challenge at the first battle of Alamein in July 1942, achieved a spectacular victory, turned the tide against the Germans in North Africa and changed the entire course of the war. Envy of Chink's unusual intelligence, resentment of his rapid promotions, dislike of his arrogant manner and sharp tongue, doubts about his ability to command troops in the field and scepticism of his military theories ("brilliant but unsound") all contributed to his demotion. Chink was unfairly blamed for the disastrous mistakes of General Neil Ritchie and his subordinate commanders, which led to the defeats at Tobruk and Gazala in June 1942—though Chink had advised Auchinleck to relieve Ritchie. Ritchie's reversals, according to John Connell, "were completely outside the limits of Dorman-Smith's control or responsibility."

Winston Churchill arrived in Cairo, after an exhausting journey from England, in August 1942, just after the first battle of Alamein. Unable to reconcile himself to a long pause before the next battle, Churchill (who had not mastered the political situation but did not tolerate contradiction) was determined to force Auchinleck into a premature offensive that would compensate for the past defeats in North Africa and save his political career.[38] The two victorious generals, wrote Connell, took him to the spartan operations caravan that served as their headquarters:

The Prime Minister gazed intently at the wall map, thrusting his thumb and fingers across it as if they were battle-tested formations. "Attack,

attack," he demanded. . . . Auchinleck explained his reasons for not putting a fresh, unacclimatized division, untrained in desert warfare, straight into the field.

The Prime Minister's mood darkened. Auchinleck was adamant. Churchill rounded on Dorman-Smith, who supported his Chief. Because these two officers acted as they did that morning, a division was not squandered and many men's lives were saved, but they set the seal on their own professional doom.[39]

In a holograph note on the endpaper of his copy of J. A. I. Agar-Hamilton and L. C. F. Turner's *Crisis in the Desert, May–July 1942*, published in 1952 (and now owned by Chink's son), Chink defended himself and wrote: "General Auchinleck and his assistant General Dorman-Smith . . . as well as General Corbett, the C.G.S. Middle East, were all dismissed on the 6th August by the Prime Minister as scapegoats, and their careers ruined. It is an odd quirk of history that those responsible for these disasters [Whiteley and Ritchie at Tobruk and Gazala] went unpunished, while those who retrieved them were punished with the utmost severity." And Chink explained his reaction in a letter to Liddell Hart of October 5, 1942: "I was and am angry, for Auchinleck has been treated shamefully and the state has not profited at all by the transaction. We have merely lost one general capable (like Rommel) of learning from his mistakes and besides the one staff officer [Chink] who would see that he didn't forget his lessons. A super victory for the forces of reaction."[40]

Churchill, who was willing to sacrifice men for an immediate victory, later quoted and tried to justify in his war memoirs, *The Hinge of Fate*, his extraordinary decision to relieve commanding generals after a decisive victory on the battlefield: "I have no doubt the changes will impart a new and vigorous impulse to the Army and restore confidence in the Command, which I regret does not exist at the present time." Chink, outraged at the suggestion of defeatism, sued for libel and forced Churchill (who feared he would lose the suit in the Irish courts) to retract his assertion and to exonerate Chink in the later editions of his memoirs: "My latter remarks are [not] to be taken as imputing personal blame to any individual. . . . Major-General Dorman-Smith . . . bears no responsibility for the fall of Tobruk or the defeats at Gazala."[41]

Chink's career, nevertheless, was destroyed. He was unjustly blamed for the defeat at Gazala and did not receive credit for the victory at Alamein. After the Cairo purge, Barnett observed, his "fall was final. . . . All those in the army who bore him ill-will, who had never forgiven him his brilliance and unorthodoxy, saw to that. On reaching London he was reduced to colonel's rank"[42] and given command of a Welsh infantry brigade in Kent. But in March 1944 he was relieved of this command and sent to Italy to avoid embarrassment when Ritchie (who had been defeated in the desert and was junior to Chink, but retained the rank of major general), took command of the XII Corps in Wales.

Chink regained the rank of brigadier and successfully commanded a brigade, after the landings at Anzio, during the attack on the well-fortified Acquabona Ridge in June 1944.[43] But after an adverse report (which Chink fiercely disputed) stated that he did not have the confidence of his commanding officers, he became embittered and retired at his own request in November 1944, in the midst of the war, at the age of forty-nine.

Chink's younger brother, Sir Reginald Dorman-Smith, always believed that Chink ran into Churchill in Rome in August 1944, immediately "picked a fight" and recklessly but characteristically told the prime minister exactly what he thought of him. He had unjustly lost three commands—in Egypt, England and Italy—and may have felt that the situation was hopeless with Churchill against him and that he had nothing more to lose in this personal confrontation.[44]

Francis de Guingand, who had changed his mind about the volatile and vulnerable Chink, convincingly concluded:

> "Chink" made a definite contribution in helping Auchinleck to stem the tide at Alamein, although in certain other directions he was apt to cause friction and disharmony. Whatever weakness Dorman-Smith may have had, I consider that it was hardly fair to lay at his feet many of the Eighth Army's shortcomings. He was certainly ambitious, perhaps too much so, but this is not an unusual trait amongst able men. . . .
>
> There is no doubt that an unnecessary and vicious vendetta was waged against him by the Army hierarchy. From being on the point of being made a Lieut.-General and V.C.G.S. [Vice-Chief of the General Staff] in Cairo he was demoted overnight to a Brigadier.[45]

The final irony—as Connell, Barnett, R. W. Thompson and Roger Parkinson state—was that Chink's battle plan of July 27, 1942, "Appreciation of the Situation in the Western Desert" (printed as an Appendix to Barnett's book), was adopted by Montgomery and provided the "blueprint" for his first success in North Africa at the battle of Alam Halfa in September 1942. Liddell Hart confirmed this point and wrote that Montgomery delayed the attack against Rommel for an even longer period than Auchinleck and Chink had recommended: "No radical change was made in the defence that had been designed by Dorman-Smith and approved by Auchinleck while he was still in command, [though] after the battle was won it was widely reported that the plan was completely recast [by Montgomery]. . . . The ironical result of these changes [in command] was that the resumption of the British offensive was put off to a much later date than Auchinleck had proposed. For the impatient Prime Minister had to give way to Montgomery's firm determination to wait until preparations and training were completed."[46]

Hemingway's Colonel Cantwell is obsessed by his humiliating demotion and mentions it at least six times in *Across the River*. His degradation explains his cruel and bitter character, which even the redemptive love of Renata cannot assuage. Cantwell fought against Rommel in World War One just as Chink did in World War Two. (Rommel praised the effectiveness of Chink's battle plans in his memoirs.[47]) Cantwell lost his regiment (a disaster hinted at but not revealed until the end of the novel) because he was forced by politics and publicity to follow impossible orders: "The order is to take it by assault. It's important because it got into the newspapers. You have to take it. 'So you leave one company dead along a draw. You lose one company complete and you destroy three others. The tanks get smacked even as fast as they could move and they could move fast both ways.' . . . 'It was a beautiful regiment until I destroyed it under other people's orders.' " But Chink lost his promotion by *refusing* to follow Churchill's impossible orders to attack with untrained men and saved the lives of soldiers at the cost of his own career.

Hemingway makes a direct allusion to his old comrade when Cantwell caustically observes: "After a man gets one star, or more, the truth becomes as difficult for him to attain as the Holy Grail was in our ancestors' time. . . . If I had lied as others lied, I would have been a three-star general."[48] For Thompson remarks that when Auchinleck was offered another post in the Middle East, Dorman-Smith, who was not careful about his own career, "reported to his chief that the new [Persia-Iraq] command was unsound and unworkable, and advised very strongly against it, though Auchinleck's acceptance would have meant Dorman-Smith's promotion to Lieutenant-General."[49]

Hemingway sent Chink proofs of *Across the River* before it was published and felt confident that his old friend would understand its more subtle meaning: "It's about Venice and it seems very simple unless you know what it is all about. It is really about bitterness, soldiering, honour, love and death." Chink, who must have felt gratified and proud, confirmed the novel's military accuracy and praised the book. "Had a letter from the Gen. in Ireland (Bellamont Forest)," Hemingway told Charles Scribner, "who has now read it three times with his lady wife. He says he now knows it is the best thing I've written."

Hemingway tried to console and justify Chink in his last letter, as he had done in his novel, and reached the same conclusion as the military historians: "Your having brains and being a fighting man would always be suspect in your Army. I have never known a fighting man with a good brain to ever come to any good end." An understanding of Chink's role in *Across the River* reveals that Cantwell's confessional mode and his regret that he is "no longer of any real use to the Army"[50] represented Hemingway's vicarious attempt to express and purge Chink's bitterness and his betrayal.

23

Death in the Family
1951–1953

> The smallest boy . . . had a dark side to
> him that nobody but Thomas Hudson
> could ever understand. . . . They recog-
> nized it in each other and knew it was
> bad.
>
> *Islands in the Stream*

I

In March 1952 Hemingway summarized the sequence of deaths that
had depressed and distracted him during the previous year. He spoke
of himself as

> some one who is trying to keep his peace of mind and work well with,
> in one year, the death of his first grand-son in Berlin where his son was
> stationed as a Capt. of Infantry; the death of his mother; serious illness
> of his father-in-law with cancer; death of his former wife and mother of
> two of his sons; suicide of the maid servant of this house (one previous
> attempt); had kept her on and tried to pull her out of it; then last the
> death of my last old friend in Africa and then the death of my very dear
> friend and publisher Charlie Scribner. All this time I have tried to work
> steadily and well.

In Oak Park hospital, Grace Hemingway banged her head when
mishandled by an attendant, lost her memory and did not even recognize Sunny during her last visit in 1951. Hemingway, who kept a safe
distance from Grace and Oak Park, had not seen her for twenty years.
He clung to the myth that she hated him and had been responsible for
his father's death, and remained resolutely hostile. As he told Scribner
in August 1949:

478

My mother is very old, her memory is more than spotty and she is addicted to fantastic statements. Lately, because she is so old, I have played the role of a devoted son in case it pleased her. But I hate her guts and she hates mine. She forced my father to suicide and, one time, later, when I ordered her to sell worthless [Florida] properties that were eating her up with taxes, she wrote, "Never threaten me with what to do. Your father tried that once when we were first married and he lived to regret it."[1]

Grace died at the age of seventy-nine on June 28, 1951, and Hemingway did not attend her funeral. He probably felt more relief than remorse, and was glad that he no longer had to support the old lady.

The death of Pauline on October 1 had more serious consequences, and led to a quarrel with Gregory that caused estrangement and great bitterness on both sides. Mario Menocal, Jr., noted that as a boy "Gregory was a real character and a charmer, delightful company for everyone. . . . Until around 1945 [or later], Gigi was the acknowledged hero, the star." Gregory confirmed that he was the most promising child, the one whose character most resembled Hemingway's, the favorite son before the fall. He had always seen others blamed by his father, but until Pauline's death *he* had never been blamed for anything.[2]

Gregory had had a destructive governess and a troubled childhood. As early as 1941, two years after Hemingway left Pauline, he told her that Gregory had "the biggest dark side in the family except me." And in *Islands in the Stream,* where Gregory appears as Andy, Hemingway wrote:

> "The meanest is Andy."
> "He started out mean," Thomas Hudson said.
> "And boy, did he continue." . . .
> There was something about him that you could not trust.[3]

Hemingway sensed that Gregory had problems, but refused to recognize or take responsibility for them.

In 1942 the ten-year-old Gregory had tied for first place in the pigeon-shooting contest in Havana; and he had been a good student at Canterbury School in Connecticut. During a fishing expedition in June 1949, Elicio Arguelles saw Gregory walking alone on the beach, holding his head in his hands. He was having an appendicitis attack and was in great pain. They radioed a coast guard cutter to pick him up and he was saved by an emergency operation. The following year, after completing his freshman course at St. John's College in Annapolis, he dropped out of school, refused psychotherapy, was attracted to the cult of dianetics and experimented with drugs. Early in 1951 (when Adriana was visiting the Finca), Gregory brought home a girl whom his father disliked and took savage pleasure in describing as an outsized concubine his son had found, floating belly up, in the Levant. He also boasted of brutally breaking up Gregory's affair with his previous girl.[4] Later that year Gregory moved to California, worked as an aircraft mechanic and married his first wife, Jane, against his father's wishes.

Ever since his father's suicide, Hemingway had associated telegrams and telephones with bad news. In 1932 he told the editor of *Cosmopolitan:* "Your goddamned long distance phone calls get me spooked—each time I think somebody is dead or I'm indicted." In September 1951 Gregory got into serious trouble, which shocked and outraged Hemingway, and was arrested in Los Angeles. Pauline, who was in San Francisco, was anxious to keep the Hemingway name out of the newspapers as well as to cure Gregory's disturbance. On the evening of September 30, Pauline called Hemingway from Jinny's house in Los Angeles to tell him what had happened. They quarreled bitterly when Hemingway blamed her and said: "see how you've brought him up!" Soon Pauline "was shouting into the phone and sobbing uncontrollably." At 1 A.M. she awoke with severe abdominal pain and internal bleeding. At noon on October 1 Hemingway received a cable from Jinny saying that Pauline, who was fifty-six, had died on the operating table of St. Vincent's Hospital.

In February 1952, four months after the funeral, Gregory took his new wife to meet his father. Hemingway could no longer blame Pauline for Gregory's problems and may have wanted to sever relations with his son. He shocked and horrified Gregory by saying that his trouble in California had killed Pauline—and they never met again. When Gregory entered the University of Miami Medical School, after attending UCLA, he learned from her autopsy report that Pauline had died of a rare tumor of the adrenal gland (near the kidney), which could fire off and malfunction in times of emotional stress. Gregory then concluded:

> It was not my minor troubles that had upset Mother but his brutal phone conversation with her eight hours before she died. The tumor had become necrotic or rotten and when it fired off that night, it sent her blood pressure sky-rocketing; a medium-sized blood vessel . . . had

ruptured. Then the tumor stopped discharging adrenaline, her blood pressure dropped from about 300 to 0, and she died of shock on the operating table.[5]

Pauline's death, in contrast to Grace's, had a profound emotional impact on Hemingway. The day after he heard the news, he confessed to Scribner (in an elaborate sea metaphor) that he could no longer dam up his feelings for her: "The wave of remembering has finally risen so that it has broken over the jetty that I built to protect the open road-stead of my heart and I have the full sorrow of Pauline's death with all the harbour scum of what caused it. I loved her very much for many years and the hell with her faults." But in 1959, when Tennessee Williams, who had known Pauline in Key West, asked about her death, Hemingway replied, with an odd mixture of banality, bitterness and wit: "She died like everyone else . . . and after that she was dead."[6] After Pauline's death, the Key West house reverted to Hemingway and her sons inherited her fortune. (In September 1951 he gave Jack $1,900 and Patrick $500 of his German royalties; in February 1952, he cancelled his payment to Gregory of $100 a month.) Gregory felt guilty about the inheritance from his mother, spent it quickly on expensive safaris and killed eighteen African elephants in one month.

Partly as a result of Hemingway's brutal accusation, Gregory had a very difficult time in the 1950s. He was discharged from the army, drank heavily, could not hold a job. He hunted in Kenya for several years, but never got a professional license. He had four children from two broken marriages. His second wife had mental problems; when they got divorced in 1966, Leicester brought up Gregory's two sons. After their irrevocable quarrel in 1952, Gregory wrote many angry and abusive letters in which he threatened to beat Hemingway, called him an ailing alcoholic, said *The Old Man and the Sea* "was as sickly a bucket of sentimental slop as was ever scrubbed off the bar-room floor" and predicted that he would never write again. In 1957, like Patrick a decade earlier, Gregory had electric shock treatments.[7]

Hemingway said equally harsh things in bursts of rage that recurred in his unpublished letters of the 1950s: that Gregory was always strange, an exploded firecracker, worthless, no good, ruined by money, a macabre and mercenary mixture of Charles Addams and the National City Bank, an absolute pathological shit, a son he would like to see hanged.

Gregory's memoir, *Papa*— which begins: "I never got over a sense of responsibility for my father's death"—is the most agonizing of all the portrayals of Hemingway. Gregory's case history expresses a sense of tragic betrayal and makes a cruel judgment on the god that failed. He contrasts the heroic father of his childhood with the bully, sick bore and professional celebrity whose drunken revels with sycophants during the last decade of his life "merely anaesthetized the pain which had accompanied the loss of his talent." Since Gregory never saw his father after their quarrel in 1952, his portrayal of the overbearing megalomaniac is not convincing. "It's fine to be under the influence of a dominating personality as long as he's healthy," though Gregory did not seem to like it even then, "but when he gets dry rot of the soul, how do you bring yourself to tell him he stinks?"[8]

A number of familiar patterns emerged from the most searing and anguished quarrel of Hemingway's life. He refused to recognize Gregory's emotional problems as he had previously refused to recognize Patrick's. He blamed Gregory for Pauline's death as he had blamed Grace for Ed's suicide. He was willing—indeed eager—to burden Gregory with his own guilt and did not worry about the effect this would have on the vulnerable young man. Self-justification was always more important to him than friends, wives and children. He was shocked when Gregory rejected his accusation and fought back, though it took his son more than a decade to free himself from guilt. After his quarrel with Gregory, as with his sister Carol, he cut him off completely and never saw him again. As with Martha, the persistent vilification of Gregory in his letters merely emphasized how much Hemingway had loved his son.

Gregory, like Leicester, tried desperately and failed to please Hemingway. As Leicester's first wife observed: "Gregory is another one who wanted to emulate Ernest and fell short. He could never seem to get Ernest's approval and that's what he craved the most. Ernest wouldn't take him seriously." Gregory felt profound relief at his father's funeral and remorsefully wrote: "I couldn't disappoint him, couldn't hurt him [or be hurt by him] anymore."[9]

II

After a fallow decade in the 1940s, which produced the unfinished *Garden of Eden* and the unsuccessful *Across the River,* Hemingway wrote as much in the 1950s as he had in the 1930s—though his later work was distinctly inferior (and most of it remained unpublished until after his death): *Islands in the Stream, The Old Man and the Sea,* the "African Journal," the "Dangerous Summer" articles and *A Moveable Feast.* Until 1940 his books concerned his current experience; after 1941 his works began to lose their immediacy.

Islands in the Stream, begun in 1946–47 and abandoned (after *Across the River*) in 1950–51, was the "Sea" book in the projected war trilogy. (The sections on the Air with the RAF in England and on the Land with the 22nd Infantry in Europe were neither planned nor written.) It is a transitional novel that connects his past and future work. It returns to the boat and barroom milieu of *To Have and Have Not,* describes violent maritime action and has a loose tripartite structure. Like the Key West novel, it is artistically weak but autobiographically interesting. It is the only novel about the destruction of his family, and illuminates his loneliness, emptiness and anguish.

Like *Across the River,* the novel is a futile attempt to write a book about World War Two that would equal *A Farewell to Arms* and *For Whom the Bell Tolls. Islands in the Stream* portrays his love for Hadley just as *Across the River* does for Adriana. Hudson, like Cantwell, is insensitive, embittered and arrogant. *Islands in the Stream* idealizes his relations with his sons (who were then too young to challenge him) just as *A Moveable Feast* idealizes his relations with his first wife. Memories of Joyce, Ford, Pound and Pascin, the association of poverty with purity and wealth with corruption, also foreshadow *A Moveable Feast.*

In *Islands in the Stream* Hemingway scarcely bothers to transform the events of his life. Hudson paints with the same dull realism that Hemingway now uses in his writing. He remembers a canvas of bathers by Cézanne, rejects the original style and wants to have it repainted by the American realist Thomas Eakins. Part I, "Bimini," which takes place in 1936, accurately portrays Jack, Patrick and Gregory, but sentimentalizes the love and loss of his sons. The shark attack on Gregory in the Gulf Stream in the early 1940s inspired the scene where Hudson rescues David (Patrick), his best-loved son, from an attack by a hammerhead shark; and the car accident that kills the boys is (as we have seen) based on their accidents in Havana and Key West. David's bloody struggle and loss of the great marlin is an adolescent anticipation of Santiago's struggle in *The Old Man and the Sea.*

Part II, "Cuba," takes place in the early 1940s and describes the ceiba tree in front of the Finca; Hemingway's paintings by Gris, Klee and Masson; his raw onion sandwiches; his insomnia; Boise and numerous other cats; his bitch of a third wife, who is reporting the Pacific war; his tedious chat with the barman and barflies at the Floridita. There are also sexual fantasies about sleeping with his friend's wife on a ship, with three Chinese whores in Hong Kong and with his actress-wife (based on Marlene Dietrich), who returns to the island for a brief encounter. In his imagination, Hemingway sleeps with the Kraut and kills the Krauts. Part III, "At Sea," based on the sub-hunting expeditions, dramatizes the chasing and killing of Germans from a sunken submarine, who have massacred the inhabitants of a remote key. Hudson, like Robert Jordan, seems to be fatally wounded.

Hemingway never completed *Islands in the Stream* and kept it in a bank vault during the last decade of his life. He was aware of its faults and realized it was more therapeutic than artistic. Long excerpts from Parts I and II appeared in *Esquire* (1970) and *Cosmopolitan* (1971); the final version was edited by Carlos Baker and Mary Hemingway. The novel, which came out in October 1970, was a Book-of-the-Month Club selection, sold 100,000 copies in the first three months and remained on the best-seller list for half a year. After Hotchner's widely read revelations about Papa (1966) and Baker's biography (1969), the public was eager for Hemingway's work. Just as *A Moveable Feast* portrays the most promising period of his life, so *Islands in the Stream* depicts the most depressing. The novel was inevitably read with the knowledge that the author had killed himself.

The critics of this deeply flawed and at times preposterous book were essentially sympathetic and slightly uneasy, as if they regretted their inability to praise the final work of an acknowledged master. There was no concurrence about which part of the novel was best or worst, but they agreed that the main faults were the same ones that had plagued Hemingway since 1940: a self-indulgent rather than disciplined attitude to art, an excessive display of vanity and self-pity, a weak structure (the islands remained separate rather than attached to the mainland of the novel), a lack of aesthetic distance between author and protagonist, an inability to create a reflective character, a tendency to try to act out his fantasies instead of portraying them in his novels.

III

The artistic impulse that inspired *Across the River* and *Islands in the Stream* continued with *The Old Man and the Sea*, which Hemingway completed on February 17, 1951, eleven days after Adriana left Cuba. He counted on the new book—*Moby Dick* for the masses—to recover his reputation after the disastrous reviews of *Across the River* and told Wallace Meyer, who had replaced Perkins at Scribner's:

> Tactically, publishing it now will get rid of the school of criticism that I am through as a writer. It will destroy the school of criticism that claims I can write about nothing except myself and my own experiences. . . . I am tired of not publishing anything. Other writers publish short books. But I am supposed to always lay back and come in with War and Peace or Crime and Punishment or be considered a bum.

Hemingway had a long history of well-justified quarrels with Jonathan Cape that led to an explosion about *The Old Man and the Sea*. Cape had bowdlerized the text of the English edition of *In Our Time*, had changed words and made deletions in *Death in the Afternoon*. Hemingway became "sick with dismay" when Cape's designers confused the marlin in the story with a tuna fish and produced a revolting dust wrapper. He called the jacket of *The Old Man and the Sea* ridiculous and sickening, more suitable for a comic book than a serious novel, and told Cape he could not have done a more effective job if he had *tried* to destroy the book.[10] Cape compounded the felony by undercutting the price of the American edition in foreign markets.

Nevertheless, the novella, whose stark simplicity eliminated the obvious faults of *Across the River,* was phenomenally successful and realized all Hemingway's hopes. He dedicated the book to the memory of Max Perkins and Charles Scribner. The Book-of-the-Month Club guaranteed $21,000 and ordered a first printing of 153,000 copies. *Life* paid $40,000 for serial rights, published the full 27,000-word text on September 1, 1952, and sold 5,300,000 copies in two days. A week later, Scribner's brought out the first printing of 50,000 and bookstores rushed advance copies to their customers. It remained on the best-seller list for half a year. The book is used as an English text in French, Italian, German and Japanese schools, and still earns $100,000 a year in foreign royalties.

Dos Passos' description of sharks attacking a marlin in the Gulf Stream suggests the excitement and drama that Hemingway conveyed in the book:

The fish are huge—a thousand pound tuna 800 pound sharks—600 pound marlin—We had the tuna on the line eight hours—Ernest finally brought him up, alive and almost landed when five sharks rushed him at once—They came like express trains and hit the fish like a planing mill—shearing off twenty-five and thirty pounds at a bite. Ernest shoots them with a machine gun, *rrr*—but it won't stop them—It's terrific to see the bullets ripping into them—the shark thrashing the blood and foam—the white bellies and fearful jaws—the pale cold eyes. I was really aghast but it's very exciting.

The novella is set in Cojímar (seven miles east of Havana), a low-roofed village extending along both sides of the bay, where men fished in their own small boats, with sails and oars. The boy, Manolin, is based on Manolito, the son of the café owner. Santiago, like Hemingway, has benign skin cancer; and like Gregorio Fuentes (the model, with Carlos Gutiérrez, for the old fisherman), he comes from the Canary Islands.

Hemingway had planned this book for more than fifteen years. He outlined the essence of the story, which had been told to him by his old mate Gutiérrez, in a paragraph of "On the Blue Water" which appeared in *Esquire* in April 1936:

An old man fishing alone in a skiff out of Cabañas hooked a great marlin that, on the heavy sashcord handline, pulled the skiff far out to sea. Two days later the old man was picked up by fishermen sixty miles to the eastward, the head and forward part of the marlin lashed alongside. What was left of the fish, less than half, weighed eight hundred pounds. The old man had stayed with him a day, a night, a day and another night while the fish swam deep and pulled the boat. When he had come up the old man had pulled the boat up on him and harpooned him. Lashed alongside the sharks had hit him and the old man had fought them out alone in the Gulf Stream in a skiff, clubbing them, stabbing at them, lunging at them with an oar until he was exhausted and the sharks had eaten all that they could hold. He was crying in the boat when the fishermen picked him up, half crazy from his loss, and the sharks were still circling the boat.[11]

Most critics—forced to make a *volte-face* after pronouncing the writer dead—fell over each other in praising the work. Most of them shared the enthusiasm of Bernard Berenson, who exclaimed, in the kind of public pronouncement that the great are called upon to make: "Hemingway's *The Old Man and the Sea* is an idyll of the sea as sea, as un-Byronic and un-Melvillian as Homer himself, and communicated in a prose as calm and compelling as Homer's verse. No real artist symbolizes or allegorizes—and Hemingway is a real artist—but every real work of art exhales symbols and allegories. So does this short but not small masterpiece."

Cyril Connolly, who had savaged *Across the River,* compared the novella to Flaubert's "A Simple Heart," called it "the best story Hemingway has ever written" and observed: "a long physical struggle is described with the dynamic right words even as the changing qualities of the static sea are portrayed in their true colours, and the soul of the old man—humble, fearless, aromatic—is described perfectly too."[12] The English advance orders reached 20,000 copies and the fine reviews inspired sales of 2,000 a week.

"Everywhere the book is being called a classic," said the influential critic Mark Schorer, who had written an appreciative review of *For Whom the Bell Tolls.* He admired the religious theme, called the work "not only a moral fable, but a parable" and believed that "Hemingway's art, when it is art, is absolutely incomparable, and that he is unquestionably the greatest craftsman in the American novel in this century." The classical scholar Gilbert Highet noted the Conradian theme and emphasized the epic pattern rather than the religious significance: "A hero undertakes a hard task. He is scarcely equal to it because of ill luck, wounds, treachery, hesitation, or age. With a tremendous effort, he succeeds. But in his success he loses the prize itself, or final victory." Joyce Cary, responding to a questionnaire in the *New York Times Book Review,* chose the novella as his favorite book of the year: "Hemingway's old man is profoundly original. It deals with fundamentals, the origins. Its form, so elaborately contrived, is yet perfectly suited to the massive shape of a folk theme." And William Faulkner's curt, mock-humble puff agreed with Schorer, Highet and Cary, stressed Hemingway's new element of pity (as opposed to toughness) and affirmed: "His best. Time may show it to be the best single piece of any of us. I mean his and my contemporaries."[13]

After the first rave reviews, a much cooler reaction was inevitable in the more considered essays in the major quarterlies. R. W. B. Lewis, writing in the *Hudson Review,* doubted "if the book can bear the amount of critical weight already piled up on it. . . . [It] is not absolutely persuasive. . . . Our assent has to be partially withheld." He praised Hemingway, however, for perceiving "the stimulating and fatal relation between integrity of character and the churning abundance of experience. His style catches this perception with a good deal of its old power." In the most penetrating review of the book, Delmore Schwartz, who had blasted *To Have and Have Not,* clarified the reasons for the enthusiastic critical response: "there was a note of insistence in the praise and a note of relief, the relief because his previous book was extremely bad in an ominous way, and the insistence, I think, because this new work is not so much good in itself as a virtuoso performance which reminds one of Hemingway at his best."[14]

The Old Man and the Sea, like all of Hemingway's late works, is closely connected to his earlier books. Like the hero of "Big Two-Hearted River," Santiago engages in the ritual of fishing and tests his inner strength while isolated in the natural element. Hemingway's great fish, like his bull, is singled out to serve as prey; man and fish are "joined together" like the man and bull at the moment of truth. The novella has the same victory-in-defeat theme as the bullfighting story "The Undefeated" (1925), in *Men Without Women:*

> "What do you keep on doing it for?" . . .
> "I was going good. . . . I didn't have any luck. That was all."[15]

In the novella Hemingway eliminated women entirely and replaced sexual conflict with the relation of a man and a marlin. The world of war and sport was attractive to him because it removed women, his greatest source of anxiety.

"The Snows of Kilimanjaro" and *To Have and Have Not,* which were written in the 1930s and deal with the theme of corruption, were balanced by *The Old Man and the Sea* and *A Moveable Feast,* which were written in the 1950s and deal with the theme of purity. It is ironic —though understandable—that in his later works Hemingway praised Santiago's spartan life and his own early poverty while living in considerable luxury. The ravenous sharks attacking the magnificent fish were his allegorical portrayal of the critics' relation to the artist. If *Across the River* was misread and condemned for external reasons, *The Old Man and the Sea*—the last of Hemingway's books to be published in his lifetime—was clearly his most overrated work.

The novella has some strengths: a tough, modest and sympathetic hero; an epic struggle whose noble values and ironic dénouement reflect the human condition. And there are vivid details of sea, boat and fish: the subtle shift from the smell of land to the smell of ocean, the line "so taut that beads of water were jumping from it," the great fish tail as sharp as a scythe, the full air sacks along the marlin's back that prevent him from going down deep to die.

The weaknesses of *The Old Man and the Sea* are radical. There is pervasive sentimentality and self-pity: the dead wife's photograph on the wall of the lonely shack, the lack of food, the tears. Santiago has Hemingway's tendency to blame others for his own faults and condemns the sharks for eating the fish. The stoicism—which was much more subtle and restrained in Jake Barnes—has become simpleminded: "They had gone one day and one night with their elbows on a chalk line on the table" during a marathon arm-wrestling match. Ponderous banalities are dressed up as peasant wisdom: "The setting of the sun is a difficult time for all fish," "The ocean is very big and a skiff is small."

The Christian symbolism—which tends to appear in the opening and closing pages, while Santiago is on land but not at sea—is forced and obtrusive. In the beginning, he is doubted, mocked, acquires a humble disciple. At the end, he is sorely wounded, shoulders his heavy mast, staggers under the weight and falls asleep with palms up in a crucified position. The inspirational theme: "A man can be destroyed but not defeated"[16] (which recalls the simplistic thematic statement in *To Have and Have Not*), resembles the pious sermons of the Congregationalist pulpit in Oak Park. And the irony, when the tourists mistake the marlin for a shark at the end of the book, is crude and obvious.

In the highly acclaimed *Old Man and the Sea,* Hemingway either deceived himself about the profundity of his art or expressed his contempt for *Life,* Scribner's, the reading public, the critics and religion by writing an ironic and mock-serious fable that gave them exactly what they wanted and expected. The story offered moral uplift, provided a pretense of culture, was admired by everyone—and earned him a fortune. In May 1952, a month before he left for Europe and Africa, *The Old Man and the Sea* won the Pulitzer Prize that had been denied to *A Farewell to Arms* and *For Whom the Bell Tolls.*

Hemingway disliked almost all the movies based on his works. Unlike Fitzgerald, Faulkner, Dos Passos, West and Agee, he never wrote screenplays for Hollywood. But when he sold Leland Hayward the rights of *The Old Man and the Sea* and his services as technical adviser for $150,000, he became directly involved in the production of the film that was eventually released in 1958.

The screenplay was written by the novelist Peter Viertel, who also did the film script of *The Sun Also Rises* (1957)—mistakenly made in Morelia, Mexico, with Robert Evans miscast as Romero. Viertel was born in Germany in 1921 and came to California five years later. His father, Berthold, was a poet, later became director of the Vienna Stadt-theater and was portrayed in Isherwood's *Prater Violet*. His mother, Salka, wrote screenplays for Garbo's films, and had a famous salon in Los Angeles that included Thomas Mann and Bert Brecht. Viertel served in the Marines in the Pacific and met Hemingway while skiing in Sun Valley in 1946. Hemingway read and liked Viertel's first book, and suggested they collaborate on a novel based on the sub-hunting expeditions. Viertel was supposed to write the scenes aboard the German U-boat, but felt he could not portray events he had never experienced. Like Durie Shevlin, Viertel thought Hemingway well past his prime in his late forties: bloated, jowly, scarred, grubby and disfigured by skin disease. But he also found him a thoughtful, charming, amusing friend, who tried out his literary and military stories in fascinating conversations before they appeared in his books of the 1950s.

Paul Greene had done a draft of the screenplay, which Hemingway and Leland Hayward did not like; and Hemingway—who had been contractually given final say on the script—asked Viertel to try another version. Viertel wanted Santiago to go to Havana in search of work, become repelled by the city and return to catch the great fish. Hemingway wanted the film to be absolutely faithful to the book and rejected this idea. So Spencer Tracy read large chunks of the novel in a voice-over narration that represented Santiago's thoughts during his fight with the fish. When Viertel said the script was too long and suggested deletions, Hemingway argued that the passages from his novella had to stay in because they were "poetry," and added: "you don't know what it cost me to use that word."[17]

Leland Hayward—who had produced *Oklahoma!* and *South Pacific* on Broadway—was a charming gentleman, with goodwill and great empathy. Hemingway rather awed and frightened Hayward, who lacked the ruthlessness of ordinary film producers and tried to do everything to please him. Hayward authorized three expensive boats and crews to do the fishing sequences, but was forced to cancel the expedition after a month of futile filming in Peru. Hemingway considered this a personal betrayal, broke off their friendship and severed his connection with the film.

Humphrey Bogart wanted the leading role and was well suited to play the fisherman, but Tracy got the part because he had bought the rights with Hayward and was co-producer. The portly, Hibernian Tracy was a complete physical contrast to the gaunt and weatherbeaten Cuban fisherman in the novel. He had promised to lose weight; when he failed to do so, Hemingway attacked his self-indulgence, criticized his Spanish accent, said he moved awkwardly on the boat and excluded him from the story conferences. Tracy, a reformed alcoholic, got drunk, lost control and was in poor condition during the first ten days of filming.[18]

Fred Zinnemann, born in Austria in 1907, was much more cultured and intelligent than the usual Hollywood director, and had just achieved considerable success with his films *High Noon* and *From Here to Eternity*. Zinnemann met Hemingway in Havana in 1955 and was impressed by his panache and flamboyance. Though Hemingway bullied Mary, Zinnemann found him interesting and entertaining, seductively charming and larger than life.

Zinnemann was honored to work with Hemingway. He admired the poetic power of the novel, but thought the religious imagery was phony and planned to reduce it in the film. He felt the individual style of the book would be difficult to enhance, and wanted to take a documentary approach that would provide visual accompaniment to the words. Zinnemann found Hemingway helpful, encouraging, eager to get the best results and to achieve the spirit—if not always the letter—of his work. He had great insight about narrative and character development, but no technical knowledge of photography and editing.[19]

The great problem was that Zinnemann could not direct a marlin. In August 1955 they fished near Havana for a month, caught sailfish, but failed to get the huge black marlin. The biggest fish they ever filmed weighed only three hundred pounds. Mayito Menocal explained: "They did not jump, the big ones rarely do. . . . They go down deep. They don't fight very much. They're too old, I guess, and too fat."

So in April 1956, while Zinnemann shot the Cojímar scenes with Tracy, a second unit—with Hemingway, Mary, Arguelles and Gregorio —flew from Havana via Miami, Panama City and Talara to Cabo Blanco, Peru. The great thousand-pound marlin were common in the cold, dark and turbulent Humboldt Current. The crew lived for a month in a luxurious hotel on the edge of a cliff overlooking the famous fishing club, trained the Peruvian sailors for filming—and then spent ten days without even seeing a fish. Hemingway offered Arguelles ten to one that Elicio would not catch a fish on his birthday, the next day, but lost $100 and paid up. They caught big marlin, but the fish would not jump. (During the filming a cameraman boxed with Hemingway. Arguelles warned him to keep away when Hemingway was drinking, but he paid no heed and appeared the next morning with a huge black eye.) Finally, they had to abandon the quest and pay a quarter of a million dollars for Alfred Glassell's film of his world-record catch of 1,560 pounds. In the film of *The Old Man and the Sea,* a real marlin from Glassell's footage jumped in the sea. But a rubber dummy was used on the side of Santiago's boat.[20]

Warner Brothers' studio created a brilliant twenty-foot-long artificial fish, with internal motors that moved its eyes, mouth and fins, and shipped it, at enormous expense, from Los Angeles to Miami and Havana. Hemingway hated it, called it the condom-atic fish and told Viertel: "No picture with a rubber fish ever made a dime!" The first time they tried the fish out in the ocean, it immediately sank. Zinnemann, Hayward and Tracy all felt they were getting nowhere. Zinnemann, who had "a whim of iron," would not shoot the film with a rubber fish in a studio tank—and resigned. Hemingway, disappointed and upset, accepted the director's decision and promised financial support when the studio threatened to sue Zinnemann to recover the million and a half dollars they had spent on the film. Very little of the footage that Zinnemann made was used in the final version. John Sturges, who completed the work in the studio, emphasized the Christian symbolism and got the director's credit.[21]

Hemingway was bitter about the filming of *The Old Man and the Sea.* In his "Situation Report" of September 1956 he contrasted fishing in the Gulf Stream and at Cabo Blanco:

> It was different in Peru where we went to try to photograph big fish for the picture. There the wind blew day and night. Sand blew in your room from the desert that makes the coast and the doors banged shut with the wind.
>
> We fished 32 days from early morning until it was too rough to photo-

graph and the seas ran like onrushing hills with snow blowing off the tops. . . .

The marlin were large and did not fight as the fish off Cuba do. But their weight and bulk in the heavy seas made it hard work, and a fish that you would bring to gaff in eight or twelve minutes you would let run again . . . [and] have Gregorio harpoon him to try for the camera shot you needed in the picture.[22]

After several months of fishing and filming on location, he was left with a fake Santiago, a fake ocean and a fake fish.

IV

Hemingway's hostility to critics, which intensified after *Across the River* and subsided after the enthusiastic response to *The Old Man and the Sea,* flared up again during his correspondence from January 1952 to April 1953 (the year of the deaths) with two scholars who were writing studies of his work. Hemingway owned all the books about him that were published during his lifetime and sent by dutiful but trembling authors. He had helped his acquaintances Louis Cohn and Lee Samuels compile a *Bibliography* in 1931 and a *Check List* in 1951. He suppressed Lawrence Kubie's psychoanalytic essay, impeded the publication of Edmund Wilson's chapter, was annoyed by Cowley's portrait, hurt by Ross' profile and irritated by McCaffery's "unreadable" anthology. He gave valuable information to Arthur Mizener, the biographer of Fitzgerald, and then condemned his book. All these works put him on guard against biographical and psychological interpretations, which he felt could be as damaging as cancer to an artist engaged in serious work.

Hemingway had been educated by war and journalism, affected a belligerent anti-intellectual stance and was scornful of academic life. He believed the university cut people off from the reality of the outside world and limited rather than increased their understanding and knowledge. Despite his violent opposition to studies of his work, which were stimulated by Cowley's efforts to "embalm" him while he was still alive, he unwillingly cooperated with critics. He answered the letters of Philip Young of New York University and Charles Fenton of Yale, and allowed them to quote from his books. He knew studies would be written about him and thought it would be better to help the authors than to stop them (though he could have done so) and perhaps provoke an attack. He liked to talk about himself, was probably pleased and flattered at the same time that he was disturbed and irritated by their attention, and very generously put their interests before his own.

Young's theory that Hemingway's fiction was inspired by his war wound of July 1918 was not likely to appeal to the author. He "had always run as an adjusted person" and rejected the idea that his solid and substantial work was based on a marsh of trauma. Four years after Young's book appeared, he blasted the critic in a letter to Harvey Breit: "It's all trauma. Sure plenty trauma in 1918 but symptoms absent by 1928 [the year of his father's suicide]—none in Spain 37-38—none in China 40-41—None at sea, none in air, none in 155 days of combat. I suppose when [the boxer] Archie Moore loses his legs P. Young will diagnose him as a victim of trauma."

In February 1952—when Young's editor, with the help of Cowley's report, was trying to publish the book—Hemingway told Wallace Meyer that he resented young English professors rattling the skeletons in his cupboard and crawling through his private life to academic success: "[They all see] gold in them dirty sheets now. Imagine what they can do with the soiled sheets of four legal beds by the same writer and you can see why their tongues are slavering." He passionately agreed with Dr. Kubie's belated conclusion that public psychoanalysis was an invasion of privacy. When Young sent him a chapter he had read at an academic conference, Hemingway felt that Young was now doing what Kubie had tried to do. As a man who valued professional expertise, he objected to the critic's assumption that he was qualified to use psychoanalytic theory and that the evidence of the works could be used as if they were the revelations of a patient: "I thought your paper, that you so kindly sent me, was very interesting; but fairly shocking in the way three critics and their critic lightly used serious medical terms without, as far as I knew, being medically qualified to pronounce such judgments even in private."[23]

Hemingway disliked and distrusted Young's method and conclusions, and felt there were many dead authors to write about. But he very decently relented (and even returned his share of Young's permission fees) when the author and his editor explained that Young's book was being thwarted, his career threatened and his living imperiled. Since Young had acted in an honorable way, Hemingway (with Young as with

Cowley) gave in to the financial rather than the intellectual argument:

> If you give me your word that the book is not biography disguised as criticism and that it is not a psycho-analytical study of a living writer I have no objection to your quoting from my books. . . . If it means your job if not published inform Wallace Meyer at Scribners you have my formal permission to quote. Hope you're happy. . . . I'm very sorry, kid, if you are up the creek financially. I can let you have $200 if you need it and you can feel free to call me a son of a bitch if you wish.[24]

Young eroded Hemingway's patience so that Charles Fenton—a more irascible personality—had a more difficult time. He was the son of a headmaster at the Hill School, had served in the RAF, published an unsuccessful novel, taught creative writing (a red flag to Hemingway) and was completing a first-rate dissertation on the apprenticeship in Oak Park, Kansas City and Toronto from 1916 to 1923. In a letter printed in Cohn's *Bibliography* in 1931, Hemingway expressed his attitude toward his early, hastily written journalism: "If you have made your living as a newspaperman, learning your trade, writing against deadlines, writing to make stuff timely rather than permanent, no one has any right to dig this stuff up and use it against the stuff you have written to write the best you can." He repeated this belief in a letter of October 1952, stated that Fenton had no right to quote youthful work which he did not choose to reprint, compared Fenton's activities to cheating at cards or reading personal mail, warned him to stop his investigations and threatened him with serious trouble.

To his lawyer Alfred Rice, Hemingway explained that Fenton, by exposing the actual sources of his fiction, made him vulnerable to legal action:

> By naming actual people with their real names he makes it impossible for me to write fiction and by saying that so and so was such and such real person he exposes me to any amount of libel suits. He has also interfered with my privacy to an unbelievable extent. I do not know how much of the shit in [recent] articles like WHY and PAGEANT comes from him or from his colleague Philip Young.

And to Fenton, who was profiting in every sense from Hemingway's letters, he wittily explained that their correspondence would have to stop: "I average between fifty cents and a dollar a word for everything that I write and I write you letters between five hundred and fifteen hundred words long which you in-corporate in material which you sell for 2½ cents a word with a royalty deal over 100,000 copies sold. Mr. Fenton I hope you will agree that this is economically unsound."[25] Astonishingly enough, Fenton became furious instead of conciliatory when Hemingway raised these telling objections; and he managed to publish his book, despite Hemingway's original opposition, in 1954. In 1961, the year of his own suicide, Hemingway wrote Carlos Baker that Fenton set a bad example to other biographers by jumping to his death from a hotel window, and wondered what he had been thinking about on the way down.

24

Second Safari
1953–1954

> This strange vice was the reading
> of one's own obituaries.
>
> "The Christmas Gift"

I

In the last decade of his life, Hemingway attempted to recapture the past by returning to Spain and Africa, and by writing again (though not nearly as well) about the places that had inspired him in the 1920s and 1930s. He also returned to his work as a journalist and arranged for *Look* to subsidize the trip with lavish fees. They paid $15,000 for a picture story of the safari, to be photographed by Earl Theisen, and another $10,000 for a 3,500-word article that appeared in the magazine on January 26, 1954.

Hemingway's son Patrick was then living in East Africa. He had attended Stanford for two years, transferred to Harvard and married after graduation in June 1950. In April of that year Hemingway told Adriana, in a condescending letter that criticized his son's marriage, that he had inspected Patrick's fiancée. He said the girl came from a good Baltimore family, was quite pretty and seemed healthy. They both wanted to marry and it was their business, not his. But, as we all know, a young man married is a young man marred. Hemingway was usually hostile to his daughters-in-law and never adopted them as his own long-sought daughters. He refused to attend the wedding, sent Gianfranco to represent him in Baltimore and (alluding to Patrick's nickname) concluded with an ironic epitaph: "Sic Transit Gloria Mousie."

Patrick had spent some time studying agriculture on Pauline's ancestral plantation in Piggott. After her death in October 1951, Patrick used his inheritance to visit Africa and buy a 2,300-acre farm at Sao Hill in the southern highlands, southwest of Dar-es-Salaam. Hemingway now praised the son who had supplanted Gregory as his favorite: "He is brave, like Pauline, and he has other of her good qualities" and proudly told Berenson that Patrick "loves Africa as though Africa were a girl."[1] Patrick farmed for a few years, broke into the exclusively English circle of white hunters with the help of Philip Percival, and in 1955 started his own company, Tanganyika Tour Safaris, near Mount Kilimanjaro. He gave up the business when his wife became ill in 1963, worked for the United Nations in Arusha for twelve years teaching game conservation and moved to Hemingway country in Montana in 1975.[2]

The Hemingways sailed from New York aboard the *Flandre* on June 24, 1953, a month after he had won the Pulitzer Prize, and spent six weeks in Pamplona, Madrid, Valencia and Paris before leaving for Africa. The ostensible purpose of the Spanish trip was to gather material for an appendix to *Death in the Afternoon* on the evolution and decline of the modern bullfight, but his encounters with Luis Miguel Dominguín and Antonio Ordóñez convinced him that there was a contemporary renaissance in the art of the corrida. Gianfranco met them at Le Havre with a Lancia driven by Adamo Simon, a mortician from Udine in northeast Italy, who was the funereal replacement for Toby Bruce and Archie Pelkey.

Hemingway had not been to Spain since November 1938 and told Berenson that for a Loyalist supporter entering Franco's country, "it was a little spooky at the border, but only for a moment. Afterward the [guards] seemed rather proud and pleased that one had the cojones to come. It really took very little as they would not harm Mary who had never been there and it was [too] late to shoot me." Juanito Quintana had lost his hotel during the Civil War. Hemingway (no longer a celebrated friend of Spain) was unable to find a room in Pamplona during the fiesta and had to stay twenty miles north in Lecumberri. Mary went to the bullfights at San Fermín like Hadley, stayed in the Hotel Florida in Madrid like Martha and then shot lions in Kenya like Pauline.

Hemingway loved to lead his troops in peace and war. In Pamplona, he picked up the crowd of friends and followers that formed his entourage in Spain: Gianfranco, Tommy and Durie Shevlin, Peter Viertel, Peter Buckley and Rupert Belleville. Hemingway warned Viertel that his pocket might be picked as the crowd pressed together to enter the bullring and Viertel cautiously clutched his wallet. When they sat down, Hemingway discovered that he had been robbed. He maintained that abuses had entered modern bullfighting after 1928, when the horses were padded, the picadors unusually cruel and the crowd forbidden to condemn these abuses by throwing bottles.[3]

The "tall and boring Peter Buckley . . . each day more unbearable," claimed to be a childhood acquaintance of Bumby and fastened onto Hemingway. He made the great mistake of writing about bullfighting, competing with the Master and asking for help with his work. In May 1957 Hemingway refused Buckley's request and said he could not write an introduction to such a confused book. He did not believe that Buckley, who knew nothing about bullfights, could eliminate the wild statements and the structural faults.[4]

In 1956 Buckley shared a room during the crowded Zaragoza *feria* with Hotchner. The latter recalled that Buckley enraged Hemingway by disturbing Ordóñez before a bullfight. Buckley's book *Ernest* (1978) contains photographs by himself and others, but his derivative and simple-minded text reveals an abysmal lack of perception: "Ernest knew the short words and the long ones; he tried different sentences with different words, and he tried different paragraphs with different sentences."[5]

Rupert Belleville, an old friend of Mary, was also part of the Spanish circus. He had been a brave pilot on the Fascist side in the Civil War, had an expert knowledge of Spain, was an alcoholic and later died—while drunk—by impaling himself on a post. Hemingway thought Rupert sober was even more repetitive than Sinsky drunk; and Gianfranco wrote a quaintly spelled description of traveling with his inebriate friend: "Rupert afther I left you was a smal problem, across the border he started very fast to make no sens, for a cople of brandys he got while I was arranging with pasaports. He got in a state he would shure have killed himself if he was driving."[6]

The return to Pamplona was a sad contrast to Hemingway's first trips to the fiesta in the mid-1920s. In his youth, when few foreigners went to San Fermín, the fiesta was fresh and exciting. Hemingway first learned about bullfighting in an electric atmosphere that combined physical danger during the running of the bulls with sexual temptation during the holidays with Duff Twysden and Pauline Pfeiffer. But *The Sun Also Rises* had transformed both the festival and Hemingway himself into tourist attractions, and he could not find a hotel room in the place he had (in a sense) created. In 1953 he returned to a country that had been devastated by Civil War as patron, expert and celebrity; his big car was driven by a chauffeur and he was surrounded by young admirers rather than by contemporaries and friends.

II

On August 6 the Hemingways sailed on the *Dunnottar Castle* from Marseilles to Mombasa, and met his friend Mayito Menocal and the *Look* photographer Earl Theisen in Nairobi. Theisen, a specialist in Hollywood movie stars, had many good stories to tell. Denis Zaphiro wrote: "He fitted in well and was a craftsman interested mostly in his assignment. Low key sort of person. He was irritated that Hemingway was not getting on with the article quickly enough or giving him enough opportunities to get photos of him in action." Like a film star, Hemingway was now expected to pose and perform.

The government of Kenya had persuaded Philip Percival to come out of retirement (he was then sixty-eight) in the hope of reviving tourism during the Mau Mau emergency—the fierce independence movement led by Jomo Kenyatta. Though this was, as Hemingway said, "an actual state of war," the danger was primarily in the Kikuyu district north of Nairobi; there was no trouble where he hunted, south of the capital. Zaphiro quoted Hemingway's ironic comment on all the young white males with pistols on their belts in the Long Bar of the New Stanley Hotel: "only way they can feel something hard between their legs."[7] Percival's assistant and Menocal's white hunter was the capable Roy Home, who, according to Mario Menocal, Jr., was back in business "after doing a stretch in jail for shooting his wife when he caught her in bed with another man (maybe it was the man whom he shot); in any case, he reported it immediately to the Game Department, writing it down on the report as 'vermin.' "

They first hunted near Percival's farm at Machakos, forty miles southeast of Nairobi; and were then granted permission to hunt during September in the game reserves at Kajiado and Magadi (south and southwest of the capital), which were under the supervision of the game warden, Denis Zaphiro. He was "the son of a specialist in the British diplomatic service. I think that his father was at one very delicate time

H.M.'s ambassador to Abyssinia. He had chosen a career in Africa, and after some years' service in the Sudan Defense Force, a crack volunteer outfit similar to the Arab Legion, had accepted a post in the Game Department of Kenya."[8]

In "Francis Macomber" as in actual life, Hemingway liked to draw analogies between hunting, masculinity and sexual performance. In 1953 Mayito Menocal's superior shooting spoiled the safari for Hemingway just as Charles Thompson's had done in 1934. Hemingway had aged and was drinking heavily, which made it difficult to shoot accurately. And he may have been afraid of not living up to his heroic image in front of Theisen, who was having problems getting the pictures he needed. When several shots were fired and it was not clear who had killed a lion and leopard, Hemingway claimed the credit and kept the trophies. Percival was deeply distressed by Hemingway's failure and kept saying: "He's a most changed man." Mario Menocal, Jr., who had many conversations with his father about the safari, observed that the poor shooting

> grew into a sort of monster that affected his character and hurt him psychologically. . . . He took it out on Roy [Home], he took it out on Mary; none of it did him any good. . . . After one particularly shameful show, Ernest came up to make some kind of excuse, and Philip stared him down, saying, "Oh, Ernest, don't give me that nonsense. The whole thing has been a disgrace!" . . .
>
> He seemed to have completely lost confidence in himself. . . . It made him drink more than usual, he took refuge in lies and statements of the most fantastic and outlandish character.[9]

This was a trying time for Mary. But she was, as usual, patient, submissive, eager to please; and she handled him well—like an Indian trainer with a domesticated elephant.

Zaphiro agreed that Hemingway's "weakest point was boastfulness, but not often displayed. Suspected he was trying to live up to a reputation. [Boastfulness] grew when he became famous and began drinking." In contrast to Menocal, Zaphiro emphasized the positive, even contemplative side of the safari, after the frustrated Hemingway had lost interest in killing the animals, no longer had to perform for the camera or meet Percival's high standards:

> Apart from Hemingway's dislike of Roy Home, who he thought had cheated him over costs of the safari and a quarrel he had with Patrick

at Shimoni, the safari went off very well indeed, particularly when Hemingway, Mary and myself were alone.

Ernest was not all that interested in shooting—except lion. He did not, for instance, shoot or even want to shoot an elephant. After everyone had left, i.e. Patrick, Menocal, Percival, Home, etc. he preferred to drive around and look at the animals. He didn't shoot his lion on either occasion. . . .

He loved Africa. He loved to sit in it and watch it. He had a natural knowledge of what animals would do and where they would be. . . . He was always reading, reading. Carried soft covers and papers and magazines in his pockets all the time. He read whenever the pace slowed.[10]

In October Hemingway visited Patrick in Tanganyika. Then, perhaps to escape from the strain of the hunting trip and from the awareness of his failure to embody the ideal image of the photomagazine, he indulged in atavistic regression and attempted to return to his grubby adolescence in Michigan, when he camped and fished with boyhood friends. Though going native was especially frowned upon during the Mau Mau period, he shaved his head, hunted with a spear, dyed his clothes the rusty Masai color and began an elaborate courtship of his African "fiancée," Debba. Zaphiro described her as "an evil-smelling bit of camp trash"; but Hemingway, using considerable imagination, connected Debba to his youthful infatuation with an Indian girl and later told the incredulous MacLeish that she was a cross between Prudy Boulton and an impudent, dark, short-haired version of Marilyn Monroe. Mary, who understood enough about his mental state to remain aloof, tolerated his absurd behavior: "she just stays the hell away from it and is understanding and wonderful."[11] There was no sexual consummation with Debba any more than there was with Prudy; she did not do what others had done better.

The second safari produced no literary work comparable to the two great African stories of 1936. Hemingway published a minor article, "Safari," to accompany Theisen's photographs and fulfill his obligation to Look. Ten years after his death, when Mary published what Hemingway had written in 1954–56 and chosen to keep back, a quarter of his 200,000-word "African Journal" appeared in Sports Illustrated (December 1971–January 1972). This lifeless boy's adventure story is an unintentional parody of the worst aspects of Green Hills of Africa. Hemingway and Percival, portly and puffing, are twenty years older; Mary instead of Pauline now stalks lion. Despite the Mau Mau, the

Africans—including N'Gui, nephew of the original M'Cola—are as faithful as ever. Nicknames and Swahili words provide *verismo,* the description of Debba is intolerably arch and there is plenty of whiskey to soften the rough life. The flat narrative—"The day that Miss Mary shot her lion was a beautiful day. That was about all that was beautiful about it"[12]— is accompanied by hideous drawings (Hemingway had no luck with portraits and illustrators). But the articles are also interspersed with nostalgic and sentimental memories (positive on Pound, negative on Ford) that begin his search for a meaningful subject and anticipate the superb writing in *A Moveable Feast.*

III

Hemingway's best essay on Africa, "The Christmas Gift," was written in Nairobi while he was recovering from extensive injuries. *Look* paid $20,000 for the autobiographical article and published it in April–May 1954. The two plane crashes that took place in January of that year and were described in the essay caused the worst wounds he had suffered since World War One, but he was now too old to recover from them quickly, as he had done in his youth. The accidents battered him physically at a time when he was drinking heavily, shooting badly and acting foolishly. They caused permanent damage and were (like his war wounds) a major turning point in his life.

In August 1922 Hemingway had flown from Paris to Strasbourg and recreated in a *Toronto Star* story the excitement, pleasure, interest and danger of a small aircraft. In January 1934 he flew from Serengeti to Nairobi to be treated for amoebic dysentery and used this experience for the superb description, at the end of "The Snows of Kilimanjaro," of Harry's dream of a plane that followed the contours of the land and would rescue him from gangrenous death: "[He saw] the camp beside the hill, flattening now, and the plain spreading, clumps of trees, and the bush flattening, while the game trails ran now smoothly to the dry waterholes, and there was a new water that he had never known of." He flew to China in 1941 and with the RAF in 1944; but he preferred ships to planes and never flew across the Atlantic in peacetime until his last trip to Spain in 1960.

In January 1954 Hemingway chartered a small plane to fly over the spectacular lakes and mountains of East Africa. The bad luck began almost immediately when the hydraulic system of their twin-engine aircraft failed to operate as they approached Kilimanjaro, and they were lucky to get back to Nairobi "without burning." The route of the next flight, in a Cessna 180 with Roy Marsh as pilot, was west from Nairobi to Mwanza on the south shore of Lake Victoria, over the Mountains of the Moon in Ruanda Urundi, and across Lake Kivu to Bukavu in the Congo. The second stage, flying north, took them over Lake Edward and Lake Albert to the impressive Murchison Falls in Uganda, where the Nile thunders down a cataract toward the fertile valleys of the Sudan and Egypt. On January 23, Hemingway nonchalantly wrote in "The Christmas Gift," they encountered a flock of large ibis above the Nile River:

> Roy Marsh dived sharply under these birds. . . . The aircraft had encountered [an abandoned telegraph] wire with its propeller and its tail assembly. It was temporarily uncontrollable and then was so obviously damaged that it was necessary to land. . . .
>
> There was the usual sound of rending metal which is audible in a forced landing [on the shore]. . . . [Mary] had two broken ribs which were causing her considerable pain and from which she was never complaining at any point.[13]

Hemingway sprained his right shoulder.

They rationed the bottle of water, bottle of Scotch and four beers, and spent the night in the open near a herd of elephants. The overwhelming noise of the falls obliterated the sound of the search plane that had spotted the wreckage and reported them dead. The next morning they hailed a launch, which had been used by John Huston during the filming of *The African Queen* and was now chartered by a surgeon from Kampala. After paying an extortionate sum to the Indian captain, they were taken to Butiaba, on the eastern shore of Lake Albert. The Hemingways and Roy Marsh planned to go by road to Masindi and Entebbe, on the north shore of Lake Victoria; but they accepted a lift from Reginald Cartwright, who had been searching for them in his H-89 de Havilland Rapide, to the capital of Uganda.

The deeply ridged washboard runway at Butiaba was similar to the airstrip on the Paris-Strasbourg flight in 1922: "the plane began to move along the ground, bumping like a motorcycle, and then slowly rose into the air." But in the second flight, on January 24, the "aircraft became violently air-borne through no fault of its own. This condition existed only for a matter of seconds after which the aircraft became violently de-air-borne and there was the usual sound, with which we were all by now familiar, of rending metal. Unfortunately, on this second occasion flames were observed coming from the starboard engine which was burning." Mary, Roy Marsh and the pilot escaped by kicking out the front window. Hemingway, who was too large for that exit, found the passenger door was jammed; instead of using his left shoulder, rear end or feet, he battered the door open with his head and gave himself his fifth concussion.

The second crash was much worse than the first and seriously injured Hemingway. His skull was fractured, two discs of his spine were cracked, his right arm and shoulder were dislocated, his liver, right kidney and spleen were ruptured, his sphincter muscle was paralyzed by compressed vertebrae on the iliac nerve, his arms, face and head were burned by the flames of the plane, his vision and hearing were impaired—but his sense of smell became more acute. He suffered internal bleeding, nausea and retching, burning pains in his back, severe headaches, and trouble with his liver and kidneys that would plague him for the rest of his life. But he was, as usual, proud of his ability to endure and survive his wounds. He told Harvey Breit that brain fluid had leaked out of his fractured skull and fortunately relieved the pressure from the hemorrhage.[14] And he joked to Peter Viertel that his cracked vertebrae had caused a permanent erection.

After an agonizing fifty-mile car ride to Masindi, where they rested overnight, they completed the journey to Entebbe. He made a statement to the Civil Aviation Board, told reporters, "My luck, she is still good" and met Patrick, who had borrowed money, chartered a plane and flown up from Dar-es-Salaam. Hemingway wryly remarked: "This is the first time any son of mine has ever arrived without being broke or, if you did not hear from him, asking you to either get him back into the Army [Jack] or get him out of jail [Gregory]." Hemingway had the courage to get into a small Cessna 170 and fly to Nairobi with Roy Marsh; Mary and Patrick followed him in a commercial airline. Hemingway's two plane crashes were unlucky, but they may also have been the fault of the pilots. Though passengers pay for and rely on a pilot's expertise, Hemingway never blamed them. Roy Marsh should have known about the telegraph wire across the falls. Reginald Cartwright may have been at fault for letting the passengers influence his judgment; he carried too much extra weight and was unable to take off.[15]

IV

Like Mark Twain, Hemingway could say: "The reports of my death are greatly exaggerated"; like Robert Graves, he was officially reported dead and publicly announced that he was still alive. He was as gratified by the early grief and late rejoicing of his friends as he had been by Jack's response after he was reported dead in the London car crash in May 1944. In a letter to Charles Fenton, he approved of the way Jack had expressed his sorrow in a Hemingwayesque mixture of sentimentality and swagger. Jack got drunk, wept and caught the clap. Hemingway's fictional hero had done the same thing in "A Very Short Story" after learning that his girl (based on Agnes) had jilted him.

In Africa he was reported dead for the second time. On January 24 at 2:28 P.M. an Associated Press bulletin announced: "Hemingway and his wife are feared to have perished in the crash of a chartered plane yesterday in Northwest Uganda." The front-page headline in the final edition of the *New York Daily Mirror* on January 25 read: "HEMINGWAY, WIFE KILLED IN AIR CRASH." On January 25 the *New York Herald Tribune* and many other newspapers around the world printed Hemingway's premature obituaries. He had been "spooked" by seeing "Hemingway's Death" on the galleys of his bullfighting book, but enjoyed reading his death notices: the first was a prediction, the second an escape from death.

He studied the obituaries and preserved them in two handsome scrapbooks, bound in zebra hide and lion skin. But he was not entirely pleased by the morbid judgments and ironically noted, in a *Sunday Express* article, "Reading One's Own Obituaries," that he incorporated into "The Christmas Gift": "One in the German press stated that I had attempted to land the aircraft myself on the summit of Mount Kilimanjaro . . . in an effort to approach the carcass of a dead leopard. . . . In all obituaries, or almost all, it was emphasized that I had sought death all my life. Can one imagine that if a man sought death all of his life he could not have found her before the age of 54?"[16]

If Hemingway had died violently in an African plane crash over a cataract or among wild elephants, his reputation would have been even greater than it is today. He would have gone out in a literal blaze of glory, just after the enormous success of his most popular novel, *The Old Man and the Sea,* and before he began to decline and waste away through accidents, alcoholism, physical disease, paranoia, electric shock treatments and depression. By surviving the two near-fatal air crashes, he strengthened the image of the indestructible tough guy and lived up to the legend of the mythical Papa.

Hemingway's African injuries—which began in October 1953 when he fell out of a Land Rover on a sharp curve, cut his face and sprained his shoulder—were not yet over. They had chartered a fishing boat at Shimoni, south of Mombasa on the Indian Ocean. When a bush fire broke out in late February he insisted on fighting it, but fell down, caught fire himself, and suffered second- and third-degree burns (in addition to the first-degree burns from the plane) from his lips to his legs.

In *Islands in the Stream* Hemingway imitated (but did not equal) the effective repetition of "and" in the opening paragraph of *A Farewell to Arms* when he described their departure from Mombasa, en route to Venice, on the *Africa:* "Then Africa was behind them, and the old white town with the great trees and all the green behind it, then the sea breaking on the long reef as they passed and then the ship gained speed and was in the open ocean and flying fish were splitting out of the water and ahead of the ship." In July he wrote Cape an amusing letter about the problems of his paralyzed sphincter and the technical skill needed to deal with this ailment. He said that he had to defecate standing up, which was not especially difficult. But on the boat from Mombasa he slid into the door of the toilet and missed the bowl. When Mary remarked that no gentleman ever shits on the floor, he told her that she'd just seen one do it.[17]

When Hemingway reached Venice in late March 1954 his friends immediately noticed his physical deterioration. His head was shaved, his hair was white, his movements were slow, his speech hesitant, his manner subdued. In contrast to the first safari, when loss of weight had improved his appearance, his massive frame now seemed shrunken after losing twenty pounds. He talked more frequently about his ailments, worried about his skin disease and his failing eyesight. He had been betrayed by his body, lost confidence and suddenly become an old man.

Mary noted that he was treated callously by the doctors who examined his wounds in Venice. They kept him waiting for half an hour while he sat naked on an icy table, they bruised his bladder during a kidney test, they did not treat his alarmingly high blood pressure. His Italian translator, Fernanda Pivano, wrote: "I remember him in Venice, surrounded by all the arms and equipment of the safari in the Gritti apartment, sitting in a sunless window, with hair suddenly white, his hands folded next to a plate which contained but one lettuce leaf . . . his great eyes surprised by his body's first treachery. . . . He would not let the photographers in: 'it's not legal,' he said, 'to surprise a defeated man.' "[18]

The one consolation was a final visit from his beloved Adriana. In the Prado Museum in Madrid in July 1953 he had fallen in love with Andrea del Sarto's *Portrait of a Woman,* which resembled and reminded him of Adriana. His imagination, which could change Debba into Prudy Boulton, could also transform a woman—or a portrait—into his ideal beauty. In Venice he confessed to Adriana that he had wanted to live so that he could see her again, that he still loved her, that leaving her was like having an amputation. As they parted for the last time, he remembered when he first saw her standing in the rain and associated her with his wounds, and wept tears of self-pity: "Look, daughter, look. Now you can tell everybody that you have seen Ernest Hemingway cry."[19] Hemingway's self-conscious and self-indulgent remark, coming after the world-wide news coverage and the pursuit by reporters, showed a hypersensitive awareness of himself as a public figure and a desire to dramatize rather than express his feelings about his lost past and lost love.

After the plane crashes, Hemingway's enormous consumption of alcohol clearly began to destroy his weakened body. Patrick said his father drank a quart of whiskey a day for the last twenty years of his life. By 1940, or 1945 at the latest, he had succumbed to the occupational disease of writers, had become a chronic alcoholic. Hemingway had said that alcohol was his great friend. He had always been a successful drinker, had a high tolerance for liquor and rarely suffered from hangovers. Though his speech became a bit incoherent and his boasting increased after heavy drinking, he never got staggering drunk. In Africa, wrote Denis Zaphiro, though he never seemed inebriated, "his drinking would have killed a less tough man. Two or three bottles of hard liquor a day. Wines etc. with meals. Gin a favorite drink. I suppose he was drunk the whole time but seldom showed it. Just became merrier, more lovable, more bull-shitty. Without drink he was morose, silent and depressed." He now depended on it to ease his pain, distract his mind and revive his spirits.

Hemingway realized his dependence on alcohol when, after the plane crashes, liquor was either unavailable or forbidden by doctor's orders, and he was suddenly deprived of the astonishing quantity he habitually consumed. For a long time liquor had no apparent effect on Hemingway's iron constitution; but when he resumed drinking heavily after rupturing his liver and kidneys, he did grievous and permanent harm to his vital organs and hastened his physical decline.[20]

V

The Hemingways left Venice with Hotchner and their driver on May 6, stopped in Aix and Carcassonne, saw the bullfights at the San Isidro *feria,* visited Dominguín and Ava Gardner at his bull ranch near El Escorial, sailed from Genoa on the *Francesco Morosini* and reached Havana in July. They had been away for more than a year and had to deal with many domestic details.

On October 28, 1954, Hemingway was awarded the $35,000 Nobel Prize for Literature. When interviewed by Harvey Breit about the Prize, he shrewdly and safely praised an art critic and two aging second-rate writers—rather than more potent contemporaries—and said that Bernard Berenson, Carl Sandburg and Isak Dinesen deserved the award. He wanted to puncture all pomposity and wrote (with odd arithmetic) to his sister Ursula that he had completed 4,500 imperishable words that week, guaranteed by eighteen Swedes who had drunk too much aquavit and immortalized him by a vote of nine to seven, with one abstention. He pleaded injuries, declined the invitation to Stockholm and sent a brief address to be read by the American ambassador at the formal ceremony. His insightful speech, which diagnosed the dangers of literary life even as he reaped its rewards, was a sad acknowledgment of solitude, uncertainty and personal failure: "Writing, at its best, is a lonely life. Organizations for writers palliate the writer's loneliness but I doubt if they improve his writing. He grows in public stature as he sheds his loneliness and often his work deteriorates. For he does his work alone and if he is a good enough writer he must face eternity, or the lack of it, each day."[21]

Yet even the Nobel Prize, as his speech suggested, could not compensate him for his disastrous accidents, his excruciating pain and his separation from Adriana in 1954. The novelist Norman Lewis, who met

Hemingway in Cuba just after he had won the Prize, perceived his condition: "There's fame. . . . Saddest man I ever met. Sated." And Hemingway himself confessed to Chink that suffering and melancholy had weakened his will to live:

> I had to look after Mary and there is always the obligation to survive, that mis-understood obligation. But I believe I would have stayed in the kite that burned at Butiaba, once Mary was out, if I could have seen the rest of 1954 as she would be and as she'd feel. We call this "black-ass" [depression] and one should never have it. But I get tired of pain sometimes even if that is an ignoble feeling.[22]

25

The Dangerous Summers

1955–1959

> Nobody ever lives their life all
> the way up except bull-fighters.
>
> ' *The Sun Also Rises*

I

The mid-fifties—the least eventful years of Hemingway's adult life—
were largely spent recovering from his African injuries and dealing
with many new illnesses. His working hours were devoted to the frus-
trating filming of *The Old Man and the Sea* in the summer of 1955 and
the spring of 1956, and to the writing of his "African Journal"—though
it must have been depressing to complete 200,000 words and realize
they were not good enough to publish. The seven undistinguished short
stories that he wrote about World War Two during this period were also
consigned to the bank vault.

Hemingway disliked formal ceremony (it was most unusual for him
to wear a tuxedo when entertaining Adriana) and did not attend the
presentation of the relatively few awards he had received: the Gold
Medal from the Limited Editions Club in November 1941, the Pulitzer
Prize in May 1953, the American Academy of Arts Award of Merit in
April 1954 and the Nobel Prize in October 1954. It was not possible to
avoid the less formal presentations in Havana, and he had accepted the
Bronze Star for meritorious service as a war correspondent at the
American Embassy in June 1947.

Hemingway was the most famous man in Cuba: he was recognized
wherever he went and people cried out "Papa, Papa" as if he were king.
He had given his gold Nobel medal to the shrine of the national saint,

the Virgen de Cobre, and was often honored by the Batista government. He received the Cuban Medal of Honor in 1952, the Order of
Carlos Manuel de Céspedes in 1954 and the Order of San Cristóbal on
November 17, 1955. During the last ceremony, he sweated under the
hot television lights at the Havana Sports Palace and then caught cold
in his right kidney, as he had done in the fall of 1929 after fishing the
icy waters of Spain. "It cut out on me and then the other kidney and
the liver were affected," he dramatically told Wallace Meyer. "The first
I knew it was bad was when my right foot swelled like a football and
the pressure brought blood out at the base of the toenails."[1] He had
nephritis and hepatitis, suffered from anemia and spent forty days in
bed from late November until early the following year. Hemingway was
seriously ill again in November 1956, during his second postwar trip to
Spain, when he was treated in Madrid by Dr. Juan Madinaveitia, who
had served as Chief of the Surgical Unit for the Twelfth International
Brigade during the Civil War. The doctor noted Hemingway's high
blood pressure, liver disease and arteriosclerosis; he prescribed a special
diet with low alcohol and forbade sexual intercourse.

Hemingway was knowledgeable about and responsive to Spanish
literature, owned seven books by the atheistic and iconoclastic Basque
novelist Pío Baroja, and was introduced to the octogenarian in Madrid
on October 9, 1956, by the Spanish journalist Castillo-Puche. He put on
a jacket and tie, brought Baroja cashmere socks and sweater, a bottle
of whiskey and an inscribed copy of *The Sun Also Rises*. In Castillo's
version of the meeting, Hemingway, though rather repetitious, was
unusually humble and respectful:

> Don Pío, I've been wanting to come to see you for a long time, because
> I feel I owe you a great debt of gratitude. I've never forgotten how
> much I owe you, how much all of us who have read your books owe you.
> . . . To us younger writers, you were our master, and we learned so much
> from your works and from the personal example you set us. . . .
> I'm convinced that you deserve the Nobel Prize much more than
> many writers who won it—myself first of all, for I am more or less just
> another of your disciples.

Hemingway had not seen a good writer for a long time. His willingness to abandon the role of Papa and play the reverential disciple of an
older, foreign, underrated novelist, who wrote well about Spain, was
motivated by a desire to express homage from America to a cultural

hero of the pre-Fascist era, to convey his respect for old age and his recognition of mortality—as he did in letters to Berenson. Hemingway came from and embodied a culture that valued youth, strength, success and money. He had had all of these things, but was now conscious of the decay of his body, the decline of his literary powers and perhaps even the loss of self-respect. So he paid emotional homage to a symbolic figure: a poor, neglected but honorable writer, full of years and dignity. When Baroja died three weeks later, Hemingway attended the funeral and wrote a moving description of "how the weather was" when they put Baroja into the land he had described in his books:

> We buried Don Pío Baroja last Tuesday. . . . Thought Dos Passos or *some* Americans could have sent some word. . . . He was a hell of a good writer you know. Knopf dropped him, of course, when he did not sell. The day was misty with the sun breaking through and burning off over the bare hills and on the way out to the un-consecrated ground cemetery the sides of the streets were jammed solid with flowers, the flower sellers stands for Nov 2—All Souls day, and we rode out to the cemetery through the country he wrote about.[2]

Hemingway had also been expressing his loyalty and offering his help to Ezra Pound—one of the few literary friends with whom he never quarreled. During World War Two, before and after Pearl Harbor, Pound had written and delivered three hundred seven-minute propaganda broadcasts from Rome. Arthur Miller described Pound's manner and content, and stated that "in his wildest moments of human vilification Hitler never approached our Ezra for sheer obscenity." As millions of Jews were being gassed in Auschwitz and Buchenwald, Pound urged a pogrom at the top, a new style of killing important Jews, and called Hitler "a saint and a martyr." He was charged with treason in July 1943 and gave a reasoned, if unconvincing, defense of his actions. Arrested by Italian partisans in May 1945, he was handed over to the American army and confined for twenty-five days in a six-by-six-by-ten-foot cage in Pisa. In July he was examined by three army doctors, who found him "psychiatrically normal." Nevertheless, he was declared insane and unfit to stand trial by a panel of psychiatrists who wanted to protect him from punishment, and was confined in St. Elizabeths Hospital in Washington, D.C., in December 1945.

Hemingway, much more politically sophisticated than is generally recognized (he never swallowed and then recanted Communist ideology, as Dos Passos, Edmund Wilson and Max Eastman did, nor became reactionary in middle age), invented Pound's insanity plea.[3] He had read the transcripts of the wartime broadcasts, decided they could be used to prove that Ezra was obviously crazy and urged Pound's influential supporters—Eliot, Frost, MacLeish, W. C. Williams—to implement this strategy. From 1943 until Pound's release in 1958, Hemingway corresponded with MacLeish, Allen Tate, Malcolm Cowley, Pound's lawyer, his editor, his wife and his mistress, attempting to defend and assist his old friend. In these perceptive letters he explained that the egoistic Pound—brilliant but intermittently abnormal—was loyal to the Fascists mainly because they were the only government who flattered him and took his work seriously. In a letter to MacLeish of August 1943, he recalled Pound's fine poetry and generous encouragement of genius in writers like Joyce, Eliot and Wyndham Lewis, condemned his pathological behavior and insane ideas, stated that he was guilty of treason and ought to be punished. But he also insisted that the crackpot broadcasts were ineffectual and that Pound should not be martyred:

> Thanks for sending the [photo]stats of Ezra's rantings. He is obviously crazy. I think you might prove he was crazy as far back as the latter Cantos. He deserves punishment and disgrace but what he really deserves most is ridicule. He should not be hanged and he should not be made a martyr of. He has a long history of generosity and unselfish aid to other artists and he is one of the greatest of liveing poets. It is impossible to believe that anyone in his right mind could utter the vile, absolutely idiotic drivel he has broadcast. His friends who knew him and who watched the warpeing and twisting and decay of his mind and his judgement should defend him and explain him on that basis.

After Pound had won the Bollingen Prize for *The Pisan Cantos* in 1949, Hemingway told Pound's wife, Dorothy: "give Ezra good wishes and congratulate him on his prize and tell him how much I admire what he has written since he has been in trouble. I am sure that he would have hanged with as much style as Roger Casement. But I am much happier that he is writing good poetry instead." As pressure to free Pound intensified in 1957, Hemingway feared that Pound's friendship with the fanatical neo-Nazi segregationist John Kasper might make it dangerous to release him. In a letter to Frost of June 1957, he mentioned the paradoxical aspects of Pound's character and career, the potential danger he presented inside (as well as outside) the hospital and his belief that Pound—as a major poet—should continue to receive special treatment. Others argued, more severely, that "a man of [Pound's] stature, learning and influence has an even greater responsibility to uphold ethical principles and serve as an exemplary model." But Hemingway defended Pound on personal and artistic rather than on moral and political grounds:

> If Pound were to die in confinement after eleven years in St. Elizabeths, it would make an impression in all of the civilized world that cultural missions and programs would not undo. . . .
>
> Great poets are very rare and they should be extended a measure of understanding and mercy.
>
> I would be glad to contribute fifteen hundred dollars toward getting him settled with his daughter.
>
> I detest Pound's politics, his anti-semitism and his race-ism. But I truly feel it would do more harm to our country for Pound to die in confinement, than for him to be freed and sent to live with his daughter in Italy.[4]

Hemingway kept his word; and in July 1956, two years before Pound was released, he sent a check for a thousand dollars. Pound was grateful, said he did not need the money, placed it in plexiglass and used it as a paperweight.

When Hemingway became embroiled in his own legal problems, he also chose the moral argument. In August 1958, when he was publishing very little, he brought suit in the New York Supreme Court to block *Esquire* from reprinting in an anthology three of his uncollected stories of the Spanish War. He felt the stories did not represent his best work, thought they were not good enough to reprint and wanted to revise them. "I reserve the right to make my prose as good as it can be," he said. "In fact, I have the obligation to do so." He claimed that he had sold only the first serial rights and that *Esquire* had no right to reprint. He angrily blamed his lawyer, Alfred Rice, for mistakenly introducing irrelevant considerations and told the *New York Times:* "I have just called him up and given him hell for it."

The real issue was whether or not *Esquire* could use the stories twice after paying for them only once. Rice explained that the law cannot prevent publication without copyright, it can only extract payment for damages afterwards. Since the courts could issue an injunction to stop publication on the grounds of irreparable injury, Rice shifted from a literary to a political argument and stated that Hemingway did not want the stories reprinted because he had changed his political views since the Spanish War. Hemingway perfectly understood Rice's tactics and knew exactly what was happening, but he became very angry and publicly criticized Rice for sacrificing the moral to the legal argument and distorting Hemingway's views. In order to prevent publication, Rice made it seem as though Hemingway were recanting the ideas that he had gone to Spain to uphold. In the end, there was a compromise. Hemingway got the return of the copyright and the magazine—which had gained excellent publicity—was allowed to publish "The Butterfly and the Tank," but not the other two stories, in *The Armchair Esquire* (1958).[5]

II

By 1957 Hemingway had become irritated by the oppressive heat and disastrous hurricanes of Cuba. In April he complained to Berenson about the destruction of the landscape that inevitably occurs when a poor country becomes industrialized. The charm and beauty of the coast had vanished. A four-lane highway now cut through the hills near the Finca and the lovely old tree-lined road had gone. The beaches had been excavated to make cement for skyscrapers, and Havana was being transformed into a cross between Barcelona and Caracas.

In August 1958 political problems hit home when a patrol of government soldiers shot his dog, Machakos. The Batista regime, in its death throes, became more repressive as the threat of revolution increased. Hemingway felt trapped in a violent and hostile atmosphere, and was pessimistic about the future of the island. "Cuba is really bad now," he told Patrick in November. "Living in a country where no one is right —both sides atrocious—knowing what sort of stuff and murder will go on when the new ones come in—seeing the abuses of those in now— I am fed [up] on it."[6]

Hemingway thought of finding a permanent refuge in case he was forced to leave Cuba. In October he drove out to Ketchum with Toby Bruce, for the first time in ten years, and stayed in a rented house. His old pals (Beartracks Williams, Lloyd and Tillie Arnold, Clara Spiegel) welcomed him—and noticed how much he had aged. He also made friends with a younger generation of sportsmen: George Saviers, who became his family doctor; Don Anderson, Williams' assistant guide; Forrest MacMullen, Hemingway's man Friday; Bud Purdy, who came from a wealthy railroad-construction family, had graduated from Washington State University, and was a rancher and owner of a farm supplies store. Purdy agreed with Williams that Hemingway was still "a hell of a shot" and could beat any of the men in trap shooting. Hemingway's mood greatly improved when he was working well, and he boasted to Purdy that he had earned a thousand dollars one morning for writing a thousand words.[7]

Hemingway also renewed his friendship with Gary Cooper (the son of a lawyer from Montana), whom he had first met in 1940, who had starred in the films of *A Farewell to Arms* and *For Whom the Bell Tolls,* and who still came to Sun Valley for hunting and skiing. When they first met, Hemingway wrote to Max Perkins: "Cooper is a fine man: as honest and straight and friendly and unspoiled as he looks." Though he still liked Cooper as a sporting companion, Hemingway now felt that Cooper loved money more than most people loved God. He was ironic about Cooper's conversion to Catholicism to please his wife (perhaps because he had done the same thing when he married Pauline) and told Viertel that Cooper now had both money and God.[8]

In November 1958, the month he saw Cooper, Hemingway invited his Polish translator, Bronislaw Zielinski, to Ketchum, and arranged for the royalties of the translation of *Green Hills of Africa* (plus an additional thousand dollars) to be used as a prize for the best novel of the year in Poland. Zielinski, like almost everyone else, was impressed by Hemingway and had fond memories of the visit:

> He nicknamed me "The Old Wolf from Warsaw" and "The Magnetic Pole." . . . His manner was simple, and even a little subdued, not in the least boisterous; he never tried to be the center of a gathering although this was just happening by itself. . . . He was listening very carefully and with real interest to what somebody else had to say. . . . Once he turned to his wife and said: "Mary, you wanted me to talk about literature with Bron; I've done it—may I stop now?" . . . On the whole my impression was that of a charming straightforward man without a trace of pretentiousness.[9]

In April 1959, three months after Fidel Castro took power in Cuba, Hemingway bought a house on seventeen acres of land at 400 Canyon Run Boulevard, one mile northwest of Ketchum, for $50,000. The two-story concrete structure stood like a fortress on a fine site above the swirling Big Wood River. It was a complete contrast to the Finca, and had neither character nor charm. Mary (who still owns the house) thought it hideously designed and coldly depressing.

That same month, after Hemingway had returned to Havana, he met Tennessee Williams and the drama critic Kenneth Tynan at the Floridita. Tynan, who shrewdly characterized Hemingway as "a gruff, gigantic boy, shy and reticent in manner," noted that he remained extremely popular during the wave of anti-American feeling that followed the Castro revolution: "He ordered a double frozen daiquiri, locally known as a 'Papa *doble*,' hugged a few waiters and signed a few autographs. A dramatic bronze bust of him stood in a niche beside the bar. 'We cover it,' he said, 'during Lent.' A trio of Negro musicians saluted him with a song called *Soy Como Soy*—'I am as I am'—about a Lesbian who cannot, however hard she tries, change her appetites to suit Papa's."

Hemingway pronounced a bitter epitaph on Batista: "Sic transit hijo de puta" (there goes the son of a whore) and was sympathetic to Castro. Dr. José Luis Herrera (brother of El Monstro) was a friend of Castro, who had not yet declared himself a Communist. Just as Mao Tse-tung had learned from T. E. Lawrence's *Seven Pillars of Wisdom* on the Long March in 1949, so, Fidel told Tynan, "We took *For Whom the Bell Tolls* to the hills with us, and it taught us about guerrilla warfare." Fidel did not break diplomatic relations with the United States until January 1961, after Hemingway had finally left Cuba.

In those early days of hope, when Fidel seemed to improve conditions on the island, Hemingway repeatedly expressed his support for the new regime. He told Tynan that he thoroughly approved of Castro: " 'This is a good revolution,' he said, 'an *honest* revolution.' "[10] In May 1960 Castro won a fishing competition and Hemingway presented him with the prize. When interviewed about Castro at Torrejon Air Force Base, Hemingway contrasted a commonplace uprising in a banana republic to this "real revolution" and stated his admiration for Fidel. In April he compared the Castro government to the Spanish Republic and expressed cautious hope in a letter to his Polish friend Zielinski: "This is a very pure and beautiful revolution so far—Naturally I do not know how it will come out. But I hope for the best—So far it is what we hoped for, in intent, when they made the Republic in Spain (and which never arrived). I hope things will go well—The people who are being shot deserve it."[11]

Hemingway had not seen the bloody fighting and the consolidation of power as Batista fled in December 1958, and his own house and property had not been harmed. After spending only a month in Cuba, he traveled to Spain and was absorbed in bullfighting from May to October. His nostalgic support for the Spanish Left and distaste for the cruelty of Batista's regime led to a rather naive, misguided and perhaps self-protective public statement when, after Castro had ruled for ten months, Hemingway flew into Rancho Boyeros airport on November 3, 1959. J. L. Topping of the American Embassy reported to the State Department that Hemingway told journalists:

1. He supported [the Castro government] and all its acts completely, and thought it was the best thing that had ever happened to Cuba.
2. He had not believed any of the information published abroad against Cuba. He sympathized with the Cuban government, and all *our* difficulties.
3. Hemingway emphasized the *our*, and was asked about it. He said that he hoped Cubans would regard him not as a *Yanqui* (his word), but as another Cuban. With that, he kissed the Cuban flag.[12]

In February 1960 even Anastas Mikoyan, the Soviet minister of trade, was drawn to Hemingway and visited the Finca for two hours. The commissar brought Russian translations of Hemingway's works and promised to give him the royalties that had been frozen in the Soviet Union. Hemingway generously said that he could not accept the money unless Mikoyan paid all the American writers published in Russia. Mary was impressed by Mikoyan's shrewdness and told Clara Spiegel that he was a sharp and astute man, who gave the Cubans $100 million credit to buy Russian tools and made them feel that the Soviet Union was very generous.[13]

Hemingway had remained on good terms with his Cuban friends who supported Franco in the Civil War. But when he praised Castro, kissed the Cuban flag and received Mikoyan, his friends Menocal, Sánchez and Arguelles—soon to be dispossessed and driven into exile by Fidel—were bitterly hurt and broke off relations with him. Hemingway left Cuba for the last time in July 1960. He was scrupulous about Ameri-

can taxes, citizenship and patriotism, and would not have remained in
Cuba if his presence there hurt American interests.

III

In the summer of 1959 Hemingway's passion for the craft and sullen art
of bullfighting became as keen as it had been during the San Fermín
fiestas of the 1920s. He had contracted with *Life* magazine to write a
series of articles on the *mano a mano* (the personal and more dangerous
combat between two matadors, instead of the usual corrida with three)
of the two greatest bullfighters since the death of Manolete: Luis Miguel
Dominguín and Antonio Ordóñez. *Life* wanted Hemingway to write
about their personal and professional rivalry, to cover what, he said,
"turned out to be the gradual destruction of one person by another with
all the things that led up to it and made it."

Because of Hemingway's self-exile after the Civil War, he had not
seen Manolete fight in Spain. In February 1947, six months before
Manolete was killed, Hemingway flew to Merida in Mexico and saw him
fight badly with "lousy bulls." Though his knowledge of Manolete was
limited to this one occasion, Hemingway denied his greatness and exalted Antonio Ordóñez as he had praised his father, Cayetano, in the
1920s. Hemingway was so popular in Spain that the crowd would stand
up and applaud as he entered the plaza de toros. But he committed the
biggest gaffe of his career and aroused the wrath of *aficionados*
throughout the country when, in "The Dangerous Summer," he insulted the memory of a national hero and his followers: "It will be years
before [people] know that Manolete was a great bullfighter with cheap
tricks and that he used the cheap tricks because his public wanted
them. He was fighting before an ignorant public that enjoyed being
defrauded."[14]

Hemingway had unwisely sold Spanish-language rights for an additional $10,000 and feared that his criticism of Manolete would provoke
an angry reaction when "El Verano Sangriento" appeared in the Spanish edition of *Life* in October–November 1960. Castillo-Puche said the
article aroused slanderous gossip, insulting letters and political hostility:

When Ernesto used the words "cheap tricks" in reference to Manolete,
the *aficionados*—and many other people—were terribly offended. It

was something like an insult to the whole country, throwing down the gauntlet to challenge every last Spaniard. The newspapers and magazines had taken out on Ernesto all their resentment for things that had happened long before. His worst sin wasn't what he had written about bullfighting; they naturally brought up again his whole [anti-Fascist] role in the Civil War.

Ordóñez defended Hemingway, ignored his use of the word "cheap" and claimed: "This was a mistranslation. *Truco* can also be a positive term when, for example, it applies to food and drink. I don't think Hemingway really meant to criticize Manolete." Dominguín cynically believed: "Hemingway wrote this as a deliberate provocation, to go against all accepted opinion [about Manolete]. He once asked me: 'what is your trick?' And I answered: 'Love for the art, a passion to be perfect.' "[15]

Dominguín, whose father had also been a bullfighter, was born in the province of Toledo in 1925. After becoming a matador in 1944, Dominguín had challenged Manolete for the supreme position in bullfighting and was competing with him *mano a mano* in Linares in August 1947 when Manolete was killed by a Miura bull. Dominguín retired at the peak of his profession in 1953, but returned to accept the challenge of Ordóñez in 1958. During the dangerous summer of 1959 they fought *mano a mano* three times: in Valencia, Málaga and Ciudad Real. Both men were seriously gored: Dominguín in Valencia and Bilbao, Ordóñez in Aranjuez and Palma de Majorca. Because of penicillin, improved surgical techniques and operating rooms in the major bullrings, all of which had developed since the 1920s, wounded matadors were much less likely to die in the 1950s. Dominguín and Ordóñez, despite their injuries, were able to continue their corridas. Hemingway told Patrick, recalling his own war wounds and nightmares: Ordóñez "has thirteen cornadas altogether and not one of them has spooked him. He is spooked sometimes in the night the way we all are and prefers to sleep in the daytime."[16]

In contrast to Ordóñez, Dominguín had led a flamboyant life outside the bullring. He was lively, witty, sharp-tongued and sophisticated. When he first retired as Spain's leading matador in 1953, he had no interests outside his profession. He tried various ventures—a bull ranch in Peru, business in Spain, education in Paris, big-game hunting in Africa—and had a well-known affair with Ava Gardner, but none of these things held his interest. In 1959 he was far more worldly and experienced than Antonio, the younger and more successful torero.

Antonio Ordóñez, born in Ronda in 1932, was the son of the matador who fought under the name Niño de la Palma, the model for the handsome Pedro Romero in *The Sun Also Rises*. By 1932 Niño had fallen from grace, and was condemned in *Death in the Afternoon:* Niño de la Palma "started to be great but after his first severe goring developed a cowardice which was only equalled by his ability to avoid taking chances in the ring. . . . If you see Niño de la Palma the chances are you will see cowardice in its least attractive form; its fat rumped, prematurely bald from using hair fixatives, prematurely senile form."[17] Ordóñez, who became the friend of the man who had written these cruel things about his father, explained: "I have read Hemingway's criticism in *Death in the Afternoon*. But I believe that a bullfighter, a public figure who is judged by a mass audience, must learn to accept and to ignore destructive criticism. If a critic is negative about you, that means he has no understanding of what you are doing. I don't know about my father's friendship with Hemingway or his response to *The Sun Also Rises*."

Ordóñez became a full matador in 1951 and was managed by Domínguín's father; he married Domínguín's beautiful sister Carmen in 1953 and was devoted to his family. Hemingway met Ordóñez in Pamplona in 1953, during his first postwar trip to Spain. He was immediately charmed by Ordóñez and later wrote: "I noticed the eyes first; the darkest, brightest, merriest eyes anybody ever looked into and the mischief urchin grin and could not help seeing the scar welts on the right thigh. Antonio reached his left hand out, the right had been badly cut by the sword on his second kill, and said, 'Sit down on the bed. Tell me. Am I as good as my father [was in his best days]?' "[18]

Hemingway and Ordóñez did not have a great deal in common, apart from their passion for bullfighting. Ordóñez, who had left school at fourteen, half-jokingly said that a great bullfighter did not have to know how to read or write: "All I need to do is to be able to sign my name on a check." Apart from bulls, his interests included cards, soccer, movies, adventure stories and sports cars. He had little knowledge of Hemingway's work and remarked: "What a great life you writers lead —all you have to do is keep pushing the pen around."[19]

But they had great respect and sympathy for each other. Hemingway was at his best with Ordóñez, who was like a son and inspired both tenderness and awe. For Ordóñez had everything that Hemingway most admired. He was young, handsome, warm-hearted, manly, rich and famous, and had a beautiful wife. He was the son of an old friend, had realized the greatness his father failed to achieve and allowed Hemingway to recapture the spirit of his own youth in Spain. Most important, he was highly skilled in an art that Hemingway greatly admired. The writer believed it was necessary to find "some people that by their actual physical conduct gave you a real feeling of admiration . . . [and] I have got hold of it in bull fighting"[20]—particularly in Ordóñez. Antonio became Hemingway's hero and received valuable publicity as the novelist spread the matador's fame to English-speaking countries.

Hemingway spent the summer of 1959, accompanied by Bill Davis and Hotchner, criss-crossing Spain in his Lancia and following the grueling schedules of the two bullfighters. The "Dangerous Summer" articles—which were originally intended to be a supplement to the second edition of *Death in the Afternoon,* but did not appear in book form until 1985—were a financial success and a literary failure. He earned $30,000 —$15 a word!—for a 2,000-word article, "A Matter of Wind," which appeared in *Sports Illustrated* in August 1959; $90,000 for the English-language rights of "The Dangerous Summer," which was drastically cut from 120,000 to 70,000 words and published in *Life* in September 1960. Just as "The African Journal" seemed to be a weak parody of *Green Hills of Africa,* so "The Dangerous Summer"—flat, wordy, smug—was a pale imitation of *Death in the Afternoon.*

In *Death in the Afternoon* the rivalry between Joselito and Belmonte had played a relatively minor role in the description of the history and ritual of the bullfight, which was placed in the context of Spanish culture. In "The Dangerous Summer" the focus was narrowed to Hemingway's personal attitude toward the competition of Dominguín and Ordóñez, and became repetitious, self-parodic and dull. His experience and expertise did not deepen his knowledge and understanding as they had done in *Death in the Afternoon.* Age did not bring serenity and wisdom, but irritation and a sense of loss.

Hemingway's bias against Dominguín was immediately apparent in the criticism of his physique and character—a strong contrast to his emotional enthusiasm for Ordóñez: "Luis Miguel was a charmer, tall, dark, no hips, just a touch too long in the neck for a bullfighter, with a grave mocking face that went from professional disdain to easy laughter." Hemingway's prejudice extended to his capework: Dominguín's "style did not move me at all. I did not like the way he handled the cape," whereas Ordóñez "was using the cape as no one alive had ever used it."[21] Hemingway also claimed, rather unfairly, that Ordóñez could handle the wind—always dangerous when it accidentally blows the cape in a bullfight—and that Dominguín could not. As soon as their personal combat started, Hemingway portrayed Dominguín as tight-lipped, white-faced and neurotic, barely escaping disaster through the relentless but tragically preordained pressure of Ordóñez.

Dominguín believed: "He was grossly unfair. He mistakenly said that the best bulls were reserved for me, the poorer ones for Antonio; that I could not handle the wind; and many other things that he knew to be false. Because he was not honest, and knew it, he never published these articles as a book or even as a supplement to *Death in the Afternoon.*" Ordóñez, however, rather simplistically justified Hemingway's personal loyalty: "A writer always praises and defends his true friends. Hemingway's main loyalty was to me, so he naturally tried to dramatize the conflict and diminish Dominguín in his description of the three *mano a manos.*" Hemingway described Dominguín's *cornadas* and printed a photograph of him in the hospital; but Ordóñez's gorings occurred offstage and were merely mentioned.

Dominguín was cool, caustic and much more critical of Hemingway than the reverential Ordóñez. He felt equal or superior to Hemingway, was irritated by his personality and was not, like Ordóñez, willing to play the son's role. Dominguín said:

I first met Hemingway in a Madrid bar, La Alemana, on the Plaza de Santa Ana in 1953. I was not aware of his reputation as a writer. At that time, I knew about nothing but bulls. Hemingway was a great personality. But I immediately knew he was an *embustero*—a liar—when he claimed he had killed water buffalo with a spear, like the Masai. He had a gigantic ego. He pretended to knowledge he did not have. I was a rebel, refused to call him Papa and used his proper name, Ernesto. That name does not have the priggish connotations in Spanish which it took on in English after Wilde's play, *The Importance of Being Earnest.* The monk makes the habit, the man makes the name. A Spaniard called Jesús might well be an imbecile.

It was difficult to converse with him, especially at his Finca in Havana [in September 1954], because his Spanish was extremely poor, even childlike; because he worked in the mornings; and because he began to drink heavily as soon as he stopped writing. There was only a brief period during the first few drinks when good talk was possible. Hemingway talked mainly about women and bragged of his sexual conquests at the Floridita, a Havana bar with an upstairs *bordello*. He once said he had made love five times that morning. This was obviously absurd. It was naive of him to think that I would believe him, would be impressed by his claims and would agree that five times was better than four times, that quantity was better than quality.

Hemingway also asked many questions about my own sexual life, especially with Ava Gardner. I thought this was insensitive and crude, and told him: "one doesn't ask a man such questions." His good relations with Ava lasted only a short while, when she was ill for a week trying to pass a painful kidney stone. Hemingway tried to play the conquistador and she soon tired of him.

In May 1957, Hemingway told Harvey Breit about the two sides of Ava's personality. She could be sweet, attractive, witty and good fun. She also had a sharp tongue and could be an absolute devil. She suffered from a sense of inferiority and reacted violently if anyone joked about her.[22]

Dominguín also spoke of his visit to Havana, his quarrel with Hemingway and Hemingway's expertise in bullfighting:

Hemingway told Cuban reporters that I had come to Havana to ask his advice about bullfighting. When they questioned me about this at the airport, I said: "That's absurd. Hemingway can't tell me anything about bulls." And when I [disparaged his achievement and] sarcastically remarked: "Hemingway won the Marshall Plan Nobel Prize," he became angry, our relations cooled considerably and he shifted his allegiance to Ordóñez. Hemingway was all or nothing about people, always demanded that they agree with him.

Hemingway had no knowledge of bullfighting. His knowledge of bulls, like one's knowledge of languages or painting, was relative. He knew more than most Americans but less than almost all Spaniards. But this is a very difficult subject to know about and I would say that only ten percent of matadors have any real understanding of bullfighting.

I never read *Death in the Afternoon*, though I've been told about it, because there is nothing I could learn from it. It is an extremely superficial book, whose defensive tone was meant to counter Anglo-Saxon cultural hostility, and was written solely for Americans. He was right, however, about Niño de la Palma. He had a brief moment, two years at most, and then went down rapidly. Sidney Franklin, the American bullfighter who helped Hemingway with that book, had absolutely no standing as a matador in Spain. I have no interest in reading Hemingway's books. He certainly never gave me any advice or encouragement about writing. I threw away his letters and all the other letters I received because I fear papers even more than I fear bulls.

Ordóñez, by contrast, genuinely admired Hemingway and was very careful not to criticize his friend. The contradictory attitudes of Dominguín and Ordóñez revealed as much about them as about Hemingway. Their responses—one hostile, the other sympathetic—were completely subjective and entirely determined by his relations with them and writings about them.

Ordóñez said that when they first met,

I knew he was a world famous writer, but I was not yet acquainted with his books. He was a fine human being: strong, sympathetic, warm and kind. He loved life. We were often alone, despite my *cuadrilla*—and his! But we talked very little about bulls. We made a pact and agreed that I would not advise him about how to write books and he would not tell me how to fight bulls. We spoke of all the things you normally talk about with comrades: food, drink, friends, love, travel, business, politics, books, art and Spain.

Hemingway's knowledge of Spanish and of Spain was very good. He knew more about the country than most educated Spaniards. I saw no sign of Catholicism in him. But he had respect for the religion of others. I always got along perfectly with him. I never felt he was possessive or domineering. His knowledge of bullfighting was virtually perfect, though Spaniards never respect the opinion of foreigners about either bulls or flamenco. The people erected a bust of Hemingway outside the Pamplona bullring, and today they respect, admire and even love him.

Hemingway's bias in "The Dangerous Summer" exacerbated the hostility of the two bullfighters. Dominguín admitted that in a gladiatorial sport where a great deal of money is at stake, "toreros are more jealous than actors, more jealous even than prima donnas in opera. It is not just part of our nature, it is also something which others push us to, deliberately." Dominguín was extremely antagonistic to Hemingway and in a biography published in 1972, called him a drunkard, liar and bore; vulgar, childish and slightly mad. And he quoted Hemingway's threat: "I'm going to ruin you for life, Miguel. . . . I'll have you kept out of the ring." Dominguín, who had been accused of forcing Manolete to take unnecessary risks, maintained that Hemingway, by provoking Ordóñez and promoting "The Dangerous Summer" for his own profit, deliberately transformed their harmless rivalry into a fanatical fight to the death. Dominguín's attack was bitter and biased; but he did expose some of the weaknesses of the aging Hemingway.

Dominguín was even more savage about Ordóñez's career, character and cowardice. Dominguín claimed, with considerable exaggeration: "My father found him and made him into a torero, but I gave him his career. I took him from nowhere to as near the top as he could get with his talents. . . . Antonio hardly had a ring left that wanted him, unless it was with me." Their hostility was intensified after Ordóñez dismissed Dominguín's father as his manager because of "dishonesty." The intelligent, quick-witted Dominguín called Ordóñez greedy and unscrupulous, consumed with jealousy, cowardly, slimy and stupid: "He knew that I couldn't give up while he was still trying to take my place as Número Uno; he knew that I was too proud to allow shit to follow on the real thing. All through the years before Hemingway got into the act it had been one long story of provoking me, cheating me, lying, trying to get ahead, climbing on people's backs."[23]

IV

Hemingway had been invited to spend the dangerous summer of 1959 at the estate of a wealthy expatriate American, Nathan (Bill) Davis, and used his luxurious home as a base between bullfight expeditions. Davis was born in California in 1907 and first visited Spain, where his father had business connections, in 1926. He greatly admired *The Sun Also Rises,* which appeared that year; after Davis met Pauline in San Francisco, he used her introduction to meet Hemingway in Sun Valley in 1941. Hemingway and Martha visited Davis in Mexico in the spring of 1942. Davis—tall, thin, ruddy-faced, quiet and well-read—had known Trotsky in Mexico, was the brother-in-law of Cyril Connolly, and collected Jackson Pollock paintings and literary celebrities. His friendship with Hemingway was based on their common interest in Spain and bullfighting; on Davis' reverential attitude toward Hemingway's work, character and conversation; on Davis' eagerness to be his driver and host. Ordóñez, staggered by the number of books in Davis' house, gave him the slang nickname *El Negro* (the ghostwriter) and the epithet stuck because of Davis' broad lips and nose, and his humble attitude toward Hemingway. According to Castillo-Puche, Hemingway would introduce Davis, affectionately rather than maliciously, as "my nigger, my slave." Davis, who felt no resentment about this, modestly called himself a "glorified yes man."[24]

Davis' estate, La Consula, built in 1835 and located in Churriana, a village near the Málaga airport, recalled the grandeur of Hemingway's Key West house and the privacy of the Finca. It had remained in Spanish hands until the Civil War, when it was neglected, abandoned and ruined. Davis bought it from an Englishman in 1951, completely restored it and lived there until 1973. The entrance to the estate was marked by a lamplit arch and a long tree-lined drive that led to the splendid two-story house. The shuttered, high-ceilinged rooms opened onto a wide balcony around the second floor and overlooked an extensive garden and park, with fountains and a sixty-foot swimming pool. Hemingway found it an ideal refuge for work and rest, and described it as "a wonderful huge cool house with cool rooms and esparto grass reed-plaited mats in the corridors and the rooms, and every room was full of books and there were old maps on the walls and good pictures. There were fireplaces for when it would be cold. There was a swimming pool fed by water from a mountain spring and there was no telephone."[25]

When Hemingway learned that his sixtieth birthday coincided with the thirtieth birthday of Carmen Ordóñez, he decided to have a lavish party at La Consula on July 21, 1959. Mary organized the details and paid for the party with the thousand dollars she had earned from *Sports Illustrated* for an article on Ordóñez's convalescence. But she had broken her toe, and seemed tense and unhappy, while Hemingway was surrounded by courtiers competing to attract his attention and satisy his needs.

Hemingway summoned his distant friends, who flew in from America and Europe. The guests included Bill and Annie Davis, Antonio and Carmen Ordóñez, Buck Lanham, Evangeline and David Bruce (who was then American ambassador to Germany), Gianfranco and Cristina Ivancich, Valerie Danby-Smith, the Maharajah of Cooch Behar (brother-in-law to the Indian ambassador to Spain and an enthusiastic *aficionado,* whom Hemingway had met in Zaragoza in 1956), George and Pat Saviers from Sun Valley, Hotchner and Peter Buckley. Gerald Brenan, who lived near Davis in Churriana and whose books on Spanish culture had been praised by Hemingway, noted that in the mid-1950s the massive, white-bearded Hemingway "suggested one of the famous sea captains of past ages who have spent their best years in the Arctic."[26]

The festivities went on through the night and included guitar players and flamenco dancers, an orchestra, photographers, fireworks that set a palm tree on fire and a shooting gallery with a caricature of Buckley as the target. Ordóñez recalled:

> The Consula party was only a party, but it was a very good one. Hemingway shot cigarettes out of my mouth with pellets from the kind of air gun you use at a fair stand. They were not real bullets, but they could damage your face. Later on, at El Escorial outside Madrid, he shot cigarettes out of my mouth with real bullets.
>
> Hemingway respected Davis more than Hotchner because he thought Hotchner was a poor writer. I named him *El Pecas:* Freckles. We dressed him up as a torero. He marched in my opening paseo but didn't take part in the actual fight.

Certain aspects of Hemingway's behavior, mentioned by Ordóñez, revealed how much his attitudes and values had changed by 1959. Gregory, who had always been taught to treat guns with the greatest care and caution, knew his father was deteriorating when he read that Hemingway took uncharacteristic risks and shot cigarettes out of Ordóñez's mouth.[27] It was also most unusual for Hemingway, who extolled the high art of the corrida and condemned the decadence of the modern bullfight, to mock the ritual by encouraging Hotchner to walk in the *paseo* during the final *mano a mano* at Ciudad Real in August 1959. At the party, when Lanham's arm accidentally grazed the back of his head, Hemingway infuriated his friend by shouting that no one was allowed to touch his head. He then rather pathetically explained to Lanham that he had combed his hair forward to hide his baldness and was afraid of revealing his bare scalp.

During this period Hemingway had the last of the injuries and accidents—though not the last of his illnesses—that had plagued him since childhood. While attempting to vault a high wire fence in Ketchum in October 1958, he sprained his ankle and damaged his heel tendon. Just after the party, while Davis was driving Hemingway and Valerie from Burgos to Madrid, Hemingway was involved in his fourth road accident.

Davis, who was not a good driver, became drowsy, lost control, bounced off a concrete barrier and damaged the car (but not the passengers). They drove on to the capital and then flew down to Málaga. In September Hemingway's pocket was picked for the third time in Spain while he was signing autographs in Murcia. In a newspaper advertisement, he sportingly appealed to the thief to return the wallet and St. Christopher's medal and keep the $150 as a tribute to his technical skill.

V

Hemingway aroused Mary's jealousy and treated her cruelly in 1959, as he had done when he fell in love with Adriana ten years earlier, by adopting Valerie Danby-Smith as his companion and secretary. Like Ben Jonson's Volpone, he attempted to renew his youth by associating with a nineteen-year-old girl. Castillo-Puche observed: "He was noticeably cold and distant and indifferent to [Mary] at times, as though he were a stranger living at her side. He made excuses for not making love to her. . . . I was surprised to see that Ernesto worried constantly about Antonio's little scratch [acquired during the running of the bulls], which required no more than a strip of adhesive tape, yet dismissed Mary's really painful injury [a broken toe] as nothing at all." Lanham, much closer to both Ernest and Mary, put it more bluntly and said Hemingway "treated Mary like a god damned dog." At La Consula, while neglecting his wife, Hemingway boasted to Lanham that Mary "would be more amenable [because] he'd irrigated her four times the night before." After Hemingway's death, when Lanham asked if his aging friend had been a magnificent lover, Mary tartly replied: "I wish to hell it were true."[28]

At the end of his life, Hemingway found Mary willing and useful, but no longer seemed to love her. According to Jack Hemingway, Mary tried to control Hemingway by excluding some of his friends, and sometimes made him unhappy by her desire to spend money and to lead an active social life. As he became old and sick, he feared that he would grow completely dependent upon Mary. And he felt that she inhibited his courtship of Valerie as she had done with Adriana. He may even have wanted to leave Mary for the young girl, but no longer had the strength and confidence to go through yet another divorce and marriage. Mary, who had done everything to please Hemingway and found it unbearable to watch him "destroying himself," stated: "The London Blitz was not so bad a strain for me as the summer of 1959, which was horrible and hideous and miserable." For the second time, she seriously thought of leaving him. She was deeply wounded and felt he no longer wanted her to be his wife, but "would not allow hurt or pique to propel [her] into hasty, hysterical action" and learned to tolerate Valerie.[29]

Valerie Danby-Smith, the daughter of an Irish building contractor, was born in 1940 and grew up in a suburb of Dublin. After finishing high school, she worked as English tutor to a family in Madrid and as stringer for a Belgian news agency. In the spring of 1959 she was sent to interview Hemingway at the Hotel Suecia, but was inexperienced and botched the job. Hemingway, the gallant old journalist, was patient and pedagogic, told her the proper way to conduct an interview and said she must come to the Pamplona festival in July. She did not think his invitation (or command) was serious until she received a letter from Juanito Quintana, who had arranged her room reservation and bullfight tickets.

During the fiesta Hemingway paired Valerie with a depressing reporter from the *Christian Science Monitor* who later committed suicide. Hemingway was obsessive about controlling her, and everyone else. She soon became weary of all the bullfights, spongers, heavy drinking, tall stories and late hours, but did not want to disappoint him. When she said she was ill as an excuse to escape and be alone, he sent Dr. Saviers to examine her. He invited Valerie to his party at La Consula and hired her as his secretary (which involved very little work) at a salary of $250 a month. She continued to work for him, after they left Spain, in Cuba and Ketchum; and worked for Mary after his death. Life was intense and frantic in Spain, but calmed down at the Finca, where Hemingway and Mary seemed happier. They all established a regular routine of dressmakers, cockfights, swimming and fishing, and of social life with friends like the American ambassador Philip Bonsal and Dr. José Luis Herrera.[30] Hemingway continued to write for a few hours each day, truly but not well.

Valerie was fair-skinned, dark-haired, intelligent and responsive. She had a vague resemblance to some of the pale noble ladies painted by Goya and was appealing rather than beautiful. Hemingway, who had a transfiguring imagination, idealized his current passion and fancied

that Valerie looked like Adriana and even the stunning Carmen Ordóñez. But Hemingway's two teenage idols were very different in appearance, character and circumstance. Adriana was aristocratic, Italian,
beautiful, tragic; she was an honored guest at the Finca, closely guarded
by her mother. Valerie, middle-class and Irish, was less attractive and
exotic. She was far from her parents, hero-worshipped Hemingway, and
became an employee and a member of his household. Valerie also
established a friendship (rather than a rivalry) with his wife. Mary accepted Valerie's relations with Hemingway, which cheered him up,
improved his behavior and made him more bearable. In February 1960
Mary wrote to Clara Spiegel, with some irony, that she was entertaining
a nice little nineteen-year-old Dublin girl, who "secretaries" (a new
verb) for him and fits gracefully into their life.

Castillo-Puche, who had a poor opinion of foreign women, noted
Hemingway's infatuation and criticized Valerie's behavior in Spain:
"He couldn't keep himself from casting covert glances at the affectionate little Irish girl with the unkempt hair, or touching her. . . . She kept
stroking herself, and constantly acted more or less like a little bitch in
heat. She was a very pretty little creature, who was to lose a great many
things at the fiesta." Despite these snide innuendos, Castillo anticlimac-
tically concludes: "In actual fact, it was all very open and aboveboard
and rather dull."[31]

Hemingway's friends were puzzled by the precise nature of his
relations with Valerie and wondered if "she put on his knowledge with
his power / Before the [ardent] beak could let her drop." Toby Bruce
doubted if she was Hemingway's mistress. Bill Davis saw no evidence
of their sleeping together at La Consula. But Clara Spiegel got the
impression from Mary (although she was never told directly) that Hemingway and Valerie were lovers. Buck Lanham and George Plimpton
also thought they slept together.[32]

Valerie knew that Hemingway was attracted to her and wanted her
to stay with him. On October 25, 1960, a month after she saw him for
the last time and a month before he entered the Mayo Clinic, he linked
their fates (as he had done with Adriana) and confessed that he loved
her very much and missed her help. It had been a difficult time of year,
and he could not work in Ketchum unless he was sure she was all right
and doing well. His last (jumbled) telegram to her from Ketchum read:
"Goodbye. Have good luck whatever you do. Forever [i.e., wherever
you] go."[33]

VI

Writing in the *Transatlantic Review* in October 1924 and perhaps thinking of Ford's hastily published memoir of Conrad, the young Hemingway stated: "It is only when you no longer believe in your own exploits that you can write your memoirs." Ten years later, writing in *Esquire* and perhaps thinking of Stein's cunningly constructed *Autobiography,* he accurately predicted: "legendary people usually end by writing their memoirs." And in 1954, examining his life and obituaries after narrowly escaping death in Africa, he showed more respect for memoirs and observed: "The most complicated subject that I know, since I am a man, is a man's life." But Stein, who knew him well, noted the moral and artistic difficulties of doing justice to that complicated subject: "What a book . . . would be the real story of Hemingway, not those he writes but the confessions of the real Ernest Hemingway."[34]

A Moveable Feast, Hemingway's nostalgic memoir of his life in Paris during 1921–26—when he was in love with his wife and writing his most original work—was partly inspired by the astonishing recovery in November 1956 of two small trunks containing typed fiction, colored notebooks, newspaper clippings, books and old clothes that he had stored in the basement of the Ritz Hotel in Paris when he left for Key West in March 1928. Though none of the memoir, apart from the chapter on Ford, belongs to the 1920s, the discovery of the trunks and the visits to some of his old haunts in the 1950s triggered his remembrance of things past. "The African Journal" and "The Dangerous Summer" were imitations and self-parodies. *A Moveable Feast* was a repossession of original material that Hemingway had hinted at but never properly developed, a self-exploration that allowed him to recreate the days of poverty and purity, before he had succumbed to the weakness and corruption predicted in *Green Hills of Africa* and "The Snows of Kilimanjaro."

The memoir was mainly written in Cuba and Idaho from the fall of 1957 to the spring of 1960. After completing the work he confirmed the topographical accuracy by retracing his footsteps in Paris. He had kind words to say about Sylvia Beach, Jules Pascin, Pound, Joyce and Shipman; but he was not loyal to most of his old friends. Though his distinguished companions and competitors were either *hors de combat* or dead, most of his portraits were venomous and brutal. After his death the book was edited and prepared for press by Mary. Passages from eleven of the twenty sketches appeared in *Life* (April 1964) a month before the publication of the book, which had a first printing of 85,000 copies. The memoir was on the best-seller list from May to December 1964, and held first place for nineteen weeks from June to October.

The critics, who used the posthumous publication to evaluate Hemingway's entire career, praised the indirect self-portrait—his imposing presence was there "by reflection"—for its clarity of recall and vividness of scene. Nearly everyone disapproved of his bitchiness and agreed that the nasty, funny and moving sections on Fitzgerald were the most interesting part of the book. Some reviewers, grateful for this gift from beyond the grave, were adulatory. George Plimpton stated, on the front page of the *New York Herald Tribune Book Week:* "The Paris sketches are absolutely controlled, far enough removed in time so that the scenes and characters are observed in tranquillity, and yet with astonishing immediacy—his remarkable gift—so that many of the sketches have the hard brilliance of his best fiction." He called the memoir a therapeutic work which still retained "a note of impending chaos and death." Morley Callaghan, who had been on the scene in the 1920s, called Hemingway "an attractive, interesting, fascinating companion, dark and brooding though he might be, with strange shrewd hunches about people that turned into grudges." He thought the power of the book came from Hemingway's recognition—in the twenties—that this would be the happiest period of his life: "when the time came to write this book, maybe he knew what he had lost. And maybe this knowledge explains the book's bitter tone . . . the quick leap for the jugular vein."[35]

The longer reviews by three English writers were more severe. In an acute analysis, Julian Maclaren-Ross (who could have drunk Papa under the table) expressed great admiration for the writer whose life and work had a considerable influence on his own career. He was not entirely uncritical, however; he remarked that "A lot of nostalgic nonsense is often written about poverty and hunger by successful authors who no longer have to experience them," and that Hadley seemed to be the model for all the "far too admiring and acquiescent" women in his fiction. Tony Tanner also thought that "Hemingway certainly reveals himself more nakedly than he can have intended. . . . The book is written with a good deal of arrogance: every episode is turned to leave Hemingway looking tougher, more talented, more honest, more dignified than anyone else." He too saw the book as a doomed idyll whose "dawn brightness is occasionally darkened by sombre intimations of twilight." Frank Kermode ironically noted that Hemingway's famous built-in shit detector "can purge not only your prose but your acquaintance." But he stated that this essentially fictional work is "about the heroic apprenticeship" of writing, that it is, "in some ways, Hemingway's best book since the 1920s" and that (like Proust) it conveys with "authority and distinction . . . the sense of time regained."[36]

In a typically tough-minded, authoritative essay, Marvin Mudrick utilized Edmund Wilson's distinction between "the early master and the old impostor." He noted: "The reputation had its lethal effect on criticism, which either attacked the public image as if it were all there was of Hemingway, or praised virtually all of Hemingway as if the public image were quite unrelated to the work." He called Hemingway's early style "as original and personal an invention as anything in literature" and concluded: "That Hemingway could have resolved to risk such a candor of private regret and longing [about his first marriage] against the grain of his so carefully cultivated reputation, less than a year before his death, is the proof of the strength he could still muster."[37]

"Movable feast" is an ecclesiastical term which applies to holidays, like Easter, that are not fixed to a specific date. Hemingway first used the phrase in *Across the River* when Cantwell says: "Happiness, as you know, is a movable feast," but he also referred to his book as "The Autobiography of Alice B. Hemorrhoid." The form as well as the content is related to his previous works, for he had alluded to his early life in Paris in "The Snows of Kilimanjaro," *Islands in the Stream* and "The Dangerous Summer." Confronted by the literary enthusiasms of the farm manager Kandinsky in *Green Hills of Africa,* he menacingly said: "I did not wish to destroy anything this man had, and so I did not go into those brilliant people in detail." But there was no such restraint in his memoir. In his Foreword to the African book he stated that he wanted to see if "an absolutely true book . . . can compete with a work of the imagination"; in the Preface to *A Moveable Feast* he again obscured the generic basis of the book and blurred the distinction between fact and fiction: "If the reader prefers, this book may be regarded as fiction. But there is always the chance that such a book of fiction may throw some light on what has been written as fact." *A Moveable Feast* finally fulfills Harry's desire, in "The Snows of Kilimanjaro," to describe his youthful expatriate life: "He remembered the good times with them all, and the quarrels. They always picked the finest places to have the quarrels. . . . He had never written any of that because, at first, he never wanted to hurt any one and then it seemed as though there was enough to write about without it. . . . Now he would never write the things that he had saved to write until he knew enough to write them well."[38]

A Moveable Feast is fictionalized autobiography, loosely based on fact but heightened by the imagination. Since subjective truth was more important to Hemingway (and to most other writers) than literal truth, he engaged in his familiar habit of reconstructing his life to fit his personal mythology and recreating his own vision of the past. Malraux observed in his essay on T. E. Lawrence: "Whoever writes his memoirs (except to deceive) judges himself,"[39] and there is more deception than self-judgment in Hemingway's memoir. He presents a retrospective view of how he began as a writer and provides essential background for *The Sun Also Rises.* He idealizes Hadley and exaggerates his poverty in his "Down and Out in Paris and Schruns." And he always portrays himself as superior to others. He is a knowledgeable and sophisticated insider, a dedicated and disciplined writer, a severe judge of his numerous friends and acquaintances. His sketches start sweetly but suddenly turn sour. They are based on a series of thematic polarities—poverty-wealth, simplicity-complexity, purity-filth, friendship-loneliness—that contrast Hemingway and Hadley to the sterile artists and decadent bohemians of the Latin Quarter.

The retrospective distortion of reality is revealed in three ways. First, Hemingway was not especially interested in food until the postwar period, when he began to frequent luxurious restaurants; but the feast often becomes quite literal as his current culinary tastes (like much else in the book) are transposed from the 1950s to the 1920s. Second, the pervasive theme of death marks the memoir as a late rather than a youthful work. Fitzgerald's face is a death mask, Ernest Walsh is marked by death, Ralph Cheever Dunning is dying, Jules Pascin hanged himself. Finally, all the characters but Ford are portrayed not as they were in the 1920s, but as Hemingway saw them after the quarrels of the 1930s. Stein was not a disgusting lesbian until after her *Autobiography* in 1933, Wyndham Lewis did not have the eyes of an unsuccessful rapist until "The Dumb Ox" in 1934, Fitzgerald was not an alcoholic failure until the "Crack-Up" articles in 1936, Dos Passos was not a sycophantic and destructive toady until after the bitter fight about José Robles in 1937, Pauline was not a predatory bitch until Hemingway left her in 1939.

Hemingway's memoir offers a bitter recreation of and nostalgic longing for the powerfully absorbing friendships of his youth. By describing how he first found his vocation and realized his talent, the aging writer was able to repossess his art and present a distorted though completely convincing account of his Paris years. *A Moveable Feast,* infinitely superior to all his postwar books, was his greatest work of nonfiction. The memoir decisively showed that Hemingway had arrested his decline and regained the full force of his literary power only months before he entered the Mayo Clinic.

26

Mayo Clinic
1960–1961

> Doctors did things to you and then
> it was not your body any more.
>
> *A Farewell to Arms*

I

Hemingway's last decade was a period of disintegration. The African plane crashes ruined his physical health and filled him with splinters of mortality. A fatal combination of physical and mental illness during the last year of his life accelerated his tragic descent from the triumphs of *The Old Man and the Sea* and the Nobel Prize to the disastrous shock treatments at the Mayo Clinic that damaged his memory, intensified his depression and led to his suicide. As Hemingway moved rather desperately from Idaho to Cuba to Spain, and from Ketchum to the Mayo, he seemed like a hunted animal, driven from his lair.

Hemingway, who was erotically aroused by women's hair and had experimented with growing and cutting his own hair to match his lover's, was acutely sensitive about baldness. He had mocked Niño de la Palma's use of hair fixatives and interpreted any attempt to disguise baldness as a sign of moral corruption. In a Spanish War dispatch of 1938, he noted that the lying correspondent who had convinced Martha Gellhorn to carry a dangerous illegal message had "strips of blond hair pasted carefully across a flat-topped bald head" and concluded: "Never trust a man who slicks hair over a bald head." And in *For Whom the Bell Tolls,* one of the Fascists slaughtered by Pablo had hair "brushed over the top of his head from one side to the other to cover a baldness."

538

Hemingway felt particularly bitter when he too lost his hair and (as he contritely told Lanham) was forced to use cosmetic subterfuge.

Hemingway, always handsome and photogenic, had satirized the hideous skin of Sinclair Lewis. Now (at the age of sixty) he was in love with a teenage girl and distressed by the disfiguring effects of chronic skin disease. Castillo-Puche gave a clinical description of "the angry red streak running from his nose to his cheek, the rash of little whitish pustules that sloughed off like dandruff . . . that bright red patch, extending from the bridge of his nose almost down to his mouth and up to his eyes, kept peeling off in scaly white flakes."[1]

Alcohol had always provided an immediate escape from distress. "The bottle becomes a sovereign means of direct action," Hemingway remarked in *Death in the Afternoon*. "If you cannot throw it, at least you can always drink out of it." Just after he returned from World War Two, he told Lanham: "You wake up in the night and things are unbearable and you take a drink and make them bearable."[2] But as he became increasingly dependent on and dominated by alcohol, his damaged organs could no longer tolerate the poison. George Plimpton noticed: "His liver was bad. You could see the bulge of it stand out from his body like a long, fat leech." In his final year, he was forced to break a lifetime habit of heavy drinking, to cut drastically or eliminate entirely his tremendous consumption of alcohol. He strictly followed the doctor's orders, but suffered greatly from the deprivation. Hadley observed, without exaggeration: "He might have survived with alcohol, but could not live when deprived of it."[3]

Hemingway, born with defective vision, felt he had inherited his mother's weak eyes. He had cut his right pupil in 1927, had serious eye problems in the summer of 1931 and had suffered intermittently since then. Trouble developed again in April 1960, as he wrote his publisher from Cuba: "The best man here says there is a progressive deterioration of the vitreous (humor) (matter) caused by much former high blood pressure etc. and the astigmatism, strain, reading without glasses."

His eye problems may have been related not only to hypertension but also to incipient diabetes mellitus, which was diagnosed at the Mayo in December 1960. He had also been frightened and depressed when told by a Cuban doctor in the summer of 1960 that he had hemo-chromatosis, a rare, chronic and fatal form of diabetes, "that makes you blind and permanently impotent." His dark urine, edema of the ankles, high blood urea and high prothrombin time (clotting), reported in his medical examination of January 19, 1961, indicated that he also had liver and kidney disease.[4]

Hemingway's main physical disease, the ostensible reason for his entering the Mayo, was high blood pressure. But reserpine and other drugs he was taking for hypertension had two harmful side effects: they increased his severe depression, which was the real reason for entering the Clinic, and (according to Gregory) paralyzed the "nerves that control the sexual mechanism." Hemingway had become impotent, for psychological and physical reasons, with Pauline just after their marriage in May 1927, with Jane Mason during their crisis in January 1936, and with Mary after his two concussions during August–November 1944. Now his diseased liver, badly damaged by heavy drinking, caused "a high concentration of estrogen in the bloodstream," reduced his libido and contributed to his impotence.[5]

II

In addition to all his physical diseases, Hemingway suffered from obsessions, delusions, paranoid fears of poverty and persecution, extreme depression, inability to work and suicidal impulses, which led to a serious mental breakdown in November 1960. It was difficult for his wife and friends to chart the scarcely perceptible changes that took place as he moved from the personal and aesthetic emphasis on truth and reality in his youth, through the fantasies and myths of his maturity, to the suspicions and terrors of old age. Mary must have been reluctant, even unwilling, to accept the reality of her husband's deterioration. She did not have the ability to probe the nuances of human motivation. She must have found it difficult to reflect on the meaning of Hemingway's thoughts, feelings and actions, and to deal with his mental problems.

All of Hemingway's friends noticed his strange behavior, but there was a natural tendency to dismiss it as a temporary aberration as well as considerable confusion about the proper medical treatment for his illness. As early as October 1958 Toby Bruce noted (or retrospectively remembered) that Hemingway was uncharacteristically hesitant and indecisive. He had difficulty deciding which shirt and belt to wear, which motel to stay at, what to do that day. His Ketchum friends, who had not seen him for ten years, observed the changes but did not understand them. Clara Spiegel sensed that his general attitude had altered and become more negative; that he was, in some way, different —worse. Tillie Arnold was surprised when Hemingway, usually polite and deferential to women when hunting, got angry at Mary and shouted: "you shot my duck." Toward the end of his life, he looked through rather than at Tillie and did not seem to hear what she said. Bud Purdy summed up everyone's feelings when he observed: "poor old Ernie, it was all downhill for him."[6]

In late July 1960 Hemingway left Cuba for the last time and went to New York. He told Mary: "They're tailing me out here already. . . . Somebody waiting out there," and was reluctant to leave the rented apartment on East Sixty-second Street. On a rare visit outside the flat, he would lunch at Toots Shor's with Leonard Lyons or Jimmy Cannon. In early August, when the first signs of mental illness had become apparent, Hemingway impulsively and rather desperately decided he was "needed" by Ordóñez (who had driven with Hemingway from New York to Ketchum the previous November). He flew to Madrid and spent August at La Consula; Mary had suffered greatly from his harsh treatment during the summer of 1959 and did not accompany him. Just as Hemingway had been reported dead after his London car crash in May 1944 and his African plane crash in January 1954, so on August 9, 1960, the wire services reported that he had (appropriately enough) collapsed in the bullring in Málaga. This story was faked by a Swedish journalist in Torremolinos; but there were few men, as Ford said of Pound, "whose deaths have so often been announced."

Hemingway had his first breakdown when he was away from Mary —who provided stability, comfort and reassurance—and was well aware of what was happening. In Spain he had cramps, nightmares and insomnia (despite the heavy doses of sleeping pills); was bored, forgetful, irascible, suspicious, lonely, frightened and guilt-ridden. In August he feared a "complete physical and nervous crack-up from deadly overwork" and complained of his "worn out head—not to mention body." On September 23 he told Mary: "I wish you were here to look after me and help me out and keep from cracking up. Feel terrible and am just going to lie quiet now and try to rest."[7] This, from Hemingway, was an extraordinary admission.

Valerie Danby-Smith had come from Dublin to Havana at Hemingway's request in February 1960 and stayed with him until he left for Spain in August. When the alarming symptoms appeared during his stay at La Consula, Mary must have felt incapable of dealing with them and in September (as Carlos Baker euphemistically put it) "sent Valerie over to help him with his mail." Valerie noticed a tremendous change in him when she reached Madrid. He was extremely worried about everything and felt his problems were hopeless. Many of his fears were irrational. Remembering the car accident near Burgos in 1959, he asked Valerie: "Did you notice how Davis is driving? He's trying to kill me." As a boy, in 1915, he had been pursued by the game warden for shooting a heron and had learned his lesson; he now had an absolute need to obey the law. When Valerie temporarily mislaid her passport and American visa, and asked if they were in his room, he became agitated (as he had been in July when they crossed from Havana to Key West), insisted that she follow all the immigration laws and worried about his responsibility if she broke the rules.[8]

Hotchner has provided the first, though incomplete, account of Hemingway's mental deterioration during the last year of his life. He flew down to the Finca in late June to help Hemingway cut eighty percent of "The Dangerous Summer" for *Life* (this was the first time Hemingway had ever asked for such assistance) and found him unusually hesitant, disorganized and confused. Hemingway kept postponing his flight from Madrid to New York in October, was worried about excess baggage and insisted, for "better security," on taking a slow propeller flight instead of a jet. He was given permission to hunt pheasant on a farmer's land in Ketchum the following month, but was unwilling to go into the field for fear of trespassing and getting shot. He had difficulty completing *A Moveable Feast*, was anxious about the loss of the Finca and distressed about the lack of money—though he sold film rights to *The World of Nick Adams* for $125,000 in January 1961 and was very well off. He had satirized a yachting capitalist who was worried about Internal Revenue Service investigators in *To Have and Have Not*, and now found himself in the same position. He had always been scrupulous about paying his high taxes when he could have reduced or avoided them (he received only $20,000 of the film money after deductions for taxes and lawyer), but was still desperately distressed about taxes. During his last years he did not enjoy his wealth, which brought great insecurity as well as the tedious complications of lawyers, servants, private planes and bad publicity.

His deepest and most disturbing fear concerned the FBI. In June 1952 he had compared Charles Fenton to an FBI agent and told him:

"Nobody likes to be tailed . . . investigated, queried about, by any amateur detective no matter how scholarly or how straight." Three years later at the Floridita, Hemingway met some students from Miami University in Ohio who were on a Navy ROTC summer training cruise in the Caribbean. After buying them drinks, he "stated that a certain person in the bar was an FBI man who was keeping him under surveillance." He reaffirmed this in his "Situation Report" of 1956 when he said the Floridita characters included "the F.B.I. [and] former F.B.I." men. Toby Bruce mentioned that "Papa got kind of neurotic about the FBI toward the end. . . . But then we used to joke about how the FBI was wire-tapping his phone all the time back in the old days."[9]

Both Mary and Hotchner have said that Hemingway imagined he was being followed and spied on by FBI agents in Ketchum and in the Mayo Clinic, and that no kind of argument or evidence could change his mind or alleviate his irrational but quite terrifying fear. Mary and Hotchner thought his fear of the FBI meant that he was losing touch with reality and heading for a mental breakdown. But a letter from the special agent in Minneapolis to Edgar Hoover on January 13, 1961, reported that Hemingway had secretly entered the Mayo Clinic and the FBI knew about his treatment: "He is seriously ill, both physically and mentally, and at one time doctors were considering giving him electro-shock therapy." Dr. Howard Rome, the psychiatrist treating him, "stated that Mr. HEMINGWAY is now worried about his registering under an assumed name, and is concerned about an FBI investigation. [The doctor] stated that inasmuch as this worry was interfering with the treatments of Mr. HEMINGWAY, he desired authorization to tell HEMINGWAY that the FBI was not concerned with his registering under an assumed name. [The doctor] was advised that there was no objection." The FBI had, in fact, tracked Hemingway to the walls of the Mayo Clinic and discussed his case with his psychiatrist. The agents *were* following him, he knew it, and was more realistic and perceptive than his wife and friend. Dr. Rome's contact with the FBI gave substance to Hemingway's fear " that one of the interns was a Fed in disguise."[10] The FBI file on Hemingway proves that even paranoids have real enemies.

It is essential, when attempting to understand Hemingway's mental illness, to distinguish between his trivial and significant symptoms, between his imaginary and real fears. Hotchner wrote that in November 1960: "He had changed so. He seemed depressed. He refused to go hunting. He carped about old friends. He no longer invited a Friday night group to watch the fights. He looked bad." Carlos Baker noted that signs of mental illness, in Hemingway's letter of January 8, 1961, were "his frequent reiteration of the same addresses, his extreme preoccupation with details, his worry over income taxes, his error on the date of his admission to St. Mary's, and his fear of 'security' leaks." All these symptoms were common neurotic traits, observable in many people who function well in the outside world, and did not constitute grounds for psychiatric treatment. Hemingway's reluctance to leave Spain—like his fear of the FBI—also had a rational basis. He was deeply attached to Ordóñez (who was the reason for his visit), was naturally reluctant to leave his close friend and instinctively felt that he would never return to Spain.

Some of Hemingway's problems were quite real. He had failing eyesight and several serious diseases. He had badly misjudged the political situation in Cuba and knew he could not return to the Finca. He had failed to sell his property and get his possessions out of the country, and was rightly worried about losing his house, boat, paintings and everything else. Ketchum did not mean as much to him as Havana; it was a holiday resort, not a home. After Castro had taken over, Elicio Arguelles' wife came to see Hemingway to get dollars and felt something was wrong with him. He was scared, said: "Shut up. Don't talk in front of the servants," and was so upset that she refused the money he offered.[11]

None of the three people closest to and responsible for Hemingway in November 1960 knew exactly what was wrong with him. Mary and Hotchner, of course, had no professional qualifications. After Hemingway's death, Mary told several people that he had been "manic depressive": "He was just exactly, almost, the opposite of what he had been before—outgoing and exuberant and articulate and full of life—and this was all inward and quiet and inarticulate." Hemingway was certainly depressive, but unlike Theodore Roethke and Robert Lowell, he never had a manic phase.

Dr. George Saviers was born in Idaho in 1915, graduated from Berkeley, served in the Navy, trained at Cornell Medical School and had a general practice in Sun Valley. Hemingway called him "Geeorge," went shooting with him, invited him to prizefights in New York, fishing in Havana and the party at La Consula. Dr. Saviers (who is called Vernon Lord in Hotchner's memoir) admitted: "I'm just a country doctor and a pretty young one [i.e., forty-five] at that. I have the responsibility of knowing that Ernest needs immediate help that I can't provide. . . . Ernest is in a serious condition that is so far out of my field that I cannot even diagnose it."[12]

Though everyone meant well, there were some questionable decisions about how to deal with Hemingway's mental illness. His sons, brother and sisters were not informed about his condition until April. There is no evidence that he saw a psychiatrist before he entered the Mayo Clinic. The obvious but vague diagnosis "depressive—persecutory" was made by Dr. James Cattell of New York after Hotchner had described Hemingway's behavior to him. Cattell recommended the Menninger Clinic in Topeka, Kansas, but Saviers felt Hemingway would not be willing to enter a mental hospital and Mary feared bad publicity if the newspapers discovered the nature of his illness. He suffered from paranoid fears and depression, and made frequent suicide threats to Valerie, Mary, Hotchner and Saviers. But it is important to emphasize that Hemingway did not actually attempt suicide until after he had been treated at the Mayo Clinic.

Hemingway had a lifelong scorn of psychiatrists and rejected their belief that every man had a breaking point. In *Death in the Afternoon* he mocked the ambitious claims of the pseudo-science and mentioned "those inner-searching Viennese eyes peering out from under the shaggy brows of old Dr. Hemingstein, that masterful deducer." In *The Fifth Column* the narcissistic Dorothy avoids the real issue and suggests a superficial remedy for Philip's irritation with her: "That's just an inhibition. You could go to an analyst and have that fixed in no time. It's easy and it's very fascinating."[13] Hemingway remained sceptical and told Lillian Ross: "Analyst once wrote me, what did I learn from psychoanalysts? I answered, very little." When asked the name of his analyst, he replied: "Portable Corona No. 3."[14] He had been furious about Lawrence Kubie's essay and was hostile to Philip Young's theory that a "wound-trauma" had inspired his work. He wanted to keep the delicate balance between his psychological state and his creative process private and protected.

Hemingway was a good patient when he was scared by blood in his urine or high blood pressure, and believed he was entering the Mayo to be treated for hypertension (which was then under control). On November 30, 1960, he flew to Rochester, Minnesota (Mary's home state), in a private plane and entered St. Mary's Hospital of the Mayo Clinic. The doctors did not originally plan to admit Hemingway under the name of George Saviers; but the "cattle-pen" admission procedure had many tedious delays and Saviers filled in the complicated forms with his own name in order to expedite matters. Hemingway was agitated at first, but calmed down when he saw the nuns at St. Mary's.[15] They must have reminded him of the kind sisters at Billings Hospital when he was recovering from the fractured arm in 1930.

Rochester is a depressing town, where the modern dance of death goes on in expensive hospitals. All visitors are either sick themselves or related to the sick. A grotesque spectacle of illness appears in the corridors and the streets as the modern pilgrims seek salvation in technology rather than in faith. Hemingway had a number of negative associations with the Mayo Clinic which, combined with his hostility to psychiatrists and the deceit necessary to get him admitted, made his prognosis poor. In 1951 Pauline had been in the Mayo and doctors had failed to diagnose the tumor that soon caused her death. Clara Spiegel and Jinny Pfeiffer also had bad experiences there. Martha Gellhorn, who remained in close touch with her stepsons, retrospectively expressed the feelings of family and friends about the Clinic when she said: "The Mayo made terrible mistakes with Hemingway."[16]

III

An aura of secrecy surrounds Hemingway's treatment at the Mayo. Dr. Irving Yalom, a psychiatrist who has written about Hemingway, recorded: "Dr. Rome informed me, with a finger across his mouth, that before treating Hemingway, he had been obliged to promise that his lips would be forever sealed."[17] Yet we know a good deal about what happened to Hemingway. He was searched when he entered his room, which had double-locked doors and heavily barred windows, in the Psychiatric Unit on the sixth floor. Mary stayed at the Kahler Hotel, ate meals alone in her room and saw him every day. Ordóñez wanted to visit Hemingway at the Mayo and Castillo-Puche convincingly suggested that Antonio "was even more important to Ernesto than Mary; he was the only person who could possibly have revived Ernesto's interest in living after his two visits to the Mayo Clinic." But Bill Davis discouraged Ordóñez and was thanked by Hemingway for doing so. Hemingway seemed conscious—to a degree—of his paranoia and told Davis, with characteristic explicitness: "Doctors say I am getting better." Davis took this to mean that Hemingway knew he was not improving.[18] According to Anthony Burgess (who gave no source), Dr. Rome "was a psychiatrist but did not present himself as one" to Hemingway. Hemingway had been reclusive in New York and Ketchum, and did not even see his own friends. But he became "pals" with the doctors, was the guest of honor at a luncheon attended by many of the doctors' friends and seemed to be treated "like a celebrity as much as a patient."[19]

Hemingway's medical problems were reflected in the titles of five books that he owned and read: William Bates' *The Cure of Imperfect Sight Without Glasses,* Harold Himsworth, *El hígado y sus enfermedades* (The Liver and Its Diseases), Alcoholics Anonymous' *Sedatives and the Alcoholic,* Marcel Lapipe's *Contribution à l'étude physique, physiologique et clinique de l'electrochoc* (1947) and (with eerie foreshadowing) Russell Elliot's *Your Shotgun vs. You.* He had seen the aftermath of Patrick's shock treatments, administered without anesthesia in 1947, which must have increased his own reluctance to submit to them.[20] But Dr. Rome recommended electro-convulsive therapy (ECT), then the best-known treatment for desperate cases, and persuaded him that it would help. In December 1960 he was given between eleven and fifteen electric shocks.

It is not known whether Hemingway or Mary signed the required "Consent for Electrotherapy" form. A sample document describes the procedure in a reassuring (but still alarming) manner and minimizes the dangers:

> Treatments are given in the mornings before breakfast, in a specially equipped treatment room. You will be attended by an anesthetist, a nurse, and a physician.
>
> A needle will be placed in your vein (like you may have had when samples were taken for blood tests) and an anesthetic will be injected. You will be asked to count backwards and you will become drowsy and fall asleep. Other medicines will be given to relax your muscles and reduce the irritability of your heart. The anesthetist will help you breathe with pure oxygen through a mask.
>
> The treatment is given while you are asleep. Momentary electric currents are passed through electrodes on the scalp to stimulate the brain. When the brain is stimulated, there are muscular contractions for up to a minute; but with proper relaxation, the contractions are barely measurable. The treatments take only a few minutes.

Electro-convulsive therapy is "a crude application of electricity to a highly sensitive part of the body" (i.e., the brain).[21] The power applied ranges from 70 to 150 volts (about the same consumed by a large light bulb) and the duration of the electric shock is usually more than one minute. These "electrical inductions of experimental epilepsy" produce seizures (euphemistically called "barely measurable" muscular contractions) that have "characteristics similar to those of the spontaneous seizures recorded from epileptic patients."[22] ECT is supposed to unsettle whatever brain patterns are causing psychopathic behavior in order to allow healthier ones to take their place, but no one understands how this mysterious process works: "Seizures have been induced in the severe mentally ill for more than forty years [i.e., since 1938], and yet no satisfactory explanation of how they elicit improvement in a patient's behavior has been accepted. . . . Current theories of the mode of action of ECT are inconclusive and the standing of the treatment remains empirical."[23]

The dangers, however, are very well known. Because of drugs, patients no longer had to be forcibly held down to prevent injury, but they still urinated, defecated and even ejaculated during ECT.[24] There were risks from anesthesia, the possibility of electrocution and the marked rise in blood pressure during the seizure (this was especially threatening to Hemingway, who had stopped taking reserpine for hypertension because it increased his depression). The most common aftereffects were: "Death, fractures, panic, fear, memory loss, postseizure delirium, spontaneous seizures, and cardiovascular complications. . . . Other complaints were of epilepsy, severe episodic pain, personality change [and] poor concentration."[25] As one would expect, this treatment for severe depressive illness often did not work, was "frequently ineffective in the presence of strong accompanying paranoid trends." And in certain cases—like Hemingway's—it made the mental illness even worse: "In some patients, paranoid ideation, suspiciousness, hostility, ideas of reference, and delusions become more marked."[26]

After 1960, when drugs were introduced in modern ECT, the main risk of the treatment was amnesia:

A unique effect of convulsive therapies compared with other treatments is the production of cognitive impairment, the best investigated component of which is a reversible retrograde amnesia. . . . [Firstly,] everyday forgetfulness such as forgetting names or faces, forgetting phone numbers or messages, forgetting things when going shopping; secondly, holes or gaps in past memories. . . . Patients who complain of [both temporary and permanent] memory impairment are not imagining their disabilities.[27]

For Hemingway, as for most other patients, serious impairment of his memory, of events both immediate to and remote from his illness and treatment, was the most serious possible side effect of the induced seizures.

An objective, clinical description of the procedure and its effects does not convey the emotional intensity of what actually happens when a patient climbs on the table, as Hemingway did, to receive ECT. They clamp the patient's wrists and ankles, put graphite salve on his temples as a conducent, give him a piece of rubber hose to bite on, fasten the electrodes to his scalp, turn the dial and release the current that passes through two layers of skin and bone and enters his brain. After a minute or so, the electricity leaves a sparky smell of burning, corrosion and battery acid.

The subjective and even poetic accounts by three psychotic writers, much more seriously ill than Hemingway was, give a vivid sense of the ghastly process that sometimes produced both convulsions and coma. Lowell compared it to a trolley pole sparking at contact. The French writer Antonin Artaud, who was subjected to this treatment in 1944, explained: "The electric shocks make me despair, take my memory away, numb my thinking and my heart, make me absent and aware of myself as absent. I see myself pursuing my own existence for weeks, like a dead man at the side of a living man who is no longer himself." Artaud begged a friend to secure his release from the hospital "because I don't want my soul, my memory, my consciousness and my personality to be murdered by a new series of electric shocks." Artaud's doctor also described the extreme effects of this terrifying electrocution: "The subanxiety on waking is, on the psychological level, even a desirable phenomenon as it obliges the patient, who has been reduced to nothingness, who has been totally obliterated, to build himself up again."[28] Sylvia Plath, who endured ECT in 1952–53, compared the effect of this horizontal electric chair to "being burned alive all along your nerves" and wondered what terrible thing she had done to deserve this punishment: "Something bent down and took hold of me and shook me like the end of the world. Whee-ee-ee-ee-ee—, it shrilled, through an air crackling with blue light, with each flash a great jolt drubbed me till I thought my bones would break and the sap fly out of me like a split plant."[29] Something like this happened to Ernest Hemingway at the Mayo Clinic.

IV

We do not know exactly what anesthetic was used and where the electrodes were placed, or about the intensity of the current, the duration of each shock, the number of shocks in each series, the convulsions produced and the physical effects of the ECT. But we do know that after the first series was abruptly stopped in January 1961, Hemingway's delusions had not altered or disappeared. He still thought his room was wired and his phone tapped, that one of the doctors was an FBI agent in disguise. He had never kept a notebook and had always been justly proud of his superb memory. Now, in the most tragic moment of his life (far more so than his suicide), he realized that his memory had been virtually destroyed. "What is the sense of ruining my head and erasing my memory, which is my capital, and putting me out of business?" he asked. "It was a brilliant cure but we lost the patient." His increasing sense of physical deterioration, his worries about failing imaginative powers, his desperate fear of losing his reputation as a major author, were now fully realized. His life had culminated in an overwhelming void.

He had hoped to return from the Mayo by Christmas 1960 but was released, in ruins, on January 22, 1961, and flown back to Ketchum in a private plane. In February he was asked to contribute a handwritten tribute to President Kennedy, took an entire week of heroic effort to write three or four simple sentences and—weeping tears of frustration and anguish—told Dr. Saviers that the words would not come anymore. Lloyd Arnold explained the tragedy in his homespun style: "He couldn't write any more, he was done at that; and though he didn't say so directly you got the message that they had tampered with his think machine back there, and loused it up, so it was no good, what he labored to put on paper."[30]

Mary had badly broken her elbow while hunting in November 1959 and had been cared for by Hemingway for several months. Now Hemingway, who had been nursed at the beginning of his adult life by Agnes, was nursed at the end by Mary. He showed little or no improvement after his first stay in the Clinic, and was brutally abusive to his wife. Mary described how he would obsessively and irrationally berate her during the three reclusive months he spent in Ketchum between confinements. He insisted, she said, that "I was not helping him find someplace safe from taxes. I was spending too much on groceries. I had neglected him throughout his stay at St. Mary's Hospital. How could I have enjoyed a TV program that evening when we were in such great danger? I was betraying our well-being." She later remarked: "Ernest was mean: M-E-A-N," but felt it was her duty to stay with him. Hadley compassionately observed: "No need to say how tragic were Ernest's last years—I weep for his sufferings. Lucky he was indeed to have such a wife as Mary."[31]

In April 1961, as conditions became unbearable for Mary, she showed the strain by falling down the stairs and cutting her head. A few weeks later, on April 21, she found Hemingway holding a shotgun and talked to him for nearly an hour until Dr. Saviers arrived to take his daily blood pressure. He persuaded Hemingway to surrender the weapon and put him under heavy sedation in the Sun Valley hospital. On April 25, only three months after his short-lived cure, he reentered the Mayo and was given ten more shock treatments. When Mary visited him in late May, he was absolutely convinced he could not be cured and told her: "You had set things up there [Idaho] so that I'd go to jail. . . . You think as long as you can keep me getting electric shocks, I'd be happy." The man who had avidly devoured books all his life did not read anything during the first six weeks of his second stay in the Clinic.

A few weeks later, after Hemingway's period of impotence had ended, Dr. Rome summoned Mary to the Mayo. Since Hemingway was not allowed to leave the hospital, their therapeutic love-making in the bare, barred room was inevitably unsatisfactory and depressing. Mary asked Dr. Rome a great many questions. Though he assured her that Hemingway's memory would return after the treatment was completed, his answers left her dissatisfied about the superficial nature of the somatic procedure and confused about the purpose and duration of the ECT: "I think the doctors did disabuse Papa of his immediate hallucinations," she told Hotchner, "but aren't there deeper things that have to be touched? I don't even know what electric shock is supposed to achieve. . . . The last time I spoke to the doctors they said they were going to start a series of them. But I don't even know how many that would be."

In June (while still in the Mayo) Hemingway again threatened suicide and told Hotchner: "If I can't exist on my own terms, then existence is impossible. . . . That is how I've lived, and that is how I *must* live—or not live."[32] On June 15 he wrote a moving, final letter to Dr. Saviers' nine-year-old son, who was dying of heart disease, that recalled his letters to the invalid children of Gerald and Sara Murphy. This letter helped to convince Dr. Rome that he was optimistic and in good mental health:

> I've had a chance to see some wonderful country along the Mississippi where they used to drive the logs in the old lumbering days and the trails where the pioneers came north. Saw some good bass jump in the river. I never knew anything about the upper Mississippi before and it is really a very beautiful country and there are plenty of pheasants and ducks in the fall.

When Elicio Arguelles called the Mayo and spoke to Mary, Hemingway took the phone and said: "I've got to speak to him. . . . I'm feeling perfect. Will be leaving here in a few days."

Mary begged Hemingway not to "con" the doctors into letting him leave the hospital before he was well. She wanted to follow Dr. Cattell's advice and transfer Hemingway to the Institute for Living in Hartford, a halfway house for the mentally ill that treated alcoholics and chronic schizophrenics (Lowell was a patient there in 1962). But she still feared publicity and felt that Hemingway, despite the ECT at the Mayo, would not agree to enter a mental institution. Dr. Cattell prophetically observed "there might be some advantages to inside-page news items about going to the Institute, in contrast to the front-page headlines about his suicide."[33]

Dr. Rome wanted to release rather than transfer Hemingway, and urged Mary to accept his decision. Without prior discussion, he summoned her to his office, where she found Hemingway dressed in street clothes, and announced: "Ernest is ready to go home." Mary "knew that Ernest was not cured, that he entertained the same delusions and fears with which he had entered the clinic, and realized in despair that he had charmed and deceived Dr. Rome." On June 26 George Brown (the boxer from New York) drove them west and they arrived in Ketchum on the thirtieth. Charles Collingwood, his journalist friend in World War Two, recalled Hemingway's kind gesture on this trip:

> When Hemingway was driving back to Idaho, from the Mayo Clinic where he was spending an increasing amount of time, he happened to watch [Collingwood's television documentary on modern art] in a motel somewhere in between. He wrote me an enthusiastic postcard saying he found it as good the second time around as the first.
>
> I cite this to show the generosity of spirit which showed through what must have been a terribly bad patch for him—to take the trouble to do that, at that time, for an old friend. In other words, with all his faults, weaknesses and so on, he could also be a very loyal and generous friend.[34]

While Hemingway was being treated at the Mayo, Dr. Rome discussed the case with the FBI agent in Minneapolis. Presumably, he took part in the luncheon party and would have lost some of his objectivity by becoming the buddy of his famous patient. He made the depressing arrangements for Hemingway's unsuccessful sex therapy with Mary. He continued the second series of shocks after the first had damaged Hemingway's memory and intensified rather than relieved his depression. He did not inform Mary about the exact nature of Hemingway's treatment. He did not recommend transferring him to the Menninger Clinic or the Institute for Living, as Dr. Cattell had suggested. He did not seem to be aware that patients often appear better after they have finally decided to commit suicide. He was deceived by Hemingway, said he was ready to go home and released him, despite Mary's pleas and against her wishes, when he was still depressed and suicidal. Hemingway's second admission to the Mayo suggested that the first procedure had been unsuccessful, just as his suicide—only two days after he reached Ketchum—proved the second treatment had also failed.

Hemingway, who usually weighed between 200 and 250 pounds, weighed only 155 when he was released in late June. Leslie Fiedler, who had made a pilgrimage to see Hemingway the previous November (just before he first entered the Mayo), was surprised to find the heroic figure doubtful, distressed and reduced to "a fragile, too-often-repaired old man . . . broken beyond repair." Fiedler was also shocked, after Hemingway's lifetime of achievement and praise, to see "his doubt and torment, his fear that he had done nothing of lasting worth, his conviction that he must die without adequate reassurance."

During Jack's last visit in April 1961, he too found the ravaged man a mere shadow of himself and was astonished that his once exuberant father no longer smiled. Bill Walton also saw Hemingway for the last time in the spring of 1961 and found him a scarcely recognizable old man, hesitant and unsure of himself, with a badly damaged liver and kidneys. Hemingway was proud of Walton's friendship with President Kennedy, drew him on the sofa and held his hand. He was sixty-one and seemed ninety.[35] A last photograph of the aged, sickly Hemingway, taken in Ketchum in April, revealed the loss of memory in the dazed and vacant stare, and the hollowness at the core of his frail frame.

Hemingway died only twelve miles from where Ezra Pound was born. Like Pound at the end of his life, he too was wasted, silent, depressed and sceptical of the value of his work. He was also tragically like Scott Fitzgerald, whom he had scorned for his weakness in the twenties and thirties. He too had become a Catholic, been dazzled by the rich, turned into a celebrity, created a legend that made his life better known than his works; he too was blocked as a writer, had failed in marriage, escaped into alcoholism, cracked up and become suicidal.

27

Suicide and Aftermath

Sleep after toyle, port after stormie seas,
Ease after warre, death after life, does greatly please.
SPENSER, *The Faerie Queene*

I

Suicide was a recurrent theme in Hemingway's life and work. Even before his father's suicide in 1928, which profoundly influenced his ideas and emotions, he was obsessed by the theme of self-destruction. Marcelline recalled that the young Ernest liked to read Stevenson's "The Suicide Club" (an appropriate name for the Hemingway family). As he was recovering from his war wound in October 1918, he expressed a belief that he held till the end of his life: "How much better . . . to go out in a blaze of light, than to have your body worn out and old and illusions shattered."

Hemingway's thoughts of suicide often coincided with his marital crises. In July 1921, two months before he married Hadley, he became apprehensive about his new responsibilities and alarmed her by mentioning suicide. Five years later, during the crisis with Pauline, he calmly told her that he would have killed himself if their love affair had not been happily resolved. He seemed strangely comforted by these morbid thoughts, remembered his recent transatlantic crossings and anticipated Hart Crane's almost aesthetic mode of suicide: "When I feel low, I like to think about death and the various ways of dying. And I think about probably the best way, unless you could arrange to die some way while asleep, would be to go off a liner at night."[1] As a young man he adopted romantic ideas about self-destruction to glamorize his feelings of anxiety, heighten his love affair and assuage his guilt. But he still believed that life would improve once the hellish mood had passed, and was not yet serious about suicide.

When he saw his father pitifully depressed by diabetes and angina, Hemingway remarked: "If I ever get that way, I'll have someone kill me—or I'll do it myself." Ed's final legacy to his son was not the Civil War tradition, the medical background, the religious training or the lore of the woods, but an impulse to self-destruction. After 1928, suicide was a serious possibility: the will and the weapons were always there. Hemingway asked his mother to send him Ed's gun, as if to animate it and involve himself in the event; then gave it a ritualistic burial in a mountain lake to exorcise the dreadful inheritance. He thought suicide was a lonely way to die. In an unpublished fragment of the 1930s, he anticipated the autobiographical themes of *For Whom the Bell Tolls,* called his father a coward, blamed Grace for Ed's death and seemed inevitably destined for a similar end: "[My old] man was a coward. [He] never had any fun and was married to a bitch and he shot himself. . . . [I] am not a coward, have had a damned good time, plenty of fun, been married to two good women and I think I will shoot myself."[2]

Hemingway's story "Indian Camp," in which the doctor is based on his father, described the suicide of an Indian during his wife's agonizing birth pain. The theme of suicide became more prominent in his work after 1928, and during the 1930s he discussed it in *Death in the Afternoon,* "A Clean, Well-Lighted Place," *To Have and Have Not* and *For Whom the Bell Tolls.* He had always been attracted to the Spanish cult of death and "much interested in suicides." In the bullfighting book he pessimistically argued: "There is no remedy for anything in life. Death is a sovereign remedy for all misfortunes." And he added that the wounded matador Gitanillo, tormented by unbearable nerve pain, would have maintained his dignity and "been much luckier to have died . . . while he still had control of himself and still possessed his courage rather than to have gone through the progressive horror of physical and spiritual humiliation."

During what Auden called the "low, dishonest decade," Hemingway frequently discussed the question of suicide with friends, in letters and in interviews as well as in his work. He told his Key West friend Jim Sullivan that he would kill himself, and even threatened to do so; but Sullivan thought that if he talked about it, he would never do it. Another factor that restrained him from the "big disgust" of shooting himself, he informed MacLeish in 1936, was the bad effect it would have on his sons. A gratuitous, light-hearted reference to suicide in an autobiographical sketch that year suggested that suicide, like sports, was an escape from the exacting tensions of writing: "Since he was a young boy he has cared greatly for fishing and shooting. If he had not spent so much time at them, at ski-ing, at the bull ring, and in a boat, he might have written much more. On the other hand, he might have shot himself."³

In *Green Hills of Africa* he extolled the almost orgasmic pleasure of a rifle: "the sweet clean pull of the Springfield with the smooth, unhesitant release at the end." Two years later, in *To Have and Have Not*, the means of sensual satisfaction was directed not at animals but at the self. The Smith and Wesson pistol, his father's suicide weapon, became a simple, permanent cure for all psychological, moral, medical and financial problems: it was one of "those well-constructed implements that end insomnia, terminate remorse, cure cancer, avoid bankruptcy, and blast an exit from intolerable positions by the pressure of a finger."⁴

During the Spanish War, he foreshadowed his own fate and told Joris Ivens that the most efficient way to do it was not with a gun at the temple but with a shotgun in the mouth. Yet in 1939, when he heard that an American friend who had flown for the Loyalists had taken his own life, he wrote his Catholic mother-in-law that he had frequently talked himself out of that drastic step and could also have knocked the idea out of Frank Tinker's head. The wounded Robert Jordan, debating suicide at the end of *For Whom the Bell Tolls*, thinks he could face quick death, but not slow degradation: "Dying is only bad when it takes a long time and hurts so much that it humiliates you."⁵

Hemingway attempted to exorcise his father's suicide by writing about it in his Spanish War novel. In the 1950s, as his self-destructive impulse increased, he struggled to find arguments against the sovereign remedy: life would get better, it would be bad for his sons, it was selfish, it was cowardly. In an undated, unfinished story, "James Allen lived in a studio," he insisted that he could not stand suicide and had no sympathy with it. In 1954 he tried to see it from a survivor's point of view and told Robert Manning: "It's everybody's right, but there's a certain amount of egotism in it and a certain disregard of others."⁶ After the dangerous summer of 1959, he unconvincingly asserted that he would never destroy himself; but he told Bill Davis, more uncertainly: "I'm going to try not to do it." In 1939 Hemingway had suggested that he and Clara Spiegel make a pact and promise to tell each other if they ever wanted to commit suicide. She could not assume the responsibility of convincing Hemingway that it was wrong to kill himself and refused. On July 1, 1961, the day after he returned to Ketchum, Clara invited him to dinner. He asked her instead to come to his house on July 2 and (she later realized) hinted at suicide by saying after that date he would have no social life—even with close friends.[7]

II

In *The Myth of Sisyphus,* Camus observed: "There is but one truly serious philosophical problem and that is suicide. Judging whether life is or is not worth living amounts to answering the fundamental question of philosophy."[8] Hemingway—remembering the suicides of Hadley's father and his own, of Jules Pascin and Charles Fenton—debated this vital question throughout his adult life. There was also an existential element in his suicide. His code—formulated in youth, based on toughness and stoicism—was not suited to old age and failed him at the end.

Hemingway's body had been broken by war and accidents, and strengthened at the fractures. The African plane crashes confirmed the legend of the hero who inscribed his experience on his body and seemed to be able to survive anything. But when his memory and ability to write were virtually destroyed at the Mayo, the only thing left to him was freedom. He had told Janet Flanner: "liberty could be as important in the act of dying as in the acts of living," and agreed with Nietzsche's belief: "Die at the right time! . . . He that consummates his life dies his death victoriously."[9] In the end, he combined the tragic roles of the bullfight and became both killer and victim. The hunter's last prey was himself. His death—a sudden, passionate, violent self-extinction—was perfectly consistent with his life.

Hemingway's suicide left the puzzling question of why a man who had looks, sporting skill, friends, women, wealth, fame, genius and the Nobel Prize would kill himself. The simple explanation is that he had a terrible combination of physical and mental illness that was caused by his neglect (even destruction) of his own health and that he had lost his memory during medical treatment at the Mayo. He suffered from weight loss, skin disease, alcoholism, failing eyesight, diabetes, suspected hemochromatosis, hepatitis, nephritis, hypertension and impotence. His body was in ruins, he dreaded a decline into invalidism and a lingering death. He could no longer remember, he could no longer write, he was severely depressed. But why did he choose to kill himself rather than live with his diseases?

"What does a man care about?" Hemingway asked in June 1961. "Staying healthy. Working good. Eating and drinking with his friends. Enjoying himself in bed. I haven't any of them." His old friend Gary Cooper, sustained by religion as he was devoured by cancer, provided a terrible warning to Hemingway. When he telephoned the actor from the Mayo in May 1961, Cooper said: "I bet I make it to the barn before you do." Cooper kept his word and died on May 13. Hemingway, also suffering terribly and dying by inches, was not afraid of death. If he could survive with dignity and honor, he would live; "when he wasn't good enough to be what he considered Ernest Hemingway the man, then he wanted to be dead."[10] His suicide had elements of self-pity and revenge, but was not inspired by desperation and derangement. It was a careful and courageous act.

All of Hemingway's numerous accidents and injuries were a form of self-destruction, but he had made only one attempt to kill himself. Lloyd Arnold wrote that on April 23, 1961, as Hemingway was about to leave on his second trip to the Mayo, he went from the Sun Valley hospital to his house to get some clothes:

> Papa said Don [Anderson] needn't come in, his things were upstairs where Mary was, he'd be down in minutes. Don was at his heels anyway, so close they practically went in as one; then Don was alone, for Papa took off like a shot. Don beckoned to Joan [Higgon, a nurse] and followed him; at the corner gun rack in the living room, from behind him, Don pinned Papa's arms as he closed the breech on his double-barrel shotgun, and managed to get a thumb on the gun's opening lever. Joan pulled out the shells and the storm subsided immediately. The struggle was brisk but short, neither man off his feet or hurt in any way.

That same day, as they stopped for fuel in Rapid City, South Dakota, Hemingway searched for a gun at the airport hangar and then walked toward a moving propeller, which stopped whirling just as he approached it.

On July 2, two days after he came home from the Mayo, Hemingway (as usual) woke up early. Though known to be suicidal, he was able to get a loaded gun. Mary, convinced that he was still mentally ill, had only a few days before urged the Mayo doctors not to release him to her care.

In Ketchum, "she had locked all the guns in the storage room in the basement. . . . But the keys, as he well knew, were on the window ledge above the kitchen sink." Mary explained that she did not hide the keys because "no one had a right to deny a man access to his possessions and I also assumed that Ernest would not remember the storeroom."[11] Though the exact meaning of this statement is unclear, Mary may have meant that Hemingway had a right to kill himself if he wished.

Mary had suffered almost unbearable tension since the previous fall, when Hemingway returned to America after his last trip to Spain, and was probably reaching her own breaking point. In the spring of 1961 she told Hotchner that a repetition of the last three months would destroy her, and later wondered "if we had not been more cruel than kind in preventing his suicide" on April 23. Patrick said the family's attitude about the problems of others was "handle it yourself," and confessed: "We left Mary with the clean-up operation and the burden on her was impossible."[12] It seems that Mary dealt with the intolerable burden she had unwillingly inherited from the Mayo Clinic by behaving with classic ambivalence: she locked the guns in the basement but left the keys in the kitchen.

Martha Gellhorn, Patrick and Tillie Arnold all believed that Mary might have committed Hemingway to a mental institution like the Menninger or the Institute for Living when she felt it was impossible to care for him herself, and that Hemingway feared this would happen.[13] In the last minutes of his life he played out the final psychodrama with his wife. He may have felt that he had no choice but to kill himself or be certified; he may have taken revenge and punished Mary for giving him the freedom to make this terrible choice.

Hemingway had always condemned his father for his cowardly suicide, but now understood how conditions could drive a man to that destructive act. Like his father, he suffered from diabetes and depression, and shot himself in the head in his own house. At about seven o'clock on that Sunday morning, Hemingway, dressed in pajamas and bathrobe, went down to the basement to get the gun and a box of ammunition. But he did not kill himself in that dark vault. Instead, he came upstairs to the foyer, near the gun rack and just inside the main entrance of the house. Knowing that Mary would find him there, he pushed two shells into the twelve-gauge Boss shotgun (made in England and bought at Abercrombie & Fitch), put the end of the barrel into his mouth, pulled the trigger and blew out his brains.

Mary had been up at about 6 A.M. for a glass of water, noticed that Hemingway was already awake, and gone back to sleep. An hour later, she wrote, "the sounds of a couple of drawers banging shut awakened me and, dazed, I went downstairs, saw a crumpled heap of bathrobe and blood, the shotgun lying in the disintegrated flesh, in the front vestibule of the sitting room." The carnage was much greater than she suggests. Hemingway's chin, mouth and lower cheeks were left, but the upper half of his head was blown away. Blood, bones, teeth, hair and flesh were blasted around the ceiling, walls and floor of the room. Mary had to step over shattered parts of his head when she came down the stairs to find him.

Mary screamed for George Brown, who was sleeping in the nearby guest house. Brown telephoned Don Anderson, who said: "Papa's finally got the job done." Brown and Anderson cleaned up the mess, and Lloyd Arnold burned it. When Sunny arrived for the funeral, she "looked around for signs of the tragedy that had happened the day before," but saw no "sign of disorder [or] stain."[14]

III

Mary, saddened and perhaps relieved by Hemingway's death, was treated for shock and stayed overnight in the hospital. Though Hemingway was an expert with guns, she told the *New York Times:* "I feel certain that this, in some incredible way, was an accident." In the early 1970s she repeated that Hemingway's death had been an "enormous surprise and shock" and (despite his previous attempt) that she did not believe the suicide would actually happen. Mary, of course, wanted to believe it was an accident; the fact that she had left the keys out and enabled him to commit suicide must have made it imperative to state that it actually was an accident. The Blaine County coroner stated that Hemingway (who left no suicide note) died of a "self-inflicted gunshot wound in the head," but he did not rule on whether it was an accident or a suicide. Under Idaho law, an inquest was not required unless there was a suspicion of foul play.[15]

The funeral was delayed until July 5 to allow Patrick to fly home from Africa. Jack came from a fishing trip in Oregon, Gregory from medical school in Miami. Mary quickly recovered, seemed to take Hemingway's death rather well and capably organized the funeral arrangements. Jack and Puck stayed in Hemingway's room, Patrick in the guest house with George Brown, Gregory and Gianfranco in Clara Spiegel's cottage, Bill Horne and his wife in Clara's house. At the cemetery in Ketchum, Mary and the three sons stood on one side of the grave, with Clara and Tillie behind Mary, and three of Hemingway's sisters (Carol did not attend) on the other. The cemetery was closed during the funeral, which began at 10:30 A.M., but people thronged outside the low chain-wire fence near the grave.

Though neither Hemingway nor Mary was Catholic, there was a Catholic burial to show that he had not committed suicide.[16] He had been excommunicated after his divorce from Pauline and was therefore "denied the privilege of the complete funeral mass." Because of Hemingway's divorces and suicide, George Brown objected to a High Mass, thwarted Mary's plans and made her furious.[17] Father Robert Waldman, the priest who conducted the burial service, said: "the church accepted the ruling of the authorities that Hemingway had died of a self-inflicted gunshot wound in the head" and would "not go beyond the ruling of the authorities." So an ambiguous compromise was reached. Hemingway had a funeral service at the graveside, but not in the church; he had a Catholic burial, but not a High Mass. Mary and the sons asked Father Waldman to read his favorite "sun also rises" passage from *Ecclesiastes;* but the priest somehow misunderstood the request and read only the first line from the quite different Catholic Douay version. Later, because of the international publicity surrounding the funeral, the lenient "priest was rather severely reprimanded by the Bishop."[18]

The behavior at the funeral was rather bizarre. The three brothers, who had not been together since the late 1940s, began laughing and joking as they had done in the old days. Marcelline carefully took notes on what everyone said in preparation for her forthcoming book and infuriated Sunny by declaring that suicides did not go to heaven. Sunny, who had missed Hadley's wedding and her father's suicide, now had a compensatory mystical experience. As if to prove Marcelline wrong, "on the carpet [of the church] was a perfect outline of Ernest's head, beard and all! It seemed as if his sad eyes were pleading." Valerie, working for *Newsweek* at that time, was treated as a journalist and ostracized by Mary. But she was courted by Gregory, who later married her. At the funeral Leicester tapped Valerie on the shoulder and asked: "Miss, do you know where my manuscript is?" She could not bear to tell him that Hemingway had burned it.

The grave, placed between two pine trees, faced the Sawtooth Mountains. Hemingway's name and dates were cut on the long gray granite tombstone, which was later placed horizontally to prevent tourists from stealing the dirt as souvenirs. In "Fathers and Sons," the little boy (based on Bumby) tells his father: "I hope we won't live somewhere so that I can never go to pray at your tomb when you are dead."[19] Jack now lives in Ketchum and passes his father's "tomb" when he drives from his house into town.

IV

The will, read by Alfred Rice soon after the funeral, produced acute shocks and disappointments. Hemingway punished his sons in his will as he had punished Mary by his suicide. On September 17, 1955, he wrote: "I have intentionally omitted to provide for my children now living or for any that may be born after this will has been executed, as I repose complete confidence in my beloved wife Mary to provide for them according to written instructions I have given her."[20] Though Hemingway had no life insurance, Mary inherited an estate worth $1.4 million, including a lucrative stock account that seemed more like a banker's than a writer's. She was also named his literary executrix. Despite her vision, Sunny was not invited to the reading of the will, did not receive the Michigan cottage that Hemingway had promised her and had to buy it from Mary. Mary refused to return Miró's *The Farm* to Hadley or to Jack, who eventually relinquished his claim to the painting for a payment of $20,000.

Hemingway's sons were disinherited; and there have been bitter feelings in the family as they struggled for their share of the valuable estate. There was no clear indication of why Hemingway cut his formidable sons out of his will, but he seemed to express disappointment and disapproval of their wives and their careers. He may have had a Lear-like superstition about dividing his estate, or trusted Mary as much as he distrusted lawyers, or believed she would be generous, or been indifferent about what happened to his money after his death.

Friends and fellow writers, shocked by the sudden loss after Hemingway fired the shot heard round the world, were eager to render homage to the titanic figure. Everyone realized that Hemingway's death had diminished his own life, that something important had gone out of the world. It seemed as though a powerful oak had suddenly been uprooted from the earth and toppled over. As Matthew Arnold wrote in his "Memorial Verses" on another charismatic figure:

> When Byron's eyes were shut in death,
> We bow'd our head and held our breath.
> He taught us little: but our soul
> Had felt him like the thunder's roll.

Hemingway was the Byron of our time. Both men were powerful and good-looking, astonishingly attractive to women. Byron was born with a clubfoot; Hemingway, born with defective vision, was seriously wounded in the leg. Both attached great importance to sporting life: boxing, shooting, sailing. Both had their own boats: Byron the *Bolívar*, Hemingway the *Pilar*. Both maintained a strange menagerie of animals. Both felt fasting intensified their mental powers, but were heavy drinkers. Both lived most of their adult lives abroad and spoke foreign languages fluently but incorrectly. Both had a frank and open character, abused their intimates and quarreled with their friends. Both had devoted servants and cultivated the company of inferiors rather than equals. Both were brilliant talkers as well as attentive listeners. Hemingway, like Byron, had "the power of attaching those about him to his person. No human being could approach him without being sensible of this magical influence." Hemingway's close friendship with Gianfranco Ivancich, the brother of the woman he loved, resembled Byron's friendship with Pietro Gamba, the brother of his mistress, Countess Guiccioli. Both were superstitious rather than orthodox in their religious beliefs.

Both men visited Constantinople in their youth and witnessed Greco-Turkish wars. Both were attracted by the glory of military life and proved by their own deeds that an author could also be a man of action. Both devoted their time, talent and money to the wars in Greece and in Spain, which they saw as a struggle between barbarism and civilization. Both achieved early fame, became heroic and legendary figures. The work of both writers had an immediate social impact. The behavior of their fictional characters was widely imitated, and they left a permanent mark on their age and culture. Both were idolized by their countrymen, who found their private lives a subject of great fascination. Like Byron, Hemingway preferred to die "than to drag on an existence with faculties impaired, and feelings blunted."[21]

Robert Frost, who had cooperated in securing the release of Ezra

Pound and still believed Hemingway died by accident, expressed the appropriate public sentiments to the *New York Times* on the day after the death:

> He was rough and unsparing with life. He was rough and unsparing with himself. It is like his brave free ways that he should die by accident with a weapon. Fortunately for us, if it is a time to speak of fortune, he gave himself time to make his greatness. His style dominated our story telling long and short. I remember the fascination that made me want to read aloud "The Killers" to everybody that came along. He was a friend I shall miss. The country is in mourning.

The response of Hemingway's friends and acquaintances was more personal. Arnold Gingrich, then married to Jane Mason, was still hostile, ignored the tragedy and fastidiously asked: "How could anybody do such a messy thing? How could you leave a mess like that for somebody to clean up?" Nathan Asch, a friend from the Paris days, was profoundly moved by the loss: "Hemingway is dead, and I don't believe it. I hated the son of a bitch, and I loved him. . . . I am proud that he liked my work at one time. I weep [for] him as if my brother was dead, I am sorry for myself because he is dead. I myself am the less for that. We are all the less for that."[22]

In Ireland, Chink Dorman-Smith thought of the suffering Hemingway must have endured before he shot himself and, since there had been no indication of suicide, was surprised by the manner of his death. In Spain, when the bullfighter Juan Belmonte was told " ' Don Ernesto has just committed suicide,' Belmonte said, very slowly and very clearly, 'Well done.' . . . A little while later Belmonte, the greatest of them all . . . shot himself in the same way. Right through the head."[23] Ordóñez, deeply distraught, at first exclaimed: "He's destroyed our lives, too. . . . I'm a dead man now. The news of his death has been a mortal blow." Later he added: "I had no hint about his suicide; he never mentioned this subject to me. I was surprised, shocked and hurt by his death. I would still like to think it was an accident; it could have been, despite his knowledge of guns." The most interesting reaction came from Edmund Wilson, one of the first critics to recognize Hemingway's extraordinary ability. He read the works in terms of the tragic end and (when he had learned the truth from the literary grapevine) specified the real cause of Hemingway's death: "It is as if a whole corner of my generation had suddenly and horribly collapsed. I knew that the desperation in his stories was real. . . . It makes it more understandable to know that he had been taking shock treatments and was part of the time quite out of his mind."[24]

In January 1961, after Castro had nationalized most of the American property on the island, the United States broke diplomatic relations with Cuba. The Bay of Pigs fiasco followed in April. A few days after Hemingway's funeral, his boat and possessions were (as he had feared) expropriated by the Castro regime. Mary explained: "I had a phone call in Ketchum from the Cuban government asking me whether I would consent to donate our home in Cuba as a museum. In exchange I would be allowed to remove all the papers from the Bank and my personal belongings. I accepted. At the time I was so grief-stricken that I didn't care about giving up the house."

Bill Walton, then working for President Kennedy, arranged through the State Department counsel for Mary to go to Cuba that July. She was forced to give up the house. But Castro, who came to the Finca to see Mary, allowed her to keep her clothes and jewelry, twenty-five precious books, the paintings by Miró, Gris, Klee and Masson (the Braque had been stolen in their absence), all of Hemingway's papers and forty pounds of manuscripts from the bank vault. On August 7 Mary, who had acted rather precipitately, told Waldo Peirce that she had burned many papers she was certain Hemingway would not want anyone to publish or to see. The *Pilar* was hauled onto the grounds and the Finca became the Hemingway Museum. John Kennedy was impressed by Mary's successful dealings with Castro. But when they later met at a White House dinner for Nobel laureates, she irritated the President by telling him how to manage Castro.[25]

In January 1962 Mary went to Key West to sort and retrieve the boxes of papers and manuscripts that Hemingway had stored at Sloppy Joe's bar in 1940, and found a treasure similar to the one Hemingway had discovered at the Ritz. Ten years later, Mary placed all his surviving letters, manuscripts, documents, scrapbooks, clippings, reviews, tapes, photographs and memorabilia in the Hemingway Collection of the Kennedy presidential library, designed by I. M. Pei and located at Columbia Point in Boston. Archibald MacLeish was asked to give the speech at the opening ceremony in July 1980, which was attended by Jacqueline Onassis and Patrick Hemingway. When MacLeish was unable to do so, George Plimpton delivered a witty talk.

Hemingway had always said that his manuscripts were his life insurance, but only two new works—*A Moveable Feast* and *Islands in the Stream*—appeared after his death. Most of the royalties have come from the astonishing sales of the books published in his lifetime rather than from his posthumous compilations: *The Wild Years* (his *Toronto Star* pieces); *By-Line: Ernest Hemingway* (a more comprehensive anthology of his journalism); *The Fifth Column and Four Stories of the Spanish Civil War; Ernest Hemingway, Cub Reporter* (the *Kansas City Star* articles); *Ernest Hemingway's Apprenticeship* (the high school pieces); *The Nick Adams Stories; 88 Poems; Selected Letters* and *The Dangerous Summer.*

V

Hemingway adopted an unusually regretful tone in "The Christmas Gift" and declared, with more truth than he realized: "my past life . . . is often very distasteful due to the mistakes that I have made and the casualties to various human beings involved in that sad affair."[26] Many of the people close to Hemingway seemed fated to have unhappy lives or suffer tragic deaths.

Richard Cooper was drowned and Rupert Belleville impaled while they were drunk. Jigee Viertel and Hemingway's journalist friend Sam Boal burned to death. Duff Twysden died of tuberculosis at the age of forty-five; Mikhail Koltzov was murdered in Stalin's prison camps; Bror von Blixen was killed in a car crash; Robert Capa was blown up in Indo-China. Jane Mason and Scott Fitzgerald had both attempted suicide during their intense involvement with Hemingway, and Charles Fenton had leaped to his death from a window. Hemingway's sister Ursula, who had survived three cancer operations, became depressed and killed herself with an overdose of drugs in 1966. Leicester continued to imitate and live under the shadow of Hemingway; he grew a beard and looked amazingly like his brother. He also had severe diabetes, endured five operations, was threatened with the loss of his limbs and shot himself in 1982. But even Leicester's suicide was not taken seriously: everyone thought it was just another imitation of Ernest.[27] Adriana Ivancich, married and with two sons, hanged herself on her farm in 1983.[28]

Pauline had lesbian relationships after her marriage to Hemingway had ended. Martha became permanently embittered about him; she divorced her second husband, the *Time* editor Thomas Matthews, and now lives in London. Mary once told Clara Spiegel that it was bad for a woman to live too long without a man, who was needed for balance as well as for bed.[29] After Hemingway's death she greatly missed her social and sexual life, and her importance as the wife of a great writer. She continued to give Hemingway's birthday party in Ketchum on July 21. Mary collected and cared for his papers, published his posthumous books, wrote her memoirs and (like Adriana) was deeply disappointed by the reception of the book. When these tasks were completed, Mary (always a hard worker) seemed to lose her purpose in life. Now in her late seventies, she has difficulty remembering things. She spends most of her time in her two Manhattan penthouses and has turned over the responsibilities of the estate to Alfred Rice. (When a friend of Mary asked Rice: "What can I do to help?" he replied: "You can take care of me.")

Hemingway's sons, with all their good looks and sporting skill, were also afflicted by tragedy. Jack was wounded and captured during the war; he lost an infant son in 1951 and his wife nearly died of lung cancer. But the glamorous Hemingway image continued with Jack's daughters, Margaux and Mariel, who have achieved fame as models and movie stars. Patrick and Gregory had electro-convulsive therapy in 1947 and 1957; and there have been four generations of mental illness in the family. Patrick's first wife, Henrietta, was a juvenile diabetic. She went blind, had kidney failure and, after a five-year illness, died in 1963, when their adopted daughter was only three years old. Gregory had two broken marriages and went through a very bad period in the 1950s. He met Valerie at the funeral and married her in 1966. Hemingway's sons lit out for the territories, and continue to fish and hunt in Idaho and Montana.

Hemingway inspired a series of seventeen personal memoirs—by Leicester, Marcelline, Sunny, Gregory, Mary, Adriana, Lloyd Arnold, Hotchner and several others—which appeared between 1949 and 1980. The authors were related by blood and friendship, connected by rivalry and hostility; their viewpoints range from reverence and awe to condescension and hostility. The memoirs—by professional journalists, exploiters and hangers-on as well as emotionally involved family and friends—are distorted by personal bias, exude a strong element of self-interest and reveal more about the authors than the subject.

When Hotchner's book was serialized in the *Saturday Evening Post,* Mary, then writing her own memoir, sued to prevent publication and lost her case in the spring of 1966 in both the New York State Supreme Court and the Court of Appeals. The courts ruled that Hotchner was free to publish their conversations unless Mary could prove that Hemingway specifically told him not to do so. Two years later, in *Hemingway: Entre la Vida y la Muerte,* Castillo-Puche called Hotchner a hypocrite, a sickening toady, an obsequious bore, a clever exploiter. Though Castillo got away with this in the Spanish edition and Mary testified for Castillo's American publisher (perhaps in retaliation for her lost lawsuit), Hotchner won $125,000 in damages. But his libel award was thrown out by the Federal Appeals Court the following year.[30]

VI

Hemingway flaunted his weaknesses and hid his strengths, took more care to conceal his wisdom than his folly. Like his heroes Twain and Kipling, he never fully matured as an artist. He maintained an anti-intellectual attitude, cut himself off from cultural centers, quarreled with fellow writers, had a messy private life, succumbed to publicity and lost his serious dedication to art. His novels appeared in alternating cycles and his finest fiction was inevitably succeeded by minor works. *In Our Time* was followed by *The Torrents of Spring, The Sun Also Rises* by *Men Without Women, A Farewell to Arms* by *To Have and Have Not, For Whom the Bell Tolls* by *Across the River,* and *The Old Man and the Sea* by *Islands in the Stream.* He did his best work between 1925 and 1940 and significantly declined during the last twenty years of his life.

Hemingway's reputation had five distinct phases and fluctuated wildly during each decade of his career. He received almost universal praise in the 1920s and reached the peak of his contemporary reputation with *A Farewell to Arms* in 1929. His books of the 1930s were severely criticized by disenchanted reviewers, but he made a major recovery with *For Whom the Bell Tolls* in 1940. He published no significant work in the 1940s, which culminated in the almost universally condemned novel *Across the River* in 1950. But two years later he achieved an astonishing critical triumph with *The Old Man and the Sea.* He brought out no books during the last nine years of his life, but regained his reputation with the posthumously published *A Moveable Feast* in 1964.

Though Hemingway has not equaled the very greatest modern novelists—Mann, Proust and Joyce—his stature, based on his innovative style, technical virtuosity and emotional intensity in three major novels and a dozen first-rate short stories, is secure. Unlike Dreiser, Lewis, Anderson, Wolfe, Dos Passos and Steinbeck, who are no longer widely read and greatly respected, Hemingway has survived his decline, his death and his detractors. He is now recognized as the most important American novelist of the twentieth century as well as a seminal influence on the modern American character.

Hemingway's life and work, which taught a generation of men to speak in stoical accents, had a profound influence on a school of hard-boiled writers—Chandler, Hammett, Cain, Caldwell, Farrell, O'Hara, Algren, Shaw, Jones, Kerouac—who were affected not only by his style and technique, but also by his violent content and heroic code, which seemed to represent the essence of American values. He has also influenced novelists as different as Saul Bellow, Morley Callaghan and Norman Mailer.

Bellow, whose Augie March is an eagle-flying hero in the Hemingway tradition, testified to the inescapable power as well as the limitations of the stoical Kiplingesque code in his first novel, *Dangling Man:* "This is the era of hardboiled-dom. Today, the code of the athlete, of the tough boy—an American inheritance, I believe, from the English gentleman—that curious mixture of striving, asceticism, and rigor, the origins of which some trace back to Alexander the Great—is stronger than ever. Do you have feelings? There are correct and incorrect ways of indicating them. Do you have an inner life? It is nobody's business but your own. Do you have emotions? Strangle them. To a degree, everyone obeys this code."

Morley Callaghan, who had punched Papa when they were young, felt that his own boxing ability had swamped his literary reputation, that his artistic individuality had been destroyed by the overpowering influence of two far greater writers: "Hemingway and Fitzgerald, they ruined me. I never had any desire to be part of any movement, but now I am probably better known for boxing with Hemingway than for anything I've written."[31]

The most important disciple was surely Norman Mailer, whose brawling character Sergius O'Shaughnessy and brilliant story "The Time of Her Time" would be inconceivable without Hemingway. Mailer was obsessed with Hemingway, fastened onto the son after he had failed to meet the father, enjoyed bouts of ram-like head-butting with Gregory and wrote a short preface to his book. In *Advertisements for Myself,* Mailer attacked his contemporaries but acknowledged the influence of the Master: "I was one of the few writers of my generation who was concerned with living in Hemingway's discipline. . . . I could not become a very good writer unless I learned first how to keep my nerve, and what is more difficult, learned how to find more of it."

After *The Naked and the Dead,* Mailer became the hip-pocket Hemingway of our time, who replaced marlin, bulls and lions with thumb wrestling, softball and jogging, though he outmarried Hemingway and had six wives and eight children. When Mailer reexamined Hemingway's public persona after his suicide, the younger writer saw his manly style as a sophisticated device for both hiding and revealing an obsession with courage that was rooted in anxiety. Mailer saw him as a tragic figure, wrestling, like the biblical Jacob, with destructive self-knowledge: "It is not likely that Hemingway was a brave man who sought danger for the sake of the sensations it provided him. What is more likely the truth of his own odyssey is that he struggled with his cowardice and against a secret lust to suicide all his life, that his inner landscape was a nightmare, and he spent his nights wrestling with the gods. It may even be that the final judgment on his work may come to the notion that what he failed to do was tragic, but what he accomplished was heroic, for it is possible that he carried a weight of anxiety with him which would have suffocated any man smaller than himself."[32]

Jean Rhys, Ford Madox Ford, Scott Fitzgerald, Martha Gellhorn, John Dos Passos, Leicester Hemingway and Philip Roth have all paid tribute to Hemingway's overwhelming personality by portraying him in their fiction.[33] Pound, Cummings, MacLeish, Roethke, Berryman, Merton and Yevtushenko recalled him in their poems. Hemingway's generation of novelists had wild, destructive, alcoholic lives, which were continued by American poets of the next generation. Roethke noted the diminution of character and talent when he ironically wrote:

> It wasn't Ernest, it wasn't Scott—
> The boys I knew when I went to pot.

John Berryman, another suicidal son of a suicidal father, took Hemingway (as Edmund Wilson and Norman Mailer had done) as the tragic model of the self-destructive artist:

Tears Henry shed for poor old Hemingway
Hemingway in despair, Hemingway at the end,
the end of Hemingway. . . .
Save us from shotguns & fathers' suicides. . . .
Mercy! my father; do not pull the trigger
or all my life I'll suffer from your anger
killing what you began.[34]

Hemingway described with unusual knowledge and authority physical pleasure, the natural world, violent experience and sudden death. He portrayed the heroic possibilities and tragic consequences of war, the psychic dislocation in battle and the stoicism of survival. He created unsurpassed images of Italy, France, Spain and Africa. As a man, he had intense idealism, curiosity, energy, strength and courage. He attractively combined hedonism and hard work, was a great teacher of ritual and technique, carried an aura of glamour and power. As an artist, he wrote as naturally as a hawk flies and as clearly as a lake reflects.

Hemingway's phrases now live in our language: grace under pressure, a separate peace, death in the afternoon, a clean, well-lighted place, a movable feast. His imagination has permanently placed in our culture a series of unforgettable scenes: the retreat from Thrace, the execution of the Greek ministers, fishing the Big Two-Hearted River, the festival at Pamplona, the arrival of the killers, the bitter couple waiting for the train in "Hills Like White Elephants," Nick's breakdown in "In Another Country," the retreat from Caporetto, his hawk-eyed father in "Fathers and Sons," the bullet tearing through the lion in "Francis Macomber," Harry's death at Kilimanjaro, the massacre of the Fascists in Pilar's village, duck shooting in the Venetian marshes, and the car journey with Fitzgerald from Lyon to Paris.

Appendix I

Accidents

Childhood: falls with stick in throat,
gouges tonsils
catches fishhook in back
1915–17: boxing injuries
football injuries
Spring 1918: fist through glass show-
case
July 8, 1918: concussed and wounded
by trench mortar and
machine gun

June 1920: cuts feet walking on glass
July 1920: falls on boat cleat, internal
hemorrhage

April 1922: burns from hot-water
heater

September 1925: tears ligament in
right foot

December 1927: Bumby cuts pupil of
good right eye

March 1928: pulls skylight on forehead; needs stitches,
welt forms
October 1929: tears muscle in groin

Illnesses

Infancy: left eye defective from birth
mysterious minor operation

October 1918: jaundice
Early 1919: tonsils removed
operation on injured leg

1920s: appendicitis operation

October 1922: malaria

June 1927: anthrax in cut foot
September 1927: swollen, itchy hands
and feet
December 1927: grippe
hemorrhoids
toothache

October 1929: kidney trouble from
cold stream

May 1930: cuts right index finger
       punching bag

August 1930: lacerations from bolting
       horse

November 1930: breaks right arm in
       car accident

Summer 1931: eye trouble, needs
       glasses

April 1932: bronchial pneumonia

October 1933: throat operation

c. January 1934: amoebic dysentery;
       prolapsed large intes-
       tine

1934: blood poisoning in right index
       finger

April 1935: shoots himself in legs
       gaffing shark

January 1935: recurrence of dysentery

February 1936: breaks big toe kicking
       locked gate

?1937–38: dropkicks foot through mir-
       ror

August 1938: scratches pupil of bad
       left eye

December 1938: severe liver
       complaint

May 1944: second concussion when
       car strikes water tank in
       blackout

August 1944: third concussion jumping
       from   motorcycle   into
       ditch; suffers double vi-
       sion and impotence

December 1944: ?pneumonia, coughs
       up blood

June 1945: car overturns; head goes
       into mirror,   knee injured

August 1947–: hypertension

December 1948: ringing in ears

March 1949: erysipelas, hospitalized in
       Padua

September 1949: clawed while playing
       with lion

February 1950: skin infection

July 1950: fourth concussion; gashes
       head falling on boat

May 1950: ?skin cancer from sun at sea

September 1950: leg pains from
       encysted shell
       fragments

October 1953: cuts face, sprains

August 1953: second dysentery

shoulder, falling out of
car

January 1954: two plane crashes in
Africa; fifth concussion,
fractured skull, internal
bleeding, paralyzed
sphincter muscle, two
cracked spine discs,
ruptured liver, right
kidney and spleen,
dislocated right arm
and shoulder, first
degree burns

January 1954: severe burns fighting fire

January 1955: rash on face and chest

November 1955: nephritis
hepatitis
anemia
swollen right foot
40 days in bed with
hepatitis

November 1956: hypertension, high
cholesterol, arterio-
sclerosis; strict diet,
no alcohol or sex

October 1958: sprains ankle, tears
heel ligaments
climbing fence

July 1959: car goes off road near
Burgos

July 1959–July 1961: skin rash
alcoholism
eye troubles
diabetes
suspected hemo-
chromatosis
nephritis
hepatitis
hypertension
impotence
mental break-
down
electroconvulsive
therapy
loss of weight
loss of memory
severe depression

Appendix II

Trips Abroad

May 23, 1918: New York to Bordeaux on *Chicago*
January 4, 1919: Genoa to New York on *Giuseppe Verdi.* Arrive January 21

December 1921: New York to France on *Leopoldina.* Arrive December 22
August 17, 1923: France to Quebec on *Andania.* Arrive August 27

January 19, 1924: New York to Cherbourg on *Antonia.* Arrive January 29
February 3, 1926: France to New York on *Mauretania.* Arrive February 9

February 19, 1926: Hoboken to Cherbourg on *Roosevelt.* Arrive February 28
March 1928: La Rochelle to Havana and Key West on *Orita*

April 5, 1929: Havana to Boulogne on *Yorck.* Arrive April 21
January 10, 1930: France to New York and Havana on *Bourdonnais*

May 4, 1931: Havana to Vigo on *Volendam.* Arrive May 16
September 1931: France to New York on *Île de France*

August 7, 1933: Havana to Santander on *Reina de la Pacífica*
November 22, 1933: Marseilles to Mombasa on *General Metzinger.* Arrive December 8
Early March 1934: Mombasa to Villefranche on *Gripsholm.* Arrive March 18
March 27, 1934: France to New York on *Île de France.* Arrive c. April 2

Late February 1937: New York to France on *Paris*
May 13, 1937: France to New York on *Normandie.* Arrive May 18

August 14, 1937: New York to France on *Champlain*
January 12, 1938: France to New York on *Gripsholm*

577

March 19, 1938: New York to France on *Île de France*
May 1938: France to New York on *Normandie*. Arrive May 31

August 31, 1938: New York to France on *Normandie*
Late November 1938: France to New York

January 27, 1941: by air from New York to Los Angeles. February 1, 1941: San Francisco to Hawaii on *Matsonia;* by air to Hong Kong, Chungking, Rangoon
May 1941: by air from Rangoon to Hong Kong, Manila, Guam, Midway, Honolulu, Los Angeles, New York

May 17, 1944: by air from New York to London
March 6, 1945: by air from Paris to London, New York, Havana

September 1948: Havana to Genoa on *Jagiello*
April 30, 1949: Genoa to Canal Zone (May 22) to Havana on *Jagiello*

November 19, 1949: New York to Le Havre on *Île de France*
March 22, 1950: Le Havre to New York on *Île de France*

June 24, 1953: New York to Le Havre on *Flandre*. Arrive June 30
August 6, 1953: Marseilles to Mombasa on *Dunnottar Castle*
March 1954: Mombasa to Venice on *Africa*
Late May or early June 1954: Genoa to Havana on *Francesco Morosini*. Arrive July

April 1956: by air from Havana to Cabo Blanco, Peru
Late May 1956: by air from Cabo Blanco to Havana

Late August 1956: New York to Le Havre on *Île de France*
Late January 1957: Le Havre to New York and Matanzas, Cuba, on *Île de France*

Late April or early May 1959: New York to Algeciras on *Constitution*
Late October 1959: Le Havre to New York on *Liberté*. Arrive October 31 or November 1

Early August 1960: by air from New York to Madrid
October 8, 1960: by air from Madrid to New York

Notes

Chapter 1: A Midwestern Boyhood

1. The ambiguous circumstances of Hall's wound and his early retirement from action may have influenced his unwillingness to discuss the war. According to Hall's Civil War records in the National Archives, Washington, D.C., he was wounded "during his term of service but not in the regular discharge of his duty; though from an enemy in arms against the authority of the U.S."
2. Quoted in Marcelline Hemingway Sanford, *At the Hemingways* (London, 1963), p. 7.
3. Letter from Hemingway to Mary Welsh, September 13, 1945, Firestone Library, Princeton University.
4. Civil War records of Anson Tyler Hemingway, National Archives, Washington, D.C.
5. Typescript obituary of Anson Hemingway, Oberlin College Archives. Hart Crane was born in Ohio on the same day and year as Hemingway.
6. Interview with Carol Hemingway Gardner, Shelburne Falls, Mass., January 31, 1983.
7. Interviews with Gregory Hemingway, Bozeman, Montana, May 22, 27–28, 1983.
8. Ernest Hemingway, *For Whom the Bell Tolls* (New York, 1940), p. 336.
9. Ernest Hemingway, "The Lost Commander," *American Dialogue*, 1 (October–November 1964), 10.
10. Frank Lloyd Wright, *Autobiography* (New York, 1943), p. 79.
11. Robert Twombly, *Frank Lloyd Wright* (New York, 1973), p. 27. Barton's comment appeared in *Oak Leaves*, June 30, 1906.
12. Madelaine Hemingway Miller, *Ernie* (New York, 1975), p. 92. During interviews with me in 1983 Sunny frequently mentioned religion, and Carol said grace before lunch.
13. Interview with Edward Wagenknecht, West Newton, Mass., November 8, 1982.
14. Ernest Hemingway, *Selected Letters, 1917–1961,* ed. Carlos Baker (New York, 1981), p. 3.
15. Letter from Hemingway to Ernest Walsh, January 2, 1926, John F. Kennedy Library, Boston.
16. Ernest Hemingway, "On Writing," *The Nick Adams Stories* (New York: Bantam, 1973), p. 215.
17. See Sanford, *At the Hemingways,* p. 50.
18. College records of Ed Hemingway, Oberlin College Archives.
19. Interview with Carol Hemingway Gardner.
20. Bill Smith, unpublished memoir "The Hunter's Eye," Charles Fenton papers, Bei-

necke Library, Yale University; letter from J. Charles Edgar to Charles Fenton, March 26, 1952, Yale.

21. Letter from Wilhelmina Corlett to Charles Fenton, June 10, 1952, Yale; Leicester Hemingway, *My Brother, Ernest Hemingway* (New York: Fawcett, 1962), p. 63.

22. Letter from Fannie Biggs to Charles Fenton, February 24, 1952, Yale.

23. Ernest Hemingway, *A Farewell to Arms* (New York, 1969), p. 72.

24. George Orwell, *Collected Essays, Journalism and Letters*, ed. Sonia Orwell and Ian Angus (London, 1968), 2:22.

25. In addition to the innumerable nicknames he invented for his boyhood friends, Hemingway devised nicknames for his wives, children and adult companions: Hash (Hadley Richardson), Mooky (Martha Gellhorn), Kitten (Mary Welsh); Bumby (Jack Hemingway), Mousie (Patrick Hemingway), Gigi (Gregory Hemingway); Butstein (Katy Smith), Jaggers (Bill Smith), Fever (Howell Jenkins), Wolfie (Winston Guest), Sinsky (Juan Dunabeitia), Monstro (Roberto Herrera), Black Priest (Father Andrés Untzaín), Negro (Bill Davis), Pecas (Aaron Hotchner), Xenophobia (Leopoldina, a Cuban whore).

26. Grace Hemingway, Scrapbooks, Kennedy.

27. Ernest Hemingway, "Now I Lay Me," *Short Stories* (New York, 1953), p. 365.

28. Gregory Hemingway, *Papa* (Boston, 1976), p. 62.

29. Ernest Hemingway, *The Wild Years*, ed. Gene Hanrahan (New York, 1962), p. 219.

30. Grace Hemingway, Scrapbooks; quoted in Sanford, *At the Hemingways*, pp. 114–115.

31. Susan Kesler, "The High School Years," *Ernest Hemingway as Recalled by His High School Contemporaries*, ed. Ina Schleden and Marion Herzog (Oak Park, 1973), p. 23.

32. Andrew Turnbull, *Scott Fitzgerald* (New York, 1962), p. 311. In Ernest Hemingway, *Across the River and into the Trees* (New York, 1950), p. 113, the cello metaphor is positive: "Her voice was so lovely and it always reminded him of Pablo Casals playing the cello that it made him feel as a wound does that you think you cannot bear."

33. Malcolm Cowley, "A Portrait of Mister Papa," *Ernest Hemingway: The Man and His Work*, ed. John McCaffery (New York: Avon, 1950), p. 37.

34. Ernest Hemingway, *By-Line: Ernest Hemingway*, ed. William White (New York, 1967), p. 189.

35. Letter from Hemingway to Ed Hemingway, n.d., Kennedy.

36. Sanford, *At the Hemingways*, p. 69.

37. Quoted in William Dawson, "Ernest Hemingway: Petoskey Interview," *Michigan Alumnus Quarterly Review*, 64 (1958), 118.

38. Hemingway, "Indian Camp," *Stories*, p. 93.

39. Hemingway, "Three Shots," *Nick Adams Stories*, p. 4.

40. Donald St. John, "Interview with Hemingway's 'Bill Gorton,' " in Bertram Sarason, *Hemingway and "The Sun" Set* (Washington, D.C., 1972), p. 172.

41. Letter from Marian Smith (Mrs. Bill Smith) to Jeffrey Meyers, April 18, 1983. See Henry Severence, *Professor William Benjamin Smith* (Columbia, Missouri, 1936).

42. Hemingway, "Fathers and Sons," *Stories*, p. 491.

43. *Ibid.*, p. 496. In 1918, when she was sixteen, the pregnant Prudence Boulton committed suicide with her lover in Charlevoix.

44. Edward Wagenknecht, *Cavalcade of the American Novel* (New York, 1952), p. 370; interview with Edward Wagenknecht, November 8, 1982. The quote of course is by Hemingway, not Shakespeare.

45. Letter from Lewis Clarahan to Charles Fenton, May 24, 1952, Yale.
46. Quoted in D. E. Wylder, "Hemingway's Satiric Vision—The High School Years," *Rendezvous* (Pocatello, Idaho), 5 (Winter 1970), 30.
47. *Ernest Hemingway's Apprenticeship: Oak Park, 1916–1917*, ed. Matthew Bruccoli (Washington, D.C., 1971), p. 62.
48. Letter from Hemingway to his family, ?Spring 1917, Kennedy.
49. Quoted in Audre Hanneman, *Supplement to Ernest Hemingway: A Comprehensive Bibliography* (Princeton, 1975), pp. 211–212.
50. Lewis Clarahan in *Hemingway Recalled by His Contemporaries*, p. 37; letter from Hemingway to Malcolm Cowley, April 25, 1949, Kennedy.
51. Edward Wagenknecht quoted in Charles Fenton, *The Apprenticeship of Ernest Hemingway* (New York: Mentor, 1962), p. 18.
52. Letter from Albert Dungan to Charles Fenton, October 24, 1952, Yale.
53. Hemingway's grades are listed in "Young Hemingway: A Panel," *Fitzgerald-Hemingway Annual 1972* (Washington, D.C., 1973), p. 128:

English 95	Science 85
85	Zoology 80
90	Chemistry 85
95	Algebra 90
93	Geometry 70
Ancient History 90	Latin 70
American History 93	75
Law 93	75
Manual Training 90	

54. Letter from Fannie Biggs to Charles Fenton, February 24, 1952, Yale.
55. Letter from Hemingway to Mary Welsh, September 13, 1945, Princeton.
56. *Letters*, p. 597.

Chapter 2: Kansas City and the War

1. *For Whom the Bell Tolls*, pp. 405–406.
2. "Crossing the Mississippi," *Nick Adams Stories*, p. 116.
3. "Summer People," *Nick Adams Stories*, p. 198.
4. Hemingway, memoir of Lionel Moise, item 553, Kennedy, quoted in Carlos Baker, *Ernest Hemingway: A Life Story* (New York, 1969), p. 35.
5. Quoted in Paul Fisher, "Back To His First Field," *Kansas City Star*, November 26, 1940, p. 1.
6. Letter from Hemingway to Charles Fenton, January 22, 1952, Yale.
7. Theodore Brumback, "With Hemingway Before *A Farewell to Arms*," *Kansas City Star*, December 6, 1936, reprinted in *Ernest Hemingway, Cub Reporter: The Kansas City Star Stories*, ed. Matthew Bruccoli (Pittsburgh, 1970), p. 7.
8. Quoted in Leicester Hemingway, *My Brother*, p. 39.
9. Quoted in Michael Culver, "The 'Short-Stop Run': Hemingway in Kansas City," *Hemingway Review*, 2 (1982), 78.
10. *Cub Reporter*, pp. 28, 30–31, 43.
11. *Ibid.*, pp. 56–58.
12. Quoted in Sanford, *At the Hemingways*, p. 157.
13. Letter from Grace Hemingway to Ernest Hemingway, May 16, 1918, Kennedy.
14. Letter from Ed Hemingway to Ernest Hemingway, May 19, 1918, Kennedy.

15. William Horne, "Letter of September 3, 1977," *The Student* (Winston-Salem, North Carolina) (Winter 1978), 35.
16. Ernest Hemingway, *Death in the Afternoon* (New York, 1932), p. 136.
17. *Letters*, pp. 10–11.
18. "A Way You'll Never Be," *Stories*, pp. 405–406.
19. Ernest Hemingway, Introduction to *Men at War* (New York, 1942), p. xxvii.
20. *Report of the Department of Military Affairs: January to July, 1918* (Rome: Department of Information, American Red Cross, 1919), p. 14.
21. Letter from Ted Brumback to Ed Hemingway, July 14, 1918, Kennedy.
22. Quoted in Harold Loeb, "Hemingway's Bitterness," in Sarason, *Hemingway and "The Sun" Set*, p. 132.
23. Letter from Bill Horne to Harold Loeb, August 31, 1961, Princeton.
24. Cited and translated in Robert Lewis, "Hemingway in Italy: Making It Up," *Journal of Modern Literature*, 9 (1982), 224.
25. Giovanni Cecchin, *Con Hemingway e Dos Passos sui campi di battaglia italiani della Grande Guerra* (Milano, 1980), pp. 121–122.
26. Quoted in Jeffrey Meyers, *Katherine Mansfield: A Biography* (London, 1978), p. 224.
27. Letter from W. R. Castle to Ed Hemingway, July 20, 1918, Kennedy.
28. *Letters*, p. 14.
29. *Ibid.*, p. 19.
30. Introduction to *Men at War*, p. xxvii.
31. Ernest Hemingway, "The Spanish War," *Fact*, 16 (July 1938), 21.
32. Letters from Hemingway to Archibald MacLeish, June 7, 1933, and to Bruce Bliven, June 19, 1933, Kennedy.
33. Quoted in Jeffrey Meyers, *A Reader's Guide to George Orwell* (London, 1975), p. 118.
34. Quoted in Malcolm Cowley, *A Second Flowering* (New York, 1973), p. 224.
35. *A Farewell to Arms*, pp. 54–56.
36. Ernest Hemingway, remarks after screening *The Spanish Earth*, 1937, TS, pp. 7–8, Library of Congress, Washington, D.C.
37. Letter from Hemingway to Harvey Breit, January 1, 1951, Kennedy.
38. *Across the River*, p. 71.
39. Letter from Hemingway to Mr. Demastus, May 31, 1950, Kennedy.
40. Quoted in John Peale Bishop, "Homage to Hemingway" (1937) in *After the Genteel Tradition*, ed. Malcolm Cowley (Carbondale, Illinois, 1964), p. 154.
41. Quoted in Turnbull, *Scott Fitzgerald*, p. 244.
42. Letter from Nurse Charlotte Heilman, November 11, 1952, quoted in Michael Reynolds, *Hemingway's First War: The Making of "A Farewell to Arms"* (Princeton, 1976), p. 195.
43. "In Another Country" and "Now I Lay Me," *Stories*, p. 268, 363.
44. Letter from Henry Villard to Carlos Baker, February 1, 1962, quoted in Reynolds, *Hemingway's First War*, p. 200; Henry Villard, "In a World War I Hospital with Hemingway," *Horizon*, 21 (August 1978), 89.
45. Letter from Bill Horne to Harold Loeb, August 31, 1961, Princeton.
46. *A Farewell to Arms*, pp. 18, 114.
47. Quoted in Michael Reynolds, "The Agnes Tapes," *Fitzgerald-Hemingway Annual, 1979* (Detroit, 1980), pp. 269, 271.
48. Sanford, *At the Hemingways*, p. 171.
49. Letters from Agnes von Kurowsky to Hemingway, December 4, October 21, December 20, 1918, Kennedy. The second letter is quoted in Bernice Kert, *The Hemingway*

Women (New York, 1983), p. 61; the third letter is quoted in Reynolds, *Hemingway's First War*, p. 203.

50. Quoted in Reynolds, *Hemingway's First War*, p. 202.
51. Quoted in Miller, *Ernie*, p. 87.
52. Quoted in Reynolds, *Hemingway's First War*, p. 204; quoted in Kert, *Hemingway Women*, p. 63.
53. *Death in the Afternoon*, p. 180. Another example of homosexual corruption appears in Ernest Hemingway, *To Have and Have Not* (New York, 1970), pp. 231–233.
54. Quoted in Reynolds, *Hemingway's First War*, p. 209; quoted in Villard, "In a World War I Hospital," p. 92.
55. Quoted in Reynolds, *Hemingway's First War*, p. 204.
56. "A Very Short Story," *Stories*, p. 142.
57. Quoted in Reynolds, *Hemingway's First War*, p. 215. Agnes was a Red Cross nurse in Bucharest and Constantia in 1920–21 and (after four years of private nursing) in Haiti in 1926. She married Howard Garner in 1928, left Haiti in 1930 and divorced him in Reno a year later. She married William Stanfield, a widower with three children, in 1934, and worked in a Red Cross blood bank during World War Two. After the war Agnes lived in Virginia Beach; and in 1955, when Hemingway was living in Havana, she became a librarian in Key West.
58. "The Snows of Kilimanjaro," *Stories*, pp. 64–65; Sofya Tolstoy, *Countess Tolstoy's Later Diary, 1891–1897*, trans. Alexander Werth (London, 1929), p. 128; Ernest Hemingway, "The Art of Fiction," *Paris Review*, 18 (Spring 1958), 68.
59. A letter from Chink's son, Christopher Dorman-O'Gowan (the family reassumed their original Irish name in 1949), to Jeffrey Meyers, March 30, 1983, explains the origin of his curious nickname: "When he joined the first battalion 5th Fusiliers in early 1914 they had just returned from India. There they had a pet chinkara (a type of Indian buck) as a mascot. Father had such a long face that when he was introduced to a brother officer in the mess that officer remarked: 'Look—we have got our Chink back.' So it stuck."
60. In August 1914 Sir John French's four divisions were outflanked and forced to retreat from Mons in Belgium—the first "bad show" of the Great War.
61. "The Spanish War," p. 22.
62. See Brigadier H. R. Sandilands, *The Fifth in the Great War: A History of the First and Second Northumberland Fusiliers, 1914–1918* (Dover, 1938), p. 119: "It was evident that if they were to escape annihilation at the hands of the enemy who were fast surrounding them, it could only be by risking immediate retirement across the open. It was thus in fact that Dorman-Smith and a handful of other ranks escaped from the position, which their companies had captured and held for nine hours."
63. Interview with Christopher Dorman-O'Gowan, Thropton, Northumberland, August 6, 1983. For more information on Chink, see Lavinia Graecen, "Friendship with Hemingway," "Turning Point of Desert War" and "The Years in Ireland," *Irish Times*, March 16, 17, 18, 1983, all on p. 10.
64. Major General Eric Dorman-O'Gowan, "When Hem Was 21—and I was Rising 25," *Today*, August 19, 1961, pp. 4–5.
65. Ernest Hemingway, *88 Poems*, ed. Nicholas Gerogiannis (New York, 1979), p. 75.
66. Letter from Rowan Boone to Carlos Baker, December 1, 1950, Yale.
67. John Dos Passos, *The Best Times* (New York, 1966), p. 156.
68. See "Christmas on the Roof of the World" (December 22, 1923), *By-Line: Ernest Hemingway*, pp. 127–132; "Skier's Only Escape" (January 12, 1924), *The Wild Years*, p. 277; "To Chink Whose Trade is Soldiering" and "Some day when you are picked

up" (both 1924), *88 Poems*, pp. 74–75; "On Writing" (written 1925), *Nick Adams Stories*, p. 216; *Death in the Afternoon*, pp. 265, 496–497; *Green Hills of Africa* (New York, 1935), pp. 280–281; Introduction to *Men at War*, p. xiv; *A Moveable Feast* (written 1957–60) (New York, 1964), pp. 53–57, 61, 74. The third and fourth interchapters of *In Our Time* (1925) were based on Chink's experience at Mons and he also provided the stoical Shakespearean quotation that the hunter Wilson lives by in "The Short Happy Life of Francis Macomber" (1936). Chink did not save Hemingway's early correspondence, but twenty letters from Hemingway to Chink, written between 1950 and 1955, were published in the *Irish Times* on March 19 and 21–24, 1983.

Hemingway expressed his admiration for Chink in the presentation copies of his first and third books (now owned by his son). *Three Stories and Ten Poems* is inscribed: "For Chink with love from Popplethwaite. Paris. August 1923"; *In Our Time* is inscribed: "To Chink with Homages Respectueus [*sic*] from his former A.D.C. and still, with the occasional permission of His Britannic Majesty, companion. Popplethwaite. Paris. October 1925." Hemingway's second book, *in our time* (1924) is respectfully dedicated to Chink, Robert McAlmon and William Bird.

Chapter 3: Hadley

1. Letter from Marcelline Sanford to Delbert Wylder, summer 1952, courtesy of Professor Wylder.
2. "Soldier's Home," *Stories*, pp. 145–146.
3. Quoted in Michael Reynolds, *Hemingway's Reading, 1910–1940* (Princeton, 1981), p. 4; *Across the River*, p. 278.
4. "Indian Camp," *Stories*, p. 92; quoted in Sarason, *Hemingway and "The Sun" Set*, p. 172.
5. Letter to Malcolm Cowley, August 19, 1948, quoted in Sotheby Parke Bernet, *Fine Modern First Editions* (New York: October 25, 1977), lot 425; *Letters*, p. 697.
6. "The End of Something," *Stories*, p. 110. Compare with pp. 170 and 177.
7. "Up in Michigan," *Stories*, p. 85. In this story, as in many others, he emphasizes men's hands and women's hair. Jim's automaton-like hands, which seem to take on a life of their own, influenced Nathanael West's description of Homer's horrible hands, which commit murder in *The Day of the Locust* (1939).
8. Quoted in Maurice Neville, book catalogue no. 6, 1982, no. 229.
9. Donald Jones, "Built by a wealthy practical joker, house once was Hemingway's home," *Toronto Star*, June 11, 1977.
10. Letter from Ralph Connable to Hemingway, January 12, 1920, Kennedy.
11. Letter from Ed Hemingway to Ernest Hemingway, February 17, 1920, Kennedy.
12. Gregory Clark, "Hemingway Slept Here," *Montreal Standard*, November 4, 1950, p. 13.
13. Quoted in Donald Jones, "Newspaper job in Toronto launched writer's career," *Toronto Star*, June 18, 1977.
14. Quoted in Fenton, *Apprenticeship*, p. 80.
15. Quoted in Baker, *Life Story*, p. 71.
16. *Letters*, p. 46.
17. Letter from Ted Brumback to Hemingway, April 23, 1920, Kennedy.
18. Frederick Spiegel, "Young Hemingway: A Panel," *Fitzgerald-Hemingway Annual, 1972* (Washington, D.C., 1973), p. 137.
19. Letter from Hemingway to Charles Scribner, March 15, 1953, Kennedy.

20. Miller, *Ernie,* p. 67.
21. Letter from Grace Hemingway to Ernest Hemingway, July 24, 1920, Kennedy.
22. Quoted in Leicester Hemingway, *My Brother,* p. 57.
23. "Soldier's Home," *Stories,* pp. 151–152.
24. *Letters,* pp. 597–598.
25. Sherwood Anderson, *Letters,* ed. Howard Jones (Boston, 1953), p. 82.
26. Letter from Hemingway to Buck Lanham, December 27, 1948, Princeton. Information about the quarrel comes from Bill Smith's taped interview with Patrick Hynan, Kennedy, and my interview with Marian Smith, April 12, 1983. Emily Hahn casts more light on Kenley in a letter to Jeffrey Meyers, October 17, 1983:

    Y. K. and Doodles met at a sanatorium where both were trying to get rid of TB. They never actually married because they had no use for outworn ceremonies, so they wrote their own ceremony and made vows. . . . After Doodles he married a Russian, Julie, who needed somehow to live in the USA. (He was an idealist: it was a kind of Auden–Erica Mann arrangement.) Then she died and he and [my sister] Helen were married.

27. Ernest Hemingway, "Will You Let These Kiddies Miss Santa Claus?" *Co-operative Commonwealth,* 2 (December 1920), reprinted in *Fitzgerald-Hemingway Annual, 1970* (Washington, D.C., 1970), pp. 105–106.
28. H. Rappaport, "False Cooperatives and a $15,000,000 Shell Game," *Nation,* 113 (October 19, 1921), 447.
29. *Letters,* p. 719.
30. Quoted in Kert, *Hemingway Women,* p. 96.
31. Interview with Hadley in Patrick Hynan's record *Hemingway* (Toronto: CBC, 1970).
32. Sanford, *At the Hemingways,* p. 201; interviews with Madelaine Hemingway Miller, Deerfield Beach, Florida, January 1, 1983, and with Carol Hemingway Gardner.
33. Quoted in Alfred Aronowitz and Peter Hamill, *Ernest Hemingway: The Life and Death of a Man* (New York, 1961), p. 57.
34. Max Eastman, "The Great and the Small in Ernest Hemingway," *Great Companions* (London, 1959), p. 36.
35. Letter from Hemingway to Bill Smith, December 6, 1924, Yale.
36. Quoted in Ruth Sokoloff, *Hadley: The First Mrs. Hemingway* (New York, 1973), p. 26, and in Sotheby catalogue, lot 429.
37. Sokoloff, *Hadley,* pp. 24, 31.
38. Quoted in Hynan, *Hemingway;* quoted in Aronowitz, *Ernest Hemingway,* p. 96.
39. "Wedding Day," *Nick Adams Stories,* p. 212.

Chapter 4: Paris

1. George Orwell, *Down and Out in Paris and London* (New York, 1961), p. 5.
2. Quoted in E. R. Hagemann, "A Preliminary Report on the State of Ernest Hemingway's Correspondence," *Literary Research Newsletter,* 3 (1978), 163.
3. Letter from Hemingway to Katy Smith, February 16, 1922, Kennedy.
4. *A Moveable Feast,* p. 4, tells this story but does not give the name of the street. Baker, *Life Story,* p. 85, Sokoloff, *Hadley,* p. 48, and many others repeat it.
5. Quoted in Harold Loeb, *The Way It Was* (New York, 1959), p. 207.
6. Dos Passos, *Best Times,* p. 143; quoted in Nancy Milford, *Zelda* (New York: Avon, 1970), p. 116.
7. *Letters,* p. 636.

8. Quoted in Allen Tate, *Memoirs and Opinions, 1926–1974* (Chicago, 1975), p. 64; quoted in Matthew Josephson, *Infidel in the Temple* (New York, 1967), p. 423; *Memoirs of Kiki: The Education of a French Model* (1929), trans. Samuel Putnam (London, 1964), p. 56.

9. *Letters*, p. 165.

10. Ernest Hemingway, "The Art of Fiction," p. 68; letter from Hemingway to Hadley Richardson, December 23, 1920, Kennedy.

11. Jean Rhys, *Quartet* (New York, 1964), p. 60; *The Wild Years*, p. 79.

12. *Death in the Afternoon*, p. 278; Morley Callaghan, *That Summer in Paris* (New York: Penguin, 1963), p. 30.

13. Dorman-O'Gowan, "When Hem Was 21," p. 5.

14. Letter from Hemingway to Charles Fenton, January 19, 1952, Yale. Aronowitz, *Ernest Hemingway*, p. 68, improbably specifies "some eighteen stories, thirty poems, and an unfinished novel."

15. Letter from Hemingway to Bill Smith, December 6, 1924, Yale; item 98, pp. 895, 888, Kennedy.

16. Item 98, p. 887, Kennedy; quoted in Luis Quintanilla, "Hemingway en mi recuerdo," *Cuadernos del Congreso por la libertad de la Cultura* (Paris), 54 (noviembre 1961), 48. My translation.

17. Quoted in Fenton, *Apprenticeship*, pp. 221 n22, 156; Sanford, *At the Hemingways*, p. 221.

18. Hemingway, *A Moveable Feast*, p. 74; item 98, p. 903, Kennedy; Cowley, "A Portrait of Mister Papa," p. 41. See also Masolino d'Amico, "Hemingway in Action," *TLS*, July 25, 1980, p. 857.

19. Letter from Robert McAlmon to Norman Holmes Pearson, February 28, 1952, Yale.

20. Quintanilla, "Hemingway en mi recuerdo," p. 51.

21. Jack Hemingway, "Memories of Papa," p. 32.

22. Quoted in Honoria Murphy Donnelly, *Sara and Gerald* (New York, 1983), p. 165; quoted in Hynan, *Hemingway*.

23. Tate, *Memoirs and Opinions*, p. 60; Dos Passos, *Best Times*, p. 205.

24. Quoted in Sarason, *Hemingway and "The Sun" Set*, p. 199; *To Have and Have Not*, p. 98.

25. The various book lists that Hemingway drew up and recommended were often whimsical, eccentric and misleading. See *Green Hills of Africa*, pp. 27, 71, 108; *By-Line: Ernest Hemingway*, p. 211; "The Art of Fiction," *Paris Review*, p. 73; and "James Allen lived in a studio," item 529a, Kennedy, which improbably states that the books he cared for most were *Alice in Wonderland*, George Moore's *Hail and Farewell*, *Huckleberry Finn*, George Borrow's *Lavengro* and W. H. Hudson's *Far Away and Long Ago*.

26. These would include Irene Goldstein, Gertrude Stein, Alfred Flechtheim, Harold Loeb, Jules Pascin, Nathan Asch, Leon Fleischman, Dorothy Parker, Donald Friede, Sidney Franklin, Louis Cohn, Maurice Speiser, Michael Lerner, Robert Capa, Milton Wolff, Werner Heilbrun, General Morris Cohen, Bernard Berenson, Alfred Rice, Harvey Breit, Lee Samuels, Leonard Lyons and Clara Spiegel.

27. *Cub Reporter*, p. 18; letter from Hemingway to Harvey Breit, October 19, 1952, Kennedy.

28. *To Have and Have Not*, p. 236.

29. Ernest Hemingway, "Homage to Ezra," *This Quarter* (Spring 1925), reprinted in *Ezra Pound: A Collection of Essays*, ed. Peter Russell (London, 1950), p. 74; Wyndham Lewis, "Ezra Pound," *Ezra Pound: A Collection of Essays*, p. 258.

30. *Letters*, p. 62.
31. "Homage to Ezra," p. 74; *A Moveable Feast*, p. 108.
32. Quoted in Noel Stock, *The Life of Ezra Pound* (London, 1974), p. 396; quoted in Baker, *Life Story*, p. 236.
33. *A Moveable Feast*, p. 132; *Death in the Afternoon*, p. 191.
34. Quoted in Gianfranco Ivancich, ed., *Ezra Pound in Italy* (New York, 1978), n.p.; quoted in Hynan, *Hemingway*.
35. Anderson, *Letters*, p. 85.
36. *A Moveable Feast*, p. 14; quoted in Sokoloff, *Hadley*, p. 50.
37. Letter from Hemingway to Ezra Pound, July 22, 1933, Yale; *A Moveable Feast*, p. 17.
38. *Letters*, p. 650.
39. Jack Hemingway, "Memories of Papa," p. 31; quoted in Gertrude Stein, *The Flowers of Friendship*, ed. Donald Gallup (New York, 1953), p. 165.
40. Martin Seymour-Smith, *Robert Graves* (New York, 1983), p. 188; *A Moveable Feast*, pp. 20, 116.
41. Quoted in Aronowitz, *Ernest Hemingway*, p. 75; quoted in Samuel Putnam, *Paris Was Our Mistress* (New York, 1947), p. 138.
42. *A Moveable Feast*, p. 17; *Letters*, p. 649.
43. Wyndham Lewis, *Time and Western Man* (Boston, 1957), pp. 51, 58, 61; Georges Braque, *Testimony Against Gertrude Stein* (The Hague, 1935), pp. 13–14.
44. See Harold Acton, *Memoirs of an Aesthete* (London, 1948), pp. 160–161, 173–175, and Nathalie Barney, *Traits et Portraits* (Paris, 1963), p. 66.
45. *Letters*, p. 411; Ernest Hemingway, *The Torrents of Spring* (London, 1966), p. 90.
46. *88 Poems*, p. 90; Ernest Hemingway, "My Own Life," *New Yorker*, 2 (February 12, 1927), 23.
47. Gertrude Stein, *The Autobiography of Alice B. Toklas* (New York, 1933), pp. 216, 218, 220; Anderson, *Letters*, p. 295.
48. Letter from Hemingway to Ezra Pound, July 22, 1933, Yale.
49. See Ernest Hemingway, *"The Farm,"* reprinted in Clement Greenberg, *Joan Miró* (New York, 1948), p. 5; Ernest Hemingway, Introduction to Jimmy Charters, *This Must Be the Place* (New York, 1965), p. 7.
50. John Chamberlain, review of *Green Hills of Africa*, *New York Times*, October 25, 1935, p. 19; *For Whom the Bell Tolls*, p. 289.
51. *A Moveable Feast*, pp. 27–29; *Letters*, pp. 649–650.
52. *A Moveable Feast*, p. 35.
53. Ernest Hemingway, *Islands in the Stream* (New York: Bantam, 1972), pp. 59–60. Richard Ellmann, *James Joyce*, revised edition (New York, 1982), p. 515, unaccountably places their meeting in the spring of 1921, when Hemingway was still in Chicago.
54. Quoted in Robert Manning, "Hemingway in Cuba," *Atlantic*, 216 (August 1965), 106; quoted in Valerie Danby-Smith, "Reminiscences of Hemingway," *Saturday Review*, 47 (May 9, 1964), 31.
55. *Letters*, pp. 789, 696.
56. Letters from Robert Hickok and Andree Hickok to Jeffrey Meyers, May 20 and April 4, 1983.
57. Wyndham Lewis, "Ezra: The Portrait of a Personality," *Quarterly Review of Literature*, 5 (December 1949), 140; *A Moveable Feast*, p. 109.
58. Letter from Archibald MacLeish to Jeffrey Meyers, October 1977; letter from Archibald MacLeish to W. K. Rose, April 25, 1960, Vassar College Library, Poughkeepsie, New York; *Across the River*, p. 115.
59. Letter from Hemingway to Ernest Walsh, [1925], Yale.

60. Quoted in Wyndham Lewis, *Rude Assignment* (London, 1950), pp. 203–204; letter from Hemingway to Pound, [late 1927], Yale.
61. Letter from Hemingway to Jonathan Cape, October 13, 1932, University of Reading; reprinted in Jeffrey Meyers, *Hemingway: The Critical Heritage* (Boston, 1982), pp. 192, 195–197, 206.
62. Lewis, *Rude Assignment*, p. 203; *A Moveable Feast*, pp. 108–109.
63. William Carlos Williams, *A Voyage to Pagany* (New York, 1970), p. 20.
64. Robert McAlmon and Kay Boyle, *Being Geniuses Together* (Garden City, New York, 1968), pp. 180, 175.
65. Letter from Hemingway to Ezra Pound, 1926, Yale.
66. Callaghan, *That Summer in Paris*, pp. 84–85.

Chapter 5: European Reporter

1. *Green Hills of Africa*, p. 193.
2. Quoted in Fenton, *Apprenticeship*, p. 113; André Malraux, *Antimemoirs*, trans. Terence Kilmartin (London, 1970), p. 116.
3. Introduction to *Men at War*, p. xxi.
4. Letter from Henry Wales, correspondent of the Chicago *Tribune*, to Charles Fenton, August 7, 1952, Yale; *By-Line*, p. 223.
5. Lincoln Steffens, *Letters*, ed. Ella Winter and Granville Hicks (New York, 1938), p. 868; letter from George Seldes to Jeffrey Meyers, April 2, 1983, and interview with George Seldes, Hartland Four Corners, Vermont, April 8, 1983.
6. Denis Mack Smith, *Italy: A Modern History*, rev. ed. (Ann Arbor, 1969), p. 372.
7. *The Wild Years*, pp. 188–190; Introduction to *Men at War*, p. xxviii.
8. *The Wild Years*, pp. 214–215; *88 Poems*, p. 63; *Letters*, p. 76.
9. *Letters*, p. 107.
10. Letter from Hemingway to Peter Buckley, June 4, 1957, Kennedy.
11. *Death in the Afternoon*, p. 192.
12. *Letters*, pp. 91–92.
13. George Abbott, *Greece and the Allies, 1914–1922* (London, 1922), p. 221.
14. *The Wild Years*, pp. 201–202.
15. Arnold Toynbee and Kenneth Kirkwood, *Turkey* (London, 1927), pp. 105–106.
16. "On the Quai at Smyrna," *Stories*, p. 88. See also *Death in the Afternoon*, pp. 2, 135.
17. Bernard Lewis, *The Emergence of Modern Turkey* (London, 1962), p. 249.
18. *The Wild Years*, p. 196.
19. *Ibid.*, pp. 204–205.
20. *Stories*, p. 97.
21. Donald McCormick, *One Man's Wars: The Story of Colonel Charles Sweeny, Soldier of Fortune* (London, 1972), p. 121; Tate, *Memoirs and Opinions*, p. 51.
22. *By-Line*, p. 222. See Scott Donaldson, "Hemingway of *The Star*," *College Literature*, 7 (1980), 267–270.
23. Salahi Sonyel, *Turkish Diplomacy, 1918–1923* (London, 1975), p. 225.
24. S. P. Phocas-Cosmetatos, *The Tragedy of Greece* (London 1928), p. 312.
25. *Stories*, p. 127.
26. See *The Wild Years*, pp. 156–158.
27. *Stories*, p. 233.
28. "The Snows of Kilimanjaro," *Ibid.*, pp. 55–56.
29. *Ibid.*, pp. 65–66.

30. *88 Poems,* p. 63.
31. *The Wild Years,* p. 147.
32. Meyers, *Hemingway: Critical Heritage,* p. 187; see Archibald MacLeish, "Post-War Writers and Pre-War Readers," *New Republic,* 102 (June 10, 1940), 789–790; *Death in the Afternoon,* p. 112.
33. Dos Passos, *Best Times,* p. 141; Edmund Wilson, "Hemingway: Gauge of Morale," *The Wound and the Bow* (New York, 1947), p. 240.
34. Quoted in Sarason, *Hemingway and "The Sun" Set,* p. 164.
35. Dorman-Smith (who later served in India and espoused imperial values) greatly admired Kipling. He had a framed copy of "If" in his study and gave his son a copy of the *Complete Poems.* Interview with Christopher Dorman-O'Gowan.
36. Introduction to *Men at War,* p. xiv.
37. Edmund Wilson, "Hemingway: Gauge of Morale," p. 239n. The two quotations from Kipling's poetry appear in "The Winners" and "The Female of the Species."
38. Jeffrey Meyers, "Rudyard Kipling: Codes of Heroism," *Fiction and the Colonial Experience* (Totowa, New Jersey, 1973), p. 122.
39. Leicester Hemingway, *My Brother,* p. 26. See also Sanford, *At the Hemingways,* p. 133.
40. Patrick Hemingway, "My Papa, Papa," *Playboy,* 15 (December 1968), 264. Carlos Baker, Introduction to *Letters,* p. xvi, revealed that young Patrick heard the censored version. Hemingway "modified a line from Kipling's 'If' to boast that he could 'walk with shits nor lose the common touch.' "
41. *Letters,* p. 260.
42. *Ibid.,* p. 277; letter from Hemingway to Owen Wister, March 11, 1929, Library of Congress.
43. Hemingway, "In Defense of Dirty Words," *Esquire,* 2 (September 1934), 158; *Green Hills of Africa,* p. 27.
44. *By-Line,* p. 218; *Letters,* p. 466. Kipling's "plays," like Hemingway's "Today is Friday" (1926), were dramatic dialogues, not meant to be acted.
45. *Ibid.,* pp. 666, 724; letter from Hemingway to Charles Scribner, December 20, 1951, Kennedy.
46. Ernest Hemingway, "Letter to a Young Man," *Mark Twain Journal,* 11 (1962), 10; *By-Line,* p. 446.
47. *88 Poems,* p. 54. For other allusions to Kipling, see pp. 111, 125. Stein, *Autobiography,* p. 213; Sokoloff, *Hadley,* p. 40.
48. Fenton, *Apprenticeship,* pp. 108, 219n; *By-Line,* p. 17, noted by Baker, *Life Story,* p. 84.
49. Rudyard Kipling, *Something of Myself* (New York, 1937), pp. 227, 225; *A Moveable Feast,* pp. 13, 75.
50. Henry James, *Letters,* ed. Percy Lubbock (London, 1920), 1: 271.
51. C. S. Lewis, "Kipling's World," *They Asked for a Paper* (London, 1962), p. 89.
52. Wilson, "The Kipling That Nobody Read," *The Wound and the Bow,* p. 168; "In Another Country," *Stories,* p. 270.
53. Rudyard Kipling, "In the Same Boat," *A Diversity of Creatures* (London, 1917), p. 73.
54. Meyers, *Hemingway: Critical Heritage,* p. 246.
55. Rudyard Kipling, "Without Benefit of Clergy," *The English in India,* ed. Randall Jarrell (New York, 1963), p. 235; "In Another Country," *Stories,* p. 272.
56. *Letters,* pp. 87–88.
57. *Death in the Afternoon,* p. 2.

58. *For Whom the Bell Tolls*, p. 364; *Stories*, p. 207. Maera was not, in fact, killed in the bullring but died of tuberculosis in December 1924.
59. *Death in the Afternoon*, pp. 91, 233.
60. McAlmon, *Being Geniuses Together*, p. 275; letter from Hemingway to Stewart's friend Father Vincent Donavan [December 1927], Kennedy. See the story that was probably sent by Bill Bird: "Bull Gores 2 Yanks Acting as Toreadores," *Chicago Daily Tribune*, July 29, 1924, p. 1.
61. Letter from Hemingway to Gertrude Stein, July 15, 1925, Yale.
62. *Letters*, p. 180.
63. "The Three-Day Blow" and "Cross-Country Snow," *Stories*, pp. 122, 187.
64. Stein, *Autobiography*, p. 213; McAlmon, *Being Geniuses Together*, p. 277.
65. *A Farewell to Arms*, pp. 139, 304, 298, 309, 320; Franz Kafka, *Diaries, 1910–1913*, trans. Joseph Kresh (New York, 1965), p. 296.
66. Jeffrey Meyers, *The Enemy: A Biography of Wyndham Lewis* (London, 1980), p. 265.
67. Letters from J. H. Cranston to Charles Fenton, August 7, 1951, and February 1, 1952, Yale.
68. Quoted in Fenton, *Apprenticeship*, pp. 201, 204; *Letters*, pp. 104, 94.
69. Interview with Jack Hemingway, Ketchum, Idaho, May 25, 1983.
70. *Letters*, p. 109; letter from J. H. Cranston to Charles Fenton, August 26, 1951, Yale.

Chapter 6: A Writer's Life

1. Stein, *Autobiography*, p. 213; Kathleen Cannell, "Scenes with a Hero," in Sarason, *Hemingway and "The Sun" Set*, p. 149; Burton Rascoe, *We Were Interrupted* (Garden City, New York, 1947), p. 186.
2. William Carlos Williams, *Selected Letters*, ed. John Thirlwall (New York, 1957), p. 294.
3. Ezra Pound, Appendix I, *Confucius to Cummings*, ed. Ezra Pound and Marcella Spann (New York, 1964), p. 327.
4. Letter from Ed Hemingway to Ernest Hemingway, January 27, 1927, Kennedy.
5. Ford Madox Ford, *Provence* (1935; New York, 1979), pp. 62, 56; Ford Madox Ford, *It Was the Nightingale* (Philadelphia, 1933), p. 295.
6. Meyers, *Hemingway: Critical Heritage*, p. 154.
7. Meyers, *Hemingway: Critical Heritage*, p. 13; Ford Madox Ford, "Some American Expatriates," *Vanity Fair*, 28 (April 1, 1927), 64.
8. Meyers, *Hemingway: Critical Heritage*, pp. 151, 156. The second sentence is: "In the bed of the river there were pebbles and boulders, dry and white in the sun, and the water was clear and swiftly moving."
9. Quoted in Alice B. Toklas, *What is Remembered* (New York, 1963), p. 113; *Letters*, p. 113.
10. Stein, *Autobiography*, p. 220; quoted in John Berryman, *Stephen Crane*, revised edition (New York, 1977), p. 251.
11. Rascoe, *We Were Interrupted*, p. 185.
12. Rhys, *Quartet*, p. 9.
13. Hemingway, item 180, p. 2, Kennedy; quoted in Callaghan, *That Summer in Paris*, p. 119.
14. *Transatlantic Review*, 2 (December 1924), 550.
15. Quoted in Stein, *Flowers of Friendship*, p. 167.
16. *Letters*, pp. 125–126.
17. *The Torrents of Spring*, pp. 101, 55, 96; *A Moveable Feast*, p. 81.

18. Quoted in Frederic Svoboda, *Hemingway and "The Sun Also Rises"* (Lawrence, Kansas, 1983), p. 85.

19. Ernest Hemingway, "The Unpublished Opening of *The Sun Also Rises,"Antaeus,* 35 (1979), 12–14. Belloc (b. 1870) and Crowley (b. 1875) were both in their fifties in 1925, but they did not look alike.

20. Meyers, *Hemingway: Critical Heritage,* p. 486; Arthur Mizener, *The Saddest Story* (New York, 1971), p. 208.

21. *Letters,* p. 244; "The Art of Fiction," *Paris Review,* p. 79. The manuscript of "Ten Indians" reveals that the story was started before May 16 and heavily revised after the initial spurt of inspiration.

22. *By-Line,* p. 218.

23. *Green Hills of Africa,* p. 108; *A Moveable Feast,* pp. 131–132.

24. *By-Line,* p. 184; Introduction to *Men at War,* pp. xvii–xviii.

25. Berryman, *Stephen Crane,* p. 6; Introduction to *Men at War,* p. xvii.

26. Joseph Conrad, *Victory* (Garden City, New York, 1957), p. 154; F. Scott Fitzgerald, *Letters,* ed. Andrew Turnbull (New York, 1963), p. 363; *Death in the Afternoon,* p. 2; *By-Line,* p. 219.

27. D. H. Lawrence, *Collected Letters,* ed. Harry Moore (London, 1962), 1: 234; "Fathers and Sons," *Stories,* p. 491.

28. *A Moveable Feast,* p. 13. See Robert Lair, "Hemingway and Cézanne: An Indebtedness," *Modern Fiction Studies,* 6 (1960), 165–168; Emily Watts, *Ernest Hemingway and the Visual Arts* (Urbana, Illinois, 1971); Meyly Hagemann, "Hemingway's Secret: Visual to Verbal Art," *Journal of Modern Literature,* 7 (1979), 87–112; and Alfred Kazin, "Hemingway the Painter," *An American Procession* (New York, 1984), pp. 357–373. For a discussion of the relation between art and literature, see Jeffrey Meyers, *Painting and the Novel* (Manchester, 1975).

29. *Letters,* p. 501; letter from Hemingway to Bernard Berenson, December 7, 1952, I Tatti, Settignano, Italy; "The Art of Fiction," *Paris Review,* p. 64.

30. *Letters,* p. 153.

31. *For Whom the Bell Tolls,* p. 230; *Death in the Afternoon,* p. 2; *Letters,* p. 837.

32. "The Art of Fiction," *Paris Review,* pp. 88, 84.

33. H. E. Bates, *The Modern Short Story* (London, 1942), p. 175; *A Moveable Feast,* p. 75.

34. Fernanda Pivano, "Hemingway, cacciatore sconfitto della preda" (hunter trapped by his prey), *Corriere della Sera,* luglio 3, 1981, p. 3. My translation.

35. *Letters,* pp. 187, 216; letter from George Seldes to Jeffrey Meyers, April 2, 1983.

36. *A Moveable Feast,* p. 74.

37. *Letters,* pp. 91–92.

38. Sandilands, *The Fifth in the Great War,* p. 14. A map showing Chink's platoon appears on p. 15; a photograph of the iron-lever drawbridge on p. 17.

39. *For Whom the Bell Tolls,* p. 367. A similar mood is expressed by W. H. Auden, "Poem XXX," *Poems* (1930): "Consider this and in our time / As the hawk sees it or the helmeted airman," and by George Orwell, "Rudyard Kipling" (1942), *Critical Essays* (London, 1946), p. 101: "No one, in our time, believes in any sanction greater than military power."

40. *Dear Scott/Dear Max: The Fitzgerald-Perkins Correspondence,* ed. John Kuehl and Jackson Bryer (New York, 1971), p. 131.

41. Ernest Hemingway, "Gattorno" (a Cuban artist), *Esquire,* 5 (May 1936), 141.

42. "Big Two-Hearted River," *Stories,* pp. 231–232. In "On Writing," *Nick Adams Stories,* pp. 213–220, a coda deleted from the original version of "Big Two-Hearted

River," Hemingway discusses the relation of imagination and reality and says of "Indian Camp," the first story in *In Our Time:* "Everything good he'd ever written he'd made up. . . . Of course he'd never seen an Indian woman having a baby. That was what made it good."

43. *Letters,* p. 128.
44. Meyers, *Hemingway: Critical Heritage,* pp. 11, 63–64; *Letters,* p. 129.
45. Meyers, *Hemingway: Critical Heritage,* p. 73.
46. Quoted in Baker, *Life Story,* p. 160; quoted in Philip Young's essay, in Jackson Benson, ed., *The Short Stories of Ernest Hemingway: Critical Essays* (Durham, North Carolina, 1975), p. 44.
47. "The Last Good Country," *Nick Adams Stories,* p. 75; letter from Grace Hemingway to Ernest Hemingway, December 4, 1926, Kennedy; interview with Carol Hemingway Gardner.
48. Sanford, *At the Hemingways,* pp. 216, 219, 241.
49. Letter from Hemingway to his family, May 7, 1924, copy in Princeton; letter from Mario Menocal, Jr., to Carlos Baker, October 1, 1964, courtesy of Señor Menocal.
50. *Letters,* p. 243; quoted in a Detroit newspaper clipping (no date) in the Marcelline Sanford correspondence, Kennedy.
51. *Letters,* pp. 885, 605; Archibald MacLeish, *Letters,* ed. R. H. Winnick (Boston, 1983), p. 123. Peter Hamilton was a wealthy American who, in 1926, had lent MacLeish his luxurious residence at 41 avenue du Bois de Boulogne.
52. *A Moveable Feast,* p. 121; *Letters,* p. 134.
53. Josephson, *Infidel in the Temple,* p. 430; *A Moveable Feast,* p. 134.
54. Dos Passos, *Best Times,* p. 158.

Chapter 7: Duff Twysden and Scott Fitzgerald

1. John Peale Bishop, "Homage to Hemingway," in *After the Genteel Tradition,* p. 149.
2. Quoted in Baker, *Life Story,* p. 178; *To Have and Have Not,* pp. 244–245.
3. *Stories,* pp. 170, 177; 340, 342.
4. *Death in the Afternoon,* p. 498; letter from Hemingway to Buck Lanham, November 24, 1948, Princeton; letter from Hemingway to Bill Smith, March 4, 1925, Yale.
5. Harold Loeb, "Hemingway's Bitterness," in Sarason, *Hemingway and "The Sun" Set,* p. 114. In *The Sun Also Rises* (New York, 1954), p. 45, Hemingway writes of Cohn: "When he fell in love with Brett his tennis game went all to pieces. People beat him who had never had a chance with him."
6. Loeb, *The Way It Was,* p. 250; quoted in Baker, *Life Story,* pp. 156, 148. Duff married for a third time in 1928 and died of tuberculosis in Santa Fe a decade later.
7. Quoted in Baker, *Life Story,* p. 148; *Letters,* p. 164.
8. Quoted in Baker, *Life Story,* p. 156; quoted in Aronowitz, *Ernest Hemingway,* p. 92.
9. Quoted in Sarason, *Hemingway and "The Sun" Set,* p. 194; Loeb, *The Way It Was,* pp. 295–297.
10. In "Portrait of Hemingway," 1961, BBC Archives, London, Arthur Moss, a journalist in Paris in the 1920s and co-editor with Jed Kiley of the *Boulevardier,* recalled that Hemingway's essay " 'The Real Spaniard' was a parody of Louis Bromfield, who was mentioned by name. It was also full of obscenities which Moss, as editor, had to take out. Hemingway was angry about this and told Moss, who was 5'1": 'If you were my size I'd knock your block off.' Moss replied: 'If I were your size maybe I'd knock your block off.' Hemingway suddenly lost his anger and said: 'Maybe you would. Let's have a drink.' "

11. *Letters,* p. 166; quoted in Baker, *Life Story,* p. 154.
12. Fitzgerald, *Letters,* p. 278; *Dear Scott/Dear Max,* p. 219.
13. Quoted in Jeffrey Meyers, *Married to Genius* (London, 1977), p. 198; Glenway Wescott, "The Moral of Scott Fitzgerald," *The Crack-Up,* ed. Edmund Wilson (New York, 1945), p. 325.
14. *A Moveable Feast,* p. 147; *Letters,* pp. 483, 689. Robert Cohn repeats Fitzgerald's remark in *The Sun Also Rises,* p. 44. And Hemingway's hero, Col. Richard Cantwell, expresses the same sentiment in *Across the River,* p. 45: "I wish I could fight it again, he thought. Knowing what I know now."
15. *Letters,* p. 438. Hemingway's famous *mot* on Fitzgerald is a paraphrase of his admired Clemenceau, who said: "America is the only nation in history which miraculously has gone directly from barbarism to degeneration without the usual interval of civilization."
16. Fitzgerald, *Letters,* p. 345; *Dear Scott/Dear Max,* p. 177; quoted in Sotheby catalogue, September 16, 1951, lot 425.
17. *Letters,* pp. 306, 528.
18. Gregory Hemingway, *Papa,* pp. 34–35; quoted in Callaghan, *That Summer in Paris,* pp. 125–126.
19. Quoted in Callaghan, *That Summer in Paris,* pp. 214–215.
20. *Letters,* p. 302; letter from Hemingway to Max Perkins, November 7, 1929, Kennedy. This fight had assumed epic proportions in Hemingway's mind by 1951, when he told Arthur Mizener: "Scott let the first round go *thirteen* minutes" (*Letters,* p. 716).
21. Quoted in Esther Arthur (a friend of Zelda), "A Farewell to Hemingway," 1961, BBC Archives; quoted in Matthew Bruccoli, *Some Sort of Epic Grandeur* (New York, 1981), p. 229.
22. Quoted in Milford, *Zelda,* p. 122.
23. H. L. Mencken, quoted in Meyers, *Married to Genius,* p. 199; *Letters,* p. 408.
24. Edmund Wilson, *The Thirties* (New York, 1980), p. 303; *A Moveable Feast,* pp. 188–189.
25. Fitzgerald, *The Crack-Up,* p. 76; Sheilah Graham, *The Real F. Scott Fitzgerald* (New York, 1976), p. 30. A more plausible resolution of a similar incident is described by John Haffenden, *The Life of John Berryman* (Boston, 1982), p. 60. Berryman wrote of a friend in "Freshman Blues": "he was afraid / his penis was too small. / We mooted it, we did everything but examine it." The problem was solved when they tactfully "repaired to their lodgings, measured themselves, and compared sizes by telephone."
26. *A Moveable Feast,* p. 182; Ernest Hemingway, "The Art of the Short Story," *Paris Review,* 79 (1981), 88–89.
27. See Ernest Hemingway, "The Original Conclusion to *A Farewell to Arms,*" in Carlos Baker, ed., *Ernest Hemingway: Critiques of Four Major Novels* (New York, 1962), p. 75; letter from Hemingway to Arthur Mizener, February 1, 1951, McKeldin Library, University of Maryland.
28. Hemingway, *"The Farm,"* in Greenberg, *Joan Miró,* p. 5; letter from André Masson to Jeffrey Meyers, December 21, 1983.
29. Five of these reviews are reprinted in Meyers, *Hemingway: Critical Heritage,* pp. 63–65, 67–69 and in Michael Reynolds, ed., *Critical Essays on Ernest Hemingway's "In Our Time"* (Boston, 1983), pp. 15–16, 20–23; *Letters,* p. 105.
30. *The Torrents of Spring,* p. 80; F. Scott Fitzgerald, *Correspondence,* ed. Matthew Bruccoli and Margaret Duggan (New York, 1980), p. 183.

31. Quoted in Fitzgerald, *Correspondence,* p. 184; quoted in Walker Gilmer, *Horace Liveright* (New York, 1970), p. 123; *Letters,* p. 183. Hemingway's letter, enclosed with the typescript, mentions the fear of offending Anderson but seems to anticipate acceptance. Liveright's biographer doubts if Hemingway deliberately wanted to break the contract.

32. *Letters,* pp. 205–206.

33. Quoted in John Brinnin, *The Third Rose: Gertrude Stein and Her World* (Boston, 1959), p. 255; "The Art of the Short Story," *Paris Review,* pp. 100–101.

34. Donald Ogden Stewart, "An Interview," *Fitzgerald-Hemingway Annual, 1973* (Washington, D.C., 1974), p. 85.

Chapter 8: Pauline

1. Callaghan, *That Summer in Paris,* p. 98; Josephson, *Infidel in the Temple,* p. 416.

2. Letter from Laura Huxley to Jeffrey Meyers, August 20, 1983.

3. Dos Passos, *Best Times,* p. 204.

4. Main Rousseau Bocher (1891–1976) was born in Chicago, edited the French *Vogue* from 1922 to 1929, opened his own salon in 1930, became a well-known clothes designer and moved to New York in 1939. See *Time,* September 27, 1963, and Phyllis Levin, *Wheels of Fashion* (New York, 1965), pp. 117–141.

5. "The Snows of Kilimanjaro," *Stories,* p. 60.

6. Miller, *Ernie,* p. 104.

7. Quoted in Kert, *Hemingway Women,* pp. 176, 178–179.

8. *A Moveable Feast,* p. 205; quoted in Baker, *Life Story,* p. 593.

9. *Letters,* p. 412; quoted in Kert, *Hemingway Women,* pp. 180–181; quoted in Baker, *Life Story,* p. 172.

10. *The Sun Also Rises,* p. 245; quoted in McAlmon, *Being Geniuses Together,* p. 201.

11. Hadley Mowrer, quoted in Hynan tapes, Kennedy; item 529a, pp. 33, 42, Kennedy.

12. Item 648a, pp. 4–5, 42, Kennedy.

13. *Death in the Afternoon,* p. 4; quoted in Hynan tapes, Kennedy.

14. *Letters,* pp. 217, 257–258.

15. Quoted in Kert, *Hemingway Women,* pp. 184, 187–188.

16. *Letters,* pp. 220, 222, 226–228.

17. *A Moveable Feast,* pp. 207–208; deleted passage quoted in Baker, *Life Story,* p. 591.

18. Jack graduated from the Storm King School in New York in 1941, joined an accelerated program at Dartmouth in 1942, and was in the army from 1943 to 1945. Interview with Jack Hemingway.

19. *Letters,* pp. 493, 537, 555.

20. *Hemingway at Auction: 1930–1973,* compiled by Matthew Bruccoli and C.E. Frazer Clark (Detroit, 1973), p. 236; quoted in Scott Donaldson, *By Force of Will* (New York: Penguin, 1977), p. 225.

21. See Cecchin, *Con Hemingway e Dos Passos,* p. 126. Hemingway was fond of inventing stories about his Catholicism. He told Edward O'Brien that he left the church while fighting with the Italian army in the Great War, after drunken Italian troops repeatedly raped girls of an Austrian village. But he did not join the Italian army, which fought on Italian (not Austrian) soil, and could scarcely have left the church before he "joined it" after his wound.

   He also told Bill Davis: "I prayed my impotence would be cured and became a Catholic when it was." Interviews with Harry Sylvester, Washington, D.C., December 26, 1982, and with Bill Davis, Alhaurin de la Torre, Spain, July 9, 1983.

22. Letter from Hemingway to Father Vincent Donavan, [December 1927], Kennedy.
23. Letter from Hemingway to Guy Hickok, July 15, 1931, Princeton; interviews with Peter Viertel, Marbella, Spain, July 2, 3, 4, 10, 1983.
24. Letter from Mario Menocal, Jr., to Jeffrey Meyers, April 18, 1983; quoted in Baker, *Life Story*, p. 220; quoted in Lillian Ross, *Portrait of Hemingway* (New York, 1961), p. 48.
25. *The Sun Also Rises*, p. 97.
26. "Today is Friday," *Stories*, p. 357; *88 Poems*, pp. 83, 148; *A Farewell to Arms*, p. 261.
27. *Death in the Afternoon*, p. 204; "A Clean, Well-Lighted Place," *Stories*, p. 383; Ernest Hemingway, *The Fifth Column and Four Stories of the Spanish Civil War* (New York, 1969), pp. 5, 25.
28. Letter from Hemingway to Mary Pfeiffer, August 18, 1938, Princeton.
29. Interview with Patrick Hemingway, Bozeman, Montana, May 23, 1983.
30. *Letters*, p. 710; Callaghan, *That Summer in Paris*, p. 251.
31. Quoted in Sarason, *Hemingway and "The Sun" Set*, p. 199; *88 Poems*, p. 87.
32. *Letters*, pp. 792, 745, 179.
33. "The Art of Fiction," *Paris Review*, p. 77; Alexander Solzhenitsyn, *Cancer Ward*, trans. Nicholas Bethell and David Burg (London, 1982), p. 558; quoted in Bruccoli, *Scott and Ernest*, p. 54.
34. *Letters*, p. 262. The real models for the other fictional characters were: Harold Loeb (Robert Cohn), Bill Smith and Don Stewart (Bill Gorton), Pat Guthrie (Mike Campbell), Ford Madox Ford and Stella Bowen (Mr. and Mrs. Braddocks), Harold Stearns (Harvey Stone), Glenway Wescott (Roger Prentiss), Kitty Cannell (Frances Clyne), Cayetano Ordóñez (Pedro Romero), Juanito Quintana (Juanito Montoya).
35. Letter from Hemingway to Owen Wister, March 11, 1929, Library of Congress; *Letters*, p. 229; *The Sun Also Rises*, pp. 41, 187.
36. *The Sun Also Rises*, pp. 168, 10; D. H. Lawrence, *The Plumed Serpent* (London, 1979), p. 20; Roy Campbell, *Lorca* (New Haven, 1959), p. 96.
37. See Meyers, *Hemingway: Critical Heritage*, pp. 89–93.
38. Malcolm Cowley, *Exile's Return* (New York, 1951), pp. 225–226.

Chapter 9: Accidents

1. Quoted in A. E. Hotchner, *Papa Hemingway* (New York: Bantam, 1967), p. 55.
2. Letter from Pauline to Hemingway, June 10, 1934, Kennedy; "The Snows of Kilimanjaro," *Stories*, p. 55; Jack Hemingway, "Memories of Papa," p. 30.
3. *Green Hills of Africa*, p. 195.
4. "The Art of the Short Story," *Paris Review*, p. 99; "The Killers," *Stories*, pp. 283, 287.
5. Quoted in Baker, *Life Story*, p. 595; *The Wild Years*, p. 257. He was especially fond of this simile and repeated it in a dispatch from Castellon in "The Spanish War," p. 68.
6. "Hills Like White Elephants," *Stories*, pp. 275, 277.
7. "In Another Country," *Stories*, pp. 267, 271; Meyers, *Hemingway: Critical Heritage*, pp. 111, 113–114.
8. "Fathers and Sons," *Stories*, p. 491; *88 Poems*, p. 25.
9. *Hemingway at Auction*, p. 170; *A Moveable Feast*, p. 18.
10. *The Sun Also Rises*, p. 20.
11. "A Simple Enquiry," *Stories*, pp. 329–330; *Death in the Afternoon*, pp. 204–205.
12. *Islands in the Stream*, pp. 219, 238, 169. For a discussion of this theme, see Jeffrey Meyers, *Homosexuality and Literature, 1890–1930* (London, 1977).

13. Quoted in Kenneth Tynan, *Tynan Right and Left* (New York, 1967), p. 332.
14. Dos Passos, *Best Times*, p. 219.
15. *Green Hills of Africa*, p. 148; quoted in Ellmann, *James Joyce*, p. 708; *Letters*, p. 15.
16. *Letters*, p. 272; *A Farewell to Arms*, p. 298; quoted in Baker, *Life Story*, p. 190.

Chapter 10: Key West

1. Dos Passos, *Best Times*, pp. 198–199; Sotheby catalogue, [1932], lot 422.
2. Letter from Hemingway to Harry Saltpeter, April 16, 1936, Maurice Neville book catalogue, 1982, no. 233; letter from Hemingway to Owen Wister, September 27, [?1928], Library of Congress.
3. *Letters*, p. 280; interview with Thorwald Sánchez, Jr., Palm Beach, Florida, December 31, 1982; quoted in Kert, *Hemingway Women*, p. 211.
4. *Letters*, p. 280; "The Snows of Kilimanjaro," *Stories*, p. 71; quoted in Scott Berg, *Max Perkins: Editor of Genius* (New York: Pocket, 1978), p. 140.
5. Quoted in Sanford, *At the Hemingways*, pp. 225–226, 228–229; interview with Carol Hemingway Gardner; interview with Madelaine Hemingway Miller.
6. Quoted in Sanford, *At the Hemingways*, p. 230; interview with Madelaine Hemingway Miller. Leicester Hemingway, a less reliable witness, gives a different and more critical account of Uncle George in *My Brother*, pp. 98–99. Leicester said the Florida land "had no resale value" and that George demanded payment of a promissory note that Ed had signed: "The relative who had issued the note had spoken unsympathetically about the facts of life and how business was business."
7. Leicester Hemingway, *The Sound of the Trumpet* (New York, 1953), pp. 182–183; "Dr. Hemingway, Writer's Father, Ends Own Life," *Chicago Tribune*, December 7, 1928, p. 41.
8. Letter from Hemingway to Mary Pfeiffer, December 13, 1928, Princeton; quoted in Miller, *Ernie*, p. 115.
9. "Fathers and Sons," *Stories*, p. 491; letter from Hemingway to Max Perkins, October 30, 1929, Kennedy.
10. *Letters*, pp. 292, 296.
11. *For Whom the Bell Tolls*, p. 337; letter from Ernest to Grace Hemingway, [April 1929], Kennedy.
12. Quoted in Meyers, *A Reader's Guide to George Orwell*, p. 20; Dos Passos, *Best Times*, p. 210.
13. *88 Poems*, p. 95; quoted in Baker, *Life Story*, p. 387; letter from Hemingway to Malcolm Cowley, July 15, 1948, Sotheby catalogue, lot 425.
14. Interview with Toby Bruce, Key West, Florida, January 5, 1983; interview with Martha Gellhorn, London, November 28, 1982.
15. Item 513, p. 9, Kennedy; quoted in Baker, *Life Story*, p. 609.
16. *For Whom the Bell Tolls*, pp. 338–340; "Indian Camp," *Stories*, p. 95.
17. Letter from Ernest to Grace Hemingway, [late May 1929], Kennedy.
18. *Islands in the Stream*, p. 224; Hemingway, Introduction to *A Farewell to Arms* (New York, 1948), p. vii.
19. *Letters*, p. 800; letter from Hemingway to Maurice Coindreau, December 31, 1930, Princeton.
20. Reynolds, *Hemingway's First War*, p. 112; quoted in Noel Fitch, *Sylvia Beach and the Lost Generation* (New York, 1983), p. 530.
21. *A Farewell to Arms*, pp. 105–106, 325. Hemingway may have been influenced by Levin's response to the birth of his child in Tolstoy's *Anna Karenina:* "Gazing at this

pitiful little bit of humanity, Levin searched his soul in vain for some trace of paternal feeling. He could feel nothing but aversion." Translated by Rosemary Edmonds (London, 1978), p. 750.

22. Letter from Hemingway to Sinclair Lewis, November 15, 1941, Yale. The escape by rowboat is rooted in Hemingway's honeymoon on Walloon Lake and his convalescent trip to Stresa. In "Wedding Day," *Nick Adams Stories*, p. 212, he wrote: "It was a long row across the lake in the dark"; and in a letter of September 29, 1918, to his family from Lake Maggiore, he said he was still limping but could row on the lake. The mountains were only a few miles away and he could see Switzerland from the garden of his hotel (Princeton).

23. Loeb, *The Way It Was*, p. 283; *A Farewell to Arms*, pp. 184–185, 249. The last passage was foreshadowed by a letter of October 1926, in *Hemingway at Auction*, p. 116.

24. See *Letters*, p. 307: "It was funny how I couldn't get into All Quiet etc. but once in it it was damned good—Not so great as they think—But awfully good."

25. Quoted in Baker, ed., *Hemingway: Critiques of Four Major Novels*, p. 75.

26. Meyers, *Hemingway: Critical Heritage*, pp. 19–20, 137.

27. Aldous Huxley, "Foreheads Villainous Low," *Music at Night* (London, 1931), p. 201; *Death in the Afternoon*, p. 191.

28. "On Writing," *Nick Adams Stories*, p. 217; letter from Hemingway to Ralph Stitt, [?November 1932], Kennedy.

Chapter 11: The Public Image

1. *Letters*, p. 351; *Green Hills of Africa*, p. 148.
2. *Letters*, pp. 330–331.
3. Gregory Hemingway, *Papa*, p. 19; interviews with Gregory Hemingway.
4. *Islands in the Stream*, p. 53; Gregory Hemingway, *Papa*, p. 18; interview with Patrick Hemingway.
5. *Letters*, pp. 346–347; interview with Marguerite Cohn, New York, December 20, 1983; interview with Jack Hemingway.
6. Interview with Toby Bruce; *Islands in the Stream*, pp. 50, 118; quoted in Marian Christy, "Life of the White Hunter Lures Patrick Hemingway," *Boston Globe*, June 2, 1982, p. 25.
7. *Letters*, p. 376.
8. *Ibid.*, p. 156; *Death in the Afternoon*, p. 517.
9. Wyndham Lewis, *Snooty Baronet* (London, 1932), pp. 213, 217. Roy Campbell, a close contemporary, was the South African Hemingway: both "populate a Nation's mind and heart." Both men spent a significant part of their childhood hunting and fishing in the wilderness, retained a lifelong passion for blood sports, violence and war. Both cultivated a heroic persona—"They blame me that I shun my fellow-doctors / To haunt the quays, the markets and the camps"—but were actually book-ish and pensive. Both lived most of their adult lives in Latin countries, became Catholic converts, were passionately committed (to opposite sides) in the Spanish Civil War. Both authors had flamboyant characters, were combative, liked to test their courage in dangerous situations, flayed their friends with venomous truths (exposing William Plomer's buggery and Dos Passos' bastardy), drank heavily, boasted of legendary achievements, declined during the last two decades of their lives and died violent deaths.
10. The reactions of his unidentified sons and friends who came to Pamplona include Patrick (P.H.), Jack (J.H.), McAlmon (X.Y.), Dorman-Smith (Capt. D.S.), Sally Bird

(Mrs. A.B.), Hadley (Mrs. E.R.), Duff Twysden (Mrs. S.T.), Bill Smith (W.G.), Don Stewart (R.S.), Pauline (P.M.), Jinny (V.R.), ?Gerald Murphy (A.U.), ?Sholom Asch (S.A.), ?Sara Murphy (Mrs. M.W.) and Bill Bird (W.A.).

11. *Death in the Afternoon,* pp. 179, 137, 140.

12. *Ibid.,* p. 275.

13. Sidney Franklin, "A Farewell to Hemingway," 1961, BBC; *Death in the Afternoon,* pp. 505, 503.

14. Interview with Luis Miguel Dominguín, Andújar, Spain, July 13, 1983; letter from Barnaby Conrad to Jeffrey Meyers, April 4, 1983. Peter Viertel and Bill Davis confirmed the truth of Conrad's letter.

15. Quoted in Leicester Hemingway, *My Brother,* p. 177; "The Spanish War," p. 27.

16. *Letters,* p. 361; interview with Tillie Arnold, Hailey, Idaho, May 27, 1983.

17. Meyers, *Hemingway: Critical Heritage,* pp. 170, 161; *Letters,* p. 374.

18. Meyers, *Hemingway: Critical Heritage,* pp. 165–169.

19. *Death in the Afternoon,* p. 94; Meyers, *Hemingway: Critical Heritage,* pp. 173–174, 176.

20. Letters from Hemingway to Archibald MacLeish, June 7 and c. June 21, 1933, Library of Congress. For a discussion of Murry's attitude to Lawrence, see Jeffrey Meyers, "Memoirs of Lawrence: A Genre of the Thirties," *D. H. Lawrence Review,* 14 (Spring 1981), 1–32.

21. *Dear Scott/Dear Max,* pp. 239–240. Perkins' desk was still in his old office at Scribner's in 1983.

22. Eastman, *Great Companions,* pp. 46–47.

23. *Ibid.,* p. 51.

24. Interview with Toby Bruce.

25. Interview with John and Carol Hemingway Gardner.

26. Letter from Hemingway to Mary Pfeiffer, March 23, 1933, Princeton; letter from Hemingway to Archibald MacLeish, June 28, [1933], Library of Congress.

27. *Letters,* p. 671; letter from Hemingway to Miss Sproul, October 15, 1950, Kennedy.

28. *Letters,* p. 663; interview with Carol Hemingway Gardner.

29. Letter from Hemingway to W. G. Rogers, July 29, 1940, printed in Gotham Book Mart pamphlet (New York, 1972); Dwight Macdonald, "Ernest Hemingway," *Against the American Grain* (New York, 1962), pp. 171–172.

30. André Malraux, *The Walnut Trees of Altenburg,* trans. A. W. Fielding (London, 1952), pp. 51–52; Ernest Walsh, "Ernest Hemingway," *This Quarter,* 1 (1925–26), 67.

31. Raymond Chandler, *Farewell, My Lovely* (New York, 1976), pp. 134–135, 138.

32. Letters from Mario Menocal, Jr., to Jeffrey Meyers, April 18, 1983, and to Carlos Baker, October 17, 1964.

33. *Letters,* p. 700; quoted in Baker, *Life Story,* p. 621.

34. *Letters,* p. 338.

35. Bruccoli, *Scott and Ernest,* pp. 101, 155. Serious errors continue to appear in recent biographical books. Anthony Burgess, *Ernest Hemingway and His World* (London, 1978), mistakenly stated that Hemingway's left leg was badly wounded at Fossalta, confused Hemingway's friend Malcolm Lowrey with the English novelist, and said Valerie Danby-Smith was Scottish. James Joyce, *Finnegans Wake* (New York, 1939), p. 57.

36. Meyers, *Hemingway: Critical Heritage,* pp. 304–305.

37. Letter from Hemingway to Louis Cohn, June 24, [1930], Princeton; Hemingway, *Letters,* p. 712.

38. Quoted in Fenton, *Apprenticeship,* p. 87; James Thurber, "A Farewell to Hemingway," 1961, BBC.

39. Eastman, *Great Companions,* p. 40; Brinnin, *The Third Rose,* p. 259.

Chapter 12: Jane Mason

1. Letter from Mario Menocal, Jr., to Bernice Kert, February 9, 1979, courtesy of Señor Menocal; quoted in Kert, *Hemingway Women*, p. 265.
2. See the announcements of Jane's engagement and wedding, *New York Times*, January 3, 1927, p. 23, and June 12, 1927, p. 25.
3. Telephone conversation with Antony Mason, April 12, 1983, and interview with Antony Mason, Tuxedo Park, New York, June 3, 1983.
4. Gregory Hemingway, *Papa*, p. 92; letter from Hemingway to Carlos Baker, February 17, 1951, Kennedy; Mary Welsh Hemingway, *How It Was* (New York: Ballantine, 1976), p. 266.
5. "The End of Something," *Stories*, p. 108.
6. Leicester Hemingway, *My Brother*, p. 107.
7. Letter from Hemingway to Archibald MacLeish, [1933], Library of Congress; interviews with Jack Hemingway, Patrick Hemingway, Antony Mason; *Islands in the Stream*, p. 183.
8. Quoted in Baker, *Life Story*, p. 607; quoted in Kert, *Hemingway Women*, p. 250.
9. *By-Line*, p. 137; Jane's date book is owned by Antony Mason.
10. Interview with Patrick Hemingway.
11. Lawrence Kubie (1896–1973) earned his medical degree at Johns Hopkins in 1921; was trained at the London Institute of Psychoanalysis during 1928–30; practiced in New York; taught psychiatry at Yale, Columbia and Hopkins from 1947 until his death; and published his best-known work, *Neurotic Distortion of the Creative Process*, in 1961. For the complete text of Kubie's essay, see Jeffrey Meyers, "Introduction to Lawrence Kubie's Suppressed Essay on Hemingway: 'Cyrano and the Matador,'" *American Imago*, 41 (Spring 1984), 1–18.
12. *By-Line*, p. 455.
13. "Fathers and Sons," *Stories*, p. 491.
14. Interview with Antony Mason.
15. Quoted in Donnelly, *Sara and Gerald*, p. 171; *Letters*, p. 446; Vernon (Jake) Klimo and Will Oursler, *Hemingway and Jake* (New York: Popular, 1972), p. 73.
16. *Green Hills of Africa*, p. 65; "The Short Happy Life of Francis Macomber," *Stories*, pp. 4, 8. Jane actually had posed for cosmetic ads.
17. "The Art of the Short Story," *Paris Review*, p. 93; quoted in Arnold Gingrich, *Nothing But People* (New York, 1971), p. 279.
18. *To Have and Have Not*, pp. 150, 189, 229, 245; item 204.8, p. 219, Kennedy.
19. *The Fifth Column and Four Stories of the Spanish Civil War*, p. 83.
20. Interviews with Antony Mason and Toby Bruce.
21. Dos Passos, *Best Times*, p. 216.
22. "The Home Front," item 477.5, p. 1, Kennedy; interview with Antony Mason.
23. Arnold Gingrich, *The Well-Tempered Angler* (New York, 1965), p. 21.

Chapter 13: Africa

1. Meyers, *Hemingway: Critical Heritage*, p. 185.
2. "The Art of the Short Story," *Paris Review*, p. 99; "A Way You'll Never Be," *Stories*, pp. 405, 414.
3. "A Clean, Well-Lighted Place," *Stories*, pp. 382–383; quoted in Arthur Power, *Conversations with James Joyce* (Dublin, 1974), p. 107.

4. "Fathers and Sons," *Stories*, p. 497.
5. *The Sun Also Rises*, p. 10; quoted in John Atkins, *The Art of Ernest Hemingway* (London, 1952), p. 88; *Green Hills of Africa*, p. 195.
6. Theodore Roosevelt, *African Game Trails, Works* (New York, 1926), 4:33; letter from Denis Zaphiro to Jeffrey Meyers, August 24, 1983.
7. *Green Hills of Africa*, p. 64; letter from Zaphiro to Meyers, August 24, 1983.
8. *Green Hills of Africa*, pp. 154, 84, 86, 293.
9. Quoted in Leicester Hemingway, *My Brother*, p. 128; item 699, Kennedy.
10. *Green Hills of Africa*, p. 4; Hemingway gratuitously attacks Emerson, Hawthorne, Whittier, Poe, Thoreau, Melville, Stein, Upton Sinclair, Sinclair Lewis, Wolfe, Válery, Rilke and Heinrich Mann. But he also praises the writers he most admired: Twain, James, Crane, Pound, Kipling, Joyce, Turgenev, Dostoyevsky, Tolstoy, Stendhal, Flaubert and Thomas Mann.
11. *Green Hills of Africa*, pp. 23, 28.
12. Meyers, *Hemingway: Critical Heritage*, p. 210; Carl Van Doren, *New York Herald Tribune Books*, October 27, 1935, p. 3.
13. Meyers, *Hemingway: Critical Heritage*, pp. 213, 215.
14. *Ibid.*, pp. 305–306.
15. Quoted in Baker, *Life Story*, p. 281.
16. Roosevelt, *African Game Trails*, 4:10, praises Patterson for dispatching the Tsavo lions. James Brasch and Joseph Sigman, *Hemingway's Library* (New York, 1982), p. 285, note that he owned two copies of *Man-Eaters of Tsavo*.

    Patterson was decorated for bravery in the Boer War, commanded the Jewish Legion in Gallipoli and Egypt in the Great War, became an ardent supporter of the Zionist cause, advocated the formation of a Jewish army to fight Hitler and died in Los Angeles at the age of 79. For information on Patterson, see: J. H. Patterson, *With the Zionists in Gallipoli* (London, 1916); J. H. Patterson, *With the Judeans in the Palestine Campaign* (London, 1922); V. E. Jabotinsky, *The Story of the Jewish Legion*, Foreword by J. H. Patterson (New York, 1945); Patterson's obituary in the *New York Times*, June 20, 1947, p. 20; Joseph Schechtman, *Fighter and Prophet; Rebel and Statesman: The Vladimir Jabotinsky Story* (New York, 1956, 1961); *Encyclopedia Judaica* (Jerusalem, 1971), 13:186–187.
17. CO 533.43. Kenya: Original Correspondence, Public Record Office, Kew.
18. Lt. Col. J. H. Patterson, *In the Grip of the Nyika* (London, 1909), pp. 205, 296, 302.
19. CO 533.57, p. 673.
20. *Ibid.*, pp. 395–396, 400.
21. *Ibid.*, p. 378.
22. *By-Line*, p. 215; Introduction to *Men at War*, p. xv.
23. Letter from Hemingway to Peter Buckley, June 4, 1957, Kennedy.
24. "The Short Happy Life of Francis Macomber," *Stories*, p. 23.
25. Quoted in Jackson Burke, "Ernest Hemingway—Muy Hombre!" *Bluebook* (July 1953), p. 7.
26. "The Short Happy Life of Francis Macomber," *Stories*, p. 17.
27. Josephson, *Infidel in the Temple*, p. 424.
28. *Letters*, p. 439.
29. *Ibid.*
30. Letter from Wallace Stevens to L. C. van Geyzel, May 16, 1945, Dartmouth College Library. See also Wallace Stevens, *Letters*, ed. Holly Stevens (New York, 1966), pp. 411–412.
31. "The Short Happy Life of Francis Macomber," *Stories*, pp. 7, 29–30.

32. "The Snows of Kilimanjaro," *Stories,* p. 53.

33. "The Art of the Short Story," *Paris Review,* p. 96; "The Snows of Kilimanjaro," *Stories,* p. 59.

34. Berg, *Max Perkins,* p. 305; "The Snows of Kilimanjaro," *Stories,* p. 72. Scott's story, "The Rich Boy," did not begin with this sentence.

35. Item 204.8, p. 203, Kennedy. Hemingway used the same phrase about Fitzgerald in *Letters,* p. 438.

36. Fitzgerald, *Letters,* p. 543.

37. "The Snows of Kilimanjaro," *Stories,* p. 54.

Chapter 14: In the Caribbean

1. Letter from Mario Menocal, Jr., to Jeffrey Meyers, April 18, 1983.

2. *The Dialogues of Archibald MacLeish and Mark Van Doren* (New York, 1964), p. 87; quoted in Baker, *Life Story,* pp. 261–262; letter from MacLeish to Baker, January 31, 1965, Princeton.

   Leicester Hemingway, who was not on the scene but loved to invent good stories, claimed in *My Brother,* p. 172: "That day fishing was poor. A discussion of personalities developed and became heated." Archie went ashore at a remote Key, swarming with insects and lacking fresh water, and Hemingway left him there. When he got home, Pauline insisted he return to rescue the castaway. But MacLeish, in Baker, *Life Story,* p. 611, denied that he was ever marooned against his will.

3. *Letters,* p. 406. See p. 438 on Fitzgerald.

4. Undated letters from Hemingway to MacLeish in the mid-thirties, Library of Congress; *Letters,* pp. 544–545.

5. Quoted in Klimo, *Hemingway and Jake,* pp. 79–80; letter from Patricia Hemingway to Jeffrey Meyers, February 5, 1983.

6. Quintanilla, "Hemingway en mi recuerdo," p. 45; Ernest Hemingway, Introduction to *Luis Quintanilla Catalogue* (New York: Pierre Matisse Gallery, 1934), n.p.

7. Dos Passos, *Best Times,* p. 211.

8. Interview with Tommy's second wife, Durie Shevlin Appleton, Palm Beach, Florida, January 3, 1983.

9. John Dos Passos, *The Fourteenth Chronicle: Letters and Diaries,* ed. Townsend Ludington (Boston, 1973), p. 472 (for a similar but derivative account, see Leicester Hemingway, *My Brother,* p. 164); *By-Line,* p. 201.

10. Interview with Harry Sylvester; Gregory Hemingway, *Papa,* p. 30.

11. Baker, *Life Story,* pp. 274–275; quoted in Eduardo Zayas-Bazán, "Hemingway: His Cuban Friends Remember," *Fitzgerald-Hemingway Annual* (Englewood, Colorado, 1975), p. 169.

12. Quoted in Berg, *Max Perkins,* p. 301.

13. *Green Hills of Africa,* p. 191.

14. *Letters,* p. 421; Ernest Hemingway, "Who Murdered the Vets?" *New Masses,* 16 (September 17, 1935), 9–10.

15. *Letters,* pp. 232, 655.

16. *Letters,* pp. 436, 434; *Green Hills of Africa,* p. 192; *Islands in the Stream,* p. 50.

17. See Gregory Hemingway, *Papa,* p. 106; interviews with Valerie Danby-Smith Hemingway, Bozeman, Montana, May 22, 27–28, 1983; item 485, Kennedy. See *By-Line,* p. 185.

18. *To Have and Have Not,* pp. 172–173, 246.

19. *Ibid.,* p. 225. In a letter to MacLeish of c. May 5, 1943, *Letters,* p. 545, Hemingway referred to the origins of his thematic statement: "a passage you quoted once—1929;

one man alone ain't got no bloody etc." And in a letter to Howard Hawks, October 18, 1943, he explained: "It is the story of a man who tried to buck this world single-handed and found it couldn't be done and that men had to stick together to win" (Kennedy).

20. Quoted in letter from Mario Menocal, Jr., to Carlos Baker, November 7, 1970, p. 12.

21. *To Have and Have Not*, pp. 186, 192, 240. Hadley had accused Pauline of knowing sexual tricks.

22. Meyers, *Hemingway: Critical Heritage*, pp. 227–228; 230–232; 233, 235.

23. *Ibid.*, pp. 241–242; 244, 251.

24. *To Have and Have Not*, p. 83.

Chapter 15: Martha and the Spanish War

1. Graham Greene, "Short Stories," *Spectator*, 156 (May 22, 1936), 950.

2. *Green Hills of Africa*, p. 64; letter from Archibald MacLeish to Carlos Baker, August 9, 1963, Princeton; letter from Prudencio de Pereda to Carlos Baker, July 18, 1967, Princeton; interview with Harry Sylvester; interview with George Seldes.

3. Pauline, quoted in Josephson, *Infidel in the Temple*, p. 428; interview with Martha Gellhorn.

4. Quoted in Kert, *Hemingway Women*, pp. 291, 294. Mrs. Kert read Martha's letters in the Kennedy Library in the 1970s. When Martha discovered their existence, she removed them from the Kennedy, gave them to Boston University and prohibited everyone from reading them.

5. Reynolds, *Hemingway's Reading*, p. 28.

6. Interview with Joseph Losey, London, August 23, 1983.

7. Letter from MacLeish to Carlos Baker, August 9, 1963, Princeton; quoted in a letter from Hemingway to Buck Lanham, May 24, 1947, Princeton.

8. *Green Hills of Africa*, p. 71.

9. Quoted in Josephson, *Infidel in the Temple*, p. 428.

10. *Letters*, p. 815; letter from Hemingway to Ezra Pound, July 22, 1933, Yale.

11. *Letters*, pp. 456–457; letter from Hemingway to Harry Sylvester, July 1, 1938, courtesy of Mr. Sylvester. Hemingway nearly got into a fist fight with Sylvester about Spanish politics, but quickly cooled down (as he did with Harold Loeb, Arthur Moss and Max Eastman).

12. Quoted in Baker, *Life Story*, p. 304; *By-Line*, p. 296. Hemingway's frequent use of "daughter" in his speech and in his fiction about Spain began at this time and was taken from the common Spanish appellation *hija*. Similarly, he adopted the tender title "Miss" (as in "Miss Mary") from familiar southern speech.

13. *Letters*, p. 480.

14. Gustav Regler, *The Owl of Minerva* (London, 1959), p. 296; Meyers, *Hemingway: Critical Heritage*, pp. 359–360; Jason Gurney, *Crusade in Spain* (London, 1974), p. 145.

15. Martha Gellhorn, *The Face of War* (New York, 1959), p. 20; "The Spanish War," p. 26.

16. Alvah Bessie caricatured Hemingway as Clem Elliman in his novel about the Spanish War, *The Un-Americans* (New York, 1957). Cecil Eby, "The Real Robert Jordan," *American Literature*, 38 (1966), 382–383.

17. Ludington in Dos Passos, *The Fourteenth Chronicle*, p. 496; *Letters*, p. 463; letter from MacLeish to Carlos Baker, November 4, 1963, Princeton. Hugh Thomas, *The*

Spanish Civil War (London, 1982), p. 706 & n, says Robles was "perhaps killed because he had been interpreter to the disgraced [Russian] General Berzin. . . . He was murdered because he knew too much."

18. Item 204.8, Kennedy; Introduction to *Men at War,* p. xvi.
19. *Letters,* p. 623; Ludington in Dos Passos, *The Fourteenth Chronicle,* p. 567.
20. Townsend Ludington, *John Dos Passos: A Twentieth Century Odyssey* (New York, 1980), p. 456; *Letters,* p. 776; *A Moveable Feast,* pp. 205–206.
21. Interview with Joris Ivens, Paris, July 20, 1983. All the following unpublished information comes from M. Ivens.
22. Joris Ivens, *Mémoire d'un regard* (Paris, 1982), pp. 146, 148. My translation.
23. Ernest Hemingway, Afterword to *The Spanish Earth* (Cleveland, 1938), pp. 55–56; "Big Two-Hearted River," *Stories,* p. 223; "Night Before Battle," *The Fifth Column,* p. 110.
24. Interview with Pedro Menocal, Coral Gables, Florida, January 4, 1983.
25. "The Spanish War," p. 13; Joris Ivens, "Spain," *The Camera and I* (New York, 1969), p. 113.
26. *The Spanish Earth,* p. 46; quoted in Baker, *Life Story,* p. 313.
27. Orson Welles, "A Trip to Quixoteland," *Cahiers du Cinéma,* 5 (November 1966), 42; letter from Prudencio de Pereda to Carlos Baker, June 22, 1967, Princeton; Hemingway actually wrote: "This is the true face of men going into action," *The Spanish Earth,* p. 23.
28. Ivens, *Mémoire,* p. 154.
29. Fitch, *Sylvia Beach and the Lost Generation,* p. 433, based on Francis Smith, "Hemingway Curses, Kicks, Reads at Sylvia Beach Literary Session," Paris *Herald Tribune,* May 14, 1937, p. 5.
30. Ernest Hemingway, "The Writer and War," *The Writer in a Changing World,* ed. Henry Hart (New York, 1937), p. 69.
31. *Letters,* p. 460.
32. Jasper Wood, end note to *The Spanish Earth,* p. 63.
33. Meyers, *Hemingway: Critical Heritage,* p. 258.
34. Herbert Matthews, *A World in Revolution* (New York, 1971), p. 29.
35. *The Fifth Column,* pp. 80, 4, 25, 84.
36. *Ibid.,* pp. 39, 58, 4.
37. *Ibid.,* pp. 44, 42, 57; quoted in Kert, *Hemingway Women,* p. 333. See "The Snows of Kilimanjaro," *Stories,* p. 55: "I went wherever you wanted to go and I've done what you wanted to do," and the source in Ruth 1:16.
38. *The Fifth Column,* p. 26; Ernest Hemingway, Note on Martha Gellhorn, *Collier's,* 113 (March 4, 1944), 43.
39. "The Last Good Country," *Nick Adams Stories,* p. 101; *Green Hills of Africa,* p. 73; *Across the River,* pp. 248, 251; letter from Hemingway to Bernard Berenson, May 27, 1953, I Tatti.
40. Quoted in Kert, *Hemingway Women,* p. 325; quoted in Hotchner, *Papa Hemingway,* p. 146; *The Fifth Column,* pp. 4, 47.
41. *For Whom the Bell Tolls,* pp. 343, 22, 344, 68.
42. Quoted in Kert, *Hemingway Women,* p. 301; Gregory Hemingway, *Papa,* p. 6.
43. "The Snows of Kilimanjaro," *Stories,* p. 64; quoted in Mary Hemingway, *How It Was,* p. 168.
44. "Hemingway on war; an essay discovered," *Miami Herald,* November 29, 1982, p. 20.
45. *Dear Scott/Dear Max,* p. 242.

46. Matthews, *A World in Revolution*, pp. 24–25.
47. Meyers, *Hemingway: Critical Heritage*, pp. 264–265; 266–267; 285, 287.
48. Letter from Hemingway to Lawrence Langner, received March 19, 1940, Yale.
49. Meyers, *Hemingway: Critical Heritage*, pp. 290, 292.
50. Ernest Hemingway, Preface to Gustav Regler, *The Great Crusade* (New York, 1940), p. vii.
51. Quoted in Kert, *Hemingway Women*, p. 299.
52. Orwell, *Collected Essays, Journalism and Letters*, 3:236.

Chapter 16: The End of Something

1. Graham Greene, *Ways of Escape* (London, 1980), p. 240; Graham Greene, *Our Man in Havana* (London, 1958), p. 63.
2. Item 204.8, p. 203, Kennedy.
3. Quoted in Mary Hemingway, *How It Was*, pp. 381–382. Constante, the Floridita bartender, invented a potent cocktail, the Papa Doble, and the dedicatee drank thousands of them. The sugarless recipe deserves to be recorded: juice of half a grapefruit and a large lime, 2½ jiggers of rum, 6 drops of maraschino and crushed ice.
4. Gregory Hemingway, *Papa*, p. 47; interview with Martha Gellhorn.
5. Letter from Mario Menocal, Jr., to Jeffrey Meyers, April 18, 1983; *Islands in the Stream*, pp. 229, 231–232.
6. Interview with Pedro Menocal; letters from Mario Menocal, Jr., to Carlos Baker, October 1 and 17, 1964; quoted in Zayas-Bazán, "Cuban Friends Remember," p. 158. Photograph no. 89 in Baker, *Life Story*, is of Mayito and not (as the caption states) of his son Mario.
7. Letter from Hemingway to Buck Lanham, June 10, 1948, Princeton.
8. Letter from Mario Menocal, Jr., to Bernice Kert, February 9, 1979; interview with Elicio Arguelles, Coral Gables, Florida, January 4, 1983.
9. James Tuite, "An Old Man of the Sea Still Casts His Net with a Young Heart," *New York Times*, March 30, 1969, sec. 5, p. 5; interview with Tina Sánchez and Thorwald Sánchez, Jr., Palm Beach, December 31, 1982. I found these three Cuban families attractive and impressive, and could easily see why Hemingway would want to spend so much time with them. His friends' sons, Pedro Menocal and Thorwald Sánchez, Jr., both became painters.
10. Leicester Hemingway, *My Brother*, p. 117; quoted in Dos Passos, *The Fourteenth Chronicle*, p. 421; letter from Mario Menocal, Jr., to Carlos Baker, November 7, 1970.
11. Letter from Mario Menocal, Jr., to Jeffrey Meyers, April 18, 1983; interview with Joseph Dryer, Palm Beach, December 31, 1982.
12. "The Art of Fiction," *Paris Review*, p. 88.
13. *Letters*, pp. 534, 514, 467. Hemingway's unpublished story "On the Garden Side" is set in the Ritz Hotel in Paris and contains a conversation with Malraux.
14. See Reynolds, *Hemingway's Reading*, p. 25. Hemingway reprinted two episodes from *Seven Pillars of Wisdom* in *Men at War* (1942) and refers favorably to Lawrence in "Homage to Switzerland" (1933) and *Islands in the Stream*, p. 213. For a discussion of the influence of Tolstoy on Lawrence and Lawrence on Malraux, see Jeffrey Meyers, *The Wounded Spirit: A Study of "Seven Pillars of Wisdom"* (London, 1973).
15. St. John Philby, *Arabian Days: An Autobiography* (London, 1948), p. 210; Bill Smith quoted in Hynan, *Hemingway*; T. E. Lawrence, *Seven Pillars of Wisdom* (New York, 1967), p. 500.

16. In a letter to Jeffrey Meyers, January 3, 1983, Hemingway's Polish translator and friend, Bronislaw Zielinski, wrote: "I asked him why many historical figures appear in 'The Bell' under their real names, and Swierczewski is neither Swierczewski nor [General] Walter? He replied: 'He was such a splendid man and splendid soldier that I wouldn't dare to present him in fictitious situations, and put in his mouth fictitious words.' "

Hugh Thomas, *The Spanish Civil War*, pp. 457–458, confirms Hemingway's judgment of André Marty.

17. *For Whom the Bell Tolls*, pp. 41, 163, 418; *Death in the Afternoon*, p. 43.

18. *For Whom the Bell Tolls*, pp. 168, 71; see Ben Finney, "The Ernest Hemingway I Knew," *Feet First* (New York, 1971), p. 197. The outdoor seduction-rape scene between the Indian Romero and Dollie Urquhart in D. H. Lawrence, "The Princess," *The Portable Lawrence* (New York, 1947), p. 209, provides an ironic contrast to Hemingway's romanticism:
"Don't you like last night?" he asked.
"Not really," she said. "Why? Do you?"

19. University of Virginia exhibition catalogue, *In Their Time, 1920–1940* (Bloomfield Hills, Michigan, 1977), no. 152.

20. In a letter to Malcolm Cowley, June 1, 1951, Kennedy, Hemingway gives a less accurate version of this incident and says he was in China (1941)—not Havana (1939)—at the time.

21. Alvah Bessie, *New Masses*, 37 (November 5, 1940), 29. Hemingway told Milton Wolff: "You have your Marty and I've married my Marty," quoted in Baker, *Life Story*, p. 357. Wolff did not think the novel was a betrayal, but believed it "fell short of what Hemingway owed the cause." Interview with Milton Wolff, Boulder, Colorado, February 27, 1985.

22. Meyers, *Hemingway: Critical Heritage*, pp. 320; 315; 319; 324.

23. *Ibid.*, pp. 331–336; 337, 340.

24. *Ibid.*, pp. 342–343; 347–348, 350; E. M. Forster, *Listener*, 26 (July 10, 1941), 63.

25. Meyers, *Hemingway: Critical Heritage*, pp. 353, 356–358.

26. Interview with Clara Spiegel, Ketchum, Idaho, May 26, 1983.

27. Interview with Jack Hemingway; quoted in Baker, *Life Story*, p. 368.

28. Interview with Tillie Arnold.

29. *The Sun Also Rises*, p. 50.

30. Letter from Harry Sylvester to Jeffrey Meyers, December 3, 1982. Baker, *Life Story*, p. 345, and James McLendon, *Papa Hemingway in Key West* (New York: Popular, 1972), p. 199, say the boys were in New York with Pauline; Kert, *Hemingway Women*, p. 336, states the boys were on the boat with their father. I believe Sylvester is most accurate. This minor incident shows the difficulty of evaluating conflicting evidence.

31. Interview with Patrick Hemingway; Gregory Hemingway, *Papa*, p. 18; letter from Hemingway to A. E. Hotchner, March 14, 1955, Kennedy.

32. *Letters*, p. 499; *Green Hills of Africa*, p. 137.

33. Quoted in Donnelly, *Sara and Gerald*, p. 187; interview with Harry Sylvester.

34. Interview with Toby Bruce.

35. Interview with Gregory Hemingway; item 580.5, p. 14, Kennedy; Anne Stevenson, *Elizabeth Bishop* (New York, 1966), p. 46, discreetly wrote: "Pauline Hemingway . . . was a close friend—apparently humane, witty and stoic—like Elizabeth Bishop herself."

36. Sybille Bedford, *Aldous Huxley: A Biography* (London, 1974), 2:300.
37. Interviews with Patrick Hemingway and Gregory Hemingway.
38. Letter from Mario Menocal, Jr., to Carlos Baker, October 17, 1964; letter from Hemingway to Adriana Ivancich, April 10, 1950, Humanities Research Center, University of Texas.
39. *Letters*, p. 554.

Chapter 17: Finca Vigía and China

1. Quoted in Josephson, *Infidel in the Temple*, p. 428; quoted in Donnelly, *Sara and Gerald*, p. 177.
2. Letter from Martha Gellhorn to Clara Spiegel, September 1, 1940, Princeton; quoted in Paul Fisher, "Back to His First Front," *Kansas City Star*, November 26, 1940, p. 1.
3. Quoted in Lloyd Arnold, *High on the Wild with Hemingway* (Caldwell, Idaho, 1968), p. 331; quoted in Berg, *Max Perkins*, p. 387.
4. Quoted in Kert, *Hemingway Women*, pp. 367, 384.
5. Letter from Hemingway to Archibald MacLeish, December 25, 1943, Library of Congress; quoted in Donnelly, *Sara and Gerald*, p. 178.
6. *Letters*, p. 877, 500; Scott Donaldson, notes on an interview with Buck Lanham, April 5, 1974, courtesy of Professor Donaldson.
7. "The Snows of Kilimanjaro," *Stories*, p. 60; *Letters*, p. 518.
8. Quoted in Baker, *Life Story*, p. 350. Baker adds that Ernest "sheepishly followed her out," and Kert, p. 319, sheepishly repeats: "Grinning sheepishly he followed her out." I am inclined to imagine a more goatish swagger to cover his embarrassment, but refrain from adding this novelistic touch.
9. *Ibid.*, p. 380.
10. Letter from Martha Gellhorn to Clara Spiegel, May 17, 1940, Princeton; letter from Martha Gellhorn to Professor Gerry Brenner, March 8, 1976, Kennedy.
11. *Letters*, p. 249; interview with Martha Gellhorn; quoted in Mary Hemingway, *How It Was*, p. 195.
12. Quoted in Donald St. John, "Leicester Hemingway: Chief of State," *Connecticut Review*, 3 (1970), 16; letter from Hemingway to Bernard Berenson, June 10, 1953, I Tatti; letters from Mario Menocal, Jr., to Carlos Baker, October 17, 1964, and to Jeffrey Meyers, April 18, 1983.
13. Letter from Robert Joyce to Jeffrey Meyers, May 2, 1983; interview with Jack Hemingway.
14. Martha Gellhorn, *The Heart of Another* (New York, 1941), pp. 38, 43–44. Felix also appears in "The German," *A Honeyed Peace* (London, 1954), pp. 131–132, where he is ambushed and beaten up for punching a Nazi.
15. Kert, *Hemingway Women*, pp. 381–382.
16. Gregory Hemingway, *Papa*, p. 92.
17. Letter from Martha Gellhorn to Clara Spiegel, March 4, [1941], Princeton; confidential interview, London, January 1984.
18. Quoted in Kert, *Hemingway Women*, p. 380.
19. Martha Gellhorn, *Travels with Myself and Another* (New York, 1978), pp. 30, 32.
20. Letter from Hemingway to Jonathan Cape, October 24, 1951, University of Reading Library, Reading, Berkshire; letter from Emily Hahn to Jeffrey Meyers, October 28, 1983. See Charles Drage, *Two-Gun Cohen* (London, 1954). *Islands in the Stream*, pp. 269–278, contains a fantastic version of his life in Hong Kong.

21. Gellhorn, *Travels,* pp. 54, 34, 40; letter from Martha Gellhorn to Bonte Durán, n.d., courtesy of Mrs. Durán.
22. Gellhorn, *Travels,* pp. 55, 57, 60.
23. *Ibid.,* pp. 35, 61, 56; Hemingway, Note on Martha Gellhorn, *Collier's,* March 4, 1944, p. 43.
24. Interview with Jack Hemingway; *Letters,* p. 864n.
25. *Letters,* p. 549.
26. Letters from Martha Gellhorn to Clara Spiegel, April 15 and May 30, 1940, Princeton.
27. Martha Gellhorn, *A Stricken Field* (New York, 1940), pp. 207–208, 288.
28. Gellhorn, *Heart of Another,* pp. 77–78.
29. *Ibid.,* pp. 137, 134.
30. Gellhorn, *Honeyed Peace,* pp. 77–78.
31. *Ibid.,* p. 83; Gellhorn, *Heart of Another,* p. 128.
32. Quoted in Kert, *Hemingway Women,* p. 390.

Chapter 18: Our Man in Havana

1. Braden adored his wife and once said that he would like to die while holding her hand in a plane crash. She was not pleased by this prospect. Interview with Bonte Durán, Cambridge, England, July 29, 1983.
2. Letter from Robert Joyce to Jeffrey Meyers, February 28, 1983; Hugh Thomas, *Cuba, or the Pursuit of Freedom* (London, 1971), p. 730; Spruille Braden, *Diplomats and Demogogues* (New Rochelle, New York, 1971), p. 283.
3. In a letter to Jeffrey Meyers on May 26, 1983, James Hall of the FBI Records Division wrote that Hemingway's intelligence reports and all other "records of our legal attaché's office in Havana were destroyed prior to the closing of that office in the year 1960."
4. Letter from Hemingway to Buck Lanham, December 22, 1948, Princeton. Joyce joined the O.S.S in September 1943, served in Cairo, and in Bari as head of the Yugoslav section. He was head of political intelligence for O.S.S at Caserta in 1945, replaced Allen Dulles in Berne after the war, and served for four years under George Kennan as a member of the State Department Policy Planning Staff. In *My Secret War* (New York, 1968), p. 197, Kim Philby, who worked with Joyce on the Special Policy Committee that opposed the Communists in Albania in 1949, called him "a convivial soul with experience of Balkan affairs." Joyce became second in command under Douglas Dillon at the Paris embassy, was deputy chief of mission in Rio, retired from the Foreign Service in 1963 and then lived in Greece.
5. Michael Straight, *After Long Silence* (New York, 1983), p. 268. All the unpublished information comes from interviews with Durán's widow, Bonte, and his daughters, Jane and Lucy (London, September 4, 1983).
6. André Malraux, *Man's Hope,* trans. Stuart Gilbert and Alastair Macdonald (New York, 1938), pp. 10, 57. See also Robert Thornberry on Durán in *Malraux et l'Espagne* (Genève, 1977) and Günter Schmigalle, "Gustavo Durán: Eine biographische Skizze," *Iberoamericana,* 19–20 (1983), 22–42.
7. Quoted in Simone Téry, "Gustavo Durán: Le General Musicien," *Front de la Liberté: Espagne, 1937–1938* (Paris, 1938), p. 149; José Martín-Artajo, Introducción a *Una enseñanza de la Guerra Española* (Madrid, 1980), p. 12. My translations.
8. "Night Before Battle," *The Fifth Column and Four Stories of the Spanish Civil War,* p. 116; letters from Hemingway to Gustavo Durán, March 5, 1940 and August 13, 1940, courtesy of Mrs. Durán.

9. Robert van Gelder, "Ernest Hemingway Talks of Work and War," *Writers and Writing* (New York, 1946), p. 98.

10. *For Whom the Bell Tolls*, p. 335.

11. Interview with Patrick Hemingway.

12. Braden, *Diplomats*, p. 299.

13. Letter from Robert Joyce to Jeffrey Meyers, February 28, 1983.

14. Letter from Robert Joyce to Jeffrey Meyers, May 2, 1983.

15. *Death in the Afternoon*, p. 82.

16. See *The Fifth Column*, p. 61, Rawlings to Dorothy: "You're doing quite well out of the war, aren't you?"

17. *Letters*, pp. 375, 360.

18. See "Arrest of 12 Accused of War Recruiting; FBI Agents Seize Men and a Woman Indicted for Acting for Spanish Loyalists; Prosecutor Says Detroiters Lured Prospective Soldiers at Communist Meetings," *New York Times*, February 7, 1940, p. 8.

19. *By-Line*, p. 450.

20. See Hemingway's ill-advised wartime assertion in his Introduction to *Men at War*, p. xxiv: prevention of future wars with Germany "can probably only be done by sterilization." For Communist attacks on Hemingway, see Meyers, *Hemingway: Critical Heritage*, pp. 35–36, 351.

21. *To Have and Have Not*, p. 82; *Islands in the Stream*, pp. 316, 203.

22. Letter from Robert Joyce to Jeffrey Meyers, February 28, 1983. Joyce was Episcopalian, not Catholic.

23. Braden, *Diplomats*, p. 289.

24. Letters from Hemingway to Buck Lanham, March 2, 1945, and January 15, 1949, Princeton.

25. Department of State file on Durán.

26. See *Time*, October 22, 1951, p. 23, which reproduces a photograph of McCarthy holding an "incriminating" picture of Durán and defends him against McCarthy's charges. For a fine defense of Durán, see David Caute, *The Great Fear* (London, 1978), pp. 332–338; for a defense of McCarthy, see William Buckley and Brent Bozell, "The Case of Gustavo Durán," *McCarthy and His Enemies* (Chicago, 1954), pp. 140–146.

27. Caute, *Great Fear*, p. 336.

28. Letter from Ernest to Patrick Hemingway, January 20, 1954, Princeton. For reports of Braden's testimony against Communist infiltration, see *New York Times*, December 23, 1953, pp. 1, 10, and March 26, 1954, p. 7.

29. While suffering these persecutions, Durán had a distinguished career with the United Nations in New York, Chile, the Congo and Greece from 1946 to 1969. He was U.N. representative in Luluabourg and Stanleyville in 1961–62 and political officer in charge of U.N. Operations in the Congo during 1962–65. In Athens, he was the U.N. resident representative and administered the technical assistance programs for the development of water, forestry and housing. Though his career was impeded by his lack of a university degree and his political troubles, he became a D-1 and nearly reached the highest level of administration. Worn down by the witch-hunters, he found it extremely difficult to accept and deal with his wife's very severe illness and with his series of heart attacks that began in 1961. He hoped to return to Spain after retirement, but died in Athens in 1969. For Durán and the Congo, see Conor Cruise O'Brien, *To Katanga and Back* (London, 1962), pp. 66, 71, 107; for his career at the U.N., see "Gustavo Durán of the U.N. Dies; Was Associate of Hemingway," *New York*

Times, March 27, 1969, p. 47, and the obituary by his friend Brian Urquhart, in the *U.N. Newsletter*, 1969.

30. Jeffrey Meyers, *A Fever at the Core* (London, 1976), p. 96; *Across the River*, pp. 51–52.
31. Ellis Briggs, *Shots Heard Round the World* (New York, 1957), p. 57; interview with Toby Bruce; interview with Patricia Hemingway, Silver Spring, Maryland, April 28, 1984; quoted in Leicester Hemingway, *My Brother*, p. 208.
32. Quoted in Briggs, *Shots*, p. 58.
33. *Islands in the Stream*, p. 251; letters from Mario Menocal, Jr., to Carlos Baker, October 17, 1964, and November 7, 1970, Princeton.

    Gregorio, Paxtchi and Saxon are portrayed as Antonio, Ara and Willie in *Islands in the Stream*.

    A good photograph of Guest appeared in Ami Shinitzsky, *The Endless Chukker* (Gaithersburg, Maryland, 1978), p. 75. See Guest's obituary in the *New York Times*, October 27, 1982, sec. 4, p. 25.
34. Quoted in Zayas-Bazán, "Cuban Friends Remember," pp. 162, 171, 179. This view was confirmed in interviews with Elicio Arguelles and Pedro Menocal, and letters from Mario Menocal, Jr.
35. Quoted in Cowley, "A Portrait of Mister Papa," p. 28. Hemingway did not get a decoration for sub hunting, but was awarded a Bronze Star on June 16, 1947, for his work as a war correspondent.
36. Letter from Robert Joyce to Jeffrey Meyers, February 28, 1983.

Chapter 19: To the Siegfried Line

1. Quoted in Hynan, *Hemingway;* quoted in Leicester Hemingway, *My Brother*, p. 175; quoted in Donaldson, *By Force of Will*, p. 67.
2. Quoted in Kert, *Hemingway Women*, pp. 391–392; Gregory Hemingway, *Papa*, pp. 91–92.
3. Interview with John Hersey (who arrived at Costello's just after this incident), New Haven, January 15, 1983.
4. Interview with Irwin Shaw, Southampton, Long Island, June 2, 1983.
5. Irwin Shaw, *The Young Lions* (New York, 1949), pp. 42, 373; 384; 514, 568.
6. Quoted in Hynan, *Hemingway;* Mary Hemingway, *How It Was*, p. 119.
7. Interview with Michael Foot, M.P., London, October 17, 1983; interview with Lael Wertenbaker, Marlborough, New Hampshire, November 8, 1982; interview with William Walton, New York, January 14, 1983; quoted in A. E. Hotchner, Postscript to *Papa Hemingway* (New York, 1983), p. 308.
8. Walton, quoted in Kert, *Hemingway Women*, pp. 403, 416; item 564c, p. 35, Kennedy; Oriana Fallaci, "Mary Hemingway," *The Egotists* (Chicago, 1968), p. 153.
9. *88 Poems*, p. 104; *Letters*, p. 572.
10. Interview with William Walton; letter from William Walton to Jeffrey Meyers, December 1, 1982.
11. Quoted in Kert, *Hemingway Women*, p. 398; *Letters*, p. 571. Lowndes Square (northwest of Belgrave Square) is not on the way to Park Lane (northeast of Belgrave Square), but the driver may have become lost in the dark.
12. Interview with Martha Gellhorn.
13. Interviews with Peter Viertel and Bill Davis, who heard this, independently, from Hemingway.
14. Letter from Roald Dahl to Jeffrey Meyers, April 22, 1983; interview with Professor

Roger Sharrock, who quoted Sir John, London, October 17, 1983; quoted in Baker, *Life Story*, pp. 392–393.

15. Letter from Nigel Hamilton to Jeffrey Meyers, March 9, 1983; Air Marshal Sir Peter Wykeham, "Hair Raising," *Times* (London), August 5, 1969, p. 8.

16. Letter from Roald Dahl to Jeffrey Meyers, April 22, 1983.

17. *By-Line*, p. 234.

18. Albert Camus, *The Rebel*, trans. Anthony Bower (London, 1954), p. 251; *For Whom the Bell Tolls*, pp. 236, 287.

19. *Letters*, p. 608; Sotheby catalogue, April 9, 1948, lot 425.

20. *New York Times*, July 22, 1978, p. 22. See item 580.5, Kennedy.

21. Interviews with Jack Hemingway, Gregory Hemingway, Valerie Danby-Smith Hemingway and Bill Davis about Lanham's character. Lanham's letters confirm his dullness. Baker dedicated his biography to Lanham, who was his prime informant, accepted him at Hemingway's valuation and put many pages of Lanham's letters and memoirs straight into his *Life Story*.

22. Quoted in C. L. Sulzberger, *A Long Row of Candles* (New York, 1969), pp. 611–612.

23. "The Spanish War," p. 14; interview with John Groth, New York, December 20, 1982.

24. Buck Lanham, "Memoir," pp. 28–30, Princeton. In August 1949 Hemingway falsely boasted to Charles Scribner that he had shot a "snotty SS Kraut" in the belly, just as he had boasted to Bonte Durán about shooting a dog in the guts (*Letters*, p. 672).

25. *Letters*, p. 584; letters from Ernest to Mary Welsh Hemingway, September 5, 1945, and May 3, 1947, Princeton.

26. Letters from Helen Kirkpatrick to Jeffrey Meyers, February 23, 1983, and from Charles Collingwood to Jeffrey Meyers, March 14, 1983.

27. *By-Line*, p. 382. Pelkey (1916–77) was born in Potsdam, New York; worked in the CCC in North Dakota; joined the army in 1933, served two terms and was recalled to duty after Pearl Harbor. He died while drinking beer in front of his television set and was not discovered for two days.

28. *By-Line*, p. 365; letter from Irving Krieger to Jeffrey Meyers, March 12, 1983; interview with Irwin Shaw.

29. David Bruce's letter to a war correspondent, 1947–48, Kennedy.

30. Andy Rooney, "One Eye on the War, One on Paris," *Overseas Press Bulletin*, August 1964, p. 4; interview with Irwin Shaw.

31. Meyers, *A Fever at the Core*, p. 165; letter from David Bruce to Hemingway, December 11, 1948, Kennedy.

32. *Across the River*, p. 133; quoted in Scott Donaldson's interview with Lanham, April 5, 1974.

33. Quoted in Baker, *Life Story*, p. 420; Lanham, "Memoir," p. 9, Princeton.

34. Interview with John Groth; Ernest Hemingway, Introduction to John Groth, *Studio Europe* (New York, 1945), p. 9.

35. Barbara Loxton, War Diary, courtesy of Polly Loxton.

36. Transcript of investigation at Nancy, October 6, 1944, Kennedy; letters from Colonel Buck Lanham, Major James Thornton and Colonel David Bruce in the "Investigation of War Activities" file, Kennedy.

37. Letter from Hemingway to Judge Paul Leahy, June 26, 1952, Kennedy, and to Charles Fenton, August 2, 1952, Kennedy; quoted in Cowley, "A Portrait of Mister Papa," p. 31. Hemingway's unpublished autobiographical story, "The day we drove back from Nancy to Paris," item 356, Kennedy, confirms this account.

38. Charles Macdonald, *The Mighty Endeavor* (New York, 1969), p. 354; Charles Macdonald, *The Siegfried Line Campaign* (Washington, D.C., 1963), pp. 434–435; quoted in Baker, *Life Story*, p. 643.

39. Interview with John Groth.

40. Interview with Lael Wertenbaker, corroborated by a letter from Hemingway to Buck Lanham, August 25, 1948, Princeton.

41. *Letters*, pp. 576, 574.

42. Letter from Buck Lanham to Carlos Baker, August 23, 1965, Princeton; interview with William Walton; letter from Hemingway to Buck Lanham, July 23, 1945, Princeton.

43. Interview with Martha Gellhorn; letter from Martha Gellhorn to Jeffrey Meyers, July 30, 1983. Martha also noted: "Under Cuban law if you divorce someone for desertion, you have a right to everything that belongs to both parties." Hemingway thus kept everything that belonged to Martha: $500 in her bank account, her car, shotgun, typewriter, tennis racket—even her long underwear (quoted in Kert, *Hemingway Women*, pp. 422–423).

44. Letters from Hemingway to William Seward, August 26, 1948, Kennedy, and to Bernard Berenson, May 27, 1953, I Tatti.

45. Interview with Robert Manning, Boston, January 20, 1983.

46. Item 525a, pp. 13, 15, Kennedy; *Across the River*, pp. 212, 95.

47. Letter from Hemingway to Harvey Breit, April 16, 1952, Kennedy.

48. Letter from Hemingway to Mary Welsh, April 10, 1945, Princeton.

Chapter 20: Mary

1. Interview with Jack Hemingway; Gregory Hemingway, *Papa*, p. 95; interviews with Gregory Hemingway.

2. Interviews with Toby Bruce; with George Plimpton, New York, December 20, 1982; and with Elicio Arguelles; Arguelles quoted in Zayas-Bazán, "Cuban Friends Remember," p. 160.

3. *By-Line*, p. 473.

4. Letter from Hemingway to Jonathan Cape, March 24, 1950, Reading; quoted in Mary Hemingway, *How It Was*, p. 607; interview with Patrick Hemingway.

5. *Letters*, pp. 609–610.

6. *Letters*, p. 645; interview with Patrick Hemingway. See also letter from Ernest to Mary Hemingway, July 8, 1947, Princeton.

7. *Islands in the Stream*, p. 92.

8. Letter from Hemingway to Buck Lanham, September 18, 1958, Princeton; interviews with Peter Viertel.

9. Letter from Ernest to Mary Hemingway, July 5, 1947, Princeton; interview with Tillie Arnold; interviews with Peter Viertel.

10. Interview with Fred Zinnemann, London, August 3, 1983; interview with Bill Davis; letter from Slim Hawks Hayward, now Lady Keith, to Jeffrey Meyers, January 30, 1983. Some good photographs appear in " 'Slim' Hawks," *Life*, January 20, 1947, pp. 67, 69–70.

11. Mary Hemingway, *How It Was*, pp. 313, 318; interviews with Peter Viertel. In 1954 Jigee accidentally lit her nightgown with a cigarette, suffered horrible burns and died after a month in hospital.

12. Interview with Durie Shevlin Appleton.

13. Quoted in Sulzberger, *Long Row of Candles*, p. 612.

14. Interviews with George Plimpton and with William Walton; quoted in Hynan, *Hemingway*.

15. Sotheby catalogue, September 5, 1948, lot 425; *Letters*, p. 658.

16. Quoted in Stephen Birmingham, *The Late John Marquand* (Philadelphia, 1972), p. 218; letter to Harvey Breit, July 20, 1952, Kennedy.

17. Letter from Hemingway to Buck Lanham, December 23, 1946, Princeton. See *Stories*, p. 59.

18. Letter from Hemingway to Waldo Peirce, June 17, 1928, Colby College, Waterville, Maine; *Letters*, p. 666.

19. *Letters*, pp. 621–622, 726.

20. Ross, *Portrait of Hemingway*, p. 62; interview with Wallace Meyer, Yorktown Heights, New York, December 19, 1982.

21. *Death in the Afternoon*, p. 173; *Letters*, p. 604; quoted in Gregory Hemingway, *Papa*, p. 102.

22. William Styron, *This Quiet Dust* (New York, 1982), p. 89; Bruce Kawin, Introduction to Faulkner's screenplay *To Have and Have Not* (Madison, 1980), p. 17.

23. James Meriwether and Michael Millgate, ed., *Lion in the Garden: Interviews with William Faulkner* (New York, 1968), p. 58; quoted in Harvey Breit, *The Writer Observed* (New York, 1961), p. 184.

24. *Letters*, p. 769; "The Art of the Short Story," *Paris Review*, pp. 96–97.

25. José Luis Castillo-Puche, *Hemingway in Spain*, trans. Helen Lane (London, 1975), pp. 82, 182–183; interviews with Toby Bruce, William Walton, Irwin Shaw, Bill Davis, Peter Viertel and Valerie Hemingway.

26. Interview with Alfred Rice, New York, December 21, 1982.

27. Sanford, *At the Hemingways*, pp. 61–62; *A Moveable Feast*, p. 208; *A Farewell to Arms*, p. 114.

28. *For Whom the Bell Tolls*, p. 67; *Across the River*, p. 80; *A Moveable Feast*, p. 14.

29. "Up in Michigan," *Stories*, p. 85; "The Last Good Country," *Nick Adams Stories*, p. 95.

30. *A Farewell to Arms*, p. 299; *For Whom the Bell Tolls*, p. 345; *Islands in the Stream*, pp. 323–324.

31. Baker, *Life Story*, pp. 454–455; Aaron Latham, "A Farewell to Machismo," *New York Times Magazine*, October 16, 1977, p. 52; Mary Hemingway, *How It Was*, p. 466.

32. *Death in the Afternoon*, p. 88, 182; quoted in Baker, *Life Story*, p. 390.

Chapter 21: Adriana

1. *The Wild Years*, p. 215; quoted in Mary Hemingway, *How It Was*, p. 515. See the culinary defense in "Ernest Hemingway's Fillet of Lion," *Sports Illustrated*, 3 (December 26, 1955), 40–42.

2. *Letters*, p. 708.

3. Adriana Ivancich, *La Torre Bianca* (Milan, 1980), pp. 316, 38. All translations from this book are by Valerie Meyers.

4. *The Wild Years*, p. 216; *Across the River*, p. 173.

5. Information from the dust jacket of Gianfranco Ivancich, *Ezra Pound in Italy*, and interview with Joseph Dryer—who shared a bachelor flat in Havana with Gianfranco. In 1943 Jack Hemingway asked Dryer, a Dartmouth friend, to take care of some of Hemingway's guns. When Dryer arrived in Cuba and mentioned the guns to Hemingway, he said: "Do you still have them? You do! Then this is the first time I ever got anything back."

6. Interview with Pedro Menocal; letter from Mario Menocal, Jr., to Jeffrey Meyers, April 18, 1983; letter from Hemingway to Adriana Ivancich, April 21, 1950, Texas.

7. Quoted in Ivancich, *Torre Bianca*, p. 207.

8. Letter from Hemingway to Adriana Ivancich, July 6, 1951, Texas.

9. *Across the River*, pp. 80, 109.

10. Ivancich, *Torre Bianca*, p. 144.

11. Interview with Charles Scribner, Jr., New York, January 14, 1983; letter from Julien Dedman to Carlos Baker, April 15, 1972, Princeton.

12. Gregory Hemingway, *Papa*, pp. 109, 100; interview with Tina Sánchez.

13. I have combined letters from Mario Menocal, Jr., to Carlos Baker, November 16, 1964, to Bernice Kert, February 9, 1979, and to Jeffrey Meyers, April 18, 1983.

14. Quoted in Gregory Hemingway, *Papa*, p. 111; Ivancich, *Torre Bianca*, p. 52.

15. Letter from Hemingway to Thomas Welsh, October 20, 1950, Kennedy.

16. Interview with Martha Gellhorn; quoted in Kert, *Hemingway Women*, p. 457.

17. Quoted in Kert, *Hemingway Women*, p. 453; Mary Hemingway, *How It Was*, pp. 348–349.

18. Letter from Mario Menocal, Jr., to Bernice Kert, February 9, 1983; Mary Hemingway, *How It Was*, pp. 354, 604.

19. Ivancich, *Torre Bianca*, p. 202; interview with Afdera Franchetti Fonda, London, May 4, 1984.

20. Quoted in Luciano Simonelli, "Povera Musa di Hemingway," *Domenica del Corriere*, 85 (aprile 16, 1983), 37. My translation.

21. Interview with Pedro Menocal, a cousin of Juan Veranes; quoted in Kert, *Hemingway Women*, p. 470.

22. Ivancich, *Torre Bianca*, pp. 170–171, 299. The paragraphs on *Torre Bianca* are based on Valerie Meyers' review-essay in *Hemingway Review*, 3 (Fall 1983), 66–69.

23. Interview with Afdera Fonda. See Fernanda Pivano, "É morta Adriana Ivancich, Fece inamorare Hemingway" (Adriana is dead, she made Hemingway fall in love), *Corriere della Sera*, marzo 26, 1983, p. 5.

Chapter 22: The Lost Hero: *Across the River and into the Trees*

1. Ernest Hemingway, "And to the United States," *Transatlantic Review*, 1 (May–June 1924), 355; Ernest Hemingway in "Joseph Conrad Supplement," *Transatlantic Review*, 2 (October 1924), 341; *Letters*, p. 162.

2. *88 Poems*, p. 93; letter from Hemingway to John Dos Passos, [late December 1928], Kennedy; *Letters*, p. 264.

3. *Green Hills of Africa*, pp. 21, 109; *Letters*, p. 471.

4. Edmund Wilson, *Letters on Literature and Politics, 1912–1972* (New York, 1977), p. 387; *Letters*, p. 557.

5. Mary Hemingway, *How It Was*, p. 310.

6. Maxwell Geismar, *Saturday Review of Literature*, 33 (September 9, 1950), 18.

7. John O'Hara, *New York Times Book Review*, September 10, 1950, pp. 1, 30–31.

8. Philip Rahv, *Commentary*, 10 (October 1950), 400–401.

9. Cyril Connolly, *Sunday Times* (London), September 3, 1950, p. 3; letter from Hemingway to Cyril Connolly, September 24, 1950, Kennedy.

10. Meyers, *Hemingway: Critical Heritage*, pp. 377, 393–395.

11. *Ibid.*, pp. 403; 378.

12. *Ibid.*, pp. 382, 384–385; 393; quoted in Mary Hemingway, *How It Was*, p. 379.

13. *The Sun Also Rises*, p. 247; *Across the River*, p. 260; Stein, *Autobiography*, p. 235.

14. *Across the River,* p. 18; "Hemingway Novel Slated for March," *New York Times,* October 13, 1949, p. 25; letter from Mario Menocal, Jr., to Carlos Baker, November 16, 1964.

15. *Letters,* pp. 247, 379.

16. Cowley, "Portrait of Mister Papa," p. 26; letter from Hemingway to Buck Lanham, December 27, 1954, Princeton.

17. *Letters,* p. 744.

18. Meyers, *Hemingway: Critical Heritage,* p. 113.

19. *Ibid.,* p. 113; *Letters,* p. 647. Mary's journalist friend Connie Bessie once introduced Hemingway to her mother, who had written a book on language, *In a Word.* He spoke in Indian talk and Margaret Ernst asked: "Mr. Hemingway, when did you lose your articles?" He at first thought she meant newspaper rather than grammatical articles, but good-naturedly accepted her criticism and returned to normal speech. Interview with Connie Bessie, New York, December 21, 1982.

20. *By-Line,* p. 218; *Letters,* pp. 624, 673.

21. Ross, *Portrait of Hemingway,* p. 35.

22. *Ibid.,* pp. 13–14; Lillian Ross, "The Hemingway Profile," *New Republic,* 145 (August 7, 1961), 30; Hotchner quoted in Hynan tapes.

23. Quoted in Baker, *Life Story,* p. 651; *Letters,* p. 744.

24. Quoted in Hotchner, *Papa Hemingway,* p. 116; Edward Burns, ed., *Staying On Alone: Letters of Alice B. Toklas* (New York, 1973), p. 194.

25. *Green Hills of Africa,* p. 8; Meyers, *Hemingway: Critical Heritage,* p. 222; Sinclair Lewis, *Newsweek,* October 18, 1937, p. 34.

26. *Letters,* pp. 531–532; Sinclair Lewis, "Mr. Eglantine," *The Man from Main Street,* ed. Harry Maule and Melville Cane (New York, 1953), p. 292.

27. Interview with George Seldes; *Across the River,* p. 87.

28. *Letters,* p. 721.

29. Meyers, *Hemingway: Critical Heritage,* p. 574.

30. *Letters,* p. 493. *The Future of Infantry* (1933) was written by Chink's friend B. H. Liddell Hart. Chink published descriptions of the Pamplona fiesta in his regimental gazette; *Elementary Tactics* (1932); "Land Warfare," *Journal of the United Services Institution of India,* 71 (January 1941), 10–26; and an Introduction to B. H. Liddell Hart, *The Strategy of Indirect Approach,* new and enlarged edition (1946).

31. Letter from Hemingway to Buck Lanham, September 3, 1947, Princeton. See Major Gen. Sir Francis de Guingand, *Operation Victory* (New York, 1947), p. 133.

32. Dorman-O'Gowan, "When Hem Was 21," p. 6; *Letters,* pp. 686–687.

33. *Across the River,* pp. 82, 125–126. Chink foreshadowed this passage in a letter to Liddell Hart of November 27, 1942 (in the Liddell Hart papers, King's College, London University): "Given enough equipment, as [Montgomery] was, he had a very simple straightforward task. We may never again in this war see a general handed success on a platter because of the prudent arrangements of his predecessor and the stupidity of his opponent."

34. *Across the River,* p. 251; letter from Hemingway to Jonathan Cape, March 24, 1950, Reading.

35. See *Across the River,* p. 134. General David Belchem, chief of Montgomery's Operations staff, wrote in *All in a Day's March* (London, 1978), p. 208: "The pincer movement to close the Falaise gap was not entirely successful because some German sub-units managed to fight their way out to the east. . . . On Monty's side, he overestimated the speed of advance of the Polish Armoured Division and of the Canadians: he had forces available to reinforce them but did not do so."

36. Correlli Barnett, *The Desert Generals* (New York, 1961), pp. 305, 307. Barnett dedicated *Britain and Her Army* (1970) "To the Memory of Eric O'Gowan."

37. Roger Parkinson, *The Auk: Auchinleck, Victor at Alamein* (London, 1977), p. 180; Sir Basil Liddell Hart, "Major-General Dorman-O'Gowan," *Times* (London), May 21, 1969, p. 10.

38. John Connell, *Auchinleck* (London, 1959), p. 551. See R. W. Thompson, *Churchill and the Montgomery Myth* (New York, 1967) and *Churchill: Taken from the Diaries of Lord Moran* (Boston, 1966), pp. 41n, 51.

39. Connell, *Auchinleck*, p. 697.

40. Liddell Hart papers, King's College, London University.

41. Winston Churchill, *The Hinge of Fate* (Boston, 1950), p. 461 and p. 378n in later editions.

42. Barnett, *The Desert Generals*, p. 308.

43. See B. H. Liddell Hart, *The Tanks* (London, 1959), 2:278.

44. Interview with Christopher Dorman-O'Gowan.

45. Major Gen. Sir Francis de Guingand, *Generals at War* (London, 1964), pp. 185–186.

46. B. H. Liddell Hart, *History of the Second World War* (New York, 1971), pp. 290–291.

47. See Erwin Rommel, *The Rommel Papers*, ed. B. H. Liddell Hart (New York, 1953), pp. 237n, 253n, 273n.

48. *Across the River*, pp. 233, 242; 117, 145.

49. R. W. Thompson, *Generalissimo Churchill* (London, 1973), p. 216.

50. *Letters*, pp. 692, 702, 844; *Across the River*, p. 306.

Chapter 23: Death in the Family

1. *Letters*, pp. 761, 670.

2. Letter from Mario Menocal, Jr., to Carlos Baker, November 7, 1970; interviews with Gregory Hemingway.

3. *Letters*, p. 524; *Islands in the Stream*, pp. 10, 135.

4. Interview with Elicio Arguelles; letter from Hemingway to Chink Dorman-Smith, quoted in *Irish Times*, March 22, 1983, p. 10; letter from Hemingway to Patrick Hemingway, September 30, 1951, Princeton.

5. *Letters*, p. 367; interviews with Valerie Danby-Smith Hemingway; Gregory Hemingway, *Papa*, pp. 6, 12. A year after Pauline's death, Hemingway told MacLeish that they had talked very tenderly an hour before she died in California (letter of October 5, 1952, Library of Congress). But Pauline was in the hospital an hour before she died and this letter seems to be an attempt to assuage his guilt. Jinny and Gregory's explanation of the events seems more convincing.

6. *Letters*, p. 737; quoted in Tynan, *Tynan Right and Left*, p. 335. This was a variation of his remark on the death of Ford Madox Ford in 1939: "People dying this year that never died before" (quoted in Baker, *Life Story*, p. 366).

7. Quoted in letter from Ernest to Patrick Hemingway, November 26, 1952, Princeton; interviews with Gregory Hemingway.

8. Gregory Hemingway, *Papa*, pp. 3, 100.

9. Letter from Patricia Hemingway to Jeffrey Meyers, February 15, 1983; Gregory Hemingway, *Papa*, p. 118.

10. *Letters*, p. 758; letter from Hemingway to Jonathan Cape, September 5, 1952, Reading.

11. Dos Passos, *The Fourteenth Chronicle*, p. 423; *By-Line*, pp. 239–240.

12. Meyers, *Hemingway: Critical Heritage,* p. 46; Cyril Connolly, *Sunday Times,* (London), September 7, 1952, p. 5.
13. Meyers, *Hemingway: Critical Heritage,* pp. 410, 412; 414; 417; 414.
14. *Ibid.,* pp. 421–422; 415.
15. "The Undefeated," *Stories,* pp. 243, 265.
16. Ernest Hemingway, *The Old Man and the Sea* (New York, 1952), pp. 44, 69, 73, 124, 103.
17. Interviews with Peter Viertel.
18. Interview with Elicio Arguelles.
19. Interview with Fred Zinnemann.
20. Zayas-Bazán, "Cuban Friends Remember," p. 185; interview with Elicio Arguelles.
21. Interview with Fred Zinnemann.
22. *By-Line,* pp. 472–473.
23. *Letters,* pp. 867, 751, 760.
24. *Ibid.,* pp. 760; quoted in Baker, *Life Story,* p. 502; *Letters,* p. 762. For Young's side of the story, see his lively Foreword to the revised edition of *Ernest Hemingway: A Reconsideration* (New York, 1966), pp. 1–28.
25. Hemingway, letter to Louis Cohn, in *A Bibliography of Ernest Hemingway* (New York, 1931), p. 112; *Letters,* pp. 819, 776.

Chapter 24: Second Safari

1. Letter from Hemingway to Adriana Ivancich, April 10, 1950, Texas; quoted in Mary Hemingway, *How It Was,* p. 389; *Letters,* p. 792.
2. Interview with Patrick Hemingway.
3. *Letters,* p. 823; interviews with Peter Viertel.
4. Quoted in Edward Stanton, "The Correspondent and the Doctor: A Spanish Friendship," *Hemingway Review,* 1 (1981), 54; letter from Hemingway to Peter Buckley, May 28, 1957, Princeton.
5. Hotchner quoted in Hynan tapes; Peter Buckley, *Ernest* (New York, 1978), p. 120.
6. Interview with George Plimpton; letter from Gianfranco Ivancich to Hemingway, July 25, 1953, Princeton.
7. Letter from Denis Zaphiro to Jeffrey Meyers, August 24, 1983; *By-Line,* p. 425.
8. Letter from Mario Menocal, Jr., to Carlos Baker, November 16, 1964.
9. Letters from Mario Menocal Jr., to Carlos Baker, October 17 and November 16, 1964.
10. Letter from Denis Zaphiro to Jeffrey Meyers, August 24, 1983.
11. *Ibid.;* letter from Hemingway to Archibald MacLeish, March 29, 1954, Library of Congress; *Letters,* p. 826.
12. Ernest Hemingway, "African Journal," *Sports Illustrated,* 36 (January 3, 1972), p. 36.
13. "The Snows of Kilimanjaro," *Stories,* p. 76; *By-Line,* pp. 432–434.
14. *By-Line,* pp. 42, 444; letter from Hemingway to Harvey Breit, April 28, 1954, Princeton.
15. *By-Line,* p. 455; interview with Patrick Hemingway, who had a pilot's license and owned a plane.
16. Letter from Hemingway to Charles Fenton, February 21, 1952, Kennedy; *By-Line,* pp. 455–456, 460.
17. *Islands in the Stream,* pp. 212–213; letter from Hemingway to Jonathan Cape, July 28, 1954, Reading.
18. Pivano, "Hemingway, cacciatore sconfitto," p. 3. My translation.
19. Quoted in Ivancich, *Torre Bianca,* p. 324.

20. Letter from Denis Zaphiro to Jeffrey Meyers, August 24, 1983; interviews with Patrick Hemingway and Jack Hemingway.

21. Letter from Hemingway to Ursula Jepson, June 24, 1955, Kennedy; Ernest Hemingway, "Acceptance" in *Nobel Lectures, 1901–1967,* ed. Horst Frenz (Amsterdam, 1969), p. 501.

22. Quoted in Caroline Moorehead, "Stories of Survival," *Times* (London), December 8, 1983, p. 15; *Letters,* p. 843.

Chapter 25: The Dangerous Summers

1. *Letters,* p. 851.

2. Quoted in Castillo-Puche, *Hemingway in Spain,* p. 261; *Letters,* p. 873. A good photograph of Hemingway at Baroja's bedside appears in Castillo after p. 222.

3. Arthur Miller, quoted in E. Fuller Torrey, *The Roots of Treason: Ezra Pound and the Secrets of St. Elizabeths* (London, 1984), p. 200. As early as 1956 Hemingway wrote: "I do not want to vote for Nixon, not because of his useful role in the Hiss case, but on his record" (*Letters,* p. 871).

4. *Letters,* pp. 548, 742, 879; quoted in Torrey, *The Roots of Treason,* p. 208. See Jeffrey Meyers' review of Torrey's book in the *Spectator,* 252 (April 28, 1984), 25–26.

5. Quoted in Jerome Beatty, "Ernest Hemingway vs. *Esquire,*" *Saturday Review,* 41 (August 23, 1958), 11; quoted in Laymond Robinson, "Hemingway Says He Will Drop Suit, Asserts That Political Fear Did Not Spur Attempt to Bar Reprints of Stories," *New York Times,* August 7, 1958, p. 27; interview with Alfred Rice.

6. Letter from Hemingway to Bernard Berenson, April 30, 1957, I Tatti; *Letters,* p. 888.

7. Interview with Bud Purdy, Picabo, Idaho, May 27, 1983.

8. *Letters,* p. 518; letter from Hemingway to Bernard Berenson, March 6, 1953, I Tatti; interviews with Peter Viertel.

9. Letter from Bronislaw Zielinski to Jeffrey Meyers, January 3, 1983.

10. Tynan, *Tynan Right and Left,* pp. 331, 333–334, 336; *Letters,* p. 890.

11. Interview with Bill Davis, who heard a tape of the Torrejon interview; letter from Hemingway to Bronislaw Zielinski, April 12, 1959, Princeton.

12. FBI file on Hemingway.

13. Letter from Mary Hemingway to Clara Spiegel, February 29, 1960, courtesy of Clara Spiegel.

14. Letter from Hemingway to Bill Lang of *Life,* March 1, 1960, quoted in Hotchner, *Papa Hemingway,* p. 261; Ernest Hemingway, "The Dangerous Summer," *Life,* September 5, 1960, p. 86.

15. Castillo-Puche, *Hemingway in Spain,* p. 73; "Jeffrey Meyers Meets Hemingway's Matadors," *Literary Review* (London), 67 (January 1984), 32–36. All direct quotations are taken from these interviews, on July 12, 1983, with Luis Miguel Dominguín, Andújar and Antonio Ordóñez, Seville, Spain.

16. *Letters,* p. 895.

17. *Death in the Afternoon,* pp. 43, 87–88.

18. "The Dangerous Summer," *Life,* September 5, 1960, p. 86.

19. Quoted in Shay Oag, *In the Presence of Death: Antonio Ordóñez* (New York, 1969), p. 85; quoted in Castillo-Puche, *Hemingway in Spain,* p. 156.

20. *Letters,* p. 117.

21. "The Dangerous Summer," *Life,* September 5, 1960, pp. 87, 88, 106.

22. Letter from Hemingway to Harvey Breit, May 17, 1957, Kennedy.

23. Quoted in Keith Botsford, *Dominguín* (Chicago, 1972), pp. 200, 190, 201, 205, 207. Dominguín has a few references to Hemingway in his recent memoirs, serialized in *Hola* (Barcelona) beginning October 15, 1983.

24. Castillo-Puche, *Hemingway in Spain*, p. 48; interview with Bill Davis.

25. "The Dangerous Summer," *Life*, September 5, 1960, p. 61.

26. Gerald Brenan, *A Personal Record* (London, 1974), p. 367.

27. Interviews with Gregory Hemingway.

28. Castillo-Puche, *Hemingway in Spain*, pp. 66, 346; Scott Donaldson's interview with Buck Lanham, April 5, 1974.

29. Interview with Jack Hemingway; Mary quoted in Hynan tapes; Mary Hemingway, *How It Was*, p. 602.

30. Interviews with Valerie Danby-Smith Hemingway.

31. Letter from Mary Hemingway to Clara Spiegel, February 29, 1960, courtesy of Mrs. Spiegel; Castillo-Puche, *Hemingway in Spain*, pp. 191, 184, 347.

32. Interviews with Toby Bruce, Bill Davis, Clara Spiegel, George Plimpton; Scott Donaldson's interview with Lanham. When asked if Valerie was Hemingway's mistress, Forrest MacMullen suggestively replied: "Hard cock has no conscience" (telephone conversation, March 16, 1983).

33. Letter from Hemingway to Valerie Danby-Smith, October 25, 1960, Kennedy; interviews with Valerie Hemingway. Valerie did not wish to clarify the nature of her relations with Hemingway.

34. Ernest Hemingway, "Pamplona Letter," *Transatlantic Review*, 3 (October 1924), 301; *By-Line*, pp. 158, 460; Stein, *Autobiography*, p. 216.

35. Meyers, *Hemingway: Critical Heritage*, pp. 444, 446; 464–465.

36. *Ibid.*, pp. 483–484; 477–478; 471, 475.

37. *Ibid.*, pp. 503, 509.

38. *Across the River*, p. 68; *Green Hills of Africa*, p. 19; "The Snows of Kilimanjaro," *Stories*, pp. 66, 54.

39. André Malraux, "Lawrence and the Demon of the Absolute," *Hudson Review*, 8 (1956), 528.

Chapter 26: Mayo Clinic

1. *By-Line*, pp. 294, 296; *For Whom the Bell Tolls*, p. 109; Castillo-Puche, *Hemingway in Spain*, pp. 36, 169.

2. *Death in the Afternoon*, p. 188; *Letters*, p. 586.

3. George Plimpton, in Dwight Macdonald, *Against the American Grain*, p. 183; Hadley, quoted in Hynan tapes.

4. *Letters*, p. 906; quoted in Gregory Hemingway, *Papa*, p. 13; Baker, *Life Story*, p. 667, quotes this technical report, which is meaningless to the layman, without explaining its significance.

5. Gregory Hemingway, *Papa*, p. 15.

6. Interviews with Toby Bruce, Clara Spiegel, Tillie Arnold and Bud Purdy.

7. Quoted in Mary Hemingway, *How It Was*, pp. 622–623; Ford Madox Ford, *Thus to Revisit* (New York, 1966), p. 168; *Letters*, p. 908.

8. Baker, *Life Story*, p. 554; interviews with Valerie Danby-Smith Hemingway. Valerie said she never attended drama school in New York or had a $1,500 tuition fee paid by Hemingway, as reported by Hotchner, pp. 291–292, and repeated by Baker, p. 555, and Kert, p. 498.

9. *Letters*, p. 765; letter from Professor Karl Ryavec to Jeffrey Meyers, March 24, 1983;

By-Line, p. 475; quoted in John De Groot, "FBI vs. Papa," *Palm Beach News-Sun-Sentinel,* October 9, 1983, p. 6A.

10. FBI file on Hemingway; Hotchner, *Papa Hemingway,* pp. 308–309.

11. Hotchner, *Papa Hemingway,* p. 296; *Letters,* p. 911; interview with Elicio Arguelles.

12. Mary Hemingway, "How It Was," *Student,* p. 23; informal interview with George Saviers, Ketchum, May 26, 1983; quoted in Hotchner, *Papa Hemingway,* p. 302.

13. *Death in the Afternoon,* p. 54; *The Fifth Column,* p. 32.

14. Quoted in Ross, *Portrait of Hemingway,* p. 36; quoted in Young, *Hemingway: A Reconsideration,* p. 165.

15. Informal interview with George Saviers.

16. Interviews with Patrick Hemingway and Martha Gellhorn.

17. Quoted in Irving and Marilyn Yalom, "Ernest Hemingway—A Psychiatric View," *Archives of General Psychiatry,* 24 (June 1971), 486. Of the doctors who treated Hemingway, Howard Rome, Hugh Butt and John Butsch did not answer letters; John Moritz and Scott Earle could not provide information; George Saviers was extremely discreet; Randall Sprague spoke only of his diabetes. The Mayo records may or may not exist, and the Clinic maintains absolute silence. According to Alfred Rice, Mary did not want to know exactly what happened and did not consider a negligence suit. Patrick had no interest in the records; Jack and Gregory showed more curiosity, but did not actually request them. Experts consulted at Harvard, Yale, Boston University and University of Minnesota medical schools agreed that it would be almost impossible to get the clinical information on Hemingway.

18. Castillo-Puche, *Hemingway in Spain,* p. 58; interview with Bill Davis.

19. Burgess, *Ernest Hemingway and His World,* p. 111; Hotchner, *Papa Hemingway,* p. 306.

20. Interviews with Gregory Hemingway.

21. Max Fink, *Convulsive Therapy: Theory and Practice* (New York, 1979), p. 221; Robert Palmer, ed., *Electroconvulsive Therapy* (Oxford, 1981), p. 290.

22. Fink, *Convulsive,* pp. 10, 85. For a vivid description of an epileptic fit, see Fyodor Dostoyevsky, *The Idiot,* trans. David Magarshack (London, 1955), p. 258.

23. Fink, *Convulsive,* p. 161; Palmer, *Electroconvulsive,* p. 288.

24. Interview with Dr. Richard Selzer, New Haven, Conn., December 15, 1982.

25. Fink, *Convulsive,* p. 12; Palmer, *Electroconvulsive,* p. 255.

26. Yalom, "Hemingway—A Psychiatric View," p. 494; Fink, *Convulsive,* p. 133.

27. Palmer, *Electroconvulsive,* pp. 97, 255, 176.

28. Quoted in Ronald Hayman, *Artaud and After* (London, 1977), p. 128.

29. Sylvia Plath, *The Bell Jar* (New York, 1971), pp. 1, 161.

30. Quoted in Hotchner, *Papa Hemingway,* p. 308; Arnold, *High on the Wild with Hemingway,* p. 331.

31. Mary Hemingway, *How It Was,* p. 629; interview with Matthew Bruccoli, Columbia, South Carolina, December 29, 1982; letter from Hadley Hemingway Mowrer to Archibald MacLeish, August 4, 1961, Library of Congress.

32. Quoted in Mary Hemingway, *How It Was,* p. 632; quoted in Hotchner, *Papa Hemingway,* pp. 321, 328.

33. *Letters,* p. 921; interview with Elicio Arguelles; quoted in Hotchner, *Papa Hemingway,* p. 333.

34. Mary Hemingway, *How It Was,* p. 633; letter from Charles Collingwood to Jeffrey Meyers, March 14, 1983.

35. Leslie Fiedler, "An Almost Imaginary Interview: Hemingway in Ketchum," *Partisan*

Review, 29 (1962), 404, 400, 402; interviews with Jack Hemingway and William Walton.

Chapter 27: Suicide and Aftermath

1. *Letters,* p. 19; quoted in Baker, *Life Story,* p. 167.
2. Quoted in David Butwin, "Turning the Keys," *Saturday Review,* 54 (February 27, 1971), 40; Sotheby catalogue, typed fragment, 1930s lot 419.
3. *Death in the Afternoon,* pp. 20, 104, 220; interview with Harry Sylvester; Ernest Hemingway, autobiographical sketch, *Portraits and Self-Portraits,* ed. Georges Schreiber (Boston, 1936), p. 57.
4. *Green Hills of Africa,* p. 101; *To Have and Have Not,* p. 238.
5. Interview with Joris Ivens; *For Whom the Bell Tolls,* p. 468.
6. Item 529a, p. 8, Kennedy; quoted in Manning, "Hemingway in Cuba," p. 106.
7. Letter from Hemingway, November 22, 1959, Knox College, Galesburg, Illinois; interviews with Bill Davis and Clara Spiegel.
8. Albert Camus, *The Myth of Sisyphus,* trans. Justin O'Brien (New York, 1955), p. 3.
9. Quoted in Janet Flanner, *Paris Was Yesterday* (New York, 1972), p. viii; Friedrich Nietzsche, *Thus Spoke Zarathustra, The Portable Nietzsche,* trans. Walter Kaufmann (New York, 1954), p. 183.
10. Quoted in Hotchner, *Papa Hemingway,* p. 330; quoted in "Hemingway Killed by Shot: 'Accident,' " *New York Herald Tribune,* July 3, 1961, p. 10; Air Marshal Sir Peter Wykeham, quoted in Hynan, *Hemingway.*
11. Arnold, *Hemingway: High on the Wild,* p. 335; Baker, *Life Story,* pp. 561, 563; Mary Hemingway, *How It Was,* p. 635.
12. Mary Hemingway, *How It Was,* p. 630; interview with Patrick Hemingway; quoted in Kert, *Hemingway Women,* pp. 502–503.
13. Interviews with Martha Gellhorn, Patrick Hemingway, Tillie Arnold.
14. Mary Hemingway, *How It Was,* p. 636; interviews with Tillie Arnold and Martha Gellhorn; Miller, *Ernie,* p. 139. The photograph of a Spanish soldier with the top of his head blown off, which Hemingway reproduced in his article, "Dying, Well or Badly," *Ken,* April 21, 1938, p. 68, gives some sense of how he looked after the suicide.
15. "Widow Describes Hemingway Manuscripts," *New York Times,* July 9, 1961, p. 45; Hynan, *Hemingway,* and "Interview with Mary Hemingway," 1977, BBC Archives. Death certificates, not a matter of public record in Idaho, are made available only to the immediate family.
16. Interviews with Jack Hemingway and Patrick Hemingway. Patrick also mentioned that Pauline was not a practicing Catholic when she died.
17. Julanne Isabelle, *Hemingway's Religious Experience* (New York, 1964), pp. 53–54; interview with Toby Bruce.
18. Quoted in Montgomery, *Hemingway in Michigan,* p. 190; "Father L. M. Dougherty Talks about Ernest Hemingway," *Rendezvous,* 5 (Winter 1970), 13.
19. Miller, *Ernie,* p. 141; interviews with Valerie Hemingway; "Fathers and Sons," *Stories,* p. 499.
20. Quoted in Ronald Maiorana, "Hemingway Wrote His Will in Legal Style," *New York Times,* August 25, 1961, p. 27.
21. *His Very Voice and Self: Collected Conversations of Lord Byron,* ed. Ernest Lovell, Jr. (New York, 1954), pp. 317, 366.

22. Quoted in "Hemingway Dead of Gunshot Wound; Wife Says He Was Cleaning Weapon," *New York Times*, July 3, 1961, p. 6; quoted in Dennis Brian, ed., "The Hemingway Hunters," *Murderers and Other Friendly People* (New York, 1972), p. 47; quoted in Eva Mills, "Ernest Hemingway and Nathan Asch: An Ambivalent Relationship," *Hemingway Review*, 2 (1983), 51.

23. Interview with Christopher Dorman-O'Gowan; quoted in James Michener, *Iberia* (New York, 1968), p. 498.

24. Quoted in Castillo-Puche, *Hemingway in Spain*, p. 168; "Jeffrey Meyers Meets Hemingway's Matadors," p. 34; Wilson, *Letters on Literature and Politics*, pp. 602, 607.

25. Quoted in Fallaci, "Mary Hemingway," p. 148; letter from Mary Hemingway to Waldo Peirce, August 7, 1971, Library of Congress; interview with William Walton. According to Valerie Hemingway, who helped Mary burn the papers, they followed Hemingway's written instructions to destroy his diary-like drafts of inferior fiction, and his letters about Martha and illness in the family (telephone conversation, February 1, 1985).

26. *By-Line*, p. 466.

27. See "A Sister of Hemingway is 'Apparent Suicide,'" *New York Times*, November 1, 1966, p. 3; Herbert Mitgang, "Leicester Hemingway, Writer and Ernest's Brother, Is Suicide," *New York Times*, September 15, 1982, sec. IV, p. 27.

28. See "Died: Adriana Ivancich," *Time*, April 4, 1983, p. 64.

29. Letter from Mary Hemingway to Clara Spiegel, February 16, 1949, courtesy of Mrs. Spiegel.

30. See "Mrs. Hemingway Loses Book Plea," *New York Times*, February 22, 1966, p. 7, and "Appeal on Hemingway Book," *New York Times*, March 18, 1966, p. 41; Arnold Lubasch, "Hotchner's $125,000 Libel Award Upheld," *New York Times*, August 3, 1976, p. 20, and "Federal Appeals Court Throws Out $125,000 Libel Award," *New York Times*, March 24, 1977, p. 28.

31. Saul Bellow, *Dangling Man* (New York, 1944), p. 9; quoted in Michael Kaufman, "The Man Who Boxed Hemingway Keeps Writing," *New York Times*, June 27, 1983, p. C-9.

32. Norman Mailer, *Advertisements for Myself* (New York, 1959), p. 265; Norman Mailer, "Punching Papa," *New York Review of Books*, 1 (August 1963), 13.

33. See Jean Rhys, *Quartet* (New York, 1929); Ford Madox Ford, *The Rash Act* (London, 1933); Scott Fitzgerald, "In the Darkest Hour," "The Count of Darkness," "The Kingdom of the Dark," "Gods of Darkness," *Redbook* (October 1934, June 1935, August 1935, November 1941); Martha Gellhorn, *The Heart of Another* (New York, 1941) and *The Honeyed Peace* (London, 1954); Irwin Shaw, *The Young Lions* (New York, 1949); John Dos Passos, *Chosen Country* (Boston, 1951) and *The Great Days* (New York, 1958); Leicester Hemingway, *The Sound of the Trumpet* (New York, 1953); David Lodge, *The British Museum is Falling Down* (London, 1965); Philip Roth, *The Great American Novel* (New York, 1973).

34. Theodore Roethke, "Song for the Squeeze-Box," *Collected Poems* (New York, 1979), p. 107; John Berryman, *His Toy, His Dream, His Rest* (London, 1969), p. 164. See also Ezra Pound, *Cantos* (London, 1975), p. 427; E. E. Cummings, "No Thanks," *Poems, 1923–1954* (New York, 1954), p. 294; Archibald MacLeish, "Years of the Dog," *Act Five* (New York, 1948), p. 53, and "Hemingway," *Atlantic*, 208 (November 1961), 46; Malcolm Cowley, "Ernest," *Blue Juniata* (New York, 1968), p. 96; Thomas Merton, "An Elegy for Ernest Hemingway," *Commonweal*, 74 (September 22, 1961), 513; Yevgeny Yevtushenko, "Encounter," *Selected Poems* (New York, 1962), pp. 79–80.

Select Bibliography

Arnold, Lloyd. *High on the Wild with Hemingway.* Caldwell, Idaho: Caxton, 1968.

Baker, Carlos. *Ernest Hemingway: A Life Story.* New York: Scribner's, 1969.

Bruccoli, Matthew. *Scott and Ernest.* New York: Random House, 1978.

Castillo-Puche, José Luis. *Hemingway in Spain,* trans. Helen Lang. London: New English Library, 1975.

Cowley, Malcolm. "A Portrait of Mister Papa," in John McCaffery, ed., *Ernest Hemingway: The Man and His Work.* New York: Avon, 1950.

Dos Passos, John. *The Best Times.* New York: New American Library, 1966.

Fenton, Charles. *The Apprenticeship of Ernest Hemingway.* New York: Mentor, 1954.

Hanneman, Audre. *Ernest Hemingway: A Comprehensive Bibliography.* Princeton: Princeton University Press, 1967; *Supplement.* Princeton, 1975.

Hemingway, Gregory. *Papa.* Boston: Houghton Mifflin, 1976.

Hemingway, Leicester. *My Brother, Ernest Hemingway.* New York: Fawcett, 1962.

Hemingway, Mary. *How It Was.* New York: Ballantine, 1976.

Hotchner, A. E. *Papa Hemingway.* New York: Bantam, 1966.

Ivancich, Adriana. *La Torre Bianca.* Milano: Mondadori, 1980.

Kert, Bernice. *The Hemingway Women.* New York: Norton, 1983.

Meyers, Jeffrey. "Ernest Hemingway's Four Wives." *Married to Genius.* London: London Magazine Editions, 1977. Pp. 174–189.

——. *Hemingway: The Critical Heritage.* London: Routledge & Kegan Paul, 1982.

——. "Wallace Stevens and 'The Short Happy Life of Francis Macomber,' " *American Notes and Queries,* 21 (November–December 1982), 47–49.

——. "Hemingway: Wanted by the FBI!" *New York Review of Books,* 30 (March 31, 1983), 17–20.

——. "A Queer, Ugly Business: The Origins of 'The Short Happy Life of Francis Macomber,' " *London Magazine,* 23 (November 1983), 26–37.

——. "Hemingway, Ford Madox Ford and *A Moveable Feast,* " *Critical Quarterly,* 25 (Winter 1983), 35–42.

———. "Jeffrey Meyers Meets Hemingway's Matadors," *Literary Review* (London), 67 (January 1984), 32–36.

———. "Hemingway's Second War: The Greco-Turkish Conflict, 1920–1922," *Modern Fiction Studies*, 30 (Spring 1984), 24–36.

———. "Kipling and Hemingway: The Lesson of the Master," *American Literature*, 56 (March 1984), 88–99.

———. "Introduction to Lawrence Kubie's Suppressed Essay on Hemingway," *American Imago*, 41 (Spring 1984), 1–18.

———. "Chink Dorman-Smith and *Across the River and into the Trees*," *Journal of Modern Literature*, 11 (July 1984), 314–322.

———. "Memoirs of Hemingway: The Growth of a Legend," *Virginia Quarterly Review*, 60 (Autumn 1984), 587–612.

———. "Tolstoy and Hemingway." *Disease and the Novel, 1860–1960*. London: Macmillan, 1985. Pp. 19–29.

———. "The Quest for Hemingway," *Virginia Quarterly Review* 61 (Autumn 1985) 584–602.

———. "Hemingway's Five Wars," *London Magazine* 25 (November 1985), 58–70.

Miller, Madelaine Hemingway. *Ernie*. New York: Crown, 1975.

Montgomery, Constance. *Hemingway in Michigan*. New York: Fleet, 1966.

Reynolds, Michael. *Hemingway's First War: The Making of "A Farewell to Arms."* Princeton: Princeton University Press, 1976.

Ross, Lillian. *Portrait of Hemingway*. New York: Simon and Schuster, 1961.

Sanford, Marcelline Hemingway. *At the Hemingways*. London: Putnam, 1963.

Sarason, Bertram. *Hemingway and "The Sun" Set*. Washington, D.C.: NCR Microcard Editions, 1972.

Sokoloff, Ruth. *Hadley: The First Mrs. Hemingway*. New York: Dodd, Mead, 1973.

Index

compiled by Valerie Meyers

625

Copyright Acknowledgments